AMERICA COMPARED

American History in International Perspective

SECOND EDITION

VOLUME I: To 1877

CARL J. GUARNERI

SAINT MARY'S COLLEGE OF CALIFORNIA

WADSWORTH
CENGAGE Learning™

Australia • Brazil • Japan • Korea • Mexico • Singapore • Spain • United Kingdom • United States

WADSWORTH
CENGAGE Learning™

America Compared: American History in International Perspective, Volume I: To 1877, Second Edition

Carl J. Guarneri

Publisher: Charles Hartford

Editor-in-Chief: Jean Woy

Senior Sponsoring Editor:
Sally Constable

Development Editor:
Lisa Kalner Williams

Senior Project Editor:
Rosemary R. Jaffe

Editorial Assistant:
Rachel Zanders

Senior Art and Design Coordinator:
Jill Haber

Senior Composition Buyer:
Sarah Ambrose

Senior Photo Editor:
Jennifer Meyer Dare

Senior Manufacturing Coordinator:
Priscilla Bailey

Senior Marketing Manager:
Sandra McGuire

Cover image: *Battle of Cerro Gordo* (Mexican War), by Carl Nebel. Special Collections, University Libraries, University of Texas at Arlington.

For product information and
technology assistance, contact us at **Cengage Learning Customer & Sales Support, 1-800-354-9706**

For permission to use material from this text or product, submit all requests online at **www.cengage.com/permissions**
Further permissions questions can be e-mailed to **permissionrequest@cengage.com**

Library of Congress Control Number: 2002109469

ISBN-13: 978-0-618-31856-8

ISBN-10: 0-618-31856-9

Wadsworth Cengage Learning
20 Davis Drive
Belmont, CA 94002-3098
USA

Cengage Learning is a leading provider of customized learning solutions with office locations around the globe, including Singapore, the United Kingdom, Australia, Mexico, Brazil, and Japan. Locate your local office at **www.cengage.com/global**

Cengage Learning products are represented in Canada by Nelson Education, Ltd.

To learn more about Wadsworth, visit
www.cengage.com/wadsworth

Purchase any of our products at your local college store or at our preferred online store **www.cengagebrain.com**

To my parents-in-law, George and Alice Weller

Printed in the United States of America
2 3 4 5 6   19 18 17 16 15

AMERICA COMPARED

CONTENTS

PREFACE

American History in International Perspective

Events have conspired to make the appearance of a second edition of *America Compared* especially timely. The attacks on the World Trade Center and the Pentagon in September 2001 shattered Americans' sense of separateness and awakened feelings of national vulnerability. When American policymakers responded by invading Afghanistan and Iraq and declaring a worldwide war on terrorism, the United States reached its highest level of global intervention since the Cold War. Pondering these developments, many journalists have called upon teachers and scholars to provide a more global context for understanding America's history. Their sense of urgency is understandable, but it is important to remember that this appeal has been voiced many times before. Throughout the twentieth century, including the time after Japan's surprise bombing of Pearl Harbor in December 1941 — an attack to which the events of 9/11 have been widely compared — calls to place American history in international perspective appeared regularly in newspapers and scholarly journals whenever Americans were reminded by momentous events that their nation's fate is entwined with the rest of the world.

If we pull back from the trauma of 9/11 to analyze longer-term trends, we can see that three modern developments have highlighted the international dimension of American history. First, in the twentieth century the United States emerged as an unusually potent world player: a "superpower" that intervened in two world wars, waged a successful cold war against Soviet communism, and undertook foreign policy initiatives that influenced the lives of people everywhere. Charting the rise of the United States from provincial backwater to world power has become an essential task for those studying its history. Second, the linking of the world's people through instant communication, open markets, multinational corporations, and mass entertainment — a phenomenon loosely referred to as "globalization" — has prompted scholars to rethink the American past. Today's global connections have their origins in revolutions begun by printing presses and oceanic sailing ships five centuries ago, when Europeans' expansion began to create an interlinked world economy. The United States, a nation settled in the first stage of globalization, has been implicated in international patterns of trade and migration from its birth. Its story must be told with these connections in mind. Third, beginning in the 1960s, the varying fortunes of America's world position, from the tragedy of the Vietnam War to the triumphant end of the Cold War to the jarring ups and downs of the nation's economy, have spurred a lively debate over America's special uniqueness. American "exceptionalism" is the belief, dating back nearly four hundred years to the era of colonization, that America is a "chosen land" that developed fundamentally apart from the rest of the world and has been exempt from its problems. This faith is so linked to Americans' national identity that it is part of the air they breathe, but in recent decades it has been questioned by many people at home and abroad as they try to examine more objectively America's place in the world.

The commitment to exceptionalism has traditionally produced insular narratives of the American past. But the United States' involvement in the world has become too obvious to ignore, and as its global impact has grown, scholars have increasingly sought larger contexts for describing its history. More and more historians are tying American events to trends elsewhere, pursuing ideas and movements across national boundaries, and analyzing American history comparatively.

America Compared gathers some of the best of these internationally informed writings for assignment in American history courses. This reader is intended for undergraduate survey classes, although it has also been used in high school Advanced Placement courses and served as a text for specialized college courses aimed at upper-division students. The topics covered are synchronized with those of most introductory courses in American history. Thus, *America Compared* takes familiar subjects and tries to see them anew through international contexts and comparisons. The primary focus is, of course, American history, but each reading that I have selected gives its topic a new dimension by relating it to comparable features in other societies or by situating it in a history of transnational contacts and exchanges. In this way, each selection is meant to contribute to the two major aims of this book: to place U.S. history in an international context and to assess the nature and extent of American uniqueness.

The Varieties of Comparative History

To illustrate the different ways that American history can be internationalized, I have used an elastic definition of comparative history. It incorporates **four "c-words"** that help to lead U.S. history outward toward larger frameworks of interpretation. First, and most obviously, there are direct **comparisons** between different national experiences. Most of the selections in *America Compared* offer focused comparisons, sometimes brief but at other times extended, between developments in the United States and elsewhere. A second way to internationalize America's history is to explore transnational **connections.** Many selections included in this reader describe contacts or connections between Americans and other peoples through such experiences as migration, trade, travel, international social movements, the transfer of technology, diplomacy, and wars. A third strategy measures specific features of American history against **concepts** that social scientists have developed to describe processes that go beyond particular societies. In this case, scholars examine overall theories or models concerning such developments as revolutions, nation building, industrialization, or imperialism to determine how well they describe the American version of these processes. Finally, encompassing the first three strategies, there is the search for larger **contexts** for understanding events that took place on American soil. Once we follow the flow of people, ideas, and goods across national borders, we begin to realize that many developments that we think of as uniquely American were not. The American Revolution, religious revivalism, the expanding frontier, and other key features of American history were variants of larger movements that proceeded simultaneously on other continents and were related through economic and cultural ties. Several readings in this collection explore these transnational contexts and systems and discuss America's place in them.

Each of these interpretive strategies expands our appreciation of the international dimensions of American history. There is also much overlap between them. Since all of the "four c's" involve international comparisons in one way or another, the selections that adopt their approaches discuss similarities and differences between America's history and that of other places.

The French historian Marc Bloch once noted that the most illuminating comparisons are those between societies with common influences and substantial basic similarities. Keeping this in mind, most of the selections in this reader relate the United States to one of three reference groups: 1) other European "settler societies" in Latin America, Canada, Australia, and South Africa that were established as colonies, confronted indigenous peoples, and attained their independence; 2) western European nations, such as Great Britain, France, and Germany, that forged transatlantic connections with the early United States and later underwent similar political, social, and industrial trends; and 3) the new political and industrial world powers of the twentieth century, Japan and Russia. The possibilities for making brief and intriguing comparisons across places and times are endless, as opinion pieces in our newspapers' editorial pages demonstrate daily. But the richer rewards that come from more sustained comparisons and deeper engagement with history are what we are after here. These are more likely to surface when focusing our attention on nations with substantial ties or basic similarities to the United States.

The Format and Features of This Book

The topics covered in *America Compared* are divided into periods and themes ranging from the Columbian encounter to Reconstruction (Volume I) and from Reconstruction to the controversy over globalization and American empire (Volume II). Each chapter of the book features two journal articles or book extracts. These **selections** represent the heart of this collection. They are not historical documents from the time period being studied, which historians call "primary sources." Rather they are works of historical interpretation, or "secondary sources," in which historians describe and analyze past events and consider their significance. As noted above, these readings have been chosen because they make fresh contributions to our understanding of American history by examining its features and events in an internationally comparative perspective.

Brief **chapter introductions** announce the topic and set it in an international or comparative context, then note the place of the selections that follow in that context. There is no single theme or approach that links every pair of selections. Some chapters ask students to distinguish between interpretations that stress American uniqueness and those that emphasize transnational similarities. Sometimes the readings offer sharply contrasting interpretations of the same event or era. In other cases, the first selection makes comparative generalizations that can be tested by a specific case study in the second. Often the selections cover different aspects of the chapter's overall topic, and they frequently feature different types of comparative approaches. The chapter introductions help to get students started in characterizing and comparing the selections that follow.

After this overview, **introductions to each selection** set the stage for its specific topic and approach. These introductions describe the broad historical issue or question the selection addresses and suggest the new dimension that comparative or transnational history brings to the topic. Offering a "sneak preview" of the selection to students, they note some ideas or arguments to look for and perhaps to contrast with other selections. When necessary, the introductions also provide basic background information on the foreign event or development that the selection uses as a comparative reference point.

Following each introduction and preceding the selection, a brief **Glossary** includes historical terms, persons, or events that appear in the reading but are not adequately described there. This will allow students to make the most of this reader without resorting to dictionaries, encyclopedias, or even an American history textbook. These glossaries are especially important for terms relating to other countries' histories, which are not likely to be identified in other books assigned in a U.S. history course. Students may want to peruse the glossary before beginning the selection, or they can simply consult it for information as they go along. Either way, the glossaries make it easier for students to grasp international references and comparisons.

At the end of each selection I have provided **Questions to Consider** to help students understand and analyze the reading. These questions are clustered into five numbered groups and are carefully constructed to guide students to increasing levels of historical understanding. The first questions help students comprehend the reading. The next questions encourage students to analyze its ideas and evidence and to relate its findings to important historical issues. The final questions ask students to compare the selection's viewpoint to those of others in the book and to assess the value of its particular kind of comparative method. These study questions are intended to integrate students' understanding of specific topics in America's past, and at the same time they invite them to explore the longer timespans and wider contexts of American history.

What's New in This Edition

This second edition of *America Compared* features **new selections** drawn especially from recent historical writings.

Volume I includes **seven new selections** that explore the international dimensions of early American history. These cover British colonial "folkways," the Atlantic economy, the Louisiana Purchase, American nationalism, the Second Great Awakening, transatlantic abolitionism, and the international women's rights movement.

Volume II includes **nine new selections** that place modern American history in comparative perspective. These feature such topics as Indian-white relations, settlement patterns on the frontier, American imperialism in the Philippines, World War I, and jazz music. They also include entirely new chapters on the Cold War and on globalization and American empire.

Consistent with the first edition, many of these readings situate domestic American events in their international context, but the new edition gives substantially increased attention to America's role in the world through diplomacy, war, and economic and cultural influence.

There are other changes that are intended to maximize the selections' impact and to deepen students' understanding of historical interpretation and method.

Expanded introductions to chapters and selections initiate more comparisons and contrasts between the selections and provide insights about the particular kinds of comparative approaches they use.

New and revised glossaries provide succinctly the most accurate and useful information on people, events, and terms found in the selections.

Expanded Questions to Consider consistently encourage students to connect, compare, and contrast different selections in the book.

More reference maps have been provided to clarify the geographic contexts of events in the United States and elsewhere.

I am gratified by the interest that teachers and students showed in the first edition of *America Compared,* and I have incorporated some of their suggestions for revisions. Partly because of their feedback, readers will find this edition more tightly organized, more focused in its approach, and more accessible in its information about events around the world.

Acknowledgments

Although I take sole responsibility for this book's contents, I am pleased to credit its existence to many people, from those who influenced my thinking over decades to others who offered specific assistance more recently. Years ago, my interest in comparative history was stimulated by inspiring teachers in graduate and undergraduate history programs: John Higham, Marcus Cunliffe, Robert Sklar, Robert Rosen, Stuart Samuels, and Jack Reece. Since then, numerous colleagues and friends have sustained our conversation on the global dimensions of American history, leading me to new insights and sources along the way as well as pointing out factual errors in my work. Among them I would like to thank Jonathan Beecher, Robert Blackey, Christopher Clark, Michel Cordillot, George Fredrickson, Jay Gordon, Nancy Green, Michael Kammen, Thomas Osborne, Jacques Portes, Allan Potofsky, Andrew Rotter, David Russo, Peter Stearns, Ian Tyrrell, and Francois Weil. I was fortunate to participate in the La Pietra conferences on Internationalizing United States History that took place from 1997 to 2000 under the joint auspices of New York University and the Organization of American Historians. At these meetings, ably conducted by NYU's Thomas Bender, several dozen scholars and teachers from around the world exchanged ideas about how American history should be rethought for a global age. Their insights profoundly shaped my thinking and are reflected in many ways in this edition of *America Compared*.

In practical terms, my plan for this reader crystallized when a curriculum development grant from the James Irvine Foundation enabled me to design an upper-division course on "United States History in Comparative Perspective" and then to revise my introductory U.S. history survey along similar lines. I am grateful to several groups of my students for testing most of the selections found here as well as others that were not chosen for the book. Saint Mary's College and its faculty have been generous in their support. An Alumni Faculty Fellowship Grant helped defray some of the first edition's permissions expenses, and the Frank J. Filippi Endowment provided some respite from full-time teaching in order to complete revisions for the second edition. My colleagues in the history department have suggested readings to include and offered encouragement for the project from the outset.

Colleagues at other institutions reviewed various drafts of this reader, in whole or in part, and made significant contributions to the final version of the first or second editions. I thank the following teachers and scholars for their thoughtful criticisms and suggestions.

For the second edition:

Amy E. Davis, University of California, Los Angeles
Anthony G. Gulig, University of Wisconsin — Whitewater
Paul A. Kramer, Johns Hopkins University
Victor Silverman, Pomona College

For the first edition:

Thomas A. Brown, Augustana College — Illinois
David B. Castle, Ohio University
Anthony Edmonds, Ball State University
Ellen Eslinger, DePaul University
Lisbeth Haas, University of California, Santa Cruz
Judith M. Ishkanian, University of California, Santa Barbara
Elizabeth A. Kessel, Anne Arundel Community College
Alexander W. Knott, University of Northern Colorado
Michael Kurtz, Southeastern Louisiana University
Everett Long, University of Wisconsin — Whitewater
James I. Matray, New Mexico State University
Elizabeth McKillen, University of Maine
Scott Nelson, College of William and Mary
T. Michael Ruddy, St. Louis University
Bruce J. Schulman, Boston University
Michael W. Schuyler, University of Nebraska at Kearney
Ron Spiller, Stephen F. Austin State University
William W. Stueck, University of Georgia
Thomas Templeton Taylor, Wittenberg University
Sara W. Tucker, Washburn University
William Woodward, Seattle Pacific University

At Houghton Mifflin, Leah Strauss, Christina Lembo, and Lisa Kalner Williams helped develop this edition of *America Compared,* which is sponsored by Sally Constable. Rosemary Jaffe oversaw the production process, while Michael Farmer, Stella Gelboin, Jan Kristiansson, Penny Peters, Lisa Jelly Smith, and Linda Sykes played important roles in various stages of the project. Special thanks again go to Menton Sveen, who got my foot in the door.

C. J. G.

AMERICA COMPARED

I

WHEN WORLDS COLLIDE

In 1492, Europeans and Native Americans discovered each other. It was a dramatic but not an isolated event. Long before Columbus, since the early Crusades set out for the Holy Land in the twelfth century and the Venetian Marco Polo returned from China in 1295, Europeans had been widening their horizons, searching for new trade routes and new territory to Christianize. Then for three and a half centuries after Columbus, European nations would continue to spread their influence around the globe. The land that eventually became the United States was one of many places where this expansion collided with the ways of indigenous peoples. As exploration evolved into conquest and colonization, rival European powers staked claims for dominion in Africa, Asia, and Australia as well as in the Americas. Although in the end the Europeans emerged politically dominant, in every place the lives of newcomers as well as natives would be transformed by their encounter.

Due to the global sweep of European expansion and the variety of places, peoples, and nations involved, there are many opportunities for comparative study that can illuminate early American history. The most direct approach is to compare societies on both sides of an encounter between natives and intruders on American soil. In the first selection of this chapter, David J. Weber uses the occasion of Francisco Coronado's gold-seeking expedition of 1540 to contrast the world view of the Zuni Indians of the American Southwest with the culture of their Spanish conquerors.

Another strategy is to compare the dynamics of European colonization in different places, even on different continents. In the second essay, George M. Fredrickson examines the impact of English and Dutch colonial policies on native peoples by comparing the British settlements in Virginia and Massachusetts with the Dutch outpost at Cape Town in South Africa.

1

Each of these essays pursues a different comparative strategy. Weber presents a static comparison that considers each group as representative: as his narrative proceeds, the Spanish become emblematic of all Europeans and the Zuni typify Native Americans. This approach highlights dramatic cultural differences between European invaders and native peoples (as well as a few similarities). But it should lead you to ask how other New World encounters, such as those between the Spanish and the Aztecs of Mexico or between the British and the Indians of North America's eastern seaboard, might present different pictures from the one Weber portrays.

In contrast to Weber's static approach, Fredrickson juxtaposes the developing histories of two different European settlements. This approach introduces a wider range of European actions and native responses, but it, too, raises questions about other cases and categories. How did Spanish settlement patterns (as opposed to the Spanish conquest) in the American Southwest compare with those of the British and Dutch? To what extent were differences in these colonies due to the colonizers' economic motives? to geography and climate? to contrasts between Catholicism and Protestantism? to the different native cultures the Europeans faced? The questions raised by the diversity of European collisions with native peoples may seem endless, but only by undertaking careful comparisons — and understanding the limits of any single case — can the most accurate picture of the North American encounter emerge.

Worlds Apart

DAVID J. WEBER

Two worlds met on American shores at the end of the fifteenth century. On one side of the Atlantic, monarchs consolidated their kingdoms and competed for domination of Europe's growing trade with Asia. On the other side of the ocean, two continents unknown to Europeans were teeming with hundreds of societies engaged in complex trading networks, yet unaware of lands beyond the seas. Columbus's voyage of 1492 bridged the gap of mutual ignorance. Soon the name "America" (derived from the Italian explorer Amerigo Vespucci) was given by Europeans to the so-called New World.

Of course, neither Vespucci nor Columbus "discovered" America, for it was already in-habited. What European explorers and colonizers called the wilderness was in fact home to as many as seven million natives north of Mexico alone, and perhaps four times that num-ber between the Rio Grande and Cape Horn. Their ancestors had crossed the Bering Strait from Asia more than ten thousand years earlier. These indigenous peoples, whom Columbus labeled "Indios" because he thought he had reached the East Indies, spread through North, Central, and South America and evolved astonishingly diverse cultures by the time the Spanish arrived. As David Weber points out, the variety of their languages, religions, and customs was greater than that of their European contemporaries. Despite these differences, most Native American societies shared common characteristics. They belonged to small polit-ical and economic units based upon kinship rather than ideology. They worked intimately with nature (which they believed was connected to God). They rewarded the use, rather than the possession, of land. And they aimed for a comfortable sustenance rather than an economic surplus.

The Spanish invaders brought with them a culture that was in many ways diametrically opposite, one increasingly organized around powerful nation-states. More systematically than Columbus, conquistadors such as Cortés, Pizarro, and Coronado imposed a powerful mix of European religious and secular notions upon Native Americans while conquering their land. Motivated by gold, glory, and the gospel, the Spanish had the confidence, organi-zation, and technology to subdue tribes that far outnumbered them. Indian peoples tried to use the alien intruders to their own advantage, occasionally with success. But as Weber points out, Europeans also had a secret weapon: disease. Perhaps the most tragic result of what anthropologists now call "the Columbian Exchange" was the unwitting transmission of European diseases such as smallpox, typhoid, diphtheria, and measles, which killed tens of millions of Native Americans. Far from a friendly encounter, the Spanish invasion was a catastrophic clash of two cultures.

One of those Spanish adventurers, the young nobleman Francisco Vázquez de Coronado, set out north of the Rio Grande in 1540 with a band of soldiers in search of the legendary Seven Cities of Gold. Like many European visions of New World riches, the cities of Antilia proved elusive. Instead, after months of wandering through the Southwest, Coronado and his sun-parched men came across the modest adobe pueblos of the Zuni people. In Weber's skilled hands, Coronado's conflict with the Zunis becomes the occasion for a sensitive — and sobering — contrast between Amerindian and European worlds in the sixteenth century.

GLOSSARY

ADELANTADO   An entrepreneur commissioned by the Spanish king to extend Christianity and Spanish rule into new territory. Financing their own expeditions, these military adventurers risked bankruptcy and death to gain titles of nobility, extensive lands, and political offices, which were the customary rewards for success.

AMAZONS   In classical mythology, a race of female warriors dwelling near the Black Sea; in the sixteenth century, a fabled tribe of women warriors in South America.

ARQUEBUS   A small-caliber long gun, predecessor to the musket and rifle.

CONQUISTADORS   The Spanish military adventurers who conquered the Native American civilizations of Mexico, Central America, and Peru.

CORONADO, FRANCISCO VÁZQUEZ DE (1510–1554)   The Spanish explorer who in 1540 pushed north of the Rio Grande in search of gold and encountered the pueblos of the Zuni tribes. Coronado reached as far as Kansas before returning to Mexico, where his expedition was regarded as a failure.

CORTÉS, HERNANDO (1485–1547)   The Spanish soldier who was chosen to command the armada sent to Mexico in 1519. He used alliances with other tribes to build his force's strength and defeated the Aztecs at the capital of Tenochtitlán (on the site of present-day Mexico City) in 1521.

ESPAÑOLA   Later called Hispaniola; the name Columbus gave to the island in the West Indies today comprising Haiti and the Dominican Republic.

IBERIA   The peninsula comprising Spain and Portugal.

INQUISITION   The court established by the medieval Roman Catholic Church to seek out and punish heretics, often brutally. Urged by Fernando and Isabel, Pope Sixtus IV endorsed the creation of an independent Spanish Inquisition in 1483. Among its eventual targets were Jewish and Islamic converts to Christianity, Protestants, and baptized Indian peoples of the Spanish colonies.

MOCTEZUMA (Montezuma II) (*circa* 1480–1520)   The last Aztec emperor of Mexico, whose indecision contributed to his people's defeat. Believing that Cortés was a legendary Aztec deity, he initially received the Spanish conquistador with gifts. Moctezuma died under mysterious circumstances during a subsequent battle with the Spanish invaders.

PATHOGEN   Any microorganism or virus that can cause disease.

PIZARRO, FRANCISCO (*circa* 1475–1541)   The Spanish soldier and explorer who came to the New World with Cortés and in 1534 conquered the Incas, claiming Peru for Spain.

RECONQUISTA   The long Spanish struggle to reconquer the Iberian Peninsula from the Muslims. Begun soon after the Muslim invasion of 711, it ended in 1492 when the last Moorish kingdom, Granada, fell.

REQUERIMIENTO   The Spanish notice to New World natives demanding that they accept the rule of the Spanish Crown and embrace Christianity. Those who refused could be conquered by force and enslaved.

ZUNIS   An Amerindian people whom the Spanish confronted in the American Southwest. Since the Zunis lived in adobe villages, the Spanish called them "Pueblos," and the Europeans associated their settlements with the mythical Seven Golden Cities of Antilia.

✸ ✸ ✸ ✸ ✸ ✸ ✸

E arly in the summer of 1540 a group of young Spanish adventurers, mounted on horseback, approached a Zuni village in what is today New Mexico. Led by Francisco Vázquez de Coronado, a thirty-year-old nobleman from the Spanish university town of Salamanca, the Spaniards had traveled for six months to reach this bleak and forbidding land of brilliant skies, broad vistas, red rocks, and sharp-edged mesas. Coronado had moved ahead of the main body of his army with a small group of mounted men, numbering little more than one hundred. Although summer was upon them, some of Coronado's men feared Indian arrows more than heat and wore protective coats of chain mail or thick buckskin. Coronado himself sported a plumed helmet and a suit of gilded armor that dazzled the eyes when it caught the rays of the sun.

The Spaniards had traveled long and hard. They had come through a stretch of uninhabited country and several men had died of hunger and thirst. "I thought we all should die of starvation if we had to wait another day," Coronado later recalled. But as the Spaniards made their way along the narrow plain of the Zuni River, they expected to be rewarded for their troubles by the sight of a splendid city — one of seven cities of a rich province that Indian informants had called "Cíbola." Instead, Coronado saw the sun-baked mud-brick walls of a modest town of multistory apartments, whose inhabitants displayed none of the gold, silver, or jewels that symbolized wealth to the Spaniards.

Unlike the Spaniards, the Zunis were dressed for the season. Coronado noted that "most of them are entirely naked except for the covering of their privy parts." Only able-bodied men remained at Cíbola. Women, youngsters, and the elderly had been sent away, for the Zunis did not intend to allow Coronado's party to enter, much less intend to provide the food and shelter that the Spaniards desperately needed. Coronado's arrival had not surprised the Indians. Their scouts had followed the strangers' movements. Even before Coronado reached the outskirts of their towns, Zunis had attempted an ambush. Now, with the Spaniards on the very edge of Cíbola, the natives sought supernatural assistance. With sacred golden cornmeal, Zuni warriors drew lines on the ground, warning the intruders not to pass beyond them.

While the Zunis waited to see if sacred cornmeal would turn back the unwelcome strangers, the Spaniards also appealed to metaphysical sources for help. Through an interpreter, probably a Pima Indian, Coronado assured the Zunis that he had come on a holy mission. The Spaniards read aloud a statement that summarized Spanish theology, explaining that Spain's monarchs had received temporal powers from a deity through one they called Pope. Spaniards issued this *requerimiento* or notification to natives throughout the New World — on occasion, legalistically reading it in Spanish to Indians who did not speak or understand their tongue. The requerimiento demanded that native peoples accept the dominion of the Spanish Crown and embrace Christianity.

If they resisted, their lands would be taken from them and they would be killed or enslaved. Although learned men in Spain had written the requerimiento and a notary probably attested to its reading at Zuni as the law required, the document failed to win the Zunis' obedience.

Instead of submitting, the Zunis fired arrows at the Spaniards. Coronado responded with orders to attack, crying out as an incantation the name of Saint James — *Santiago!* In the bloody battle that followed, the Zunis took several Spanish lives and Coronado himself almost perished. As he explained, "the Indians all directed their attack against me because my armor was gilded and glittering." Struck by rocks and arrows and thrown to the ground, only Coronado's sturdy helmet and the quick action of a companion saved his life. Within an hour, Spaniards armed with guns and steel swords fought their way into the natives' homes. The vanquished defenders fled, leaving behind storehouses of corn, beans, turkeys, and salt, to the delight of their hungry visitors.

Why the Zunis refused to permit Coronado's band to enter their town may never be fully understood, but it seems likely that they already knew enough about the mounted, metal-clad strangers not to welcome them. Like natives throughout northwestern Mexico, Zunis must have heard reports of Spanish slave hunters operating to the south. Then, too, a small Spanish scouting party headed by a black former slave, Esteban, had reached Zuni the year before Coronado arrived. The Zunis killed the black man, they explained to Coronado, because of liberties he had taken with their women. The natives, then, had ample reason to reject the overtures of the bizarrely costumed, bearded interlopers. Their resolve to keep the Spaniards out, however, may have been strengthened by the timing of Coronado's visit. He arrived during the culmination of the Zuni sacred summer ceremonies; his presence threatened to interrupt the return of Zuni pilgrims from the sacred lake and to endanger the prospects for abundant summer rains and a good harvest.

Whatever the reason for Zuni resistance to Coronado's soldiers, one essential fact seems clear. Nothing in either group's previous experience had prepared them to comprehend the other. Coronado's translators could convert words from one language to another, but they could not convey the deepest meaning of the requerimiento to the Zunis. Nor could Zunis convey to the Spaniards the meaning of lines of sacred cornmeal or the significance of their summer ceremonies. The two peoples who met at Zuni in 1540 came from different worlds.

I

The worlds of the sixteenth-century Iberians and their contemporaries in North America differed profoundly, but neither can be easily characterized because neither Iberians nor native North Americans constituted a uniform group. Physically, Amerindians were relatively homogeneous, having descended from waves of hunter-gatherers who had crossed the Bering Strait from Asia, beginning certainly as long as 14,000 years ago. Although they probably came in more than one migration and may have represented different populations, native Americans shared a number of physical, dental, and genetic characteristics that suggest their common ancestry in eastern Asia. Well over 90 percent of native North Americans, for example, have type O blood [a trait they share with East Asians]. As early immigrants from Asia dispersed throughout a hemisphere devoid of previous human occupants, their numbers grew and their cultures and languages became astonishingly diverse and complex. By the time Europeans first encountered them, even those natives who appeared to outsiders as a single "tribe," such as the peoples whom the Spaniards called Pueblos, often differed more than initial impressions suggested.

At Zuni, Coronado met the first of many peoples who lived in compact communities of esplanades, courtyards, and apartment houses, some rising to three and four stories. Spaniards called these prosperous urban-dwelling farmers Pueblos because in contrast to their nomadic neighbors they lived in towns, or *pueblos*. No central government linked the autonomous towns of the Pueblos, but they seemed to the earliest Spanish visitors to be one people. They grew maize, beans, cotton, and gourds in irrigated fields, dressed in cotton blankets and animal skins, and appeared to Coronado's men to have "the same ceremonies and customs." Despite superficial similarities, significant differences in Pueblo religious practices, and in political, social, and family organization probably existed then as they do now. Indeed, Pueblos spoke and still speak several mutually unintelligible languages. For example, Zunis speak Penutian, a language of some California peoples. Hopis, who live in what is today Arizona, speak a Uto-Aztecan language. Neither of these is related to the languages of the many Pueblo towns — numbering perhaps over ninety at the time of Coronado's arrival — that flourished farther east. In the watershed of the Rio Grande, residents of certain pueblos speak at least three mutually unintelligible forms of Tanoan (Tewa, Tiwa, and Towa, all of the Kiowa-Tanoan language family); Indians from still other pueblos speak Keresan, a language apparently unrelated to any other. Still other languages, such as Piro and Tompiro, were spoken by Pueblo groups that have become extinct.

The Pueblos offer only one example of the diversity of native North Americans. In California alone, with an indigenous population of perhaps 300,000 in the mid-eighteenth century, one linguist has estimated that Indians spoke "no fewer than 64 — and perhaps as many as 80 — mutually unintelligible tongues, further differentiated into an unknowably large number of dialects." These differences in language suggest differences in culture, but we will never know the full variety of native languages and cultures that existed in North America when Spaniards first arrived. Only two dozen or so of the languages of California natives have survived and many Indian languages[,] particularly in the Southeast, became extinct without having been recorded.

The variety of languages, religions, and customs of native North Americans in the sixteenth century appears to have been greater than that of their European contemporaries. Some Native Americans lived in large urban centers and others in family homesteads, and their social structures, governments, economies, religious beliefs, technologies, histories, and traditions ranged across a wide spectrum. They engaged in a variety of economic activities, from hunting, fishing, and gathering to irrigating fields and manufacturing tools and wares. Native trading networks ranged from the local level to the transcontinental. Yumas on the Colorado River, for example, knew of Coronado's arrival at Cíbola, nearly four hundred miles to the east, soon after the event, and Coronado's contemporary in the Mississippi Valley, Hernando de Soto, met Indians who owned turquoise that came from the direction of the sunset — from the Pueblos.

Notwithstanding the great variety of their cultures, it appears that many native North Americans held certain attitudes in common, some of which set them apart from Europeans in general and Spaniards in particular. In contrast to Spaniards, for example, most North American Indian people interacted more intimately with the natural world, placed less emphasis on the accumulation of surpluses of food and other goods, and tended to regard the users of land as possessing greater rights than the nominal owners of land.

At the time of Coronado's arrival, natives throughout North America lived in small units, none of which seems to have approached in size what Europeans would come to call a "state." Larger political or economic units existed in Arizona and New Mexico centuries before Coronado's arrival, but we know these so-called Anazasi and Hohokam peoples very imperfectly, largely through physical remains of their great urban centers and cliff dwellings (such as the ruins known today as Mesa Verde, Chaco Canyon, and Casa Grande) and through artifacts unearthed and interpreted by archaeologists. The same may be said of the great chiefdoms of what archaeologists call the Mississippian tradition, which reached its apogee throughout southeastern America between 1200 to 1450 A.D.

The native American bands, tribes, and chiefdoms that the Spaniards encountered were not only smaller than states but lacked some of the institutions of the emerging states of Europe, especially those designed to enforce social order — armies, police, and bureaucracies. As one anthropologist has reminded us, Amerindian communities were not "smaller, backward versions of European villages," but rather unique, nonwestern cultures "rooted in the obligations of kinship rather than the appeal of political ideology." Beyond this, few generalizations about native Americans at the time of Coronado's visit have value; it is more useful to consider individual tribes than to speak inaccurately of Indians in the aggregate.

II

In contrast to the cultures of native Americans, which had grown increasingly diverse since their ancestors crossed the Bering Strait, the cultures of the various peoples who inhabited the Iberian peninsula had begun to amalgamate by the sixteenth century. Unlike native Americans, who probably had a common group of ancestors, the peoples of Iberia descended from a wide variety of tribes and genetic strains from outside the peninsula, including Phoenicians, Greeks, Romans, Visigoths, Franks, Jews, and Muslims. Indeed, even these broad categories included still smaller tribes and bands, each with its discrete culture. Among the Muslim invaders of Spain, for example, were Arabs, Syrians, and Berbers from North Africa who were themselves splintered into subgroups.

Like North American Indians in the early sixteenth century, Spaniards were not a unified people and did not compose a single nation. The nation state that came to be called Spain had consisted of many tribes organized into kingdoms, such as Castile and Catalonia, which spoke distinct languages. These realms vied with one another for power, and factions within them fought ruinous civil wars.

In 1469, the marriage of Queen Isabel of Castile to Prince Fernando of Aragón brought two powerful kingdoms together in a condominium that laid the foundations of the modern Spanish state. Under these so-called Catholic Monarchs, the realms that would become Spain moved toward greater political and cultural homogeneity, although they never fully achieved it. Isabel and Fernando, for example, sought to insure Christian orthodoxy by establishing the Inquisition and prohibiting Jews and Muslims from living in Spain. Just as Castile came to dominate the other kingdoms, so its language, Castilian, became the most widely used in the peninsula and in America. Because Castile's monarchs took the position that the Spanish pope, Alexander VI, "gave" the New World to Castile in the celebrated papal donations of 1493, its monarchs believed themselves to have exclusive sovereignty over the newly discovered lands (excepting the east coast of South America, which they inadvertently gave to Portugal in the Treaty of Tordesillas in 1494).

Spain remained politically disunited and culturally heterogeneous in the sixteenth century (and in many ways it remains so yet today), but by 1492 its peoples possessed greater organizational unity and common hierarchical and religious values than did the peoples of North America. This relative political and cultural unity worked to Spain's advantage when its seafaring sons discovered another world. In North America, where decision making in most native societies depended on what one anthropologist has described as "a slow process of achieving consensus," Spaniards and other Europeans enjoyed a great advantage. Unencumbered by democratic constraints, Spanish leaders had authority to take quick, concerted action.

So, too, did Spaniards' prior experience with "infidels" from North Africa work to their benefit in the New World. A prolonged struggle to reconquer the Iberian Peninsula from Muslim invaders profoundly influenced Spanish values and institutions, making Spaniards uniquely suited among European nations to conquer, plunder, and administer the New World. The reconquest, or *reconquista,* of Iberia began soon after the Muslim invasion of 711; it did not end until 1492, when the combined forces of Isabel and Fernando entered the Alhambra in triumph as the last Moorish kingdom, Granada, capitulated. More than seven centuries of intermittent warfare along a shifting Christian-Muslim frontier had honed Spanish fighting skills and exalted the soldier to a status alongside the lawyer and the priest in Spanish society. Spanish warriors had fought to free their homeland from an alien religion as well as an alien people. Nourished by contention with Moors and Jews, Spanish Catholicism became uniquely vital and intense, its appetite for expansion unsatisfied by the expulsion of Moors and Jews from Spain.

Even before the fall of Granada in 1492, church and state had supported expansion beyond Iberia — into the western Mediterranean, Africa, and far out into the Atlantic. In conquering the Canary Islands (1478–96), which became the starting point for

Columbus's venture into the unknown, Spaniards had invoked the values of the reconquest and gained valuable experience in conquering infidels and colonizing overseas territory. With Columbus's return, it seemed only natural for Spaniards to carry their holy war to new frontiers across the sea, and to appeal to Saint James, the Killer of Moors — "Santiago Matamoros!" — against infidels in America, as Coronado did at Zuni. By the time Coronado entered the Pueblo world, Spaniards had refined their fighting skills and modified the institutions of conquest to adapt to new peoples and conditions in Española, Puerto Rico, Jamaica, Cuba, Mexico, and Peru, but the militant values of the reconquista continued to obtain. Indeed, for the next three hundred years, Hispanic soldiers in North America would continue to call upon the patron saint of the reconquest when they went into battle, and some Hispanic frontiersmen would regard Indians as synonymous with "Moors."

The Spanish struggle to control the New World and its peoples became, in effect, an extension of the reconquista — a moral crusade to spread Spanish culture and Catholicism to pagans in all parts of the Americas. Optimism born of religious zeal, ignorance, and intolerance gave Spain's onward-moving Christian soldiers another powerful advantage in their encounters with native Americans. Spaniards believed in a supreme being who favored them, and they often explained their successes as well as their failures as manifestations of their god's will. Was it not providential, for example, that Spaniards discovered America, with its fresh supply of infidels, in the same year they completed the long struggle against the Muslims in Iberia?

With or without the reconquista, Spaniards of the early sixteenth century would have believed that Providence sided with them. They knew that persons radically unlike themselves, who neither held Christian beliefs nor lived like Christians, were inferior human beings, perhaps even bestial, deserving of slavery or whatever other ills might befall them. Like other Christians, Spaniards understood that their god had given them "dominion" over all creatures on the earth, including these infidels. The god of the Christians, according to their holiest text, had ordered them to "be fruitful and multiply, and replenish the earth and subdue it: and have dominion over the fish of the sea, and over the fowl of the air, and over every living thing that moveth upon the earth." Pope Alexander VI, in a famous decree of 1493, asserted that he had the right, "by the authority of the Almighty God," to "give, grant, and assign" the New World to Isabel and Fernando so that they might convert its inhabitants. In a similar document, an earlier pope had cited biblical justification for such a papal donation of so-called pagan lands: "See, I have this day set thee over the nations and over the kingdoms, to root out, and to pull down, and to destroy, and to throw down, to build, and to plant."

Christianity thus imbued Spaniards with a powerful sense of the righteousness of their aggression against those natives in North America who threatened to block their advance. Nowhere was this clearer than in the requerimiento that Coronado read to the Zunis. Conquistadores had read this summons to countless indigenous Americans since it was drawn up in 1513. The requerimiento commanded Indians to "acknowledge the [Catholic] Church as the ruler and superior of the whole world, and the high priest called Pope, and in his name the king and queen of [Spain]." Those natives who did so, the document said, would be treated well. Those who did not were assured that "with the help of God we shall forcefully . . . make war against you . . . take you and your wives and your children and shall make slaves of them . . . and shall do to you all the harm and damage that we can." More zealous than any other European power in its attempt to fulfill what it saw as its legal obligations to the natives, Spain put them on notice that if they failed to obey, "the deaths and losses which shall accrue from this are your fault, and not that of their highnesses, or ours." True to their word, Coronado and his companions invaded Zuni and other recalcitrant pueblos, permitted their animals to eat the natives' crops, appropriated food and clothing as needed (no matter whether Indians went hungry or cold), and destroyed towns that offered armed resistance.

Christian belief contrasted sharply with the religious views of many of the natives of North America. Instead of the extraterrestrial god of the Spaniards, who had created nature but was not in nature, the North American natives generally believed in the interconnectedness of god and nature. Natives believed spirits resided in the natural world and not outside of it. The spiritual world of the Zunis, for example, was and is earth-centered. Zunis believe that their ancestors entered this world through a hole in the earth, and that after death a Zuni's spirit continues to reside in the world, in clouds or other natural phenomena depending on the role the deceased played while walking the path of life. Instead of offering prayers and sacrifices to a deity in a distant "heaven" as Christians do, Zunis direct their prayers and offerings toward the natural world. They seek to maintain harmony with earth, sky, animals, and plants, all of which are regarded as living beings capable of taking on several forms. Coronado was close to the mark when he noted that the Zunis "worship water, because they say that it makes the maize grow and sustains their life." Like other native North Americans, Zunis had apparently received no divinely inspired message to subdue the earth. Instead, they sought to live in harmony with it, although in practice they, like other native Americans, contributed to environmental degradation. Similarly, although they engaged in warfare, Zunis sought harmony with their neighbors, preferring accommodation and compromise to aggression (by no means a universal trait among North American Indians). The Pueblos, two members of the Coronado expedition correctly noted, seemed "more given to farming than to war."

Spaniards had material as well as spiritual motives to subdue the earth. Like other Europeans, Spaniards placed high value on gold and silver and were willing to suffer extraordinary hardships to obtain these minerals. Cortés exaggerated only slightly when he sent a message to Moctezuma saying that the Spaniards had a disease of the heart that only gold could cure. In contrast, gold and silver held little intrinsic value for most native North Americans until they discovered the value of those metals to Europeans. "These Indians do not covet riches," one seventeenth-century observer wrote of the natives of Florida, "nor do they esteem silver or gold."

For Spaniards, the accumulation of gold and silver was not merely a means to an end, but an end in itself. Thus, men with means to live comfortably gambled all they had in order to acquire more, and the Spanish Crown encouraged their risk taking. Free enterprise had fueled Castile's reconquest of the Muslims and had set precedents that would carry over to the New World. In fighting the Muslims the king of Castile licensed an entrepreneur, or *adelantado* (what the English would later call a proprietor), to push forward the frontiers of Christianity. These military chieftains risked their own capital, knowing that success would bring titles of nobility, land, broad governmental powers over the conquered domain, and the right to part of the spoils of war. Under this arrangement, the rewards for the adelantado could be considerable. So could rewards for those warriors whom he engaged to follow him, many of them villagers whose poverty heightened their ambition and whose experience taught them that honor and wealth could be more easily won through plunder than through manual labor. Since these commissioned bands of warriors enabled Spain's monarchs to add to their realm without risking their own capital, they extended the system to the New World. Typically, then, Coronado financed his own expensive invasion of New Mexico. Since he had no personal fortune, however, he relied upon his patron, the viceroy, and his wealthy wife, Beatriz de Estrada, daughter of the treasurer of New Spain, as Mexico was then called.

Thus, even before the discovery of America, a peculiarly Spanish institution and ethos had developed that would enable the future conquerors of America, most of them predatory young men like those who accompanied Coronado, to serve God, country, and themselves at the same time — with no sense that these goals might be contradictory. To the contrary, if Spaniards served their god well, it seemed only right that he should reward them. One soldier who fought in the conquest of Mexico explained the matter clearly: Spaniards had left Europe "to serve God and his Majesty, to give light to those who were in the darkness and to grow rich as all men desire to do."

In addition to this ethos, hardened in the crucible of the reconquest of Iberia, the conquistadores brought to the New World overheated imaginations, fired by the popular literature of their day — romantic novels posing as history. Literate and illiterate alike knew the stories contained in these widely circulated romances. The novels extolled knight-errantry in exotic lands, where brave men found wealth and glory. They exalted courage, stoicism, and heroism, and glorified the warrior as the ideal of Spanish manhood. Manifestly works of fiction, these romances came to be regarded as fact by their ordinary readers or listeners. As the line between fantasy and reality blurred in the popular imagination, it became easy to believe in the existence of the fabulous places described in these "lying histories," as some critics termed them. Who could doubt that beyond the horizon there existed enchanted islands, Amazons, and fountains of youth? Then, too, like many other Europeans of their time, Spaniards imagined the existence of an earthly paradise in some faraway place, inhabited by peoples who still lived in an Edenic state of grace. Sophisticated critics might scoff. One chronicler, for example, noted that it was not the fountain of youth that made men young, but the search itself, which caused a "reversion to infantile actions and intelligence." But among most sixteenth-century Spaniards raised in an age of faith, skepticism remained subordinate to the will to believe.

Reports of the Seven Cities had beguiled Coronado, leading him to abandon the comforts of home and position to venture into the unexplored interior of North America. The Seven Cities of Antilia, said to have been founded by seven Portuguese bishops who had fled across the Atlantic during the Muslim invasion of Iberia, existed so firmly in the popular imagination that fifteenth-century mapmakers drew an imaginary island in the Atlantic called Antilia. At first, Europeans believed that Columbus had landed on Antilia in 1492, and so the West Indies came to be called the Antilles. Five years after Columbus, John Cabot landed on the shores of New England and named that area the "Seven Cities." The cities proved elusive, but that seemed no reason to doubt their existence. Thus, when reports reached Mexico in the late 1530s of seven cities to the north, Coronado willingly risked his life and his wife's fortune to find them. Coronado expected to find seven cities, and he refused to be disappointed. He reported to the viceroy that seven Zuni towns existed, although archaeological evidence suggests only six Zuni pueblos in Coronado's day.

Like his Spanish contemporaries, Coronado's view of reality had been shaped by literature and lore. He projected his fantasies onto an unfamiliar world, where they became superimposed on the garbled translations of stories that Spaniards heard from the natives. But the dreams of Coronado and his fellow conquistadores floated over a bedrock of reality. Coronado knew of the extraordinary discoveries of Cortés and Pizarro, where fact seemed more fantastic than fiction. In this new world, dreams had come true. It seemed reasonable to suppose that beyond the horizon a new Mexico might await discovery.

So it was that fact and fantasy intertwined to shape the minds and motives of those Iberians who came to the New World in the first decades after its discovery. Today's conventional wisdom holds that the native Americans lived in a world of myth and legend while Europeans inhabited a world of rationality and well-grounded religious faith. In truth, each world contained elements of the mythic and the rational, but those worlds did not harmonize well with one another.

III

The coming together of Spaniards and Indians in North America represented more than an encounter of peoples with different values and institutions. Spaniards arrived in the New World with a variety of practical advantages that enabled them to turn many of their dreams into realities. One advantage was technology. Europeans living in an age of iron and steel entered a hemisphere where technology remained in the stone age.

At the time of their first encounter with outsiders from across the sea, native Americans living in the Southeast knew how to build and navigate large, swift dugout canoes that could carry people and goods along coastal waters and from island to island in the Caribbean. Spaniards, however, sailed more sophisticated craft than the natives had ever known. In the century before the discovery of America, the Europeans, with Iberians in the vanguard, had mastered the winds. Innovations in reckoning latitude, shipbuilding, and rigging had made Spanish vessels suitable for blue-water sailing, beyond the continental shelf. No matter how cramped, crowded, filthy, or vermin-infested their vessels and how much the uncomfortable passengers and often-mutinous mariners suffered from spoiled food, acrid water, illness, and monotony, Spaniards could cross the Atlantic void and return again to Spain. The disparity between European and

Indian mastery of the seas determined that encounters between the two peoples would take place in the New World, rather than in the Old.

Carried to American shores by the new technologies and navigational know-how, Spaniards found that the technological superiority of their weaponry — steel swords, guns, and explosives — gave them tactical and psychological advantages that helped them defeat overwhelming numbers of natives on their home ground. Weapons, for example, seemed to give Coronado the edge in storming Zuni, where the Pueblos held a defensive position with superior numbers. "God," a Spanish priest in New Mexico later observed, "hath caused among the Indians so great a fear of [Spanish soldiers] and their arquebueses that with only hearing it said that a Spaniard is going to their pueblos they flee." Or, as a Spanish priest in Florida put it, "Gunpowder frightens the most valiant and courageous Indian and renders him slave to the White man's command."

Sixteenth-century Spaniards, some of whom were literate, also enjoyed an advantage in what one writer has called the "technology" of manipulating symbols. "Your Majesty, language is the perfect instrument of empire," the Bishop of Avila reportedly told Queen Isabel upon presenting her with the first grammar of a modern European language. Not only could Spanish leaders read and write, but those skills may have honed their analytic abilities and produced superior modes of gathering intelligence. Spaniards, then, may have been more adroit than certain Indians at interpreting symbols or signs and using them to manipulate the natives. As Hernando de Alarcón made his way up the Colorado River in search of Coronado, for example, an Indian asked "whether we had sprung from the water or the earth or descended from the sky." Alarcón, like other Spaniards who were eager to convince the natives of their extraworldly powers, answered that he had come as a messenger from the sun, and that he was the son of the sun. North American natives, however, also used symbols to manipulate Spaniards, as Coronado and other explorers soon discovered. Many Spanish explorers in North America came to believe, in the words of one chronicler, that Indians were "born liars and in the habit of always telling falsehoods," even as they themselves lied to Indians.

Europeans gained further advantages from animals, plants, and microbes that were commonplace in the Old World but not previously known in the New. Columbus's voyage marked the beginning of a lengthy and profound biological exchange between the two worlds. Although the exchange went both ways, it initially facilitated the European domination of North America.

North American natives, for example, had only one domestic four-legged animal, the dog. Whatever their virtues as man's best friend, dogs clearly are inferior sources of food and leather and less effective beasts of burden than two European domestic quadrupeds — horses and cattle. Without competitors or predators in the new American environment, some European animals flourished and played a vital role in the military campaigns of their Spanish masters. Herds of pigs and cattle provided a mobile larder for the Spanish invaders. Horses, some of them trained for war, increased the range and speed of the conquistadores' movement on land, just as their vessels increased their mobility on the water, and also gave Spaniards a psychological advantage. "The most essential thing in new lands is horses," one of Coronado's soldiers wrote upon returning to Mexico. "They instill the greatest fear in the enemy and make the Indians respect the leaders of the army." Similarly, greyhounds, unknown in America but long trained by Europeans for hunting and warfare, guarded the Spaniards' camps, tore limbs from Indian adversaries, and frightened others into submission. Although it was a rare occurrence on Coronado's expedition, one of his lieutenants set dogs loose upon an Indian in order to extract information from him.

Invisible organisms, unknown in the western hemisphere before the 1500s, took passage on Spanish ships and committed silent carnage. Native Americans certainly did not live free of illness before the arrival of Europeans. In Southwestern America, for example, they suffered the ravages of parasites, tuberculosis, and dental pathology. Contagious "crowd" diseases endemic to Europe, however, seem to have been unknown in America — including smallpox, measles, diphtheria, trachoma, whooping cough, chicken pox, bubonic plague, typhoid fever, scarlet fever, amoebic dysentery, and influenza. These became epidemic killers in the New World, where natives had no prior exposure and, therefore, had acquired no immunities against them. In central Mexico alone, some 8 million people, perhaps one-third of the native population, perished within a decade of the Spaniards' arrival. The vast majority of those who died probably succumbed to disease. Pathogens, then, served as valuable if accidental allies of the Spanish conquistadores.

Among Europeans, Spaniards held no monopoly on the introduction of disease to the New World, but far more natives apparently perished from diseases introduced by Spaniards in the first half of the sixteenth century than at any other time. Two common European maladies, smallpox and measles, struck this virgin population with deadly force, producing what one specialist has described as "possibly . . . the greatest demographic disaster in the history of the world." The most extreme estimate suggests that during a great pandemic of 1519–24, smallpox alone took the lives of three of every four Indians who came in contact with it. A more conservative estimate places the death rate at one out of every three. Disease not only took native American lives but demoralized grieving survivors and weakened their resolve to resist if not to live. The same diseases that devastated and dispirited Indians raised the spirits of Europeans and strengthened their faith in a divine providence. One of Cortés's followers put it succinctly when he explained the fall of the Aztec capital of Tenochtitlán: "When the Christians were exhausted from war, God saw fit to send the Indians smallpox."

No one doubts that a large number of native North Americans died from diseases of European origin, but scholars disagree about the rapidity and extent of the disaster. Estimates of the number of natives living in North America when Europeans first arrived vary considerably. The question may he unanswerable, but scholars in the twentieth century have tended to accept increasingly higher figures. Many experts believe the native population of the entire hemisphere in 1492 exceeded 100 million although more conservative estimates put the total at half that number and below. In America north of Mexico, recent estimates range as high as 18 million with 7 million representing a more conservative conjecture (5 million in the area of the present-day conterminous United States). In comparison, the combined kingdoms of Castile and Aragón probably did not exceed 7 million in 1492, and the population of all Europe, eastern and western, may have stood at about 70 million in 1500.

Ironically, then, it may be that disease, the least visible trans-Atlantic baggage, was Spain's most important weapon in the conquest of America. Had diseases worked against them, Spaniards might have found North America as impermeable as sixteenth-century West Africa — a "white man's grave" where indigenous diseases formed a deadly shield against encroaching Europeans and their animals. Instead, disease in North America worked so much in the favor of Europeans in thinning the native population that it is more accurate to think of subsequent generations of "settlers" as re-settlers of the continent.

Although it might be argued that disease was the single most important element in assuring the Spaniards' quick victory over the natives, such an assertion cannot be proved. In practice Spaniards took advantage of a combination of circumstances — institutional, technological, and natural — that they believed their god had presented to them. These circumstances became a potent mixture when blended with the powerful motives of individual Spaniards who journeyed into a new world to pursue particular religious, imperial, and personal goals. This heady mixture of motives and circumstances enabled the sons and daughters of Iberia to penetrate a world that they dimly understood and to make a stunningly rapid series of discoveries and conquests in lands where natives vastly outnumbered them. In the process, Spaniards began to transform that new world, even as it began to transform them.

QUESTIONS TO CONSIDER

1. Describe some features of the Native American cultures that existed in the Southwest before the arrival of the Spanish. Were they homogeneous or diverse? How did Native American social and cultural patterns compare with those of Europeans?

2. What were Spain's reasons for conquering the Americas? Was there a conflict between spiritual and material motives? In what ways did the Spanish transfer the ideas and practices of the *reconquista* (their campaign against Muslims in Spain) to their encounter with Amerindians?

3. Despite the conventional contrast between myth-centered Native Americans and rational Europeans, "each world contained elements of the mythic and the rational, but those worlds did not harmonize well with one another." Using examples from the reading, explain what Weber means by this.

4. It seems astonishing that within a few generations a small invading force of Europeans successfully subjugated millions of Native Americans. What political, cultural, technological, and biological advantages did the Spanish have over Indian peoples in the contest of worlds? How do these advantages help explain Spanish dominance? How might other factors that Weber omits, such as divisions between Native peoples, have contributed to the Spanish conquest?

5. How would other New World collisions, such as those between the Spanish and the Aztecs of Mexico or between the British and North American Indians, produce similar or different comparisons from the one that Weber presents?

2

Two Colonial Frontiers

George M. Fredrickson

In the century and a half after Columbus landed, Spain vied with Portugal, France, England, and Holland for territorial empire in the "New World." England was among the later entrants in this race for colonies. Only after the settlement at Jamestown established by the Virginia Company in 1607 had survived its precarious infancy could England exhibit a permanent foothold in the Americas. By that time, Spain ruled most of Central and South America except Brazil (declared by the pope to be Portugal's) and boasted a great cathedral and a thriving university in Mexico City. One year after the Jamestown landing, Samuel Champlain claimed Quebec for the French, and two decades later the Dutch, in their bid for a stake in the New World, bought New Amsterdam (later New York City) from the Indians.

Each of the European rivals operated under different colonizing plans, which affected the indigenous peoples in divergent ways. Historians often contrast the Spanish, French, and English domains in the New World as empires of conquest, commerce, and settlement, respectively. Whereas the Spanish tried to incorporate Indians into a hierarchical social system run by an Iberian elite, the French were content to exchange furs with hunting tribes at profitable trading posts, and the British generally forced Indians aside in order to plant white settlements. In the following essay, historian George Fredrickson pushes such comparisons beyond the New World. Noting that colonies in the Americas were founded at the same time that Europeans were penetrating Africa and Asia, Fredrickson casts a more global net for his study. His comparison groups are the English colonies on the North American seaboard and the Dutch colony at Cape Town in South Africa. Both were established in the 1600s and became "white settler societies" of northern Europeans. And in both places the struggle between colonists and indigenous peoples for possession of the land created the conditions under which "white supremacy" was defined and enforced.

Things did not start out exactly that way. Cape Town was founded not as an extensive colonial settlement, but as a supply station for Dutch ships engaged in the lucrative East Indies trade. The British, also interested in trade with Asia, initially probed the North American coast for a "northwest passage" through the continent to the Pacific Ocean and Asia. In the early 1600s, however, they began to establish settlements at Virginia and Massachusetts Bay that were intended to grow into full-scale agricultural colonies. Thus, Fredrickson distinguishes between an English plan of settlement and a Dutch perspective of commercial enterprise. In the British case, trade with the indigenous peoples (the eastern Indian tribes) was less important than the desire to establish territorial claims and expropriate land. Pursuing this goal led the English colonists to decimate the natives and suppress their culture. Settlers in New England justified this policy by proclaiming the superiority of "civilized" Christians over "savage" heathens. For the Dutch, on the other hand, a trading motive did not require large-scale conquest of territory. Instead, it encouraged the South African colonists to tolerate coexistence with the natives (the Khoikhoi, also known as Hottentots) as long as they cooperated in the commercial relationship.

Eventually, whites who were determined to expand the limits of both colonial frontiers — farmers in backcountry North America and "trekboers," or herders, in southern Africa — brought diseases that killed many natives and provoked wars that took away most of their land. To those who were victimized by the whites' encroachment, Fredrickson admits, it mattered little that the plans and racial ideas of the English and Dutch colonists differed somewhat. In both cases the end result was tragically similar: dispossession and dependence for the natives. Still, Fredrickson's account shows how ideology and economics led to different forms of subjugation in the two colonies, with important implications for the future. In South Africa the Khoikhoi were taken on as a cheap and exploitable labor force by the Dutch colonists. Their mixed-race descendants formed the core of a population group known as the "Cape Coloreds." Surviving North American Indians, on the other hand, were kept apart from white society and compelled to migrate westward to a moving frontier, where the battle between "savagery" and "civilization" would be reenacted again and again.

GLOSSARY

ASSIMILATION   The process by which one group adopts the cultural norms and social patterns of another group.

BOERS   Descendants of the Dutch colonists in South Africa.

DUTCH EAST INDIA COMPANY   The company granted a monopoly on Dutch trade east of the Cape of Good Hope. Chartered by the Dutch government in 1602, the company had its own military and naval forces and was authorized to wage war or make peace within its domain. By compelling local Asian rulers to grant it trading privileges, the company routed its Portuguese rivals and dominated the spice trade for over a century.

ETHNOCENTRISM   Belief in the superiority of one's own ethnic group.

INDENTURED SERVANTS   Men or women bound to a master for a period of years, normally from three to seven. The master owned their labor and in return often paid for their passage to the colonies and provided food and shelter. Following their service, they were given money, tools and clothing, or land.

KHOIKHOI   A native tribe of South Africa, called Hottentots by whites. They were a pastoral, transhumant society whose population was decimated as Dutch colonists took over their lands in the seventeenth century. Over time, many intermarried with whites and Asians to form a mixed-race group known as the Cape Coloreds. Others fled northward, where their descendants live in villages in present-day Namibia.

KING PHILIP'S WAR (1675–1676)   A war pitting a coalition of eastern tribes led by the Wampanoag chief Metacomet (Philip) against the New England colonists and their tribal allies. Indian raids burned many New England towns and killed as many as a thousand settlers. But colonial forces eventually crushed their adversaries, effectively ending Indian resistance in the area.

MERCANTILISM   An economic policy followed by the major European trading nations from the sixteenth through the eighteenth centuries. Mercantilist governments sought to increase exports and restrict imports with the hope of dominating international trade and accumulating gold and precious metals. Colonies were supposed to provide crops and raw materials and serve as markets for the home country's products.

NARRAGANSETTS   An Indian tribe of Eastern Algonkian linguistic stock who occupied much of Rhode Island when English colonists arrived. The Narragansetts joined the Wampanoags in King Philip's War against the English.

NORTHWEST PASSAGE   A route from Europe to Asia through the northern regions of North America, which various European explorers sought from the 1530s to the 1850s. It eluded them because of the facts of geography and the frigid Arctic climate.

POWHATAN (*circa* 1550–1618)   The Algonkian chief who headed the confederacy of thirty tribes living in settlements along Virginia and Chesapeake Bay at the time the Jamestown settlers arrived. The English seized his best land but secured temporary peace through John Rolfe's marriage to Powhatan's daughter Pocahontas in 1614.

RALEIGH, SIR WALTER (1552–1618)   An English naval commander and writer and favorite of Queen Elizabeth I. She gave him vast estates in Ireland and a patent authorizing colonization in North America. Raleigh organized the unsuccessful attempt to found a settlement at Roanoke Island.

ROANOKE ISLAND   An island off the coast of present-day North Carolina that was the site of the earliest English colony in North America. The colony was established in 1585–1587 under the absentee direction of Sir Walter Raleigh. Its settlers had vanished without a trace by the time additional supplies were brought from England in 1591.

TRANSHUMANT   Moving seasonally in search of pasture for livestock.

TREKBOERS   Itinerant Dutch herdsmen who pushed inland on the South African frontier, displacing and often provoking conflict with the native Khoikhoi.

VATTEL, EMMERICH (1714–1767)   The Swiss diplomat and legal philosopher who codified much of international law. His theories justified the land rights of "civilized" cultivators over "savage" hunters and gatherers.

WAMPANOAGS   An Indian tribe of Eastern Algonkian linguistic stock who inhabited territory in Rhode Island and Massachusetts. Their leader Massasoit welcomed the English and remained at peace with them despite land disputes and epidemics. His son Metacomet (Philip) organized an intertribal coalition that sought to drive away English settlers in King Philip's War.

✯ ✯ ✯ ✯ ✯ ✯ ✯

In May of 1607, three small ships sailed up the James River from Chesapeake Bay in search of a site for the first permanent English colony in North America. The prospective settlers chose a peninsula that had the clear disadvantage of being low and swampy. But it did provide good anchorage, and the fact that it was a virtual island made it defensible against possible attacks by hostile Indians. By giving a high priority to their physical security, the colonizers showed an awareness that this was not an empty land but one that was already occupied by another people who might well resist their incursion. Unlike earlier attempted settlements, Jamestown was not so much an outpost as a beachhead for the English invasion and conquest of what was to become the United States of America.

Forty-five years later, another three ships, flying the flags of the Dutch Republic and its East India Company, anchored in Table Bay at the Cape of Good Hope. Their purpose was to establish a refreshment station where ships could break the long voyage between the Netherlands and the Company's main settlement at Batavia in Java. The expedition of 1652 was under the command of Jan van Riebeeck, who was instructed to build a fort, plant a garden that would provide fresh fruit and vegetables for the scurvy-ridden sailors, and obtain meat through an amicable cattle trade with the local indigenes — the yellowish-skinned herders known to the Europeans as "Hottentots." By carrying out these orders, Van Riebeeck unwittingly initiated the train of events that would result in the emergence and expansion of a white-dominated society in southern Africa.

From the perspective of the seventeenth century, these occurrences were simply two examples among many of the early penetration by Europeans into Africa, Asia, and the Americas. But for the modern historian of comparative colonization, they have the special significance that they constituted the beginnings of two of the first "white settler societies" emanating from northern Europe. Unlike the tropical "exploitation colonies" being established by the Dutch, the English, and the French in the East and West Indies, both the Cape of Good Hope and the regions claimed by the English on the eastern coast of North America were temperate in climate and potentially attractive to white colonists as permanent homes rather than uncomfortable and unhealthful places where fortunes could be made and then brought back to Europe. Furthermore, the indigenous populations, at least those encountered in the early stages of settlement, lacked the population density and the developed forms of political and economic organization that were to preserve most Asian and African societies from large-scale European settlement. Since these regions also lacked the readily available mineral resources that stimulated Spanish colonization of South and Central America, as well as the opportunities for lucrative trade in scarce commodities that existed in the East, land for agriculture and grazing quickly became the source of wealth or sustenance most desired by the European invaders. The struggle with the original occupants for possession of the land constituted the essential matrix for a phase of race relations that began when the first colonists disembarked and persisted along a moving frontier until late in the nineteenth century. . . .

. . . [T]he Elizabethan Englishmen who cast covetous eyes on the New World were not at first entirely clear in their own minds about how best to profit from this new sphere of activity and what role the indigenous peoples would play in their enterprises. For some, North America was regarded as a geographical obstacle to be overcome by the finding of a "northwest passage" to the Orient and its precious commodities. Only after the fruitless attempts of Martin Frobisher and John Davis to discover such a passage in the 1570s and 80s did their attention focus on the establishment of settlements in the coastal areas between Canada and Florida that were claimed by England. Colonization of this region would break the Spanish monopoly on the New World and give the English a base from which to counter the expansionism of an arch-rival in the struggle for world power.

The individuals and companies that showed an interest in exploiting this opportunity saw two possible ways to do it. Some of the early promotional literature emphasized trade as the greatest source of potential profit. Entrepreneurs who sought to encourage investment in expeditions designed to establish mercantile relationships with the American Indians envisioned the barter of English woolens for a variety of desirable commodities that indigenous societies might be capable of producing, including perhaps the gold and silver that the Spanish had extracted from Indians elsewhere in the Americas. . . . But some of the most influential proponents of colonization saw native society as too primitive and limited in economic capacity to produce what the English wanted. The elder Richard Hakluyt, who, along with his nephew of the same name, was one of the principal spokesmen for expansion to America, wrote a paper for the guidance of Sir Walter Raleigh in 1585 arguing that the development of American resources required the English to "conquer a countrey or province in climate & soil of Italie, Spaine, or the Islands, from whence we receive our Wines and Oiles, and to man it, to plant it, and to keepe it, and to continue the making of Wines and Oiles able to serve England."

This image of an English agricultural colony producing crops that England could not raise at home and was currently forced to import from its enemies was flawed in its notion of what could actually be grown in places like Virginia but prophetic in its anticipation of the principal role that New World colonies would play, or were supposed to play, in the development of a mercantilist empire. In such a scheme, the Indians could serve only two conceivable functions — either they would be exterminated and driven away to make room for an exclusively English agricultural population or they would be converted and "civilized" so that they could become productive workers under English supervision. The elder Hakluyt and his contemporaries clearly anticipated the latter result; the only question in their minds was whether or not it would be necessary to use force to bring the Indians "in subjection and to civilitie." But what if the indigenes proved unwilling or unable to shed their own way of life and adopt that of the English? . . .

The dreams of the Elizabethan promoters came to fruition in the early seventeenth century when a permanent colony was established in Virginia. Unlike the earlier and abortive settlement of the 1580s on Roanoke Island, the Jamestown colony soon came to be regarded as "a permanent community" — "an extension of England overseas." After the failure of early attempts to find precious minerals, the struggling settlement turned primarily to agriculture carried on by the colonists. The local Indians — a confederation of Algonkian tribes under the paramount chieftainship of Powhatan — were the object of confused and conflicting attitudes and policies during the first fifteen years of settlement. During the early "starving times," the indigenes sometimes offered a model of cooperation by providing food from their own reserves that enabled the colony to survive. But the recipients of their charity manifested an early version of the stereotype of "the Indian giver" by suspecting some ulterior motive or treachery in this generosity. As a cosmopolitan man of the Renaissance who had observed cultural diversity in many parts of the world, Captain John Smith manifested an intelligent and sometimes sympathetic interest in the Indian way of life, but he was also an early advocate and practitioner of the view that the native Americans were inherently untrustworthy and responded better to force and intimidation than to friendly persuasion. Other early spokesmen for the colony deplored the Indians' "gross defection from the true knowledge of God," but conceded that their culture showed the rudiments of a "civilized" existence.

The belief that Indians were potential raw material for assimilation into an English-dominated society was an influential viewpoint in Virginia before 1622, and a process of acculturation actually began that might conceivably have led to a bi-racial community if conflicts of interest had not intervened. Plans were made for Indian conversion and education that went so far as to encourage the adoption of Indian children by white settlers. Indians were permitted to work in white settlements as day laborers, and some Englishmen — in defiance of the law — equipped themselves to be cultural intermediaries by fleeing from the settlement and taking up residence in Indian villages. But the spirit of voluntarism and persuasion that could have made for some form of accommodation was counteracted by a belief that Powhatan was too strong and independent for the safety and security of the colony and that his power must be broken. In 1609, Sir Thomas Gates was dispatched to Virginia as governor with instructions to conquer the Chesapeake area and make the Indian tribes direct tributaries of the English, who could then use essentially feudal precedents to require chieftains to make annual payments of corn, skins, and other commodities and also submit to labor requisitions. The smallness of the English settlement made this policy difficult to enforce, but it did provide the stimulus for such coercive and unfriendly actions as the kidnapping of Powhatan's daughter Pocahontas in 1613 as a way of bringing the paramount chief to tolerate the English presence. Pocahontas' subsequent marriage to the colonist John Rolfe created the basis for an uneasy peace that lasted until the Indian uprising of 1622.

The vacillation between accommodation and coercion that characterized this earliest phase of Indian–white relations in British North America was due less to confusion about whether the "savages" were well-disposed and tractable or naturally hostile and unreliable than to the actual state of power relationships between the two peoples. The

C Smith taketh the King of Pamavnkee prifoner 1608

*Against the background of fighting between Indian warriors and the badly out-
numbered English, Captain John Smith of Jamestown captures the Pamunkey
chief Opechancanough, Powhatan's elder brother, who refused to supply the
Virginia colonists with corn in 1608. (Rare Books and Manuscripts Division,
The New York Public Library, Astor, Lenox and Tilden Foundation.)*

dominant view was that the Indians, however friendly they might seem, were not to be
trusted. A member of the first expedition up the river from Jamestown in 1607 showed
the power of prejudice to master direct experience when he wrote that the Indians
were "naturally given to trechery, howbeit we could not finde it in our travell up the
river, but rather a most kind and loving people." Perhaps the fact that Indians had
apparently wiped out the earlier English settlement on Roanoke Island had strengthened the stereotype of savage treachery that already had a strong hold on the European
mind. But so long as the English lacked the numbers to impose their will directly on the
Indians, they had good reason to deal cautiously and pragmatically with communities
that still had the potential strength and cohesion to drive them into the sea. (The
English were fortunate that Powhatan refrained from making a full-scale attack on the

settlement while he still had the probable advantage. It appears that he hoped to use an alliance with the whites to extend his own authority over tribes of the Chesapeake region that remained outside his confederacy.) But the "Great Migration" of 1618–23, which reportedly increased the population of the colony from 400 to 4,500, altered the balance of power. Furthermore, the simultaneous rise of tobacco cultivation gave the colony an economic foundation in the form of a profitable staple for export and stimulated rapid territorial expansion at the expense of the Indians. As a result, the earlier acceptance of a limited degree of coexistence and interdependence was replaced by a growing sense of the Indian as intolerable obstacle to white ambitions.

The Indians quite naturally viewed the rapid expansion of white settlement with alarm. Their own hopes for cooperation and coexistence were being shattered by the encroachment of tobacco farms on their hunting lands and by the increasing arrogance and disrespect manifested by the colonists. Consequently, they struck back in 1622 by attacking the settlements and wiping out about a third of the total population of the colony. But the "massacre" of 1622 turned out to be more disastrous for the Indians than for the colonists; for the colony survived and launched a devastating counterattack on Indian society. Thereafter, all thoughts of "civilizing" the natives and sharing the land with them on some mutually agreeable basis were jettisoned in favor of a naked policy of aggression. According to one colonial spokesman, "Our hands which before were tied with gentlenesse and fair usage are now set at liberty by the treacherous violence of the Sausages [savages]. . . . So that we . . . may now by right of Warre, and law of Nations, invade the Country, and destroy them who sought to destroy us: whereby we shall enjoy their cultivated places. . . . Now their cleared grounds in all their villages . . . shall be inhabited by us, whereas heretofore the grubbing of woods was the greatest labour."

. . . [T]he resistance of the indigenous people to English encroachment and domination was countered by policies of extermination and expropriation, and . . . the image of the treacherous savage who perversely resisted the benefits of civilization could be invoked to justify genocide and dispossession. The events in Virginia were to be recapitulated in most of the other English colonies of North America. An early phase during which the beginning of white agricultural activity was accompanied by trade, mutual assistance, and diplomacy was quickly superseded by a period of accelerated white expansion which threatened the territorial base of the indigenous societies. The fact that land was sometimes acquired by methods that met European standards for legitimate purchase did not alter the destructive nature of the process from the Indian perspective.

The intensely ethnocentric English community that was planted in New England in the 1630s went further and subjected the Indians to a peculiarly harsh disparagement and repression of their culture and way of life. More than other colonists, Puritans were animated by the belief that Indian religion was not simply an unfortunate error of the unenlightened but quite literally worship of the Devil. Hence they believed that they had a God-given duty to stamp it out wherever possible. . . . A few Indians might be saved — the Puritans did not believe that God's awful majesty in choosing his elect was limited by a material fact such as physical appearance — but the fate of most who fell under colonial jurisdiction or control was simply to be governed by laws forbidding the heathenish and "sinful" practices that were in fact integral to Indian culture. In other colonies threats to the integrity of the Indians' way of life came less from systematic cultural intolerance than from the ravages of European diseases against which they had no immunity and the demoralizing effect of contact with traders who plied native Americans with alcohol, made them dependent on European trade goods, and induced them to carry on the disastrous practice of extirpating the wildlife within their territories to provide furs and skins for the white market. These epidemiological and economic pressures were not lacking in New England, but at times they were overshadowed by a more direct assault on Indian culture.

As elsewhere, the resistance of the New England Indians to territorial loss and cultural disintegration was severely limited by tribal rivalries that inhibited common action against the invaders; but when Plymouth authorities executed three Wampanoags accused of murdering another Indian in 1675, they touched off an uprising in which four tribes cooperated in a last desperate effort to preserve what remained of their independence and traditional way of life. The Narragansetts and others joined the Wampanoags partly because the Puritans were attempting to enforce laws requiring observance of the Sabbath and prescribing capital punishment for blasphemy. "King Philip's War" of 1675–76 resulted in the total destruction of twelve New England towns and the death of over a thousand whites, but approximately five thousand Indians were killed, and the ultimate white victory signaled the end of the last vestiges of Indian autonomy in Massachusetts, Connecticut, and Rhode Island. Furthermore, it resulted in the virtual abandonment of a peculiarly Puritan Indian policy that might be described as acculturation without assimilation. Unwilling to absorb Indians directly into their own society, the Puritans had nevertheless felt an obligation to bring the message of reformed Christianity and the discipline of a "civil" existence to as many Indians as possible. To accomplish this purpose they had organized the Indians directly under their control into fourteen separate "praying towns" where the gospel was preached and the inhabitants encouraged to imitate the practices of the white colonists. As a result of the stresses of King Philip's War, most of these villages were disbanded, and the missionary impulse that had brought them into existence waned perceptibly, both because there were so few Indians left to proselytize in the vicinity of the white settlements and because the racial animosities stirred by the conflict encouraged a conviction that all Indians were incorrigible slaves of the Devil whose sole function had been to serve as a vehicle for divine wrath against the backsliding of the colonists.

The general pattern of settler encroachment and increasing friction leading to a major war of extirpation was repeated in North and South Carolina in the early eighteenth century. Here again, the Indians' resistance resulted in the destruction of their societies and the loss of their land. By the 1720s, all the coastal tribes from Massachusetts to South Carolina had either been exterminated by warfare and European diseases, pushed westward, or reduced to more or less detribalized fragments surviving on the fringes of white society. –

The story of early indigene-white relations in the Dutch colony at the Cape of Good Hope is a simpler one because of the smaller scale of settlement and the existence of a single native policy dictated by relatively modest territorial ambitions. Any comparison with the American experience requires a recognition that this was, or at least was meant to be, colonization of a different type. While American settlement represented an effort to plant English communities that would produce important commodities for the mother country, the colony at the Cape of Good Hope had no other purpose than to serve as a provisioning station for the ships of the Dutch East India Company. Where the English Crown claimed much of North America by the right of discovery, the Dutch had neither a basis for such claims in southern Africa nor an interest in acquiring more land than they needed for the maintenance and protection of their fort and garden in the shadow of Table Mountain. All the manpower the founders anticipated needing was a relatively small number of company servants and slaves. In 1657 the directors of the Company instructed Commander van Riebeeck to keep the establishment "as confined and . . . small . . . as possible." But in that same year a decision was made that would have unforeseen expansionist consequences. To increase agricultural production to a level that would enable the colony to fulfill its mission, a small number of company servants were freed and allowed to take up land as freehold farmers. Thus a class of free burghers [citizens] was created that would gradually grow in number as company servants and soldiers fulfilled their terms of service and were induced to remain at the Cape as free colonists.

In accordance with the general policies of the East India Company, the founders of the settlement were enjoined not to conquer or enslave the indigenous inhabitants. The primary relationship was to be one of trade; for the people Europeans called Hottentots — but who are more properly designated as Khoikhoi, the name they gave themselves — had vast herds of cattle and sheep which could be a vital source of fresh meat for the ships that put into Cape Town. The Company's oft-repeated instructions were to treat them with gentleness and forebearance in order to encourage the cattle trade. . . . [T]here were also the usual professions of an intention to convert them to true Christianity, but almost nothing was done along these lines — partly because of a lack of clergymen and partly because there was no practical advantage in it since the Khoikhoi did not have to be Christians to fulfill their role as suppliers of livestock.

The Khoikhoi did not initially regard the Dutch intrusion with alarm because they had a long experience of trading with ships of various European nations that had put into Table Bay in search of fresh provisions. Only gradually did they begin to realize that the Dutch, unlike the earlier visitors, had come to stay and were slowly increasing in numbers and enlarging their land holdings. Tension developed in what might otherwise have been a successful symbiotic relationship when the expansion of white farming began to encroach on Khoikhoi pasture lands. The first Khoikhoi-Dutch war of 1659–60 resulted in part from this expansion and was resolved by a treaty acknowledging white rights to occupancy of the disputed territory. Despite their limited numbers and the low morale and disloyalty of the Company's white servants and imported African and Asian slaves, the Dutch were able to gain a firm foothold by the end of Van Riebeeck's tenure in 1662 because the Khoikhoi in the immediate vicinity of the original settlement were divided into small and loosely organized tribes whose mutual jealousies and animosities could be manipulated by the invaders for their own advantage.

Furthermore, their transhumant way of life offered them a relatively painless alternative to direct confrontation with the Dutch; they could simply walk away. Indeed a main source of Dutch grievance in the early years was not the presence of the Khoikhoi but their absence. They were not always available to provide livestock at the right time and in the quantities that the Company desired.

What the Dutch failed to understand was that the Khoikhoi valued their cattle as permanent sources of wealth and status rather than as articles of commerce and were usually willing to part only with their older and less healthy animals. The failure of the neighboring tribes to provide adequate numbers of cattle induced Commander Van Riebeeck to contemplate seizing their herds and enslaving the herdsmen. But the directors of the Company rejected such drastic and inhumane policies, so the governor was compelled to try to establish contact with inland tribes whose larger herds promised a more substantial commerce. At first, Company officials could only gain access to the cattle of the inland Khoikhoi by working through local native intermediaries who were astute enough to limit the supply in order to keep the prices high. Although ways were eventually found to eliminate these middlemen from the neighboring tribes and deal directly with the source, the more remote tribes also refused to part with most of their healthy breeding stock, and the process of exhausting the surplus quickly repeated itself.

The continued unreliability of the Khoikhoi cattle trade encouraged two important deviations from the original policy of reliance on peaceful trade. The first was to encourage cattle-raising by the colonists themselves, thereby setting up a competing livestock economy. The second was to use coercion to divest the Khoikhoi of their remaining cattle. The Khoikhoi-Dutch war of 1673–77 was provoked by the alleged murder of some white elephant hunters by a tribe known as the Cochoqua, but the result of this conflict was the Company's seizure of at least 1,765 cattle and 4,930 sheep. The Dutch did not again declare war on any Khoikhoi tribes, but their well-armed trading expeditions increasingly resorted to intimidation or threat of force to compel the exchange of cattle. At the same time, the growth of a private white interest in cattle-raising and the cattle trade encouraged illegal expeditions by burghers which further depleted Khoikhoi holdings by methods ranging from unequal barter to outright raiding.

Under such pressures the Khoikhoi economy and way of life disintegrated. By the early eighteenth century the indigenes of the south-western Cape had not only lost much of their cattle but were unable to prevent white graziers from occupying their best interior pasture lands. Those who still had some livestock tended to migrate to remote semi-desert regions. The large proportion who had lost all their cattle either retreated to mountainous areas and adopted the hunting, gathering, and raiding habits of a closely related people, the San or "Bushmen," or hung around white farms and settlements in search of casual labor. In 1713 a devastating smallpox epidemic annihilated most of the surviving Khoikhoi population in or near the areas of white concentration.

In many ways, therefore, their fate was similar to that of the coastal Indians. Again a weaker and less organized people gave way to a more powerful and unified invader. In both instances there was a pattern of trade that turned out to be destructive to the indigenes. Once the Indians had exhausted their supply of furs and skins for the white market and the Khoikhoi had lost their ability to provide cattle to the Company, their continued survival as independent societies no longer made any contribution to the success of white settlement. At that point the trading interest was overshadowed by the desire of white colonists to expropriate for their own use the land still occupied by the indigenous population. Force was employed when necessary to satisfy white territorial ambitions. The end result was dispossession of the indigenes and their loss of power, independence, and cultural cohesion.

Yet there were some differences in the precise way this process occurred and how it was rationalized. Almost from the beginning in the American case, purely commercial relationships were subordinated to the aim of establishing white settlements that would produce something on their own for the English market. Not all the colonies succeeded in doing this; settlement for religious reasons in areas like New England and Pennsylvania that lacked the capacity to produce staples needed in England led to a pattern of mixed agriculture and commerce that provided a basis for local prosperity but did not fit well into a mercantilistic imperial economy. But whatever the actual pattern of colonial economic development, the Indian trade rapidly became a marginal and sectional aspect of it that was readily dispensable. The desire for territorial expansion and land acquisition became paramount, and violent Indian resistance against gradual encroachment was made the occasion for huge land grabs.

In South Africa, on the other hand, the official ideology of the colonizers put a much greater premium on trade than on control of the land. The Company's original intention was to restrict the colonists to growing cereals, other foodstuffs, and wine in the immediate vicinity of Cape Town and to leave the vast and semi-arid interior to the Khoikhoi herders who would supply most of the necessary meat. This division of labor broke down by the beginning of the eighteenth century mainly because the Khoikhoi were not culturally conditioned to produce for a growing market, and because their economy and society were too fragile to sustain the pressures of an unequal commercial relationship with the Dutch. Even then the Company did not encourage the migration of white graziers into the interior. They preferred to build up more intensive forms of livestock-raising as an aspect of mixed agriculture in the settled and relatively well-watered hinterland of Cape Town and to exploit what remained of the Khoikhoi trade in a controlled and monopolistic fashion. The actual displacement of most of the independent Khoikhoi by the itinerant white herdsmen known as trekboers, which took place during the eighteenth century, was, from the Company point of view, an unplanned and troublesome development that promised to weaken the cohesiveness of the colony and make it more difficult to administer. But by 1730 the destruction of the Khoikhoi economy had made the Cape market dependent on white pastoralists, and a more permissive attitude toward their movements inevitably resulted. Somewhat reluctantly, the government extended the borders of the colony when necessary to accommodate white expansion and established a system for the leasing of frontier grazing lands to trekboers. But the enlargement of the Cape Colony beyond a very limited area remained at best a necessary evil as far as the authorities were concerned. It required no official rationalization because it was more an accident than an official policy.

It is even doubtful that the trekboers themselves felt much need for an ideological sanction for taking possession of territory previously occupied by Khoikhoi tribes; for they had little practical need to extinguish Khoikhoi title to it or even to recognize that such a thing had ever existed. This easy state of mind resulted from the fact that the indigenous herders were transhumant, which meant that they moved seasonally in pursuit of pasture. Although their patterns of migration took the form of regular beats that were respected by the different tribes or hordes, they lacked established villages or fixed habitations that whites would recognize as establishing any kind of possessory rights. Because of the aridity of the interior pastoral areas, the white graziers often became semi-nomadic themselves. Not allowed by the government to establish freehold farms on the frontier (as colonists had earlier been permitted to do in the vicinity of Cape Town), they held large parcels as "loan places" where they established rude homesteads. These habitations were readily deserted, either temporarily for purposes of transhumance, or permanently with the intention of acquiring a new loan place which offered the prospect of better pasture and surer supplies of water. In a thinly populated pastoral environment where migration was often necessary for survival because of the uncertainty of grass, rainfall, and wet waterholes and where most of the land was actually vacant most of the time, precise claims to land did not assume the same importance as on an agricultural frontier. Although the Dutch regarded the Khoikhoi as abject savages — indeed reports coming out of the Cape of Good Hope gave the "Hottentots" the general reputation of being the most bestial people yet encountered by Europeans in the course of discovering and conquering new lands — the circumstances were such that the concept of savagery was seldom used ideologically to rationalize territorial dispossession of the indigenous people. Such use was perhaps implied by Van Riebeeck when he proposed in 1654 to seize the persons and cattle of local tribes which he had earlier described as a "dull, rude, lazy, and stinking nation." But, as we have seen, this scheme was vetoed, and thereafter an extremely unfavorable stereotype of the Khoikhoi floated freely in the white consciousness without being linked to any calculated or comprehensive policy of dispossession and domination. In fact most Khoikhoi remained in theory members of free and independent tribes until they became an important source of servile labor during the eighteenth century.

In North America, the Indians' claim to the land constituted a real obstacle to white ambition, with the result that a strong need was felt to rationalize their dispossession. Unlike the Khoikhoi, the coastal Indians lived in permanent or semi-permanent villages, cultivated crops, and had more or less fixed tribal boundaries. Although they lacked the concept of private property in the European sense, many tribes had a highly developed system of users' rights which served to allocate land to families or kinship groups for indefinite periods. The very fact that the coastal Indians were an essentially sedentary people whose forms of land use and allotment actually approximated "civilized" norms created a real problem for settlers who wished to remove them and carve up their domain into freehold farms on the English model. The best solution that colonists and colonial governments could come up with was to seize on the fact that most land in Indian possession remained uncultivated and was used for hunting. According to John Winthrop, the first governor of the Massachusetts Bay Colony, almost all of the land in North America was *vacuum domicilium* [devoid of legal residences] because the Indians had not used it for agriculture. This meant that it was not private property in the legal or civil sense and could be expropriated by anyone who would put it under the plow. The notion that the Indians had only "savage title" because they used most of their land for hunting and therefore left it thinly populated and undeveloped became the standard rationalization for extinguishing their territorial claims and replacing them with white agriculturalists who would follow the Biblical injunction to "increase and multiply, replenish the earth and subdue it" in the way that the Indians allegedly could not. By the early eighteenth century the principle that civilized cultivators took precedence over those "savage" hunters and gatherers had become an established principle of international law as codified by the Swiss jurist Vattel. Later in the century it was incorporated into a widely accepted theory of social evolution that gauged human progress in terms of a great transformation from "barbarism" to "civilization" that was characterized primarily by the advent of sedentary agriculture.

In order to make this ideology persuasive it was necessary to distort reality by exaggerating the Indians' reliance on hunting and by interpreting their occasional movements and migrations as genuine nomadism. Furthermore, the desire to seize whole blocks of Indian territory, including both cultivated and uncultivated areas, required the further argument that English political sovereignty over the "savage" inhabitants of territories the English had "discovered" had superseded tribal rights to possess or allocate land. All Indian landholding was thus without ultimate legal sanction and existed only on the sufferance of the King. The coastal Indians actually lost their land through legitimate purchase, fraud, treaties in which coercion was often involved, and land settlements resulting from wars. But behind all these policies was the settlers' conviction that they had a natural or God-given right to the soil because they were civil and the Indians were not. Hence the persistent notion that the frontier was a moving zone of conflict between "savagery" and "civilization" became central to Americans' expectations about the progress and development of their society from a very early period. . . .

For those who were the victims of white occupation of the area east of the Appalachians before the Revolution or of the trekboer movement that simultaneously divested the Khoikhoi of most of their pasture land in the northern and eastern Cape, these differences in the precise meaning that whites attributed to what was occurring could hardly have mattered very much. But there were economic and demographic influences on the South African frontier that made the ultimate fate of the Khoikhoi different from that of the Indians east of the Appalachians. Besides those who were decimated, clustered on small reservations, or impelled to migrate westward, some Indians were enslaved in the colonial period; but most of these were either shipped to the West Indies or absorbed into the Afro-American slave population. Consequently Indians as a group were not integrated into the European economy as a source of labor. Once the whites had their land, they had no further use for them; for the labor needs of the colonists were met by white indentured servants and, by the eighteenth century and especially in the South, by imported African slaves.

The Cape Khoikhoi suffered a demographic disaster of equivalent proportions. As in the case of the Indians, diseases brought by the Europeans probably accounted for a greater proportion of their mortality than the wars that were fought either with the colonists or among themselves for control of the trade that the whites had inaugurated. The smallpox epidemics that broke out in 1713, 1735, and 1767 apparently resulted in the disappearance of entire tribes. But the largely detribalized Khoikhoi who survived these and other disasters resulting from the white invasion did find an important niche in the settler economy. Before the coming of the Dutch, Khoikhoi who had somehow lost their cattle had customarily become clients of those who still possessed them and had acted as herdsmen in return for payment in kind that might allow them gradually to regain their status as livestock owners. When the Khoikhoi as a people had lost most of their cattle, it was quite natural for many of them to enter into similar clientage arrangements with white pastoralists. Hence they became the herdsmen, ox-trainers, and wagon drivers for the Boers, occupations for which they were eminently qualified. Indeed they became indispensable; for without their tutelage, the Boers would have had much difficulty in adjusting to a harsh environment. But their hopes for regaining independence were thwarted by white control of the land and by the tendency of the Boers to exploit their vulnerability by transforming the terms of their employment from genuine clientage, involving a voluntary and mutually advantageous exchange of labor for sustenance and protection, into a pastoral form of serfdom. Hence the Khoikhoi were not simply shoved aside or exterminated like the Indians, but often became economic collaborators with the white frontiersmen.

There was also a military aspect to white-Khoikhoi interdependence. When the Boers encountered major resistance from other indigenous groups in the mid-to-late eighteenth century, they were forced to arm their Khoikhoi clients and use them as an important part of their militia. In the bitter conflicts with the hunting and gathering "Bushmen" or San, which slowed white expansion into the northern Cape in the late eighteenth century, large numbers of Khoikhoi served in the "Commandos" that meted out brutal retribution to the marauding hunters. In the wars with the Bantu-speaking Africans that began along the eastern frontier in the 1780s, they played an equally significant military role, although they did not always prove to be loyal or reliable. In the course of their intimate economic and military association with frontier whites the Khoikhoi eventually lost not only their indigenous culture but even their biological identity from a process of racial mixing. . . . It would be misleading, however, to say that they became extinct; for their mixed descendants were the most important of the constituent elements that went into the formation of the population group that became known as the Cape Coloreds.

QUESTIONS TO CONSIDER

1. What features did British North America and Dutch South Africa have in common as "settler colonies"? How, according to the author, were they different from tropical "exploitation colonies"? In what ways did contrasting Dutch and English ideologies of colonization create different social and economic patterns in North America and South Africa? How did these patterns compare with Spanish colonization in Latin America?

2. Describe the evolution of relations between white settlers and indigenous peoples in the North American and South African colonies. Why, according to the author, were early Indian-white relations in North America so inconsistent? What does Fredrickson mean when he calls Puritan policy toward the Indians "acculturation without assimilation"? Why did the British in Massachusetts and Virginia make few attempts to enslave Native Americans? How did trading relations between the Dutch and the Khoikhoi in South Africa deteriorate into warfare over land? From the natives' perspective, did it make any difference that the English and Dutch had contrasting ideologies of colonization?

3. Why, according to the author, did North American colonists develop an elaborate ideological justification for taking away the natives' land, while the South African colonists did not? In what way did this justification depend upon a distortion of Indian culture?

4. Some historians argue that national differences between the colonizers are less important in explaining the dynamics of colonization than conflicting attitudes held by different white colonial interest groups regardless of their nationality. In other words, traders, missionaries, farmers, and imperial administrators held opposing viewpoints whose clash determined the colony's history. Is there evidence in this essay to support this interpretation?

5. Critics contend that comparative studies of European colonization policies sometimes portray indigenous peoples as the passive victims of powerful European settlers. Does Fredrickson's essay fit this description? What strategies did the Indians and the Khoikhoi adopt to accommodate or resist colonial domination?

II

FORMING AMERICAN SOCIETY

Since the American colonies were peopled through overseas migration, an appropriate way to examine their history is to ask whether and how conditions in the New World transformed the institutions that colonists brought with them. What was the cultural inheritance of the groups who established themselves on American soil in the 1600s and 1700s? How quickly and how completely did they adopt a distinctively American social pattern? Was that pattern the same everywhere? These are comparative questions. They involve generalizations about the European (and, in the case of slaves, the African) background against which to measure changes; they require careful description of the process of transformation that followed; and they compel us to recognize the various ways that region, class, and race shaped the pattern that resulted.

The tasks of weighing continuity versus change and unity versus variety are among the most important, and most difficult, requirements of historical analysis. It is not surprising that historians often reach differing conclusions. One traditional view of colonial America emphasizes unity and change, portraying its inhabitants as a homogeneous people and their history as a fundamental break from the past. According to this interpretation, the British colonists, seeking freedom and prosperity on the New World frontier, quickly discarded the Old World's hierarchical ways and developed new democratic forms of political and social life. Calling themselves "Americans" in contrast to their European relatives, they put aside minor differences and easily coalesced into a new people. If we listen closely to this interpretation, we can hear echoes of American "exceptionalism," the enduring and popular notion that America's history has proceeded separately from trends elsewhere and has exempted its people from problems that plague the rest of the world.

33

The two readings in this chapter disagree with the stark Old World–New World dichotomy of exceptionalist approaches. Instead, they describe important continuities between societies on both sides of the Atlantic. Recognizing that migrants to the colonies brought distinctive ways of life that they tried to transplant, these essays convey a richer sense of the inherited ideas and customs that shaped their lives. In the first selection, David Hackett Fischer traces the origins of four different societies in colonial Massachusetts, Pennsylvania, Virginia, and the West to four waves of settlers who hailed from different regions in Great Britain. More than any other factor, Fischer contends, the contrasting British "folkways" carried by these migrants determined regional patterns in the colonies, and they defined conflicts over key concepts such as "liberty" that persist to this day.

In the second essay, Stephanie Grauman Wolf likewise notes customs carried over from the Old World, but in place of Fischer's single-factor thesis she explains colonial differences by pointing to multiple variables. Noting that much depended upon when, from where, and how the colonists came as well as where they settled, Wolf suggests that forming American society involved continual negotiation between the colonists' inherited ideals and the situation in which they found themselves. Her specific subject is the American family, whose features she traces in the diverse geographic and economic environments of the thirteen colonies. Ranging across lines of class and color as well as colonial boundaries, Wolf differs from Fischer by taking a truly multicultural approach that incorporates the experience of Native Americans and African Americans as well as European colonists into her story. More than Fischer's essay — and in contrast to an exceptionalist fixation upon Americans' unified culture — her account emphasizes that despite pressures toward a single cultural pattern, eighteenth-century Americans remained "as various as their land."

Note that while Fischer and Wolf both oppose the separatist tendencies of exceptionalist history, their essays model different strategies for internationalizing the colonial story. Fischer's approach is broadly *transnational* rather than comparative: his thesis documents the transatlantic migration of British folkways and relies upon this single factor to explain colonial development. Wolf, on the other hand, employs a *comparative* approach that uses both domestic and international reference points. She sees family arrangements determined by race, region, culture, and class within the colonies, but she also measures colonial patterns against Old World family models. Unlike Fischer, Wolf lists a variety of factors at work to create different colonial outcomes, and her findings support no overarching theory. Her localized analysis may lack Fischer's clarity and force, but it covers a greater range of cases. What do you think are the strengths and weaknesses of each of these approaches?

Albion's Seed

DAVID HACKETT FISCHER

"What, then, is the American, this new man?" asked Hector St. John de Crèvecoeur, a French visitor who settled in colonial New York and wrote the celebrated Letters from an American Farmer *(1782). In his rose-colored response, Crèvecoeur identified America as a place where Old World prejudices and manners evaporated and anything was possible. The newcomer "no sooner breathes our air," he swooned, "than . . . he begins to feel the effects of a sort of resurrection." Ignoring traditional class lines and ethnic boundaries, putting aside inherited political ideas and economic constraints, Americans, according to Crèvecoeur, were building an entirely new democratic culture.*

Were the British colonists on the eastern seaboard "new men" (and women)? Did their Old World ways truly disappear in the new American environment? In this excerpt from a larger study, David Hackett Fischer, an American historian well versed in the European background of colonization, answers these questions with a resounding "no." He argues that instead of disappearing, the ideas and customs of those who founded the thirteen colonies are the key factor that explains the configuration of colonial society and, in the longer run, the emergence of the United States as a contentious but stable democracy.

Fischer identifies four regions of the British Isles that sent men and women to the North American colonies in successive waves. From England's eastern counties came Puritan migrants of the 1630s who arrived in Massachusetts to build their godly commonwealth. Virginia's immigrants of the mid-1600s were less concentrated in origin, partly because that colony's landed gentry and indentured servants had different backgrounds, but most came from counties that stretched along a crescent from southwestern England to areas north of London. In the late 1600s and early 1700s, thousands of Quakers left England's North Midlands to seek refuge in the Pennsylvania colony. Finally, throughout the 1700s a massive flow of "border migrants," often Scottish Presbyterians, left the England-Scotland border region and northern Ireland to seek freer lives on America's western frontier. All these migrants were British, but each group, according to Fischer, carried distinctive regional folkways to their destination that lent a unique flavor to the way each colony's settlers spoke, dressed, built families and houses, worked, and worshipped. In the excerpt that follows, Fischer devotes particular attention to four different concepts of liberty that British migrants invoked to govern their colonies and to regulate social relations. The transplanting of Albion's (Britain's) regional seeds blossomed into competing world views among the settlers of New England, the Mid-Atlantic, the South, and the West. And even though most Americans today have no British ancestry at all, Fischer claims that the contest among these inherited "freedom ways" continues to define Americans' social attitudes and political debates.

Fischer's insistence upon the colonists' cultural ties to the Old World calls into question not only Crèvecoeur's praise of American newness but also much of traditional historical writing. At the beginning of his essay, Fischer briefly situates his theory among competing interpretations of American origins: the "germ theory" (or Teutonic thesis), which unearths democracy's roots deep in the European past; the "frontier thesis" (or Turner thesis), which, like Crèvecoeur, praises the transformative effects of the American environment; and the "migration model," which credits ethnic diversity for the foundation of America's pluralist institutions. As you read Fischer's essay, consider where its interpretation fits in this cluster of theories.

You might also consider similarities and differences among these approaches and even potential combinations of them. Is it possible, for example, that the interaction between inherited culture and environmental conditions determined regional patterns in the colonies? Was it merely a coincidence that each of Fisher's groups settled on lands appropriate to their vision of the good society? To what extent did the climatic, geographic, and economic situations of each colony determine its customs rather than bend to them? (This is a question you should return to after you read Selection 5.) To what degree did ethnic and racial diversity — a factor that Fischer virtually ignores — push the colonists toward religious toleration and expanded notions of freedom and citizenship? Fischer has given us a clear and ambitious new theory of American origins, one that acknowledges, rather than ignores, transatlantic ties. As you analyze his essay, you should judge for yourself how convincingly he argues for it.

GLOSSARY

ALBION   The first recorded name for Britain, which the Greeks called the "island of the Albiones" in the sixth century B.C.

BURKE, EDMUND (1729–1797)   An influential British parliamentary leader and political thinker who sought to reduce the king's powers and urged a policy of compromise toward the American colonies. Despite his sympathy for the colonists, Burke was no revolutionary. His *Reflections on the Revolution in France* (1790) favored tradition and hierarchy over the promotion of radical change and equal rights.

ENGLISH CIVIL WAR (1642–1651)   A series of battles in which supporters of Parliament defeated those loyal to the monarchy (Royalists) during the reigns of Charles I and Charles II. The victors, led by the Puritan Oliver Cromwell, proclaimed England a republican commonwealth. Charles II was restored to the throne not long after Cromwell's death in 1658.

FOUR FREEDOMS   A list of basic human rights formulated by President Franklin Roosevelt in 1941 to justify American assistance to nations opposing Germany and Japan in World War II. The four were freedom of expression, freedom of worship, freedom from want, and freedom from fear.

GENERAL COURT   The elected legislature of colonial Massachusetts.

MAGNA CARTA   The "great charter" issued by King John of England in 1215 guaranteeing that the king would not curb feudal privileges, proclaiming freedom of the church, and extending civil rights to royal subjects. It is the founding document of British constitutional government.

MIGRATION MODEL   An interpretation that attributes the development of American democracy, voluntary citizenship, and ethnic diversity to the nation's peopling by immigrants, especially those from outside England.

PENN, WILLIAM (1644–1718)   An English Quaker leader and champion of religious freedom who was granted vast lands in North America because of a debt the king owed his father. There Penn set up the Pennsylvania colony in 1682 to model religious toleration and fair dealings with Native Americans. Penn governed the colony personally during two trips to America in 1682–1684 and 1699–1701.

QUAKERS   The common name for the Society of Friends, a dissenting sect originating in seventeenth-century England. Quakers stood out for their beliefs in simplicity, equality, and pacifism, and they were often subject to persecution. The colony of Pennsylvania was established as a refuge for Quakers and a "holy experiment" in religious toleration.

TEUTONIC THESIS (germ theory)   A theory popular among American historians of the late nineteenth century that traced America's democratic institutions to British and, ultimately, medieval German predecessors.

TURNER THESIS (frontier thesis)   The influential theory of historian Frederick Jackson Turner. He asserted in 1893 that the existence of a western frontier was the most important factor in American history because it broke down Old World habits and encouraged the growth of democracy and individualism.

WHIGS   During the eighteenth century, a faction or party in the British Parliament that favored a limited constitutional monarchy rather than an all-powerful king. Originally an aristocratic group, the Whigs evolved after the 1780s to represent industrialists, religious dissenters, and advocates of electoral reform.

✻ ✻ ✻ ✻ ✻ ✻ ✻

We Americans are a bundle of paradoxes. We are mixed in our origins, and yet we are one people. Nearly all of us support our republican system, but we argue passionately (sometimes violently) among ourselves about its meaning. Most of us subscribe to what Gunnar Myrdal called the American Creed, but that idea is a paradox in political theory. As Myrdal observed in 1942, America is "conservative in fundamental principles . . . but the principles conserved are liberal and some, indeed, are radical."

We live in an open society which is organized on the principle of voluntary action, but the determinants of that system are exceptionally constraining. Our society is dynamic, changing profoundly in every period of American history; but it is also remarkably stable. The search for the origins of this system is the central problem in American history. . . .

The organizing question here is about what might be called the determinants of a voluntary society. The problem is to explain the origins and stability of a social system which for two centuries has remained stubbornly democratic in its politics, capitalist in its economy, libertarian in its laws, individualist in its society and pluralistic in its culture.

Much has been written on this subject — more than anyone can possibly read. But a very large outpouring of books and articles contains a remarkably small number of seminal ideas. Most historians have tried to explain the determinants of a voluntary society in one of three ways: by reference to the European culture that was transmitted to America, or to the American environment itself, or to something in the process of transmission.

During the nineteenth century the first of these explanations was very much in fashion. Historians believed that the American system had evolved from what one scholar called "Teutonic germs" of free institutions, which were supposedly carried from the forests of Germany to Britain and then to America. This idea was taken up by a generation of historians who tended to be Anglo-Saxon in their origins, Atlantic in their attitudes and Whiggish in their politics. Most had been trained in the idealist and institutional traditions of the German historical school.

For a time this Teutonic thesis became very popular — in Boston and Baltimore. But in Kansas and Wisconsin it was unkindly called the "germ theory" of American history and laughed into oblivion. In the early twentieth century it yielded to the Turner thesis, which looked to the American environment and especially to the western frontier as a way of explaining the growth of free institutions in America. This idea appealed to scholars who were middle western in their origins, progressive in their politics, and materialist in their philosophy.

In the mid-twentieth century the Turner thesis also passed out of fashion. Yet another generation of American historians became deeply interested in processes of immigration and ethnic pluralism as determinants of a voluntary society. This third approach was specially attractive to scholars who were not themselves of Anglo-Saxon stock. Many were central European in their origin, urban in their residence, and Jewish in their religion. This pluralistic "migration model" is presently the conventional interpretation.

Other explanations have also been put forward from time to time, but three ideas have held the field: the germ theory, the frontier thesis, and the migration model.

This [essay] returns to the first of those explanations, within the framework of the second and third. It argues a modified "germ thesis" about the importance for the United States of having been British in its cultural origins. . . .

THE FOUR GREAT MIGRATIONS

During the very long period from 1629 to 1775, the present area of the United States was settled by at least four large waves of English-speaking immigrants. . . . The first wave (1629–40) was an exodus of English Puritans who came mainly from the eastern counties and planted in Massachusetts a very special culture with unique patterns of speech and architecture, distinctive ideas about marriage and the family, nucleated settlements, congregational churches, town meetings, and a tradition of ordered liberty.

The second wave [ca. 1642–75] brought to Virginia a different set of English folkways, mainly from a broad belt of territory that extended from Kent and Devon north to Northamptonshire and Warwickshire. This culture was characterized by scattered settlements, extreme hierarchies of rank, strong oligarchies, Anglican churches, a highly developed sense of honor and an idea of hegemonic liberty.

The third wave (ca. 1675–1715) was the Friends' migration, which carried yet another culture from the England's North Midlands to the Delaware Valley. It was founded on a Christian idea of spiritual equality, a work ethic of unusual intensity, a suspicion of social hierarchy, and an austerity which Max Weber called "worldly asceticism." It also preserved many elements of North Midland speech, architecture, dress and food ways. Most important, it deliberately created a pluralistic system of reciprocal liberty in the Delaware Valley.

The fourth great migration (1717–75) came to the backcountry from the borderlands of North Britain — an area which included the Scottish lowlands, the north of Ireland and England's six northern counties. These emigrants were of different ethnic stocks, but shared a common border culture which was unique in its speech, architecture, family ways and child-rearing customs. Its material culture was marked by extreme inequalities of condition, and its public life was dominated by a distinctive ideal of natural liberty. . . .

These four groups shared many qualities in common. All of them spoke the English language. Nearly all were British Protestants. Most lived under British laws and took pride in possessing British liberties. At the same time, they also differed from one another in many other ways: in their religious denominations, social ranks, historical generations, and also in the British regions from whence they came. They carried across the Atlantic four different sets of British folkways which became the basis of regional cultures in the New World.

By the year 1775 these four cultures were fully established in British America. They spoke distinctive dialects of English, built their houses in diverse ways, and had different methods of doing much of the ordinary business of life. Most important for the political history of the United States, they also had four different conceptions of order, power and freedom which became the cornerstones of a voluntary society in British America.

Today less than 20 percent of the American population have any British ancestors at all. But in a cultural sense most Americans are Albion's seed, no matter who their own forebears may have been. Strong echoes of four British folkways may still be heard in the major dialects of American speech, in the regional patterns of American life, in the complex dynamics of American politics, and in the continuing conflict between four different ideas of freedom in the United States. The interplay of four "freedom ways" has created an expansive pluralism which is more libertarian than any unitary culture alone could be. That is the central thesis of this [essay]: the legacy of four British folkways in early America remains the most powerful determinant of a voluntary society in the United States today.

MASSACHUSETTS FREEDOM WAYS: THE PURITAN IDEA OF ORDERED LIBERTY

The public life of New England was . . . shaped by an idea of liberty which was peculiar to the Puritan colonies. To understand its nature, one might begin with the word itself. From the generation of John Winthrop (1558–1649) to that of Samuel Adams (1722–1803), the noun "liberty" was used throughout New England in at least four ways which ring strangely in a modern ear.

First, "liberty" often described something which belonged not to an individual but to an entire community. For two centuries, the founders and leaders of Massachusetts wrote of the "liberty of New England," or the "liberty of Boston" or the "liberty of the Town." This usage continued from the great migration to the War of Independence and even beyond. Samuel Adams, for example, wrote more often about the "liberty of America" than about the liberty of individual Americans.

This idea of collective liberty, or "publick liberty" as it was sometimes called, was thought to be consistent with close restraints upon individuals. In Massachusetts these individual restrictions were numerous, and often very confining. During the first generation, nobody could live in the colony without approval of the General Court. Settlers even of the highest rank were sent prisoners to England for expressing "divers dangerous opinions," or merely because the Court judged them to be "persons unmeet to inhabit here." Others were not allowed to move within the colony except by special permission of the General Court. For a time, the inhabitants of Dedham, Sudbury and Concord were forbidden to move out of their towns, because the General Court believed that those frontier settlements were dangerously under-populated. . . .

New Englanders also used the word "liberty" in a second way which is foreign to our own time. When it referred to individuals, it often became a plural noun — "liberties" rather than "liberty." These plural liberties were understood as specific exemptions from a condition of prior restraint — an idea which had long existed in East Anglia and in many other parts of the western world. In the manor of Hengrave (Suffolk), for example, tenants were granted a specific "liberty" of fishing in the river Lark. Such a liberty was not universal or absolute; the river was closed to all other people. There were a great many of these liberties in East Anglian communities during the early seventeenth century. A person's status was defined by the number and nature of liberties to which he was admitted.

The idea of plural liberties as specific exemptions from a condition of prior constraint was carried to Massachusetts. The General Court, for example, enacted laws which extended "liberties and privileges of fishing and fowling" to certain inhabitants, and thereby denied them to everyone else. One person's "liberty" in this sense became another's restraint. In Massachusetts, as in England, a person's rank was defined by the liberties that he possessed, and vice versa.

The laws of the Bay Colony granted some liberties to all men, others to all free men, and a few only to gentlemen. For example, a "true gentleman" and "any man equal to a gentleman," was granted the liberty not to be punished by whipping "unless his crime be very shameful, and his course of life vicious and profligate." Other men had a lesser liberty, not to be whipped more than forty stripes. Other liberties were assigned not to individuals at all, but to churches and towns and other social groups. . . .

New England Puritans also used the word "liberty" in a third meaning, which became urgently important to the founders of Massachusetts. This was the idea of "soul liberty," or "Christian liberty," an idea of high complexity. Soul liberty was freedom to serve God in the world. It was freedom to order one's own acts in a godly way — but not in any other. It made Christian freedom into a form of obligation.

The founding generation in Massachusetts often wrote of "soul liberty," "Christian liberty" or "liberty of conscience." Many moved to the New World primarily in hopes of attaining it. What they meant was not a world of religious freedom in the modern sense, or even of religious toleration, but rather of freedom for the true faith. In their minds, this idea of religious liberty was thought to be consistent with the persecution of Quakers, Catholics, Baptists, Presbyterians, Anglicans and indeed virtually everyone except those within a very narrow spectrum of Calvinist orthodoxy. Soul liberty also was thought to be consistent with compulsory church attendance and rigorous Sabbath laws. Even the Indians were compelled to keep the Puritan Sabbath in Massachusetts. To the founders of that colony, soul freedom meant that they were free to persecute others in their own way. . . . To others of different persuasions, the Puritans' paradoxical idea of "soul freedom" became a cruel and bloody contradiction. But to the Puritans themselves "soul liberty" was a genuinely libertarian principle which held that a Christian community should be free to serve God in the world. Here was an idea in which the people of Massachusetts deeply believed, and the reason why their colony was founded in the first place.

The words "liberty" and also "freedom" were used in yet a fourth way by the builders of the Bay Colony. Sometimes, the people of Massachusetts employed the word "freedom" to describe a collective obligation of the "body politicke," to protect individual members from the tyranny of circumstance. This was conceived not in terms of collective welfare or social equality but of individual liberty. It was precisely the same idea that a descendant of the Massachusetts Puritans, Franklin Roosevelt, conceived as the Four Freedoms. That way of thinking was not his invention. It appeared in Massachusetts within a few years of its founding. The Massachusetts poor laws, however limited they may have been, recognized every individual should be guaranteed a freedom from want in the most fundamental sense. The General Court also explicitly recognized even a "freedom from fear." Its language revealed a libertarian conception of social problems (and solutions) that was characteristic of English-speaking people as early as the seventeenth century.

These four libertarian ideas — collective liberty, individual liberties, soul liberty and freedom from the tyranny of circumstance — all had a common denominator. They were aspects of a larger conception which might be called ordered liberty. This principle was deeply embedded in Puritan ideas and also in East Anglian realities. It came to be firmly established in Massachusetts even before the end of the great migration. For many years it continued to distinguish the culture of New England from other parts of British America. Even today, in much modified forms, it is still a living tradition in parts of the United States. But this principle of "ordered liberty" is also opposed by other libertarian ideas, which were planted in different parts of British America.

VIRGINIA FREEDOM WAYS:
THE ANGLICAN IDEA OF HEGEMONIC LIBERTY

"How is it," Dr. Samuel Johnson asked, "that we hear the loudest yelps for liberty among the drivers of negroes?" That famous question captured a striking paradox in the history of Virginia. Like most other colonists in British America, the first gentlemen of Virginia possessed an exceptionally strong consciousness of their English liberties, even as they took away the liberty of others. Governor William Berkeley himself, notwithstanding his reputation for tyranny, wrote repeatedly of "prized liberty" as the birthright of an Englishman. The first William Fitzhugh often wrote of Magna Carta and the "fundamental laws of England," with no sense of contradiction between his Royalist politics and libertarian principles. Fitzhugh argued that Virginians were both "natural subjects to the king" and inheritors of the "laws of England," and when they ceased to be these things, "then we are no longer freemen but slaves."

Similar language was used by many English-speaking people in the seventeenth and eighteenth century. The fine-spun treatises on liberty which flowed so abundantly from English pens in this era were rationales for political folkways deeply embedded in the cultural condition of Englishmen.

These English political folkways did not comprise a single libertarian tradition. They embraced many different and even contradictory conceptions of freedom. The libertarian ideas that took root in Virginia were very far removed from those that went to Massachusetts. In place of New England's distinctive idea of ordered liberty, the Virginians thought of liberty as a hegemonic condition of dominion over others and — equally important — dominion over oneself.

The Virginia idea of hegemonic liberty was far removed from the New England system of communal restraints which a town meeting voluntarily imposed upon itself. The English traveler Andrew Burnaby observed that "the public and political character of the Virginians corresponds with their private one: they are haughty and jealous of their liberties, impatient of restraint, and can scarcely bear the thought of being controlled by any superior power."

Virginia ideas of hegemonic liberty conceived of freedom mainly as the power to rule, and not to be overruled by others. Its opposite was "slavery," a degradation into which true-born Britons descended when they lost their power to rule. The idea was given its classical expression by the poet James Thomson (1700–1748) in a stanza that everyone knows without reflecting on its meaning:

> When Britain first, at Heaven's command,
> Arose from out of the Azure main,
> This was the charter of the land,
> And guardian angels sang this strain:
> Rule, Britannia, rule the waves;
> Britons never will be slaves.

In Thomson's poetry, which captured the world view of the Virginians in so many ways, we find the major components of hegemonic liberty: the concept of a "right to rule"; the notion that this right was guaranteed by the "charter of the land"; the belief that those who surrendered this right became "slaves"; and the idea that it had been given to "Britain first, at heaven's command."

It never occurred to most Virginia gentlemen that liberty belonged to everyone. It was thought to be the special birthright of free-born Englishmen — a property which set this "happy breed" apart from other mortals, and gave them a right to rule less fortunate people in the world. Even within their own society, hegemonic liberty was a hierarchical idea. One's status in Virginia was defined by the liberties that one possessed. Men of high estate were thought to have more liberties than others of lesser rank. Servants possessed few liberties, and slaves none at all. This libertarian idea had nothing to do with equality. Many years later, John Randolph of Roanoke summarized his ancestral creed in a sentence: "I am an aristocrat," he declared, "I love liberty; I hate equality."

In Virginia, this idea of hegemonic liberty was thought to be entirely consistent with the institution of race slavery. A planter demanded for himself the liberty to take away the liberties of others — a right of *laisser asservir,* freedom to enslave. The growth of race slavery in turn deepened the cultural significance of hegemonic liberty, for an Englishman's rights became his rank, and set him apart from others less fortunate than himself. The world thus became a hierarchy in which people were ranked according to many degrees of unfreedom, and they received their rank by the operation of fortune, which played so large a part in the thinking of Virginians. At the same time, hegemony over others allowed them to enlarge the sphere of their own personal liberty, and to create the conditions within which their special sort of libertarian consciousness flourished. . . .

One acute English observer in the eighteenth century clearly perceived the special meaning of hegemonic liberty in what he called the "southern colonies." Edmund Burke declared in Parliament:

> a circumstance attending these colonies . . . makes the spirit of liberty still more high and haughty than in those to the northward. It is, that in Virginia and the Carolinas, they have a vast multitude of slaves. Where this is the case in any part of the world, those who are free are by far the most proud and jealous of their freedom.
>
> Freedom is to them not only an enjoyment, but a kind of rank and privilege. Not seeing there that freedom, as in countries where it is a common blessing and as broad and general as

the air, may be united with much abject toil, with great misery, with all the exterior of servitude, liberty looks amongst them like something that is more noble and liberal.

I do not mean, Sir, to commend the superior morality of this sentiment, which has at least as much pride as virtue in it; but I cannot alter the nature of man. The fact is so; and these people of the southern colonies are much more strongly, and with a higher and more stubborn spirit, attached to liberty than those to the northward. . . . In such a people, the haughtiness of domination combines with the spirit of freedom, fortifies it, and renders it invincible.

Burke understood very well this system of hegemonic liberty in Virginia — perhaps because it was also shared by so many English gentlemen in the eighteenth century. He correctly perceived that liberty in Virginia was both a right and a rank, with a good deal of "pride" in it, and many contradictions. He also understood that this conception of hegemonic liberty contained larger possibilities which would expand in years to come.

One of these larger libertarian possibilities lay in its conception of self-government and minimal government. Hegemonic liberty was not an anarchical idea, opposed to all government. The preservation of liberty was thought to require the protection of the state. But the function of the state was largely limited to that minimal role. These ideas were introduced at the very beginning of Virginia's history. In the critical years from 1649 to 1652 the people of Virginia agreed to stand by Governor Berkeley and the Royalist cause only on condition that light taxes and loose restraints would be guaranteed to them. This wish was granted. Berkeley agreed to a general reduction of taxes, to the abolition of poll taxes altogether, to the principle of no taxation without representation, and to the idea of equitable assessments — "proportioning in some measure payments according to men's abilities and estates." Berkeley's tax policy lay at the root of his popularity. The burgesses acknowledged a debt of gratitude for themselves and their descendants. "This is a benefit descending unto us and our posterity," they declared, "which we acknowledge [is] contributed to us by our present governor." . . .

Hegemonic liberty was a dynamic tradition which developed through at least three historical stages. In the first it was linked to Royalist cause in the English Civil War. The Virginia gentleman Robert Beverley boasted that the colony "was famous, for holding out the longest for the Royal Family, of any of the English Dominions." Virginia was the last English territory to relinquish its allegiance to Charles I, and the first to proclaim Charles II king in 1660 even before the Restoration in England. Speeches against the Stuarts were ferociously punished by the county courts. The Assembly repeatedly expressed its loyalty to the Crown, giving abundant thanks for "his Majesty's most gracious favors towards us, and Royal Condescensions to anything requisite."

In the second stage, hegemonic liberty became associated with Whiggish politics, and with an ideology of individual independence which was widely shared throughout the English-speaking world. In Virginia, many families who had been staunch Royalists in the seventeenth century became strong Whigs in eighteenth century; by the early nineteenth century they would be Jeffersonian Republicans. Their principles throughout tended to be both elitist and libertarian — a clear expression of a cultural ethic which was capable of continuing expansion. . . .

In the nineteenth and twentieth centuries, the tradition of hegemonic liberty entered a third stage of development, in which it became less hierarchical and more egalitarian. Such are the conditions of modern life that this idea is no longer the exclusive property of a small elite, and the degradation of others is no longer necessary to their support. The progress of political democracy has admitted everyone to the ruling class. In America and Britain today, the idea of an independent elite, firmly in command of others, has disappeared. But the associated idea of an autonomous individual, securely in command of self, is alive and flourishing.

Delaware Freedom Ways: The Quaker Idea of Reciprocal Liberty

In 1751 the Assembly of Pennsylvania celebrated an anniversary. The Charter of Privileges, which William Penn had granted his settlers in 1701 to guarantee their liberty, was exactly half a century old. To mark the occasion, the legislature ordered that a great bell should be purchased for the Pennsylvania State House.

Today, that building is better known as Independence Hall, and the great Quaker bell is called the Liberty Bell. Both of these symbols are associated in the popular mind with the American Revolution. But in fact they were the products of an earlier period of Anglo-American history; and they were meant to celebrate a special idea of liberty which was unique to the Quaker founders of Pennsylvania.

The original resolution to purchase the great Quaker bell was voted by members of the Society of Friends, who made up 70 percent of the Pennsylvania Assembly in 1750. The inscription was selected by the Quaker speaker, who chose a passage from the book of Leviticus which seemed particularly meaningful to Christians of his denomination. The quotation referred to the liberty that God had given not merely to a chosen few, but to all his children, so that they might be safe in the sanctity of their families and secure in the possession of their property. The full biblical text seemed perfectly suitable to the anniversary of William Penn's Charter of Privileges:

> Ye shall hallow the fiftieth year, and proclaim liberty throughout *all* the land unto all the inhabitants thereof: and ye shall return every man unto his possession, and ye shall return every man unto his family.

Here was a libertarian idea that differed very much from the Puritan conception of ordered liberty for God's chosen few, and also from the cavalier notion of hierarchical liberty for the keepers of slaves. Quakers believed in an idea of reciprocal liberty that embraced all humanity, and was written in the golden rule.

This Christian idea was reinforced in Quaker thinking by an exceptionally strong sense of English liberties. As early as 1687, William Penn ordered the full text of the Magna Carta to be reprinted in Philadelphia, together with a broad selection of other constitutional documents. His purpose was to remind the freeholders of Pennsylvania to remember their British birthright. . . .

On the subject of liberty, the people of Pennsylvania needed no lessons from their Lord Proprietor. Few public questions were introduced among the colonists without being discussed in terms of rights and liberties. On its surface, this libertarian rhetoric seemed superficially similar to that of Massachusetts and Virginia. But the founders of Pennsylvania were a different group of Englishmen — a later generation, from another English region, with a special kind of Christian faith. Their idea of liberty was not the same as that which came to other parts of British America.

The most important of these differences had to do with religious freedom — "liberty of conscience," William Penn called it. This was not the conventional Protestant idea of liberty to do only that which is right. The Quakers believed that liberty of conscience extended even to ideas that they believed to be wrong. Their idea of "soul freedom" protected every Christian conscience.

The most articulate spokesman for this idea was William Penn himself. Of nearly sixty books and pamphlets that Penn wrote before coming to America, half were defenses of liberty of conscience. Some of these works were among the most powerful statements ever written on this subject. One ended with a revealing personal remark: ". . . tis a matter of great satisfaction to the author that he has so plainly cleared his conscience in pleading for the liberty of other men's."

Penn's idea of liberty of conscience was a moral absolute. It was summarized in many of his epigrams:

> Conscience is God's throne in man, and the power of it his prerogative.

> Liberty of conscience is every man's natural right, and he who is deprived of it is a slave in the midst of the greatest liberty.

> There is no reason to persecute any man in this world about anything that belongs to the next. . . .

These ideas of liberty of conscience were grounded in Penn's Quaker faith. He once remarked that there was an "instinct of a deity" within every human soul which needed no forcing from the hand of mortal man. Further, the idea of the inner light led him to believe that everyone possessed the power of telling truth from error. The optimistic fatalism of Quaker faith persuaded him that truth would inevitably overcome error if it were left free to do so. . . .

William Penn's personal experience of religious persecution gave him other reasons for believing in religious liberty. His own sufferings convinced him that the coercion of conscience was not merely evil but futile, and deeply dangerous to true faith. "They subvert all true religion," Penn wrote, ". . . where men believe, not because 'tis false, but so commanded by their superiors."

These memories and experiences were not Penn's alone. In the period from 1661 to 1685, historians estimate that at least 15,000 Quakers were imprisoned in England, and

In keeping with their belief in human equality and freedom of conscience, Quakers dressed simply and gathered in plain meetinghouses rather than ornate churches. This British painting shows an elder standing to address the congregation after an "inner light" inspired him to break the customary silence of Quaker worship. Quaker women could also speak at meetings and become elders, an egalitarian practice that prepared them to take leading roles in the abolitionist and women's rights movements of the nineteenth century. (Museum of Fine Arts, Boston. Bequest of Maxim Karolik.)

450 died for their beliefs. As late as the year 1685, more than 1,400 Quakers were still languishing in English jails. Most "books of sufferings" recorded punishments that continued well into the eighteenth century — mostly fines and seizures for nonpayment of tithes. . . .

Many Quaker immigrants to Pennsylvania had experienced this religious persecution; they shared a determination to prevent its growth in their own province. The first fundamental law passed in Pennsylvania guaranteed liberty of conscience for all who believed in "one Almighty God," and established complete freedom of worship. It also provided penalties for those who "derided the religion of others." The Quaker founders of Pennsylvania were not content merely to restrain government from interfering with rights of conscience. They also made it an instrument of positive protection. Here was a reciprocal idea of religious liberty which they actively extended to others as well as themselves.

Liberty of conscience was one of a large family of personal freedoms which Quakers extended equally to others. William Penn recognized three secular "rights of an Englishman": first, a "right and title to your own lives, liberties and estates; second, representative government; third, trial by jury." In Pennsylvania, these liberties went far beyond those of Massachusetts, Virginia and old England itself. In regard to the right of trial by jury, Penn insisted that every free-born Englishman had a right to be tried by his peers; that a jury had the right to decide questions of both fact and law; and that the law could not be used to punish a jury for its verdict. The laws of Pennsylvania also guaranteed the right of every freeman to a speedy trial, to a jury chosen by lot in criminal cases, and to the same privileges of witnesses and counsel as the prosecution. These ideas went far beyond prevailing practices in England and America. . . .

As regards the right of representative government, the Quaker colonies also went beyond other provinces in British America. One of the fundamental laws of Pennsylvania required that taxes could be imposed only by consent of the governed, and that all tax laws expired automatically after twelve months. These rules expressed the Quaker principle of reciprocal liberty, and their libertarian application of the golden rule, in the idea that no taxes should be levied upon the people except those which they were willing to impose upon themselves. . . .

The Quakers of the Delaware Valley also differed from other English-speaking people in regard to race slavery. The question was a difficult one for them. The first generation of Quakers had been deeply troubled by slavery, but many were not opposed outright. The problem was compounded in the Delaware Valley by the fact that slavery worked well as an economic institution in this region. Many Quakers bought slaves. Even William Penn did so. Of the leaders of the Philadelphia Yearly Meeting for whom evidence survives, 70 percent owned slaves in the period from 1681 to 1705.

But within the first decade of settlement a powerful antislavery movement began to develop in the Delaware Valley. As early as 1688, the Quakers of Germantown issued a testimony against slavery on the ground that it violated the golden rule. In 1696, two leading Quakers, Cadwalader Morgan and William Southeby, urged the Philadelphia Yearly Meeting to forbid slavery and slave trading. The meeting refused to go that far, but agreed to advise Quakers "not to encourage the bringing in of any more Negroes." As antislavery feeling expanded steadily among Friends, slaveowning declined among leaders of the Philadelphia Yearly Meeting — falling steadily from 70 percent before 1705, to only 10 percent after 1756.

The Pennsylvania legislature took action in 1712, passing a prohibitive duty on the importation of slaves. This measure was disallowed by the English Crown, which had a heavy stake in the slave trade. In 1730 the Philadelphia Yearly Meeting cautioned its members, but still a few Friends continued to buy slaves. Other Quaker antislavery petitions and papers followed in increasing number. . . . The argument came down to the reciprocal principle of the golden rule. Quakers argued that if they did not wish to be slaves themselves, they had no right to enslave others.

The turning point came in 1758. The Philadelphia Yearly Meeting recorded a "unanimous concern" against "the practice of importing, buying, selling, or keeping slaves for term of life." This was the first success for the cause of abolition anywhere in the Western world. "The history of the early abolitionist movement," writes historian Arthur Zilversmit, "is essentially the record of Quaker antislavery activities." . . .

. . . In 1773, non-Quakers joined Friends within the Pennsylvania legislature in trying to stop the trade in human flesh by imposing a prohibitively high duty on slaves. Once again it was disallowed by British imperial authorities. In January 1775, one of the first acts of Pennsylvania's Provincial Convention, when freed from British oversight, was to prohibit the importation of slaves. After a protracted legislative process, the Assembly also passed a bill in 1780 for the gradual abolition of slavery. Here was yet another expression of the idea of reciprocal liberty which Quakers made a part of the political folkways of the Delaware Valley. . . .

The Quakers radically redefined the "rights of Englishmen" in terms of their Christian beliefs. But they never imagined that they were creating something new. Penn and others in the colony wrote always of their rights as "ancient" and "fundamental" principles which were rooted in the immemorial customs of the English-speaking people and in the practices of the primitive church.

In the conservative cast of their libertarian thinking, the Quakers were much the same as Puritans and Anglicans. But in the substance of their libertarian thought they were very different. In respect to liberty of conscience, trial by jury, the rights of property, the rule of representation, and race slavery, Quakers genuinely believed that every liberty demanded for oneself should also be extended to others. . . .

BACKCOUNTRY FREEDOM WAYS:
THE BORDER IDEA
OF NATURAL LIBERTY

The backsettlers, no less than other colonists in every part of British America, brought with them a special way of thinking about power and freedom, and a strong attachment to their liberties. As early as the middle decades of the eighteenth century their political documents contained many references to liberty as their British birthright. In 1768, the people of Mecklenberg County, North Carolina, declared, "We shall ever be more ready to support the government under which we find the most liberty."

No matter whether they came from . . . England or Scotland or Ireland, their libertarian ideas were very much alike — and profoundly different from notions of liberty that had been carried to Massachusetts, Virginia and Pennsylvania. The traveler Johann Schoepf was much interested in ideas of law and liberty which he found in the backcountry. "They shun everything which appears to demand of them law and order, and anything that preaches constraint," Schoepf wrote of the backsettlers. "They hate the name of a justice, and yet they are not transgressors. Their object is merely wild. Altogether, natural freedom . . . is what pleases them."

This idea of "natural freedom" was widespread throughout the southern back settlements. But it was not a reflexive response to the "frontier" environment, nor was it "merely wild," as Schoepf believed. The backcountry idea of natural liberty was created by a complex interaction between the American environment and a European folk culture. It derived in large part from the British border country, where anarchic violence had long been a condition of life. The natural liberty of the borderers was an idea at once more radically libertarian, more strenuously hostile to ordering institutions than were the other cultures of British America. . . .

In North Britain this idea of natural liberty as something which "every animate creature does naturally desire . . ." was rapidly in process of decay during the eighteenth century. But in the hour of its extinction, it was carried to the American back settlements, where conditions conspired to give it new life. The remoteness of the population from centers of government and the absence of any material necessity for large-scale organization created an environment in which natural liberty flourished.

A leading advocate of natural liberty in the eighteenth century was Patrick Henry, a descendant of British borderers, and also a product of the American backcountry. Throughout his political career, Patrick Henry consistently defended the principles of minimal government, light taxes, and the right of armed resistance to authority in all cases which infringed liberty.

In the first great issue that brought him to notice — the court case called the Parsons Cause — Patrick Henry amazed his audience in the backcountry courthouse of Hanover County, Virginia, by arguing that the King, in disallowing an obscure act of 1758, had "degenerated into a tyrant and forfeit[ed] all rights to his subjects' obedience." The tidewater gentry were astounded by this argument. An eyewitness on that occasion remembered that "amongst some gentlemen in the crowd behind me, was a confused murmur of 'treason, treason!'" But the backcountry jury was "highly pleased with these doctrines." . . .

He is even better remembered for his headlong assault upon the Stamp Act, in a speech that threatened the King of England with tyrannicide: "Caesar had his Brutus," he declaimed, "Charles the First his Cromwell, and George the Third . . ." — and he was stopped short by the tidewater gentry who had felt Henry's lash upon their own backs. Patrick Henry went on to introduce the Virginia Resolves, which ended by declaring that all who dissented from his view of the question should be treated as an "enemy to this his Majesty's Colony" — a classical expression of the intolerance for contrary opinions which was part of the backcountry's idea of natural liberty. . . .

Patrick Henry's ideas of natural liberty were not learned from treatises on political theory. . . . [They] were drawn from the political folkways of the border culture in which he grew up. He embibed them from his mother, a lady who described the American Revolution as merely another set of "lowland troubles." The libertarian phrases and thoughts which echoed so strongly in the backcountry had earlier been heard in the borders of North Britain. When the backcountry people celebrated the supremacy of private interests they used the same thoughts and words as William Cotesworth, an English borderer who in 1717 declared: ". . . you know how natural it is to pursue private interest even against that Darling principle of a more general good. . . . It is the interest of the Public to be served by the man that can do it cheapest, though several private persons are injured by it."

This idea of natural liberty was not a reciprocal idea. It did not recognize the right of dissent or disagreement. Deviance from cultural norms was rarely tolerated; opposition

A frontier gentleman descended from a well-to-do family on the English border with Scotland, Patrick Henry gave classic expression to backcountry ideals of natural liberty. Henry shocked leaders from other American colonies with his vehement rhetoric and fierce opposition to British "tyranny." One described him as "in religious matters a saint; but the very Devil in politics." Henry went on to lead opposition to the new national constitution of 1787, claiming that its strong government threatened Americans' liberty. (Mead Art Museum, Amherst College, Bequest of Herbert L. Pratt, Class of 1895.)

was suppressed by force. One of Andrew Jackson's early biographers observed that "It appears to be more difficult for a North-of-Irelander than for other men to allow an honest difference of opinion in an opponent, so that he is apt to regard the terms opponent, and enemy as synonymous."

When backcountrymen moved west in search of that condition of natural freedom which Daniel Boone called "elbow room," they were repeating the thought of George Harrison, a North Briton who declared in the borderlands during the seventeenth century that "every man at nature's table has a right to elbow room." The southern frontier provided space for the realization of this ideal, but it did not create it.

This libertarian idea of natural freedom as "elbow room" was very far from the ordered freedom of New England towns, the hegemonic freedom of Virginia's county oligarchs, and the reciprocal freedom of Pennsylvania Quakers. Here was yet another freedom way which came to be rooted in the culture of an American region, where it flourished for many years to come.

QUESTIONS TO CONSIDER

1. Describe the four colonial-era migrations from Britain highlighted by the author. Compare and contrast their geographic origins, timing, destinations, religious beliefs, and concepts of freedom.

2. How did the migrant groups' different concepts of liberty shape contrasting regional cultures in Massachusetts, Pennsylvania, Virginia, and the western frontier? What role, if any, does Fischer attribute to such factors as climate, geography, and economic activity in the development of regional differences? In what ways do African slaves, Native Americans, and non-British immigrants figure in Fischer's regional comparisons?

3. To modern minds, concepts such as the "ordered liberty" of Puritan Massachusetts and the "hegemonic liberty" of Virginia appear self-contradictory. What assumptions held by colonial-era settlers allowed them to consider these terms logical and consistent? How are these assumptions similar to or different from those held by many twenty-first-century Americans?

4. Fischer labels his interpretation of colonial society a "modified 'germ thesis.'" In what ways does his account of British folkways return to the germ theory developed by historians in the nineteenth century? How does he modify it? How does his theory differ from the frontier thesis and the migration model? How might these theories supplement, rather than compete with, one another?

5. Despite the fact that less than 20 percent of today's Americans have any British ancestors, Fischer claims that British folkways lie behind "the continuing conflict between four different ideas of freedom in the United States." How might disagreements over the separation of church and state, individual privacy, taxation, and the role of government illustrate this? To what extent are conflicts over these issues still rooted in ancestral ties, religious beliefs, or regional differences?

As Various as Their Land

Stephanie Grauman Wolf

To capture in one theory how American society took shape in the colonial period is a daunting task when we recognize the huge differences among Puritan villagers in Massachusetts, German immigrants in Pennsylvania, and slave-owning planters in South Carolina. To make things even more difficult, any generalization about "Americans" must also encompass the experience of Native Americans and African Americans who were pushed to white society's periphery or forced to provide much of its menial labor.

In this selection, Stephanie Grauman Wolf views the transformation of colonial society through the prism of family and household, which were considered the basic building blocks of the preindustrial social structure. Beginning with traditional European concepts of "dynastic" families and "domestic" households, Wolf conducts a vivid tour of colonial households of all races, classes, and regions. Unlike exceptionalist historians, Wolf finds no sharp Old World–New World dichotomy. And in contrast to David Hackett Fischer in Selection 3, she does not offer one factor that explains American development. Instead, she portrays the formation of American society as a process in which the colonists' Old World "cultural baggage" combined with their labor status, economic means, place of settlement, and other factors to create a broad spectrum of family types. There was, she says, no single American household pattern. Rather, there was a rich multicultural mosaic. Southern planters developed a "pseudo-dynastic" family and New England Puritans advocated a biblical domestic household, while slaves and convict laborers had little chance to establish any stable family life. Native American tribal customs were so different that Euro Americans found them almost incomprehensible.

One pervasive change, however, began to course through family life during the eighteenth century. Because of increased city dwelling, the spread of labor for wages, the growing numbers of immigrants, and new familial bonds of affection, the nuclear family of parents and children increasingly replaced the extended household's jumble of relatives, boarders, and servants. By the century's end, the Middle Colonies' social profile of private nuclear families and unattached individuals was becoming the American norm. The triumph of a more individualistic society made colonial life more dynamic and modern, but it disappointed colonists who had brought the ideal of a tightly knit community with them across the Atlantic.

Astute readers will notice that Wolf's survey is domestically as well as internationally comparative. It portrays family patterns as shaped by region, class, culture, and race within the colonies, and it also assesses colonial households against inherited European models. Combine this with the impact of immigration and urbanization during the 1700s, and you have a complex story indeed. But Wolf's account artfully blends historical generalization with telling details, and it is unified by her respectful attention to the daily experience of common people in the past.

GLOSSARY

ALMSHOUSE   An institution in which paupers were maintained at public expense; a poorhouse.

APPRENTICESHIP   An arrangement in which a person was bound by legal agreement to work for an employer for a specified time in exchange for instruction in an art or trade.

CREOLES   A group designation that has had different meanings according to time and place. In this essay, it refers to blacks born in colonial America, as distinguished from those brought from Africa.

CULTURAL RELATIVISM   The concept that all cultures are ordered and rational systems of belief and behavior and should be judged on their own terms.

ENTAIL   A legal provision limiting the passage of a landed estate to a specified line of heirs.

EXTENDED HOUSEHOLD   A household including relatives beyond the nuclear family, servants, hired laborers, or others under one roof.

FEUDALISM   A political and social system in medieval and early modern Europe that featured landholding in return for dues and military service to a lord or king, and that concentrated power in the hands of lords based at castles.

GRIOT   In African kingdoms of the tenth through the twentieth century, a professional musician who recounted the history of tribes and offered counsel to rulers.

INDENTURED SERVANTS   Men or women bound to a master for a period of years, normally from three to seven. The master owned their labor and in return often paid for their passage to the colonies and provided food and shelter. Following their service, they were given money, tools and clothing, or land.

JOURNEYMAN   A worker who has completed an apprenticeship and labors for wages.

LINGUA FRANCA   A mixed language widely used as a means of communication among speakers of other languages.

MATHER, COTTON (1663–1728)   An influential Puritan minister in Massachusetts whose prolific writings promoted church authority and biblical learning.

MATRILINEAL   Tracing descent or family membership through women.

NUCLEAR FAMILY   A family unit consisting only of a mother and father and their children.

PATRIARCHAL   Ruled by a patriarch; that is, a man who is the head of a household or clan.

PATROONSHIP   A large estate given to Dutchmen who brought fifty immigrants to New Netherland to become their tenants.

PENN, WILLIAM (1644–1718)   The English Quaker leader who founded the Pennsylvania colony.

POLYGYNY   The practice of having more than one wife at a time.

PRIMOGENITURE   The system of inheritance by the firstborn, specifically the eldest son.

REDEMPTIONERS   Bound servants, similar to indentured servants, who sold themselves upon arrival in the colonies to pay for the cost of their passage.

SCOTS-IRISH   Scottish settlers in northern Ireland, mostly Presbyterians, many of whom migrated to the American colonies in the eighteenth century.

★ ★ ★ ★ ★ ★ ★

A reputable individual — alone — was almost unthinkable in the everyday world of America in 1700. From a practical point of view, a solitary human being had little chance of survival on the wild frontier or in the thinly settled agricultural regions and rural villages that made up the vast majority of the colonial lands. Even in rapidly growing cities such as Boston, New York, Philadelphia, or Kingston, Jamaica, where laborers were in short supply and desperately needed, newcomers were suspected and disliked. It is not surprising. Although the computer age gives us numerous ways of checking on a stranger's identity, from passports, driver's licenses, and other picture IDs to social security cards and credit cards, we still get fooled by a sharp line of talk or an ingratiating smile.

How much easier it was in the eighteenth century to prey on the gullible when most people had no "papers" at all to prove their identities. There were only a few documents that might be expected of a newcomer, and any of these could easily be forged, faked, or altered. The most common forms of legitimation included: signed indentures that indicated the satisfactory completion of an apprenticeship; redemption papers given to those who had finished the labor required when they sold themselves to gain passage to the New World; proof of freedom dues paid by blacks who had bought their way out of slavery; certificates of removal offered by some religious groups like the Quakers to ease the introduction of their members to a new community of worshippers; or a letter of introduction from a well-known person to a local resident.

Occasionally, there were less trustworthy, one-of-a-kind written documents attesting to the worthiness of a stranger. Such was the "parchment" carried by John Hill in 1733, when he attempted to earn a living as a panhandler on the streets of Boston. His "wife" Rachel did his speaking for him since, the parchment testified, he had been captured by the Turks and tortured, his arms burned by irons and his tongue torn out by the roots. Their act fooled many respectable Yankees despite the reputation of New Englanders for sharp judgment. It was not until one of the Hills' potential victims became suspicious, grabbed him by the throat, and forced him to "produce his Tongue or be choaked" that the couple ended up in the Boston prison, convicted of fraud. . . .

While the true exploits of run-of-the-mill con men were far from amusing to their many victims, it was not merely fear of being swindled or laughed at that made unattached individuals an anathema to eighteenth-century Euro-Americans. A conviction that people belonged in families was basic to their deepest culture. As an institution, the family in Europe had always been on a par with the church and the state, the third pillar on which the whole social system rested. Like the church and the state, the organization of families was patriarchal, headed by a man who not only controlled the private lives of those who depended on him, but also represented them in the public arena. Not all men shared in this power, however; those who were not at least the head of an individual family were considered subordinates along with all women and children.

If the duty of the state was to keep the peace and that of the church was to protect the soul, the family was charged with responsibility for the basic necessities of everyday life. Within the parameters of the walls and fields of the "Domestick oeconomie," crops and goods were produced, the young were educated in practical skills and moral behavior, and social services for "unproductive" members of the community — the old, the orphaned, the handicapped, the insane, and the just plain unruly — were provided. The first full-blown economic census of England, taken in 1688 by "Gregory King, Esqr, Lancaster herald at Armes," was organized by family, subsuming all individuals with the exception of "Vagrants; as Gipsies, Thieves, Beggars, &c."

Over the centuries, the traditional European institution of the family had come to include, roughly, two kinds of organization: the "House" with a capital "H" as in the Royal House or the House of Gloucester, which might be called the "dynastic" family; and the "household" with a small "h," which might be referred to as the "domestic" family. While each of these frameworks incorporated some of the meanings still included in our definition of the word "family," neither was based on the crucial modern criteria of a family: immediate blood ties and/or emotional nurturance and intensity.

The concept of the dynastic family was derived from both biblical and feudal ideas and practices. Essentially rural in nature, it embraced a complex set of relationships, functions, and responsibilities best characterized by the three "L's": land, lineage, and labor. It had less to do with our definition of blood relationship than it did with land and economics; more to do with power and control than it did with modern concepts of intimacy and affection. While the head of the House as well as his dependents recognized the special affinities of blood and emotion expressed by the titles of wife and child, parent, brother and sister, grandparents, aunt, uncle, or cousin, these were "relatives" rather than "family." Beyond them, the preferred term for more distant relatives was "kin," a word with no deeper overtones than "kith" (neighbor, friend, or ally), with which it was often paired.

The law stood behind the continuation of Houses through the apparatuses of primogeniture and entail, by which only the oldest male heir could inherit the lands and title. He, in turn, held them in trust for the next generation, and was legally forbidden to sell out or abdicate responsibility for the rest of his family. This family of obligation was made up of all those who lived on his land: his wife and children, of course; domestic "live-in" servants; farm laborers, bound or free; husbandmen who lived on scattered farms around the estate, and their live-in servants and laborers; and cottagers and artisans who lived in villages on the property. Whether or not the landowner even recognized them by sight, they were all considered to be part of his "family." In return for their labor and submission, all the members of the dynastic family down to the lowliest disabled and widowed cottager, in theory at least, were protected at the most basic level by an economic and social safety net of the master's devising.

In the everyday world, the dynastic family model was, for the most part, an ideal rather than a reality. Most members of Western society lived in domestic households — the alternative form of traditional family — circumscribed by the single farmstead, the craftsman's house and workshop, or the shopkeeper's apartments and store. Family members included those who lived and worked within these confines: the head of the household, his wife and resident children, his servants and apprentices. The grand alliances of dynastic families were mirrored on a small scale by the rural cooperation of neighboring farm households through resource sharing, labor pooling, and intermarriage. Urban merchant families did business with relatives, in-laws, and coreligionists in far-off places because they were felt to be known, and therefore more reliable and trustworthy than strangers.

The idea of "family" as blood or affectionate relationship was nearly as irrelevant to the domestic household as it was to the dynastic House. Individuals came and went, leaving one family and joining another as they grew from children in their fathers' houses to apprentices or servants in the houses of their masters; became heads of their own households when they finished their training, married, and went into business on their own; and finally, when widowed or elderly, entered the families of others, as dependents. They were always "kin," of course, to their birth relatives, emotionally and nostalgically attached, perhaps, but that was not part of the family domain.

While the dynastic family was based on the three L's of land, lineage, and labor, it was the third of these — labor — that really defined the parameters of the domestic household. The position of every member was determined by his or her ability to contribute to the economic goals of the enterprise. While the man at the head of the house was not necessarily the oldest male, he was the publicly acknowledged economic man of action, of legal maturity and in the fullest flower of his abilities, vigor, and energy. He headed the family unit as husband, father, and employer; his wife was wife, mother, manager of domestic arrangements, and, usually, a worker or supervisor in the business as well. The sons and daughters of the family were workers in the domestic economic venture as well as children of the household; apprentices and servants were usually young, and were treated as children of the household as well as workers.

"Out-servants" — adult journeymen or farm laborers who were married and lived outside the household walls — received some cash wages, but they, too, got much of their pay in "kind," taking their meals at the household table and regarded as quasi-members of the family. At either end of the life cycle were the inevitable, but less productive, members. Everyone loved the baby perhaps, but there was no "fat" in the budget for unproductive mouths and that baby had better get working as soon as possible. The elderly widow or, more rarely, widower who had given or lost control of the farm or workshop to a son or son-in-law occupied once more a position of dependence, assigned whatever tasks he or she could still manage, but of less significance even than the infant, who would eventually improve with age.

These bald outlines of dynastic House and domestic household, as well as the basic relationship of family to state and church, applied in most areas of the Western world from which settlers to the new colonies emigrated. Many of them brought with them the ideal of institutional families along with the actuality of a society largely made up of individual, autonomous households. When they came — from early in the seventeenth century to late in the eighteenth — and where they came from determined the cultural baggage they carried and influenced the kinds of family patterns they established in America. Where they settled, in terms of geography, climate, and isolation from other communities and from the Old World, was of prime importance as well. But who they were, the nature of their crossing and their reasons for undertaking it, were factors that loomed at least as large. Did they arrive with a group of friends, neighbors, and relatives from the Old Country, hoping to reestablish a purified form of Old Testament society that they felt had been abandoned or debased in Europe? Did they come in large, well-established households with enough money to guarantee settlement on their own land with plenty of equipment, intending, perhaps, to create a new nobility in the feudal style? Were they young married couples, with perhaps a baby or toddler in tow, whose plans included an economic sufficiency and independence they could never have achieved on the overcrowded soil of their homelands? Were they underage children of the poor, selling themselves or being sold into servitude for the price of their passage or convicts who considered indentured servitude abroad preferable to prison for crimes and misdemeanors? The mixture of all these elements created many varieties of ideal and real families with traits that shared some common values within regions, classes, and ethnic/religious identities and were loosely tailored to American experiences, but never to a single American pattern.

Totally different patterns of family life existed among the indigenous people of the American continent. While staple crops, living arrangements, and even population growth varied widely across the Western hemisphere, and the term "Amerindian" subsumes a great number of language groups, confederations, and tribes — Tlingits in the Northwest, Hopi in the Southwest, Iroquois in the Northeast, and Muscogulges in the Southeast, to name just a few — they possessed the same kind of basic similarities that united Swedes, Germans, English, French, Italians, or any of the other nation/state/language groupings under the single rubric "European." Anthropologists refer to this similarity where peoples share a common cultural heritage, if not a collective culture, as a "grammar of culture."

Generally, relationships within Native American families, clans, and tribes were far more supportive than were the frequently adversarial activities of landed families and nation-states in Europe. Extended families among the Amerindians carried most of the responsibility for organization, order, and diplomatic decisions. While women were surely not "leaders" in our sense of the word (this kind of linguistic problem is what makes cultural differences so hard to discuss), they clearly played an important, sometimes central, role in Amerindian public affairs. Among the Iroquois in the North, for example, family membership was determined through the mother rather than the father, in what we call a matrilineal pattern. Groups of families related through the mother's side made up *ohivarcheras;* several of these made a clan; a number of clans constituted a village; and constellations of villages made up the Iroquois Nation, or "kinship state." The ohivarcheras and the senior women who headed them had real political power. They chose the men who represented the clans in the larger meetings of villages and tribes, and who, in turn, picked the chiefs of the ruling council of the Nation. These men were always subject to being "dehorned," or removed, if they ignored the wishes of the women who had appointed them. Among the people in the Southeast, political succession followed matrilinear clan lines, so descent was through the eldest child of the eldest sister of the chief, leading to a number of women becoming chiefs in their own right.

Within the household, Amerindian women also wielded considerable power. While membership in the clan or totem of the Chippewas was inherited through the father, domestic life was organized through the bloodline of the mother. The important events of everyday life were controlled by hunting bands made up of matrilineal family units who lived next door to each other in individual wigwams belonging to the wife. When the son of an Iroquois family married, he left his own mother, sisters, and cousins to join his wife's household. If the couple could not work out a successful union, it was up to the wife to initiate divorce by setting her husband's belongings outside the door of their house. Muscogulge husbands were not themselves members of their wives' clans, but their children were, and while husbands might leave or be sent away, the children remained and were educated and disciplined by the mother's brother or another male relative.

Increasingly frequent intrusive and brutal contacts with European explorers and settlers forced alteration in the everyday family lives of Amerindians to meet the new situations. By the time the Muscogulge peoples — who were among the first to greet de Soto when he arrived in the southeastern part of the continent in the sixteenth century — had been renamed Creeks and Seminoles by the English in the early eighteenth century, their way of life had diverged far from its original settled agricultural patterns. They had, in fact, become professional hunters, closely tied to the international fur market. On the other hand, at the end of the century, the Mississauga tribes in the Great Lakes region learned through hard experience that they could only survive the European tidal wave by transforming their economy, and therefore their cultural patterns, from hunting and gathering to herding and farming.

The newcomers were not even aware of the deepest ways in which they influenced Amerindian life. By the time the Pilgrims landed in New England in 1620, the technology of the resident Algonkian tribes had already begun to be displaced by

European trade goods, and the issue was far more serious than a taste for a few new consumer items like beads, bells, rings, and mirrors. Goods that had once been manufactured within the domestic economy of the village were replaced by imports that served the same purpose but were made of materials considered more desirable. For example, brass and iron kettles were deemed preferable to vessels of soapstone or birch-bark, and glass bottles were selected over gourds and wooden bowls. Iron-edged tools and guns were clearly superior to flint axes, spears, and arrow points; while fashion dictated the replacement of dressed rawhide and fur clothing with woven textiles. While such substitutions were cultural adaptations rather than changes, the loss of the productive economic function of the family within the tribe struck a decisive blow at Amerindian domestic life.

The radical differences between Native American definitions of family and those of European colonials played a large part in the settlers' opinion that Indians were "savage" and "uncivilized." Since cultural relativism as a mode of thinking played virtually no part in the eighteenth-century mentality, neither side was able to recognize underlying similarities even when they existed. William Penn, for example, could not see (although we may) how closely the native custom among the Delaware Indians of refusing young men the right to marry "[until they had] given some proofs of their manhood by a good return of Skins" paralleled the insistence by Western society that marriage had to be delayed until one could support a wife. Native Americans relied principally on oral traditions of religion and myth, and on ritual performance of rites and ceremonies as the underpinning of their government. In a way, they lived within a system that was just the opposite of Europeans, downplaying the status of wealth, birth, and gender; rewarding individuals who were, at once, independent yet loyal to the tribe. These basic values of Indian society, when combined with power sharing between men and women, permissive methods of childrearing, and a legal process that did not "rationalize" nor write down its laws and decisions, created the impression among Europeans that Indians had no social controls, rules, or regulations at all. The very word "Indian," used as a verb, suggested terrifying anarchy: "Now, is it not . . . an Horrible Thing, for so many English . . . to Indianize [by adopting] the Indian Vices of Lying, and Idleness, and Sorcery, and a notorious want of all Family-Discipline . . . ," wrote Cotton Mather in *Things for a Distress'd People to Think upon,* at the dawn of the eighteenth century.

It was possible for some colonists to discern elements of nobility in Amerindians and to regard their savagery or lack of civilization as merely a function of their failure to be converted to Christianity. As early as 1700, on the other hand, blacks were found to be — as Thomas Jefferson later expressed it — "inferior to whites in the endowments both of body and mind, [which] inferiority is not merely the effect of their condition of life (slavery)." Added to this growing racial rationale for the justification of slavery was a lively perception of the danger posed to white society by a large population of slaves joined by strong family ties and kinship networks within their own communities. Although white colonists failed to suppress the complex, supportive patterns of domestic and personal relationships that flourished among blacks during the eighteenth century, the twin evils of theoretical racism and actual slavery tainted much of the process of family formation among African-Americans.

Attempts to prevent the transmission of African patterns of culture to the New World derived initially from fears of shipboard uprisings such as the one that took place on the *Ferrar Galley* when "[three hundred] Negroes of one Town Language" mutinied three times between Africa and Jamaica, killing the captain in the process. It was considered worth the slavers' while to wait four months or more, enduring the terrible conditions of the African shore, to assemble a cargo from different places since, as one mariner explained in his travel report: "[We choose the Negroes] from severall parts of ye Country, of different Languages; so that they find they cannot act joyntly, when they are not in a Capacity of Consulting on an other, and this they can not doe, in so far as they understand not one another." These tactics frequently failed, as the runaway slave ads in the *Virginia Gazette* repeatedly testified. In 1770, for example, within one month of his sale to an owner in Amherst County, Virginia, the slave Charles ran away to join three other African men who had arrived with him on the slave ship *Yanimarew*, but had been separated from him and sent to Richmond. . . .

In general, our knowledge and understanding of the development of African-American life in the eighteenth century is hampered by the white observers and record-keepers who either lacked interest in the everyday life of their slaves (except insofar as it affected their ability to work) or whose own cultural blinders caused them to misinterpret what they saw. Still, even through the veil of indifference, self-interest, and ethno-centricity, we can discern black determination to create unique domestic patterns that drew from elements of the European culture of their enslavers as well as from similarities among their varied African backgrounds. We must not forget, however, that their lives were also significantly shaped by the cruelties, vagaries, and arbitrary nature of both the individual slaveholder and the general laws governing slavery.

The grammar of African culture provided a surprising number of similar patterns of family life among blacks who, by the eighteenth century, not only lived under a wide variety of conditions but whose relationship to their roots diverged sharply from one another. There continued to be immigrants newly arrived direct from Africa, or those who had been briefly "seasoned" by a stay in Jamaica or the Indies; there were more and more Creoles, blacks born in colonial America with an African descent that was generations removed from their original roots; and there were those first-generation Africans who were "Creolized," adapted or assimilated to New World life by years or decades of residence among native African-Americans. . . .

Many basic family patterns of African life were apt to be directly attacked or contradicted by white owners or by the conditions of slavery itself. Most important for family formation was the ability to create stable marriages, whether in the African or European mode. On the one hand, the Christian morality of white Americans would seem to have argued for European marriage rites, and it is known that in New England such marriages were celebrated by African-Americans as early as the 1650s. Yet the African custom of polygyny (multiple wives for one man) and the fact that it was sometimes difficult to ascertain whether an African immigrant had, in fact, already been married before his or her capture and transportation led to an easing of sexual codes and matrimonial practices as they applied to blacks in the New World, although Yankee clergymen tried desperately to prevent such sinful behavior. In other colonies, the concern

This unusual painting from the late eighteenth century shows the resilience of family life among slaves as well as the mixing of African and European practices in the New World. The ceremony is most likely a wedding where, by African custom, the bride and groom jump over a stick. The slaves' clothes and musical instruments combine African and Euro-American influences. (Abby Aldrich Rockefeller Folk Art Center, Williamsburg, Virginia.)

was more that slave marriage might be a "desecration of the Holy Rites," as one New York Anglican minister worried when his literate slave "got the trick of marrying slaves with the office in the Common Prayer Book."

In the South, throughout the century, there was acceptance, if not actual encouragement, of the use of African marriage ceremonies. One North Carolinian, in the first half of the century, described the rite in a somewhat amused and condescending way: "Their Marriages are generally performed amongst themselves, there being very little ceremony used upon that Head; for the Man makes the Woman a Present, such as a *Brass Ring* or some other *Toy*, which she accepts of, becomes his wife; but if ever they part from each other, which frequently happens, upon any little Disgust, she returns his Present. These kinds of Contracts no longer binding them, then the Woman keeps the Pledge given her. . . ."

It is not surprising that there was reluctance on the part of African-Americans to make lifelong commitments when they had no control over their ability to remain together. While white owners, like Zephaniah Kingsley, a Florida planter, insisted that they "never interfered in [slave] connubial or domestic affairs, but let them regulate those after their own manner," slavery itself created the most intense interference, of course. Black couples were separated for a multitude of reasons that made sense only to the owners: as part of an inheritance settlement; to rationalize the business development of a distant, newly purchased quarter; to pay off debts; or just to cash in on the capital investment of a slave with top market value. Sometimes separation of a man and his wife was effected to punish the one or the other, commonly when they lived on neighboring plantations and persisted in visiting each other without permission. Many owners who did not actually follow through threatened to split husbands and wives as a way of exacting obedience.

Although slave masters frequently expressed sorrow at having to break up families, they also expressed amazement that, as Edward Shippen of Lancaster, Pennsylvania, put it, "blacks have natural affections as well as we have," and the Boston *Evening Post*, in 1746, headlined it "A very surprizing Tragedy" when a black couple carried out a suicide pact on hearing that the woman was to be sold "into the Country." Most seemed to take an attitude like that of Charles Ball's master when he turned down the slave's request for travel time to visit his wife and children on a nearby plantation before he was sold hundreds of miles away. It was a waste of time, the master decided since "[Ball] would be able to get another wife in Georgia."

More perceptive masters understood more clearly the fearsome nature of the separation of slave families. When Thomas Jefferson decided to make an example of his slave, Cary, who had deliberately injured another slave, he explained that if "[Cary] was sold in any other quarter so distant as never more to be heard of among us, it would be to the others as if he were put out of the way by death." Slaves saw the issue in exactly the same light, as Frederick Douglass, once a slave himself, expressed it many years later: "[He] was like a living man going into a tomb, who, with open eyes, sees himself buried out of sight and hearing of wife, children, and friends of kindred tie."

These "friends of kindred tie" were far more important across African cultures than Europeans could have possibly imagined. In the Old World, griot castes devoted themselves entirely to the perfection of memory skills to keep track of the significant dates, events, and members of enormous extended families. All of this richness and meaning in life were wiped away in the very instant of capture and transportation, but slowly and painfully over the course of generations in the New World, new kinship patterns were woven, unwittingly extended by the nature of slavery itself. Between 1740 and 1780, carefully constructed naming patterns began to establish special relationships that could be sustained through repeated household destruction and reformation. Whenever masters moved, or set up married children on new estates, or died, dividing their slaves among their heirs, new networks of extended slave families including aunts, nieces, nephews, and cousins developed across ever broader geographical boundaries. For many African-American families, memory and blood ties played the part in their lives that land and lineage fulfilled for the dynastic houses of Euro-Americans.

The idea of the dynastic family in its pure form, although it was rare and growing rarer in its original European setting, had a certain theoretical charm for some proprietors, recipients of large colonial land grants in the New World. The prospect of enormous tracts of unclaimed land that might be organized from scratch suggested that feudalism might be resurrected and given a fresh start. The eight wealthy noblemen who received title to all the land of the Carolinas from Charles II created a constitution based on just this concept. With the help of the famous philosopher John Locke, they devised an elaborate hierarchy of hereditary "seignors," "land-graves," "caciques," and "commoners," for those who actually settled in the colony, while the proprietors, who remained in England, retained control under such titles as "Lord Palatine" or "Lord

High Chamberlain." In New York, settled first by the Dutch, investors in the Dutch West India Company tried to lure settlers by setting up their own version of the feudal system of "lords and manors," promising a huge "patroonship," or land grant, to anyone who would come with at least fifty workers and establish a working estate. Maryland implemented an early system of land grants in the form of medieval baronial manors.

The failure of these schemes to achieve their ideal societies only highlighted the fact that the New World was scarcely fertile soil on which to reestablish the moribund conventions and expectations of the institutional feudal family. There was no tradition of ties to the land, no ancient relationships of patronage and deference that had made family more indicative of dependency than of kinship. Even the great families of New York were unwilling to adopt the legal strictures of primogeniture and entail, and took pride in providing large inheritances for every one of their children rather than availing themselves of those rules necessary for the maintenance and perpetuation of fiefdoms. Stephanus Van Courtlandt, one of the most prominent of New York's patroons, stipulated in his will, written in 1700, that his oldest son, Johannes, was to receive a share that was no more than "equall in worth" to those of his brother and nine sisters. In recognition of his position as the oldest, however, Johannes was given first choice of the gristmills, sawmills, farms, and city houses, as well as of the millions of acres of real estate investment that made up his 9 percent share of his father's property.

A distinctively American pseudo-dynastic family type did, indeed, develop and flourish on the large plantations of the southern colonies, and while we may see, with the benefit of hindsight, an almost grotesque transmogrification of the English model, eighteenth-century slaveholders saw nothing false or inappropriate in their identification with the medieval/Christian ideal. Like their counterparts in the Old World, the underpinnings of these upstart dynasties were rural, dependent on the ownership of large tracts of land from which they derived both economic wealth and political power. Interwoven networks of kin, based on notions of lineage rather than personal affection, held offices at every level of government — sheriffs or vestrymen at the local level, justices of the peace at the county level, and assemblymen and burgesses at the colony level — to protect their wealth and their social control of the less well-connected yeomen and small planters around them.

Great landed southerners were, perhaps, the only colonists who continued to extend their concept of family to all who lived on their property, however far-flung their quarters from the home plantation, however temporarily or impersonally connected to the household. In the early part of the century, William Byrd II, a member of one of Virginia's most influential dynastic families, kept a diary that provides a rare glimpse into the mind of at least one of these planters. . . . In the brief three-year period between 1709 and 1712, Byrd referred to over ninety members of his family, several of whom he could not even name, such as "the Frenchman" or "the old joiner." He made it quite clear that while his definition of family did not exclude his wife and children, it certainly did not accord them any particular distinction. Not only were they mentioned far less frequently than retainers, servants, and slaves, but they were also referred to in exactly the same terms, including concern for their illnesses and grief over their deaths.

In contrast to slaves, white middle-class colonists had the opportunity to raise large families. This painting of the Cheney family, circa 1795, shows how a lifelong pattern of giving birth every few years blurred the lines between generations. Note that the Cheney family, and perhaps its household, included a son-in-law, placed on the female side of the portrait. (Gift of Edgar William and Bernice Chrysler Garbisch, © 1996 Board of Trustees, National Gallery of Art, Washington, D.C.)

It was the substitution of a family of slaves of a different race and from an alien culture for servants, however circumscribed by old obligations, that separated dynastic family structure in America from its Old World model. An uneasy recognition of the incongruity led many southerners to refer to the Bible for their precedent, where slaves were common, rather than to feudal Europe, where they were not. As William Byrd II explained in a letter to the Earl of Orrery in 1726: "I have a large family of my own. . . . Like one of the patriarchs, I have my flocks and my herds, my bond-men and bond-women. . . . I must take care to keep all my people to their duty, to set all the springs in motion, and to make everyone draw his equal share to carry the machine forward. . . ." It was not until one hundred years later, when the last vestiges of feudalism were disappearing from England and southern slavery was thoroughly institutionalized by generations of plantation masters with a work force entirely made up of Creole African-Americans, that an English visitor could note with some nostalgia: "There is an hereditary regard and often attachments [of the slaves to their owners] more like that formerly existing between lords and their retainers in the old feudal times of Europe. . . ." Eighteenth-century planters knew better as they worked unremittingly to protect themselves against poisonings, arson, and uprisings among their black slaves.

In many ways, after all, it was slavery that made it possible for a rural dynastic social and economic organization to remain viable in the increasingly fast-paced economy of an industrializing world. While English landlords rethought the family nature of their relationship with their tenants and laborers, cutting them off from ancient rights and evacuating them from the land to rationalize the business of agriculture and produce the wealth they needed to maintain social and political power, southern slave owners could make business decisions secure in the knowledge that they could reorganize and manipulate their workers to suit changing economic opportunities and needs. Although it required some tact, some blinking at infringement, and the frequent use of coercion and force, to say nothing of continual vigilance for sabotage and violence, the masters could, more or less, make decisions free of labor constraints.

After the Revolution, for example, many planters in the Chesapeake saw the need to move from a staple crop of tobacco to mixed farming in cattle raising and grain production. Since this change allowed use of the plow instead of the hoe, planters were able to reduce the number of their field hands. Some workers were transferred to non-agricultural tasks and others were hired out to neighbors as carpenters, millers, or the like, but since plow culture used male slaves predominantly, the successful plantation required a new mix in the work force, involving a higher proportion of men. This purely business decision had a devastating effect on the black family. Prime adult male slaves were retrained to use the plow, while women and children who were no longer needed were disposed of through sales to distant places where hoe culture was still practiced, or retrained for town work, particularly in home or shop service. Those planters who were reluctant to break up slave families faced the prospect of diminished profits.

Nothing could seem further removed from the dynastic plantation family of the colonial south than the vision and actuality of the domestic household in Puritan New England, although here, too, it had its grounding in the Bible. The earliest colonists in Massachusetts had no interest in perpetuating feudal ideas, but were intensely committed to returning to the purity of the Old Testament vision of family and community. Isolated men or women were seen to tear at a social fabric based on the sixth verse of Psalm 68: "God setteth the solitary in families." If God worked from this principle, surely New Englanders could do no less. An early law of Plymouth Plantation stated that "Whereas great inconvenience hath arisen by single persons in the Colony being for themselves and not betaking themselves to live in well-governed families, it is enacted by the Court that henceforth no single person be suffered to live of himself. . . ." In Massachusetts Bay, groups of unattached white male servants were organized into artificial family units, while stray "bachelors and maids" were placed under the discipline of local households. Connecticut ordered that "no young man that is neither married nor hath any servant . . . shall keep house by himself. . . ." John Littleale of Haverhill was found by the Massachusetts Court in 1662 to "lay in a house by himself contrary to the law of the country, whereby he is subject to much sin and iniquity, which ordinarily are the companions and consequences of a solitary life." He was ordered to get out of town, find himself some "orderly" family, accept that one that the selectmen found for him, or be placed in the house of correction.

Local communities in New England also kept a close eye on family units once established, continuing to support the older English system where governance, socialization, social welfare, and economic activities all fell within the purview of the domestic household. Town fathers felt free to interfere when a family seemed unable to manage on its own. In 1667, for example, in Springfield, Massachusetts, they had found it necessary to take James Osborne in hand after he had spent several years making bad deals and incurring debts he could not pay. It was reported at a town meeting that it was "mutually aggreed by the Inhabitants that . . . James Osborne doth prejudice him self and his family by disadvantagious bargaynes. It is . . . voted and concluded that none of the Inhabitants of this Town shall or will make any bargayne with the said J———— O———— without the consent of two or three of the Select men that shall amount to above 10s[hillings] value." While this kind of intense oversight waned during the eighteenth century, the ideal continued to be sought and partially practiced in many newly "planted" or isolated rural settlements.

The Puritan church was organized by families as well, with the head of each domestic household held responsible for the moral and religious well-being of each member, along with his or her economic viability. Servants, therefore, received baptism into the Christian covenant as part of the master's family, and this applied to black slaves as well, as Cotton Mather, the quintessential New England Puritan, noted in 1706: "[Our black slaves are] of our own household . . . [and] more clearly related to us than many others are." Although the primacy of Puritan thought and control sank under the diverse pressures of population increase, new economic priorities, fragmented religious organizations, and political fractiousness that increasingly penetrated the fastness of New England throughout the eighteenth century, many of the early ideals and a fair number of seventeenth-century practices continued to dominate family life, particularly in the more rural areas of the region. The word "family" remained a term of household intimacy rather than blood relationship while "kin" referred to those of near or distant blood or marriage ties on whom one could count for co-operation. Neighbors were often more important than "kin," although in the context of small isolated rural towns and villages the two were frequently the same.

New England farm households contained a fairly large number of people under one roof, perhaps as many as seven or eight at any given time, some blood relatives, some not. The basic labor force of the domestic economy most commonly included one's own children and those of neighbors, although the family could also traditionally contain one or another kind of servant, attached more or less permanently and due differing kinds of compensation. The nature of the servitude and the acceptance of nonblood household residents as "familiars" varied both over time through the eighteenth century and according to the rural, village, or urban setting of the household. In all times and places one could find apprentices, youngsters living in a family to learn the "art and mystery" of a craft or trade, from husbandry to silversmithing. At the beginning of the century, families in rural communities or villages regularly contained servants who received only the necessities, and were working to pay off debts or as punishment for crimes committed. One also found numbers of indentured servants who could look forward to a set of tools and a suit of clothing at the end of their terms, which were most often set at seven years. Both of these types of family laborers became less and less frequent during the century and were largely replaced by hired servants on yearly contract, who received not only the basic room and board, but additional compensation in the form of wages.

Sometimes the cost of their upkeep was subtracted from their wages, sometimes not. Particularly where there were no children left in the household, or where there were no boys old enough, the "hired hand" became a family fixture, remaining year after year, growing old, dying, mourned, and buried within the domestic household of work, even if he had blood relatives in the vicinity. This became, along with the labor of one's own children, the most lasting, characteristic form of rural labor on small farms in New England, described as a still-existing phenomenon in an early twentieth-century poem by Robert Frost, "The Death of the Hired Man."

The unmarried female "retainer" was an even more ubiquitous and integral part of the New England family circle, since every farm household needed at least one woman to do jobs outside the male domain such as laundry, cleaning, and needlework. In general, the women received less than half the wages of the men. Hired male servants who were married were, as they were in England, in a somewhat anomalous position, since their wives and children were expected to live elsewhere and were not generally part of the family in which the servant himself was accepted. He stood as head of his own blood household, a marginal one at best, probably with few roots in the community; one of the many throughout New England who could be seen in April if he failed to negotiate a contract for the coming year, moving along the country road with his family, goods piled high on a cart, hoping to find work in another community to carry him through the next harvest.

Slaves, whether Amerindian or black, formed only a tiny part of the New England family scene — 2 to 3 percent by the time of the Revolution — yet their place in those families and the manner of their lives is significant for an understanding of the vast gulf that lay between the cultural style and values of northern and southern states by the end of the eighteenth century. . . .

Since wealth was not to be dragged from the stony soil in the harsh climate of the northern colonies, the question of large plantation dynasties arose only infrequently, and slaves made little sense as capital. Wealthy merchants frequently got rich trading in blacks as merchandise, but rarely by exploiting them as labor. New Englanders, attempting to provide for their heirs through business as southerners did through land-holding, needed new financial instruments — testamentary trusts, charitable foundations, and holding companies — rather than easily destructible human beings who required constant upkeep in the form of food, clothes, and shelter. However, while slaves were of little use *en masse* to the New England merchant, a few were trained for specialized business purposes, and status was given a boost through a quaintly dressed black slave acting as coachman, footman, doorman, or butler. Blacks held by rural masters, artisans in town or country, or those of few pretensions who merely needed an extra pair of working hands around the place usually did the same work as grown children, white retainers, or hired help, and were similarly regarded as members of the family. For the most part, even where there were several blacks living in a neighborhood, there were never more than a very few in any single household. As a result, northern slaves lived lonely lives as enslaved members of white families rather than more sociable ones as part of whole families of slaves on southern plantations.

This difference seriously hindered the ability of northern blacks to form the strong family ties and patterns that gave southern slaves a modicum of independent choice and control over their own destinies. On the other hand, it was more likely that individual blacks in the north were treated like human beings by their white owners and had at least some feelings of self-worth as members of their household families. . . .

The best description of the violation of black family life that occurred in the north is found in a petition for freedom presented to the Massachusetts General Court by a group of slaves in 1774:

> . . . we are deprived of every thing that hath a tendency to make life more tolerable, the endearing ties of husband and wife we are strangers to for we are no longer man and wife than our masters or mistresses thinkes proper married or onmarried. Our children are also taken from us by force and sent maney miles from us wear we seldom or ever see them again there to be made slaves of for Life which sumtimes is vere short by Reson of Being dragged from their mothers Breest . . . how can a slave perform the duties of a husband to a wife or parent to his child How can the wife submit themselves to their husbands in all things How can the child obey thear husbands in all things. . . .

In their plea for freedom, these Massachusetts slaves presented another definition of "family" that neither relied on the ideal of the great southern planter's biblical dynasty nor on the model of domestic household expressed by the Puritan farmer. It was a definition that had begun to be articulated in the mid-seventeenth century in England when the *Oxford English Dictionary,* ultimate arbiter in the search for the meaning of words and their change through time, first dropped all reference to outsiders working within a household as part of the family, and included only "the group consisting of parents [and] their children whether living together or not." What this left was a core or nucleus: a father, mother, and their children, tied together by blood rather than by economic necessity and organization. It was this so-called nuclear family that became the reality of most of America, and the wave of the future. It was not the nineteenth-century sentimental vision of cuddly babies, loving, selfless mothers, and proud, protective fathers, but a new ordering of personal relationships that read children and parents into an inseparable unit even when the children no longer lived at home, and read strangers out even when they passed their lives on the premises. By the end of the eighteenth century, it had become the common form of family life in every corner of the new nation, although pockets of New England farmers and southern planters hung on to their old ways into the nineteenth century and beyond.

The desire to remove unrelated household members from the bosom of the family came early in the Chesapeake, among the small planters of Maryland and Virginia, and had to do with feelings about race and class more than it did with wage labor. In fact, the workers they so assiduously excluded right from the start of the eighteenth century were not wage workers at all, but bound servants, black or white, who were legally attached to their households — either forever, in the case of black slaves, or for a long term of years, as in the case of white convict labor. Black slaves may well have fared worse than in most other colonies. Viewed through the racial prism of southern attitudes, they were isolated on small farms without the kind of support system that came from being part of a slave family on a plantation; yet they did not become a family slave in the manner of New

England's single black servant within a household. As slaves became at once more skilled and more expensive during the eighteenth century, small farmers in the Upper South turned to a new kind of bound white labor, finding that they could more easily afford to buy convicts imported into the colonies under a statute of Parliament in 1717 "for the further preventing robbery, burglary, and other felonies, and for the more effectual transportation of felons. . . ." Through this law, which remained in effect until the Revolution, Maryland and Virginia absorbed most of the fifty thousand-plus convicts transported to the colonies, effectively "Draining [the mother country] of its offensive Rubbish, without taking away their lives," as the policy was described by a British pamphlet in 1731. . . .

. . . The vast majority of these unwilling immigrants were poor, unattached young men in their early twenties. Each had committed some fairly serious crime, often more than once, and had had no friend or family connection with enough influence to get the sentence commuted. Convict transports were apt to be untrained, at least in anything but criminal activity, or trained inappropriately for the needs of the masters who bought them. . . . Convicted felons were certainly seen as dangerous enough to keep away from one's wife and daughters, especially since, according to the *Maryland Gazette* in 1767, they were carriers of "the foulest Poluttions" and were likely to transmit all kinds of diseases, presumably venereal, through proximity to Maryland families.

Like slaves, convict laborers had little opportunity to establish stable families of their own. Since there were at least four men to every woman among those who were transported, even casual sex was difficult to come by, and marriage partners almost impossible. For the most part, bound laborers were permitted to marry only with the master's approval, which was rarely forthcoming, completing a family "catch-22" where convicts were not really part of a domestic household, yet were unable to form nuclear units of their own. The harsh nature of their treatment — they were seen to be even more exploitable than slaves, partly because they had been less expensive — and the restricted lives and opportunities available to them even after their period of servitude was over encouraged a life-style of gambling, alcoholism, and brawling. During the century, laws were enacted in both Maryland and Virginia that further restricted the convicts' access to civil rights and placed them in a position before the courts that was closer to that of slaves, although their own racism prevented them, in most cases, from seeking any kind of common cause with African-Americans.

Middle Colony farmers much preferred white labor to black, voluntary indentures to convicts, and free wage labor to any of the above; yet it was neither race nor class aversion that led to the firm establishment of the nuclear family as the basic pattern of domestic life in this region by the second half of the century. Rather, the difference was made by a complex combination of [the] . . . beliefs of Quakers and Germans, the changing nature of the German and Scots-Irish immigration over the course of the eighteenth century, and the development of a rationalized economy that found wage labor to be more profitable than bound labor.

Among New England Puritans, a shift to contract labor had often meant that these workers, along with any slaves, became members of the family circle. To the Quaker settlers of Pennsylvania and New Jersey, however, this kind of intimacy presented a danger. They believed that religious regeneration was manifested by an "Inner Light" aided by "holy conversation" between people who had already achieved the "Truth." Those who were not part of holy conversation not only suppressed the Light for themselves, but also tended to corrupt others, and should not be part of a household in which Quaker parents tried to protect their children from such "carnal talkers." Rich Quaker farmers, therefore, were apt to isolate their workers, slave or free, from the innermost circle of the hearth, and although the reason for exclusion was spiritual rather than social, the effects on the servants themselves were not dissimilar to those of the Chesapeake. Quakers made some use of slaves in their fields, houses, and shops until the predominance of wage labor was clearly established and scruples concerning the system of bondage caused the Meeting to put teeth into their abolitionist rhetoric.

German immigrants, within their own cultural frame of reference, had no background of contact with either Africans as a race or slavery as a system. Their distaste and unfamiliarity with black bondage was clearly stated in a protest issued by a newly arrived group of German Quakers, living in Germantown, Pennsylvania, in 1688: "We hear that the most part of such negers are brought hither against their will and consent, and that many of them are stolen. Now, though they are black, we cannot conceive there is more liberty to have them slaves, as it is to have other white ones. . . . And those who steal or rob men, and those who buy or purchase them, are they not all alike?" Acculturation to the New World led to a growing incidence of racial antipathy among Germans toward such "idle, slothful people" and for this reason as much as for their earlier philosophical stance they tended to eschew slaveholding in favor of the use of white indentured servants and tenant families.

The second reason for the early development of nuclear families in the Middle Colonies had to do with the changing shape of its immigrant population. Unlike New England, where immigration almost ceased during the eighteenth century, or the Chesapeake and Deep South, where most new arrivals came as forced labor, black or convict, the key feature of Middle Colony demographic life throughout the period was an abundant flow of non-English European settlers who eventually made up one-third to one-half of the total inhabitants. In the early decades of the eighteenth century, immigrants of many ethnic backgrounds — but primarily Germans and Scots-Irish — arrived as single young men or teenagers, younger sons who could not be provided for by their families at home, and who sought, through the indenture system, to establish independent lives for themselves in the New World. Pennsylvania was particularly attractive, since a servant who worked out his time was entitled to land as well as to the traditional small sum of cash and "two suits of cloathes" as "freedom dues." . . .

Beginning in the 1730s, poor economic conditions in Germany and Ireland caused the migration of whole families rather than healthy young men looking to improve their lot. Called "redemptioners" because they usually sold themselves into servitude to redeem the loan for their passage, these families were generally poorer and less well connected than earlier immigrants had been. They arrived in small units: Most commonly families consisted of a young married couple with a small child or perhaps two; older couples who brought teenage children, sold separately to pay ship's passage for the whole family; or occasionally small numbers of adult siblings, hoping to save enough to send home for aged parents. During these same years, Pennsylvania ended the practice of distributing land to servants at the conclusion of their indentures, and the arrival of so many new workers caused a cyclical glut of labor on the market. The unfortunate latecomers were often moved in gangs by "soul drivers" to less settled parts of the colony where questions of ability or stamina were overridden by the consuming need to get the land cleared and planted.

By mid-century, the economic advantage of binding whole families of servants into a household was beginning to disappear in favor of hiring individuals as wage laborers, leaving immigrant families to shift for themselves, and creating what we might call cast-off nuclear families. Living separately in assigned cottages on large farms, by the end of the century these families were far from independent. Unlike tenants who merely rented land and house for a set fee, paid the taxes on it, and were free to pursue their interests, cottagers had no such control over their own lives. They received their house, a set amount of firewood, a small plot on which they could raise some of their own food, and the right "to keep a cow and run a pig in the lane" for a small sum written off against the labor they and their families provided the farmer. They could also expect to be able to "rent the use of a plow and horses in the spring for their own little patches, a wagon and team to haul their wood or, on moving day, their family goods." They were "promised wages as harvest hands," farm work by the day at other times of the year, and if they had a skill such as weaving, they were paid wages by the piece for the work they did. Their wives and children might earn extra money by helping with the harvest, by spinning, or by performing domestic services for the farmer's wife. The rates for all of this work were generally fixed by custom, as were deductions from wages for things like liquor when it was provided along with meals during work. Most importantly, the employer set the amount of work done: he had no obligation to use his "cottagers" for a guaranteed amount of time, and they were responsible for finding other jobs to tide themselves over when their services were not required. On the other hand, he could monopolize their time for low rates, leaving them no opportunity to plant their own plots or work their trades to their own advantage.

Some landowners, of course, continued to maintain old-style domestic households, sheltering within their walls and at their tables a domestic servant, an apprentice, a single laborer, and/or a bound servant. The gulf between these workers and the farmer's own "flesh and blood" tended to be wider than it had been in the Old Country or the old days. They were regarded as "inmates" rather than intimates, and their room and board were not provided as part of a family exchange, but were charged at a commercial rate. In addition, their living spaces tended to be isolated from those of the "real" family, like "the west end of the house and garden," assigned to Greenwag and Cuff, single farm workers on the property of Caleb Brinton in Chester County, Pennsylvania, in 1781. Frequently inmates were bedded down in barns or sheds, or even as boarders with the cottagers.

It is in the cities of eighteenth-century America that we find the greatest number of cast-off nuclear families, independent because they had been cut adrift by the changeover from term labor to wage labor rather than because they had made any conscious decision to create a home for wives and children. They occupied the lowest rungs of the economic ladder where there was no safety net in the form of a master who owed them any personal obligation. The change that had taken place in reading servants out of the domestic family, paying them a wage, and giving them the freedom to set up their own households, marry, and rear children of their own is documented in the pages of the diary of Elizabeth Drinker, wife of a wealthy Philadelphia Quaker. During the 1790s, several women who had worked for the family from eleven to twenty-one years before applied to Mrs. Drinker for help when they or their husbands became disabled, or fell on hard times and were unable to support their families. It is clear that these former servants evidently felt something of the old entitlement to membership in the Drinkers' family, but it is equally clear that the Drinkers felt no such reciprocal responsibility. Although Elizabeth treated Betty Burge, for example, as she would have done any beggar, giving her "some victuals and some money," she did not see that there was any further obligation, noting that ". . . I don't expect H[enry] D[rinker] will give her a good character [recommendation], he can't, tho' perhaps she may be recommended as a proper object of charity."

The lives of laboring families in the city were far more precarious than those of rural cottagers. They had to find their own housing and generate enough income or credit to cover their food, rent, fuel, and clothing even when they received no wages because they were laid off. Men, women, and children all worked. Children of the laboring poor often disappeared from the small core family, indentured away by the Guardians of the Poor, an eighteenth-century version of a public welfare agency, since there was no one at home to care for them. One of the vaunted advantages of nuclear families, that of privacy, was almost always denied to urban wage workers, who either took in boarders or rented space and became boarders themselves as a principal way of lowering their housing costs or acquiring a little cash. Shared housing did not, however, mean a blending of family units; there is a good bit of evidence that attempts were made to provide internal divisions within the house, and even, where possible, two separate hearths for heating and cooking. When two unrelated mariners and their families occupied the same house in Boston "under the same roof" from 1754 through 1755, one part of the house was known as "the said McCartys end of the house."

At the end of the century, the individual without a family and the couple without a home were still as unacceptable to colonial society as they had been in the early 1700s. They had become, however, an established part of a system in which families were no longer expected to number among their members all those who lived within their walls or provide housing for those who merely worked by the day in the woodworking shop or shipyard. Each of the major cities had to cope with great numbers of continually shifting, single, young people of few skills, fewer resources, and no family ties at all. Young men with jobs and mariners between voyages boarded with families in cramped back-alley tenements or in boardinghouses along the wharves. Single women, whose work was almost surely domestic, continued to live in the homes of their employers under family regulation as long as they held their jobs. Prostitutes were the principal exceptions, living on their own in the nooks and crannies of the city, from inns to stables to open alleyways.

Urban communities (rural areas as well, if they were past the frontier stage) began to come to grips with the idea that the private sector, as we would call it today, was not able to cope with the effects of unemployment and underemployment resulting from the changed institution of the family. They fell back on the old British model of the almshouse, or bettering house, as a refuge for the "perishing poor," in addition to the custom of outdoor relief whereby a cash-short family might be tided over with a judicious handout of flour or firewood. In the Old World, these institutions had been intended only for the benefit of local, worthy indigents, but in the larger, more anonymous world of the young Republic, it was necessary to provide social services, in the name of humanity, even to those who seemed clearly unworthy. So the clerk of the Philadelphia Almshouse grumbled about Ruth and Henry Kendall in the summer of 1789:

> [These are the] most Notorious Strolling Ramblers generally known from Boston to Baltimore. . . . They appear to have scarce any necessary Cloathing. But are very artful in appearance, frequently leaving their cloathes & other property at different places through the Country & though they may have Money, came here [the poorhouse] in such wretched plight & swarming with Vermin so as immediately to extort clothing. They are both lame & both subject to Fits, of which with their wretched plight extorts Commiseration and Charity.

He grumbled, but he took them in.

QUESTIONS TO CONSIDER

1. Compare Native American concepts of family and household with those of the European colonists. In what ways did the colonists misinterpret Native American customs? How did contacts with European settlers change Amerindian domestic life?

2. Discuss the ways that Euro American family and household patterns varied by region and class. Why did attempts to plant feudalism in New York and Maryland fail? Why does the author call the southern plantation family an "almost grotesque" transformation of the English dynastic family? How was the Puritan domestic household influenced by religious concepts of community? Why did the mixture of nuclear families and footloose individuals first become the norm in the Chesapeake and Middle Colonies? In what ways did the evolution of economic and domestic life in the 1700s contribute to an increase in individualism? How were Americans likely to feel about this trend?

3. Describe the problems besetting African American slaves as they tried to create a stable family life. How did their domestic patterns reflect their African heritage? the European culture of their masters? the colonial region they lived in? the disruptions of slavery?

4. What dimensions does Wolf's survey of colonial families add to David Hackett Fischer's portrayal (in Selection 3) of British folkways in the colonies? Does Wolf agree with Fischer's emphasis upon the colonists' "cultural baggage," or does she attempt to modify or supplement it? How successfully does she incorporate race, region, and class into her account? What are the strengths and weaknesses of Fischer and Wolf's different approaches?

5. What overall differences do you see between eighteenth- and twenty-first-century families in America? Discuss such aspects as the extended household, the importance of kinship, the role of women, and the education and socialization of children. Do any elements of the dynastic family or domestic household survive today?

THE ATLANTIC SYSTEM

Until the age of world wars and jet travel, many Americans thought of the oceans that separate them from the rest of the world as formidable barriers. This perception bolstered Americans' faith in their national uniqueness and encouraged their isolationist sentiments. In important respects, however, it was misleading. Considering the flow of goods, people, money, and ideas that crossed to and from the New World in the centuries after Columbus, it makes greater sense to think of these oceans — especially the Atlantic — as lakes that lined the shores of several continents or highways that linked them together. An integrated Atlantic world began forming during the era of European exploration, and by 1700 it had evolved to become a dense network of trade and migration. The joint creation of European, African, and Native American enterprise, this world replaced the Mediterranean Sea and rivaled the Indian Ocean as a central highway on which Europeans, Africans, and native peoples traveled, exchanged goods, negotiated identities, and vied for power.

Britain's North American colonies originated on the edge of this world, but they were quickly brought into its orbit. Although the earliest colonists in Virginia and Massachusetts lived in precarious isolation from Europe, contacts across the Atlantic increased dramatically by the 1700s. A population explosion in Europe spurred the overseas migration of whites from Britain, Holland, and Germany. Meanwhile, the phenomenal growth of the slave trade from Africa made possible the expansion of staple-crop production in sugar, rice, and tobacco in Britain's Caribbean and southern mainland colonies, just as it had already done in Latin America. By 1750, Britain's thirteen mainland colonies had almost two million residents, nearly ten times the number of 1700. No longer isolated, the North American colonists had become part of a vast Atlantic circuit, a human network of ports and passages linking them to merchants, consumers, and laborers in Europe, Africa, and the Caribbean. Often called the "triangular trade," it was in fact a far more complex web of two-way voyages that created an integrated transoceanic economy and encouraged frequent exchanges of religious and scientific ideas as well (see map on p. 78).

The two essays that follow explore this eighteenth-century Atlantic system of economic and cultural ties at different levels. In the first selection, Charles Bergquist takes a *macroscopic* view that links the American continents to European mercantile centers. Beginning by noting the divergent fates of rich and poor New World settlements, Bergquist compares the roles played by British and other European colonies in the evolving Atlantic economy. According to Bergquist, the key to long-term economic success, as opposed to immediate wealth, can be found in whether each colony relied upon free or unfree labor. Free-labor societies encouraged economic development, while plantation economies retarded it, with consequences that outlived slavery itself.

Since slave labor was a cornerstone of the Atlantic economy, it is appropriate that Winthrop D. Jordan, author of the second selection, examines colonial slave societies on a more *microscopic* level. Jordan's particular subject is race; he compares the dynamics of black-white relations in Britain's mainland colonies against the situation in the West Indies, where a tiny English elite oversaw huge sugar plantations worked by armies of imported slaves. Jordan's essay suggests that a closer analysis can reveal important differences between Britain's plantation colonies that Bergquist's broad dichotomy between free and slave societies overlooks. Nevertheless, both essays demonstrate how comparison can highlight distinctive colonial patterns in the Atlantic world and how those colonial beginnings returned to haunt future nations.

The Paradox
of Development
in the Americas

CHARLES BERGQUIST

The Atlantic trading system that connected Europe, West Africa, and the Americas provides the context for Charles Bergquist's panoramic essay, which weaves together the various threads that formed this system. Bergquist frames his discussion by addressing a striking paradox: why did the wealthy Caribbean colonies eventually become the poorest independent nations of the Americas, while the poorest New World colonies, those of British North America, developed into the richest nation in the world?

Bergquist finds one key to understanding this paradox by comparing the roles played by the Iberian (Spanish and Portuguese) and British colonies in the Atlantic economy. New World settlements became integrated into the Atlantic system in different ways. Iberian provinces were forced to provide precious minerals and staple crops for their mother country, but British colonies gained their livelihoods in more diverse fashion. In South Carolina, Virginia, and the British Caribbean, cultivation of rice, tobacco, and sugar encouraged booming plantation economies broadly resembling those of the Spanish Caribbean or Portuguese Brazil. Farther north, however, colonists on the eastern seaboard accumulated wealth in slower but ultimately more lasting ways. In the Middle Colonies, free white settlers grew wheat and corn for local consumption and employed wage laborers or indentured servants in their fields and workshops. In New England, which lacked good climate and soil for cultivation, colonists' shrewd investment in shipping and manufacturing enterprises enabled them to copy England's success. Eventually, these "Yankees" competed with the mother country in the triangular trade, providing the West Indies with manufacturing goods in return for sugar, which, when processed into rum, was then exchanged for slaves in West Africa.

Above all, says Bergquist, the different labor systems adopted by colonies in the Americas, not their national, racial, or cultural composition, best explain their divergent economic outcomes. Rapid expansion of the African slave trade after 1600 offered white settlers a cheap, exploitable labor force to replace Indians lost to disease. Colonies with warmer climates took full advantage by concentrating upon export crops and relying more and more on slaves to

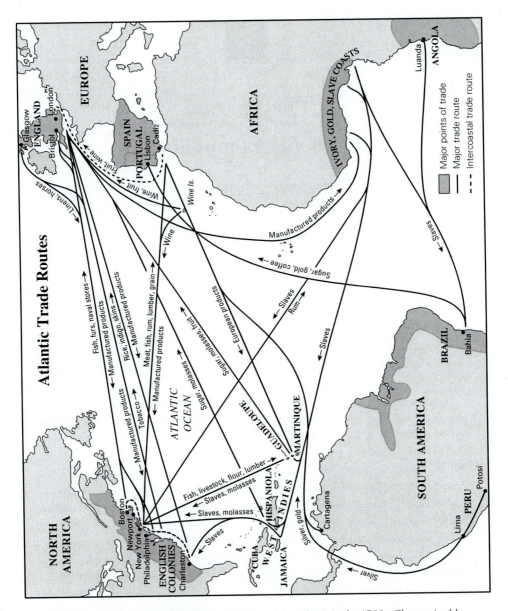

Atlantic Trade Routes

NORTH AMERICA

EUROPE

AFRICA

SOUTH AMERICA

ENGLISH COLONIES
Boston
Newport
New York
Philadelphia
Charleston

ENGLAND
Glasgow
London
Bristol

SPAIN
PORTUGAL
Lisbon
Cadiz

Wine Is.

IVORY, GOLD, SLAVE COASTS
Luanda
ANGOLA

ATLANTIC OCEAN

WEST INDIES
CUBA
JAMAICA
HISPANIOLA
GUADELOUPE
MARTINIQUE
Cartagena

BRAZIL
Bahia

PERU
Lima
Potosí

Linens, horses
Fruit, Wine
Wine, fruit
Wine
Manufactured products
Sugar, gold, coffee
Slaves
Rum
Slaves
Slaves
Slaves
Manufactured products
Fish, furs, naval stores
Manufactured products
Rice, indigo, skins
Manufactured products
Tobacco
Meat, fish, rum, lumber, grain
Manufactured products
European products
Sugar, molasses
Sugar, molasses fruit
Fish, livestock, flour, lumber
Slaves, molasses
Slaves, molasses
Slaves
Silver, gold
Silver

Major points of trade
Major trade route
Intercoastal trade route

An elaborate trade network linked peoples on both sides of the Atlantic in the 1700s. Characterized by direct exchanges as well as triangular trade, this system depended heavily upon slavery and the products of slave labor. It laid the foundation for transfers of religious and cultural practices, too.

produce them. The line between slave- and free-labor economies did not coincide with the division between Spanish and British lands; it was visible between Britain's southern and northern mainland colonies, too. Slave labor, Bergquist implies, acted as an economic stimulant with effects similar to the sugar, coffee, and tobacco it cultivated: an immediate burst of energy and wealth was followed by a depressant effect when production expanded and prices fell, then by a lasting and debilitating dependence. In contrast, colonies in temperate zones relied upon a steadier diet of grain or the more reliable output of domestic manufactures — in addition to their profits from the slave trade (a factor that Bergquist does not mention). Whereas slavery repressed innovation and southern colonies' dependence upon export crops retarded their economic development, free-labor settlements like New England were positioned to industrialize and eventually to exploit their own trading partners as economic colonies.

Bergquist ends by underscoring the irony that colonies initially less useful to Europe's mercantile system ended up the most able to profit from it. His analysis provides insight into inequalities within the Atlantic system: disparities in wealth and power that emerged between plantation and free-labor settlements, divided the British colonies, enriched Europe's imperial centers, and sent West African economies into a downward spiral. But Bergquist's is only one view. His heavily economic perspective on how Britain's North American colonies diverged from one another differs from the more culture-based interpretations of David Hackett Fischer and Stephanie Grauman Wolf in Selections 3 and 4. Also, Bergquist's stark dichotomy between slave and free societies may obscure important contrasts within the domain of colonial slavery, one of which — race relations — is highlighted in the essay by Winthrop Jordan in Selection 6. And Bergquist does not address other forces and factors that allowed the United States, although half-slave and half-free at its founding, eventually to become industrialized and wealthy. In short, comparison with other readings and a broad historical perspective will help you to assess the strengths and weaknesses of Bergquist's sweeping synthesis.

GLOSSARY

BACON'S REBELLION (1676) A revolt of colonial Virginia's farmers and freed indentured servants led by Nathaniel Bacon. Begun as an attempt to seize Indian lands, it developed into a rebellion against the colonial government that required British troops to quell. The uprising prompted Virginia landowners to import large numbers of African slave laborers in place of indentured servants.

CONTRABAND TRADE Unlawful or prohibited trade, in this case British trade with Spain's New World colonies.

IBERIAN Spanish and Portuguese.

TRIBUTE A tax paid by subjugated people to their conquerors. Spanish colonial officials often set a quota of valuable raw materials or precious metals required annually from each Indian.

✶ ✶ ✶ ✶ ✶ ✶ ✶

Most US citizens, if pressed to explain why their country developed into a powerful industrial democracy while Latin American countries remain weak, unstable, and poor, would probably respond with vague references to different cultural values, including attitudes toward work. Remembering our history textbooks, many of us would go on to contrast the predominantly Protestant English settlers who peopled the British colonies along the Atlantic seaboard of North America with the Catholic Spanish conquerors who colonized the southern part of North America, the islands of the Caribbean Sea, and, along with the Portuguese, the whole of South America.

These observations would be made in the context of some understanding of the racial geography of the Americas. Most of us are aware of the fact that the British colonies of North America (once most of the indigenous people had been exterminated or pushed west, and despite the existence of slavery) were predominantly of white, European descent. And most of us know that the majority of people in the Spanish and Portuguese colonies (despite drastic decline of a vastly more numerous indigenous population than existed in British America, and because of even greater reliance than the British colonies on slaves from Africa) were of mixed Indian, African, and European ancestry. These days most of us would not explicitly use race to explain the different historical evolution of the United States and Latin America. But behind the cultural explanations we depend on to explain this question lurks the issue of race nonetheless.

These ideas about the development of the Americas are not "wrong" in themselves. In fact, they point to some of the central elements in any explanation of the divergent histories of the American colonies. But the way these ideas are generally used to explain the different historical fates of the British and Iberian colonies in the Americas is fundamentally misleading.

This essay tests the logic of our commonsensical understanding of these matters and posits an alternative explanation for the divergent development of the Americas. . . .

[R]ace, and [climate, and] culture are [indeed] fundamental to understanding the divergent development of the societies of the Americas. But each was mediated historically by the economic roles the colonies came to play in the wider Atlantic trading system. The nature of those roles, in turn, structured the evolution of the labor systems that defined the developmental potential of each colony. Although a variety of labor systems existed in all of the American colonies, and all of them experienced free labor as well as forms of coerced labor, over time one type of labor system or the other, free or coerced, came to typify each of them. Around these systems of free or coerced labor developed characteristic patterns of social stratification, income and land distribution,

Charles Bergquist, "The Paradox of Development in the Americas," from *Labor and the Course of American Democracy: U.S. History in Latin American Perspective* (London: Verso, 1996), pp. 9–10, 14–25, 32–33. Reprinted by permission.

political institutions, and cultural attitudes. Together, these factors structured the developmental potential of the colonies, and that of the independent states they became.

The divergent development of the American colonies is sharply framed by the paradox signaled in the title of this [essay]. How did the wealthiest American colonies become the poorest nations of the hemisphere, and the poorest colonies become the core of the nation that became the richest in the world? Answering that question reveals the fallacies in explanations of United States and Latin American development that make culture, race, and climate the determining factors. The extreme examples of divergent development sketched below point instead to the centrality of colonial labor systems in the development of the United States and Latin America.

Saint Domingue/Haiti.   By the end of the eighteenth century, the French colony of Saint Domingue, situated on the western third of the Caribbean island of Hispaniola, was the largest sugar producer in the world. Measured in terms of the wealth it generated, it was also the richest colony in the Americas. In 1791 its 480,000 black slaves (in a total population that included a mere 40,000 whites and some 25,000 mulattos) were producing more than 78,000 tons of sugar a year, which accounted for more than half of the value of France's colonial trade. Today independent Haiti is the poorest nation (measured in income per person) in the Western Hemisphere.

Upper Peru/Bolivia.   During the sixteenth and seventeenth centuries, silver made Upper Peru the most lucrative Spanish colony in South America. Most of the silver was extracted by Indians forced by Spanish authorities to labor in the mines. In 1570, the population of Potosí, located at the richest mine, numbered some 160,000, making it the largest city in the Americas. Silver was by far the most important export of colonial Spanish America, and, along with Mexico, Upper Peru produced almost all of it. Yet today independent Bolivia has the lowest per capita income of Spain's ex-colonies in South America.

New England.   In contrast, the British colonies of New England were initially the poorest of the Americas. Having neither precious metals, nor the warm climate to produce agricultural staples in demand in Europe, they met their subsistence and local needs largely through small-scale diversified farming and craft production based on family and free wage labor. By the end of the colonial period, however, these societies were among the most prosperous and dynamic in the Americas. Following independence, and the victory of the North over the South in the Civil War, their institutions shaped the nation that became the richest and most industrialized in the hemisphere.

South Carolina.   Quite different was the experience of the British colonies of southern North America. The rice-exporting region of eastern South Carolina, for example, an economy based on slave labor, had the highest white per capita wealth of any part of British North America in the late eighteenth century. Yet by 1900 this region was the poorest part of the poorest census zone in the United States.

These are extreme examples, but they highlight broader patterns of colonial development in the Americas. They show how climate, natural resources (particularly precious metals), and labor supplies deeply influenced the economic possibilities of the American colonies, and the role each would play within the wider Atlantic system.

The European powers created the Atlantic system as a consequence of their chronic trade deficit with Asia. Except for precious metals, which they mined in limited quantities, Europeans produced little that they were able to exchange for the spices and luxury items they imported from the East. Mercantilism, the theory that guided the economic policies of the European states in the sixteenth and seventeenth centuries, was a direct response to these balance-of-trade problems. Acting on mercantilist principles, governments sought to maximize the nation's exports, minimize its imports, and accumulate bullion (gold or silver) in the hands of the state. Colonies outside Europe came to play a central role in mercantilist strategy. They served as sources of the bullion and raw materials European nations could not produce for themselves. Colonies also consumed exports, preferably high-value manufactures, of the metropolis. Each European power sought to acquire an empire, and, by monopolizing trade within it, pursued maximum advantage against its European rivals. War between the powers was often the result. The colonies were the spoils.

The European explorers of the fifteenth and sixteenth centuries sought new sources of gold more than anything else. Exploration also aimed at reducing the cost of Asian imports by seeking a way around the Near-Eastern middlemen who controlled the trade between Europe and Asia. Beginning in the fifteenth century, the Portuguese located supplies of gold in Africa, and by the end of that century they had discovered the way around Africa to Asia. It was the Spaniards, however, searching for a shorter, more direct western route to Asia, who discovered America and appropriated its most valuable parts.

Once in the New World, the Spaniards' quest for gold quickly led them to the great highland agrarian civilizations of Mexico and Peru. There they discovered the most numerous and most tractable labor force in the Americas. In Mexico, as was to happen all over the Americas, European contact led to rapid population decline among the native Americans. Indians died resisting European conquest and settlement. They lived shorter lives as a result of labor exploitation and reorganization of patterns of land use and settlement. Most of all they died from European diseases, from which they had no immunity. The result was a demographic disaster of a magnitude unequalled in recorded human history. In central Mexico alone an indigenous population estimated at 25 million on the eve of conquest in 1519 fell to little more than a million a century later. The Spaniards extracted tribute and labor service from this rapidly declining Indian population. Slowly they consolidated the large rural agricultural estates worked by dependent labor that came to characterize Spanish colonial society throughout the Americas.

But mining, not agriculture, was to be Spanish America's primary role in the Atlantic system during the colonial period. By the mid-sixteenth century the Spanish had discovered great silver mines in Mexico and Upper Peru, and silver became the main export of Spanish America to Europe during the next two and a half centuries. American silver had a major impact on European development, contributing to the economic decline of Spain and the rise of Spain's Western European rivals, especially Britain. Silver-driven price inflation undercut the competitiveness of Spanish manufactures and financed Spain's costly and ultimately fruitless military pretensions in Europe. Manufactures from Britain, funnelled legally through Spanish merchant monopolies, or illegally through the contraband trade, eventually supplied the bulk of the import needs of Spanish America, and those of Portuguese Brazil as well.

The Portuguese in Brazil encountered Indian peoples much smaller in numbers than those the Spaniards found in Peru and Mexico. These lowland peoples were also more egalitarian in social structure and less sedentary and dependent on agriculture than the Indian societies of the highlands. For all these reasons the Indians of Brazil — like their counterparts in the rest of lowland South America, the Caribbean, and North America north of central Mexico — proved much more resistant to European encroachment and labor demands. They fought a running battle to maintain their way of life along the advancing frontier of European settlement. Eventually, all these peoples — in Brazil and in the rest of the Americas outside the South and Central American highlands — were virtually exterminated.

The Portuguese then turned to African slaves for labor. They already controlled the West African coast and had developed a trade with Europe in African slaves. Slaves provided the labor for the large sugar estates the Portuguese established in northeast Brazil in the sixteenth century. Slaves produced all the major exports of Brazil during the next three centuries. They mined the fabulous gold and diamond reserves discovered in central Brazil in the eighteenth century. They produced the coffee, grown in the south-central region, which by the time of abolition in 1888 supplied roughly two-thirds of world demand. Brazil alone consumed almost half of the estimated ten million African slaves shipped to America.

On the Caribbean islands, many of which, like Saint Domingue, were originally claimed by Spain but fell to other Western European powers in the seventeenth and eighteenth centuries, the pattern was much the same. The indigenous people were rapidly exterminated and eventually huge numbers of African slaves (almost half those sent to America before the nineteenth century) were brought in to produce staples, primarily sugar, for export to Europe.

Table 1, drawn from Ralph Davis, *The Rise of the Atlantic Economies,* reveals the timing and magnitude of reliance on slave labor in the European colonies of the Americas. Readers should be aware that these figures are estimates. The precise numbers of slaves imported into the Americas remain in doubt.

TABLE 1 Imports of Slaves to America (in thousands), 1600–1781

	Before 1600	1600–1700	1700–1781	Total
British North America	—	—	256	256
Spanish America	75	293	393	761
Brazil	50	560	1,285	1,895
Caribbean				
British	—	261	961	1,222
French	—	157	990	1,147
Dutch and Danish	—	44	401	445
Total	125	1,315	4,286	5,726

While the Spanish and Portuguese were the first to rely on slave labor, by the seventeenth century and, especially, the eighteenth the other European powers, the British primary among them, were importing massive numbers of slaves into their colonies in the Americas.

Before they turned to slave labor, however, the non-Spanish European colonies of the Caribbean — as well as those of the North American mainland — depended on another form of coerced labor, indentured servitude. Under this system workers (primarily young males) contracted in Europe to come to America on the condition that they work for three to five or more years. Following their service they were to be granted land, a wage (often paid in kind as a quantity of sugar or tobacco), or tools and clothing. They could then aspire to become independent farmers or artisans, or at least free wage workers. Indentured servants, like slaves, had no political rights and were often subjected to brutal exploitation. Like slaves they could be punished for insubordination or attempted flight with whippings or even mutilation.

Reliance on the labor of indentured servants differentiated the American colonies of the other European powers, especially those of Britain, from the colonies of Spain and Portugal. During the seventeenth and eighteenth centuries population growth and the rapid commercialization of the British and Western European economies created a large pool of uprooted poor, many of whom seized the opportunity to improve their situation by binding themselves in temporary servitude in the New World. Spain and Portugal, in contrast, experienced no such fundamental internal transformation. The modest number of immigrants they sent to the New World were usually free and often of considerable means. Unable to take advantage of coerced white labor drawn from the mother country, the Spanish and Portuguese depended from the beginning on coerced Indian labor and African slaves in their American colonies.

But while the other European colonies in America initially depended heavily on the labor of white indentured servants, only some of them eventually came to rely on African slaves to meet their labor needs. Why did some of these colonies come to depend on slave labor, while others did not? The answer to this question holds the key to understanding the paradox of American development. It is revealed most clearly in the experience of the British American colonies, especially those that eventually formed the United States.

From virtually the beginnings of settlement, all of the American British colonies depended on indentured servants to meet part of their labor needs. Most of these colonies — from New England to the West Indies — developed initially as diversified agricultural economies, in which patterns of landholding and income distribution were, certainly by European standards of the day, relatively egalitarian.

Wherever there was a shift in these colonies to large-scale production of agricultural staples for export, however, African slaves, not white indentured servants, came to supply the bulk of the labor force. Scholars estimate that during the whole period up to the time of the declaration of US independence in 1776, a million and a half slaves were imported into the British colonies in America. Roughly a million and a quarter of these slaves went to the sugar colonies of the West Indies, most of the rest to the southern colonies of the North American mainland. The best estimate of the number of indentured servants who came to British America during the same period is 350,000, more than a quarter of the slaves imported.

The decision by planters in the British colonies to rely increasingly on African slave labor was a complex one, and the relative weights of the numerous considerations involved are still debated by historians. Contrary to modern myth, white servants proved capable of hard agricultural labor in the tropics. Yet Europeans never considered enslaving their own kind. Racial and cultural attitudes reserved the brutality of outright slavery for black, initially non-Christian, aliens. The temporary bondage of Europeans from the laboring classes did, however, prove an attractive alternative to African slavery, at least at the beginning. As noted above, in Britain during the seventeenth and eighteenth centuries there was an abundant supply of unemployed or poor farmers, artisans, and laborers who were willing to indenture themselves in America in the hope of eventually improving their condition. Indeed, indentured servants continued to stream into the southern as well as the northern mainland British colonies until the end of the colonial period.

Initially, at least, the cost to planters of a servant's passage to America was similar to the cost of an African slave. And unlike owners of slaves, masters of servants had special reasons for working their servants to death, which many seem to have done. During the seventeenth century most indentured servants in North America died before their service was up, eliminating any need to compensate them. Toward the end of that century, however, in places like Virginia, mortality rates declined and the option of buying a slave for life, rather than contracting with a servant for a few years, became more attractive.

The decision by planters to shift away from reliance on white indentured servants toward African slave labor seems to have been decisively affected by their judgments of the relative capacity of their laborers to resist. Unlike slaves, servants could appeal to the courts. And because they were white, and shared the culture and spoke the language of the free people in these societies, they had special reasons to insist on their rights and even to believe they might escape. Indentured servants were also armed psychologically by the fact that they had voluntarily submitted themselves to temporary bondage in order to improve their situation in life. When those expectations were frustrated they could become an explosive social force.

This dynamic has been documented most clearly in the shift toward slave labor in Virginia. The shift began in earnest in the tobacco-producing region of the colony in the 1680s, following a major revolt known as Bacon's Rebellion. That rebellion began as an assault on Indian lands by land-hungry whites. It ended in a movement that challenged royal authority and the planter elite itself. The rebels included some slaves promised freedom by the insurgents, but the majority were whites, primarily debt-ridden small farmers and indentured servants.

Plantation export agriculture dependent on slave labor eventually transformed all the British American colonies with warm enough climates to grow commodities that Western Europe wanted but could not produce efficiently itself. Beginning in the West Indies in the early seventeenth century, export agriculture enveloped the British colonies all the way to Maryland by the end of that century. Between 1700 and 1781 these colonies alone consumed well in excess of a million African slaves (see Table 1). As export agriculture transformed these colonies, African slaves replaced white indentured servants as the primary labor force, and land became highly concentrated. White small farmers were forced to sell out to big planters and migrate to areas where opportunities were greater. As sugar transformed the British Caribbean colony of Barbados in the early seventeenth century, for example, thousands of small farmers sold out and migrated to British North America. As tobacco transformed the tidewater area of Virginia a century later, smallholders were forced to migrate inland.

These trends were especially pronounced in sugar production, the most important American agricultural export to Europe during the colonial period. Sugar production for export required heavy investment in expensive milling machinery, which in turn encouraged extreme concentration of landholding and extreme reliance on slave labor. The same pattern of large-scale production, land concentration, and dependence on slave labor occurred in rice cultivation in eastern South Carolina, which involved large investments in irrigation.

Tobacco, the major export from the British mainland colonies, had more limited capital requirements and could be grown competitively for export by both large and small producers. Large-scale production developed where planters had sufficient capital to purchase prime land and a labor force that could be permanently denied access to it. Planters in tidewater Virginia, many of them European investors, provide the clearest example. In contrast, small-scale white tobacco producers using relatively few slaves were able to survive in the interiors of Virginia and the Carolinas.

Wherever this transition to export agriculture and slavery occurred within British America, the relatively egalitarian distribution of land and wealth, products in part of the indentured labor system, began to break down, and society became polarized into a small wealthy elite of white planters and a large class of impoverished black slaves. Land, wealth, education, literacy, and political power were monopolized by the few and denied to the vast majority. This polarization went furthest in the small sugar-producing islands of the Caribbean like Barbados and Jamaica. But it is readily discernible in the larger, geographically and economically more diverse colonies of the North American mainland such as tobacco-producing Virginia. On the mainland, however, it was rice-producing South Carolina that most closely resembled the Caribbean sugar colonies. There, blacks became a majority as early as 1708.

Nothing of this sort happened in the British colonies of New England and the mid-Atlantic seaboard, although slavery was present there as well. Despite important differences in the economies of these two groups of northern colonies, all of them depended throughout the colonial period on farming and craft production oriented toward domestic consumption. Fishing provided an important supplement to the economy of New England, and eventually shipbuilding became an important addition to the economies of both regions.

Production in these northern British colonies was based on family labor and an ever-growing proportion of free wage workers. Indentured servants continued to flood into the northern colonies during the eighteenth century, the vast majority going to the mid-Atlantic colonies of Pennsylvania, New York, New Jersey, and Delaware. The small numbers of slaves in the northern colonies were employed mainly as urban domestic servants and artisans. As production grew and society became more prosperous, the northern colonies experienced prodigious internal population growth and, in relative terms, relied less and less on the importation of labor from abroad. These population and labor trends, which sharply differentiate the development of the northern British colonies from those of the south, are graphically illustrated in Table 2. (The table is also adapted from Davis, and carries the same warning about the reliability of the absolute numbers.)

TABLE 2   Population of the British Colonies in America Excluding Canada (in thousands; slave population in parentheses), 1640–1775

	1640	1700		1775	
New England	20	130		676	(25)
New York, New Jersey, Pennsylvania, Delaware	—	65		623	(50)
Virginia, Maryland	8	87		759	(230)
Carolinas, Georgia	—	12		449	(140)
Barbados	—	54	(42)	86	(68)
Jamaica	—	53	(45)	210	(197)
Other British West Indies	20	43	(31)	113	(97)

Comparison of the British colonies, northern and southern, helps us to understand the relationship between culture, climate, race, and labor systems in the divergent development of all the European colonies of the Americas. In the British colonies the influence of British culture was a constant, so it is easier to assess the independent action of climate, race, and labor. All the British colonies were products of the same colonizing power, all were peopled initially by immigrants from British society, all were subject, more or less, to the same imperial institutions.

It is true that significant differences existed in the manner in which the British colonies were initially organized and settled. Some began as collective efforts by people of some means to establish societies based on religious tenets, others were granted to a single proprietor, who proceeded to distribute land to others at a price, and others were run for profit by companies of investors. But by the start of the eighteenth century, the two distinct economic and labor systems that would decisively affect their subsequent development were firmly set in place. The southern colonies from Virginia to the Caribbean specialized in producing export crops, especially sugar and tobacco, with slave labor for the world market. The northern colonies from New England to the mid-Atlantic produced food and manufactures largely for the domestic market using family and free labor.

The southern British colonies became the great economic success stories of Britain's mercantilist American empire. The more specialized they were in export production, the more heavily dependent on slave labor, the more concentrated and undemocratic their landholding patterns, the wealthier they became. These, not their poor northern neighbors, were the colonies that contributed handsomely to the British metropolis.

They provided sugar and tobacco for the rapidly growing British internal market. They furnished commodities for industrial processing and for re-export. And they generated, through these transactions, sizeable tax revenue for the state. On the eve of the independence of the colonies that became the United States, exports per person averaged £4.75 for the British West Indies, £1.82 for the Virginia-Maryland region, £1.78 for the Carolinas and Georgia, £1.03 for the mid-Atlantic colonies, and only £0.84 for New England. Figures on average wealth per person in the thirteen colonies at the same point in time were £54.7 for the southern colonies, £41.9 for the middle colonies, and £36.6 for New England. As these figures reveal, the northern colonies were of limited use to Britain. What exports they had generally competed with British goods. And far from producing revenue for the government, their administration and defense were an absolute drain on the imperial treasury.

Comparison of the British colonies in America helps us isolate the determining role of labor systems in the divergent development of all the European colonies in America. Slavery, and other forms of coerced labor — and the concentration of land and wealth that accompanied them — had similar effects in all the colonies where they took hold, whether they were Spanish or British, Portuguese or French. Coerced labor took hold in the Americas everywhere the Europeans found viable indigenous labor supplies, or opportunities to produce precious metals or tropical agricultural exports. To stress this point is not to deny real differences in the culture and institutions of the European colonizing powers. It is simply to point to the overwhelming similarities that coerced labor and large-scale production of export commodities created despite these initial differences.

New England and the mid-Atlantic colonies were exceptions to the pattern of coerced labor that influenced the development of all the European colonies to their south. It was not some unique cultural or racial attribute that explains their exceptionalism. It was their fortuitous location on lands lacking precious metals and with a climate unsuited to cultivation of the agricultural commodities Europe wanted. Their inability to produce primary commodities for export to Europe, their relative isolation from the main circuits of trade within the Atlantic system, allowed them to preserve and develop their unique free-labor system.

Paradoxically, however, by the eighteenth century New England and the mid-Atlantic colonies were able to assume a function within the Atlantic economy that in some ways resembled the role of European metropolis more than it did that of American colony. Unable to produce much that Britain needed, yet dependent on imports of British manufactured goods, these northern colonies began to balance their trade with Britain by provisioning the slave-based economies of the southern North American mainland and the Caribbean. This new role set the northern colonies on a path toward industrialization and political democracy that sharply distinguished their development from the other colonies of the Americas. To understand how that happened we must look more closely at the relationships between the American colonies and the workings of the Atlantic system as a whole.

The Atlantic system, as it operated from the sixteenth through the eighteenth centuries, can be usefully described as a great triangular trade between Europe, Africa, and the Americas. Europeans traded manufactures in Africa for slaves, then sold them in America. Slaves in America produced staples, primarily sugar and tobacco, and along with other workers, free and coerced, they mined the precious minerals that were America's other major export to Europe. European nations, especially Britain as time went on, sold America manufactures and financed the commerce of the whole triangular trade.

The role each point of the triangle played in this vast Atlantic trading network fundamentally influenced its economic and social evolution over time. Imports of European manufactures undercut African artisan industry, while the slave trade deprived African societies of many of their most productive members. With the infusion of slave labor the American plantation societies grew rapidly. Their economies, like those of the mining colonies of the American interior, came to revolve around the production of primary commodities for export. Meanwhile, imports of European manufactures and mercantilist restrictions stunted the growth of their manufacturing sectors. European commerce benefited from the influx of precious metals, and imports of agricultural commodities lessened the importance of domestic agriculture. Europe's exports to Africa and America stimulated the development of its manufacturing industry. Finally, because Europe controlled Atlantic commerce, it reaped profits and tax revenues on virtually every exchange within the triangular trade. It also furnished the ships, warehousing, and the insurance that made the trade possible. In elemental terms, if economic development is defined as the emergence of an expanding industrial economy, then the triangular trade fostered economic development in Europe, economic growth but not development in America, and economic retrogression in Africa. . . .

. . . [Although some historians have traced north-south colonial differences to the effects of temperate versus tropical zones,] climate does not directly explain the divergent development of the European colonies in America. That is, it did not in some mysterious way imbue the predominantly white population of the northern British colonies with "climatic energy" that somehow explains their subsequent ability to develop manufacturing industry and stable democratic political institutions. What climate explains is the *inability* of the northern British colonies to respond, as did the British, French, Spanish, and Portuguese colonies to their south, to the demand for tropical and subtropical agricultural commodities in Europe.

Nor does "culture," as we commonly use the term, explain the vast differences in the historical development of American societies. If British cultural values and institutions account for the subsequent development of the northern British colonies, why did not Virginia and South Carolina, or Barbados and Jamaica, develop in similar ways? Slavery and other forms of coerced labor had profound cultural consequences in all the American societies where those labor systems became prevalent, regardless of the European power that settled and controlled them. These labor systems created or hardened class and racial attitudes which gravely compromised the potential for industrial and democratic development. Among these cultural attitudes was widespread disdain for manual labor and the people who performed it, and the idea that people of African, Indian, or mixed descent were congenitally inferior to whites, if not subhuman.

Finally, race, in and of itself, does not account for the fact that the economy and politics of the United States evolved in such a different way from those of Latin American nations. The failure of the British colonies of the Caribbean and the southern North American mainland, like that of the Spanish and Portuguese colonies, to develop in the manner of the northern British colonies was the result of their success in using coerced labor to produce agricultural and mineral exports for Europe during the centuries of colonial rule. These societies failed to develop in the post-independence era in the way their once-poor, predominantly white, northern neighbors did not because they had too many blacks, but because they had too many slaves. . . .

QUESTIONS TO CONSIDER

1. How, according to Bergquist, do contrasting labor systems explain the divergent development of colonies in the Americas? In what ways were these labor systems related to the roles that colonies played in the Atlantic trading system? What arguments does Bergquist use to show that race and culture were less important than economics for understanding "the paradox of development" in the Americas?

2. What trends or developments led the Spanish and Portuguese to replace Native American coerced labor with imported African slaves? Were similar or different forces at work in Britain's plantation colonies? Why did British planters increasingly prefer African slave laborers to European indentured servants?

3. How did the New England and the Mid-Atlantic colonies become exceptions to the pattern of slave-labor production that Bergquist finds elsewhere? How did their exceptional situation change their role in the Atlantic economy? How, on the other hand, did the triangular trade foster "economic retrogression" in Africa?

4. In what ways does Bergquist's analysis supplement or question the reasons for regional differences among Britain's thirteen colonies that are offered by David Hackett Fischer (Selection 3) and Stephanie Grauman Wolf (Selection 4)? Would Bergquist criticize Fischer's thesis as a cultural, rather than an economic, explanation? Would Fischer agree with Bergquist that the influence of British culture was "a constant" in all the colonies? Would Bergquist find Wolf's survey more consistent with his views? How so?

5. How effectively does Bergquist's dichotomy between free- and slave-labor societies explain the paradox of American development? How exactly did slavery retard economic development, according to Bergquist, and how did its harmful economic effects persist after slaves were freed? Does slavery explain why Brazil is richer today than Haiti? Why is it that Virginia, a North American slave society, became a developed and prosperous state after emancipation? Can you suggest other possible reasons that temperate "settlement colonies" became more economically developed than tropical "exploitation colonies"? that the United States became more prosperous than Latin America?

6

Mulattoes and Race Relations in Britain's New World Colonies

Winthrop D. Jordan

In the course of the seventeenth century the Spanish and Portuguese brought nearly a million Africans to the New World as slaves. The English colonies at first were marginal participants in the slave trade, but, as Charles Bergquist noted in the preceding essay, several eventually made the transition to slave-based production. The sugar colonies of the West Indies were most deeply implicated. By 1650, there were ten thousand African slaves on the British Caribbean island of Barbados, a majority of the population. Planters in North American colonies such as Virginia and Maryland were slower to adopt the practice, largely because white indentured servants were for a time a cheaper and easily available alternative. But at the end of the 1600s, when Anglo-American merchants entered the slave trade, the supply of slaves increased, their prices dropped, and mainland colonies in the American South shifted decisively to slave labor. By 1776 approximately a million and a half slaves had been imported into the British colonies, five-sixths to the British West Indies, and one-sixth to the North American mainland.

Not all New World slave societies were the same. Unlike the Iberians, the English evolved a full-fledged racial justification for slavery. Winthrop Jordan's monumental study White Over Black *(1968) examined how English cultural notions shaped the workings of British slavery and the racially divided society the colonists built around it. Drawing upon literary sources such as Shakespeare's* Othello, *Jordan demonstrated that even before the first boat-load of Africans arrived at Jamestown in 1619, Englishmen's prejudice against "heathenism" and "blackness" laid the groundwork for unequal treatment of these involuntary newcomers. In the following selection, Jordan takes a somewhat different, and more directly comparative, tack. Tracing the fate of mixed-race colonists in different settings, he argues that black-white population ratios, more than the effect of the English cultural heritage, influenced the way that British North Americans created a rigid racial barrier between blacks and whites.*

Americans today are the product of a long tradition that lumps together persons with any trace of black ancestry and calls them black. But other New World nations define race differently. In Brazil, for example, there are an enormous number of mixed-race categories between black and white, with the steps between them marked by subtle gradations of color

91

and economic status. To account for this, some scholars of colonialism have distinguished between the racially inclusive culture the Iberians exported to Latin America and the exclusive culture the English transplanted in North America. Jordan, on the other hand, finds a similar distinction within British dominions. Race relations, he finds, differed dramatically between England's North American and Caribbean colonies. The key is the status of mulattoes, the offspring or descendants of unions between black Africans and Europeans. (These unions took various forms, such as masters with slaves, free whites with free blacks, or white servants with slaves or free blacks.) Piecing together the fragmentary record, Jordan discovers that West Indians not only used a variety of terms to describe mixed ancestry; they also viewed interracial relationships as expressions of human nature rather than threats to slave society. By contrast, Englishmen on the continent — soon to call themselves Americans — outlawed racial intermixture and identified mulattoes in status with "Negroes." Jordan concludes that population ratios between whites and blacks and between men and women explain the difference between the two patterns.

Jordan's essay is a good example of how historians must sometimes generalize from fragmentary evidence, and his comparative findings are admittedly speculative. As you follow his argument, you should be aware of its premises. Can racial distinctions be discussed separately from the issue of slavery? Was the looser pattern of Caribbean race relations always beneficial to people of color? Do numbers alone explain the American racial divide? Whatever your conclusions, Jordan's comparative approach teaches the valuable lesson that racial categories are not immutable facts of life but social constructions, human definitions capable of changing — perhaps for the better — over time and place.

GLOSSARY

BLANCHING   According mixed-race persons the rights and privileges of white persons.

CONCUBINE   A woman who cohabits with a man to whom she is not married.

DEMOGRAPHIC   Relating to population or social statistics.

MANUMITTED   Freed from slavery by one's owner.

MISCEGENATION   Sexual intercourse between members of different races.

MULATTO   A person of mixed black-white parentage or ancestry.

MUSTEE   A term used in certain American colonies to describe a person of mixed Indian-black or Indian-white ancestry.

NOUVEAU RICHE   A disparaging label for a person who is newly rich and thought to be vulgar and ostentatious.

PASSING   A process, usually silent and informal, by which a person of mixed race is permitted to identify himself or herself as white.

✵ ✵ ✵ ✵ ✵ ✵ ✵

The word *mulatto* is not frequently used in the United States. Americans generally reserve it for biological contexts, because for social purposes a mulatto is termed a *Negro* [or Black]. Americans lump together both socially and legally all persons with perceptible admixture of Negro ancestry, thus making social definition without reference to genetic logic; white blood becomes socially advantageous only in overwhelming proportion. The dynamic underlying the peculiar bifurcation of American society into only two color groups can perhaps be better understood if some attempt is made to describe its origin, for the content of social definitions may remain long after the impulses to their formation have gone.

After only one generation of European experience in America, colonists faced the problem of dealing with racially mixed offspring, a problem handled rather differently by the several nations involved. It is well known that the Latin countries, especially Portugal and Spain, rapidly developed a social hierarchy structured according to degrees of intermixture of Negro and European blood, complete with a complicated system of terminology to facilitate definition. The English in Maryland, Virginia, and the Carolinas, on the other hand, seem to have created no such system of ranking. To explain this difference merely by comparing the different cultural backgrounds involved is to risk extending generalizations far beyond possible factual support. . . . There is evidence with some nations that the same cultural heritage was spent in different ways by the colonial heirs, depending on varying conditions encountered in the New World. The English, for example, encountered the problem of race mixture in very different contexts in their several colonies; they answered it in one fashion in their West Indian islands and in quite another in their colonies on the continent.

As far as the continental colonies were concerned, the presence of mulattoes received legislative recognition by the latter part of the seventeenth century. The word itself, borrowed from the Spanish, was in English usage from the beginning of the century and was probably first employed in Virginia in 1666. From about that time, laws dealing with Negro slaves began to add "and mulattoes." In all English continental colonies mulattoes were lumped with Negroes in the slave codes and in statutes governing the conduct of free Negroes: the law was clear that Mulattoes and Negroes were not to be distinguished for different treatment — a phenomenon occasionally noted by foreign travelers.

If mulattoes were to be considered Negroes, logic required some definition of mulattoes, some demarcation between them and white men. Law is sometimes less than logical, however, and throughout the colonial period only Virginia and North Carolina grappled with the question raised by continuing intermixture. In 1705 the Virginia legislature defined a mulatto as "the child, grand child, or great grand child of a negro," or, revealingly, merely "the child of an Indian." North Carolina wavered on the matter, but

Winthrop D. Jordan, "American Chiaroscuro: The Status and Definition of Mulattoes in the British Colonies," *William and Mary Quarterly*, 3d Ser., 19 (1962), pp. 183–200. Reprinted by permission of the author and the Institute of Early American History and Culture.

generally pushed the taint of Negro ancestry from one-eighth to one-sixteenth. There is no reason to suppose that these two colonies were atypical, and in all probability something like these rules operated in the other continental colonies. What the matter came down to, of course, was visibility. Anyone whose appearance discernibly connected him with the Negro was held to be such. The line was thus drawn with regard to practicalities rather than logic. Daily practice supplied logic enough.

Another indication of the refusal of the English continental colonies to separate the "mixed breed" from the African was the absence of terminology which could be used to define a hierarchy of status. The colonists did, it is true, seize upon a separate word to describe those of mixed blood. They were forced to do so if they were to deal with the problem at all, even if they merely wished, as they did, to lump "mulattoes" with Negroes. If, however, an infusion of white blood had been regarded as elevating status, then presumably the more white blood the higher the social rank. Had such ranking existed, descriptive terminology would have been required with which to handle shades of distinction. Yet no such vocabulary developed in the American colonies. Only one word besides *mulatto* was used to describe those of mixed ancestry. The term *mustee* (*mestee, mustize, mestizo, mustizoe*) was used to describe a mixture which was in part Indian, usually Indian-Negro but occasionally Indian-white. The term was in common use only in the Carolinas, Georgia, and to some extent New York, that is, in those colonies where such crosses occurred with some frequency. Its use revealed the colonists' refusal to identify Indians and Negroes as the same sort of people, a refusal underlined by their belief that the two groups possessed a natural antipathy for each other. Yet while the colonists thus distinguished persons of some Indian ancestry by a separate word, they lumped these *mustees* with mulattoes and Negroes in their slave codes.

Although legislative enactments provide a valuable index of community sentiment, they do not always accurately reflect social practice. An extensive search in the appropriate sources — diaries, letters, travel accounts, newspapers, and so on — fails to reveal any pronounced tendency to distinguish mulattoes from Negroes, any feeling that their status was higher and demanded different treatment. The sources give no indication, for instance, that mulattoes were preferred as house servants or concubines. There may well have been a relatively high proportion of mulattoes among manumitted slaves, but this was probably due to the not unnatural desire of some masters to liberate their own offspring. Yet all this is largely negative evidence, and the proposition that mulattoes were not accorded higher status than Negroes is as susceptible of proof as any negative. Perhaps the usual procedure of awaiting disproof through positive evidence may be allowed.

A single exception to these generalizations stands out sharply from the mass of colonial legislation. In 1765 the colony of Georgia not only undertook to encourage immigration of free colored persons (itself a unique step) but actually provided that free mulatto and mustee immigrants might be naturalized as white men by the legislature, complete with "all the Rights, Privileges, Powers, and Immunities whatsoever which any person born of British parents" could have, except the right to vote and sit in the Commons House of Assembly. Thus a begrudging kind of citizenship was extended to free mulattoes. That Georgia should so distinguish herself from her northern neighbors was a measure of the colony's weak and exposed condition. A small population with an increasingly high proportion of slaves and perpetual danger from powerful Indian tribes made Georgians eager for men who might be counted as white and thus strengthen the colony. The legislature went to great lengths in its search — perhaps too far, for it never actually naturalized anyone under the aegis of the 1765 law.

Only rarely in the colonial period did the subject of mulattoes receive any attention from American writers. Mulattoes were so fixed in station that their position apparently did not merit attention. The subject did come up once in the *South-Carolina Gazette,* yet even then it was casually raised in connection with an entirely different topic. An anonymous contributor in 1735 offered the public some strictures on Carolina's *nouveau riche,* the "half Gentry," and attacked especially their imitative and snobbish behavior. For illustration he turned to the character of the mulatto.

> It is observed concerning the Generation of *Molattoes,* that they are seldom well beloved either by the Whites or the Blacks. Their Approach towards Whiteness, makes them look back with some kind of Scorn upon the Colour they seem to have left, while the Negroes, who do not think them better than themselves, return their Contempt with Interest: And the Whites, who respect them no Whit the more for the nearer Affinity in Colour, are apt to regard their Behaviour as too bold and assuming, and bordering upon Impudence. As they are next to Negroes, and but just above them, they are terribly afraid of being thought Negroes, and therefore avoid as much as possible their Company or Commerce: and Whitefolks are as little fond of the Company of *Molattoes.*

The writer's point, of course, was not that mulattoes were in fact superior to Negroes, but that they alone thought they were. Apparently mulattoes thought white blood to be a source of elevation, a proposition which whites (and Negroes as well) were quick to deny. White blood secured one's status only if undiluted.

A somewhat different aspect of this problem came up in 1784 when it was forced on the attention of a Savannah merchant, Joseph Clay. As executor of a will Clay became responsible for the welfare of two young mulattoes, very possibly the children of his deceased friend. Because the young people were both free, Clay's letter to a gentleman in Ireland offers valuable evidence of what a combination of personal freedom and some white ancestry afforded in the way of social position in Georgia. "These young Folks are very unfortunately situated in this Country," Clay wrote, "their descent places them in the most disadvantageous situation, as Free persons the Laws protects them — but they gain no rank in Life, White Persons do not commonly associate with them on a footing of equality — so many of their own Colour (say the mixt breed) being Slaves, they too naturally fall in with them, and even the Negro Slaves claim a right to their acquaintance and Society." For Clay the situation was one of unrelieved gloom, even of horror: "thus a little reflection will present to you what their future Prospects here must be — neglected by the most respectable Class of Society, [they] are forced to intermix with the lowest, and in what that must end — we would wish to draw a Veil — all the Care that can be taken of them cant prevent it, it arises from our peculiar situation in regard to these people." Clay went on to recommend as "the most eligible plan" that the children be sent to Europe if his correspondent would accept them as wards. "The

Boy might be Bound to some business . . . and the Girl might make a very Good Wife to some honest Tradesman." It was essential that they cross the Atlantic: "this alone can save them . . . I think they might both be made usefull Members of Society, no such distinctions interfere with their happiness on your side the Water." Clay added finally that several of his friends endorsed his proposal. Apparently America offered little opportunity to blacks to become whites through intermixture. American society, wedded as it was to Negro slavery, drew a rigid line which did not exist in Europe: this was indeed "our peculiar situation in regard to these people."

The existence of a rigid barrier between whites and those of Negro blood necessarily required a means by which the barrier could on occasion be passed. Some accommodation had to be made for those persons with so little Negro blood that they appeared to be white, for one simply could not go around calling apparently white persons Negroes. Once the stain was washed out visibly it was useless as a means of identification. Thus there developed the silent mechanism of "passing." Such a device would have been unnecessary if those of mixed ancestry and appearance had been regarded as midway between white and black. It was the existence of a broad chasm which necessitated the sudden leap which passing represented.

Fortunately it is possible to catch a glimpse of this process as it operated in the colonial period by following the extraordinary career of a family named Gibson in South Carolina. In 1731 a member of the Commons House of Assembly announced in the chamber that several free colored men with their white wives had immigrated from Virginia with the intention of settling on the Santee River. Free Negroes were undesirable enough, but white wives made the case exceptionally disturbing. "The house apprehending [this prospect] to be of ill Consequence to this Province," appointed a committee to inquire into the matter. Governor Robert Johnson had already sent for what seemed to be the several families involved, and the committee asked him to report his findings to the house.

"The people lately come into the Settlements having been sent for," Johnson duly reported, "I have had them before me in Council and upon Examination find that they are not Negroes nor Slaves but Free people, That the Father of them here is named Gideon Gibson and his Father was also free, I have been informed by a person who has lived in Virginia that this Gibson has lived there Several Years in good Repute and by his papers that he has produced before me that his transactions there have been very regular, That he has for several years paid Taxes for two tracts of Land and had seven Negroes of his own, That he is a Carpenter by Trade and is come hither for the support of his Family." This evident respectability so impressed the governor that he allowed the Gibson family to remain in the colony. "The account he has given of himself," Johnson declared, "is so Satisfactory that he is no Vagabond that I have in Consideration of his Wifes being a white woman and several White women Capable of working and being Serviceable in the Country permitted him to Settle in this Country upon entering into Recognizance for his good behaviour which I have taken accordingly."

The meaning of Johnson's statement that "they are not Negroes nor Slaves but Free people" is not entirely clear. Certainly Gideon Gibson himself was colored; it seems likely that he was mulatto rather than Negro, but it is impossible to tell surely. At any rate Gideon Gibson prospered very nicely: by 1736 either he or a son of the same name owned 450 acres of Carolina land. He continued to own Negroes, and in 1757 he was described as owning property in two widely separated counties. By 1765 the status of Gideon Gibson (by this time definitely the son of the original carpenter) was such that he was appointed administrator of an estate. His sister married a wealthy planter, and there is no evidence to indicate that Gibson himself was regarded by his neighbors as anything but white. In 1768 he was leading a band of South Carolina Regulators on the field of battle. The commander dispatched to arrest Gibson was a planter and colonel in the militia, George Gabriel Powell, who ignominiously resigned his commission when his men sided with the Regulators. This latter worthy, apparently a kind master to his own Negroes, sought vindication by attacking Gibson's ancestry. The exact nature of the attack is unclear, but the matter came up on the floor of the Commons, of which Powell was a member. The prominent merchant-patriot of Charles Town, Henry Laurens, recorded the conflict in a letter written some years later. Laurens was writing from England of his own conviction that slavery ought to be brought to an end, a conviction that inevitably raised the question of color.

> Reasoning from the colour carries no conviction. By perseverance the black may be blanched and the "stamp of Providence" effactually effaced. Gideon Gibson escaped the penalties of the negro law by producing upon comparison more red and white in his face than could be discovered in the faces of half the descendants of the French refugees in our House of Assembly, including your old acquaintance the Speaker. I challenged them all to the trial. The children of this same Gideon, having passed through another stage of whitewash were of fairer complexion than their prosecutor George Gabriel [Powell]. — But to confine them to their original clothing will be best. They may and ought to continue a separate people, may be subjected by special laws, kept harmless, made useful and freed from the tyranny and arbitrary power of individuals; but as I have already said, this difficulty cannot be removed by arguments on this side of the water.

Laurens showed both sides of the coin. He defended an individual's white status on the basis of appearance and at the same time expressed the conviction that colored persons "may and ought to continue a separate people." Once an Ethiopian always an Ethiopian, unless he could indeed change his skin.

Gideon Gibson's successful hurdling of the barrier was no doubt an unusual case; it is of course impossible to tell how unusual. Passing was difficult but not impossible, and it stood as a veiled, unrecognized monument to the American ideal of a society open to all comers. One Virginia planter advertised in the newspaper for his runaway mulatto slave who he stated might try to pass for free or as a "white man." An English traveler reported calling upon a Virginia lawyer who was "said to be" and who looked like a mulatto. But the problem of evidence is insurmountable. The success of the passing mechanism depended upon its operating in silence. Passing was a conspiracy of silence not only for the individual but for a biracial society which had drawn a rigid color line based on visibility. Unless a white man was a white man, the gates were open to endless slander and confusion.

That the existence of such a line in the continental colonies was not predominantly the effect of the English cultural heritage is suggested by even a glance at the English colonies in the Caribbean. The social accommodation of racial intermixture in the islands followed a different pattern from that on the continent. It was regarded as improper, for example, to work mulattoes in the fields — a fundamental distinction. Apparently they were preferred as tradesmen, house servants, and especially as concubines. John Luffman wrote that mulatto slaves "fetch a lower price than blacks, unless they are tradesmen, because the purchasers cannot employ them in the drudgeries to which negroes are put too; the colored men, are therefore mostly brought up to trades or employed as house slaves, and the women of this description are generally prostitutes." Though the English in the Caribbean thought of their society in terms of white, colored, and black, they employed a complicated battery of names to distinguish persons of various racial mixtures. This terminology was borrowed from the neighboring Spanish, but words are not acquired unless they fulfill a need. While the English settlers on the continent borrowed one Spanish word to describe all mixtures of black and white, the islanders borrowed at least four — *mulatto, sambo, quadroon,* and *mestize* — to describe differing degrees. And some West Indians were prepared to act upon the logic which these terms implied. The respected Jamaican historian, Bryan Edwards, actually proposed extension of civil privileges to mulattoes in proportion to their admixture of white blood. Such a proposition was unheard of on the continent.

The difference between the two regions on this matter may well have been connected with another pronounced divergence in social practice. The attitude toward interracial sex was far more genial in the islands than in the continental colonies. In the latter, miscegenation very rarely met with anything but disapproval in principle, no matter how avid the practice. Sexual intimacy between any white person and any Negro (that "unnatural and inordinate copulation") was utterly condemned. Protests against the practice were frequent. A traveler in New York reported that the citizens of Albany possessed a particular "moral delicacy" on one point: "they were from infancy in habits of familiarity with these humble friends [the Negroes], yet being early taught that nature had placed between them a barrier, which it was in a high degree criminal and disgraceful to pass, they considered a mixture of such distinct races with abhorrence, as a violation of her laws." About 1700 the Chester County Court in Pennsylvania ordered a Negro "never more to meddle with any white woman more uppon paine of his life." Public feeling on this matter was strong enough to force its way over the hurdles of the legislative process into the statute books of many colonies. Maryland and Virginia forbade cohabitation of whites and Negroes well before the end of the seventeenth century. Similar prohibitions were adopted by Massachusetts, North and South Carolina, and Pennsylvania during the next quarter-century and by Georgia when Negroes were admitted to that colony on 1750. Thus two Northern and all Southern colonies legally prohibited miscegenation. Feeling against intercourse with Negroes was strengthened by the fact that such activity was generally illicit; Americans had brought from England certain standards of marital fidelity which miscegenation flagrantly violated.

The contrast offered by the West Indies is striking. Protests against interracial sex relations were infrequent. Colored mistresses were kept openly. "The Planters are in general rich," a young traveler wrote, "but a set of dissipating, abandoned, and cruel people. Few even of the married ones, but keep a Mulatto or Black Girl in the house or at lodgings for certain purposes." Edward Long of Jamaica put the matter this way: "He who should presume to shew any displeasure against such a thing as simple fornication, would for his pains be accounted a simple blockhead; since not one in twenty can be persuaded, that there is either sin; or shame in cohabiting with his slave." Perhaps most significant of all, no island legislature prohibited extramarital miscegenation and only one [Montserrat] declared against intermarriage. The reason, of course, was that white men so commonly slept with Negro women that to legislate against the practice would have been merely ludicrous. Concubinage was such an integral part of island life that one might just as well attempt to abolish the sugar cane.

Mulattoes in the West Indies, then, were products of accepted practice, something they assuredly were not in the continental colonies. In the one area they were the fruits of a desire which society tolerated and almost institutionalized; in the other they represented an illicit passion which public morality unhesitatingly condemned. On the continent, unlike the West Indies, mulattoes represented a practice about which men could only feel guilty. To reject and despise the productions of one's own guilt was only natural.

If such difference in feeling about miscegenation has any connection with the American attitude toward mulattoes, it only raises the question of what caused that difference. Since the English settlers in both the West Indies and the continental colonies brought with them the same cultural baggage, something in their colonial experiences must have caused the divergence in their attitudes toward miscegenation. Except perhaps for climatic dissimilarity, a factor of very doubtful importance, the most fundamental difference lay in the relative numbers of whites and Negroes in the two areas. On the continent the percentage of Negroes in the total population reached its peak in the period 1730–65 and has been declining since. It ranged from about 3 percent in New England, 8 to 15 percent in the middle colonies, 30 to 40 in Maryland and Virginia, 25 in North Carolina, 40 in Georgia, to a high of some 60 percent in South Carolina. The proportion of Negroes in the islands was far higher: 75 percent in Barbados, 80 in the Leeward Islands, and over 90 in Jamaica.

These figures strongly suggest a close connection between a high proportion of Negroes and open acceptance of miscegenation. South Carolina, for example, where Negroes formed a majority of the population, was alone among the continental colonies in tolerating even slightly conspicuous interracial liaisons. Thoroughly disparate proportions of Negroes, moreover, made it inevitable that the West Indies and the continental colonies would develop dissimilar societies. The West Indian planters were lost not so much in the Caribbean as in a sea of blacks. They found it impossible to re-create English culture as they had known it. They were corrupted by living in a police state, though not themselves the objects of its discipline. The business of the islands was business, the production of agricultural staples; the islands were not where one really lived, but where one made one's money. By contrast, the American colonists maintained their hold on the English background, modifying it not so much to accommodate slavery as to winning the new land. They were numerous enough to create a new culture with a validity of its own, complete with the adjustments necessary to absorb non-English Europeans. Unlike the West Indians, they felt no need to be constantly running back to England to reassure themselves that they belonged to civilization. Because they were conscious of the solid worth of their own society, forged with their own hands, they vehemently rejected any trespass upon it by a people so alien as the Negroes. The islanders could hardly resent trespass on something which they did not have. By sheer weight of numbers their society was black and slave.

This fundamental difference was perhaps reinforced by another demographic factor. In the seventeenth century the ratio of men to women had been high in America and higher still in the West Indies, where the ratio was about three to two, or, as the sex ratio is usually expressed, 150 (males per 100 females). In the following century it dropped drastically. New England's sex ratio went below 100 as a result of emigration which was as usual predominantly male. Elsewhere on the continent the bounding birth rate nearly erased the differential: in 1750, except on the edge of the frontier, it was probably no more than 110 and in most places less. Perhaps not so well known is the fact that the same process occurred in most of the English islands. Emigration sapped their male strength until Barbados had a sex ratio in the 80's and the various Leeward Islands were balanced in the neighborhood of 100. A significant exception was Jamaica, where in mid-eighteenth century a plentiful supply of land maintained a sex ratio of nearly two to one.

Male numerical predomination was surely not without effect on interracial sexual relations. Particularly where the white population was outnumbered by the black, white women formed a small group. Their scarcity rendered them valuable. The natural reaction on the part of white men was to place them protectively upon a pedestal and then run off to gratify passions elsewhere. For their part white women, though they might propagate children, inevitably held themselves aloof from the world of lust and passion, a world associated with infidelity and Negro slaves. Under no circumstances would they have attempted, nor would they have been allowed, to clamber down from their pedestal to seek pleasures of their own across the racial line. In fact the sexual union of white women with Negro men was uncommon in all colonies. When it did occur (and it did more often than is generally supposed) it was in just those areas to which the demographic factors point — America north of South Carolina, especially in New England, where white women even married Negroes. Such a combination, legitimized or not, was apparently unknown in the West Indies.

If a high sex ratio contributed to the acceptability of miscegenation, it may well have enhanced the acceptability of mulatto offspring. For example, there is the striking fact that Jamaica, the only colony where the sex ratio continued high, was the only colony to give legislative countenance to the rise of mulattoes. In 1733 the legislature provided that "no Person who is not above Three Degrees removed in a lineal Descent from the Negro Ancestor exclusive, shall be allowed to vote or poll in Elections; and no one shall be deemed a Mulatto after the Third Generation, as aforesaid, but that they shall have all the Privileges and Immunities of His Majesty's white Subjects of this Island, provided they are brought up in the Christian Religion." In this same period Barbados was barring any person "whose original Extract shall be proved to have been from a Negro" from voting and from testifying against whites. Beginning in the 1730's the Jamaican legislature passed numerous private acts giving the colored offspring (and sometimes the colored mistress) of such and such a planter the rights and privileges of white persons, especially the right to inherit the planter's estate. There was objection to this blanching of mulattoes, however, for in 1761 the Assembly restricted the amount of property a planter might leave to his mulatto children, saying that "such bequests tend greatly to destroy the distinction requisite, and absolutely necessary to be kept up in this island, between white persons and negroes, their issue and offspring. . . ." The law failed to destroy the acceptability of the practice, however, for the private acts continued. It was in Jamaica, too, that Bryan Edwards called for extension of civil privileges to mulattoes. And Edward Long, in his history of the island, wrote that those beyond the third generation were "called English, and consider themselves as free from all taint of the Negroe race." Thus Jamaica, with the highest proportion of Negroes and highest sex ratio of all the English colonies, was unique in its practice of publicly transforming Negroes into white men.

The American continental colonist refused to make this extension of privilege. He remained firm in his rejection of the mulatto, in his categorization of mixed-bloods as belonging to the lower caste. It was an unconscious decision dictated perhaps in large part by the weight of Negroes on his society, heavy enough to be a burden, yet not so heavy as to make him abandon all hope of maintaining his own identity, physically and culturally. Interracial propagation was a constant reproach that he was failing to be true to himself. Sexual intimacy strikingly symbolized a union he wished to avoid. If he could not restrain his sexual nature, he could at least reject its fruits and thus solace himself that he had done no harm. Perhaps he sensed as well that continued racial intermixture would eventually undermine the logic of the racial slavery upon which his society was based. For the separation of slaves from free men depended on a clear demarcation of the races, and the presence of mulattoes blurred this essential distinction. Accordingly he made every effort to nullify the effects of racial intermixture: by classifying the mulatto as a Negro he was in effect denying that intermixture had occurred at all.

QUESTIONS TO CONSIDER

1. Describe the varying definitions of white-black mixed-race persons that Jordan found in British New World colonies. What key differences existed between North American and Caribbean race relations? What evidence does the author use to demonstrate them? What factors, according to Jordan, account for these differences? Was the Caribbean pattern of race relations better or worse for persons of color? How does Jordan explain the apparent contradiction between examples of "passing" and the existence of a rigid color barrier between blacks and whites in the American South?

2. How, according to Jordan, do sex ratios in the population help to account for the varying social and legal status of mixed-race colonists? What does the example of Jamaica suggest? What was the impact of sex and race population ratios on the status of white women? How might this explain the stereotype of the pure and fragile southern lady?

3. British colonists, says Jordan, refused to identify Indians and blacks as "the same sort of people." Why might the colonists view Africans more readily than Native Americans as likely candidates for slavery? What "logic of racial slavery" did the English colonists use to justify the institution? Was this rationale similar to or different from the colonists' rationale for taking Indians' land, as described by George Fredrickson in Selection 2?

4. To what extent do fragmentary evidence and biased selection of comparative cases call into question the author's conclusions? What additional information would you like to have about racially mixed persons in these colonies, and why? Does Jordan generalize too far beyond the evidence he presents? Would a more focused comparison between Barbados and South Carolina, whose black-white ratios were similar, support or call into question Jordan's conclusions?

5. Jordan claims that "the content of social definitions may remain long after the impulses to their formation have gone." Do Americans still draw a rigid color line between blacks and whites? How, if at all, have such developments as Asian and Hispanic immigration, black-white interracial marriages, and government antidiscrimination policies affected our racial categories?

THE REVOLUTION

Ralph Waldo Emerson wrote that the colonists who confronted British soldiers at Concord, Massachusetts, on April 19, 1775, fired a "shot heard round the world." The impact of the American Revolution was felt almost immediately abroad. Latin American colonists organized movements to free themselves from Spanish rule. Across the Atlantic, French citizens proclaimed their rights in words echoing the American Declaration of Independence and eventually discarded their monarchy for a republic. Their success inspired a wave of nationalist outbreaks that swept through Europe between 1789 and 1848.

How was the American Revolution similar to or different from other popular struggles during the Age of Revolution? When we move forward in time, how does it compare to anticolonial revolutions in Africa and Asia in the twentieth century or to such historical landmarks as the Russian and Chinese Revolutions? In what sense was the American war for independence a "revolution"? These are controversial questions whose answers are crucial for understanding American history and for clarifying whether our institutions can or should be imitated elsewhere. They are also comparative questions. They involve measuring the American Revolution against various models of revolution catalogued by historians and social scientists, and they also suggest comparisons with specific revolutionary movements.

In the following selections, two historians who specialize in non-U.S. fields offer different reference points from which to assess the American Revolution comparatively. In the first essay, R. R. Palmer tries his hand at both strategies just mentioned. First he introduces the notion that there are different types or categories of revolutions; then he settles into more focused national comparisons. Palmer finds important parallels between the American and French Revolutions, despite their undeniable differences, and he suggests that the grand and universal messages of the Declaration of Independence and the U.S. Constitution remain relevant to anticolonial struggles in our own time. In the second essay, Anthony McFarlane compares the Latin American wars for independence with that of the North Americans. According to McFarlane, the widely divergent institutions of New Spain and of the thirteen colonies explain why the British colonists were better prepared for independence and democracy than were their neighbors to the South.

Palmer's essay glides quickly over huge chunks of history in order to extract provocative questions and insights, while McFarlane offers a denser and more focused comparison. Their essays also create different impressions about the legacy of the American Revolution. Whereas Palmer believes that the democratic principles of the Revolution remain relevant to contemporary struggles, McFarlane seems to suggest that American democracy was the result of special and perhaps unrepeatable conditions. What do *you* think is the enduring message of the "shot heard round the world"?

The American Revolution
in Comparative Perspective

R. R. PALMER

In this succinct and dispassionate essay, R. R. Palmer ranges broadly through space and time to find appropriate comparisons to the American Revolution. Palmer begins by outlining various kinds of revolutions, ranging from "conservative" and "bourgeois" revolts to more radical varieties, but also including national independence movements. After considering which types might best describe the American experience, Palmer then settles upon two cases to relate to our own: first, the wave of revolutions that began in France and spread through Europe from 1789 to 1848 thanks, in part, to the American example; and second, the outbreak of anticolonial movements in the Third World that have redrawn the world's political map since World War II.

When the Marquis de Lafayette, who had fought beside Washington against the British, sent the first American president the key to the Bastille, he acknowledged that the French had followed our lead in toppling the "fortress of despotism." American independence and constitution-making inspired the famous Tennis Court Oath, in which the Third Estate (representing all Frenchmen who were not noblemen or clergy) vowed that it would not disband before a constitution was accepted by the king. But the French Revolution proceeded in phases whose violence and radicalism left its American cousin far behind. France's constitutional monarchy ended in 1791 after Louis XVI was caught attempting to flee the country. By 1793, the newly elected National Convention set up a republic and the king was executed. But as royalist uprisings threatened to halt the revolution and as France became embroiled in European wars, the dictatorial Reign of Terror ensued. The ruthless Jacobin leader Maximilian Robespierre triumphed over the more moderate Girondists and ruled France through decrees issued by his Committee of Public Safety. Robespierre and his zealous followers confiscated large estates and sent several thousand enemies to the guillotine. When the National Convention finally tired of his excesses, it overthrew him in 1794 and set up rule by a five-man Directory, which bogged down in corruption and ineptitude until 1799. At that point, the military hero Napoleon Bonaparte, recently returned from victories in Italy and Egypt, conspired to have himself appointed consul. Representative government ceased to function as Napoleon created a centralized state bureaucracy and diverted popular revolutionary fervor into military campaigns abroad. By the time he declared himself emperor in 1804, the French Revolution had given way to Napoleon's dreams of world conquest.

It speaks volumes that Tom Paine, the professional revolutionary who prodded the American colonists toward independence with his bestselling pamphlet Common Sense *(1776), was denounced as too radical by many Americans but barely escaped execution in France for being too moderate. There is no doubt that the French Revolution veered between extremes of the Left and Right (labels taken from delegates' positions in its assembly), was strongly anticlerical, tore down medieval social structures, and gave birth to modern socialist ideas — none of which was true for its American predecessor. But Palmer finds important similarities between the two revolutions, especially the powerful set of principles endorsed in their founding documents. "Ideas of political liberty and legal equality, . . . the principle of representation by numbers rather than by classes or corporate groups, the rejection of hereditary office and privileged status, . . . and the separation of state and church" were embodied in the new American and French constitutions. They became the common rallying cry of revolutionaries throughout the Western world in the 1800s.*

It is these democratic principles, Palmer contends, that made the American Revolution relevant to twentieth-century anticolonial struggles, despite undeniable differences in circumstances between it and (for example) the Algerian war for independence from the French (1954–1962), Gandhi's nonviolent crusade against British rule in India (concluded successfully in 1947), or the fall of the apartheid regime in South Africa (1990). What historian Richard B. Morris calls the "first successful decolonization movement of the modern world" was undertaken by Americans against imperial authority in England. And the Americans' belief that all men are created equal and have the same right to life, liberty, and the pursuit of happiness, Palmer suggests, still has the power to transform the world.

You will want to assess Palmer's categories and comparisons carefully. You should also study Selections 8 and 11 before deciding whether the American Revolution can be a model for other nations. Whatever your conclusions, Palmer's stimulating comparisons are a welcome reminder that the American colonists' rebellion represented not just the birth of a nation, but also a major event in world history.

GLOSSARY

ALGERIAN REVOLUTION A war for independence from French rule in the North African colony of Algeria that broke out in 1954. Led by the National Liberation Front, the Algerians achieved their goal in 1962 after years of bitter fighting.

BARRUEL, ABBÉ (1741–1820) A former Jesuit and an antirevolutionary who became the classic formulator of the conspiratorial causes of the French Revolution. He blamed it and the revolutions that followed on a secret international sect allegedly composed of Jacobins, Freemasons, and a brotherhood of agitators called "Illuminati."

BASTILLE A medieval fortress in Paris used by the French king to hold political prisoners. On July 14, 1789, a Parisian mob stormed the prison and freed its seven occupants. This marked the start of popular participation in the French Revolution.

BELGIAN REVOLT OF 1789 The revolt by the United Belgian States against rule by the Austrian emperor Joseph II. Inspired by the French Revolution, the revolt succeeded with French help in 1794, but at the price of annexation to France.

CHINESE REVOLUTION The product of a civil war between Chinese Nationalists led by Jiang Jieshi (Chiang Kai-shek) and his Communist foes led by Mao Zedong (Mao Tse-tung). Begun in 1927, this struggle was put aside for an anti-Japanese coalition during World War II but resumed thereafter, with the United States supporting the Nationalists. In 1949, Beijing (Peking) and other major cities fell to the Communists, who created the People's Republic of China with Mao as chairman. Jiang fled to Taiwan, where he established the Nationalist Republic of China.

CICERO, MARCUS TULLIUS (106–43 B.C.) The Roman orator and philosopher who counseled the Republic against the Cataline conspiracy and the tyrannical plans of Julius Caesar and Mark Antony. He was executed by Augustus.

CUBAN REVOLUTION The 1959 overthrow, by guerrillas led by Fidel Castro, of the U.S.-supported dictatorship of Fulgencio Batista y Zaldívar in Cuba. Advocating Marxist-Leninist ideology, Castro confiscated foreign-owned property, nationalized Cuban industry, collectivized agriculture, and led the nation into an alliance with the Soviet Union.

DE GAULLE, CHARLES (1890–1970) The French general who became first president (1959–1969) of the Fifth Republic. He was known in the United States for his independent stance toward the Cold War and for his nationalistic pride.

DECLARATION OF THE RIGHTS OF MAN AND CITIZEN (1789) The document drafted by Emmanuel Sièyes and adopted as the preamble to the French constitution of 1791. Influenced by the American Declaration of Independence, the French declaration asserted the equality of all men, the sovereignty of the people, and the rights of individuals to liberty, property, and security.

ENLIGHTENMENT The name given to the rationalist, liberal, humanitarian, and scientific trend of eighteenth-century Western thought during what is often called the Age of Reason. American representatives of this trend included Benjamin Franklin, Thomas Jefferson, and Thomas Paine.

FRANKFURT PARLIAMENT The popularly elected National Assembly convened as a result of the liberal revolution that swept Germany in 1848. It attempted to unify the German states under a constitutional monarchy, but Frederick William IV of Prussia refused the crown, and the Frankfurt Parliament disbanded.

FRENCH CONSTITUENT ASSEMBLY OF 1848   After the Revolution of 1848, which toppled the July Monarchy of Louis Philippe, the body elected by universal manhood suffrage to draft a constitution for the Second Republic.

GIRONDIST   Pertaining or belonging to the moderate faction of French revolutionaries opposed to social equality and advocating a "federalist" or decentralized government. The Girondists reached the height of their popularity under the constitutional monarchy in 1792, but were bypassed after Louis XVI was executed and the Jacobins centralized power under Robespierre. More than twenty Girondist leaders were executed during the Reign of Terror.

GROTIUS, HUGO (1583–1645)   The Dutch jurist whose book *Concerning the Law of War and Peace* (1628) was the first widely accepted text on international law. He argued that natural law prescribes rules of conduct for nations, as for individuals.

HAITIAN REVOLUTION   Begun as a slave rebellion in 1791, the revolt that grew into a war for independence led by the free black Toussaint L'Ouverture. Haitian forces forced the British to withdraw, quelled a mulatto uprising, and repelled a French invasion. Toussaint gained control over the island in 1801; three years later Haiti became an independent country ruled by Toussaint's successor, Jean Jacques Dessalines.

JACOBINS   A French political club whose members, mostly middle class, grew increasingly republican and radical as the French Revolution progressed, eventually supporting the Reign of Terror.

LIVY (59 B.C.–A.D. 17)   A Roman historian whose life's work was an enormous history of Rome from its founding to 9 B.C.

LOCKE, JOHN (1632–1704)   An English philosopher of the Enlightenment whose theories about natural law and the social contract influenced eighteenth-century political thought in Europe and America. Locke maintained that the state should guarantee the inalienable rights of "life, health, liberty, and possessions," and he proclaimed revolution a duty when governments failed to preserve these rights. He argued for checks and balances among branches of government (later embodied in the U.S. Constitution) and for broad religious freedom.

MANORIAL SYSTEM OR SEIGNEURIAL SYSTEM   The medieval social system based on the holding of lands from a lord (seigneur) in return for fixed dues in goods, money, and services. Unlike feudalism, the manorial system lacked military or political obligations, though the lord presided over a court and levied taxes.

MEXICAN REVOLUTION   The successful revolt begun in 1910 against the dictatorship of President Porfirio Díaz. Within a few years, the revolution became a civil war between the army of Venustiano Carranza, a rich landowner supported by the United States, and armies of cowboys and peasants led by Pancho Villa and Emiliano Zapata. Carranza prevailed when Zapata was killed in 1919 and Villa surrendered the following year.

PLUTARCH (*circa* 46–*circa* 120)   The Greek moralist and biographer whose *Parallel Lives* paired the life stories of great Greek and Roman leaders in order to demonstrate the influence of character and morality in history.

PUFENDORF, SAMUEL (1632–1694)   A German historian and legal scholar whose writings on natural and international law became standard works in the eighteenth century.

REIGN OF TERROR (1793–1794)   The period of the French Revolution that established a virtual dictatorship to preserve the republic during domestic strife and foreign wars. Led by Robespierre, the Committee of Public Safety executed counterrevolutionaries, set wage and price controls, instituted new patriotic rituals, and mobilized the military. When popular discontent grew, the Reign of Terror was ended by the overthrow of Robespierre.

ROBESPIERRE, MAXIMILIAN (1758–1794)   The radical French lawyer who became the leader of the Jacobins in the National Assembly. In 1793, he was elected to the Committee of Public Safety, and he dominated it throughout the Reign of Terror. In July 1794, independent and rightist members of the National Convention overthrew Robespierre and had him guillotined.

ROUSSEAU, JEAN JACQUES (1712–1778)   The Swiss-French Enlightenment philosopher and political theorist, author of *Social Contract* (1762), who contended that proper political institutions resulted when citizens voluntarily and temporarily delegated their sovereignty to leaders. Rousseau's writings inspired leaders of the French Revolution and profoundly influenced later political and educational theories.

RUSSIAN REVOLUTION   The violent upheavals in Russia ending in the overthrow of the czarist government in 1917. A revolution in 1905 created a parliament, which the czar suppressed, but military defeats and civilian suffering in World War I rekindled revolutionary protest. In February 1917, a new parliament forced Czar Nicholas II to abdicate and formed a provisional government. In October 1917, the Bolsheviks, led by V. I. Lenin, captured government buildings in Moscow. After a three-year civil war, they consolidated control of the new Soviet Union under the Communist Party.

ST.-JUST (OR SAINT-JUST), LOUIS ANTOINE DE (1767–1794)   A French Jacobin leader who was executed with Robespierre by the National Convention.

TACITUS, CORNELIUS (56–*circa* 120)   A Roman historian whose celebrated *Histories* and *Annals* chronicled the Roman Empire in the first century A.D.

✫ ✫ ✫ ✫ ✫ ✫ ✫

The United States of America, as a political organization, was undoubtedly created by a revolution, which found its expression in the Declaration of Independence of 1776. The experience of revolution is therefore one which Americans share with others. . . . [I]t is important to try to see the American Revolution in a comparative light, assessing both resemblances and differences between it and other revolutions, and the effects it may have had on revolutionary developments in other parts of the world.

The task is not easy. Nor is it new, for Americans have been concerned with their special relationship to the rest of the world from the time of the Revolution itself, and indeed since the first settlement of the country. Europeans, and others also, have found much in the American experience to illuminate their own. But though old, the question has its relevancy today, when some see the United States as the great conservative power opposed to twentieth-century revolutions, while others . . . believe that the American revolutionary example should be carried to Latin America and elsewhere. It may be added that . . . [today's] struggle for equality for American citizens of whatever race . . . may be seen as a contemporary manifestation of principles deriving from the American Revolution.

There are many possible views. Some have thought that there was really no revolution in America at all, in any modern sense of the word, but only a successful war of independence, which removed British control but left the country internally much the same. Closely related is the idea that the American revolt was really a conservative movement, to protect old liberties against novel demands by Great Britain, somewhat like the revolt of the Belgian estates in 1789 against the attempted reforms of the Emperor Joseph II. This idea, which later found favor in conservative circles in the United States, appeared in Europe as early as the 1790's, when Friedrich Gentz, for example, praised the conservatism of the American Revolution in order to attack the French. Other European conservatives of the time, however, for example the Abbé Barruel, insisted that the French Revolution had been anticipated in America. It was in America, said Barruel, that a "sect" of secret revolutionaries had first announced "its code of equality, liberty, and sovereignty of the people." Though no one now agrees with Barruel's conspiratorial theory of the Revolution, he nevertheless shared in a third view, indeed the classic view, common to persons of both conservative and liberal inclination, that the American Revolution was the first episode in a long revolutionary period extending from about 1770 through the European revolutions of 1848, and principally marked by the great French Revolution of 1789. Within this view many nuances exist, depending on how much one wishes to stress similarities or national differences. George Lefebvre, the eminent French historian, thought that the American Revolution had more in common with the English revolution of the seventeenth century than with the French, believing that the Anglo-Saxon revolutions, as he called them, were primarily concerned with liberty, while the French Revolution aimed most especially at equality. While the idea of equality took on a far wider range of meanings in the French Revolution, it seems certain that Lefebvre greatly underestimated its importance in America. For Alexis de Tocqueville, writing his *Democracy in America* in the 1830's, the United States offered the world's leading example of "equality," though it is true that Tocqueville did not relate his observation to the American Revolution.

The various revolutions up to 1848, including the American, and that of England in the seventeenth century, have sometimes been put together as the "bourgeois revolution," a view congenial to Marxists but not limited to them, and one in which everything depends on what is meant by the "bourgeoisie." Since, in brief, the English revolution was an affair of fairly aristocratic landowners, the American of small farmers, planters, and country lawyers, and the French of a large composite urban middle class reinforced by peasants and workers, with occasional nobles and priests, the conception of a bourgeoisie must for this purpose become excessively generalized, and signify hardly more than persons who possessed or aspired to possess private property, in land or in goods, in amounts either very large or very small. Indeed, strong emphasis on the concept of a "bourgeois revolution" is likely to imply a future stage of development in which the bourgeoisie is to be succeeded by a new dominant group, with private property in income-producing goods abolished. Such came to be the message of revolutionary or Marxist socialism in Europe after the mid-nineteenth century. In the rise of this movement, the American Revolution was of little significance. There has been little affinity between the American Revolution and the Russian Revolution as it developed after 1917, or the Chinese Revolution as it developed after World War II.

There is another category of revolutions, those aiming at national independence, in which the American Revolution is seen as a precedent, since, whatever else it may also have been, it was clearly a struggle for independence against Great Britain. In general, such revolutionary movements ran their course in Latin America through the nineteenth century, and in Europe through the close of World War I, producing such newly independent states as Czechoslovakia and Ireland. They have been in progress since that time in Africa and Asia, in the form of resistance to the European colonial rule. The leaders of such movements of national independence have often looked to the American Revolution as an example to follow, and have characteristically been befriended by the government of the United States. The situation becomes confused when movements of national independence take on a strong social character, and are directed against foreign capitalism, foreign economic control, or foreign ideas, influence, or privileges, as in the Mexican Revolution after 1910, the Cuban Revolution since 1959, and indeed in the Russian and Chinese revolutions also. . . .

Let us consider at greater length only two matters suggested by the preceding survey: first, the relationship of the American Revolution to the French and European revolutions of almost two hundred years ago; and second, the relationship of the American Revolution, whether in resemblance or by contrast, to the anticolonialist revolutionary disturbances in the Asian–African–Latin American world in recent times.

As for the first, the view taken here is a form of what has already been called the "classical" interpretation. There was one great revolutionary period from about 1770 to 1848; this was *the* European revolution or revolution of Western civilization. The American Revolution was part of this process, was indeed the opening movements of this general European or "Atlantic" phenomenon. On the other hand, the American Revolution was directed *against* Europe — Europe as a whole, and not merely Great Britain. Hence it has a positive significance for anticolonialist revolutionaries today, who are fundamentally anti-European, and can with some justice see the American Revolution as the opening movement of *their* revolution also. But in both cases we run into difficulties and paradoxes. The American Revolution of 1776 was different from the French Revolution of 1789, if only because Americans were not Europeans. But it is different also from later anticolonial and anti-European movements because the Americans are, after all, a species of Europeans — the "colony of all Europe" as Thomas Paine said in 1776, the "daughter of Europe," as General Charles de Gaulle remarked in 1965.

Similarities between the revolutions in America and in Europe in the eighteenth century are impossible to deny. It is idle to pretend that the uprising in America was not truly revolutionary, or to see it as primarily a conservative protest. The Americans rebelled against the legal authority of the British crown and Parliament, they passed from more moderate to more radical stages, reaching the point of armed conflict and a secession from the British empire which many Americans were unwilling to accept, so that the war of independence was at the same time a civil or revolutionary struggle between native Americans, in the course of which, as a few years later in France, there was a good deal of intimidation, if not actual "terror," emigration of tens of thousands who remained loyal to Britain, and confiscation of the property of these political émigrés. Victorious after a long struggle, thanks to the intervention of France, the revolutionary Americans set up new governments according to new principles, and to a large extent operated by new men, of a kind who could not have achieved prominence had the colonies remained British. This is true not only of such notables as George Washington or John Adams. A study has . . . been made of men who sat in legislatures of the colonies just before independence, and of the corresponding states just after, according to the classifications of "wealthy," "well-to-do," and "moderate." In New York, New Jersey, and New Hampshire, between 1770 and 1784, the proportion called "moderate" — i.e., in wealth, not opinion — rose from 17 to 62 percent, with corresponding loss of the "wealthy" and "well-to-do." Even in the South the "wealthy" lost their predominance in the legislatures. When classified by occupation, the proportion of merchants and lawyers greatly declined, whereas the proportion of farmers doubled. In short, the revolt in America meets the external criteria of a true revolution, and of a revolution in a democratic direction, since it was a former upper or "aristocratic" class that was displaced.

It is in principles, purposes, and ideas, or what may be called "ideology," that the resemblance between the American and the French or European revolutions is most evident. On the plane of actual politics, the modern doctrines of liberty and equality, or natural rights and the sovereignty of the people, were first proclaimed by the American Revolution. The Declaration of Independence . . . announced that "all men are created equal," with an equal right to "life, liberty, and the pursuit of happiness." There has been much discussion of what Jefferson meant by inserting "happiness" into this document; the Americans had not really been "unhappy" under British rule, and "happiness" makes a vague political program; but all students of the eighteenth century will recognize that "happiness," *le bonheur, la félicité publique*, was a common idea of the European Enlightenment. It was the revolutionary belief that men may take action to improve their conditions of life, even against the established authorities of law, state, church, or society — as St.-Just remarked a few years later, at the height of the French Revolution, "Happiness is a new idea in Europe." The Declaration of Independence went on to assert that government exists only to protect the rights thus affirmed, and that when government failed in this function, the people "may alter or abolish it." They might then "institute new government" as they chose. This is a pure formula of revolution.

As a matter of fact, it was not the Declaration of Independence which first attracted attention in Europe, or which best illustrates the resemblances in ideas between America and Europe at the time. A complaint by disaffected provincials against the king of England, rehearsing his real and alleged misdoings, however adorned with familiar eighteenth-century generalizations, could have little universal appeal. The connection between the American and European revolutions is more apparent in the constructive part of the American program, the way in which the Americans "instituted new government." They instituted it, or "constituted" it, first of all in each of the thirteen states, each of which received a new written constitution (except that in Connecticut and Rhode Island the colonial charters were retained, being virtually republican anyway), and then by establishing the federal union with the Constitution written in Philadelphia in 1787, which, as amended, remains the Constitution of the United States today. For this purpose, at the state and federal levels, the Americans devised the mechanism of a special convention or constituent assembly, which was held to exercise the sovereign power of the people, and which characteristically did two things. First, it issued a declaration of rights, listing the "rights of man" in a series of numbered articles, and setting limits beyond which the powers of government could not go. Second, it produced a written constitution, one short single document, by which the people were supposed to create a government for themselves, all public power was held to be merely a revocable and delegated authority (as in the *Social Contract* of Rousseau), various political bodies and offices were defined, and the executive, legislative, and judicial powers were separated and balanced, so that abuse of government, despotism, or dictatorship might be prevented. The American constitutions and declarations of rights gave a practical embodiment to ideas of political liberty and legal equality, to the principle of representation by numbers rather than by classes or corporate groups, the rejection of hereditary office and privileged status, the opening of careers to merit rather than birth, and the separation of state and church, or at least of citizenship from religious affiliation.

This machinery and these ideas — the constituent convention, the declaration of rights, the written constitution, the separation of powers, the new basis for political representation, the equality of rights, the career open to talent, the separation of church and state — soon became common to the great European or "Atlantic" revolution, from the French Constituent Assembly of 1789 and the French Convention of 1792, through the new regimes in Holland, Switzerland, and Italy — that is, the Batavian, Helvetic, Cisalpine, and other republics that arose during the wars of the 1790s — to the French Constituent Assembly of 1848, the German Frankfurt Parliament, and other European developments of that same year.

Yet the American Revolution was very different from the European, and especially the French Revolution, for the good reason that America in the eighteenth century was a very different kind of country from Europe, more so than it is today. The astonishing thing is that any parallel in political behavior or ideology could exist at all. In the Thirteen Colonies, at the time of their revolution, there was no feudalism, no seigneurial or manorial system, and no peasantry — for the mobile and property-owning American farmers were hardly peasants. There were no lords or nobility, no magnificent and privileged church, and one might almost say no monarchy, though the distant king and his agents were long respected. Before the troubles with England the Americans lived virtually without problems of taxation, civil service, armed forces, or foreign policy. There were no craft guilds or other medieval economic survivals. The Americans had no developed capitalism, as in Europe, no banks, no corporations or trading companies, no great wealth, and no extreme poverty. The exceptions were the Negro slaves, who were numerous in the South but played no political role (except to give importance to their owners) and whose very existence accentuated the difference between the two continents. There were no large cities and no significant network of roads. There were a handful of small colleges but no universities; and although many Americans, such as Franklin, Adams, and Jefferson, were well read and well informed, there was in truth no intellectual class. Almost no books were written in America; the book trade was part of the import trade from England. There was as yet hardly any distinctive national culture or political unity. How could such a country give lessons to Europe, or even share in European ideas?

The answer, of course, is that for many revolutionary developments in Europe, America offered no parallel. It is obvious that the French Revolution was a vaster and more profound social upheaval, involving more violent conflict between classes, more radical reorganization of government and society, more far-reaching redefinition of marriage, property, and civil law as well as of organs of public authority, more redistribution of wealth and income, more fears on the part of the rich and more demands from the poor, more sensational repercussions in other countries, more crises of counterrevolution, war, and invasion, and more drastic or emergency measures, as in the Reign of Terror. From very early in the French Revolution the American Revolution came to seem very moderate. Thomas Jefferson, who was then in France, feared that the French were going to dangerous extremes as early as June 1789. For the advanced democratic leaders of France and Europe, from 1789 or 1793 down through the nineteenth century, the Americans seemed "Girondist" or "federalist." They failed to see the need of a powerful, enterprising, centralized, unitary, democratic state as a means not only of carrying on war but of reducing inequalities against strong opposition. Only in our own time, as the federal government intervenes locally, to protect the rights of Negroes, or to assure more equality in such matters as schools and highways, are Americans learning what has long been known to Europeans.

Yet the parallels between the American and European revolutions, as already indicated, remain. Apart from the fact of rebellion itself against an older authority, the parallels have mostly to do with constitutional principles, and with the essentially ethical goals summed up in the ideas of liberty and equality. At this level there was undeniably a transatlantic ideology common to the revolutionary era of Western civilization. The Americans thought like Europeans because they were transplanted Europeans. Their only culture was an English and European culture, modified and diluted by the experience of living in a new and simpler environment. They drew their ideas from the same sources as Europeans, from their own experience in affairs, from their churches in part, and from Greek and Latin classics read in school, from Cicero and Plutarch, from Livy and Tacitus, and from the modern philosophers of natural law, such as Grotius, Pufendorf, and John Locke. Social conditions, social structures, problems, and grievances were very different on the two sides of the Atlantic. But a political philosophy is not merely the product of specific social conditions, or an instrument devised to meet immediate practical needs. There are many kinds of restraints from which a desire for liberty may arise, and many kinds of inequalities or injustices from which equality may be made an ideal. Different though the circumstances were, the American Revolution could announce a revolutionary program for Europe.

By the same token, the American Revolution has its relevancy to the contemporary anticolonialist movements, despite immense differences in circumstances, not only between the United States today and the ex-colonial countries, but between the Thirteen Colonies of 1776 and the British, French, Dutch, and Portuguese "colonies" in Asia and Africa [after World War II]. . . . These differences are very great, and involve first of all a difference of meaning in the word "colony" itself. "Colony" in recent usage has meant no more than a "possession." The colonies which became the United States were colonies in the classical and Latin sense, new communities established by the migration and settlement of persons from a mother country, with which they shared the same language, culture, inheritance, and race. In this respect, the parallel of the American Revolution might be to the Europeans in Algeria before its independence, or to the white population in Rhodesia [now Zimbabwe]. . . . The white Rhodesians, in fact, in their unilateral assertion of independence of 1965, adopted some of the language of the American Declaration of Independence, though carefully avoiding any reference to human equality. There is actually no significant parallel here. In the American colonies of the eighteenth century the whites were not newcomers among a much larger indigenous population. The native Indian population of eastern North America had always been very sparse. The attitude of the white population to these Indians may be called ruthless, but the two million whites in the Thirteen Colonies in 1776 probably outnumbered the aborigines by some magnitude such as ten or twenty to one. There were also the Negroes, some half million in number, almost all slaves. Like the whites, they were immigrants or the descendants of immigrants. . . . [But] [n]either slavery nor racial questions were ever at issue between Britain and America at the time of the Revolution, as they might have been if the white Americans had rebelled a half-century later. It may be noted in passing that many white Americans were already uneasy about the enslavement of Africans and that they suppressed the question in order to maintain unity among themselves. It was not the Americans, but the French, at the height of their own revolution in 1794, who were the first to abolish slavery. In this respect, as in others, the French Revolution went further than the American in equalitarian and humanitarian principles, though it was easier for the French to abolish slavery, which existed only in their colonies, than it would have been for the Americans to do so in their own country.

The point is that for practical purposes, at the time of the American Revolution, the Americans meant the white Americans of European and mainly English descent, and that these ex-Europeans, unlike those of [twentieth-century] Rhodesia, South Africa, or Algeria . . . , were far from being a minority in their own country. But of course by the anticolonial revolution today we mean the movements of the black Africans of Africa, the Arabs of North Africa, the peoples of Asia and the former Dutch East Indies and the . . . independent republics of Latin America, especially those in which the aboriginal or non-European element is very large. How does this modern "anticolonialism" compare with the American Revolution?

Certainly the differences are obvious and considerable. For one thing, it is not clear how many such anticolonial revolutions, in a strict sense, there have ever been. Algeria is a special case, Mexico has had a real revolution, and Cuba entertains a revolutionary ideology. On the whole, however, and with exceptions as in Vietnam, the British, French, and Dutch liquidated their empires without waiting for revolution, and not many Africans or Asians have actually had the American experience of rebellion and war to obtain their political independence.

In any case, the problems are different. In the Afro–Asian–Latin American world the problems are poverty, overpopulation, economic underdevelopment, and exploitation by foreign capital or the forces of a world market. There are difficulties of language and communication, and a lack of trained personnel for positions in government and the economy. There is the cultural problem posed by Western civilization — is this foreign culture to be rejected, resisted, made use of, or imitated? And there is the racial problem, inflamed by the humiliation of having been condescended to, segregated, or ostracized by a white ruling class.

On these matters, parallels to the American Revolution are shadowy or nonexistent. The Thirteen Colonies did not suffer from poverty. The average American at that time probably enjoyed better food, lodging, and conditions of work than the average European. There was no overpopulation; quite the reverse. Though the British colonial system was operated for British commercial and strategic advantage, and though Americans had begun to chafe at certain restrictions, the Thirteen Colonies had not been exploited. The Americans had always enjoyed a large measure of genuine self-government, and could draw on their own political experience after independence. The Thirteen Colonies were economically undeveloped, though in some cases they rivaled England itself, as in fisheries and ship-building; but in any event they had the means of rapid development in their human and natural resources and in their institutional setting, a development aided in the generations following the Revolution by the continuing investment of British capital and influx of European immigration, which brought skilled labor and professional talents to the new country. This influx was made possible by the racial and cultural affinity between white Americans and Europeans. For Americans, Europe with its older and richer civilization, and more elaborate social classes, might pose a psychological problem. Americans might at times suffer from an "inferiority complex" toward Europe, or complain of European condescension. But there was hardly the same social distance as for Asians or Africans. America was the daughter of Europe, never its slave girl or its captive.

Given such differences, what can be the parallels? What relevancy can the American Revolution have for non-Europeans and for the anticolonial movements of the twentieth century? Perhaps it might be wise to give up the very idea that there are any such parallels or resemblances. Americans today might have a more realistic view of the world, and more real sympathy, understanding, and tolerance for other peoples, if they expected no resemblance whatsoever to the American pattern. Perhaps, for some peoples in Africa, the revolution of the 1790's in Haiti offers a more significant precedent than the revolution which produced the United States. At that time the blacks of the French colony of San Domingo, in conjunction with the French Revolution, established the second oldest independent republic in the Americas. But the subsequent history of Haiti was very troubled, and the precedent would be a discouraging one, except for the fact that the Africans of today are more advanced than the slaves of eighteenth-century San Domingo, and enjoy far more support from the white man's world than the blacks of Haiti ever obtained.

Yet, in conclusion, something can be said for resemblances between the American Revolution and the twentieth-century anticolonial revolutionary upheavals. The independence of the United States did signify, after all, the first case of breakup of a European empire. It set a precedent for the act of rebellion; it showed men fighting, living dangerously, and dying for their rights. The Americans, after their independence was recognized, were the first "new nation" in a certain modern sense of the word, and they faced the problems of a new nation. Emerging from the old British Empire, they soon embarked on a successful economic development. They also had to establish their national unity and identity, and they did so with difficulty, for in the early years of the federal constitution it seemed that the country might fall apart into separate fragments, and all compromises broke down in the great Civil War of 1861. If formal unity was thereafter restored, it was at the expense of the Negroes; but . . . [the movement for racial equality gathered force in the twentieth century], and the Americans, in attempting to create an interracial society, are still at work on a problem of national unity of a kind, in general, which other "new nations" also face.

But it is at the highest level, that of abstract ideas, that the American Revolution has something to say to the anticolonialists of the twentieth century, as to European revolutionaries at the time of the great revolution in France. The Americans justified their independence by the grandeur and universality of a revolutionary message. The idea that peoples should choose their own government, and determine the forms and powers of this government by constituent assemblies, is not yet exhausted. The old eighteenth-century "rights of man," though much criticized by philosophers from that day to this, and now known more tamely as "human rights," are still very much alive. As a matter of fact, a more lucid and balanced statement of these rights was given in the French Declaration of the Rights of Man and Citizen of 1789. Some of the first American state constitutions likewise expressed the idea in more definite form. But for the belief that all men are "created equal," and have an equal right to life, liberty, and the pursuit of happiness, whose protection is the function of good government, we still turn, with good reason, to the American Declaration of Independence.

QUESTIONS TO CONSIDER

1. Palmer outlines different kinds or "categories" of revolutions: "conservative," "bourgeois," and "true" revolutions; anticolonial movements; and national independence movements. What does he mean by these terms? How are these kinds of revolutions similar or different? Where does the American Revolution fit in these categories? In what ways was it conservative? To what extent was the American Revolution a social revolution — that is, one that sought to restructure society by

redistributing wealth or abolishing privilege? What does Palmer think of the notion of the American Revolution as a "bourgeois revolution"?

2. It is common to compare the American and French Revolutions with simple dichotomies: the Americans were peaceful, the French violent; the Americans championed liberty, the French equality; the Americans were conservative, the French radical. How accurate are these generalizations? To what extent does Palmer's essay support this view?

3. What does Palmer mean when he says that the thirteen colonies "had not been exploited" by England? Do you agree? If Palmer is right, then why did the American colonists rebel?

4. Palmer notes that despite equalitarian principles, the American revolutionaries, unlike the French, did not abolish slavery. Why not?

5. How was the situation of the American colonists of 1776 similar to or different from twentieth-century colonial peoples in Africa or Asia? In what ways, if any, could the American Revolution be held up as a model for them? Why did the United States, a country that began with a revolution, oppose so many revolutions in the twentieth century?

8

Independence and Revolution
in the Americas

ANTHONY McFARLANE

From R. R. Palmer's rather abstract treatment of revolutions in Selection 7, we move to a detailed comparison between the American Revolution and the independence movements of Latin America. As Anthony McFarlane's informative essay reminds us, ours was not the only anticolonial revolution in this hemisphere. Between 1789 and 1828, nearly all the colonies of Central and South America broke away from their rulers in Spain and Portugal and confirmed their independence through military victories.

As in the British colonies, attempts to tighten royal control brought isolated protests in Spain's New World possessions in the 1760s and again in the 1780s. By the latter time, liberal intellectuals could look north with envy on the infant United States. But it was the French Revolution and its Napoleonic aftermath that triggered the Latin American independence movements. By toppling the French king and outlawing slavery in their colonies, the French set off a rebellion, led by the charismatic ex-slave François Dominique Toussaint L'Ouverture, that eventually won independence for Haiti. Then in 1807, Napoleon's armies invaded the Iberian Peninsula and deposed Ferdinand VII of Spain. Homegrown colonial elites throughout Spanish America seized the chance to push aside the Peninsulares, or ruling class from the mother country, and institute new governments. Their most heroic liberator was the articulate Venezuelan Simón Bolívar. Taking George Washington as his model, Bolívar snatched military victories from the jaws of defeat, called upon the masses to practice virtue and restraint, and declined to turn the new republics into his personal kingdoms. Although the United States government did little to aid the rebels, it did quickly recognize their new states. In 1823, President James Monroe, rejecting Britain's call for a joint Anglo-American statement on free trade, warned European governments to leave the new nations alone and to cease all further efforts at colonizing the New World.

All this suggests, as some historians have argued, that the Americas have a great deal of history in common. But, says McFarlane, after their revolutions the United States and Latin America quickly parted ways. The young United States enjoyed domestic tranquility, increased democracy, and economic growth, but in Latin America society remained rigidly unequal and governments proved undemocratic and notoriously unstable. The difference, according to McFarlane, goes back to profoundly contrasting colonial political and economic arrangements. Whereas the British colonists enjoyed a long apprenticeship as legislators, the Spanish suffocated under unrepresentative institutions. While British Americans practiced a rough equality among themselves and could simply outnumber the native population, the Creole elite of Latin America, determined to protect its property and privileges from the masses of Indians and slaves, accepted democracy only in name. Freed by Britain's "salutary neglect," the North American colonies built a commercial infrastructure that would support economic development in the young United States, whereas new Latin American nations simply exchanged Spanish royal monopolies for a less formal but equally galling dependence upon British goods and capital. McFarlane's discussion of the origins of today's wide economic gulf between the United States and Latin America shares similarities with Charles Bergquist's analysis of the paradox of development in the Americas in Selection 5, a comparison you will want to explore.

Perhaps fearing that his essay might encourage complacency among American readers, McFarlane ends ironically by noting that the modern United States has replaced Spain as Latin America's imperialist albatross. Even for the nineteenth century, you might consider whether McFarlane's contrast between a stable, democratic North America and a volatile, authoritarian South America would look as stark if he discussed slavery in the southern United States and continued his narrative to the Civil War. Somewhere between the notion of a common history of the Americas and the Mexican poet Octavio Paz's claim that the Latin American tradition is "essentially and radically alien" to the United States lies the complex truth of comparative history. The trick is to find it.

GLOSSARY

ANCIEN RÉGIME   The "old order," or established monarchical government, in France.

BOURBONS   The Catholic royal family that ruled Spain and France in the eighteenth century. The Bourbon dynasty was deposed by the French Revolution and its aftermath, but returned to power in 1814 when Napoleon was defeated. Bourbon monarchs ruled France until 1830 and Spain until 1931.

CATHOLIC COUNTER REFORMATION   The movement in the sixteenth and seventeenth centuries to reform the Catholic Church, largely in response to the Protestant Reformation. In 1542, Pope Paul III initiated a Papal Inquisition to root out heretics; three years later he convened the Council of Trent, which reorganized church practices to avoid corruption.

CAUDILLO   A military leader; the name given to nineteenth-century Latin American dictators who came to power during times of political instability. Capitalizing on their military abilities and personal charisma, *caudillos* often claimed to represent the rights of the masses and to oppose the wealthy.

COMUNEROS   Leaders of an unsuccessful Creole revolt in 1781 against Spanish rule in New Granada (comprising present-day Colombia, Venezuela, and Ecuador).

CREOLES   As used in this essay, colonists born in the West Indies or Latin America, but of European ancestry.

DOM PEDRO I (1798–1834)   The first emperor of independent Brazil. Son of the Portuguese prince regent, he fled with the royal family to Brazil when Napoleon invaded the Iberian Peninsula in 1807. After his father became King John VI of Portugal, Pedro remained in Brazil and, under popular pressure, declared it an independent monarchy in 1822. A disastrous war with Argentina and a revolt in Rio de Janeiro led to his abdication in 1831.

HETERODOX   Holding unorthodox doctrines or opinions, especially in religion.

HIDALGO REBELLION   A revolt against Spanish rule led by the Mexican priest and revolutionary leader Miguel Hidalgo y Cortilla in 1810. Commanding a huge army of Indians, Hidalgo won some initial battles, but was defeated by a royalist army in 1817 and executed.

ITURBIDE, AGUSTÍN DE (1783–1824)   A defender of the Mexican Creole elite who fought the Hidalgo rebels and then, fearing that Spain would introduce liberal reforms, declared Mexico's independence from Spain in 1821. Iturbide proclaimed himself emperor in 1822, but revolutionary forces led by Santa Anna forced him into exile the following year.

LOYALISTS   Also called Tories; American colonists who refused to renounce their allegiance to the British Crown after 1776. Approximately five hundred thousand colonists, 20 percent of the white population, actively opposed independence. Many suffered physical abuse, disfranchisement, or confiscation of property, and about one hundred thousand were forced into exile in Canada, England, or the Caribbean.

MERCANTILIST MONOPOLIES   Exclusive trading privileges required by imperial powers from their colonies.

MESTIZO   In Latin America, a person of mixed Indian and white ancestry.

METROPOLITAN STATES   Parent states or "mother countries" of colonies.

NAPOLEONIC WARS   The series of wars between France under Napoleon I and various coalitions of European opponents, including Britain, Austria, Russia, Prussia, and Sweden. Beginning in 1803, these conflicts preoccupied Europe until Napoleon was finally defeated at Waterloo in 1815.

SAN MARTÍN, JOSÉ DE (1778–1850)   A South American revolutionary leader and professional soldier who joined the revolution against Spain in his native Argentina in 1812. San Martín liberated Chile and captured Lima, Peru, then yielded power to Bolívar.

SEVEN YEARS' WAR (1756–1762)   Called the French and Indian War in the American colonies; a worldwide conflict between imperial nations fought in Europe, North America, and India. On one side were Great Britain, Prussia, and Hanover; on the other were France, Austria, Russia, Saxony, Sweden, and Spain. Two main issues were involved: the struggle between Prussia and Austria for supremacy in central Europe, and French and English colonial rivalries in North America and India. Prussian and English victories led to the Treaties of Hubertusburg and Paris in 1763, which confirmed Prussia's power on the Continent and gave Britain all of French Canada.

STAMP ACT (1765)   A law passed by the British Parliament requiring publications and legal documents to bear a tax stamp. As a tax intended to produce revenue for the king rather than to regulate commerce, the Stamp Act was denounced and resisted by the American colonists. It was repealed in 1766.

STUARTS   The royal family that ruled England (with some interruption) from 1603 to 1714. The first two Stuart monarchs, James I and Charles I, asserted the divine right of kings against the growing power of Parliament, precipitating the English Civil War in the 1640s.

SUZERAINTY   A nation whose international affairs are controlled by another nation, but is allowed sovereignty in domestic affairs.

TOUSSAINT L'OUVERTURE, FRANÇOIS DOMINIQUE (1743–1803)   Leader of the Haitian Revolution. A self-educated freed slave, he joined the rebellion of 1791 to liberate the slaves and played a key role in uniting the colony's blacks first against English and Spanish interference, then in an independence struggle against the French. He died in a French prison a year before the republic of Haiti became a reality.

TÚPAC AMARU (*circa* 1742–1781)   An Inca leader who in 1780 led a revolt against Spanish suppression of the Indians in Peru and New Granada. He was captured and executed, and the insurrection was brutally put down by Spanish troops.

UNICAMERAL LEGISLATURE   A single-chamber lawmaking body, unlike the U.S. Congress, whose Senate and House of Representatives make it bicameral.

★ ★ ★ ★ ★ ★ ★

During the half-century from 1776 to 1826, the political map of the Americas was dramatically redrawn. Over a vast arc of land stretching from the Great Lakes to Cape Horn, the boundaries of empire gave way to the borders of sovereign states as British, French, Spanish and Portuguese dominion retreated before the advance of revolution. Within fifty years, the great colonial empires in the West had largely disintegrated; on their ruins the modern community of American nation-states, formed by the United States and the countries of Latin America, began to take shape.

This transcontinental process of liberation from colonial rule began in the thirteen colonies of British North America where, between 1775 and 1783, colonial rebels waged a successful war against their parent power, seceded from the British empire, and formed the first independent government in the Americas. The American Revolution had an influence which ultimately spread far beyond its immediate geographical context, for it was to be the primary link in a chain of political changes which reshaped the Atlantic World of Western Europe and its American dominions. Not only did the political concepts of the American Revolution offer a source of ideological inspiration for opponents of the established order in Europe (particularly in France) but, by bankrupting the *ancien régime,* the American war of independence also helped to trigger the second of the great revolutions of the eighteenth-century Atlantic world, that in France itself.

Anthony McFarlane, "Independence and Revolution in the Americas," in *History Today* 34, March 1984, pp. 40–49. Copyright © 1984. Reprinted by permission of *History Today*.

OREGON
COUNTRY
(Joint U.S.-British
occupation)

BRITISH NORTH AMERICA
(Gr. Br.)

UNITED STATES

*ATLANTIC
OCEAN*

MEXICO
1821

San
Antonio

Gulf of Mexico

Mexico City

Veracruz

BAHAMA IS.
(Gr. Br.)

Havana

HAITI 1804

CUBA
(Spain)

PUERTO RICO (Spain)

BRITISH
HONDURAS
(Gr. Br.)

JAMAICA (Gr. Br.)

GUATEMALA
Guatemala

Caribbean Sea

UNITED PROVINCES OF
CENTRAL AMERICA
1823–1839

Panama

Caracas

TRINIDAD (Gr. Br.)

VENEZUELA

BR. GUIANA (Gr. Br.)

Socorro

DUTCH GUIANA (Neth.)

Bogotá

FRENCH GUIANA (France)

GRAN COLOMBIA
1819–1830

*Galápagos
Islands*

Quito

ECUADOR

Amazon

EMPIRE OF BRAZIL
1822

PERU
1821

Lima

Bahia

*PACIFIC
OCEAN*

BOLIVIA
1825

La Paz

Sucre

PARAGUAY
1811

São Paulo

Rio de Janeiro

CHILE
1817

Valparaíso
Santiago

UNITED
PROVINCES OF
LA PLATA
1816

URUGUAY
1828

Independence in
Latin America

ARGENTINA
Buenos Aires
Bahía
Blanca

Montevideo

1811 Year independence gained

Colony

PATAGONIA
(Disputed between
Argentina and Chile)

*Islas Malvinas
(Falkland Islands)*

0   500   1000 Km.

0   500   1000 Mi.

The French Revolution and its Napoleonic aftermath stirred a political conflict in Europe which had momentous consequences in the Americas. Its direct impact was felt immediately in French colonial territory in the Caribbean. On the island of St. Domingue, one of the richest colonies in the world, the collapse of the *ancien régime* set in motion a series of events which undermined French government and smashed the slave society created by French colonialism. After a series of insurrections, foreign interventions and abortive attempts to restore French control, St. Domingue was finally severed from France in 1804, when it became the independent black republic of Haiti.

In the decade which followed, the decline of European colonialism in the Americas quickened and spread. In 1810, the Hispanic empire which stretched from the Californias to Cape Horn felt the first spasms of a political convulsion which, though briefly checked by the forceful reassertion of Spanish authority following the Bourbon restoration in 1814, could not be contained. In 1821, Mexico, the greatest of Spain's American colonies, was lost; by 1825, the last bastion of Spanish rule in South America fell, when Simón Bolívar's campaign of continental liberation culminated in the capture of Upper Peru. Even Brazil, which had remained loyal to the Portuguese crown throughout these troubled years, grew impatient of imperial government and, in 1822, broke away from its metropolis to become an independent constitutional monarchy under a Portuguese prince. By 1826, only pockets of colonial rule remained in the Americas, in the largely unpopulated fastnesses of Canada, in the archipelago of the West Indies, and on the isolated Atlantic shoulder of South America in the Guianas. Throughout continental North and South America, colonial government had been superseded by a constellation of new, independent states which, released from the overarching authority of metropolitan monarchies, generally embraced republican ideals and institutions.

Clearly, the overthrow of European colonial regimes marked a major turning point in the political history of the Americas. The principal areas of European colonial rule in the continental Americas were transformed into a community of nascent states which proclaimed the sovereignty of the people as the sole legitimate source of political authority, based their governments on written constitutions, and emphasized, in theory at least, the rights of citizens to freedom and equality before the law. Equally, the collapse of European colonialism promised new departures in the economic life of the Americas. Released from the constraints of mercantilist monopolies, the new states were free to participate in the international economy, to take charge of their own commerce, and to develop their resources in accord with domestic interests. Such economic freedom, the corollary of political emancipation, appeared to provide the key to prosperity and progress.

The promise of independence was not, however, always fulfilled. Although the emancipation movements employed a similar rhetoric, there were marked differences in the social and political character of the states which they engendered and in the trajectory of their development after independence. In the ex-British colonies in North America, the republican United States established a stable, liberal form of government, achieved rapid economic development and became one of the great industrial powers. In Latin America, this pattern was not repeated. Most of the new states were afflicted by political confusion and chaos, by economic stagnation and decline, and became no more than minor regional powers with little influence beyond their own borders. These differences may, in large part, be attributed to the distinctive legacies left by European colonialism in the Americas. In both their origins and their outcomes, the revolutions for independence in the New World were profoundly influenced by the colonial cultures in which they were conceived and developed.

In their genesis, the American revolutions share a basic characteristic: the first impulse towards emancipation emanated from outside the colonies themselves, springing from changes in the character and policies of their metropolitan states in Europe. In this sense, they arise from a similar background, since such changes in the colonial systems were associated with a general realignment in the balance of economic and political forces in the Atlantic world during the eighteenth century. Throughout this period, and especially after mid-century, the leading colonial powers engaged in a long and exhausting struggle to protect and to extend their empires, a struggle that involved continuous economic competition and periodic, sometimes prolonged, military combat. This inter-imperialist competition affected the American world in a number of ways. First, it exposed the colonies to new economic influences, as European trade opened new frontiers for commercial expansion; secondly, it brought them into closer political and cultural contact with Europe, as more frequent and regular communication quickened the exchange and interaction of information and ideas; thirdly, it generated political tensions in the colonies, as the metropolitan states, seeking to strengthen their hold over their dominions, introduced economic and administrative reforms which disturbed the colonial *status quo* and loosened traditional loyalties.

The modification of imperial economic regulation and fiscal administration was the most immediate and potent source of colonial disaffection. Its corrosive effects on colonial loyalty were demonstrated in both Spanish and British America when, following the Seven Years' War (1756–62), their imperial governments introduced measures to rationalize the economic and political apparatus of their colonial regimes. Challenged by French economic and territorial ambitions in the New World, the British government abandoned its traditional "salutary neglect" of its thirteen mainland American colonies and, during the early 1760s, introduced measures to curtail colonial infringements of imperial commercial regulations, to control the colonial money supply, to constrain the movement of settlers onto western lands, and to increase revenues from taxation. These measures aroused first colonial complaint and then, following the Stamp Act of 1765, open and cumulative colonial resistance which led towards armed conflict from 1775. The Spanish Bourbon government, humiliated by defeat at the hands of the British during the Seven Years' War, also initiated an overhaul of its colonial system in these years. In 1765, the same year that North Americans rioted against the new Stamp tax, the city of Quito in South America witnessed riot and rebellion in response to tax reforms; in 1766 and 1767, there were similar outbursts of violent protest in central Mexico, again precipitated by fiscal reform.

These were, however, minor local problems compared to the great rebellions which took place in the early 1780s, when administrative and fiscal reorganization triggered the uprising of the *Comuneros* in New Grenada and the insurrection of Túpac Amaru in Peru. Coming at the very moment that Spain was embroiled in a Franco-Spanish alliance on the side of Britain's rebellious colonists, these rebellions naturally aroused fears for the stability and integrity of Spain's empire. It was, however, only in British North America that protests against new policies were converted into a general assault on imperial authority, leading to the overthrow of the colonial state and the rapid transformation of its political structures.

At first, its seems paradoxical that the reformist measures introduced by the British government should have provoked such a serious response in its colonies. Compared to the Bourbon reforms in Spanish America, British policies were relatively innocuous and unambitious. However, because social and political conditions in Anglo-America were very different from those which prevailed in Hispanic America, the impact of imperial reform was more disruptive, and the colonial response was more coherent, coordinated and radical.

From its inception, Anglo-American society diverged from the patterns of colonialism laid down by earlier European settlement in the Americas. In the territories of the Iberian powers, colonial settlement rested on the exploitation of non-European peoples in social structures which were both hierarchical and authoritarian. The Spanish-American colonies were created by the conquest of large Amerindian societies, and had developed social and economic structures in which superordinate white minorities dominated a subordinate mass of Indian and mixed-race peasants and workers. In Portuguese Brazil (and later in the Caribbean also), colonial society took another form, distinct from that of Hispanic America, but also divided between a dominant white minority and an exploited mass of people of color. In Brazil, as in Spanish America, the great estate was a basic cell of social and economic organization; but in Brazil it was geared to the production of sugar for world markets rather than foodstuffs for domestic markets, and was worked by imported African slave labor rather than semi-servile Indian labor.

English North America was, by contrast, neither a conquest society, nor a slave society. In its origins, it was a colony of farmers, a predominantly white society of European immigrants who established a relatively egalitarian system of social and economic organization as small, independent landowners living in self-governing communities. By the mid-eighteenth century, this society had undergone some important changes. Demographic and economic growth resulted in greater social and economic inequality, and the egalitarian dispositions of the classic New England settlement were increasingly submerged in a society where wealth was generally becoming more concentrated and social difference more marked. The growth of plantation agriculture, based on black slavery, was another important change, but one which mainly affected the South, where the vast majority of American blacks were located. Elsewhere, blacks were a small minority within a predominantly white and fundamentally English culture.

The political culture of Anglo-America was as distinctive as its society. Unlike the Iberian colonies, which inherited the institutions of autocratic, Catholic Counter-Reformation monarchy, the communities created by English settlement in North America were the heterodox, dissenting offspring of a metropolitan society that was itself divided by a struggle for religious and political freedom. In the Iberian colonies, freedom was residual: it existed in the interstices of theoretically absolutist states, arising from the practical difficulties of imposing full centralized control in distant dominions and from the collusion of colonial bureaucracy with local interests. In Anglo-America, it was a matter of doctrine: the English colonies inherited a system of limited, constitutional government, developed in England under the first two Stuarts and nurtured by a body of Whig political thought which stressed the contractual basis of royal government, and emphasized the need for constant vigilance to defend English liberties against the tyrannical, corrupting proclivities of monarchy. Accustomed to a considerable measure of self-government exercised through elected assemblies, and to mild and ineffective restrictions on their economic activities, North Americans had developed largely autonomous economies and polities, managed by independent mercantile and landed élites who saw themselves as separate and equal partners in empire. In short, Anglo-Americans regarded the empire as a federal structure, united by allegiance to a common crown, in which they enjoyed the rights and liberties of Englishmen and the prerogative of representative government through assemblies which they saw as the coordinates rather than the subordinates of the imperial Parliament.

Thus, within the context of British North America, imperial innovation met with a response which differed significantly from that encountered by the Spanish crown in its dominions. In Spanish America, there was no tradition of constitutional government to defend, and no representative institutions through which to focus and organize opposition to imperial government. The rebellions of the early 1780s remained as uncoordinated regional uprisings which lacked any strong institutional base or coherent ideology and, in societies deeply divided by race and class, found no lasting basis for united, cross-class opposition to Spanish rule. The creole leaders of the *Comuneros* soon reached an accommodation with the crown by the customary means of negotiation with the royal bureaucracy, and abandoned the movement's popular, radical elements; the Túpac Amaru rebellion, though it initially blended creole, mestizo and Indian discontents, broke up into a series of separate Indian insurgencies which, by posing a threat to the social order, reunited creole society and colonial government in a violent counter-revolution. In North America, however, the protests of different social groups, each with its own specific grievances, came together in a cross-class, multi-regional alliance. While rich merchants, urban artisans and laborers, and small farmers each had their own discontents, the institutional and ideological framework of American politics allowed these disparate discontents gradually to fuse around common issues and to unite behind common goals. The colonial assemblies provided a vehicle for political discussion, organization and mobilization; the defense of traditional American liberties provided a common cause, linking the discontents of rich and poor; and, finally, the presence of a politicized stratum of urban artisans provided leadership for the lower orders, and helped to merge their agitations with the constitutionalist cause.

The American War of Independence began, then, with the defense rather than the repudiation of the political system created under colonial rule. But it involved more than simply a break with the imperial power: popular mobilization against Britain also entailed a radicalization of American politics and, when the struggle for home rule was settled, fueled a struggle over who was to rule at home. Both during and after the war, urban artisans and "mechanics" played a prominent part in local politics and the growing influence of popular elements accentuated the participatory and democratic dimensions of American political life. While the state constitutions adopted between 1776 and 1780 proclaimed the doctrines of popular sovereignty and natural rights, extension of the franchise gave these doctrines a practical meaning. It broadened the social basis of politics and, by bringing large contingents of small farmers and artisans into provincial legislatures, eroded the power of established élites. Hence independence brought more than a simple transfer of power from imperial government to a colonial oligarchy of the wealthy and privileged: at the provincial level, political institutions often became more genuinely representative of, and responsive to, popular needs and aspirations. Indeed, in some states, the adoption of virtually universal manhood suffrage and the creation of unicameral legislatures gave American republicanism a distinctly radical hue.

Popular politicization and the efflorescence of radical politics did not, however, lead to large-scale violence or prolonged instability, nor shatter the unity of the new republic. Despite the disturbance caused by military and political conflict, there were important and stabilizing strands of continuity with the colonial past. The war of independence, costly and disruptive though it was, had not disintegrated the authority of the state, nor dissolved respect for law and its procedures. Violence had been relatively restrained and, directed against British armies, had rarely spilled over into domestic political disputes; even the evacuation of the Loyalist counterrevolution was achieved peacefully. Colonial assemblies were converted into state legislatures, thereby permitting the smooth transfer of authority from royal to republican government. Equally, the association and co-operation of these bodies in the Continental Congress (formed to coordinate resistance to Britain) provided the foundations for the formation of a republican confederation, eventually enshrined in the Federal Constitution of 1787. Thus the colonial experience of government gave a flexible but stable framework for the establishment of a republican regime which, by widening access to power for newly mobilized groups, contained and channeled the tensions that had helped to topple the colonial order. Change was, moreover, confined to the political system. The redistribution of confiscated Loyalist property had little effect on the distribution of wealth, while in the South, the Revolution did not disturb the social system based on slavery. So long as Southern slavery was undisturbed, there was sufficient social cohesion, in a society characterized by fluidity and mobility rather than rigid ethnic and class division, to permit the dispersal of political power without violent domestic conflict. Thus the state which emerged as one nation, unified under the Federal Constitution as the United States of America, blended political innovation with social continuity.

Among the European colonies in Latin America and the Caribbean, the transition to independence and the creation of a stable alternative to colonial government proved much more problematic. In societies divided by deep social inequalities, and with legal and political systems characterized by coercion and lack of personal freedom, broadly based movements for independence were much less readily formed and new states less easily created. Throughout the Caribbean, the identification of white supremacy with colonial rule long forestalled any movement towards independence. Only the French colony of St. Domingue broke away from imperial rule in this period, due to the unique intersection of political conflict in France with social rebellion in the colony. In Spanish

America, the collapse of imperial rule also began, as it had in St. Domingue, with a crisis in the metropolitan state which activated latent tensions and precipitated autonomist movements. However, these societies moved to independence without strong and effective political institutions and without any clearly developed heir to imperial authority; the new states which they created were, with few exceptions, afflicted by violence and disorder. Their government was by "the law of force rather than the force of law."

In St. Domingue rebellion was occasioned, not by the pressure of metropolitan authority, but by its sudden collapse in 1789. The destruction of colonial government was preceded by the fall of the *ancien régime* in France, and the colonial revolution was an extension of revolutionary events in the metropolis itself. In the setting of a slave society, where the vast majority of the population was composed of black slaves (at least half of whom were Africans), political conflict had unprecedented repercussions. First, white society divided in response to the revolution in France; then the free colored minority sought to take advantage of discord to press its claims for equality; finally, the mutinies of whites and free coloreds were overtaken by slave insurrections. With the onset of slave rebellion in 1791, the character of the conflict changed. Under the leadership of Toussaint L'Ouverture, the slaves acted to overturn slavery, and thereby threatened the very basis of the social order. Between 1791 and 1800, there was an intense struggle for power between opposing social groups, complicated by foreign intervention and by the shifting alliances of white planters and slave owners who were incapable of imposing their own control and generating new institutions. By 1800, the slaves, aided by Toussaint's astute manipulation of a complex entanglement of alliances, had emerged as the leading military and political force on the island. Their victory signaled the beginning of a new era. It did not mark an immediate end to French rule: Toussaint was prepared to accept French suzerainty in return for recognition of slave emancipation and effective autonomy under his command as governor-general. But Napoleon refused to countenance slave freedom and colonial autonomy under "this gilded African," and sent his armies to restore French slave society by military force. Now that France had re-identified with the counter-revolution of planter slavery, and sought to restore the old society, free coloreds and blacks united against the metropolis and black social rebellion became an armed movement for independence. The independent black republic of Haiti, proclaimed by the ex-slave Jean-Jacques Dessalines and his generals on January 1st, 1804, was the outcome.

In several ways, the independence of Haiti marked a sharp break with the past. The revolutionary wars had mobilized the free coloreds and blacks — both groups which had no place in the colonial political order — and their participation transformed the character of colonial politics. Slavery, the keystone of the French colonial system, was abolished, legal distinctions based on color were outlawed, and the economic and political power of the white colonists was broken. The end of slavery also entailed the gradual breakdown of the colonial economic structure based on the plantation system. Freed slaves were reluctant to work on plantations, even when they were no longer forced to do so by white owners, and both during and after the war, both private and state lands were redistributed on a large scale, among blacks and mulattos alike. Furthermore, after independence, Haiti became a symbol of black freedom, fully committed to the abolition of slavery, not simply within Haiti but throughout the American world.

The revolution failed to extinguish completely the political, economic and social inequalities inherited from the colonial past. Although the redistribution of land taken from the whites created a class of small peasant landholders among the freed blacks, it generally favored the free coloreds, who had been permitted to own property under the colony. White estates often passed intact to the coloreds, who sought to revive the plantation system and to rebuild an export agriculture. By 1826, this group was sufficiently powerful to enact new laws to ensure that peasants provided labor for the plantations. Indeed, under President Boyer the sale of state lands was halted and rural workers forcibly assigned to plantation work. Distinctions in color also continued to play a significant part in social and political life. The mulattos, who held a disproportionate share of economic resources and political power, still tended to treat European culture as their model, and to look down on the blacks and their African customs. Having forged a national revolution from a slave rebellion, the peasantry retreated from politics and accepted authoritarian regimes which promised to protect their hard-won claims to independent ownership. At the national level, politics was increasingly dominated by competition within sectors of the new propertied élites of freed blacks and mulattos who sought political power concomitant with their new economic status. The organization of government reflected both the legacy of French rule and the traumas of war. Under the French, government had been concentrated in the hands of a military governor-general; after independence, militarism and authoritarian, centralized government became even more pronounced. Without a framework of representative institutions, and led by men accustomed to a military structure of command, Haitian politics assumed a decidedly militaristic air, described by one rather jaundiced observer as "a sort of republican monarchy sustained by the bayonet."

If the French Revolution had delivered its first great blow to European colonialism by nurturing the revolution in Haiti, the "French Revolution in its Napoleonic expression" opened the way for the political emancipation of Latin America. For, in his campaign to carry French revolutionary institutions across Europe by military conquest, Napoleon overturned the governments of both Portugal and Spain, and thereby stirred political crises which did irreparable damage to their empires in the Americas.

In Spanish America, as in Haiti, the mutation of the colonial order derived directly from the disintegration of the *ancien régime* in the metropolis. When Napoleon invaded Spain and usurped the throne in 1808, the "decapitation" of the Bourbon state and the insurrection of the Spanish nation against French rule provoked a major political crisis in the colonies. Now that the monarchy had collapsed, creoles were free to express the grievances accumulated under Bourbon government during the later eighteenth century and to give rein to the feelings of a "creole patriotism" which . . . reflected growing disaffection with Spanish imperial rule. In the imperial emergency created by the French invasion of Spain, the creoles at first proclaimed their loyalty to the crown, while calling for a greater measure of participation and autonomy in the colonies. Then, as the Spanish crises deepened in 1810, they moved to overturn discredited colonial authorities which resisted their autonomist aspirations.

In Mexico, the richest and most complex of Spanish American societies, the political crisis triggered a massive popular upheaval. In 1810, creole disaffection was overtaken by peasant insurrection, driven by land hunger and high food prices, and the great Hidalgo rebellion swept over the provinces of central Mexico. Confronted by this threat from below, creole landowners and the Church — both critics of Bourbon government — rallied to support the colonial authorities, joining with it to crush the insurgency by armed force and to preserve Spanish rule. In Peru, another society with a large and impoverished majority of Indians and mestizos, the forces of creole conservatism also prevailed. Although there were small regional uprisings, creole fears that political conflict would provoke social disorder helped to keep the colony firmly under Spanish control. Elsewhere in Spanish America, a series of urban coups removed colonial governments in 1810, detaching Chile, Río de la Plata [later Argentina], New Granada [later Colombia and Ecuador] and Venezuela from imperial rule. These creole coups were, however, largely improvised, disorganized reactions to the collapse of the metropolis and they failed to generate stable alternative forms of government. Power tended to disperse among local oligarchies which failed to arouse popular support, or to overcome regional antagonisms. Narrowly based and disunited, all except Río de la Plata fell victim to Spanish reconquest after the Bourbon restoration in 1814. Thus the first steps towards autonomy foundered among a series of introverted regional rebellions which lacked clear organization, common aims or any practical blueprint for government. There was no sense of a common, national identity to unite the parallel agitations of different social groups. On the contrary, racial and social division fostered mutual suspicion and distrust. Indeed, in both Mexico and Venezuela, conflict with Spain was submerged in class and ethnic warfare.

The achievement of independence in Spanish America, a goal that was only gradually defined, was not the work of a cross-class coalition of the Anglo-American type, nor the outcome of a social revolution as in Haiti. In Mexico, it was secured by counterrevolution, by the same creole conservatives who, having preserved Spanish government against the insurgency, turned against it when it was commandeered by the liberal revolution of 1820, and used the army of the colonial state to overthrow it. In South America, independence was won by the military campaigns of Bolívar and San Martín who, from bases in Venezuela and Argentina, mounted a war to extirpate Spanish rule throughout that continent. Following San Martín's march into Chile in 1817 and Bolívar's breakthrough into New Granada in 1819, the struggle against Spain was relayed from region to region, bringing independence in the train of the revolutionary generals' liberating armies. The liberation of South America was, then, the work of military men, and its course was defined by the movement of armies and the clash of battle. In this process, the mass of the population were generally passive bystanders who simply awaited the decisions of war. However, although the generals decided the issue of home rule, the creation of independent states presented a problem which was less easily resolved; namely, how they were to be governed and who was to control them.

The problems of creating a new political order were greatly complicated by the abrupt and violent break in the continuity of the state and the absence of political institutions which might inherit the authority of the dispossessed Spanish crown. The colony did not bequeath political institutions and procedures to ease the transition to independence: new institutions had to be created to embody the ideals and to organize the political life of the new states. The active, creole groups in politics were divided on this fundamental issue. Some favored constitutional monarchy, others were committed to republicanism; some wanted a strong, centralized state, others preferred weak, federal forms of government which dispersed power among the provinces. In most countries, no single group was sufficiently powerful to create a new political order in its own image. In Mexico the conservative coalition led by Agustín de Iturbide, which declared independence in 1821, created a constitutional monarchy with Iturbide as its first emperor. But Iturbide had no substantial or enduring support from any social group, and his shallowly rooted monarchy was toppled in 1823 by a *mélange* of competing forces. It was succeeded by a prolonged conflict between military leaders, conservative and liberal, each seeking either the spoils of office, or command of the state to protect or project incompatible interests. In South America, due partly to Bolívar's influence, the new states took up republican forms of government, based on constitutions which imitated those of France and the United States. But this political change was more striking in appearance than in substance. Although based on popular sovereignty, embodied in elective government, the social basis of political life remained narrow and exclusive. In countries where illiteracy was normal and wealth and property were highly concentrated, the restriction of the franchise by property and literacy qualifications ensured that democratic forms were purely cosmetic.

Nevertheless, while power remained largely in the hands of creole minorities, this did not guarantee stability. The collapse of royal authority left a power vacuum which drew centrifugal forces into play, and released local and regional rivalries in an unrestrained struggle for power. And, because politics had been militarized during the wars of independence, it had incorporated military leaders, *caudillos,* who were inured to the use of violence as an instrument of political persuasion, and who, after independence, mobilized it in pursuit of personal or regional group interests. Thus, with creole society divided into competing groups, none of which was sufficiently strong to monopolize state power, and with no effective political institutions and procedures to mediate intersectoral disputes, the new republics were plagued by disunity, instability and disorder. Only in Chile, where society was dominated by a small, interrelated and cohesive creole élite of landowners and businessmen concentrated in one region, was such chronic instability avoided. There, within the framework of a republican constitution, a highly centralized and strongly personalized system of government, based on a concentration of power in the executive, served to provide a stable succession to Spain.

The disorder of Spanish America may also be understood in contrast with the experience of Brazil. Portugal, like Spain, suffered a French invasion and Napoleonic takeover. However, when this occurred in 1807 the Portuguese crown and court abandoned the metropolis in favor of the colony and, escorted by a British convoy, fled to Brazil. Thus, though the metropolitan state collapsed, the continuity of royal government was undisturbed and constitutional crisis avoided. The transfer of the crown to Rio de Janeiro not only muted the impact of imperial crisis; it also brought the colony to virtual independence under royal government. The Portuguese monopoly over the colony's trade was lifted, opening Brazil to trade with all friendly nations and removing one source of friction between the crown and the colonial élites; furthermore, in 1815, Brazil was granted the status of a separate kingdom and moved towards full autonomy within the empire. When, in 1820–21, a Portuguese government sought to reassert its control, the Brazilian élites refused to relinquish these gains and, in 1822, declared their independence. This did not, however, unleash a struggle for power within the white élite of the kind experienced in Spanish America. The white planter élites were much more united. They shared a fundamental identity of economic interests and, as a dominant minority with a fragile hold on the black and colored masses, they were acutely conscious of the social dangers of political disunity. Their unity was, moreover, strengthened by shared attitudes: most of the politically active members of the élites had been educated at the same university — Coimbra — in Portugal, and, united by strong social and intellectual ties, provided a stable political leadership for the emergent state. The unity of the élites was compounded by the advantages of institutional continuity. Authority passed to the Portuguese prince regent resident in Brazil, and his assumption of the role of constitutional monarch avoided a crisis of legitimacy of the kind experienced in Spanish America. Under Dom Pedro, Brazil made a virtually bloodless transition from colonial rule and, having evaded the travails of war, remained united under a centralized and generally accepted authority.

The political dislocation and dismemberment of Spanish America, which contrasted sharply with the stability and unity of both Brazil and the United States, was aggravated by economic problems. In British North America, an independent commercial infrastructure, managed by American merchants and shippers, existed before independence. This provided the new state with a degree of economic autonomy absent in Spanish America, where external trade had been monopolized by peninsular Spanish merchants. And, after an initial phase of economic dislocation and depression, the Napoleonic Wars provided North American merchants with an opportunity for a rapid expansion of their trade. Underwritten by the financial stability created by the Federal government, this generated a commercial boom of unparalleled proportions and propelled the new Republic forward on a wave of prosperity. In Spanish America, conditions were much less favorable for economic development. After a brief boom in commercial and financial speculation in the early 1820s, Spanish American trade faltered, governments defaulted on both foreign and domestic debts, and foreign interest in Spanish American markets and resources faded. Left on the margins of international commerce, the economies of the new republics — which had also been disrupted by internal war — stagnated and declined, exacerbating political disillusionment and undermining hopes that independence would generate prosperity and accelerate economic development.

Thus, beneath the upheaval of the colonial order and the movement to independence in the American continents during the late eighteenth and early nineteenth centuries lay patterns of considerable diversity and complexity. . . . Independence brought an accentuation, rather than an attenuation of colonial tendencies. In the Anglo-American territories of the North, political traditions of personal freedom and self-government, and the social realities of mobility, cultural integration and economic autonomy, all provided solid foundations for the independent state. At independence, the notion of an integrated community or "nation," in which individual interests might harmonize with social progress, was readily conceived and understood and, after independence, the tendencies towards commercialization, urbanization and increased political participation become more pronounced. In much of Latin America, by contrast, hierarchical, authoritarian societies tended to become more inegalitarian, more autocratic and more divided. Regional, racial and class differences impeded the emergence of integrated nations, and independence opened rather than ended the political conflict begun by the struggle against the imperial power.

Throughout the Americas, independence brought limited social change. Only in Haiti was the new state created amidst a social revolution. In both Anglo-America and Latin America, colonial social structures remained largely untouched, though for different reasons. In the United States, where wealth and economic opportunity were relatively evenly distributed and labor respected, the bases of a liberal, individualistic society already existed at independence, and politics was not infused with an urgent need for social reform. When political ideals clashed with entrenched economic interests, as in the slave states of the American South, reform was avoided. The same was true of Latin America, where the dominant classes in a social system which concentrated wealth and power resisted the fundamental reforms required to turn republican, liberal images into a practical reality.

There were equally marked divergences in the economic sphere. In the United States, a strong domestic merchant class developed trade and accumulated capital; at the same time, good communications and high domestic incomes provided a strong and integrated national market. Both conditions favored a movement towards autonomous, self-sustaining industrial development. In Latin America, by contrast, commerce was increasingly taken over by British rather than local merchants, and the colonial pattern of trade, based on the exchange of primary products for imported manufacturers, was reinforced. With the competition of cheap British goods, and with impoverished, poorly integrated markets, early efforts at industrial development soon evaporated. Increasingly, the Latin American economies became dependent on the industrial economies for their growth and prosperity, first as the economic dependencies of Britain, and, during [the twentieth] century, as the satellites of the United States.

Independence has, then, led the Americas in distinct and divergent directions. For the United States, it opened the way to liberal democracy, industrial development and global power; for Latin America, it foreshadowed oligarchy and dictatorship, as well as political and economic dependency in international relations. Ironically, the United States, the forerunner of independence in the Americas and the political model for many of the new republics has, for many Latin Americans, come to embody the antithesis of its early ideals. For them, the issues of freedom and equality opened by the American Revolution remain urgent concerns. Now, however, the demands for independence and revolution are not modeled on the United States, but are responses to its domination and economic imperialism.

QUESTIONS TO CONSIDER

1. What basic similarities do you see in the origins of the British American and Spanish American revolutions? Why was the colonists' resistance to imperial control stronger in British America than in Spanish America? How did colonial institutions and cultures differ in the British and Spanish dominions? Explain how this affected the way the revolutionary movements began and proceeded. How accurate is it to say that the British North Americans made their revolution, whereas the Latin Americans had theirs made *for* them?

2. Describe the various social, economic, and racial groups in the Latin American colonies, and analyze the role they played in achieving independence. Do the same for the thirteen British colonies. Which new nations received the highest level of popular support for their new governments? the lowest? What divisions between settler groups created conflict and instability in new Latin American nations? Why did democratic governments prove more stable in the United States than in most Latin American countries? Why did commercial and industrial development in the young United States outpace that of the Latin American nations? (You should compare McFarlane's response to the last question with that of Charles Bergquist in Selection 5.)

3. McFarlane claims that "when the struggle for home rule was settled" in the British colonies, it "fueled a struggle over who was to rule at home." Did Spanish America experience a similar internal struggle for power? In what sense were several Latin American revolutions led by "creole conservatives"? To what extent did the British and Latin American revolutions democratize political and social arrangements in the former colonies?

4. Some modern commentators contend that the Haitian Revolution was more radical than the American Revolution and a fitter model for today's Third World. Compare the American and Haitian Revolutions in origins, aims, leadership, and outcome. Why did slaves rebel in Haiti but not in the American colonies? Why, according to McFarlane, did Haiti fail to sustain democracy?

5. McFarlane ends his essay by implying that Latin Americans have come to see the United States less as a "sister republic" than as an economic oppressor. Has the United States contradicted its revolutionary ideals in becoming the dominant power in the Western Hemisphere? Why, according to McFarlane, is the American Revolution less relevant than modern anti-imperialist movements as a model for today's Latin Americans?

SECURING THE
REPUBLIC

According to one story, as Benjamin Franklin was leaving the Constitutional Convention in Philadelphia, he was approached by an elderly woman who asked, "Well, Doctor, what have we got, a Republic or a Monarchy?" "A Republic, madam," Franklin replied, "if you can keep it."

The conventional wisdom of the eighteenth century held that republics were fragile creations, too unwieldy for governing large areas and requiring their citizens to sustain an impossibly high standard of virtue. Added to this was the struggle that contemporary republics such as Venice and Holland faced to secure their independence while surrounded by powerful monarchies and empires. Beset by domestic divisions and preyed upon by imperial giants, republics were given poor odds of survival by political observers of the day.

In its early years, the American republic seemed to be fulfilling this pessimistic forecast. Once rid of the British king, the former colonists set up a weak central government that watched helplessly as a postwar economic depression drove farmers into rebellion against local authorities. Failing to maintain a decent army, the national government faced continued resistance from the British and their Indian allies on the western frontier. Off the nation's shores, American ships were raided by pirates or harassed without mercy by French and English sailors eager to force the young nation to take sides in the nearly constant wars between these two imperial powers. In sum, the fledgling United States was little more than a theoretical nation in the 1780s, seemingly unable to control its own citizens, police its borders, or avoid becoming engulfed by foreign wars. What, then, enabled the infant republic to survive?

The two chapters that follow address this question in different ways. Chapter VI will analyze the domestic process of making a viable nation. This chapter discusses the ways that the new American republic navigated the treacherous waters of foreign relations, where its most pressing problem was to survive in a world torn by conflicts between rival European powers. The first essay approaches this problem comparatively. Jonathan R. Dull contrasts the young United States with one of its few contemporary republics: the United Provinces of the Netherlands. In the 1780s both were beleaguered nations, divided by internal conflicts and vulnerable to interference by powerful France and England. Yet the United States thrived while Holland declined. Dull finds a mixture of luck and skill, internal and external factors that allowed young America not only to survive, but also to prosper.

In the second essay, Jon Kukla recounts the drama and intrigue of the Americans' negotiations with Napoleon Bonaparte over the Louisiana Purchase of 1803. This is diplomatic history rather than systematic comparative analysis, but Kukla deftly describes the contrasting views of American, English, and French policymakers and captures their clashes of ideas, personalities, and interests. Even more than Dull's essay, Kukla's story reminds us that the infant United States was far from the world's center of power and hardly in charge of its own destiny. While the Louisiana episode backs Dull's findings about the positive effects of America's distance from Europe and its leaders' diplomatic skills, it also shows the young nation's fate being determined by the whims and calculations of an ambitious foreign ruler. It would take nearly a century for the infant United States to become an equal to Europe's "Great Powers."

9

Two Republics in a Hostile World

JONATHAN R. DULL

Lord Cornwallis's crushing defeat at Yorktown in 1781 assured victory to the American revolutionaries. By exploiting British fears of a new French empire in North America, congressional commissioners won a generous peace treaty that not only recognized American independence but also extended the new republic northward to the Great Lakes and westward to the Mississippi. It was one thing to win independence, however, and quite another to secure it. The infant United States was confronted with a host of international problems severe enough to threaten its existence. Great Britain dominated American trade, dumped cheap manufactured goods on the new country's depressed market, and refused to evacuate its forts on the frontier until Loyalists were compensated for property taken or damaged during the war. Spanish colonies surrounded the young republic to the south and west, menacing American commerce on the Mississippi and in the Caribbean. Meanwhile, Britain's rival, revolutionary France, expected Americans to join its wars against European monarchies as repayment for French assistance during the American Revolution and threatened to paralyze America's trade if this did not happen. Even pirates from the Barbary coast of North Africa regularly preyed on American ships in the Mediterranean and off the Iberian coast. At home, the Articles of Confederation, which defined the federal government, left the national congress so weak and divided that members could not agree on where to locate the capital, much less on how to address international crises shaping the nation's destiny. No wonder many foreign observers expected the new republic to be a flash in the pan.

We have become so accustomed to America's position as a twenty-first-century superpower that it may come as a shock to learn how fragile the new nation was in the 1780s. Diplomatic historian Jonathan Dull says that this nation's closest counterpart in the 1780s was not England or France, but tiny Holland. The United Provinces of the Netherlands had once been the leading shipping and banking nation of the world. By the mid-1700s, however, it was weakened by internal discord and a costly commercial rivalry with England, was vulnerable to land invasions by France and Prussia, and was too small to control its overseas empire. At first neutral during the Revolutionary War, Holland was attacked by England for trading with France and the United States. Despite gallant fighting, the Dutch failed to hold their territories in India and the West Indies and were humiliated when France shut them out of the peace process. Holland's troubles continued with the French Revolution. French forces invaded in 1795, and France controlled the country for the next two decades, first as a republic, then a monarchy (with Napoleon's brother Louis as king), and finally as part of France itself. After Napoleon's defeat, the stadholder (or hereditary chief executive) returned as a constitutional monarch; Holland was no longer a republic or an important European power.

In the late 1700s the young United States and the Netherlands were internally divided republics. Both were vulnerable military and economic targets, and both were caught in the crossfire between two great powers, France and England. Why did the United States survive and prosper while the Netherlands declined? America's size and resources had something to do with it, says Dull. So did its distance from the main arenas of European conflict. The nearly constant wars between England and France made the New World republic useful as a trading partner to both belligerents and gave it some leverage as a neutral power. But Dull credits America's leaders, too. The Founders shrewdly procured a favorable treaty from Great Britain, compromised among themselves to draw up a constitution that has endured for more than two centuries, and then pursued a mostly successful course of neutrality in the face of foreign wars. Their skillful statesmanship, says Dull, proved that "the wisdom of its people" was the new republic's greatest strength.

GLOSSARY

ADAMS, JOHN (1735–1826)   One of the American negotiators of the Treaty of Paris ending the Revolution. Adams served as envoy to Great Britain from 1785 to 1788. He became George Washington's vice president in 1789 and succeeded him as president in 1797. Although partial to Great Britain, Adams prevented war with France by pursuing peaceful resolution of trade and diplomatic disputes as president.

BARBARY PIRATES   Pirates from the north coast of Africa who preyed on American ships in the Mediterranean and off the coasts of Spain and Portugal. In the 1790s, the United States signed treaty agreements with the Barbary states of Morocco, Algiers, Tripoli, and Tunis that required U.S. payments to those North African states to prevent attacks on American ships.

CONFEDERATION PERIOD   The years from 1781 to 1789, during which the United States was governed by the Articles of Confederation. The Articles created a loose union of states, each with one vote in a weak national legislature that required at least nine of thirteen states to agree.

EARL OF SHELBURNE (WILLIAM PETTY FITZMAURICE) (1737–1805)   The British prime minister who negotiated the Treaty of Paris and was criticized for being too conciliatory toward the Americans.

FEDERALIST   A collection of eighty-five essays published by Alexander Hamilton, James Madison, and John Jay under the name of "Publius" in 1787–1788. Written to support ratification of the U.S. Constitution, *The Federalist* endured as a classic analysis of that document and of political philosophy in general.

NANTUCKET   A small island off the coast of Massachusetts belonging to that state.

SEVEN YEARS' WAR (1756–1762)   Called the French and Indian War in the American colonies; a worldwide conflict between imperial nations fought in Europe, North America, and India. On one side were Great Britain, Prussia, and Hanover; on the other were France, Austria, Russia, Saxony, Sweden, and Spain. Two main issues were involved: the struggle between Prussia and Austria for supremacy in central Europe, and French and English colonial rivalries in North America and India. Prussian and English victories led to the Treaties of Hubertusburg and Paris in 1763, which confirmed Prussia's power on the Continent and gave Britain all of French Canada.

SHAYS' REBELLION (1786–1787)   An uprising of debt-ridden farmers in western Massachusetts led by Daniel Shays. The rebellion was put down by the state militia. Shays was eventually pardoned, and the state legislature enacted debtor-relief measures. The rebellion was widely cited as a reason to create a stronger federal constitution, which would preserve the rule of law.

STATES GENERAL   The bicameral parliament of the Dutch republic.

TREATY OF PARIS (1783)   The treaty between the United States and Great Britain ending the Revolutionary War. Great Britain formally acknowledged the independence of the United States with boundaries at the Mississippi River and the Great Lakes. Britain granted the United States fishing rights off Newfoundland and guaranteed freedom of navigation on the Mississippi. In return, the United States promised to recommend that state governments return confiscated Loyalist property.

WAR OF AUSTRIAN SUCCESSION (1740–1748)   A European war over the balance of power in the mid-eighteenth century. It was prompted by the succession of Maria Theresa as head of the Hapsburg empire of Austria. Prussia joined with France and Spain to challenge Maria Theresa's power, while England and Holland became Austrian allies. The war ended with Maria Theresa and her husband, Francis I, safe on the throne, but Prussia augmented in power and territory.

WAR OF 1812   An armed conflict between the United States and Great Britain caused by American insistence upon neutral shipping rights during the Napoleonic

Wars and by disputes over land on the western frontier. The low point of the war, from the American viewpoint, was the British capture of Washington, DC, in August 1814. Succeeding American victories brought the war to an indecisive end the following year.

☆ ☆ ☆ ☆ ☆ ☆ ☆

John Adams must have been in a pugnacious mood that first day of March in 1776. His diary for that day contains a warning that if France were not willing to help his fellow Americans it should beware for the security of its West Indian colonies. He went on to brag of how warlike and powerful America had become, of how skilled and disciplined were its armies. Were it to join forces with Britain the two in combination, Adams claimed, could conquer the French colonies within six months.

Twelve days later the count de Vergennes, the French foreign minister, presented his king a memoir warning of precisely that danger. There is little evidence, however, that Vergennes took seriously the possibility of an Anglo-American reconciliation. He soon presented an argument for aiding the Americans that portrayed them very differently. This argument virtually ignored any hypothetical threat to the West Indies. Instead it was based on considerations of the balance of power, particularly of the importance of America to the continuation of Britain's strength. To the possible objection that the Americans themselves might pose a threat to French interests, Vergennes argued that the current war would exhaust them. Moreover, he said,

> There is every reason to believe that if the Colonies attain their end, they will give to their new government the republican form, and that there will even be as many small republics as there are at present provinces: now, republics rarely have the spirit of conquest, and those which will be formed in America will have it all the less, as they know the pleasures and advantages of commerce, and have need of industry, and consequently of peace, to procure for themselves the commodities of life, and even a quantity of things of prime necessity. It may, then, be said that the fear of seeing the Americans sooner or later make invasions on their neighbors has no apparent foundation, and that this fear deserves no consideration.

The prediction that American unity would not survive the war, although widely shared in Europe, would not have met agreement among Adams and his friends, but Vergennes's other points — that republics were basically peaceful and that a desire for commerce and a desire for conquest were mutually exclusive — already were clichés in

---

Benjamin West's painting of the Treaty of Paris peace negotiators remained unfinished because the outma-
neuvered British delegates refused to sit for their portraits. Left to right: John Jay, John Adams, Benjamin
Franklin, Henry Laurens, and William Temple Franklin, his grandfather's secretary. (The Henry Francis
du Pont Winterthur Museum.)

America as well as Europe. Events of the next few years seemed to confirm that even if the United States survived it was hardly likely to be much of a threat to its neighbors. The United States lacked the resources to expel the British from its own territory, let alone to renew its attempts to add Canada to the union. Massive infusions of French capital proved necessary to prevent the collapse of American currency and subsequent government bankruptcy, and French troops and warships were needed before the military stalemate with Britain was finally broken in 1781. Although American confederation was approved the same year, political unity remained elusive. Even peace failed to resolve the problems of weakness and disunity, problems that both contributed to . . . postwar anxiety . . . and helped to lead to the constitutional convention.

European statesmen naturally saw little reason to change their opinion of the new republic during these years. Even the brilliant peace of 1782–83 offered little evidence of any real American power. France, which had provided indispensable financial, naval, and military support to the United States, nevertheless left the American negotiators free to reach their own agreement with Great Britain. The British government, anxious to split the Franco-American alliance, showered concessions on the Americans in hope they would make a compromise peace. Franklin, Jay, and Adams, the American peace commissioners, happily obliged (the agreement they signed in November 1782 being conditional in theory, although not in practice). While the American triumph reflected the shrewdness of its diplomats, it was a measure of neither present nor potential military strength. Indeed, the earl of Shelburne, whose government had made the agreement, was soon driven from office in punishment for what Parliament perceived as needless surrender of British interests. Succeeding governments showed little inclination to conciliate the United States, refusing full compliance with the terms of the peace treaty and inflicting severe damage on American trade.

The statesmen of the major European powers could hardly have been surprised by America's difficulties. They generally were accustomed to associating republics with weakness and disunity. Europe's own republics, such as the Swiss cantons, the Mediterranean trading states of Genoa, Venice, and Ragusa, and, most important of these, the United Provinces of the Netherlands, cut a poor figure in international affairs. Americans were far less likely to see the similarity, generally viewing their country as far different than any European state and associating Europe with decadence and corruption. Notwithstanding this sense of superiority, Americans nonetheless occasionally displayed a sense of solidarity with the republics of Europe, particularly the Netherlands. This was particularly true during the early years of the Revolution, when the Dutch experience was regarded as an example to be emulated. Thomas Paine, for example, in arguing for American independence cited the Netherlands as a model of successful foreign policy: "Holland, without a king hath enjoyed more peace for this last century than any of the monarchical governments in Europe." Paine had good reason for his praise. The Dutch had escaped the brunt of the War of Austrian Succession (1740–48) and had remained neutral throughout the entire Seven Years' War (1756–63). Americans, believing their trade vital to the European balance of power, thought that they too could remain neutral in future wars and prosper through trade with all the belligerents. Indeed, initially they thought their trade so valuable that France would come to their aid without even requiring a treaty of military alliance.

The War for American Independence soon introduced Americans to the realities of power politics. The war demonstrated not only American weakness, but also that of the Netherlands. Both Britain and France exerted great pressure to procure Dutch support in the war. The British interrupted Dutch trade in hope of intercepting naval stores being sent to France or munitions being sent to America via the Dutch colonies in the Caribbean. France in turn applied selective pressure on Dutch towns and provinces so they would form a common front against British demands. When the Dutch tried to find an escape in a league of neutral shippers led by Russia, the British in 1780 declared war on them. By war's end the Dutch found most of their colonies occupied by either their British enemies or their French allies. The peace negotiations largely ignored them until finally the French foreign minister arranged terms with Britain on their behalf and forced their compliance.

Their failings in war and diplomacy were in part the result of serious flaws in the Dutch political and social system, flaws which were observed at first hand by statesmen like John Adams. By 1787 the Netherlands had come to serve a cautionary purpose for

American political thinkers. During the constitutional convention the Dutch political system was a subject of discussion; later, in *Federalist* Number 20, James Madison used the Netherlands as an example of the failings of a confederacy of republics, implying that the American confederacy faced similar dangers unless it could achieve greater unity through the newly drafted constitution.

The comparison between the Netherlands and the United States can serve purposes beyond the study of American political thought, however. It also can help us place in clearer perspective the relative strengths and weaknesses of the new republic. By showing us how America's problems resembled or differed from those of the Netherlands it can help us better differentiate between problems stemming from America's political institutions and those coming from other causes. Finally, it can help to explain why pessimists about the American experiment eventually were confounded by America's survival and growth to world power.

At first glance the comparison may seem far-fetched. The Netherlands was a tiny country compared even to the United States of 1783. Slightly smaller than it is today, it occupied an area comparable to Connecticut, Rhode Island, and Massachusetts combined (not counting Maine, then a part of Massachusetts). Its population of approximately two million was somewhat more than half that of the United States. Like the thirteen American states, the seven provinces of the Netherlands varied enormously in population; the most powerful and populous, Holland, dominated the country to a much greater extent than did any of the American states. (Indeed, the Netherlands as a whole frequently was called by the name of this province.) In spite of its smaller size and population, the Netherlands appeared in many ways more advanced than the United States. It was more developed economically, more powerful militarily, and more sophisticated politically. As we shall see, these advantages were more apparent than real and were counterbalanced by American advantages that eventually proved more important.

Perhaps the most striking difference between the two countries was the relative development of their economies. The Netherlands had been the most economically powerful state of mid-seventeenth-century Europe. During the intervening century and a quarter its position relative to larger neighbors like France and Britain had deteriorated, but the Netherlands still was more advanced than most of Europe. It was heavily urbanized, contained a large and sophisticated mercantile community, and was both a major shipper and exporter of finished goods. It was still one of the world's great banking centers and by the mid-1780s had become one of the leading creditors of the United States.

By contrast, the United States was chiefly an exporter of food and raw materials to Europe and the Caribbean (although it did have a respectable merchant marine and a sizable mercantile community scattered among the small cities of the Atlantic seaboard). As such it was extremely vulnerable to foreign market conditions (except, of course, in times of war or scarcity). True, America was self-sufficient in food and in many other needs of a predominantly rural economy. On the other hand, American agriculture, fisheries, timber, and shipbuilding were dependent on access to foreign markets, particularly the European colonies in the West Indies. Moreover, the United States, unlike the Netherlands, produced few manufactured goods and could provide little credit for its merchants. The part of the American population that lived in small cities along the Atlantic coast was highly dependent on foreign trade, but even many plantation owners and farmers needed foreign manufactured goods or credit.

To compound the difficulty, America was more dependent than the Netherlands on a single trading partner. Despite its political independence, the United States remained an economic satellite of Great Britain. During the decade after the war American statesmen like Thomas Jefferson attempted with little success to foster trade with France and other European states. In 1790 America was still dependent on Britain and the British West Indies for the bulk of its imports and sent them nearly half of its exports. Britain did not hesitate to use this dominance in its own interest, severely restricting American trade with Britain, Ireland, Canada, and the West Indies, and thereby inflicting great damage on American merchants, fishermen, farmers, and shipbuilders. The problem of American dependence on Britain, unresolved by the adoption of the new constitution, was largely responsible for the fierce debate between the followers of Jefferson and those of Hamilton, as well as for the War of 1812. In today's terminology, the United States was in a neocolonial relationship to Britain that did not end until the American industrial revolution in the decades preceding the Civil War (and in the case of the American South that relationship was still existent in 1861).

In spite of their differences, the United States and the Netherlands had much in common. Neither possessed the economic basis for an independent foreign policy. The same was true of their military situation. Each lacked the military and naval strength to participate with full autonomy in international affairs. The Dutch did possess a peacetime army comparable in size to Britain's, but it lacked the British army's capacity for wartime expansion. Moreover, unlike Americans, the Dutch were not protected by an ocean's distance from potential enemies. They proved unable to defend themselves at the approach of foreign armies, like those of France in 1748 and 1794 and those of Prussia in 1787. Their navy, the fifth largest in Europe (behind that of Britain, France, Spain, and Russia) was theoretically more respectable. In spite of extraordinary Dutch bravery, however, it performed abysmally in the war of 1780–83. The Dutch could hope for safety only by balancing between competing great powers.

The United States had even less military strength. Depending on America's geographical isolation, Congress at war's end reduced the army to negligible size and eliminated the navy altogether. This step led to humiliations like those suffered by the Dutch. In order to pressure Americans to pay their debts to British creditors, the government of Great Britain refused to evacuate nine frontier forts within the United States, including such posts as Niagara and Detroit. The United States was helpless to compel their evacuation. The American Army also proved unable either to coerce Indian tribes along the frontier or to prevent tens of thousands of settlers from overrunning Indian hunting grounds. Although Britain showed restraint in its dealings with the Indians, the combination of British-held frontier posts, angry Indian tribes, and uncontrolled American settlers posed an obvious danger. The United States also was unable to prevent Spanish closure of the Mississippi River to American shipping, a move that created severe economic and political repercussions along the frontier. Fortunately, the Spanish military presence in Florida and Louisiana was very weak, but the

Spanish held close contacts with the dangerous Indian tribes along the Georgia and Carolina borders. At sea the United States was unable to defend its shipping from Barbary pirates, let alone any European power in case of war.

The lack of an effective army or navy or even of the funds to establish them mocked America's claims to an autonomous place among the powers of the Western world. During the war the French diplomatic representatives in Philadelphia had been able to exercise great influence over Congress, dependent as it was on France for financial and military support. Had any European state declared war in the 1780s, America, unable to pay its debts to France (and barely able to pay the interest on loans from the Netherlands), would have found it difficult to raise the funds to defend itself. Instead, its failure to pay its debts might have given America's creditors an excuse to intervene against it. (By the end of the decade the French minister to the United States was entertaining such ideas.) Only its distance from Europe, its difficult and extensive terrain, and the previous example of British failure gave the United States any greater security than the Netherlands.

In theory, the Netherlands even possessed considerable political advantages over America. The Dutch had a well-established government bureaucracy, the United States only the most rudimentary. (The American foreign office, for example, resembled in size and complexity that of a European state of the seventeenth century.) The Netherlands had a fixed capital at The Hague, while Congress suffered the humiliation of wandering from city to city. Whereas during the Confederation period the presidency of Congress was a largely ceremonial office with a rapid turnover of occupants (fifteen men in an equal number of years), the Dutch possessed a hereditary chief executive, the stadholder, with powers exceeding those the new American constitution would give the president. In spite of all these advantages, however, the Netherlands suffered from many of the same problems that plagued its sister republic. The major European powers treated the Dutch with contempt, deriding not only their economic dependence and military weakness, but also their acute political divisions and their cumbersome and ineffectual system of government. The Dutch were deeply divided by competition among cities, among provinces, and among social classes. In the battle for political and economic dominance, the merchants of Amsterdam held great advantages, but they met bitter opposition from other cities such as Rotterdam, provinces such as Zeeland, and classes such as the nobility, which dominated the inland provinces. Eventually the battle between the conservatives and the "patriots" led by Amsterdam resulted in armed Prussian intervention — in 1787 the king of Prussia, brother-in-law of the stadholder, felt compelled to terminate the budding Dutch revolution.

The United States, too, was marked by political, social, and sectional disagreements. Competition among the states, for example, undercut American resistance to British bullying. Here Connecticut was particularly blameworthy, frustrating attempts to form a common front on trade policy by its desire to surpass neighboring states. Entire geographical sections were divided by conflicting value systems, habits, and economic interests. The most obvious split was between the plantation (staple) economies of the South and the farming and fishing economies of the North. There were significant variations, however, even within these larger regions. The interests of New England, for example, differed from those even of its most immediate neighbors. Another basic split, evident even within individual states, was between East and West. The frontier and seaboard held differing views on subjects ranging from currency to Indian relations (a divergence not totally dissimilar from that between the Netherlands' coastal region and its agricultural hinterland). One historian has seen in these differences the embryonic development of American political parties. The split between newer and more established areas led to separatist movements, whose leaders sometimes flirted with the idea of foreign assistance, Vermonters looking toward British Canada, inhabitants of Kentucky toward either Spain or Britain. A movement for independence from the United States even developed on tiny Nantucket.

The political divisions threatening America often were manifestations of underlying social tensions — between debtor and creditor, merchant and farmer, the landed and the landless. At least America was spared the battle over the privileges of a hereditary nobility that helped embitter Dutch political life, although this was counterbalanced by the problem of the growing number of slaves and their increasing concentration in the American South. The United States also held a second advantage: the bitter battle between patriot and Loyalist during the Revolution had ended with the departure of perhaps 60,000 to 100,000 supporters of Great Britain and the reintegration of the remainder. In spite of the human costs, Americans could find a bond of unity in their support of the Revolution, however they might interpret the meaning of that Revolution.

The effects of disunity and conflict were worsened in both the Netherlands and the United States by the lack of an effective central government. The States General of the Netherlands and the American Continental Congress were each almost paralyzed by severe limits on their authority. In theory, and often in practice, the States General could proceed only with the concurrence of all seven of the Dutch provinces. Affairs moved with maddening slowness as issues were referred to the assemblies of the various provinces for debate and decision. The Continental Congress faced a nearly identical problem. After years of effort, the opposition of New York blocked its attempt to secure an independent revenue. The Dutch advantage in having the stadholder as a central authority was nullified in practice because the stadholder during this period, William V, was weak, unpopular, and a source of political discord.

The disunity and disorganization of the Dutch and American political systems profoundly affected their conduct of foreign policy. Factions in the Netherlands characteristically divided into pro-British and pro-French parties, a situation that would be duplicated in the United States of the 1790s. Debates on foreign policy in the States General retarded negotiations, as was shown by the ridiculous figure cast by the Dutch representatives at the 1782–83 peace negotiations. Luckily, the American peace commissioners were far enough distant from America to negotiate for themselves. Congress had been deeply divided over foreign policy as different factions contended over who would occupy various diplomatic posts and as representatives of different regions of the country debated war objectives. Worst of all, America had been so dependent on French assistance that in 1781 Congress had ordered the commissioners to acquiesce to French desires about negotiation of the peace. Franklin, Adams, and Jay largely ignored their orders and, rather apprehensively, took advantage of the opportunities of the moment. As already mentioned, the Dutch lacked a similar opportunity and saw the French make peace on their behalf. The advantageous American peace of 1783 was less a triumph of American foreign policy than the result of good fortune and the individual abilities of the American negotiators. Indeed, Congress failed to ratify and return the treaty by the prescribed time and had to depend on British willingness to look the other way.

The postwar period demonstrated that the United States could no longer depend on good fortune. We have already seen some of the results of American disunity, as state rivalries blocked formation of a common front against British trade policies. Congressional weakness permitted the states to act almost as individual sovereign governments. Virginia itself ratified individually the peace treaty with Britain, Georgia undertook negotiations with Spain about border issues involving Spanish Florida, and various states negotiated with Indian tribes and contracted foreign loans. The 1778 Franco-American treaty of commerce was violated by Massachusetts and New Hampshire, which levied tonnage duties on French goods. Most dangerously, the terms of the peace were violated repeatedly by state restrictions on payment of debts to British merchants and by evasions of the provisions relating to Loyalists. These violations gave Britain an excuse to retain frontier posts within the United States. Not even the States General could be defied with such impunity.

It is not surprising that the United States, like the Netherlands, was the object of the contempt of such foreign powers as France and Britain. Both America and the Netherlands were characterized by a divided polity, inefficient government, backward economy, military weakness, social conflict, and lack of leadership. With considerable justification, Hamilton described the United States as reaching "almost the last stage of national humiliation." Nevertheless the fate of the two countries would be far different. The Dutch soon lost their independence and remained under French control for almost twenty years. During most of the same period the United States managed to balance between Britain and France. The brief War of 1812 with Britain, however ill-considered, at least resulted in neither diminution of American independence nor loss of American territory. During the succeeding half century, the United States industrialized, expanded to the Pacific, survived a civil war, and entered, at least potentially, the ranks of the great powers. The Netherlands, restored to independence in 1815, resumed its lackluster role among the secondary powers of Europe. Why, in spite of their similarities in the 1780s, did the history of the United States and the Netherlands diverge so drastically? What advantages of the United States proved so decisive?

The answers in hindsight are fairly obvious. The greatest of America's advantages was its virtually limitless extent of territory. By European standards, even the land east of the Mississippi was gigantic. America's size alone gave it relative immunity from conquest. Britain had tried unsuccessfully for more than six years to solve the logistics of conquering so vast a country. Protected by its great distance from Europe, a mountainous and wooded terrain, and a dispersed population, the United States had survived the attacks of one of Europe's most wealthy and powerful states. America's greatest vulnerability had been its economy. Its trade was disrupted greatly by the war, its currency saved from collapse only by massive French loans and grants, its people subjected to severe privation. In case of future hostilities America might again lose its foreign trade, might even be driven by economic pressure or internal division to make a disadvantageous peace, but there was relatively little danger of wholesale foreign occupation. The

Netherlands, protected only by obsolete forts and a small army, was far more vulnerable; its last resort was to open its dikes and flood the countryside (as it had done in 1672), but nothing was able to protect it from the armies of revolutionary France.

America's great size also meant that the United States could support an increasing population without social dislocation. The Europe of the 1780s contained perhaps fifty times the population of the United States in only four times the area. The favorable climate and soil of the United States also added to America's promise. Benjamin Franklin had predicted, not unrealistically, a doubling of population every twenty-five years; by 1860 the United States surpassed Great Britain in numbers and had almost caught up to France. A population of thirty-one and a half million permitted it to raise armies comparable to those of the major powers of Europe, although sadly these American armies were raised to be used against each other. The Netherlands of 1860 contained fewer than three and a half million people. While the United States had tripled in area and reached the Pacific Ocean, the Netherlands had made only tiny gains against its neighbors, the Germans and the waters of the North Sea. America, moreover, had well begun its rise to become the greatest industrial power in the world.

America's growth in area, population, resources, and industry was still a dream in the 1780s, however. For the moment, its survival was based less on its ability to compete with the states of Europe than on its capacity to be useful to them. As a still predominantly agricultural country, it was a source of raw materials and markets for Britain and, to a far smaller extent, France. (This economic usefulness would alter British attitudes in America's favor, particularly after the outbreak of a new war with France.) America's agricultural surplus, moreover, was extremely important to the wealthy sugar-producing European colonies of the Caribbean and, in time of need, to Canada. Even though the United States itself posed little immediate military threat to the West Indies, American bases could be a great aid to any European forces operating in the Caribbean. In 1782, for example, a French fleet had sailed to Boston to escape the Caribbean hurricane season. America's usefulness to both France and Britain helped it to balance between the two great powers. In contrast, the Netherlands had little to offer as an ally and a huge and virtually undefended colonial empire to pillage as an enemy. Hence, both Britain and France bullied it. Divided by factionalism, the Dutch could barely resist, let alone extract diplomatic advantage from a policy of neutrality.

America's political situation, moreover, was not as similar to that of the Netherlands as had appeared in the 1780s. Its political problems proved less intractable and its political divisions less unbridgeable than many had expected. The debate over the adoption of the Constitution and social upheavals like Shays' rebellion obscure the degree of political consensus in the early United States. The power of the hereditary executive was a bitter issue in the Netherlands; the power of the American presidency proved far less divisive. Americans also were spared the Dutch debate over the privileges of the aristocracy. Divisions between American social classes were muted by the existence of almost unlimited cheap land, political divisions by common consent on issues like the validity of the recent Revolution and the desirability of republican institutions. Because of this relative consensus, a political change of revolutionary scope could occur in 1787–88 without bloodshed or the summoning of foreign troops, as happened in 1787 in the Netherlands.

Finally, the United States survived in a hostile world in part by good fortune. As we have seen, the American peace commissioners of 1782 had benefited from the British desire for separate peace. It was America's good fortune that during the 1780s, when it was most vulnerable, its potential enemies were exhausted from the recent war. The French Revolution then diverted Europe's attention and led France and Britain to court America's support. Wise statesmanship by Washington, Adams, and Jefferson helped the United States take advantage of its neutrality and avoid war. Madison, less prudent, led America into war against Britain, but again good fortune aided it in avoiding any permanent damage. The Netherlands, neither lucky nor well-led, became for twenty years a French puppet state, as did such other European republics as Genoa, Venice, Ragusa, and the cantons of Switzerland.

America thus possessed advantages that the Netherlands and the other republics of Europe did not. We must not assume, however, that America's survival in a hostile world was inevitable. The failure of America to reform its political institutions, its entrance into an unwise war, or its failure to resolve its internal disputes could have greatly altered American history. Its greatest danger came not from foreign threat, but from internal weakness and division. In overcoming that danger, the wisdom of its people proved to be America's greatest strength.

QUESTIONS TO CONSIDER

1. Why did Europe's leaders believe that the United States would remain weak after independence? What weaknesses did the early American republic actually demonstrate?

2. How does the comparison between the Netherlands and the United States highlight the relative strengths of the young American republic? What does Dull mean by "good fortune," and how did it assist the United States to survive and prosper in the 1780s? What enabled the United States to escape domination or destruction by the Great Powers (especially France or England) in the 1780s and 1790s?

3. Skillful leadership helped the early American republic to survive. How did the American commissioners obtain a favorable treaty ending the Revolutionary War? What position did the United States take in the Napoleonic Wars between France and Great Britain? How did American leaders address the nation's internal disunity in the 1780s? (You may want to recheck your response to the last two questions after reading Selections 10 and 11.)

4. Beyond making the United States difficult to conquer, what were some effects in early American history of the nation's huge extent of territory and its considerable distance from Europe? Consider such issues as attitudes toward European wars, relations with Native Americans, and population growth.

5. Have there been times in our history besides the 1780s when the survival of the United States was threatened? the War of 1812? the Civil War? the Great Depression? World War II? the Cold War? What similarities or differences do you see between these episodes and the 1780s?

Napoleon Bonaparte and the Louisiana Purchase

JON KUKLA

Following Jonathan Dull's comparison between the young United States and the Netherlands in Selection 9, we turn to Jon Kukla's case study of a single episode in American foreign relations: the Louisiana Purchase of 1803. Kukla's colorful story of diplomacy and intrigue at the court of Napoleon validates Dull's claim that the United States enjoyed comparative advantages in maintaining its independence. Not only did the Americans survive the Napoleonic era; they also managed to score gains by playing France and England against each other, as U.S. diplomat Robert Livingston did so effectively in the Louisiana episode. But there are darker implications to Kukla's story as well, for it shows how completely the fate of the weak new nation lay in the hands of powerful foreign rulers. This dependence did not always turn out well. In 1803 Napoleon's sudden decision to sell all of Louisiana gave the Americans an unexpected bonus, but several years later England's decision to continue its raids on American ships led directly to the nearly disastrous War of 1812.

Political independence did not extract Americans from the Atlantic matrix of trade and imperial power in which they had been embedded since colonial times. In fact, nationhood deprived the Americans of British protection. As long as the infant republic remained a military and naval nonentity and depended heavily upon trade with the West Indies and Europe, its fate hinged on the course of European wars and diplomacy. Faced with nearly constant wars between France and England, the Americans tried to steer a safe course of neutrality that had been marked out by President Washington when full-scale European conflict erupted in 1793.

This was more easily said than done. England and France put relentless pressure on the United States to take sides, and for two decades Americans lurched from one war scare to another. In the mid-1790s America's relations with France took a decided turn for the worse. The Jay Treaty (1794), which smoothed over American differences with Britain, provoked retaliation from the French, who began seizing American ships carrying British cargo. Negotiations between the United States and France broke down when French agents demanded a huge bribe and President John Adams released this information to Congress in the notorious XYZ Affair (so called because Adams withheld the agents' names and gave them alphabet substitutes). Outraged by this revelation, Congress authorized American ships to seize French vessels, and in 1798 Americans embarked upon an undeclared naval war (often called the Quasi-War) against French privateers operating in the Caribbean Sea. By 1800, however, both Adams and the new French ruler, Napoleon Bonaparte, were ready for peace, and a convention signed by both parties that year declared a truce.

Meanwhile, secret negotiations between France and the declining monarchy in Spain threatened to reopen hostilities between Napoleon and the American republic. By terms of the Treaty of San Ildefonso (1796), Carlos IV of Spain returned the Louisiana Territory of North America to the French, who had ceded it to Spain following the Seven Years' War (1756–1763). When rumors of this secret deal reached newly elected President Thomas Jefferson in 1801, he immediately sensed the threat to America's western settlers and their vital access down the Mississippi River to the Gulf of Mexico. If the rumors were true, Jefferson warned, "it would be impossible that France and the United States can continue long as friends." Since the products of America's interior farms and plantations passed to market through New Orleans, whoever possessed it was "our natural and habitual enemy." Jefferson dispatched Ambassador Robert Livingston to Paris with orders to prevent the cession of the territory to France, if it had not already happened, or else to try to purchase New Orleans. This is the point where Kukla picks up the fascinating story of the Louisiana Purchase.

As finally agreed upon, the purchase was a great boon to Americans. The United States received not just New Orleans but also the entire watershed of the western Mississippi; the young nation was able to double its size for the bargain price of $15 million, or four cents an acre. Although the U.S. Treasury could not afford this price, British banks were happy to underwrite the purchase for a profit of 6 percent interest and the pleasure of shrinking the French empire. The deal so delighted Jefferson that he put aside his constitutional scruples — the treaty was signed before Congress was given a chance to approve — and presented it to Americans as a matter of executive privilege. The territory's enormous expanse of western land seemed to guarantee that the United States would remain a nation of independent farmers, as Jefferson had hoped, and it opened the way for America's own "empire of liberty." The ink on the treaty was hardly dry when Jefferson dispatched Meriwether Lewis and William Clark on an expedition to explore the vast Louisiana territory and then push westward all the way to the Pacific.

Although the brilliant, ambitious, and powerful emperor of France, Napoleon Bonaparte, was a terrifying presence on the world scene, in hindsight it is clear that he deserves to be named an honorary American Founding Father. Not only did Americans benefit from his blunder of selling them the vast lands of Louisiana; they also profited from his plans to conquer all of Europe. As was noted in Selection 8, Napoleon's invasion of the Iberian Peninsula in 1807 liberated the Spanish colonies of Latin America by deposing their king. Moreover, for more than two decades of the early republic's life (1793–1815) the Napoleonic Wars in Europe preoccupied Great Britain and scaled down its imperial ambitions in North America. Even when the Americans drifted into war with England in 1812, they could fend off the British army partly because it was stretched so thin by fighting simultaneous battles on American and European soil. If, as the saying goes, politics makes strange bedfellows, America's profitable relationship with Napoleonic France shows that the complex world of international diplomacy often does it one better.

GLOSSARY

CARLOS IV (1748–1819) The king of Spain who opposed the French Revolution but after 1796 allied Spain with France against England and, later, Portugal. In 1807 Carlos was forced by an aristocratic revolt to abdicate in favor of his son, Ferdinand VII. Shortly afterward Napoleon intervened to depose Ferdinand and proclaimed his brother, Joseph Bonaparte, king of Spain.

CLERMONT Robert Livingston's family estate on the Hudson River in New York.

CONVENTION OF 1800 An agreement between France and the United States that released the United States from its 1778 treaty of alliance with France in return for America's dropping claims against France for damages to American shipping during the naval Quasi-War of the 1790s.

DU PONT, PIERRE SAMUEL (1739–1817) A French economist and diplomat who emigrated to the United States in 1799 and then returned to France in 1802 when Jefferson enlisted his aid in negotiations over Louisiana.

HELLEVOETSLUIS A port in French-controlled Netherlands where early in 1803 ice hemmed in French ships preparing to reinforce Napoleon's troops in Saint Domingue.

JACOBINS A French political club whose members, mostly middle class, grew increasingly republican and radical as the French Revolution progressed, eventually supporting the Reign of Terror.

KING, RUFUS (1755–1827) A member of the Constitutional Convention of 1787 who served as minister to Great Britain in 1796–1803 and again in 1825–1826. He ran unsuccessfully for president in 1816 as the Federalist candidate.

LAFAYETTE, MARQUIS DE (1757–1834) A French general and political leader who joined George Washington's Continental Army and aided its victory at Yorktown. Lafayette became a hero to Americans and a popular symbol of republican bonds between France and the United States.

LIVINGSTON, ROBERT (1746–1813) A wealthy New York landowner who helped draft the Declaration of Independence and served as the nation's first secretary of foreign affairs (1781–1783). Appointed as Jefferson's minister to France in 1801, Livingston played a key role in negotiations leading to the Louisiana Purchase. In his later years Livingston financed Robert Fulton's invention of the steamboat and experimented with scientific agriculture.

MADISON, JAMES (1751–1836) The Virginia lawyer and "Father of the Constitution" who served as Jefferson's secretary of state (1801–1809) during negotiations over Louisiana and rising tensions with Britain over American neutral rights. Elected president in 1808, Madison was unable to prevent the War of 1812 against England, a military stalemate that nevertheless confirmed American independence.

MONROE, JAMES (1758–1831) The Virginia lawyer and political leader who served as American minister to France from 1794 to 1796 and was sent by President Jefferson as a special envoy to assist Robert Livingston during negotiations over Louisiana. Elected president in 1816, Monroe served two relatively calm terms in office.

PINCKNEY'S TREATY (1795) A treaty between the United States and Spain, named after American envoy Thomas Pinckney. It established commercial relations between the two nations, provided free navigation of the Mississippi River by American citizens and Spanish subjects, granted Americans the right of deposit (temporary storage of goods) at New Orleans, and set the boundary of the United States with Spanish Louisiana and West Florida.

TALLEYRAND, CHARLES MAURICE DE (1754–1838) A cunning French aristocrat and diplomat who was once the bishop of Autun. Talleyrand, a wily survivor of several regimes, sided with the French Revolution but briefly sought exile from the Reign of Terror in Britain and the United States. Returning to France in 1796, Talleyrand hitched his career to the rising star of Napoleon Bonaparte, who made him minister of foreign affairs. Capable and shrewd, Talleyrand survived Napoleon's downfall and served later French kings.

TREATY OF SAN ILDEFONSO (1796) A secret treaty of alliance between Spain and France against Britain. Spain agreed to return Louisiana to France in exchange for the small kingdom of Etruria in northern Italy, which Carlos IV wanted for his daughter. Official confirmation of the exchange did not occur until 1802.

VIRGIL'S *AENEID* An epic Latin poem written *circa* 30–19 B.C. by Virgil. The *Aeneid* portrayed the legendary journey of the Trojan prince Aeneas to Italy, where his descendants founded Rome.

WHITEHALL The British government's offices, located on Whitehall Street in London.

✯ ✯ ✯ ✯ ✯ ✯

Just seven days after the House of Representatives confirmed Jefferson as president on its thirty-sixth ballot, [Robert] Livingston accepted the post of ambassador to France. "No one," wrote the French chargé d'affaires [ambassador] Louis André Pichon, "could receive this mission with qualities more apt to maintain and increase the good understanding which has just been re-established so happily between the two nations."

Delaying his departure in accord with the president's wish to secure formal ratifications of the Convention of 1800 that ended the naval Quasi-War with France, Chancellor Livingston had ample time to explore every conceivable option in detail with Jefferson and Madison. Livingston knew the president's goals as well as anyone could when he sailed for Paris in October aboard the frigate *Boston*. . . .

. . . Livingston and his entourage arrived in Paris early in December and were greeted by the marquis de Lafayette, a frequent visitor to Clermont during the Revolutionary War, and François Barbé-Marbois, former chargé d'affaires to the United States and now Bonaparte's minister of finance. Livingston met with Talleyrand on the 5th, and was formally presented to the first consul on the 6th. Bonaparte asked Livingston whether he had visited Europe before. Livingston answered that he had not. "You have come," replied the first consul, "to a very corrupt world."

Excerpt from Jon Kukla, "Napoleon Bonaparte and the Louisiana Purchase," from *A Wilderness So Immense: The Louisiana Purchase and the Destiny of America* (New York: Alfred A. Knopf, 2003), pp. 237–258.

Against a backdrop of routine consular business, including American claims for ships and property seized during the Quasi-War, Livingston became a full player in the American guessing game about Bonaparte's plans. There were three questions: Whether France had accepted Louisiana from Spain (which Talleyrand resolutely denied). Whether the Floridas were included in the cession that Talleyrand denied. And whether Bonaparte was sending troops beyond St. Domingue [Haiti] to secure New Orleans. Gathering intelligence about these matters, however, was incidental to Livingston's basic objective. Depending on how far things had gone with Spain, Jefferson wanted Livingston to persuade France to forgo the retrocession [of Louisiana]. Or, if it was too late for that, he wanted Livingston to persuade France "to make over to the United States the Floridas . . . or at least West Florida." Or finally, if the retrocession had not included the Floridas, he wanted France to persuade Spain to cede them to the United States. In short, Livingston's chief task was to press the American case against Bonaparte's ambitions in the Caribbean and Louisiana.

As events unfolded between December 1802 and the spring of 1803, Jefferson, Madison, Livingston, Du Pont, and Monroe all would contribute to the American acquisition of Louisiana, with important support from Rufus King in London. Throughout the long and complicated process of diplomacy, however, it was Livingston who did the heavy lifting. With so many uncertainties in play, his written instructions had been perfunctory from the beginning. Jefferson had explained his goals in broad terms. He and Madison kept Livingston abreast of their reactions to changing situations, but they counted on Livingston to size things up in Paris and exercise broad discretionary powers if necessary. Livingston, in turn, kept them candidly informed of both obstacles and opportunities — and his constant communication with Rufus King prevented either Britain or France from sowing confusion in the American camp.

Affable in temperament, Livingston was also hard of hearing — a potential disadvantage in his dealings with the witty and inscrutably subtle Talleyrand. But the French minister's legendary knack for discovering and exploiting an opponent's weaknesses was nearly worthless in the face of Livingston's unusual self-confidence. Despite his firm attachment to republican values that Bonaparte regarded as dangerously Jacobin, Livingston was a Hudson Valley squire to the manor born, unruffled by the hauteur of the former bishop of Autun.

Talleyrand tried to keep the American minister at arm's length with trifling ploys — pretending all the while that France had no claim to Louisiana. Soon after arriving in Paris, Livingston suggested that France offer Louisiana in settlement of the nation's debts to American merchants. "None but spendthrifts satisfy their debts by selling their lands," Talleyrand objected. Then he added, after a short pause, "but it is not ours to give." Livingston found ways to work around him.

No Frenchman was willing to admit that Spain's retrocession was in the works, so Livingston prepared a forceful memorandum addressing the question, "Whether it will be advantageous to France to take possession of Louisiana?" He had twenty copies of his memorandum privately printed. He sent one to Madison, and he sent copies to Talleyrand and Bonaparte. The rest he carefully distributed to influential men around the first consul. The genius of Livingston's pamphlet lay not in its obvious conclusion but in its careful demolition of Bonaparte's mercantilist vision of Louisiana as a bread-basket for the sugar islands. France "is no longer a republic," he advised Madison, "it is the government of one man whose will is law." In one respect Bonaparte's secrecy about Louisiana made Livingston's diplomatic task easier: if the retrocession had not been concluded, then his question was safely hypothetical.

Since France, "like every other country, possesses a limited capital" for investment, "the sole object of inquiry should be, where can this capital best be placed? At home? In the islands? At Cayenne? In the East Indies? Or in Louisiana?" The question was *not* whether France should have "any colonies" but whether she needed Louisiana.

> France possesses colonies . . . and she is bound in good faith to retain and protect them. But she is not bound to create new colonies, to multiply her points of defense, and to waste [investment] capital which she needs both at home and abroad.

In arguments that fill fourteen printed pages and that echo Jefferson's suggestions, Livingston demonstrated that France did not need Louisiana in order to reap the benefits of St. Domingue. In peacetime the sugar islands could readily buy food, manufactured goods, cloth, wood, and other commodities on the open market. In time of war, however, "the mouth of the Mississippi will be blocked up and the planters of the French Colony [will] be reduced to the utmost distress."

Nor could France expect to benefit by exporting its manufactured goods up the Mississippi into the western states. "Nothing could give birth to this idea," Livingston wrote, "but the most perfect ignorance of the navigation of the river; and of the wants of the inhabitants." French wines found no favor with "the palates or purses of the inhabitants," who preferred "their own liquors, cider, beer, whisky, and peach brandy; the last of which, with age, is superior to the best brandy of France." Glass, tableware, hardware, and dry goods all reached the west through Baltimore or Philadelphia "on cheap and easy terms," never by "the slow and expensive passage up the river against the current."

"In a commercial view, the settlement of Louisiana shall not be advantageous to France, but, on the contrary really injurious," Livingston concluded. "In a political one, it will be found still more inconsistent with her interests." Here, too, Livingston put forward arguments that he had discussed with President Jefferson, taking care neither to "leave unsaid what truth requires to be spoken" nor to "give umbrage by freedom which haughty spirits may construe into menace." The United States and France "are so happily placed with respect to each other, as to have no point of collision," Livingston wrote, in yet another echo of his conversations with Jefferson:

> How strong, how powerful, should the inducement be that compels France to lose these advantages, and convert a natural and warm ally into a jealous and suspicious neighbor, and perhaps, in the progress of events, into an open enemy!

"If there is a situation in the world," Livingston warned, again echoing Jefferson, "that would lead to these melancholy consequences, it would be that of France in possession of New Orleans."

In his cover letter to Madison, Livingston explained the purpose of his memorandum. "I have had several conferences on the subject of Louisiana," he reported, "but can get nothing more from them than I have already communicated," so "I have thought it best by conversation and by writing to pave the way . . . till I know better to what object to point." Talleyrand promised to give his memorandum "an attentive perusal after which . . . I will come forward with some proposition." As Du Pont had recognized, setting the right price was tricky, and Livingston hoped Madison could offer "some directions on this head and not leave the responsibility of offering too much or too little entirely at my door." Weighed against the costs of "guards and garrisons, the risk of war, the value of duties and [the revenue that] may be raised by the sale of lands," he ventured that the Floridas and New Orleans might be "a cheap purchase at twenty millions of dollars."

The summer passed with few developments, for as Livingston told Rufus King in August, "every body of fashion is now out of town." By October, however, Livingston had opened a new channel around Talleyrand when he gave a copy of his printed memorandum to Joseph Bonaparte, the first consul's elder brother. "My brother is his own counsellor," Joseph confided to Livingston, "but we are good brothers . . . and as I have access to him at all times, I have an opportunity of turning his attention to a particular subject that might otherwise be passed over." At their next encounter, Joseph Bonaparte told Livingston that both he and the first consul had read Livingston's memorandum "with attention," and that Napoleon had told him "that he had nothing more at heart than to be on the best terms with the United States."

While waiting for guidance from Jefferson or Madison about how much he might offer for New Orleans or Florida, in December 1802 Livingston concocted a scheme that required no money at all. In a series of conversations with Napoleon's elder brother, Livingston suggested that although Louisiana would be a ruinous burden for the French nation, it offered a lucrative haven for the Bonaparte family in the event of Napoleon's death. Napoleon could transfer sovereignty over Louisiana to the United States and transfer the ownership of its lands to his own family. Then the United States could buy half the land from the Bonapartes for, say, $2 million.

Livingston's scheme was useful, and it was actually less bizarre than it may seem. Family interests, after all, had prompted Carlos IV [the king of Spain] to exchange Louisiana for the throne of Etruria for his queen's nephew — a deal that had been brokered by Napoleon's brother Lucien. The Bonapartes were not yet an imperial family, but they were beginning to act like one. "There are duties which a man owes to himself and his family," Livingston advised, "which ought not to be overlooked when they can be performed without the smallest injury to the public." Why not barter Louisiana to the United States to underwrite "the present splendour of your family," he asked Joseph Bonaparte, and "secure to your posterity a property [in America] which nothing attainable in France would in any degree equal."

Regardless of the merits of his scheme, Livingston used it to keep Napoleon thinking about the arguments advanced in his memorandum about Louisiana while he waited for guidance from Jefferson about how much to offer and for what. Livingston's December conversations with Joseph Bonaparte also forced Talleyrand back into play.

Talleyrand did not want Napoleon's brother taking the lead in foreign affairs, and he was not about to watch from the sidelines while anyone else explored lucrative opportunities for graft. In this respect, Livingston knew he had scored a direct hit when Joseph Bonaparte informed him, early in January, that all future negotiations about Louisiana must go through Talleyrand, "who alone could inform you of the intention of the government."

Livingston also used his December conversations with Joseph Bonaparte to reemphasize the British threat. If France persisted in its efforts to reclaim Louisiana and the Floridas, her actions were certain to force America into an alliance with Great Britain. Livingston's personal Anglophobia and his affection for France were well known, but through his intrigue with Joseph Bonaparte he reminded Talleyrand and the first consul that his own republican sympathies, and those of his countrymen, had limits.

Livingston's conversations with Joseph Bonaparte in December had attracted Talleyrand's attention. Early in January he reinforced this message by openly conversing with the British ambassador about Louisiana and the Floridas. If France persisted, Charles, Earl Whitworth, reported back to his superiors at Whitehall, Livingston "gave it as his decided opinion that . . . it would have the immediate effect of uniting every individual in America, of every party, and none more sincerely than himself, in the cause of Great Britain." In light of Livingston's "known political bias" toward France, Lord Whitworth concluded that Britain would have "few enemies" in America if France took possession of Louisiana. Whitworth also noted "that the little intercourse which has arisen between [Livingston] and myself gives a considerable degree of jealousy to Mr. Talleyrand."

During the autumn of 1802, before and during his conversations with Joseph Bonaparte, Livingston also advanced America's negotiating position in one additional, crucial way. Ever since they got wind of the secret Treaty of San Ildefonso, American officials had been striving to discover whether its terms provided for the retrocession of East and West Florida from France to Spain. In August 1802, Livingston discovered that "all the old French maps mark the river Perdi[d]o as the boundary between Florida and Louisiana." Livingston knew, of course, that the Perdido River (now the westernmost boundary of the State of Florida) marked the border between the Spanish provinces of East and West Florida. He now realized that Talleyrand's and Bonaparte's evasions about the retrocession of the Floridas derived in part from their inadequate knowledge of the geography of the Gulf Coast.

Livingston, Jefferson, and Madison generally distinguished between "Louisiana proper" (by which they meant the western watershed of the Mississippi), and the city or isle of New Orleans east of the river and West Florida along the Gulf Coast. Perhaps as a result of their reliance on outdated maps, the French seem never fully to have understood the importance that the Americans attached to West Florida — that "narrow slip of very barren lands" that controlled the Alabama, Chattahoochee, Mobile, and Tombigbee Rivers, which extended north into the American frontier settlements in Tennessee and the Mississippi Territory.

The Americans' superior knowledge of their own geography gave them a greater advantage over the French than Livingston or anyone else realized. Time and again the

Americans targeted New Orleans and West Florida as their chief objectives, while shrugging with indifference about the "immense wilderness" of the western watershed. Jefferson's letter to Livingston on April 18, 1802, sought "the island of New Orleans and the Floridas." His cover letter to Du Pont demanded "the cession of New Orleans and the Floridas" as the price of peace. Similarly, the news of Spain's intended retrocession of Louisiana to France had prompted Secretary of State James Madison to "turn the present crisis to [our] advantage" by directing Charles Pinckney, the American minister to Spain, to seek "a cession . . . of the two Floridas or at least of West Florida, which is rendered of peculiar value by it containing the mouths of the Mobile and other rivers running from the United States." America had plenty of land between the Appalachians and the Mississippi, and the nation had no need to fight for more. Western farmers and planters did need, and were prepared to fight for, secure access to the world market via the Mississippi.

Until Livingston began his conversations with Joseph Bonaparte, the American objective was always limited, as Madison wrote in January 1803, to "a cession of New Orleans and Florida to the United States and consequently the establishment of the Mississippi as the boundary between the United States and Louisiana." The idea of extending the American territory beyond the Mississippi arose during Livingston's unscripted conversations with Joseph Bonaparte. In October 1802, when Bonaparte asked him "whether we should prefer the Floridas or Louisiana," Livingston replied that America "had no wish to extend our boundary across the Mississippi." America sought only "security," he said, "and not an extension of territory." As Livingston pitched his scheme to enrich the Bonapartes by the sale of American lands, however, he concocted the idea of an American colony north of the Arkansas River and west of the Mississippi. It could be justified as a buffer to protect French Louisiana from attack by British Canada, but its real purpose was to attract American farmers as the most plausible way to assure the Bonaparte family that Louisiana lands would quickly appreciate in value. Livingston dropped his quirky scheme when it had served his purposes and brought Talleyrand back into the game. Nevertheless, the idea of transferring land west of the Mississippi to the United States was a lagniappe [bonus] first voiced in Livingston's conversations with Joseph Bonaparte.

By early January 1803 Robert Livingston had everything in place for the success of the diplomatic mission that Jefferson had entrusted to him two years earlier. Bonaparte and Talleyrand knew exactly what Jefferson wanted — New Orleans, West Florida, and control of the Mississippi — and exactly why. They knew that Jefferson welcomed friendship between France and the United States. They also knew that if they took possession of New Orleans, America would regard France as its "natural and habitual enemy." With persistence and imagination over the course of many months, Chancellor Livingston had set the stage for the Louisiana Purchase, effectively conveying to the first consul and his advisors every subtle nuance of the strategy Jefferson defined in his famous letter of April 18, 1802. "Every eye in the U.S.," Jefferson had written, "is now fixed on this affair of Louisiana."

As the new year began, American eyes were watching closely to see how Bonaparte would react to Livingston's overtures. They were watching, as well, to see how

Bonaparte *and* Jefferson reacted to a flurry of recent events that brought Spain, France, Great Britain, and the United States once again to the brink of war.

On Saturday, October 16, 1802, Juan Ventura Morales, a zealous and headstrong forty-six-year-old career bureaucrat, hurled a stone into the Mississippi. He closed the port of New Orleans to Americans — an action that started a wave of indignation that . . . spread to Kentucky, Washington, and the capitals of Europe. "From this date," Acting Intendant Morales proclaimed on October 16, "the privilege which the Americans had of importing and depositing their merchandise and effects in this capital, shall be interdicted." Since the age of twelve, when Morales started working as a clerk in the customhouse of Málaga on the Mediterranean coast, he had built a reputation for meddlesome efficiency. As acting intendant at New Orleans since 1796, Morales had demonstrated a strong antagonism toward Americans and a predilection for controversy. Often working at cross purposes with the Spanish governors, Morales was an inflexible secular counterpart to the self-righteous Père Antoine [a combative Spanish priest in New Orleans]. "The intendant places more obstacles in my way than the enemy," Louisiana governor Manuel Gayoso de Lemos had complained in 1799, for "his unmitigated ambition forces him to intervene in military and political matters . . . [against] the true interests of the king."

By the terms of Pinckney's Treaty of 1795, the right of deposit had been established at New Orleans for a period of three years. After 1798 the treaty permitted Spain to designate "another part of the banks of the Mississippi [as] an equivalent establishment." Morales's proclamation — which Gayoso's successor, Manuel Juan de Salcedo, denounced as "a direct and open violation of the Treaty" — asserted that the period of "privilege" could be extended no longer "without an express order of the King."

Within two days, the news of Morales's suspension of what Americans regarded as their *right* of deposit, not privilege, had reached Natchez. From there it spread rapidly upriver to Kentucky and Ohio. By October 26 the news of the closing of the port had reached Lexington, Kentucky, and the following Wednesday it was on the front page of Frankfort's weekly *Guardian of Freedom*. "Whether this order was given by the Spaniards, or by the French," the *Guardian* reported, "was [a] matter of uncertainty," but after months of speculation about Bonaparte's intentions, many westerners were ready to believe the worst. Early in November rumors flew through the bluegrass country, embellishing the story of the closing of the port with claims "that a French army had actually taken possession of Orleans." The next Wednesday's *Guardian* happily contradicted that rumor, "on the authority of a gentleman late from Natchez," who assured the editor "that no army has arrived . . . but that the French would take possession of the Colony shortly." Newspapers throughout the west also buzzed with information from another gentleman "just arrived from Bordeaux, who stated that arrangements were making by France to take possession of the colony, with 10,000 troops" commanded by General Victor.

More immediately alarming were the reports of Spanish officials turning away flatboats laden with cotton, which gave all Kentucky farmers reason to fear that their autumn harvests "will be in the same predicament." A subsequent letter stating that some boats arriving at the closed port were being allowed "to land their cargoes, on paying a duty," offered *Guardian* readers a moment for optimism early in December, until they read in the next column that the situation at Natchez was one of "very great and general consternation," with Americans and Spanish alike "much agitated, fully expecting a war." . . .

It took five weeks for news of the New Orleans crisis to reach Washington, but as soon as it arrived Jefferson and Madison adopted the position that Morales had acted on his own. Only a prompt reopening of the port could dissuade the western states from marching on New Orleans as they had been ready to do many times in the past. Since it is easier for a sovereign to disavow an overzealous subordinate than to be seen reversing his own policy, ascribing the closing of the port to a maverick Spanish bureaucrat gave the Jefferson administration room for diplomatic and political maneuvering toward a peaceful resolution of the crisis.

The closing of the port "is so direct and palpable a violation of the Treaty of 1795," Madison wrote, "that in candor it is to be imputed rather to the Intendant solely, than to instructions of his Government." Equally surprised by the proclamation, the Spanish ambassador in Washington had hastily assured Madison that Morales had overstepped his authority, while firsthand reports from New Orleans indicated "that the Governor did not concur with the Intendant" either. On the other hand, Kentucky's *Guardian of Freedom* regarded the text of Morales's proclamation itself as convincing "evidence that the shutting the port of New Orleans was not an act of the Intendant's, but of the Spanish government" — and the *Guardian's* editor called upon the president and Congress to do everything in their power to avenge the "insult" and "redress the grievance thus created."

"From whatever source the measure may have proceeded," Madison advised Charles Pinckney, the American envoy to Spain, "the President expects that the Spanish Government will neither lose a moment in countermanding it, nor hesitate to repair every damage which may result from it." The wrath of America's western citizens, Madison believed,

> is justified by the interest they have at stake. The Mississippi is to them every thing. It is the Hudson, the Delaware, the Potomac, and all the navigable rivers of the atlantic states formed into one stream. The produce exported through that channel last year amounted to $1,622,672 from the Districts of Kentucky and Mississippi [alone], and will probably be fifty per cent more this year . . . a great part of which is now or shortly will be afloat for New Orleans and consequently exposed to the effects of this extraordinary exercise of power.

After writing to Pinckney, Madison also met with the French chargé d'affaires, Louis André Pichon. It was anyone's guess, he warned Pichon, what the five or six thousand Americans who were at that moment floating their harvest downriver might do when they reached New Orleans and found the port closed to their exports. "We have rumours flying through the woods from Pensacola to St. Louis," General James Wilkinson informed Kentucky senator John Brown, "that inflame our latent combustibility." Unless the port is quickly reopened, "our citizens will *kick up a dust*," James Morrison wrote from Lexington to Virginia senator Wilson Cary Nicholas. "They already *talk of war*." Kentucky was "all in a Hubbub," Robert Barr advised Kentucky senator John

Breckinridge, "all ready and waiting to step on board and sail down and take possession of New Orleans."

With French troops expected to arrive in New Orleans at any moment, the timing of the Spanish intendant's action was especially alarming. Many Americans jumped to the conclusion that Bonaparte had pressured Spain to close the port. Northern Federalists began clamoring for war — less because they cared about Louisiana than because their enemy would be France. Congressman John Stratton, of Northampton County on Virginia's Eastern Shore, reflected the exasperation of southern Federalists when he decried "the timidity of our executive in meeting this flagrant violation of our Treaty with Spain." New Orleans could be taken by "the Kentucky Militia alone," Stratton exclaimed. "No better opportunity ever can occur for furnishing . . . a pretext for seizing the East Bank of the Mississippi." Stratton and other southern Federalists believed that "Securing perminantly the free Navigation of that River" was "all important to America." Angry westerners were in full agreement. They were ready to oust "the reptile Spaniards" from New Orleans before Bonaparte took possession.

With demands for war coming from either side, the Jefferson administration upheld the convenient fiction that Juan Ventura Morales's revocation of the American right of deposit and closing of the port of New Orleans was simply a colossal blunder by one overzealous, avaricious, bigoted, and probably stupid colonial official. A colossal but perhaps reversible blunder.

Withdrawing the American right of deposit may have been short-sighted, but it was not the work of a maverick local official. On July 14, 1802, the order to close the port had been issued by Carlos IV himself. . . . Earlier that spring Intendant Morales and other colonial officials had complained to the ministers of the Spanish treasury that Americans were abusing the right of deposit and heavily engaged in smuggling. Upon the advice of his chief minister . . . Carlos IV had secretly directed the intendant of Louisiana to prohibit the deposit of American goods in New Orleans — and Carlos had specifically instructed Morales not to justify his action as "the order of the king." Instead, he was to pretend that he had reviewed the terms of Pinckney's Treaty on his own initiative "and found that the limit of three years fixed by article XXII bound his hands so that he could not allow the introduction and deposit of American goods without the express permission of the king." By following his secret instructions to the letter, Juan Morales deflected responsibility from the king to himself so effectively that a full century passed before historian Edward Channing discovered and published the direct order from Carlos IV that precipitated the Mississippi crisis of 1802.

Bonaparte was delighted when the news of Morales's proclamation arrived in a letter from his American envoy early in January 1803. By closing the port, Talleyrand wrote to his ambassador in Madrid, "Spain had taken a step equally in accordance with its rights and with the interests of France." The American right of deposit was incompatible with Bonaparte's plans to nurture trade between Louisiana and the French West Indies, "replace" the Americans, and "concentrate [Louisiana's] commerce into the national commerce." The first consul and his foreign minister welcomed Morales's proclamation as a measure that would curb American competitors and encourage French commerce. The closing of the port, however, was the only bit of good news from the New World that reached Bonaparte that winter.

During the first week of January 1803, as troops assigned to reinforce General Charles Leclerc in St. Domingue waited in the cold at Hellevoetsluis, news of General Leclerc's death on November 2 — and of the catastrophic losses and dismal failure of the Caribbean expedition — reached the first consul. Bonaparte's dream of reviving the French sugar empire in the West Indies died with his brother-in-law. His anger burst forth after a dinner party on Wednesday, January 12 — just two days after Pierre Clément Laussat and the *Surveillant* cleared the harbor at La Rochelle for New Orleans. "Damn sugar, damn coffee, damn colonies!" Bonaparte exclaimed. (These were the "exact words of the First Consul," Pierre Louis Roederer, director general of public education, noted in his diary.)

At the end of January the government newspaper in Paris, *Le Moniteur*, published a story hinting that the first consul was turning his attention to the east and thinking about reconquering Egypt. Great Britain reacted promptly to this threatened breach of the year-old Treaty of Amiens, by which Great Britain had promised to surrender the island of Malta to France and Bonaparte had agreed to return Egypt to the Ottoman Turks. On March 2, George III informed Parliament of Bonaparte's "very considerable military preparations . . . in the ports of France and Holland." The king advocated "additional measures of precaution" against the possibility, which Bonaparte was in fact entertaining, that the French troops and vessels assembled for Louisiana and St. Domingue might be redirected toward an invasion of England. As the ice melted in the harbor of Hellevoetsluis, British warships moved into the English Channel, trapping General Victor's forces in their harbors as they made ready for war.

On Sunday afternoon, March 12, Chancellor Livingston and the foreign diplomatic corps attended a salon held by Josephine Bonaparte. "After going the usual round of Ladies in one room," her husband exchanged a few polite words with Livingston, a few more with the Danish ambassador, "and then went to the other end of the room . . . and went up to Lord Whitworth," the British ambassador. Bonaparte told Whitworth "that they would probably have a storm." Whitworth replied that he "hoped not."

"I find, my Lord, your nation wants war again," said Bonaparte.

"No, sir," Whitworth replied, "we are very desirous of peace."

"You have just finished a war of fifteen years," Bonaparte said.

"It is true, sir, and that was fifteen years too long," Whitworth replied.

"But you want another war of fifteen years," Bonaparte asserted.

"Pardon me, sir," Whitworth replied, "we are very desirous of peace."

Bonaparte then expressed "a few more very strong terms evoking the vengeance of heaven upon those who broke the treaty."

"I must either have Malta or war," he declared. Then, being told that "Madame B[onaparte] and the ladies in the next room expected him," Bonaparte departed. . . .

Within days of the first consul's confrontation with Lord Whitworth at Josephine Bonaparte's salon, Joseph and Lucien Bonaparte sent an intermediary . . . to suggest that in return for "a valuable consideration" the Bonapartes might be able to persuade their

This character study of Napoleon Bonaparte (around 1803), who was then first consul of the French Republic and soon to be crowned emperor of France, projects genius and ambition. The latter is accentuated by an outline of the pyramids that commemorates Napoleon's invasion of Egypt in 1798. In 1803, after French troops were defeated by disease and rebellious ex-slaves in Saint Domingue (Haiti), Napoleon abandoned plans for a New World empire and redoubled his efforts to conquer all of Europe. After extending his empire across the Continent to the gates of Moscow, Napoleon was finally defeated by a coalition of European nations in 1815. (Musée Condé, Chantilly/Réunion des Musées Nationaux/Art Resource, N.Y.)

brother to relax his insistence on Malta or war. Whitworth immediately reported the proposal to the British foreign secretary, Robert Banks Jenkinson, Lord Hawkesbury. "I lose no time in informing you," Hawkesbury replied three days later, "that if an arrangement could be concluded which should be satisfactory to His Majesty, and by which His Majesty should retain the Island of Malta, the Sum of one Hundred thousand Pounds might be distributed as Secret Service."

The sum of £100,000 — worth about $16 million today — was indeed a valuable consideration, but with so many men around Bonaparte "partaking in the Pillage of this country," Whitworth determined that more money was required, especially if the British hoped to enlist Talleyrand's support. "I have no fixed Idea of what Sum may be necessary," Whitworth wrote on March 24, "but on calculating what we may expend in one month of War, the sacrifice of a Million, or even two Millions, would be economy." By the middle of April, the British were secretly negotiating with Joseph and Lucien Bonaparte, Talleyrand, and even Napoleon's fearsome chief of secret police, Joseph Fouché.

In the end, the war was not averted and no money changed hands. Nevertheless, the British attempt to bribe Napoleon's brothers and ministers, which probably came to the first consul's attention through Fouché, underscored Talleyrand's and the Bonapartes' opposition to Napoleon's decision to sell Louisiana. Talleyrand . . . had been advocating colonization since his lectures at the National Institute in 1797. He and Napoleon's brothers hoped that the first consul's projects in St. Domingue and Louisiana might divert his interest in Malta and Egypt. The attempted bribery also helps to explain both the famous bathroom encounter between Napoleon and his brothers as well as the first consul's eventual decision to negotiate with the Americans through his incorruptible finance minister, François Barbé-Marbois, rather than Foreign Minister Talleyrand.

The bathroom episode began one evening when Lucien Bonaparte came home to change clothes for the theater. Joseph was waiting for him. "Here you are at last," Joseph said, "I was afraid you might not come. This is no time for theater-going; I have news for you that will give you no fancy for amusement. The General wants to sell Louisiana."

"Come now," Lucien replied, "if he were capable of wishing it, the Chambers would never consent."

"He means to do without their consent," Joseph answered. "What is more," he continued, "this sale would supply him the first funds for the war. Do you know that I am beginning to think he is much too fond of war?" — an opinion that Talleyrand shared. The brothers resolved to talk with Napoleon the next morning.

Lucien reached the Tuileries [the royal palace] first, where he found the first consul soaking in a bath of rosewater. They exchanged pleasantries until Joseph arrived, whereupon Napoleon asked their opinion of his determination to sell Louisiana.

"I flatter myself," Lucien warned, "that the Chambers will not give their consent."

"You flatter yourself," Napoleon answered sarcastically. "That is precious, in truth!"

"And I flatter myself," Joseph interjected, "as I have already told the First Consul."

"And what did I answer?" Napoleon growled.

"That you would do without the Chambers," said Joseph.

"Precisely!" said Napoleon. "And now, gentlemen, think of it what you will; but both of you go into mourning about this affair — you, Lucien, for the sale itself; you, Joseph, because I shall do it without the consent of any one whatsoever. Do you understand?"

"You will do well," Joseph snarled as he stepped toward the tub, "not to expose your project to parliamentary discussion; for . . . I will put myself first at the head of the opposition."

Napoleon laughed scornfully. "You will have no need to lead the opposition, for I repeat that there will be no debate."

Months of relentless advocacy by Chancellor Livingston now paid off, as the first consul claimed the New Yorker's arguments as his own. "It is my idea," Napoleon declared as he rose from the tub. "I conceived it, and I shall go through with it, the negotiation, ratification, and execution, by myself. Do you understand? by me who scoffs at your opposition."

"Good!" Joseph shouted in a rage. "I tell you, General, that you, I, and all of us, if you do what you threaten, may prepare ourselves soon to go and join the poor innocent devils whom you . . . have transported to Sinnamary," site of the infamous prison colony near Cayenne in French Guiana.

"You are insolent!" Napoleon thundered as he fell back into the tub, dousing Joseph and Lucien with a torrent of rose-scented water.

Soaked to the skin, Lucien Bonaparte had the presence of mind to invoke the words of Neptune from Virgil's *Aeneid,*

> I will show you . . . ! But no, first I had better set the waves at rest; after that you are going to pay dearly for your offence.

As Napoleon's valet fainted and fell to the floor, the three brothers regained their composure.

After Joseph left to change his clothes, Lucien and Napoleon continued the argument. "Do you want me to tell you the truth?" Napoleon asked. "I am today more sorry than I like to confess for the expedition to St. Domingue." His decision to sell Louisiana stemmed from his realization that the dream of reviving the French empire in the Caribbean had indeed died with their brother-in-law General Leclerc. "Our national glory," Napoleon told Lucien, "will never come from our marine."

The exact date of this conversation among the Bonaparte brothers is uncertain, and the incident itself may well be apocryphal. Nevertheless, by April 10, 1803, Napoleon had resolved to offer Louisiana to the Americans — and he would not be dissuaded. His timing was exquisite. Chancellor Livingston had put everything in order, and James Monroe had landed at Le Havre. He would arrive in Paris on April 12.

After mass on Easter Sunday, April 10, 1803, Bonaparte summoned Denis Decrès, minister of marine and colonies, and François Barbé-Marbois, minister of finance, to his palace at St. Cloud. A well-educated nobleman from the province of Champagne, Decrès had served with Admiral de Grasse in the West Indies and breached the British blockade at Malta during Bonaparte's Egyptian campaign. Gruff and authoritarian in his manner, hardworking and unswervingly loyal to the first consul, forty-two-year-old Rear Admiral Decrès was one of the few sailors to whom Bonaparte presented a sword of honor. For the previous two years he had been coordinating, with mixed success, preparations for the intended expeditions against St. Domingue, Louisiana, and now perhaps England.

At fifty-eight, Barbé-Marbois was a career diplomat and administrator with a literary and scientific bent and proven affection for the United States. Serving in the 1780s as secretary to the French legation in Philadelphia and later as chargé d'affaires, he had worked with Livingston, Monroe, Jay, and many other American leaders. Barbé-Marbois had compiled the twenty-two questions circulated to the thirteen American states that inspired Thomas Jefferson to compose his *Notes on the State of Virginia* in answer to his queries. In 1784 he had married Elizabeth Moore, daughter of the president of Pennsylvania's executive council. Although he had never seen Louisiana, Barbé-Marbois had traveled north to the Mohawk River in upstate New York. He had also served four years as Louis XVI's last intendant in St. Domingue, where "the ability and the virtue he practices in both public and private life" earned him "a host of enemies in the colony."

A moderate in the French Revolution, Barbé-Marbois was exiled during the Terror and then imprisoned by the Directory for twenty-six months at Sinnamari and Cayenne, in French Guiana. Returning to France after [Napoleon's] coup d'état . . . , Barbé-Marbois took charge of the public treasury in February 1801. Recognized as "a man of talents and integrity," Barbé-Marbois worked closely with Bonaparte for the next five years, amazed by the first consul's "capacity for comprehending everything, [and] the quickness and depth of his reflections."

"I know the full value of Louisiana," Bonaparte told Decrès and Barbé-Marbois, "and I have been desirous of repairing the fault of the French negotiator who abandoned it in 1763." Nevertheless, he continued, effective French control of Louisiana would be threatened by the British navy in the event of war, so "I must expect to lose it." The British had twenty ships in the Gulf of Mexico, Bonaparte said, "whilst our affairs in St. Domingue have been growing worse every day since the death of Leclerc." Rather than letting the British capture Louisiana, the first consul announced, "I think of ceding it to the United States."

"They only ask of me one town in Louisiana," Bonaparte said, echoing the arguments that Jefferson had advanced through Livingston, "but I already consider the colony as entirely lost." Once again echoing the arguments he had read in Livingston's printed memorandum, Bonaparte concluded "that in the hands of this growing power, [Louisiana] will be more useful to the policy and even to the commerce of France, than if it should attempt to keep it."

"We should not hesitate to make a sacrifice of that which is . . . slipping from us," Barbé-Marbois replied.

War with England is inevitable; shall we be able with very inferior naval forces to defend Louisiana against that power? . . . Can we restore fortifications that are in ruins, and construct a long chain of forts upon a frontier of four hundred leagues?

The expense would drain French resources, Barbé-Marbois continued, again echoing Livingston's arguments, giving Britain "a secret joy in seeing you exhaust yourself in efforts of which she alone will derive the profit." Louisiana has been settled for one hundred years, the finance minister observed, borrowing yet another argument from Livingston, "and in spite of efforts and sacrifices of every kind the last accounts of its population attest its weakness."

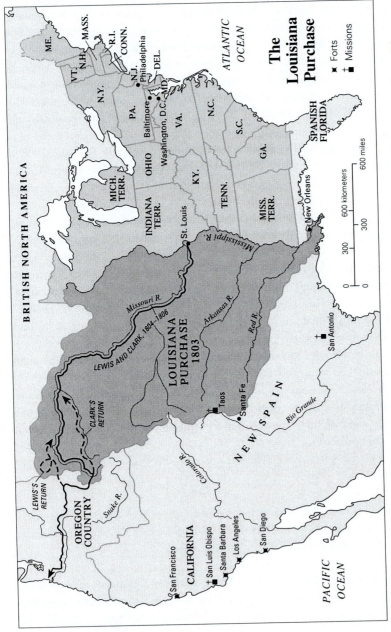

The Louisiana Purchase (1803) doubled the area of the United States and opened the trans-Mississippi West for American settlement. That year President Jefferson dispatched the Lewis and Clark Expedition to extend American control over trade and Indian relations westward into the new territory and beyond. (Adapted by permission of Houghton Mifflin Company.)

Admiral Decrès disagreed. "We are still at peace with England," he said, and "the colony has just been ceded to us." If peace continued, the sale of Louisiana would be seen as a "premature act of ill-founded apprehension," contrary to the honor of France. "There does not exist on the globe," the minister of marine and colonies asserted, "a single city susceptible of becoming as important as New Orleans." Its proximity to the American west already made it one of the most commercial ports in the world, Decrès asserted. "The Mississippi does not reach there till it has received twenty other rivers, most of which surpass in size the finest rivers of Europe." Gazing a century into the future, Admiral Decrès imagined the construction "at the isthmus of Panama [of] a simple canal . . . to connect one ocean with the other." Louisiana, he said, "will be on this new route, and it will then be . . . of inestimable value." If France were forced to abandon St. Domingue, he concluded, "Louisiana will take its place."

Having heard the candid advice of his ministers, Bonaparte ended the conversation and the three men retired to their rooms.

Early Monday morning, April 11, Bonaparte sent for Barbé-Marbois. "Irresolution and deliberation are no longer in season," he declared.

> I renounce Louisiana. It is not only New Orleans that I will cede, it is the whole colony without any reservation. I know the price of what I abandon, and I have sufficiently proved the importance that I attach to this province. . . . I renounce it with the greatest regret. To attempt obstinately to retain it would be folly.

"I direct you to negotiate this affair with the envoys of the United States," the first consul said. "Do not even await the arrival of Mr. Monroe: have an interview this very day with Mr. Livingston." The conflict with Great Britain was about to resume. "I want fifty millions" for Louisiana, Bonaparte said, "and for less than that sum I will not treat. . . . I require money to make war on the richest nation of the world."

Now it was the first consul's turn to gaze far into the future. "In two or three centuries," he observed, "the Americans may be found too powerful for Europe . . . but my foresight does not embrace such remote fears. . . . It is to prevent the danger, to which the colossal power of England exposes us, that I would provide a remedy."

Barbé-Marbois listened carefully as Bonaparte outlined his strategy for the negotiation. "Mr. Monroe is on the point of arriving," and was surely carrying secret instructions from President Jefferson about how much money to offer for New Orleans. The first consul anticipated that neither Livingston nor Monroe was "prepared for a decision which goes infinitely beyond any thing that they are about to ask of us." Therefore, he instructed Barbé-Marbois:

> Begin by making them the overture, without any subterfuge. You will acquaint me, day by day, hour by hour, of your progress. . . . Observe the greatest secrecy, and recommend it to the American ministers.

The treaty talks that culminated in the Louisiana Purchase commenced that evening, while James Monroe's carriage was still rolling toward Paris.

QUESTIONS TO CONSIDER

1. Describe Robert Livingston's arguments about why France should not take possession of Louisiana. What were the disadvantages of Louisiana to France? What were the advantages of purchasing New Orleans to the United States? To what extent did Livingston exaggerate the former and understate the latter? How did Livingston demonstrate that "innocent" Americans could hold their own in the "corrupt" world of Europe?

2. Analyze the motives and actions of the key players in the Mississippi crisis of 1802. Why did Juan Morales, the Spanish official in New Orleans, close the port? Was he acting on his own? How did Americans react to Spain's closure of the port of New Orleans in 1802? How did Napoleon react? Did this confrontation help or hinder American negotiations with France over Louisiana?

3. Assess the various factors and considerations that led Napoleon to sell the entire Louisiana Territory to the United States. How important were American actions and arguments? the French army's failure in Saint Domingue? Napoleon's estimate of the chances of keeping Louisiana? his desire for war with Britain? Were other factors also involved?

4. In what way did the policy of neutrality in the wars between France and England help the young United States during the Louisiana controversy? How different would your conclusion be if the War of 1812 were your case study?

5. Analyze America's successful diplomacy in the Louisiana Purchase against Jonathan Dull's account of the survival of the infant United States in the 1780s (Selection 9). Was America's success in 1803 due to its size, geography, distance from Europe, luck, skillful leadership, or some combination of these?

VI

MAKING A
NATION

The United States was a new nation in multiple ways. Not only was the country newly independent, but its leaders had also invented a central government to replace the thirteen colonial regimes that had coordinated the rebellion. Those who opposed the federal constitution of 1787 — the antifederalists — argued that it would merely substitute a new tyranny for the one the colonists had shed. The new government faced the task of convincing its citizens that their individual freedoms and regional differences would be respected by the new Constitution and that their disagreements could be expressed peacefully through a system of political parties. Then, too, there was the issue of cultural independence, for the American people had as yet only an embryonic sense of group identity. As historian John Murrin has written, their leaders had "erected their constitutional roof before they put up the national walls." Without a long history and common ancestral lands or ethnic origins, Americans lacked many of the building blocks of nation-making that were relied upon elsewhere and were trumpeted by nineteenth-century spokesmen as the only legitimate basis for nationhood.

For the new nation to cohere, America's republican government had to establish its authority and its people needed a sense of national identity. The intertwined problems of institutional allegiance and cultural identity are the subject of the following two essays, both of which keep comparative cases in mind. To understand the difficult political situation of the 1790s and early 1800s, according to Seymour Martin Lipset, it helps to see the United States as analogous to the postcolonial regimes of Asia and Africa after World War II. Like newly independent peoples of the Third World, Americans had to struggle to achieve a credible government, national unity, and multiparty democracy. Peter J. Parish uses a different comparative benchmark to assess the Americans' road to nationhood. Examining theories of nationalism that are grounded in

European experience, he argues that the United States achieved nationhood on a different timetable and used alternative ingredients that compensated for its peoples' lack of common blood or history.

Both authors adopt theories developed by sociologists and political scientists in order to highlight important features of the early republic that enhanced its prospects for survival. Lipset, who follows the young United States to the 1820s, develops the "new nation" analogy to reveal similar patterns across continents and centuries. Parish, on the other hand, charts the American experience of nationalism all the way to the Civil War and shows how it proved "an exception to most of the rules" about the ways nations emerge and cohere. In short, Lipset stresses transnational similarities while Parish argues for American uniqueness. In other ways, however, their accounts complement each other. Both acknowledge that Americans enjoyed crucial advantages at the outset of their republican experiment, and both recognize that it took the Civil War to resolve the issue of national unity. As you analyze these readings, ask yourself which essay more effectively places the new nation's situation in larger perspective. Comparing the two, you should also explore the advantages and disadvantages of using social science models to study history.

11

The United States as a New Nation

SEYMOUR MARTIN LIPSET

The United States, says historical sociologist Seymour Martin Lipset, was the first major colony to mount a successful revolt against colonial rule and in this sense became the first "new nation." One way to interpret America's early national history comparatively is to note that the problems it faced are common to all postcolonial societies. Thus, keeping in mind an analogy with today's emerging nations in Asia and Africa, Lipset analyzes the conflicts and controversies that surrounded our early presidents and political parties as they addressed issues central to establishing a democratic system.

One issue all new nations face is the problem of winning the allegiance of the masses to their governing system. Charismatic leaders often emerge from revolutions to embody the people's hopes, but they can easily become dictators who destroy democracy. The special achievement of George Washington, Lipset shows, was to use his enormous popularity not for self-aggrandizement but for easing Americans' transition to political stability. A second problem, the achievement of national unity over regional or political cleavages, was handled less deliberately and decisively. The Founders feared political parties. Their Constitution contains no provisions for them; in fact, it was explicitly designed to prevent what James Madison called "factions" from gaining power. Nevertheless, when the Founders organized in groups to draft and debate the new Constitution, they planted the seeds that would eventually sprout into a two-party system. Instead of promoting the dangerous factionalism that the Founders feared, the party system absorbed all shades of political opinion into the peaceful democratic process — at least for several decades. The third problem Lipset discusses is the rights of opposition parties. It is very tempting, leaders of new nations discover, simply to remove pesky opponents by condemning them as traitors, denying them free speech, or putting them in jail. In the 1790s, Lipset shows, the Federalists tried just such tactics. In 1800, however, they lost the presidency to Thomas Jefferson and the Democratic-Republicans, who proved so popular that they found such measures unnecessary to ensure reelection.

Establishing democratic political institutions was not an easy or inevitable process, even for a new nation with many advantages. In the early republic, Lipset writes, "it was touch and go whether the complex balance of forces would swing in the direction of a one- or two-party system, or even whether the nation would survive as an entity." That it did survive — albeit with a bloody civil war on the horizon — was due to the restraint of heroic leaders such as Washington and the victory of Jeffersonians at the polls as much as to advantageous conditions that today's emerging nations do not possess. Lipset implies that the history of our first three decades as a new nation should leave us a good deal more humble and patient with the halting progress of democracy among the world's newly independent peoples today. His use of sociological concepts and historical analogies creates a stimulating new perspective on Washington, Jefferson, and their political parties, and suggests comparative insights relevant to the new nations of our own time.

GLOSSARY

ALIEN AND SEDITION ACTS (1798)   Partisan laws passed by Federalists in Congress to silence their Jeffersonian critics. The Alien Act authorized the president to deport any foreigner deemed "dangerous to the peace and safety of the United States." The Sedition Act outlawed publications or speeches that brought the government or its officials "into contempt or disrepute." Both laws expired in 1801.

AUTOCRAT   A person claiming to exercise absolute authority.

CHARISMATIC LEADER   One who leads through the power of personality or a special personal quality giving him or her influence or authority over large numbers of people.

CONGO   A former colony of Belgium in central Africa that was granted independence in 1960 as the Republic of Congo. Ethnic and regional divisions caused secessionist movements and a three-year civil war in which the United Nations intervened to restore order. Continuing threats of rebellion led General Joseph Mobutu to seize power in 1965 and to rule as a dictator.

CONSTITUTIONAL CONVENTION   A convention of state delegates that met in the summer of 1787 in Philadelphia to discuss revision of the Articles of Confederation. The outcome of their debates and compromises was a new federal constitution, which was ratified by the states in 1788.

DEMOCRATIC-REPUBLICAN PARTY   A party centered around Thomas Jefferson, opposed to the Federalists, and emphasizing personal liberty, an agrarian vision, limitation of the federal government, and preference for France in foreign affairs. After Jefferson's election in 1800, the party retained the presidency until 1825.

FEDERALIST PARTY   A party evolved from the federalist, or pro-Constitution, faction in the ratification debates of 1787–1788 that favored strong centralized government, encouragement of commerce and industry, and preference for Great Britain in foreign affairs. Its leaders included Alexander Hamilton and John Adams.

"HOBBESIAN JUNGLE"   The view of the world according to the English philosopher Thomas Hobbes (1588–1679), which presents life in the state of nature as "nasty, brutish, and short."

JAY'S TREATY (1794)   A treaty between the United States and Great Britain negotiated by John Jay. Britain agreed to evacuate forts in the northwest and to guarantee unrestricted navigation of the Mississippi River. But because the treaty restricted American trade with France and the West Indies, and failed to protect American seamen from impressment (forced service in the British navy), it aroused opposition in the United States.

LEGITIMACY   In political terms, the extent to which a government is perceived by its citizens to be lawful or legal and entitled to their allegiance.

MARPLOTS   Persons who interfere without justification to defeat a plan or project.

MISSOURI COMPROMISE (1820)   Measures passed by Congress to end the first of a series of crises concerning the westward extension of slavery. By terms of the compromise, Maine was admitted as a free state and Missouri as a slave state, and slavery was prohibited from the Louisiana Purchase north of 36°30'.

"NATIONALISTS"   Those delegates at the Constitutional Convention who favored a strong central government. They were also referred to as the "Continental" caucus.

NKRUMAH, KWAME (1909–1972)   The prime minister, then president (1960–1966) of the west African nation of Ghana. Nkrumah had helped to spark the independence struggle against Britain, but his national leadership grew increasingly dictatorial before he was ousted in 1966.

NULLIFICATION ORDINANCES   Resolutions declaring that states could declare null and void objectionable federal laws. In 1798 and 1799, the Kentucky and Virginia legislatures opposed the Alien and Sedition Acts. The Kentucky Resolutions, written by Thomas Jefferson, stated that the federal government had no right to exercise powers not expressly delegated to it by the Constitution. The Virginia Resolutions, written by James Madison, were similar. Both were the first notable statements of states' rights doctrine.

PAROCHIALISM   Allegiance to narrow, localized interests or views.

PLEBISCITE   A direct vote of the people on an important public question.

POLITY   The constitutional government of a nation or state.

VIRGINIA PLAN   A plan for a federal government introduced by the Virginia dele-
gation at the Philadelphia Constitutional Convention in 1787. It marked a shift away
from revising the Articles of Confederation and toward a wholesale reorganization of
the national government. The plan called for a government with legislative, executive,
and judicial branches to replace the old National Congress. States were to be represented in a bicameral legislature in proportion to their population.

★ ★ ★ ★ ★ ★ ★

There is a tendency for older nations to view with impatience the internal tur-
moil of new ones, and to become especially alarmed at the way oligarchical-
dictatorial and revolutionary forces shake their tenuous foundations. Coupled
with this is a tendency to expect them to accomplish in a decade what other nations
have taken a century or more to do. A backward glance into our own past should
destroy the notion that the United States proceeded easily toward the establishment of
democratic political institutions. In the period which saw the establishment of political
legitimacy and party government, it was touch and go whether the complex balance of
forces would swing in the direction of a one- or two-party system, or even whether the
nation would survive as an entity. It took time to institutionalize values, beliefs, and
practices, and there were many incidents that revealed how fragile the commitments to
democracy and nationhood really were.

But it was from this crucible of confusion and conflict that values and goals became
defined, issues carved out, positions taken, in short *an identity established.* For countries,
like people, are not handed identities at birth, but acquire them through the arduous
process of "growing up," a process which is a notoriously painful affair. . . .

The Crisis of Legitimacy and the Role of the Charismatic Leader

A basic problem faced by all new nations and post-revolutionary societies is the crisis of
legitimacy. The old order has been abolished and with it the set of beliefs that justified
its system of authority. The imperialist ogre upon whom all ills were blamed has now
disappeared, and there has been a slackening of the great unifying force, nationalism,
under whose banner private, ethnic, sectional, and other differences were submerged.
The new system is in the process of being formed and so the questions arise: To whom
is loyalty owed? And why?

Legitimacy of any kind is derived from shared beliefs, that is, from a consensus as to what constitutes proper allegiance. Such a consensus develops slowly. In the words of Ernest Renan in a lecture in 1882: "To have done great things together in the past, to wish to do more of them, these are the essential conditions for being a people. . . . The existence of a nation is a daily plebiscite." In the early period of a nation's history, the results of this plebiscite are never a foregone conclusion.

According to [the German sociologist] Max Weber, there are basically three ways in which an authority may gain legitimacy, that is, an accepted "title to rule":

(1) It may gain legitimacy through *tradition,* through "always" having possessed it — the title held by monarchical societies is essentially of this type.

(2) *Rational-legal* authority exists when those in power are obeyed because of a popular acceptance of the appropriateness of the system of rules under which they have won and hold office.

(3) *Charismatic* authority rests upon faith in a leader who is believed to be endowed with great personal worth: this may come from God, as in the case of a religious prophet, or may simply arise from the display of extraordinary talents.

Old states possess traditional legitimacy, and this need not concern us further, beyond suggesting that new nations may sometimes be in a position to enhance their own legitimacy by incorporating the already existing legitimacy of subordinate centers or persons of authority. Thus, new nations which retain local rulers — for example dukes, counts, chiefs, clan heads, etc. — and create a larger national system of authority based on them, may be more stable than those which seek to destroy such local centers of authority. . . .

But where traditional legitimacy is absent, as it was in post-revolutionary America or France and in much of contemporary Asia and Africa, it can be developed only through reliance on legal and/or charismatic authority.

Legal domination, resting on the assumption that the created legal structure is an effective means of attaining group ends, is necessarily a weak source of authority in societies in which the law has been identified with the interests of an imperial exploiter. Charismatic authority, on the other hand, is well suited to the needs of newly developing nations. It requires neither time nor a rational set of rules, and is highly flexible. A charismatic leader plays several roles. He is first of all the symbol of the new nation, its hero who embodies in his person its values and aspirations. But more than merely symbolizing the new nation, he legitimizes the state, the new secular government, by endowing it with his "gift of grace." . . . Chrismatic authority can be seen as a mechanism of transition, an interim measure, which gets people to observe the requirements of the nation out of affection for the leader until they eventually learn to do it out of loyalty to the collectivity.

Charismatic leadership, however, because it is so personalized, is extremely unstable. The source of authority is not something distinct from the various actions and agencies of authority, so that particular dissatisfaction can easily become generalized disaffection. The charismatic leader must therefore either make open criticism impermissible or he must transcend partisan conflict by playing the role of a constitutional monarch. Even where opposition to specific policies on an individual — or informal factional — basis may be tolerated, there cannot be an Opposition to him that is organized into a formal party with its own leader. But the difference between these options can have fateful consequences for the entire nation.

The early American Republic, like many of the new nations, was legitimized by *charisma*. We tend to forget today that, in his time, George Washington was idolized as much as many of the contemporary leaders of new states. As Marcus Cunliffe, the English author of a brilliant biography of the first President, points out:

> In the well-worn phrase of Henry Lee, he was *first in war, first in peace and first in the hearts of his countrymen*. . . . He was the prime native hero, a necessary creation for a new country. . . . Hence . . . the comment . . . made by the European traveler Paul Svinin, as early as 1815: "Every American considers it his sacred duty to have a likeness of Washington in his home, just as we have the images of God's saints." For America, he was originator and vindicator, both patron saint *and* defender of the faith, in a curiously timeless fashion, as if he were Charlemagne, Saint Joan and Napoleon Bonaparte telescoped into one person. . . .

Washington's role as the charismatic leader under whose guidance democratic political institutions could grow was not an unwitting one. . . .

> With me . . . [he wrote] a predominant motive has been, to endeavor to gain time for our country to settle and mature its yet recent institutions, and to progress without interruption to that degree of strength and consistency, which is necessary to give it, humanly speaking, the command of its own fortunes.

Like latter-day leaders of new states, Washington was under pressure from those close to him actually to become an autocrat. However, he recognized that his most important contribution to the new state was to give it time to establish what we now call a rational-legal system of authority, a government of men under law. He permitted the members of his cabinet to form hostile factions under the leadership of Hamilton and Jefferson, even though he personally disliked the views of Jeffersonians. Before leaving office in 1797, he brought together Hamilton and Madison (leader of the Jeffersonians) to prepare drafts for his Farewell Address. And in the final sentence of the address he expressed the hope that his words "may be productive of some partial benefit, some occasional good; that they may now and then recur to moderate the fury of party spirit."

Washington wished to retire after one term in office, but the conflict between his two principal collaborators would not permit it. And on the urging of many, including Hamilton and Jefferson, he agreed to serve another term — thereby unwittingly permitting the further peaceful extension of party conflict while he was still President, though, of course, he bitterly regretted the emergence of such parties. This turned out to be a crucial decision, since during his second administration, the country was torn apart by opposing opinions of the French Revolution, and between pro-British and pro-French sentiments.

There seems little question that Washington was treated like a charismatic leader. But his refusal to take full advantage of his potential charisma — he withdrew from the presidency while seemingly in good health — doubtless pushed the society faster toward a legal-rational system of authority than would have been the case had he taken over the charismatic role *in toto* and identified himself with the laws and the spirit of the nation. This particular halfway type of charismatic leadership had a critical stabilizing effect on the society's evolution. Of particular importance in this regard is the fact that the first succession conflict between John Adams and Jefferson took place while Washington still held office, enabling him to set a precedent as the first head of a modern state to turn over office to a duly elected successor. If he had continued in office until his death, it is quite possible that subsequent presidential successions would not have occurred so easily. . . .

The importance of Washington's role for the institutionalization of legal-rational authority in the early United States can be summarized as follows:

1. His prestige was so great that he commanded the loyalty of the leaders of the different factions as well as the general populace. Thus, in a political entity marked by much cleavage he, in his own person, provided a basis for unity.

2. He was strongly committed to the principles of constitutional government and exercised a paternal guidance upon those involved in developing the machinery of government.

3. He stayed in power long enough to permit the crystallization of factions into embryonic parties.

4. He set a precedent as to how the problem of succession should be managed, by voluntarily retiring from office.

In most new nations the charismatic leader has tended to fulfill only the first of these tasks, acting as a symbol which represents and prolongs the feeling of unity developed prior to the achievement of independence. The neglect of the other three important aspects of Washington's role results[, according to Edward Shils,] in "charismatic personalities . . . [who do] not ordinarily build . . . the institutions which are indispensable for carrying on the life of a political society" — personalities whose disappearance raises again, as did the achievement of independence, the difficult problem of maintaining national unity among a conglomeration of groups and interests.

The Problem of National Unity

One of the problems shared by all new nations is that of creating a feeling of national unity among diverse elements. [According to Shils and James Coleman,] "The parochialism of the constituent segments of the societies of the new states has been commonly observed. The sense of membership in the nation, which is more or less coterminous with the population residing within the boundaries of the new states, is still very rudimentary and very frail." This tendency toward parochialism is common because the boundaries of new national communities are artificial, in the sense that they follow those "established by the imperial power rather than those coincident with precolonial socio-political groups." . . .

. . . A recent study . . . suggests that in order to create genuine stable new nations, "the first prerequisite is a sense of national unity, a political consensus. . . ." [Its authors] go on to urge that "the issues of national unity represent basic constitutional problems. Only as they are resolved can a society develop its policy and create the means for grappling with social and economic problems of modernization."

The problems of national unity and consensus alluded to by the various writers cited above are clearly more complex than those faced by the United States when it broke with Britain. Many African and Asian states are the home of numerous linguistic groups and tribal units, several of which have histories of bitter antagonism to each other. India has been unable to resist demands that its internal state boundaries be drawn along linguistic lines, a development which can place severe strains on its ultimate national unity. . . . Indonesia has faced the difficulty of resolving differences between the Javanese and those living in the outer islands, as well as ethnic and religious cleavages. Burma has had at least five different separatist movements struggling for autonomy or independence. . . . The various efforts to create a federated structure out of the successor states of the French African Empire . . . failed. This has been true also with respect to attempts to unite any two or more of the Arab nations. And the tragic story of the Congo presents the most extreme example of the difficulties inherent in winning the loyalty of areas and groups with diverse cultures and histories to a new political authority.

Early American history presented similar problems and reactions. True, its Western European heritage "established certain common traditions in advance, facilitating the task of harmonizing differences of language, culture, religion, and politics." Nevertheless, "throughout the colonial period, Americans had tended to assume that these differences of language, culture, and religion would prevent the growth of a common loyalty."

. . . Early America possessed social bases for political cleavage which cut across the established political units, the states. After the revolution, equalitarian pressures — albeit in different forms — grew up in most states. In many of them, demands emerged for broader voting rights and for greater representation in the legislatures of rural and western counties. These cleavages provided the basis for trans-state parties.

However, before parties based upon these cleavages could play a role in unifying portions of the polity across state lines, interest groups in the different states had to learn to see beyond the particular issues with which they were concerned. They had to recognize that they had something in common with other groups advocating different forms of equality. . . .

Above all, a political arena in which the individual rather than the state was the political unit had to be created. Nevertheless, in spite of working and fighting together in a seven-year struggle for independence, the best governmental structure which the Americans could devise was a loose federal union under the Articles of Confederation. This union lacked any national executive and, in effect, preserved most of the sovereignty and autonomy of each state.

The pressure to establish a unified central authority in contemporary new states comes mainly from the nationalist intellectual elite who are concerned with creating an important arena of effective operation through which the new nation, and they, can demonstrate competence. The main instrument for such action has been the revolutionary party.

After 1783, a national party that unified interests across state lines was approximated[, according to John P. Roche,] by

the advocates of central authority, who set up the plans for a convention on federal authority, to be held in Philadelphia. . . . A small group of political leaders with a Continental vision and essentially a consciousness of the United States' *international* impotence, provided the matrix of the movement. . . . Indeed, an argument with great force — particularly since Washington was its incarnation — urged that our very survival in the Hobbesian jungle of world politics depended upon a reordering and strengthening of our national sovereignty.

Many of those who served as delegates in what became the Constitutional Convention had served in the Revolutionary Continental Congress. This experience [, say historians Stanley Elkins and Eric McKitrick,] "left a deep imprint on those connected with it . . . [since it had been] a continental war effort. If there is any one feature that most unites the future leading supporters of the Constitution, it was their close engagement with this continental aspect of the Revolution. . . . All of them had . . . formed commitments, which dissolved provincial boundaries; they had come to full public maturity in a setting which enabled ambition, public service, leadership, and self-fulfillment to be conceived for each in his way, with a grandeur of scope unknown to any previous generation."

John P. Roche has argued that there was no ideological rift within the Constitutional Convention because almost all the delegates belonged to the central government party. He suggests that the differences of opinion which did emerge were specific or tactical rather than ideological. That is, there was no conflict between "nationalists" versus "states-rightists" but rather an argument over representation, the small states versus the big states. "The Virginia Plan[, which] envisioned a unitary national government effectively freed from and dominant over the states[,] . . . may . . . be considered, in ideological terms, as the delegates' Utopia. . . ." However, "the delegates from the small states . . . [a]pparently realizing that under the Virginia Plan, Massachusetts, Virginia and Pennsylvania could virtually dominate the national government — and probably appreciating that to sell this program to the 'folks back home' would be impossible . . . dug in their heels and demanded time for a consideration of alternatives. [There followed a series of compromises on the issue of equal versus proportional representation in Congress.] . . . The result was a Constitution which the people, in fact, by democratic processes, did accept, and a new and far better national government was established."

The energy behind the "nationalistic" aims of the Constitutional Convention came from leaders of a young generation whose careers, having been launched in the continental war effort of the Revolution, depended upon the survival of a nationalistic outlook. In age and aspiration, they resembled the leadership of many contemporary new states. On the other hand, those opposed to a strong central American government, who had little if any representation at the Constitutional Convention, came from an older generation whose careers were not only state-centered but had been formed prior to the Revolution. . . .

In this respect, the difference between the anti-Federalists and the "Continental" Federalists is suggestive of [Thomas] Hodgkins's classification of the structure of African parties into primitive and modern:

> Parties of the former type [primitive] are dominated by "personalities," who enjoy a superior social status, either as traditional rulers or members of ruling families, or as belonging to the higher ranks of the urban, professional elite (lawyers, doctors, etc.). . . . Their political machinery, central and local, is of a rudimentary kind. . . . They have little, if anything, in the way of a secretariat of full-time officials. . . . They depend for popular support less upon organization and propaganda than on habits of respect for traditional authority, or wealth and reputation. . . .
>
> Parties of the second type [modern] aim at . . . a much more elaborate structure. Since their chief claim and function is to represent the mass, they are committed to a form of organization that is (certainly on paper and to some extent in practice) highly democratic. . . . [T]he "mass" party . . . depends for its strength not on the backing of traditional authority but upon propaganda, designed to appeal particularly to the imagination of the young, to women, to the semi-urbanized and discontented; to those who are outside the local hierarchies, and interested in reform and change.

Early America differed from the nations in Africa in that there did not anywhere exist "modern" parties which a political leader could take as a model. These emerged as a result of needs in the American situation — some of which, however, parallel those which stimulate "modern" party organization in Africa and Asia today.

The continental "caucus" at the Constitutional Convention did not represent a full transition to a modern political party. Such a transition implies the growth of an organization that is rationally oriented toward vote-getting. It also implies that this organization is connected to a social base with common ideological interests. In contrast, the struggle for ratification was particular to each state. In some the upper classes were for it while in others they were against it, according to the peculiarities of politics in each. The "Constitutionalists" relied on old political techniques, including the manipulation of notables, cliques, and coteries to get ratification through.

However, insofar as the transition to modern parties implies the rational calculation of what policies are necessary to get votes, the Constitutional Convention did mark a step in this direction. First, it created an organ in which policies touching on the interests of persons in all of the states were to be debated. Secondly, it marked a movement away from the politics of notables and coteries who were deeply tied to the old political structure of state supremacy. By establishing the principle of rationally calculating how to marshal public support for national policy, it opened the door for policies that addressed themselves directly to specific interest groups in all states. It was only a step further for Hamilton to create a coherent fiscal program designed to mobilize interests on behalf of national power and economic development. His attempts to manage politics in the capital to get his plans through Congress then[, says historian William Chambers,] "brought strong responses across the country. In the process, what began as a *capital* faction soon assumed status as a *national* faction and then, finally, as the new *Federalist* party."

The Federalist party organization could be described as parallel to those patron parties in Africa that are national but which represent a linking of local notables rather than an organization designed to mobilize the common people. The first "modern" party, in the sense that there was a "coordination in activity between leaders at the capital, and leaders, actives and popular followings in the states, counties, and towns," was to come with the crystallization of the Jeffersonian Democratic-Republican party. . . .

The Democratic-Republicans developed party organizations for some of the same reasons that leaders develop such organizations in Africa today. They were opposed to the established authorities whose policies largely dominated public affairs through the Federalist organization. When the Jay treaty caused popular indignation, and provoked concern on the part of some merchants that the British would not pay their war debts, the Republicans took advantage of this disaffection to organize an opposition based on popular support. They appealed to social categories that cut across existing political boundaries, just as the African mass-based parties do. In so doing, the Democratic-Republican party served as a means of uniting the citizens of the several states in national citizenship by mobilizing their common interests in the national arena.

However . . . the evolution of national political parties could not erase differences in regional interests. Nor did the ratification of the Constitution serve to legitimate the new governmental structure, even though it provided a basis for national unity. Only with time, and after many attempts to thwart its powers, was the federal government finally able to achieve a high degree of political legitimacy. . . . Almost every state and every major political faction and interest group attempted, at one time or other between 1790 and 1860, to weaken the power of the national government or to break up the Union directly.

There were many threats to secede in the first decade of national existence, and the threats came from both northern and southern states. In 1798 two future presidents, Jefferson and Madison, sought the passage by a state legislature of nullification ordinances which proclaimed the right of each state to decide the extent of national authority to be tolerated within its boundaries. After leaving national office in 1801, various Federalist leaders sought in 1804, 1808, and 1812 to take the New England or northern states out of the Union.

Later, when the slavery issue became important, both abolitionists and defenders of slavery talked of destroying the Constitution and the Union. The activities of the Southerners are, of course, well known, but it is often forgotten that in the early period of the controversy, when the abolitionists despaired of eliminating slavery because of constitutional guarantees, the Constitution was described by some as a "slave-holders'" document and called . . . "a covenant with death and an agreement with hell."

Thus, in the early United States, as in contemporary new states, the achievement of national unity, and of respect for a national authority, was no easy task.

The possibility of secession remains one of the basic problems facing many new states in our century. Their unity immediately after gaining independence[, according to Harry Benda,] "is largely explained by the negative, anti-Western, anti-colonial content of non-Western nationalism. One need not be a prophet of doom to anticipate that this negative unity may in time, and perhaps before long, weaken, and that the newly independent non–Western nation-states may then find themselves confronted by some of the dissensions and antagonisms which nationalist aspirations have so often brought in their wake elsewhere."

OPPOSITION RIGHTS AND THE ESTABLISHMENT OF NEW POLITIES

The issues involved in the emergence of legitimate national authority and a sense of national unity, and those which pertain to the establishment of democratic procedures, are . . . separate problems — although they are sometimes confused in discussing the politics of new nations. Democracy may be conceived of as a system of institutionalized opposition in which the people choose among alternative contenders for public office. To create a stable, representative, decision-making process that provides a legitimate place for opposition, that recognizes the rights of those without power to advocate "error" and the overthrow of those in office, is extremely difficult in any polity. It is particularly problematic in new states which must be concerned also with the sheer problem of the survival of national authority itself.

In a . . . Ghanese White Paper [1962] seeking to justify legislation and police actions which involved restrictions upon (and actual imprisonment of) opposition politicians, the Ghana government suggested that these actions were necessary because of plots, saboteurs, subversion, and threats of foreign intervention. The White Paper argues that "the strains experienced by an emergent country immediately after independence are certainly as great as, if not greater than, the strains experienced by a developed country in wartime." According to [President] Nkrumah, a new state "is still weakly expressed as a national unity," and its frail structure must be protected by "identifying the emergent nation with the party," that is, by denying the possibility of a legitimate opposition, since the latter would endanger the stability of the nation. . . .

The early history of the United States reveals many of the same problems — and the resulting pressures to eliminate democratic rights — as do those of contemporary new states. During Washington's first administration, all important differences of opinion could be expressed within the government, since both Jefferson and Hamilton, the leaders of what were to become the two major parties, were the most influential members of the Cabinet. After Jefferson's withdrawal, at the end of Washington's first term, and the subsequent formation of an opposition party around 1797 the restraints on the tactics of both sides weakened greatly. . . .

Hamilton, the political genius behind the first incumbents, organized the first party to insure popular support for governmental policies. It was a "government party" on a national scale, as opposed to the previous state politicking. It was[, according to William Chambers,] "a party of stability, dedicated to the idea that the first imperative for government in a new nation was that it must govern and sustain itself." As such, the legitimate existence of organized opposition to it was contrary to its conception.

Opposition to its policies did not arise initially as a party matter but as individual protests both on the popular level and within the political elite. Opposition gradually crystallized, however, into a political movement around the leadership of Madison and Jefferson. Its adherents were maintaining "in effect, that the new polity should also [in addition to maintaining its stability] provide room for counteraction, for effective representation of interests and opinions that were slighted or discountenanced in the government party."

> [T]he emerging Republicans were "going to the people" in a virtually unprecedented attempt not only to represent popular interests and concerns, but to monopolize popular opposition to those who held power. If they had their way, if their appeal to planters, farmers, and "mechanics" was broadened sufficiently to succeed, it would end by displacing the Federalists in power and substituting a new set of governors.

The Federalists[, according to Marshall Smelser,] viewed such organized opposition in much the same light as many leaders of the contemporary new states view their rivals:

> [T]he Federalists took an intolerant position regarding the opposition party, which seemed to be a race of marplots characterized by excessive ambition, unwholesome partisanship and a dangerous reliance upon the judgment of the voters. At best the Republicans often seemed governed by obstinacy, envy, malice or ambition. At worst they were seditious and treasonable. Federalist private correspondence was peppered with references to Republican disloyalty, insincerity, intrigue and demagoguery. . . . The conclusion almost forced upon the reader of these and hundreds more of Federalist condemnations is that the *two-party system is immoral. . . . It became almost normal to consider opposition as seditious and, in extraordinary cases, as treasonable.*

The strains endemic in the establishment of a new structure of authority were increased by the fact that the nation and the embryonic parties were divided in their sympathies for the two major contestants in the European war, Revolutionary France and Great Britain. Each side was convinced that the other had secret intentions to take the country into war in support of its favorite. The French terror was a particular evil to the Federalists, and they, like conservatives in other countries, were persuaded that French agents were conspiring with sympathetic Americans to overthrow the government here. The Federalists were therefore opposed to any form of organized opposition. They were much more violent in their denunciations of the treasonable activities of the Republicans than were the Jeffersonians in return. And given the tremendous moral indignation which characterized Federalist private opinions, it is not surprising that they attempted to repress their opponents. The Alien and Sedition Acts passed in 1798 gave the President "the power to order out of the country any alien whom he thought dangerous to the public peace or whom he had reasonable grounds to suspect of plotting against the government" and left such aliens without recourse to the courts. The Sedition Act "was intended to deal with citizens or aliens who too severely criticized the government. . . . In its final form it was made a high misdemeanor 'unlawfully to combine and conspire' in order to oppose the legal measures of the government . . . ,

An example of factionalism in the early republic: Congressman Matthew Lyon of Vermont was sentenced to ten months' imprisonment under the Sedition Act of 1798 for publishing an attack on President John Adams. This cartoon shows Lyon (with tongs) fighting with a Federalist congressman who had insulted him. (Library of Congress.)

[t]o publish a false or malicious writing against the government of the United States, the President, or Congress with the purpose of stirring up hatred or resistance against them. . . ."

That the law was designed for partisan purposes was obvious. All those arrested and convicted under it were Republicans. Basically, Federalist officials and Federalist juries enforced the law against their political opponents. These efforts to undermine democratic rights gave Jefferson and Madison a major issue, which historians believe played an important role in defeating the Federalists in 1800.

Once defeated for the Presidency in 1800, the Federalists never were able to regain office on a national scale and virtually disappeared after 1814. The causes for the downfall of the Federalists are complex, and cannot be detailed here. However, one reason was undoubtedly their unwillingness or inability to learn how to perform as an opposition party in an egalitarian democracy. Some historians suggest that they failed basically because, as men convinced of their "natural" right to rule, they did not believe in parties which appealed to the people.

The civil liberties record of the Jeffersonians, in office, is a better one than that of the Federalists. How much of this may be explained on the assumption that they believed more firmly in the virtues of democracy than their opponents, it is difficult to say. Certainly their years of opposition had led them to make many statements in favor of democratic rights, but oppositionists in other lands have forgotten such programs once in power and faced with "unscrupulous criticism." Perhaps more important is the fact that the Democratic-Republicans did believe in states' rights and did oppose using federal courts to try common-law crimes. Also, the federal judiciary remained for some time in the hands of Federalist judges, who presumably were loath to permit convictions of their political sympathizers for expression of belief. Finally, there was a difference in the nature of the opposition. The Federalists were fighting a growing party that could realistically hope for eventual victory; the Democratic-Republicans, when in office, were opposed by a rapidly declining party, whose very lack of faith in extending the scope of the democratic process was to undermine any chance it had of returning to office. Since the Federalists were committing political suicide, there was no need for the administration to find means to repress them. . . .

Yet it should be noted that on the level of state government, Democratic-Republicans did use their power to crack down on Federalist opinion. [According to historian John C. Miller,] "Jefferson was no advocate of a 'licentious' press; like Hamilton and Adams, he believed that the press ought to be restrained 'within the legal and wholesome limits of truth.' He differed from the Federalists chiefly in insisting that this restraint be imposed by the states rather than by the Federal government. . . ."

Where the Federalists controlled a state government, as in the case of Connecticut, and hence prevented the application of the Democratic doctrine that seditious libel was a state offense, Jefferson was not averse to inaugurating prosecutions in the federal courts. In 1806, six indictments were drawn against four Connecticut Federalist editors and two ministers on the charge of seditious libel on the President. The ministers were charged with committing the libel *in sermons.*

Leonard Levy concludes his survey of freedom of speech and press in early American history by arguing that the Democrats, like the Federalists, did not believe in these freedoms when confronted with serious opposition. Each was prepared to use principled libertarian arguments when his "ox was being gored." . . .

The various efforts by both Federalists and Democratic-Republicans to repress the rights of their opponents clearly indicate that in many ways our early political officials resembled those heads of new states in the twentieth century who view criticism of themselves as tantamount to an attack on the nation itself. Such behavior characterizes leaders of polities in which the concept of democratic succession to office has not been institutionalized. . . . [N]ational officers who hold effective power for life often interpret criticism as libelous and treasonable. To accept criticism as proper requires the prior acceptance of the view that opposition and succession are normal, and that men may be loyal to the polity and yet disapprove of the particular set of incumbents. This view does not come easily to men who have themselves created a polity, and cannot, therefore, conceive of it functioning properly without them or in ways other than they think best.

Yet, though the behavior of members of both early American parties indicate that they, too, reacted to criticism as being damaging to the nation, it must also be recognized that both parties permitted a great deal of opposition, much more than is tolerated in most of the new states of Asia and Africa. In some part, this may reflect the fact that much as they disagreed, the heads of both groups had worked together to make the

Revolution and establish the Constitution. They had known and trusted each other for some decades. In a real sense, the United States began with a small, highly educated political elite, the members of which recognized each other as belonging to the ruling club. Both Adams and Hamilton demonstrated this when, on different occasions, each put adherence to the rules of the game ahead of party advantage or personal feelings. The defeat of the Federalists in the elections of 1800 represented *the first occasion in modern politics in which an incumbent political party suffered an electoral defeat and simply turned over power to its opponents.* This acceptance of the rules of the electoral game has not occurred in many new states.

The decline of the Federalists after 1800 meant that the United States did not experience a real succession problem again until 1829, with the inauguration of Andrew Jackson. The Virginia Dynasty of Jefferson, Madison, and Monroe governed the country for twenty-four years, each President succeeding the other without real difficulty. From 1809, when Madison took over from Jefferson, to 1829, when John Quincy Adams was succeeded by Jackson, each President was followed in office by his chief cabinet officer, the Secretary of State. And a national two-party system did not emerge anew until the 1830's, when Jackson's opponents united in the Whig party.

In effect, the country was dominated on the national level for close to three decades by a loosely structured one-party system. Although the analogy may appear far-fetched, in a certain sense the political system resembled that which has grown up in recent decades in Mexico, and perhaps in some other underdeveloped countries. Interest groups and sectional concerns led to serious divisions within the country — over the purchase of Louisiana, relations with the warring powers of Europe, the War of 1812, and the Missouri compromise of 1819 over slavery. Any of these issues could have resulted in the dissolution of effective national authority. However, all of them were resolved, not so much at the ballot box as by negotiations conducted under the authority of the three great Virginians — men who carried with them the prestige stemming from their role in founding the nation, and from their leadership of the all-powerful Democratic-Republican party. On the national level, conservatives and radicals all came to belong to the same party, formally at least, and gave formal allegiance on the same liberal doctrines and leaders.

Thomas Jefferson had anticipated the complete triumph of his party following the electoral defeat of Federalism, and looked forward to political divisions among those who believed in the "correct," that is, Republican, principles. And presumably so long as all effective participants in politics were on the "good" side, the temptation to repress criticism within the party would be less:

> I had always expected that when the Republicans should have put all things under their feet, they would schismatize among themselves. I always expected, too, that whatever names the parties might bear, the real division would be into moderate and ardent republicanism. *In this division there is no great danger.* . . . It is to be considered as apostasy only when they purchase the vote of federalists, with a participation in honor and power.

The almost unchallenged rule of the Virginia Dynasty and the Democratic-Republican Party served to legitimate national authority and democratic rights. By the time the nation divided again into two broad warring factions which appealed for mass support, the country had existed for forty years, the Constitution had been glorified, and the authority of the courts had been accepted as definitive. . . .

CONCLUSION

All states that have recently gained independence are faced with two interrelated problems, legitimating the use of political power and establishing national identity. And if it is a democratic polity they seek to establish, they must develop . . . constraints upon efforts to inhibit organized opposition or to deny civil liberties to individual critics of those in power.

This [essay] has explored ways in which these problems were confronted in the early history of the United States. National identity was formed under the aegis, first of a charismatic authority figure, and later under the leadership of a dominant "left wing" or revolutionary party led successively by three Founding Fathers. The pressures in new nations to outlaw opposition movements were reduced in America by the rapid decline of the conservative opposition. The revolutionary, democratic values that thus became part of the national self-image, and the basis for its authority structure, gained legitimacy as they proved effective — that is, as the nation prospered. . . .

In specifying those processes in the evolution of the first new nation that are comparable to what has been taking place in the societies of Asia and Africa in our own time, I am relying upon analogy. It ought to go without saying that[, as Karl Deutsch writes]: "We cannot assume that because conditions in one century led to certain effects, even roughly parallel conditions in another century would lead to similar effects. Neither can we be sure, of course, that the conditions were even roughly parallel." It is fairly obvious that conditions in the early United States were quite different from those faced by most of the new nations of today. Many of the internal conditions that hamper the evolution of stable authority and a unifying sense of national identity in the new nations of the twentieth century were much less acute in the early United States. But the evidence suggests that despite its advantages, the United States came very close to failing in its effort to establish a unified legitimate authority. The first attempt to do so in 1783, following on Independence, was a failure. The second and successful effort was endangered by frequent threats of secession and the open flaunting of central authority until the Civil War. The advantages which the early United States possessed, as compared with most of the contemporary new states, then, only show more strongly how significant the similarities are.

There were other American advantages that should be mentioned. . . . The absence of rapid mass communication systems meant that Americans were relatively isolated, and hence did not immediately compare their conditions with those in the more developed countries. The United States did not so urgently face a "revolution of rising expectations" based on the knowledge that life is much better elsewhere. The accepted concepts of natural or appropriate rights did not include a justification of the lower classes' organized participation in the polity to gain higher income, welfare support from the state, and the like. And whatever the exaggeration in the effects frequently attributed to the existence of an open land frontier, there can be little doubt that it contributed to social stability.

Internal value cleavages, which frustrate contemporary new nations, were comparatively less significant in young America. [Edward] Shils points out that in today's new nations "the parochialism of kinship, caste and locality makes it difficult to create stable and coherent nation-wide parties." None of these parochialisms was as strong in the United States, which was formed by a relatively homogeneous population with a common language, a relatively similar religious background (although denominational differences did cause some problems), and a common cultural and political tradition.

American social structure did not possess those great "gaps" which [according to Shils] in the contemporary new states "conspire to separate the ordinary people from their government." The culture with which the educated identified contrasted less strongly with that of the uneducated. The ideology in the name of which America made its revolution was less alien to prevailing modes of thought than some of today's revolutionary creeds. Perhaps most important, the class structure of America, even before the establishment of the new nation, came closer to meeting the conditions for a stable democracy than do those of the new nations of our time — or, indeed, than those of the Old World at that time. . . .

In this respect, the political traditions that the American colonists held in common were of particular importance since they included the concept of the rule of law, and even of constitutionalism. Each colony operated under a charter which defined and limited governmental powers. Although colonial subjects, Americans were also Englishmen and were thus accustomed to the rights and privileges of Englishmen. Through their local governments they actually possessed more rights than did most of the residents of Britain itself. In a sense, even before independence, Americans met a basic condition for democratic government, the ability to operate its fundamental institutions.

QUESTIONS TO CONSIDER

1. Why did early Americans idolize George Washington? What popular or political needs did tributes to him address? In what way did Washington embody the transition from "charismatic" to "rational-legal" authority in the new republic?

2. In what sense were the Founders a "nationalist elite"? According to Lipset, who won the struggle between "nationalists" and "states-rightists" over shaping the federal Constitution of 1787? How did the nationalist "caucus" open the way for modern political parties? How did the Democratic-Republicans develop the first "modern" party?

3. In what ways did the reigning Federalist Party of the 1790s restrict the rights of its opponents? How did the Democratic-Republicans' position on civil rights compare with that of their Federalist predecessors? On what basis does Lipset claim that America's national government was dominated for three decades by "a loosely structured one-party system"? Why were opposition rights greater in the early United States than in most twentieth-century new states in Asia and Africa?

4. Lipset notes that achieving national unity is a separate problem from establishing democratic procedures. To what extent was there "negative unity" (that is, unity based upon opposition to foreign control or threats) in the early United States? Why were there so many threats by northern and southern states to secede? Why did the democratic process fail to prevent the Civil War?

5. What features of early American national history does Lipset's analogy with modern "new nations" illuminate, and how? What advantages did the young United States enjoy over today's emerging new nations? How did these advantages help to secure democratic institutions? Why did they fail to prevent our early national history from being so full of conflict? Should we expect new nations *without* a tradition of popular rule to establish democratic political institutions?

What Made American Nationalism Different?

Peter J. Parish

"What is a Nation?" the French scholar Ernest Renan asked in a celebrated lecture of 1882. It is a bond of destiny between people, he concluded, cemented especially by "the possession of a rich heritage of memories." A nation not only "implies a past," Renan asserted; it also is "the fruit of a long past spent in toil, sacrifice, and devotion." Most nineteenth-century statesmen and philosophers agreed that ancestral ties and a common history were essential ingredients of a viable nationalism. The problem was that the United States, just a teenager in 1800, had precious little of these. With the exception of Native Americans, its people had recently come from some other place. They had coalesced from various nationalities and ethnic groups, and they had no long past in common to celebrate. If such inheritances were the glue of collective life, what sort of national identity could American citizens share?

Unlike Renan, today's scholars tend to view nationalism less as an accretion of history than as something humans have invented. In modern times nations have constructed group identity by building a powerful central government, then using the army, schools, and printing presses to woo — and sometimes coerce — citizens' allegiance. According to this view, strong governments have been necessary and state religions useful to detach individuals' loyalties from their region or ethnic group and claim them for God and country.

Both of these theories of nationalism, says historian Peter J. Parish, are based on European models, and both fail to appreciate what made American nationalism distinctive. In two crucial ways, Parish contends, American nationalism calls into question the formulas that scholars have used to discuss national allegiance and cohesion. First, when measured against modern theories, the development of American nationalism followed an unusual chronology. Americans built a constitutional structure before they developed a common peoplehood; they extended voting rights and popular literacy before centralizing their government. Thus, they reversed the sequence that modern scholars have found elsewhere, turning the effects of nationalism into its causes.

Second, contrary to Renan and other nineteenth-century nationalist spokesmen, Americans managed quite well to find alternatives to the long history and the ethnic and religious ties they lacked. In short order their writers and artists conjured up a glorious past for the American public, stocking it with heroes such as Washington and Lincoln and mythologizing memorable events from the Pilgrims' landing to the crossing of the Delaware. Their orators built national identity around virtuous America's contrast with the corrupt and decaying Old World and its anticipation of a glorious future. Instead of a national church, Americans promoted religion through competition between churches, and they successfully blended Christianity and patriotism in presidential speeches and the Pledge of Allegiance. Above all, says Parish, Americans developed a concept of "voluntaristic nationalism" that made their allegiance especially compelling. Instead of being united by blood or residence, Americans subscribed to a loose set of democratic principles and practices. This American creed — which Parish never defines, perhaps appropriately — was open and flexible enough for immigrants to endorse, for citizens to expand the boundaries of who was included, and for debate to continue over the nature of the American "experiment." In sum, neither inherited nor imposed, American nationalism was freely chosen and thus unusually resilient.

Parish's careful and even elegant presentation places American nationalism in the larger context of nation-building in European and world history. If it is true, as he writes, that political theorists of nationalism have ignored the United States, it is equally true that American historians have often taken American nationalism for granted or else made unexamined or exaggerated claims for its uniqueness. Parish's analysis makes a measured and specific case for Americans' distinctive brand of nationalism. It has the added virtue of helping to explain paradoxical beliefs that have puzzled foreign observers of Americans, such as the way they combine fierce individualism with national pride, or strong patriotism with seemingly vague national ideals.

Still, when digesting Parish's insights or catching his enthusiasm for American nationalism, we may overlook admissions that damage his case. How does his praise for the ethnic inclusiveness of American nationality square with nineteenth-century Americans' history of enslaving African Americans, organizing movements against immigrants, and excluding nonwhites from citizenship? Why did it take a horrific civil war, which forced southern states to return to a Union that was supposed to be voluntary, to finally cement American nationhood? Does it weaken Parish's claim for American uniqueness to acknowledge that centralized government and military coercion finally united Americans in the 1860s? Perhaps American nationalism was not so different after all.

Note that while Parish addresses social scientists' theories of nationalism, he does not offer any new model of nationalism that can join the American example with others. Like most (but not all) comparative historians, Parish uses theories from the social sciences to illuminate specific cases rather than to formulate general laws or improve explanatory models. As you read Parish's essay and review the previous essay by Seymour Martin Lipset (Selection 11), consider how effectively this disciplinary relationship, where social scientists use history to build models and historians use the models to examine particular cases, advances our understanding of the past.

GLOSSARY

ANTEBELLUM PERIOD   The three decades before the Civil War; that is, from 1830 to 1860.

DRED SCOTT DECISION   The Supreme Court decision, *Dred Scott* v. *Sandford* (1857), that declared blacks ineligible for citizenship and Congress powerless to prevent the extension of slavery into American territories. This decision's restriction of citizenship was reversed by the Fourteenth Amendment (1868), which granted citizenship to all persons born or naturalized in the United States.

ESTABLISHED CHURCH   A church recognized by law as the official church of a state or nation. The U.S. Constitution recognized no national church. Although some states, such as Massachusetts, had established churches, all separated church and state by 1833.

ETHNIC HOMOGENEITY   A situation where the entire population is composed of members of the same or similar ethnic groups.

EUROCENTRIC   Using Europe as a central frame of reference or standard for assessing other places.

MEXICAN WAR (1846–1848)   A war between the United States and Mexico as a result of which the United States acquired California and the territories of the Southwest. (See Selection 16.)

NATIVISM   Opposition to immigrants or immigration.

POLITY   A society with an organized government or constitution.

POSTMILLENNIAL   Optimistically anticipating a thousand-year kingdom of heaven on earth according to biblical prophesy. Nineteenth-century Protestants often combined this belief with the notion of America's mission or destiny.

★ ★ ★ ★ ★ ★ ★

When and how did the United States become a nation? What kind of nation did it become? The American example has always presented a problem to those who have examined the phenomenon of nationalism in the modern world. Too often they have responded by averting their gaze from the American experience and concentrating on European or third world examples. It would seem that the historical evolution of American nationalism does not fit neatly into any of the patterns or models presented by the theoreticians and generalizers on the subject. Yet the United States is surely far too important to be ignored by those who seek to understand the role of nations and nationalism in the making of the world as we know it. The question remains: what did American nationalism have in common with nationalism elsewhere, and where did it differ?

American nationalism in the nineteenth century had several conspicuous — and perhaps distinctive — characteristics. Can they be accommodated within any of the currently available theories of nationalism? In particular, the relationship of American

From Peter J. Parish, "An Exception to Most of the Rules: What Made American Nationalism Different in the Mid-Nineteenth Century?" *Prologue* 27 (Fall 1995): 219–229. Reprinted by permission.

nationalism to Benedict Anderson's concept of the nation as an "imagined community" deserves closer examination. As Anderson sees it, the nation is an imagined political community in the sense that, although even in a small nation no individual can know all his fellow nationals, each person still feels a sense of community with them. Education, literacy, mobility, modern technology and communications, and political democracy all combine to stimulate a sense of simultaneity — an awareness of thousands or millions of others leading lives simultaneously with one's own as citizens of the same nation.

The search for what is distinctive in American nationalism may be conducted in two stages. First, there are certain matters of chronology, which challenge the European nationalist model. These refer to the development in the United States earlier than elsewhere — or in a sequence different from elsewhere — of a number of circumstances and conditions conducive to the growth of an imagined national community. Second, there is the process by which Americans found ways of overcoming the absence, or the short supply, of many of the conventional raw materials of nation-building.

In the matter of chronology, a crucial formative influence in the American experience was the establishment of a political framework, with the potential to become a national framework, even before a vigorous national self-consciousness had developed. In the making of the American nation, the winning of independence and the framing of the Constitution were the beginning, and not the end, of the story. According to John Murrin, "Americans had erected their constitutional roof before they put up the national walls." There was a world of difference between Union and nation, and the one did not inevitably lead to the other. Thirty years ago, Daniel Boorstin described the newly independent United States as "little more than a point of departure. The nation would long profit from having been born without ever having been conceived."

Liah Greenfeld comments that, after independence, it was a matter for debate whether a single nation or several nations would be best suited to American needs and an American identity. "Americans," she says, "held some things to be self-evident, but the Union was not among them." The Union was an experiment — and often a fragile one at that. Kenneth Stampp has reminded us of the slow evolution over half a century and more of the idea of a perpetual union. Carl Degler has described the Union as "more a means to achieve nationhood than a nation itself." Even by 1860, he claims, only a truncated nationalism existed among Americans. "The Civil War," he concludes, "was not a struggle to save a failed Union, but to create a nation that until then had not come into being."

In other words, whereas there are many examples of a national movement seeking to achieve the status of a separate polity, the order of things was reversed in the American experience. From the outset, the United States had a political structure with the potential — no more than that — for nationhood but took several decades to evolve a full national self-consciousness: that is to say, to become in the full sense an imagined national community. In one of his rare lighter moments, Ernest Gellner presses the argument that every vigorous culture seeks a political infrastructure to support and define it. He paraphrases the character in the novel *No Orchids for Miss Blandish*, who observes that every girl ought to have a husband, preferably her own; every culture, he says, wants a state, preferably its own. But he ignores the example of the United States in its formative years, when it had a political framework but needed time to evolve a fully fledged national culture of its own. One might be tempted to reverse the old cliché about Italian unification: "We have made Italy; now we must make Italians." In the case of the United States, it was more a matter of saying: "We have made Americans; now we must make America."

Other instances where developments in the United States were ahead of events elsewhere — or where the chronology was simply different — are quite familiar. The achievement of something like universal white manhood suffrage by . . . 1830 is one such example. The right to vote may have been one of the best available indexes of citizenship in the antebellum United States. Most authorities, including Anderson, see a relationship between modern nationalism and political democracy but often fail to note the peculiar importance of the American example. Writing of the transformation of nationalism in the period after 1870, Eric Hobsbawm identifies the spread of political democracy and mass politics as one key factor, without pausing even to acknowledge that this development was well advanced in the United States half a century earlier.

Similarly, most recent work has emphasized the combined effects of the spread of literacy, broader access to education, and advances in communication (especially in print technology) in promoting national sentiment and commitment — above all in promoting the imagined community on the Anderson model in which citizens are aware of the simultaneous existence of millions of fellow nationals whom they will never meet. However, few writers have drawn attention to the lead that the United States enjoyed in all these areas — and which was all the more important in an imagined community covering a vast geographical area. It can hardly be disputed that the United States was the most literate society, with the most widespread popular education, in the mid-nineteenth-century world. Americans were the champion newspaper readers and the champion letter-writers of the nineteenth century. Benedict Anderson has depicted the newspaper as the concept of simultaneity laid out in parallel columns of print; he could have added (but did not) that this was nowhere more true than in the United States in the nineteenth century.

For both newspapers and letter-writers, the mail service was crucial to the making of an imagined American community. It is an illuminating comment on the strictly limited scale and functions of the federal government that its civilian employees numbered only 36,700 on the eve of the Civil War. But even more remarkably, of those 36,700, some 30,000 were local postmasters. At first sight this might seem a strange order of priorities, but in the context of nation-building, it made a good deal of sense. Gerald Linderman has noted that, during the Civil War, some forty thousand letters a day passed through Washington from soldiers to family and friends, and a similar number in the opposite direction. In the roster of builders of the American national community, schoolteachers and newspaper editors, letter-writers and postmasters, deserve a very high place indeed.

There is a common feature linking the early arrival of political democracy (however flawed) and developments in literacy, education, and communication — and also rapid economic growth, a high degree of mobility, a high material standard of living for the majority, and the expectation of continuing expansion. The common feature lies in something that was absent. None of these things was directed or dictated by a powerful central authority. In other words, the growth of nationalism was not accompanied by rapid centralization, although some authorities, notably Gellner, identify such centralization as one of the key features of nation-making. Indeed, Gellner goes so far as to argue that the crucial power and function of the modern national state is its centralized control over education — over a particular kind of education at that, which will equip citizens with the basic skills that their national community needs. Here the United States is clearly an exception to the rule. Popular education was essential to both its democracy and its sense of nationhood, but that education was not controlled and directed from the center. In a striking phrase, Gellner asserts that "at the base of the modern social order stands not the executioner but the professor." (Such an observation may come as something of a surprise to members of the professoriat today, whether in the United States or elsewhere.)

The phenomenon of nationalism without centralization may have a broader significance. It may suggest that, in the nineteenth century, the federal system enshrined in the Constitution was more than just a stepping stone on the way to building a national community. It served also as a political metaphor or analogy for the concept of simultaneity that is so important to Anderson's nation as imagined community — and a political device that made it workable and meaningful for a population scattered over hitherto unimaginable distances. In a paraphrase of Anderson's comment on the role of newspapers, one might say that federalism, with a limited central government operating alongside thirteen or twenty or thirty state governments, was the concept of simultaneity laid out in parallel lines of political authority.

So much for examples of how the United States was ahead of the game in the evolution of modern nationalism. If this were the whole story, one would be left to wonder why, as Degler and others have indicated, the process of making the nation lasted at least until 1865 and was finally achieved at such cost. But there is another side to the coin. It is almost a truism to observe that, in the first century of its history, the United States lacked many of the building-blocks of nation-making that were commonly available, and relied upon, elsewhere.

The catalog of what was missing or in short supply in the American context is long and varied. It includes such matters as the lack of a long history going back into the mists of antiquity; the lack of a separate American language or literary and cultural tradition; the lack of an established church or a state religion; the lack of a powerful central government; the absence of a strong and menacing neighbor; and the absence of the kind of ethnic homogeneity that was at the core of many European nationalisms. Separately and cumulatively, these would seem to have been severe brakes on the growth of any real or imagined national community, and there is no need to belabor the point. (However, they may also reflect an essentially Eurocentric view of what makes a nation.) What is much more interesting and revealing is the way in which Americans sought, often successfully, to compensate for these inbuilt handicaps — or indeed, to turn them to advantage. It was a protracted, and sometimes painful, process.

Compensation for the lack of an ancient history, and of the mythology that often arises from it, came in two main forms. First, the more recent past — and often the very recent past — was invoked to take the place of a more distant antiquity. Glorification of the Revolutionary heroes is the most obvious example — and it was annually rehearsed in thousands of Fourth of July ceremonies. George Washington was scarcely cold in his grave before the process of converting him into a marble monument began. Thomas Jefferson

*This historical allegory, painted by an unknown folk artist after Washington's
death in 1799, illustrates the new nation's hunger for symbols of its own: the
pine tree, the liberty pole and cap, the flag, the bald eagle, and Liberty herself
trampling the crown of tyranny and adorning the Father of His Country
with a simple wreath of laurel. (New York State Historical Association,
Cooperstown, N.Y.)*

became the guiding spirit of American democracy, but Americans had to wait eighty years for the martyrdom of Abraham Lincoln to complete their secular trinity of household gods. The other strategy for overcoming the lack of a long history was to focus attention upon the national future — for example, upon the fulfillment of the national destiny in the west. The strong postmillennial emphasis in American Protestantism gave an extra dimension to the concept of the missionary nation, or the nation with a God-given destiny, or indeed of a particular nation as exemplar or model or standard-bearer, which others would choose to follow.

Again, because of its lack of powerful and threatening neighbors, the nineteenth-century United States did not need a massive accumulation of military power. It enjoyed something approaching "free security" from outside attack. In terms of external stimuli to American nationalism, compensation for lack of a credible military threat could be sought in deep suspicion of Britain as the former imperial power or in propagation of the contrasting notions of decadent Europe and virtuous America. More generally, in relation to the outside world, American nationalism could rely upon the power of its example rather than the demonstration of its power.

State religion was one of the basic props of traditional European national or imperial authority, but the American revolutionaries chose to dispense with it, along with monarchy, in the establishment of their new republic. However, in the nineteenth century, there was more than adequate compensation for the lack of an established church in the achievement of the various Protestant denominations in intertwining Protestantism so closely with Americanism. Formal institutional connection was replaced by popular commitment.

Something of the same process took place in the arena of government and politics. Reference has already been made to the conspicuous lack of a strong central governmental authority in the nineteenth-century United States. The federal government was small in size, limited in functions and resources, and very limited in its impact on the everyday life of the citizen. But once again, the weakness of formal governmental structures was compensated by a network of informal, unofficial, nongovernmental institutions and agencies, from political parties through churches to endowment trusts, charitable and philanthropic societies, and voluntary associations of all kinds — many of which played important public roles. A nagging question remains as to why individual citizens in their local communities should feel any attachment to this loose-limbed Union. One ingenious answer has been provided by Phillip Paludan, who has argued that Americans were devoted to the Union not in spite of the remoteness and limited functions of its government, but for that very reason. The Union was the essential framework for participation in democracy at the local community level. Local self-rule and national unity were interdependent. When that sense of interdependence (which is not far removed from Anderson's imagined community) broke down, as it did in much of the South in 1860, the nation was in crisis.

There remains one further striking example of the way in which the American national model was constructed by substituting something very different for one of the basic props of traditional European nationalism. Ethnic homogeneity was the foundation or the goal (often realized only imperfectly) of many European nationalisms. This was not close to the American reality even before the Revolution and became much less so in the face of the large-scale immigration of the mid-nineteenth century. On the one hand, that immigration triggered from time to time a nativist backlash, which proposed an exclusive definition of who and what constituted the nation. On the other hand, out of this challenge came a dramatic reinforcement of the concept of nationality by choice: an American was someone who chose to be an American.

In other words, the collective historical memory of the moment in the quite recent past, when British colonists had chosen to become American citizens, was paralleled in the family history of an increasing proportion of the population by the moment when a choice had been made to stop being something else and to become an American. The peculiar quality and strength of the voluntary principle at work in American nationalism derives from this convergence of the collective and the individual experience. From the mid-nineteenth century onward, each new generation reenacted the nation-making experience.

In a broader sense, too, the keys to appreciation of the distinctiveness of American nationalism may be found in the combination of the nation as choice and the nation as process. It might be thought that "the American nation as choice" is simply one example of what Gellner labeled the voluntaristic definition of the nation. But there are important points to be made about the particular American experience. First, it flatly contradicts the claim of Benedict Anderson that nations were able to inspire self-sacrificing devotion precisely because nationality, like skin color, gender, and parentage, was unchosen. For ordinary people, he says, "the whole point of the nation is that it is interestless." Whatever the applicability of this argument in other parts of the world, it does not fit the American case. The key element of choice in American nationalism meant that citizens had an interest, a stake, in the national community. Their actual or prospective success as individuals, as families, and as communities was closely intertwined with the actual or prospective success of the nation. With characteristic perception, David Potter identified common interest as one of the mainsprings of the evolving American nationalism of the antebellum period.

The other important aspect of the American version of voluntaristic nationalism is that it is part of a process that takes place over time. It is not just a matter of a once-for-all decision. All nationalisms are to a greater or lesser extent inventions or artifacts. The point about the American example is the intense and sustained self-consciousness of what proved to be a lengthy process. The Union was established in the 1780s; the nation was conceived or invented or imagined — and constantly re-conceived, re-invented, re-imagined — over the next eighty years at least, and probably much longer.

The middle decades of the nineteenth century — say, from 1840 to 1870 — are a critical period in this process. This period is marked by the intensification and definition of American nationalism in response to a series of dramatic challenges, which went to the very heart of the matter. After all, there could have been few more fundamental questions than: Where was the United States on the map? Who was or was not, could or could not be, an American? Was the United States to be one nation or not?

Ever since the founding of the republic, American borders had been expanding and elastic. The surge of expansionism in the 1840s made it harder than ever for Americans to point to a map and say: This is the shape of the United States, and this is how it will

remain. The geographical identity of the United States was still in the process of definition. Only hindsight enables us to see that the geographical mold of the continental
United States was quite firmly set by 1850.

The population of the territories acquired as a result of the Mexican war, and then
the huge influx of immigrants, especially Irish Catholic immigrants, renewed and intensified the debate over who could be, or could qualify to be, an American. The acceptability as American citizens of much longer established inhabitants who happened
to have black skins was denied by the Supreme Court in the Dred Scott decision in
1857; but within a decade, a constitutional amendment established the principle (if it
could not guarantee its consistent application) that all those born or naturalized within
the United States were American citizens.

Then came the greatest of all challenges to the integrity and durability of the nation
in the shape of sectional crisis, secession, and internal conflict on a massive scale. The Civil
War, rather than the War of Independence, was the great struggle for the American
nation. If the war and its outcome did not mark the conclusion of the process of
nation-making, they certainly marked the end of a very important chapter. It fell to
Abraham Lincoln to define the meaning of that process and its climactic moment. In his
inaugural address in March 1861, he spoke repeatedly of the Union and its salvation; in
the Gettysburg Address, two and a half years later, he interpreted the war as the supreme
test of the nation. Garry Wills has recently characterized the Gettysburg Address as "the
words that remade America." It is notable that, almost half a century after the Civil War,
in the course of a tribute to Lincoln, Herbert Croly could write that "for the first time,
it was clearly proclaimed by a responsible politician that American nationality was a
living principle rather than a legal bond."

On the one hand, the Civil War strengthened popular nationalism in the North and
reinforced the links between the local and the larger "imagined" national community.
In his study of the attitudes of Union soldiers, Reid Mitchell writes:

> When a Northern recruit joined the army to protect American institutions, his idea of those
> institutions came from his own, usually limited, experience. The institutions, the values for
> which he fought were those with which he had grown up. Democracy meant the town hall;
> education meant the schoolhouse; Christianity meant the local church. As for broader
> concepts — freedom, Constitution, democratic rule — so frequently had they been mediated
> by local figures that even they might be thought of as community values. In the North, local-
> ism aided rather than hindered national patriotism. The Northern soldier fought for home
> and for Union, for family and for nation. For him, the Civil War experience made sense only
> in relation to both the domestic and the civic components of his world.

On the other hand, of course, the war also compromised the voluntary principle at
the root of the American nation by the resort to compulsion in order to save the Union.
In the moment of extreme crisis, voluntarism was not enough. Karl Deutsch, another
of the leading authorities on the phenomenon of nationalism, has observed that "a nationality becomes a nation when it possesses the additional power to *compel* its members,
and to back up their group aspirations."

The process of definition and intensification of American nationalism in the mid-nineteenth century survived this series of challenges and crises. This was achieved not so much by once-for-all resolution of problems but by their management or containment within the national framework. What is striking is the rejection, or at least the avoidance, of totally negative or exclusive answers. Nativism did not die, but immigration was not seriously checked or restricted. Black Americans continued to be the victims of discrimination and injustice, but they ceased to be slaves and became citizens. Southern separatism was crushed, and the South reintegrated into the Union. In short, if the meaning of American nationalism was redefined or reinforced during this critical period, this was not achieved by resort to any one simple criterion, whether of frontiers or ethnicity or race or color or, for that matter, of region or section. Immigrants or blacks or white Southerners were not excluded; indeed, in the Southern case, they were not allowed to leave. One did not have to be an ardent expansionist or a nativist or a racist or a champion of strong central government in order to qualify as an American nationalist (although it may sometimes have appeared advantageous to be one or other, or a combination of these things!).

This inclusive approach was the product of the very distinctive brand of American voluntaristic nationalism — nationalism by choice. Its distinctiveness owed much to the unusual combination of conditions that have been the main theme of this essay: the existence of a political union at the beginning rather than the end of the protracted process of making a nation; the early arrival of other elements such as political democracy, modern communications, and economic growth; resourcefulness in compensating for the lack of traditional national foundations with a formidable set of new ones; the replication of the national experience in the immigrant experience; and flexibility and resilience in riding out the challenges of the mid-nineteenth century. Much emphasis is often placed upon the ideological content of American nationalism. It is true enough that commitment to the ideals enshrined in the Declaration of Independence served as a focal point of American nationalism. But this offers a description rather than an explanation of the process that produced America's distinctive brand of voluntaristic nationalism. The explanation — or at least a substantial part of it — lies in the complex of forces discussed in this essay.

Writing in the *North American Review* six months after Appomattox, Samuel Fowler reflected on the enormous changes in the United States since the era of Thomas Jefferson. In the immediate afterglow of victory, there is an understandable note of triumphalism in his remarks. However, he does convey something of American nation-making as process and as choice, and there is even a fleeting reference to the broader comparative context:

> Continued association under favorable circumstances is powerful enough to fuse even the diversities of race, and to create a new birth, — the genius of a nation. . . . This is the day of great nations. . . .
>
> No example of the strength of this law of attraction has ever been presented equal to this nation of eighty years growth. It has not only impressed a national character upon a population of different races and languages, but has shown the surrender of a national life to be impossible, except at the sacrifice of one of the dearest instincts of the heart. Not a new body only, but a new soul, has been added to the family of nations. We are at an immeasurable distance from

the times when Jefferson could describe us as "one nation towards others, separate governments among ourselves. . . ." The most casual acquaintance with our recent history will disclose the perfect difference in the undercurrents of thought prevailing at the time when our government commenced its experiment and at present. Beginning in darkness and doubt, national interests and policy have insensibly conquered the first place in the estimation of the people.

The theorists and generalizers about the phenomenon of nationalism have ignored the United States at their peril. The history of American nationalism is distinctive, and it frequently breaks the rules of the established Eurocentered models. But it is not altogether exceptional or unique, and it should not be divorced from the history of nationalism elsewhere. At the very least, it poses a series of tests or challenges to some of the assumptions and generalizations of those who have written about nationalism in broad conceptual or comparative terms. . . .

QUESTIONS TO CONSIDER

1. What does Parish mean by the term "nationalism"? In what ways, according to Parish, did the United States develop the conditions for nationalism earlier than people elsewhere or in a different sequence? What does it mean to say that "Americans had erected their constitutional roof before they put up the national walls"? How did popular literacy and widespread suffrage foster the growth of nationalist sentiment in the nineteenth century? When, according to Parish, did American nationalism emerge, and why? In what ways was the Civil War more important than the American Revolution for defining the nation?

2. How, according to the author, did Americans compensate for their lack of several ingredients, such as an ancient history, ethnic unity, or an established church, that European nationalists claimed were essential to nationhood? How can one square Parish's emphasis on the voluntary and inclusive nature of American nationality with the nation's nineteenth-century record of slavery, anti-immigrant movements, and racial exclusion from citizenship?

3. How does Parish explain the paradox that America's weak, decentralized government fostered strong feelings of attachment to the nation? Why did these sentiments fail to prevent secession and Civil War?

4. Parish's comparison of American history with prominent theories of nationalism highlights unusual features of the American experience. Using Parish's findings, how might you modify one of the theories of nationalism he presents in order to take into account the American case?

5. Compare the ways Parish and Seymour Martin Lipset (Selection 11) use social science theories and models to illuminate American history. Which essay or model better explains particular developments of the early American republic? Which helps us to understand cultural patterns that persisted into later centuries? Which author emphasizes America's similarities to other nations, and which stresses American uniqueness? What are the advantages and disadvantages of using social science models in historical analysis?

VII

Age of the
Common Man

In the election of 1828, American voters swept out the old gentlemanly style of politics and swept in a new era of mass parties and popular democracy. The self-made westerner Andrew Jackson was its charismatic symbol. By now, few historians accept the claims of a half-century ago that Jacksonian democracy equalized American society. Jackson brutally imposed removal to the West upon American Indians, and his followers disfranchised free blacks in the North. Urbanization and explosive economic growth actually widened the gap between rich and poor during the "Age of the Common Man." There is no disputing, however, that Jackson and his followers brought a democratic revolution to American politics. They expanded the white electorate, mobilized popular support against the "special privileges" of the rich, and created the first mass political party in the United States.

While the Jacksonians set about democratizing American politics, American religion underwent a similar transformation. In the first three decades of the nineteenth century, mainstream Christianity was challenged by new leaders and methods more attuned to the styles and values of ordinary Americans. A wave of Protestant "revivals" swept through the countryside and arrived in towns and cities, transforming the way people worshipped and lived. Plainspoken preachers stirred this "Second Great Awakening" by conducting huge public meetings where men and women were told that they could be "born again" by accepting Christianity of their own free will. The promise of "salvation open to all," delivered in emotional tones and promoted by elaborate publicity campaigns, refashioned religion for a democratic culture, boosted church membership, and mobilized popular crusades against Sabbath-breaking, prostitution, alcohol, and slavery.

Although not always in agreement, these movements toward religious and political democracy shared the same egalitarian impulse and advanced hand in hand. Furthermore, this twin democratic revolution was not uniquely American. The forces transforming America in the 1820s and 1830s — the spread of a market economy, revolutions in transportation and communication, the rise of "public opinion" and grass-roots movements, and the ascendance of evangelical Protestantism — were transforming Europe, especially Britain, at the same time. As the selections here suggest, both Jacksonian democracy and the Second Great Awakening can be viewed as manifestations of a broader, transatlantic advance of peoples into the democratic age.

In the first essay, Paul Johnson parallels the rise of Andrew Jackson and the Democrats with the victory of another populist hero, Irish reformer Daniel O'Connell and his Catholic Emancipation movement. Johnson finds common "factors and forces" behind the two movements, and while he celebrates "the coming of the *demos*," he also echoes the alarms sounded by their enemies.

In the second selection, Richard Carwardine, who, like Johnson, is a British historian, reminds us that Americans successfully exported the Second Great Awakening to Great Britain. There it became part of a larger evangelical movement that challenged the power of the Anglican social and religious establishment. In contrast to Johnson's alternating story of American and British political change, Carwardine takes an analytical approach that directly compares the origins and impact of the British and American revivals.

Taken together, these essays describe common transatlantic ideas and social changes that supported the democratization of politics and religion. Both show that popular movements relied, ironically, on the actions of symbolic, larger-than-life leaders. Both authors also imply that political and religious democrats faced greater opposition in Britain and were able to take a more advanced position in the young United States. Yet there are important differences, too. Unlike Johnson, who portrays political democracy as a revolutionary force, Carwardine is careful to point out the limits of evangelical religion's challenge to the status quo and its moderating effect on social conflicts. And whereas Johnson rests his case on the essential unity of transatlantic political democracy, Carwardine suggests that religious changes had profoundly different impacts in the United States and Britain. After you read these essays, you ought to explore the areas of overlap and disagreement between their findings about the Age of the Common Man.

The Coming of the Demos

PAUL JOHNSON

Once in a while, historical figures become so powerful and influential, or so symbolic, that they lend their names to an entire era. This was the case with Napoleon, Queen Victoria, and Joseph Stalin. In nineteenth-century America, it was true for Andrew Jackson. When this rough-hewn backwoods lawyer, hero of the War of 1812, and Indian fighter took over the White House in 1829, he expanded the power of office so greatly that the presidency would never be the same. Even more important, his sweeping electoral victory and undignified inauguration signaled that "the people" had arrived. Jackson's organization, the Democratic Party, invented American mass politics by eliminating property requirements for voting and officeholding, saturating newspapers with favorable coverage, making up catchy campaign songs and slogans, and distributing the spoils of office to supporters. During Jackson's tenure, modern democracy and the two-party system, both nightmares to the Founders, became American realities.

But the Age of the Common Man happened elsewhere, too. Across the Atlantic there was a simultaneous rise of democratic movements. During Jackson's first term, Irish Catholics won the right to hold office, middle-class Englishmen got the vote, the French overthrew their king, and the Belgians broke off from Dutch rule. Most of these agitations were not directly connected to American developments, but others, such as the growth of trade unions and the rise of movements against slavery, were fed by transatlantic exchanges of people and ideas. This remarkable flowering of the ideals of liberty and equality calls into question the notion that uniquely American factors such as the frontier created democracy. Instead, it points us toward transnational developments of the 1820s and 1830s, such as the impact of economic depressions, the rise of "public opinion," the spread of revolutionary ideas, and the effect of dramatic improvements in transportation and communication.

Preoccupied as we are with our own history, our textbooks usually ignore foreign parallels to Jacksonian democracy, despite the reminders of European and, especially, British writers. In this selection, Paul Johnson, a British historian who believes that the 1820s witnessed "the birth of the modern," interweaves the colorful rise of Andrew Jackson with the equally astonishing tale of another "outsider," Irish reformer Daniel O'Connell. O'Connell's Catholic Emancipation movement and Jackson's Democratic Party, says Johnson, were the first democratic mass political movements. He credits the growing power of the popular press and the creation of sophisticated political party machinery with much of their success. But

Johnson believes that democratic innovations, like other institutions, are produced not just by impersonal "forces" but also by "the actions of great men." With their larger-than-life personalities and their ability to seize decisive moments, Jackson and O'Connell transformed Anglo-American politics and became heroic symbols of the rise of common people to power.

As you read Johnson's narrative, keep in mind the limits of democratic rights in the 1830s. Jackson's narrow, ethnocentric concept of democracy did not include blacks, Native Americans, or women. In fact, the same Democratic Party that eliminated property requirements for white male voters increased them for many free blacks. And although Catholic men in Ireland became eligible for Parliament in 1829, fewer than one in twenty met the property test for voting. The "common man" was defined restrictively. Fortunately, democratic ideals continued to challenge the status quo and to inspire "outsiders" on both sides of the Atlantic to wrest their political rights from dominant elites.

GLOSSARY

ACT OF UNION (1800)   A law promoted by Britain's chief secretary for Ireland, Robert Castlereagh, after he suppressed an Irish rebellion in 1798. The act united England and Ireland governmentally by abolishing the Irish Parliament and providing for Irish representatives in the British Parliament. Catholics were still banned from holding political office.

ADAMS, JOHN QUINCY (1767–1848)   A Federalist and former senator from Massachusetts who served as secretary of state under President Monroe and was instrumental in formulating the Monroe Doctrine. Elected president in 1825 through the House of Representatives with the support of Henry Clay, Adams had an ineffective administration. He won new respect as a congressman in the 1830s and 1840s, however, eloquently opposing the extension of slavery.

ASCENDANCY   Protestant domination of Ireland following the removal of Britain's Catholic king, James II, in the Glorious Revolution of 1688. After James was succeeded by William III, the Irish Protestant elite consolidated its victory by enacting penal laws designed to exclude Catholics from property and power.

BENTON, THOMAS HART (1782–1858)   A powerful Democratic senator from Missouri who supported Andrew Jackson's attack on the National Bank and favored western development, but, unlike Jackson, opposed the extension of slavery.

BÊTE NOIRE   Someone a person dislikes or detests.

CALHOUN, JOHN C. (1782–1850)   A South Carolina senator and vice president under John Quincy Adams and Andrew Jackson who was an ardent defender of southern agrarianism, slavery, and states' rights. He directed South Carolina's resistance to the Union in the Nullification Crisis of 1832–1833, promoted the extension of slavery into western territories, and defended the South's right to secede.

CLAY, HENRY (1777–1852)   An influential statesman and longtime congressional leader from Kentucky who was one of the western "war hawks" who brought on the War of 1812. He served as secretary of state for President John Quincy Adams and opposed the succeeding Jackson administration. Clay's "American system" was a program for federal aid to internal improvements, a protective tariff, and a national bank. He ran for president against the Democrats in 1832 and 1844 but lost.

CONGRESS OF VIENNA (1814–1815)   The international congress that restored the monarchies of France and Spain and redrew the map of Europe to assure a balance of power in the wake of Napoleon's defeat.

CRAWFORD, WILLIAM (1772–1834)   A Georgia senator who served as a cabinet member under Presidents Madison and Monroe and was himself nominated for president in 1824. With support only in the South, he finished third in a four-man race.

DEMOS   Derived from ancient Greek: the common people.

DISRAELI, BENJAMIN (1804–1881)   A British statesman and author who achieved literary fame with the novel *Sybil* (1845) and rose to leadership of the Tory (later the Conservative) Party. He pushed the party to support the Reform Bill of 1867, which led to the enfranchisement of urban working men and more than doubled the electorate.

ERIE CANAL   Human-built waterway, completed in 1825, that connected Buffalo on Lake Erie and Albany on the Hudson River, hence linking New York City to the West. Attempts by other states to duplicate the canal's success began a "canal boom" in the Jacksonian era.

MONROE, JAMES (1758–1831)   The last of the "Virginia dynasty" of presidents and a staunch Jeffersonian who had served in the Continental Congress and later negotiated the Louisiana Purchase. He was easily elected president in 1816 and again in 1820. His administration was characterized as an "era of good feelings."

O'CONNELL, DANIEL (1775–1847)   An Irish landowner and lawyer who led the fight in the 1820s to end British restrictions on Catholic officeholding. He was elected to Parliament in 1828, but only allowed to take his seat when the British government declared Catholic Emancipation in 1829. In Parliament, O'Connell worked to repeal the union of Great Britain and Ireland, to end official privileges for the Protestant Church of Ireland, and to gain greater access to landholding for the Irish.

ORANGEMEN   Members of the Loyal Orange Institution (or Orange Lodge), a society established in northern Ireland in 1795 to maintain the Protestant ascendancy. Its name was taken from the family name of William III, who defeated the Catholic James II in 1690.

PAKENHAM, SIR EDWARD (1778–1815)   The British commander who was killed and whose troops were decisively defeated by General Jackson's in the Battle of New Orleans in January 1815. Coming two weeks after the Treaty of Ghent, this great American victory did not affect the outcome of the War of 1812, but it made Jackson a military hero.

PEEL, ROBERT (1788–1850)   A leading British conservative statesman who served as chief secretary for Ireland before returning to England to become a cabinet member and eventually prime minister. Although he initially opposed Catholic Emancipation, Peel secured its passage in Parliament in 1829 and urged conservatives to support other reforms such as free trade.

RANDOLPH, JOHN (1773–1833)   A Virginia planter and statesman who served five terms in Congress and who vigorously opposed Federalist Party policies in the name of individual liberty and states' rights.

REPEAL MOVEMENT   Irish agitation beginning in the mid-nineteenth century to repeal the union with Britain. It took the form of boycotts of British goods, attacks on British officials, and disruption of parliamentary practices by Irish members of Parliament.

TORIES   Members of the conservative British party that generally represented the interests of the Church of England and the landed gentry. Tories vehemently opposed the French Revolution and lost strength in the nineteenth century as the electorate expanded.

TUILERIES   The royal palace and gardens to which Louis XVI was forced to move from Versailles in 1789 at the outbreak of the French Revolution. In the Revolution of 1848, the palace was sacked by an angry mob that deposed King Louis Philippe.

WALPOLEIAN SYSTEM   The traditional system of parliamentary rule in Britain, identified with Robert Walpole, who defined the role of prime minister in the 1720s and 1730s. Standard procedures included the exchange of patronage for votes in Parliament and the manipulation of elections through bribes and even outright purchasing of seats.

WATERLOO   The battle fought near Brussels, Belgium, in 1815 in which British and Prussian forces routed Napoleon's army, resulting in the French emperor's abdication and the end of the Napoleonic Wars.

WELLINGTON, DUKE OF (1769–1852)   The British soldier and statesman who directed the Peninsular War that drove Napoleon's armies out of Spain and then defeated Napoleon at Waterloo. He served as prime minister from 1828 to 1830, when he and Robert Peel pushed Catholic Emancipation through Parliament. He later served in other cabinet posts under Peel.

WESTMINSTER (PALACE)   The houses of the British Parliament in London.

✼ ✼ ✼ ✼ ✼ ✼ ✼

Toward the end of the 1820s, the world moved a decisive stage nearer the democratic age. This advance came about not through one dramatic incident, such as the storming of the Bastille, whose results were bound to be ephemeral, but by a combination of many factors and forces — the growth of literacy, the huge increase in the number and circulation of newspapers, the rise in population and incomes, the spread of technology and industry, the diffusion of competing ideas — and, not least, by the actions of great men. Governing elites began to realize that the right of the few to monopolize political power was no longer graven in stone. With various degrees of reluctance, they faced the likelihood that the magic circle would have to be expanded and more people admitted. So the process began whereby first some, then most, and finally all found themselves participating in the political process. . . . [Whether] welcome or alarming, the entry of the *demos* onto the great stage of history in the late

"The Coming of the *Demos*" from *The Birth of the Modern* by Paul Johnson. Copyright © 1991 by Paul Johnson. Reprinted by permission of HarperCollins Publishers, Inc.

1820s was a grand and unmistakable fact, the culminating event in the way the matrix of modernity was forged.

The prime theater of experiment was, perhaps naturally, the new world of the Americas where, between the 1770s and the 1820s the first great wave of decolonization had swept away the old monarchical order of Europe. In the south and center, paper constitutions, often radical, written and approved in the first flush of independence, proved largely worthless in the face of naked power conveyed by land, money and, above all, guns and sabers. In the north, and above all in the United States, where the roots of constitutionalism and the rule of law were deep and tenacious, it was a different matter. . . .

Discontent with the political establishment, which amounted, in effect, to a rejection of oligarchy and the system of indirect election, had been growing for some years. [James] Monroe had been 60 when he became President in 1817 and still wore breeches and top boots. . . . In the 1816 election he got the votes of all the states except Massachusetts, Connecticut and Delaware, being elected, as one newspaper put it, "with less bustle and *national* confusion than belongs to a Westminster election for a Member of Parliament in England." He was called "the last of the Revolutionary farmers," and shortly after taking over in Washington, he went on a three-month tour of 13 states to reunify the country after the stress of the war years and to boost its morale. "He wore a plain blue coat, a buff under-dress, and a hat and cockade of the revolutionary fashion. . . . The demon of party for a time departed and gave place to a general burst of National Feeling." . . .

The phrase caught on. The times were often called, then and later, the Era of Good Feelings. But if any such spirit of harmony ever prevailed, it did not last, and it certainly did not survive the bank crisis of 1819. The period was already marked by a growing feeling, especially beyond the eastern littoral, that something was fundamentally wrong with the way the system operated and that dark and sinister forces were at work, especially in Washington itself. A case can be made for describing the Monroe presidency, and the rule of John Quincy Adams who formed its appendage, as the first great era of corruption in American history. Indeed, the word itself was used with increasing frequency. Many Americans came sincerely to believe that their government, both administration and Congress, was corrupt, and this at a time when, in Britain, the traditional corruption of the 18th-century Walpoleian system was being slowly but surely extruded from public life. Of course, by corruption Americans of the 1820s did not mean simply the use of bribes and stealing from the public purse. They also meant the undermining of the constitutional system by secret deals, the use of public office to acquire power or higher office, and the giving of private interests priority over public welfare. . . .

. . . Many members of the administration, it was claimed, had been given "loans" by businessmen seeking favors — loans which were never paid. But Congress, it was said, was corrupt, too. Senator Thomas Hart Benton of Missouri served as "legal representative" to the great operator of the fur trade and real estate tycoon John Jacob Astor and managed to push through the abolition of the War Department's "factory" system, which provided Indians with clothing and tools and so competed with Astor's own posts. The fact that the War Department's system was corrupt, as Benton easily demonstrated in 1819, was not the point: What was a senator doing working for a millionaire? Benton was not the only one. The great Massachusetts orator, Daniel Webster (1782–1852), received a fee for "services" to the hated Second Bank of the United States (SBUS). One modern historian described Webster as "a man who regularly took handouts from any source available and paid the expected price." . . .

It was in 1822, when these goings-on in the capital became the subject of angry public debate, that General Andrew Jackson first seriously contemplated running for president. It was clear that he wanted office. But he would not seek it. He thus contrived a pose which was to become a postural cliché for countless candidates to come. Seeing himself as a national hero, summoned by public opinion to rule, he said: "I give the same answer — that I have never been a candidate for any office. I never will. But the people have a right to choose whom they will to perform their constitutional duties, and when the People call, the Citizen is bound to render the service required." However, Jackson had many passionate supporters, chiefly from his army days, and two in particular saw to it that the people did call. They were both former majors, who had married sisters: William Berkeley Lewis, Jackson's quartermaster in the southern wars, and John Henry Eaton, who had written his campaign biography. They served as his campaign managers — the first in presidential history — and as part of their jobs, they had the Tennessee legislature elect him to the U.S. Senate, where he served from March 1823. Jackson went the 900 miles to Washington partly by stage and by steamboat, when available, but mainly on horseback. People turned out to gape and question him when they heard he was passing through, the first stirrings of a mighty engine of populism. . . .

Jackson no longer thought it possible to return to the Jeffersonian notion of a pastoral America run by enlightened farmers. "Experience has taught me," he wrote in 1816, "that manufactures are now as necessary to our independence as to our comfort." But the bank crisis of 1819, and the overwhelming corruption (as he saw it) to which it was the prelude, made him sure that "a general cleansing" of Washington was imperative if the Union was to survive. He was the first candidate to grasp with both hands what was to become the most popular theme in American campaigning history: "clean the rascals out."

Jackson saw himself as an outsider against the insiders, and since most Americans felt themselves to be outsiders, too, he could if he chose play the democratic card. And he did choose. When Governor of the Florida Territory, he had ruled that mere residence was sufficient to give an adult male the vote. He reiterated this view in 1822. Every free man in the nation or state should have the vote, since all were subject to the laws and punishments, both federal and state, and so they "of right, ought to be entitled to a voice in making them." He added, however, that each state legislature had the duty to adopt such voting qualifications as it thought proper for "the happiness, security and prosperity of the state." The more people who had the presidential vote, the better, since if, as he believed, Washington was rotten, it gave them the means of remedy: "The great constitutional corrective in the hands of the people against usurpation of power, or corruption by their agents, is the right of suffrage; and this when used with calmness and deliberation will prove strong enough — it will perpetuate their liberties and rights." Jackson, then, was instinctively a democrat, and it is no accident that he created the great Democratic party, which is still with us. He thought the people were instinctively right and moral, and Big Government, of the kind he could see growing up in Washington, instinctively immoral. His task was to liberate and represent that huge, moral popular force by appealing to it over the oligarchic heads of the ruling elite. Here was a winning strategy, provided the suffrage was wide enough.

How far the strategy and its articulation were Jackson's own is hard to assess. He had read little. His grammar and spelling were shaky. The "Memorandoms" he addressed to himself are an extraordinary mixture of naïveté, shrewdness, ignorance, insight and prejudice. His tone of voice, in speech and writing, might be termed subbiblical. . . . By contrast, Eaton was a skilled, even sophisticated writer, and it was he who worked the "clean up Washington" theme into an integrated national campaign, the first modern election campaign, in fact. In early summer 1823, Eaton wrote a series of 11 articles, signed "Wyoming," for the Philadelphia paper, the *Columbian Observer*. These articles attracted wide attention, were reprinted in pamphlet form as *The Letters of Wyoming*, and were reproduced in newspapers across the country. The theme, worked out in impressive detail and couched in powerful rhetoric, was that the American government had fallen into the hands of Mammon, and the voters must now ensure that it returned to the pure principles of the Revolution. It was by far the most impressive electioneering tract laid before the voters anywhere. . . .

. . . Jackson was an outstanding candidate. Tall, slender, handsome and fierce, he looked tremendous, but his consumptive cough, white face, hair going from gray to white and the fact that he often seemed ill and frail, helped; it made people feel protective. He had a reputation for wildness, rages and severity, but when men actually met him, they found him courteous as well as awesome. "He wrought," wrote Josiah Quincy, "a mysterious charm upon old and young." . . .

In short, Jackson had that most valuable of all qualities for a presidential candidate, charisma. He was also known throughout the nation, and that, too, was important in a crowded field. Originally, there were five candidates: Jackson, [Henry] Clay, [John C.] Calhoun, [William] Crawford and Adams. But a stroke in 1823 made Crawford a weak runner, and Calhoun withdrew to become vice presidential candidate on both the Adams and Jackson tickets. Clay was powerful in the new West but nowhere else, so in practice it was a race between Adams and Jackson.

The election of 1824 was an important landmark in American constitutional history. . . . [W]ith a total of 356,038 votes cast, Jackson, with 153,544, emerged the clear leader, and Adams, the runner-up, was over 40,000 votes behind with 108,740. Jackson was also well ahead in electoral college votes, having 99, against 84 for Adams, 41 for Crawford and 37 for Clay. He carried 11 states, against 7 for Adams and 3 each for the other two. By any reckoning, then, Jackson was the winner. However, under the Twelfth Amendment, if no presidential candidate secured a majority of the electoral votes, the issue had to be taken to the House of Representatives, which picked the winner from among the top three, voting simply by states. That, in practice, made Clay the broker. As the fourth runner, he was excluded from the play-off. But as Speaker of the House, he determined who would win it. . . .

. . . According to rumors, Clay's people put out feelers to Jackson, asking what offices would be given to them if Jackson was elected. Andrew Wylie, President of Washington College, later asked the General to confirm this rumor: "Is that a *fact?*" Jackson: "Yes, Sir, such a proposition *was* made. I said to the bearer, 'Go tell Mr Clay, tell Mr Adams, that if I go to the chair, I go with clean hands.'"

Adams and Clay were less squeamish. . . . Clay called on Adams twice, on 9 January 1825, at 6 P.M., spending the whole evening there, and again on 29 January. The first meeting was probably the decisive one, though Adams's diary, while recording it, is un-characteristically reticent about what took place. . . . In view of Adams's character, there are two possible explanations for what took place. One is that there was no ex-plicit bargain, but an understanding that if Adams could bring himself to think Clay suitable, he would give Clay a great office; the other was that a bargain was struck, and the normally high-minded Adams could not bring himself to write about it. In all events, the story of a Clay-Adams bargain was already circulating by mid-January, John Campbell of Virginia writing to his brother David: "Letters from Washington inform us that Adams is certain to be the president. Clay & him have compromised. . . . Bargains & sales are going on . . . as infamous as you can imagine. This office and that are held out provided you vote this way and that, etc, etc. What is this but bribery and corruption?"

Nonetheless on 9 February Clay got Adams the White House [by lining up the votes of thirteen states in the House of Representatives]. . . .

. . . The cry, "corrupt bargain," was taken up all over the country. The way in which Jackson, having got most suffrages, most electoral votes, and most states, was robbed of the presidency by a furtive deal seemed, to many people, to confirm exactly what Jackson had said in his campaign was wrong with Washington and what he had been elected to change. It was the voters, as well as Jackson, who had been swindled.

Foreigners saw it differently. For the first but not for the last time, Europeans were struck by the mysterious workings of American public morality. Bargaining for office in return for votes was an absolute commonplace of British politics and occurred in every other country where parliamentary constitutions had been tried. Yes, replied the Jacksonites, and that is precisely what is wrong with the Old World and unacceptable in the New. . . .

Jackson and his supporters were determined to reverse the result as soon as they law-fully could. So the 1828 election campaign effectively began in spring 1825. The Tennessee legislature immediately renominated Jackson for President. In a 15-minute discourse, "perhaps the longest political speech in his career," Jackson accepted, giving the "corrupt bargain" as his chief reason for doing so. Indeed, the bargain gave the Gen-eral his route into the politics of the masses, under the banner of Popular Sovereignty, since the essence of the charge he leveled against Adams and Clay was that the will of the voters had been defied by corrupt politicians. These politicians thought the fuss would die down. But it never did. Jackson and his men ensured it was kept alive.

From its very inception, Jackson declared war on the Adams administration. . . . A huge, unbridgeable fissure opened between the administration and the Jacksonites. From this point opposition in Congress became systematic. The modern American two-party system began to emerge. All over what was already an enormous country, and one which was expanding rapidly, branches of a Jacksonite popular party were formed in 1825–26, and scores of newspapers lined up behind the new organization, including important new creations like Duff Green's *United States Telegraph*. As the political system polarized, more and more established politicians swung in behind the General: [Martin] Van Buren came, bringing his New York machine. So did the remains of the old Crawford faction, Randolph of Roanoke, McDuffie of South Carolina, Livingstone of Louisiana, Sam Houston of the West, Calhoun and Benton. Thus assembled what was to become one of the great and enduring popular instruments of the modern age, the Democratic party.

It was not, however, the first fully organized and financed democratic mass movement. The credit for the first must go to Ireland and to Daniel O'Connell, and we must break off for a space from Jackson's progress to the White House to see how the Liberator, as he was known, did it. Ireland was a chronically discontented country which, from time to time, became actively ungovernable. Castlereagh's plan to solve the Irish problem by the Act of Union failed when George III refused to accompany it with Catholic Emancipation — that is, removing the disabilities which banned Roman Catholics from political office, Parliament and most official jobs. The Irish birthrate was probably the highest in the world at this time. Some relief was provided by emigration to Britain.

[T]he Irish were emigrating to North America in great numbers, too. Even so, the home population was over 7 million by 1820 and heading quickly for 8 million, in a country which in times of poor harvests could barely feed 5 million. Three-quarters of these masses, including all the poorest, were Catholics. That was the main reason why Ireland could not be absorbed into the British system, as Scotland and Wales had been. Irish poverty was envenomed by the feeling that it was caused by what was seen as alien rule. The fact that the seat of royal government was still called Dublin Castle — it was, and is, not so much an actual castle as a rambling collection of dingy buildings — was symbolic of the defensive and indeed military nature of sovereignty.

. . . Much of ordinary Irish life, then as now, was lighthearted, warm, free and easy and fun, lit by flashes of brilliant wit and creative passion. But the business of governing was a morass of corruption, lies, hatred and fear. The Protestant Irish enjoyed the privileges of what was called the Ascendancy and howled for patronage day and night. But they did little in return. It was difficult to get Irish members of Parliament, even if they were members of the government, to attend twice a year at Westminster. . . . Even after Waterloo, Lord Whitworth, the Viceroy, had to lock up what he called "blackguards running about the streets in the night denying the victory and asserting that Buonaparte was the conqueror." The *Dublin Evening Post* gave joyful prominence to any French success. Like the other popular papers, it was vociferously anti-British and nationalist. All the popular papers were unscrupulous, full of libel and falsehood, and flatly refused to report the actions of the government truthfully. . . .

. . . But the government itself was unscrupulous. In the predominantly Presbyterian north, it furtively encouraged the growth of Orange Lodges, which dated from the 1790s, while preventing them from emerging as an alternative power structure. [Chief

Secretary to the Viceroy, Robert] Peel admitted, in a letter to the Viceroy in July 1814, that his object was to keep the lower classes in the north and, indeed, in the whole of Ireland disunited, since if they came together, the Protestants would be bound to adopt Catholic nationalism "and therefore a cordial concurrence in hating the British connection." He hoped they would always be divided: "The great art is to keep them so, and yet at Peace or rather not at War with one another."

Dublin Castle was rather like what Talleyrand said of Tsarist Russia: never as strong as it looked, never as weak as it looked. In the last resort, it could invoke the Irish Convention Act of 1793, which made unlawful the election and assembly of any unauthorized bodies purporting to represent the people. But it was not a despotism. Indeed, it was very much subject to the rule of law, and so vulnerable to partisan juries and a nationalist movement led by brilliant and far-from-scrupulous barristers.

The most gifted of these barristers was Daniel O'Connell (1775–1847), Peel's particular bête noire. Peel came from a strongly Protestant family, but he was far from being an Orangeman; indeed, when he first arrived in Dublin, he changed all the family facings on his servants' livery, which fortuitously had been orange. So it was a bitter point that O'Connell promptly dubbed him "Orange" Peel, a name that stuck. O'Connell . . . was born a favored member of a swarming clan which inhabited a remote peninsula in County Kerry, traditionally the poorest part of Ireland (and its people rated by other Irishmen as the stupidest). Here, in the wild southwest, it was possible for a family like the O'Connells, who traced their gentry status back to Edward III's time but had remained Catholic, to survive the fiercest phase of the Ascendancy simply because their land was so poor and undeveloped. . . .

In short, O'Connell belonged to the indigenous and, to some extent, unconquered Irish aristocracy. His status was important to him and was ignored by his Ascendancy and English opponents who saw him as a counter-jumping attorney. For most of his life, he was a substantial landowner, his lands bringing him in nominally about £4,000 a year, though not much in cash. . . . Initially, his upbringing was Celtic, in that he was fostered out to the wife of a herdsman, lived in a mud cabin and spoke Gaelic. All his life he moved and conversed at ease among the peasants, indeed, among men and women of all classes in the countryside; this facility was one of the sources of his strength both as a barrister and as a politician. But at a time when nationalists all over Europe, from Finland to Hungary, were turning to the native vernacular as a source of unity, he rejected Gaelic. He used it only when there was no other means of making himself understood. He thought English would be the first world language and for the Irish to opt against it would be to reject their entrance ticket to the modern world: "The superior utility of the English tongue, as the medium of all modern communication," he said, "is so great that I can witness without a sigh the gradual disuse of Irish."

His emotional loyalty was, rather, to a larger concept: Ireland as part of European Catholic civilization. His national idea was . . . the proselytizing Ireland of the Dark Ages, sending out Latin-speaking scholars and saints to the world. In the 17th and 18th centuries, the Irish Catholic gentry had to seek their fortunes on the Continent, chiefly as soldiers. His Uncle Daniel was a count of France and a general in the Bourbon army. His own outlook was cosmopolitan, internationalist, turning instinctively to Paris,

Vienna and even New York as much as to London. His boyhood dream was to be his country's Washington. Later he saw Bonaparte as Ireland's friend. Later still, he identified with Simón Bolívar, another "Liberator," and proudly dispatched his son Morgan, aged 14, to join the Irish Legion fighting for freedom against Spain.

O'Connell's Europeanism was reinforced by his schooling in the Jesuit colleges run for the sons of British Catholic gentry in Flanders. . . . [There he was] an eyewitness to the turmoils and terror created by the French Revolution. Just as Lord Liverpool never forgot the horror of the fall of the Bastille, O'Connell formed from these events a lifelong conviction that violence was evil and ultimately futile. His constitutionalism was reinforced by luck, often a decisive factor in politics. During the disastrous Irish rebellion of 1798, O'Connell was bedridden with rheumatic fever. This illness not merely prevented him from taking part, but allowed him to view the rising with detachment and learn the lesson — the folly of armed conspiracy and the salient truth that the Irish masses could not be trusted except under firm leadership. By instinct and conviction, he supported hierarchical order. He not only joined but enjoyed the militia, and he developed a profound respect for monarchy, which led to accusations of flunkeyism during George IV's highly successful state visit to Dublin in 1821. But he was justified by events in his belief that nonviolent mass agitation was the right way for Catholic Ireland to progress toward equality. . . .

O'Connell rose to power through the Bar, to which he was called in 1798. He became one of the most hard-working and successful advocates in Irish history. He was wonderfully at home in court, a magisterial examiner in chief, a deadly cross-examiner, more learned in the law than the great majority of judges and never afraid to stand up to them. . . . But as a Catholic he was not only banned from Parliament and thus from high legal office, not only excluded from a judgeship, but he could not even take Silk (become a King's Counsel), which disabled him from accepting briefs in the most important cases. As a Silk he could have earned £20,000–£30,000 a year in Westminster. It was this kind of discrimination which made the ablest Catholics so bitter. . . .

Nonetheless, his political rise was rapid. As early as 1808, he was the leading spokesman for Catholic Ireland. A political leader, especially a nationalist, can to some extent master events, but equally he is a victim of them, too, and O'Connell is a case in point. When Bonaparte bestrode Europe like a colossus and England's cause faltered, the chances of rapid Emancipation looked good. O'Connell consolidated his reputation with a tremendous forensic triumph during the Magee libel trial of 1813, when he crushed the Protestant Attorney General with a vituperative display of rhetoric such as had never before been heard in Dublin. This trial made him a national figure. An eyewitness recorded his morning walk in Dublin, [noting how] . . . "his celebrity as an agitator began to ensure him a tail of admiring followers whenever he appeared in public."

However, in the decade that followed the Magee case, O'Connell's political career and the cause of Emancipation both marked time, as England was everywhere triumphant. On both sides of the Channel, the bulk of the middle classes, whatever their religion, joined the ruling class in resisting reform. The repressive laws and police power were one factor, but it was primarily the spirit of the times which favored the existing order. In Ireland an additional element was the skill with which Peel, despite all his grumblings, operated the Dublin Castle machine. As long as Peel was in charge, there was little chance of O'Connell getting the better of it.

In the bitter contest between the two men, there appears to have been real dislike on O'Connell's side, matched by contempt on Peel's. . . . Peel . . . despised O'Connell, whose family had held their lands since the 14th century, as a vulgar comic, little better than a stage Irishman.

Unfortunately, there was a tiny element of truth in this view. O'Connell was a tall, handsome man, with flashing blue eyes and jet-black hair, and at times he carried himself like a prince. But he had weaknesses, characteristic of his time, place and race. For one thing, . . . there was his propensity to get himself involved in duels, often with friends, colleagues and relatives as much as with enemies — a habit which harmed his reputation as much as it did Jackson's. Then again, O'Connell was always in constant trouble over money. However hard he worked, however much he earned and got from . . . other members of his family, he was always in debt. . . . His financial problems and his efforts, both serious and comic, to solve them were well known to Dublin Castle, through its spies, and so to Westminster, and this helps to explain the derision he often evoked in English ruling circles.

Yet in a way it was O'Connell's very Irishness, with its weaknesses, as well as its strengths, which enabled him to speak for his country as no one had ever spoken before and to become the first modern populist politician. He was an Irishman in the way Jackson was an American: Both expressed, in a heightened and exaggerated manner, some characteristic traits, prejudices, attitudes, likes and dislikes of their countrymen. Both were quintessentially of their time and place. But O'Connell, while lacking Jackson's huge will and fierceness, had a political brain of great originality and showed organizational skills of no mean order. It was these qualities which enabled him to create the first modern machine of mass politics.

O'Connell's machine rested on three forces. The first was a rabid and coordinated press. In 1823, sensing that the spirit of the age had moved again and that a more liberal spirit was in the air, O'Connell founded the Catholic Association to work for emancipation from legal disabilities. The 1820s, in the United States, Britain, France and Germany, was the first great age of newspaper power. Ireland was no exception. Once Peel left Dublin Castle, the system of subsidized governmental newspapers began to collapse. By the early 1820s it was nonexistent. From 1823 four out of the six large-circulation newspapers were 100 percent behind the association. Three of them, the *Dublin Evening Post,* . . . the *Morning Register* and the *Weekly Register* . . . were completely in O'Connell's pocket. These were highly political papers, which reported the speeches of O'Connell and his satraps in immense detail and were read out loud in gatherings and public houses all over Catholic Ireland. O'Connell's domination of the Catholic media ensured that his association's propaganda reached into every chink and cranny of the south.

The second leg of the tripod was finance. O'Connell repudiated violence; instead, he introduced peaceful mass agitation, and his newspapers told the Irish peasants how they should set about it. As far back as 1784, a proposal had been made of levying a

"Rent" of £1 a year over every Catholic family to provide funds for the emancipation movement. On 4 February 1824, O'Connell launched a new and simple form of this idea through his newspapers. Each Catholic household should put in a penny a month, something which even the poorest could afford. Together these contributions brought in £50,000 a year. This sum was to be spent on legal aid for the Catholic poor, especially those appearing before "Orange" magistrates; on subsidizing and expanding the Catholic press; on educating the poor; on church and school buildings; and on parliamentary business, particularly the presentation of mass petitions drawing attention to Irish grievances. What O'Connell had not initially perceived, but which he soon grasped as the Rent was launched, was that the very act of collecting and contributing not only raised funds but bound militants and the people together into a mass organization, operating from a nationwide network of committee rooms, and forming the third leg of the tripod. Giving their pennies transformed the sentimental support of the peasants into genuine commitment. Collecting turned thousands of middle- and lower-middle-class Catholics into active campaigners. The priests were drawn in, for collections had to be taken at church doors to get the pennies of those without their own homes, such as house servants. Within two years of first organizing the Rent, O'Connell found himself the master of an octopuslike machine, whose tentacles stretched into every village of Catholic Ireland and which could easily be transferred from financial to electoral purposes.

The effects of the financial crash of 1825, and the depression which followed the next year, gave O'Connell his political opportunity. . . .

. . . Ireland, even more than Britain, sank into deep distress, as landlords ceased to spend freely and even raised rents and commerce went into sharp decline. The optimism disappeared. At the 1826 general election, O'Connell's new organization swept all before it at a trial run in Waterford. The peasant 40-shilling freehold voters, overwhelmingly Catholic, deserted governmental candidates in droves, not only in Waterford, but all over the country. Once the Irish Catholic tenantry stood united, shoulder to shoulder, landlordism as the electoral framework of the Ascendancy ceased to work. It was O'Connell's association and its Rent which brought this unity into existence. No movement of this kind, and certainly not on this scale, had ever before been launched in the British Isles or even in France. In the United States, it was still in embryonic form in 1826. It was at this point that O'Connell's repudiation of violence paid handsome dividends. Dublin Castle had no real answer to the man who played the constitutional game. O'Connell did not break the law, but he challenged it by exposing its basic inequity. His candidate at Waterford was necessarily a Protestant sympathizer, for a Catholic, being unable to take the oaths, could not occupy his seat in Parliament. But if a Catholic could not sit in Parliament, he could put up for it.

During 1827, as his movement grew, O'Connell determined to make the gesture himself. An opportune by-election vacancy in Clare the next year provided the opportunity. For the first time, O'Connell, as candidate, was able to put himself publicly and lawfully at the head of a mass movement. He began to address huge gatherings, which came not only from all over Clare but from all over Catholic Ireland. Later, in the early 1840s, one of them was to total over a million men, women and children — the largest political gathering, so far, in world history. Those days were not yet, but the gatherings in Ireland during the Clare election were already vast. Much of the mobilizing was done by parish priests, who tore off their vestments at the end of mass and led their parishioners in demonstrating. For the final gathering for the vote, in June–July 1828, which took place in the county town, Ennis, each group of tenant farmers, sometimes 100 or 200 strong, marched from their landlords' estates in column, and when they reached the county town, solemnly and publicly repudiated their masters' instructions to vote for the Ascendancy candidate, Vesey Fitzgerald. Their solidarity was their strength. A landlord might kick out one tenant for disobedience, but he could not expel them all.

Moreover, all the 3,000 men who had the vote were accompanied by perhaps 10 times as many wives and children, friends and supporters. O'Connell had 150 priests in the town, plus his own lay militants, who saw to the housing and feeding of the throng and to their discipline, for it was vital that the law be kept and violence avoided. . . . When the polls closed, O'Connell led by 2,057 to 982, having secured 67 percent of the votes cast — by the standards of the early 19th century an overwhelming victory. As Fitzgerald put it, "I have polled all the gentry . . . to a man[, but otherwise] the desertion has been universal." He was writing to Peel, who saw the event, quite rightly, as a watershed in history: "We were watching," he informed Sir Walter Scott, "the movements of tens of thousands of disciplined fanatics, abstaining from every excess and every indulgence, and concentrating every passion and feeling on one single object." Here, indeed, was the demos taking the center stage of history. . . .

What was the British government to do, faced with this unmistakable breakdown in its system for ruling Ireland? . . .

Disgusted with the liberal, or "wet" Tories, George IV [had] turned [early in 1828] . . . to the unbending or "dry" ones in the shape of Wellington and Peel. Wellington became Prime Minister, with Peel as his right-hand man in the Commons. This promised to be the strongest government since the Younger Pitt in his heyday. . . .

O'Connell, like Peel, realized a watershed had been passed. As he put it, immediately after the Clare by-election on 10 July 1828: "What is to be done with Ireland? What is to be done with the Catholics? One of two things. They must either crush us, or conciliate us. There is no going on as we are." His somber belief was that with Wellington in power, the choice would be: crush. . . . O'Connell had written to a colleague in alarm: "We are here in great affright at the idea of the Duke of Wellington being made Prime Minister. If so, all the horrors of actual massacre threaten us. That villain has neither heart nor head." In fact, Wellington had both heart and head, and nothing was more likely to persuade him of the necessity for a timely concession than the lawful and emphatic expression of public opinion in Ireland — not the rabble, as he saw, but sober and industrious tenant farmers — which the Clare election constituted. The Duke, indeed, soon convinced himself that change must come; his problem was to convince his colleagues, especially Peel, and his sovereign. He worked on Peel through the summer and autumn and by November, Peel agreed to surrender a lifelong conviction. . . .

In moving the Emancipation Bill through the Commons, Peel was adamant that he was doing the right thing, taking the occasion to state a philosophical doctrine which was to become of ever-growing importance as the 19th century ushered in the modern age. However attached a conservative statesman might be to a particular position, he argued, the need to maintain national order, impossible without a general consensus, was paramount. He would not admit, therefore, that his previous opposition to Emancipation was "unnatural or unreasonable." But nor was his decision to end such opposition. "I resign it, in consequence of the conviction it can no longer be advantageously maintained; from believing that there are not adequate materials or sufficient instruments for its effectual and permanent continuance. I yield, therefore, to a moral necessity which I cannot control, unwilling to push resistance to a point where it might endanger the Establishments which I wish to defend." The King proved more difficult, partly because he kept changing his mind and retracting any agreement to submit to the Duke's earnest persuasions. But finally he yielded, remarking bitterly: "Arthur [the Duke of Wellington] is King of England, O'Connell is King of Ireland and I suppose I am Dean of Windsor."

So the demos triumphed, and the Catholics got their rights. Britain was a liberal parliamentary regime under the rule of law and, once Clare had spoken, Emancipation was inevitable. The event was critical to Ireland, for it not only put O'Connell, with his matchless eloquence, into the Commons, but led, in time, to the creation of the Irish Parliamentary Party, to the Repeal and Home Rule movements, and finally to the creation of the Irish Free State in 1922. But it was central to Britain, too, for it set a key precedent, of government bowing to the clearly expressed will of a national majority, whether it had the vote or not, and so to parliamentary reform.

By the time O'Connell won the Clare election, General Jackson too was well on the way to harnessing the demos to his presidential chariot and sweeping triumphantly into Washington. As with O'Connell, the principal engine driving him to power was the expanding popular press. . . . Shortly after the "corrupt bargain" row began, Jackson, who advanced $3,000; Eaton, James K. Polk and other supporters amassed money to enable one of the General's favorite journalists, Duff Green, to buy out the old *Washington Gazette,* rename it the *United States Telegraph,* and turn it into the principal Jacksonian newspaper. This paper became the model for all the Democrat papers, of which there were soon 50 throughout the country. The level of argument was no higher than that advanced . . . at the Clare hustings. It was envenomed by a degree of personal abuse and malice which make present-day American elections seem tame. There was a particular concentration on what went on in the White House. . . .

. . . A White House inventory revealed that it now contained a billiard table and a chess set. Both had been paid for, as it happened, out of Adams's own pocket. Nonetheless, Representative Samuel Carson of North Carolina, a Jacksonian, demanded to know by what right "the public money should be applied to the purchase of Gambling tables and Gambling furniture?" — a question quickly parroted in the *Telegraph* and its satellite journals. For good measure, these journals added that Adams, who was now portrayed as a raffish fellow, instead of the grim stick he actually was, had pandered to the Tsar while ambassador in Saint Petersburg, by supplying him with a young American girl. Adams was referred to as "the pimp of the coalition."

Jackson's opponents hit back just as hard. The *National Journal* asserted: "General Jackson's mother was a *Common Prostitute,* brought to this country by British soldiers! She afterwards married a *Mulatto Man,* with whom she had several children, of which number *General Jackson is one!*" When Jackson read this statement, he is said to have burst into tears, but he was still more upset by attacks on his wife and the validity of their marriage. These attacks could have led to murder. The attacks on Mrs. Jackson's chastity had started during the 1824 election. As early as 6 January 1825, the General had written to a friend, "with a pen that fairly stabbed the paper," that he was prepared to challenge her accusers to a duel: "I know how to defend her!" Clay was thought to be behind these rumors, and Jackson's supporters swore revenge. One of Clay's Kentucky supporters warned him: "For God's sake be on your guard! A thousand desperadoes . . . would think it a most honourable service . . . to shoot you." . . .

The rumor about Mrs. Jackson finally got into print in an election handbill, . . . and it was printed again in Adams's paper, the *National Journal.* Jackson got a committee of 10 prominent men in the Nashville area to draw up a statement of the facts, accurate as far as can now be ascertained, and it filled 10 columns in the *Telegraph* and Jackson's nationwide press. [Pro-Clay editor Charles] Hammond replied with a pamphlet, *A View of General Jackson's Domestic Relations,* in which he asked: "Ought a convicted adulteress and her paramour husband to be placed in the highest offices of this land?" At this point, Jackson wrote a long, deliberately insulting letter to Clay which, if sent, would have resulted in a duel. But having got his feelings off his chest, he was persuaded by his friends, who knew that yet another duel would have been fatal to the General's electoral chances, to lock it in his desk. Instead, the *Telegraph* printed a report asserting that Mr. and Mrs. Adams had lived in sin together before they were married, adding for good measure that the President was an alcoholic and a sabbath breaker. . . .

Gradually, the Jackson machine developed the capacity to respond quickly, calmly, and factually to attacks on the General and to get their answers printed in the press all over the Union. Indeed, having won the midterm elections and so deprived the administration of its majorities in both houses of Congress, the Jacksonian Democrats had clearly got the upper hand by the time the campaign began in earnest in 1828. They had, to put it bluntly, the more salable candidate. Such items as campaign badges and fancy party waistcoats had first made their appearance in 1824, but it was in 1828 that the real razzmatazz began. The Jackson campaign slogan was cleaning up Washington and stopping high government spending, but the real thrust was a combination of the General's reputation as a military hero and the slogan's mass presentation by a strong media force.

This media contingent was increasingly led by an exceptionally cunning journalist, Amos Kendall (1789–1869), editor of the *Argus of Western America,* who in 1827 had deserted Clay and joined the Democrats. Jackson had long been known by his soldiers as Old Hickory, after what was generally thought to be the hardest wood in creation. This nickname was now used, by Jackson's journalistic advisers, under Kendall's inspiration, as a kind of campaign symbol. "Hickory Clubs" were created all over the country. Hickory canes and hickory sticks were sold to Jackson's supporters and flourished at meetings. Hickory trees were planted in pro-Jackson districts of towns and cities, and hickory poles were erected in the villages — some were still standing in 1845. There were parades, barbecues, and street rallies. The beginning of election gimmickry included the first campaign song, *The Hunters of Kentucky,* which proved enormously successful. It told of the great victory of January 1815 and of "Packenham [*sic*]" and "his brags" — of how he and his men would rape the girls of New Orleans — the beautiful girls "of every hue" from "snowy white to sooty" — and of how Old Kentucky had frustrated his dastardly plans and killed him.

The General himself made few campaign speeches. The aim of his minders was to keep him in the background, fearful that he might say something violent and indiscreet. In fact, the General was happy with these tactics. He argued that it was hard to "bear things with calmness and equanimity of temper," but that he could and did so. . . .

Not only was the General an ideal candidate; he also had the ideal second in command in the shape of the small, fiercely energetic, dandified figure of Martin Van Buren (1782–1862), with his reddish-blond hair, snuff-colored coat, white trousers, lace-tipped orange cravat, broad-brimmed beaver-fur hat, yellow gloves, and morocco shoes. If Van Buren dressed as self-indulgently as the young Disraeli, he had something the latter never possessed: a modern-style political machine. With Van Buren, the age of American machine politics opens. By 1828 Van Buren was the most powerful man in New York State at a time when ambitious politicians hesitated between running for governor there and running for president in Washington. . . .

Van Buren was the first political bureaucrat. He was a quiet-spoken man with no rhetorical gifts, but he had a subtle lawyer's mind and an immense capacity for hard work. . . . [In New York] he constructed an entire statewide system of the party. His main party newspapers in Albany, the state capital, and New York City, propagated the party line and supplied printed handbills and ballots for statewide distribution. The line was then repeated in the country newspapers, of which Van Buren controlled 50 by 1827. The line was set by the party elite, who consisted of lawyers and placemen. . . . Van Buren's own political views sprang from the nature of his organization. The party identity must be clear. Loyalty to majority vote in political councils must be absolute. All measures must be fully discussed and agreed on, and personal interests must be subordinated to those of the party. As his biographer put it: "Van Buren's ideas were innovative in that he identified all of the parts and integrated them into a unified political structure which, once it came into being, supplied its own momentum and its own ideology, an organic mass responding to change yet usually under control."

Was this new kind of political machine, then, totally amoral? Not exactly. . . . [For example,] though Van Buren now had the power to smash it, he supported [DeWitt] Clinton's great project of the Erie Canal because he thought it was in the interests of New York and the United States, despite the fact that the canal, triumphantly completed on 2 November 1825, enabled Clinton to regain the governorship. . . .

. . .The canal, as Van Buren saw it, involved tens of thousands of jobs and countless contracts, all controlled by New York State and therefore at the disposal of its governing party machine. And that is the principal reason he threw his resources behind Jackson. Adams made it clear during his presidency that he was a big-government, big-federal-budget man, who believed that Washington should be the prime engine behind public works projects — roads, canals, ports, welfare services, education and culture: the infrastructure and the superstructure which would turn the increasingly wealthy United States into the greatest nation on Earth. Jackson hated such ideas because he associated big government with George III and colonial rule, and he believed that Adams and his elitist, East Coast allies would turn America into a tyranny run in the interests of landowners and bankers. Van Buren joined forces with Jackson not because he opposed such projects, but because he wanted them planned and carried through by the individual states and by the party machines which controlled them. . . .

Most of 1827 Van Buren spent building up the new Jackson Democratic party nationally, exercising prodigies of tact to win support from difficult men like Benton of Missouri, a great power in the West, and the great but bibulous orator John Randolph, who was often "exhilarated with toastwater." He traveled along poor roads in jolting carriages through Virginia; down to Georgia to conciliate old, sick Crawford; through North and South Carolina; and then back to Washington, commuting between there and Albany. Thus, for the first time, the Democratic "solid South" was brought into being. In February 1828 Clinton died of a heart attack, clearing the way for Van Buren to become Governor of New York State. Van Buren campaigned vigorously to keep the job. Indeed, he spent seven weeks in July and August electioneering in the sticky heat of grim new villages in upstate New York, carrying basic provisions with him in his carriage, for none were to be had, complaining of insects, humidity, and sudden storms which turned the tracks into marshes. He brought with him entire cartloads of posters, Jackson badges, bucktails to wear in hats, and hickory sticks. He was the first American politician to assemble a team of professional writers, not just for speeches but to be lent to newspapers to write election propaganda. . . .

Thus America swung into its first modern election. Adams made a lackluster candidate and the times were against him. The crash of 1825–26 in Europe had hurt even America, isolated though it increasingly was from the storms and stresses of Europe by its own huge expansion inland. Cotton had been badly hit. The 1820s saw the first major strikes in the United States, culminating in a carpenters' strike in Philadelphia which led to the formation of the Mechanics Union of Trade Associations, the earliest American workers' federation covering an entire city. Workingmen were as opposed to bankers as was Jackson himself. They hated being paid in bank notes. A particular grievance of theirs was that if an employer went bankrupt, they had no lien on him for wages, sometimes paid monthly or even semiannually. And the number of employers who went bankrupt was enormous. The *National Gazette* reported on 15 November 1827, that in New York alone there were 1,972 men in prison for debt, some for less than $3. These debtors were given neither food nor bedding, just a quart of soup every 24 hours. In the second half of the 1820s, it was estimated that the number of people who were imprisoned annually for debt in the United States reached 75,000. Moreover, in the four years since the 1824 election, vast numbers of voters, many with little or no property, had been added to the electoral rolls. Most of these people, without quite knowing why, leaned toward Jackson, whom they saw as their champion. There were no real issues in 1828, but Jackson successfully identified Adams with the established order, with property, privilege and oligarchy. His victory was part of a much wider movement, a spirit of the age, which at the end of the 1820s, in Europe as well as America, was displacing those in possession.

This was the first popular presidential election. In Delaware and South Carolina the state legislatures chose the electors of the college, but in the other 22 states, they were selected by all the voters, who were roughly equivalent (except in Virginia, Louisiana, and Rhode Island) to the adult white male population. Thus, the demos came to America. A total of 1,155,340 white males voted, over 800,000 more than in 1824, and in all the circumstances Adams did well to get 508,064 suffrages, carrying the New England states, New Jersey and Delaware and getting a single college vote in Illinois and a majority in Maryland. Even in New York he got 16 out of 36 college votes, for Van Buren was only able to carry the state for Jackson, despite all his efforts, by a plurality of 5,000. That gave Adams a total of 83 electoral college votes. But Jackson took all the rest, 178, and his popular vote was 647,276. There was also evidence that America was moving toward a national two-party system. In 1824 no one voted for Jackson in Massachusetts, Connecticut, New Hampshire or Rhode Island, and no one voted for Adams in North Carolina or Kentucky. In 1828 there were substantial minorities in all the states. The vote, however, was decisive enough to send Jackson to the White House with a clear popular mandate and to end the old indirect, oligarchical system forever.

In those days voting for President started in September and ended in November, but the new incumbent did not take office until March. Jackson arrived in Washington on 11 February, a sad and bitter man. Early in December his wife had gone to Nashville to buy clothes suitable to her new position. While waiting, she picked up a campaign pamphlet defending her against charges of adultery and bigamy. Hitherto the General had concealed from her the true nature of the smear campaign waged against her honor, and the shock of grasping its enormities was too much. She took to her bed and died on 22 December. . . .

Hence, Jackson came to Washington . . . a widower. But he was not alone; from all over the 24 states, his followers congregated on the capital — a huge army, more than 10,000 strong, of the poor, the outlandish, the needy, the hopeful. Washington in the 1820s was by no means an elegant city. . . . But the city was stuffy in its own way, especially after four years of the saturnine presence of Adams. Now the Apostolic Succession of elite presidents had been ended and a man of the people had been chosen. Washington society was appalled as his followers crowded in, many in dirty leather clothes, "the inundation of the northern barbarians into Rome," as someone put it. . . .

. . . [T]he inaugural itself was a demotic saturnalia, reminiscent of scenes from the early days of the French Revolution but enacted against a background of the strictest constitutional legality — Demogorgon tamed, as you might say, but not yet taught good manners. It was sunny and warm. The inauguration took place on the East Portico of the Capitol, and by 10 A.M., a vast crowd had assembled there, held back by a ship's cable. At 11 A.M., Jackson emerged from his hotel and, escorted by soldiers, walked to the Capitol in a shambling procession of New Orleans veterans and politicians, flanked by "hacks, gigs, sulkies, woodcarts and a Dutch waggon full of females." By the time he had walked up Pennsylvania Avenue, the Capitol was surrounded by 30,000 people. At noon, the marine band played *The President's March;* there was a 24-gun salute; and Jackson, according to one critical observer, Mrs. Margaret Bayard Smith, "bowed low to the people in all their majesty." The new President had two pairs of spectacles, one on the top of his head and the other before his eyes, and read from a paper, but nobody could hear a word of the swearing in. Then he bowed to the mob again and mounted a white horse to ride to the presidential mansion. "Such a cortege as followed him," gasped Mrs. Smith, "country men, farmers, gentlemen mounted and dismounted, boys, women and children, black and white, carriages, waggons and carts all pursuing him."

Suddenly, to the dismay of all the gentry watching from the balconies of their houses, it became obvious that this vast crowd was all going to enter the White House. To some, it seemed like the mob taking over the Tuileries; "raving democracy" would enter — without a formal invitation card — "the President's palace." One watching Supreme Court Justice said that those who poured into the building ranged from "the highest and most polished" to "the most vulgar and gross in the nation — the reign of *King Mob* seemed triumphant." Soon the entire ground floor of the White House was crammed. Society ladies fainted, others grabbed what they could get. . . . Clothes were torn in the melee; barrels of orange punch were knocked over; men with muddy boots jumped on "damask satin-covered chairs," worth $150 each, to see better; and china and glassware "worth several thousand dollars" were smashed. To get rid of the mob, the White House servants took huge stocks of liquor onto the lawn, and the hoi polloi followed, "black, yellow and grey," wrote Van Buren's correspondent, "many of them fit subjects for a penitentiary." Jackson, sick of it all, climbed out by a rear window. . . . The scenes at the White House were the subject of much pious moralizing in Washington's many places of worship that Sunday. At the posh Unitarian church, the pastor preached indignantly from Luke 19:41: "Jesus beheld the city and wept over it."

There was more weeping and gnashing of teeth over Washington jobs as Jackson men ousted the old guard. Mass firings and new appointments had long been the custom in Pennsylvania and other states, as well as in New York, but it was Jackson who first applied it to the federal government. One of Van Buren's sidekicks, Senator William L. Marcy, told the Senate that such "removals" were part of the political process, adding "To the victors belong the spoils of the enemy." The term stuck, and Jackson will forever be associated with the spoils system at a national level. . . .

One of the most fascinating aspects of history is the way power shifts from formal institutions to informal ones, where it is really exercised. This happened in England, in the 17th and 18th centuries, when the decision-making process gradually moved from the Royal Council to the cabinet, originally a furtive and rather disreputable body. When the Americans set up their own government, they adopted the cabinet from Britain, though in strict constitutional terms they gave the institution little status. Nonetheless, it survived for the early generations after Independence, as part of the governing system, and it was still functioning effectively under John Quincy Adams. Jackson, however, was the first president to be elected by an overwhelming popular vote and this fact, in a sense, gave him an unprecedented mandate to exercise the truly awesome powers which the U.S. Constitution confers on its chief executive. From the outset of his tenure, an informal group of cronies had begun to confer with him in the White House. They included [Jackson's son-in-law, Andrew] Donelson; Major Lewis; Isaac Hill, the former editor of the New Hampshire *Patriot;* and Amos Kendall, now working in the Treasury. This "kitchen cabinet," as its enemies called it, also included two members of the formal cabinet, Eaton and Van Buren. . . .

. . . The new cabinet held no meetings. It had no agenda. Its membership varied. People thought its most important member was Kendall. Certainly, Kendall wrote Jackson's speeches. The General would lie on his bed, smoking and uttering thoughts. The ex-editor would then dress them up in presidential prose. The Jacksonian congressman Henry A. Wise termed him "the President's *thinking* machine, and his *writing* machine — aye, and his *lying* machine." . . .

. . . Kendall symbolized to observers what was happening to government. The old cabinet had been designed to represent interests from all over the Union. Its members were a cross section of America's ruling class, in so far as it had one — they were gentlemen. The kitchen cabinet, by contrast, brought into the exercise of power hitherto excluded classes, such as journalists. . . . The idea that men such as Kendall were now helping to rule the country horrified Adams and all who thought like him. But what could they do? It was the march of the masses. Jackson, by wooing them successfully, by conjuring them from out of the ground, not only set up a new political dynasty which was to last, with one or two intervals, almost up to the Civil War, but changed the power structure of America permanently. The kitchen cabinet, which proliferated in time into the present enormous White House bureaucracy and its associated agencies, was the product of the new accretion of presidential power made possible by the personal contract drawn up every four years between the President and the mass electorate. That a man like Kendall came to symbolize these new arrangements was appropriate, for if Jackson was the first man to sign the new contract of democracy, the press was instrumental in drawing it up.

QUESTIONS TO CONSIDER

1. Analyze the basic tenets of Andrew Jackson and the Democrats. How did their notion of democracy differ from those of the Founders? How did the Democrats differ from Jefferson and Monroe? What did they see as corruption in government? Why did they seek to extend suffrage to all white males? What, in their view, was the proper role of the federal government?

2. Compare the Democratic Party of the American 1830s with Daniel O'Connell's Catholic Emancipation movement. What similarities or differences do you see in their leaders, aims, constituents, tactics, and opposition? Which do you think was more of a threat to the status quo? In what ways did the different contexts that American and Irish democrats faced shape their actions?

3. Comment on the paradox of democracy's coming into being through "the actions of great men." Does Johnson overstate the roles of Jackson and O'Connell? Did they lead the people, or were they led by them? How did Jackson and O'Connell express, "in a heightened and exaggerated manner, some characteristic traits, prejudices, attitudes, likes and dislikes of their countrymen"?

4. Using the example of Jackson and Van Buren's organization, explain how the American mass political party of the nineteenth century functioned. How was it organized? How did it publicize its candidates? How did it reward supporters? To what extent was it an amoral organization? Did it rely on issues, images, or self-interest for its appeal? What similarities or differences do you see between it and today's political parties?

5. Describe how democratic leaders such as Jackson and O'Connell used the power of the expanding popular press. Did newspapers *represent* or did they *create* popular opinion? To what extent did print journalism lower the standards of political debate or redirect attention from ideas to personalities? Discuss the strengths and weaknesses of the free press in democratic polities.

14

The Second Great Awakening in the United States and Britain

RICHARD CARWARDINE

As the ordered and deferential world of the Founding Fathers gave way to the egalitarian free-for-all of a democratic society, American Christianity underwent a powerful revolution. The Second Great Awakening swept through American Protestant circles in the early nineteenth century, the boisterous grandchild of an earlier outbreak of religious emotion that had stirred the colonies in the 1740s. As in the First Great Awakening, religious "revivals" were led by roving preachers who delivered fiery sermons to crowds gathered at outdoor meetings that sometimes lasted several days. Listeners were told that if they confessed their sins and accepted God into their lives, they could be "born again" as Christians.

Much more than the colonial revivals, as the following essay by Richard Carwardine shows, the evangelical outburst of the early 1800s was geared to democratic currents that were sweeping through American society. Whereas the First Awakening had been intended to bolster the sagging authority of existing churches, the Second expanded the power of dissenting sects such as the Methodists and Baptists and inspired new religions such as Mormonism. And while colonial revivalists were strongly Calvinist in their theology, in camp meetings of the 1820s the chilling doctrine of predestination, which left individuals "damned if you do, and damned if you don't" (according to a popular jingle of the time), gave way to the idea that individuals had the free will to seek their own salvation. Optimistic preachers predicted that Christ's millennial kingdom could appear on earth within a few years if the revival spirit spread, and converts were encouraged to set up reform societies that would rid the world of such evils as prostitution and alcohol. Here was a new democratic religion that paralleled and reinforced "the coming of the demos" in politics. Charles Finney, the preacher who brought revival campaigns to the cities, unabashedly compared his methods to those of professional politicians attempting to stir up votes for their party. Appealing directly to the masses, religious organizers who proclaimed "salvation open to all" could agree with Andrew Jackson and his followers that all white men should be allowed to vote. Both movements sprang from the conviction that "the voice of the people" was, or at least could become, "the voice of God."

Transatlantic ties were another important similarity. Like democratic ideas, religious revivalism crisscrossed the Atlantic in the Age of the Common Man. American Protestants

225

were part of an Anglo-American Protestant connection that shared denominational ties, ministers' visits, and theological trends. During the First Great Awakening the English preacher George Whitefield made seven trips across the Atlantic to electrify colonial audiences with his fire-and-brimstone sermons. After 1800 this pattern reversed as charismatic American evangelists Lorenzo Dow, James Caughey, and Charles Finney brought the Second Awakening's methods to Britain. There, as Carwardine notes, they faced greater resistance than at home. "It is our judgment," Britain's Methodist Conference pronounced after a barnstorming tour by Dow in 1807, "that even supposing such meetings to be allowable in America, they are highly improper in England, and likely to be productive of considerable mischief." Anglican clergyman and landed elites were even more hostile. Nevertheless, the common people of northern Ireland, northwest England, and elsewhere on the "Celtic fringe" found the homespun language and emotional appeal of revivals irresistible, and they flocked to camp meetings by the thousands.

Such immensely popular "awakenings" were bound to have far-reaching effects in the Anglo-American world, for "mischief" or otherwise. Historians have differed sharply over whether the rise of evangelical Protestantism posed a challenge to the existing social order in Britain and the United States, or whether its impact was predominantly conservative. Some scholars have emphasized the role the revivals played in drilling order and discipline into individuals torn away from family or community and set adrift into a world of constant mobility and competition. According to this view, evangelical religion's emphasis on self-help and Christian community encouraged "respectable" middle-class behavior that conformed to the demands of the market economy. In the rapidly growing United States, evangelical Protestants established "home missions" to civilize frontier settlements; in Britain, according to one prominent theory, Methodist preaching "tamed" the potentially unruly industrial working classes, thus preventing a social revolution like those that shook the rest of Europe in 1848.

On the other hand, many scholars have stressed the revivals' potentially explosive effects. When evangelical preachers bypassed established churches, they encouraged the spread of unorthodox sects and doctrines. Revival audiences in border regions such as Wales or the American West felt empowered to press for greater autonomy or political rights. Anglo-American workers mobilized by revival preaching used biblical rhetoric to decry the "rule of Mammon" under capitalism. Women welcomed to revival benches began to venture outside the home for church activities or charitable work. Most dramatically, they and others inspired by the evangelicals' crusading moral fervor joined an antislavery movement that eventually shook the United States to its foundations. It was no coincidence that two of the most effective Anglo-American abolitionists, America's Theodore Weld and Britain's Charles Stuart, were converts of Charles Finney's revivals.

Was the impact of the revivals conservative or revolutionary? Carwardine's careful comparative approach suggests that the effects of the evangelical "awakening" varied among different groups and from place to place. Within the evangelicals' basic democratic message there were injunctions to conform as well as inspirations to rebel. Overall, however, he implies that religious changes led to dramatic contrasts. In the United States, the revivals accentuated the growing cleavage between the North and South over the issue of slavery, forcing sectional schisms among American Methodists and Baptists that prefigured civil war. For Britain, on the other hand, Carwardine seems to emphasize the role evangelical religion played in tempering the social conflicts and dislocations of the nineteenth century's democratic and industrial revolutions. As you follow his comparison, ask yourself why revivals promoted a "Peaceable Kingdom" in Britain yet helped spur the Civil War in the United States.

GLOSSARY

ANGLICAN   Relating or belonging to the Church of England, the established church of Great Britain. Anglicans made up most of Britain's social and political elite, and they generally opposed religious revivals.

ARMINIANISM   The doctrine identified with the Dutch Protestant theologian Jacobus Arminius (1560–1609) according to which Christ died for all humans, not just those "elected" or predestined for heaven. Thus, a person could earn salvation through piety or good works.

CALVINISM   The teachings of Reformation theologian John Calvin (1509–1564), which emphasized human depravity, predestination, and the sovereignty of a wrathful God.

CELTIC FRINGE   Scotland, Wales, and Cornwall, the "fringe" areas of Britain where ancient Celtic languages and folkways persisted into the modern era.

CORN LAWS   Regulations dating from medieval times restricting imports of grain to England in order to maintain high prices. A popular campaign to repeal the restrictions of 1815 succeeded in 1846.

DEISM   The belief, widespread during the eighteenth-century Age of Reason, that a benevolent God knowable by reason created the world. Deists generally opposed formal religion and disputed biblical revelation. They included such prominent figures as Benjamin Franklin, Thomas Jefferson, and Jean Jacques Rousseau.

DOW, LORENZO (1777–1834)   A tireless and controversial Methodist evangelist who conducted thousands of revival meetings from New England to Alabama and toured the British Isles twice. Dow's unkempt hair, flashing eyes, and dramatic gestures enhanced his effect upon revival audiences.

ELECTION AND REPROBATION   Those aspects of the doctrine of predestination that hold that God has predetermined the salvation ("election") and damnation ("reprobation") of individuals.

EMBOURGEOISEMENT   The process of becoming bourgeois, or middle class.

EVANGELICAL PROTESTANTISM   A version of Protestantism that stresses the authority of scriptures over church traditions, the personal experience of sin and conversion, and zealous preaching to the unconverted.

FINNEY, CHARLES (1792–1875)   A prominent American evangelical preacher who successfully brought the Second Great Awakening from rural regions to urban middle-class audiences. His *Lectures on Revivals of Religion* (1835) spread revival techniques at home and abroad, and Finney himself traveled to England in 1844 and 1859 to conduct meetings. His preaching led many converts into reform crusades such as temperance and abolitionism.

JEREMIADS   Sermons, following the example of the Old Testament prophet Jeremiah, that summoned listeners to moral reform, backed by threats of doom if their sinfulness continued.

LAISSEZ FAIRE   The doctrine that an economic system functions best without any interference from government.

MILLENNIALISM   The belief that a thousand-year reign of the kingdom of heaven on earth is coming soon, in fulfillment of biblical prophecy.

NONCONFORMISTS   Dissenters who broke with the Church of England to join other Protestant denominations, including Presbyterians, Congregationalists, Methodists, and Baptists.

PIETISM   Emphasis upon religious observance or personal holiness rather than social improvement.

REVIVALS   Meetings led by charismatic preachers who moved from place to place stirring renewed enthusiasm for Christianity in large numbers of people. Revival preachers exhorted hearers to accept forgiveness of their sins through faith and be "born again" as Christians.

TEMPERANCE   A movement advocating voluntary abstention from alcohol.

TORYISM   The monarchist, pro-Anglican, and generally conservative beliefs promoted by Britain's Tory Party.

YOUNG MEN'S CHRISTIAN ASSOCIATION (YMCA)   An organization founded in London in 1844 by George Williams, a convert of Charles Finney's revivals, and appearing in the United States in 1851. The YMCA's original intent was to foster the spiritual welfare of young men who had moved to cities.

★ ★ ★ ★ ★ ★ ★

In the early decades of the nineteenth century, successive tremors of religious revival rearranged the contours of the social and ecclesiastical landscape of the United States. Evangelical Protestant churches, on the defensive against Deism and rational religion through the Revolutionary era, recovered their confidence during what is known as the Second Great Awakening and established themselves as the primary religious force in the country. During the urgent later stages of the Awakening, in the 1830s and 1840s, hundreds of thousands of new converts became full members of Protestant churches, many of them convinced that the Kingdom of God was at hand. By mid-century evangelical Protestantism was the principal subculture in American society. Although the decade of the 1840s marks something of a fault line, the awakening's

From Richard Carwardine, "The Second Great Awakening in Comparative Perspective: Revivals and Culture in the United States and Britain," in Edith L. Blumhofer and Randall Balmer, eds., *Modern Christian Revivals*. Copyright © 1993 by University of Illinois Press. Reprinted by permission of the author.

influence persisted in a variety of ways, including the renewed outcropping of revivals in 1857–58.

[Historians] of the Awakening, with varying emphases, [have] tended to explain it as a response to changes in the wider culture and also to a new momentum within the churches themselves. The general story line traces the movement of evangelicalism from political empowerment to economic progress to cultural integration. In the first place, this burgeoning, self-confident evangelicalism can be seen as only one expression of profound social changes that occurred between the Revolution and the Jacksonian period. The accelerating development of a national market economy and the geographical mobility of a rapidly growing population, both aided by a revolution in transportation networks and technology, inevitably eroded traditional social relationships. Families broke up, servants ceased to live in the households of their masters, systems of patronage were eroded, and established routes of social progress were closed as new ones opened up. A Revolutionary spirit of egalitarianism challenged — if it did not exactly remove — old social distinctions, eroded eighteenth-century patterns of deference, and fashioned new democratic and republican codes of manners and behavior. New certainties, new communities, new social networks, and new patterns of living were needed in this world of flux and disintegration. For thousands of Americans evangelical religion provided the answer.

That religion was itself changing. Unable to depend on formal state support in the fashioning of a Christian society, enterprising evangelicals turned with formidable energy to the tasks of church-building and soul-saving, reshaping their theology and methods in the process. Influenced by the extraordinary success of . . . Methodism, many in the older Protestant denominations sought to enhance their popular appeal by neutralizing "the repulsive force of the Calvinist doctrines of election and reprobation," the symbols — in this culture — of an elitist, aristocratic society, and shifted toward a democratic Arminianism. . . . "New measure" revivalists emphasized the sinner's free will and ability actively to seek his or her own salvation, and sought to introduce God's kingdom through the systematic application of the laws of religious psychology.

Until very recently, American historians have remained remarkably unimpressed by what was in fact one of the most profound popular movements in the whole of their country's history, and their neglect undoubtedly deserves an essay in itself. For, as Gordon Wood has remarked, the power and range of the Awakening deserves comparison with the religious upheavals of seventeenth-century England and even with the European Reformation itself. Our understanding of the Awakening derives largely from a variety of local and regional studies. . . . In their focus on the local and the particular, the most recent historians of the Awakening have typified much of the best of "new social history," with its painstaking reconstruction of community and social context, and conviction that broad generalizations are best challenged and constructed at the local or regional level. This "rush to the localities" . . . would seem to be vindicated by the fact that there was not one experience of revival, but several; the revivalism of Cane Ridge[, Kentucky,] was not that of Rochester[, New York,] and both could claim only a distant relationship to the institutionalized camp meetings of the Old South of the 1850s or to the prayer-meeting revivals of 1857–58.

Revivals, such as the 1837 Methodist revival meeting in the American countryside depicted here, featured dramatic preaching by roving ministers who set up temporary outdoor camps. Such revivals spread through the South and West after 1800. This lithograph portrays a range of audience reactions, from tearful repentance to drunkenly disregard. It also suggests the large part that women played as converts and recruiters for revivals. Charles Finney, an American evangelist popular in Britain as well as the United States, brought toned-down revival techniques to New York and London, making evangelical Protestantism respectable to urban middle-class audiences on both sides of the Atlantic. (The Granger Collection, New York.)

Local studies, however, through the very closeness of their focus, tend to the celebration of characteristics that are particular and unique to the immediate culture; but the Awakening in its origins and cultural ramifications extended beyond the confines of America. For it is clear from British experience in the early decades of the nineteenth century that the United States was not alone in experiencing a "reformation" in popular religion. Extraordinary as this rolling wave of American revivals was, we necessarily limit our understanding of the phenomenon unless we set it in a much wider cultural context.

Britain, too, had its own Second Great Awakening in the later years of the eighteenth century and the first few decades of the next. Contemporaries did not call it by that name, and neither have later historians, yet these years saw an extraordinary flowering of evangelical religion, most especially in parts of the Celtic fringe and of the industrializing areas of England. Thanks to the labors of Robert Currie, Alan Gilbert, and Lee Horsley we have a good idea of the statistical dimensions of this Awakening. Methodism, in its various manifestations, enjoyed a sustained and rapid expansion at a rate much greater than that of the adult population as a whole up to the late 1830s; in 1840 "the relative strength of Methodism within English society was greater than at any period before or since." At the same time those traditional dissenting denominations that had been energized by Methodist example, especially Baptists and Congregationalists, enjoyed a similar buoyancy if not quite such spectacular expansion. In conjunction with the consolidation of an evangelical party in the established church, these developments provide the context in which to understand the emerging sensibilities commonly associated with Victorian Britain.

Both the [external and internal] factors in this remarkable British awakening evince substantial points of similarity with the experience of North America. In the first place, it is evident that industrialization, more advanced of course than in the United States, set in train social and economic changes very similar in their impact on the lives of ordinary men and women to those occasioned by the market revolution in American society. The demand for industrial labor operated, in conjunction with periods of agricultural depression, to pull people from rural society and smaller centers of population into rapidly growing towns and cities. Suffering from social disorientation and rootlessness, many — though by no means all — struggling miners, colliers, laborers, and artisans found in the warmth and community of enthusiastic religion a source of comfort and self-respect. Not all particulars of the pattern of British evangelical growth match the American. Currie and his co-laborers argue that economic depression limited, and political excitement stimulated, the growth of the most revivalist of denominations, the Methodists. If true, this was quite the reverse of the experience of American evangelical groups in the new republic, whose vexed ministers in flush times resorted to jeremiads about the enervating effects of prosperity and luxury, and who regarded most political excitement, especially that surrounding elections, as a spiritual bromide; the coincidence of high points of church growth with the economic downturns after 1819, 1837, and 1857 could not be clearer. In the main, however, it is not these incongruities that should register, but the broad similarities in the external pressures on British and American evangelicals as they tried to come to terms with a new social and economic order.

Similarities in transatlantic experience were equally apparent in the developments within evangelical churches as they sought to respond effectively to external change. The significant shifts in the thinking and practice of American churches, to meet the human needs and deprivations resulting from wider cultural change, were paralleled in Britain as evangelicals Arminianized their theology and devised agencies of evangelism that acknowledged more overtly the role of human instrumentality. As in America, it was Methodism that did so much to undermine established Calvinist thinking . . . , to "democratize" evangelical theology, to throw up both new forms of evangelistic activity and a church organization that blended discipline, urgency, local participation and central direction, and to promote a new approach to religious revival.

The complementary character of the evangelical upsurge on both sides of the Atlantic was at its most evident in reciprocated contributions, as British evangelical emigrants found a welcome in American churches and, more memorably, as exponents of American revivalism sought to evangelize the Old World. [The American preacher] Lorenzo Dow was an undoubted eccentric, but by no means so peculiar that his visionary zeal could not generate a powerful sympathy among rural Methodists in Ireland, or the indigenous revivalists of Lancashire, Cheshire, and the Potteries. Calvin Colton, through his *History and Character of American Revivals* (1832), Nathan Beman,

William Patton, and Edward N. Kirk all helped popularize protracted meetings and itinerant evangelism in the late 1830s and early 1840s, a time of accelerating revivalism on both sides of the Atlantic. No one did more to advance the "new measures" revivalism among Calvinist evangelicals, especially in Wales and Scotland, than Charles Finney . . . ; his ubiqitous *Lectures on Revivals of Religion* ensured that the revival of 1839–43 in Wales, for instance, would be known popularly as "Finney's Revival." As harvesters of converts in special meetings, however, none enjoyed the formidable success of James Caughey, a Methodist itinerant of little status among historians, but known within the overlapping subcultures of mid-Victorian British dissent as "the king of the revivalist preachers." In this context of transatlantic awareness, it came as little surprise to contemporaries that the revival of 1857–58 in the United States should soon be followed by spectacular revivals in Ulster, Wales, and many parts of Britain.

We should not, of course, attempt blandly to homogenize the experiences of two countries possessing marked cultural dissimilarities as well as congruities. Neither should we seek to avoid the complexities of classification raised by the all-purpose term "revival," which clearly encompassed a number of meanings from one chronological and cultural context to another, ranging from expansive outreach to ritualistic reaffirmation of community values. Nor is it accurate to imply that religious revivals and the subsequent "ism" held as central a place in British society as they did in the United States. Finney's experience indicated that by no means were all evangelical nonconformists receptive to his revivalism; his first visit to England was hindered by the reluctance of many nonconformist ministers to open their pulpits, and for most of his later visit during the revival of 1859–60 his work was peripheral and largely anticlimactic. American Congregationalists and Presbyterians were much readier than their English namesakes to embrace revivals; their gathered churches had generally welcomed and legitimized the "outpourings of the Spirit of God" of the eighteenth-century Awakening. Periodic regeneratory revivals became ingrained in the thinking and practice of the major American Calvinist denominations in a way that was never true of their English namesakes, who quite simply lacked the experience of revivals. As Chauncey Goodrich remarked, "If I were asked why revivals are so frequent in America, and so rare in Europe, my first answer would be, that Christians on one side of the Atlantic expect them, and on the other side they do not expect them."

This contrast was even more significant in the case of the Methodist churches. American Methodism had been at the cutting edge of the Second Great Awakening; such too was its role in Britain. But the commitment of the Wesleyan [Methodist] connection as a whole to revivalism was uncertain at best. . . . The [divisive effect] of revivals [on churches], their association in the minds of many with "enthusiastic" disorder, and doubts over the spiritual changes they evoked, made many exceedingly nervous. Wilbur Fisk was not impressed to be asked by a Wesleyan preacher "whether I thought *revivals* were, on the whole advantageous to the church"; he reflected that "what we in America term revivals are comparatively rare" in Britain.

External pressures also kept revivalism at bay, particularly those deriving from the Anglican establishment and its cultural diaspora [network]. When the United States was faced by the challenge of the new revivalism in the early nineteenth century there were no institutions of sufficient ecclesiastical and social authority to repel it; Old School Presbyterians protested, Congregationalists checked the entry of Methodists into New England, but the structure of church authority was too loose and the power of the once-established churches too limited for the new revivalists to be restrained for long. In Britain, by contrast, the Church of England seemed to American and British advocates of aggressive evangelism to be "an incubus resting on the nation to a great extent, so far as revivals and piety are concerned." Calvin Colton was appalled at how Anglican wealth, social status, and patronage, together with its guarantee of state support, dissipated its drive to save souls. The doctrine of conversion had only limited currency in Anglican circles; as the national church, membership was open to all people as a right. But the Anglican liturgy crushed the free spirit of evangelical worship; the Anglican church lacked the sectarian exclusiveness and sense of separation from the world characteristic of the most urgently revivalist churches of the period.

Moreover, the Anglican church was not just one church among others, but the church of the socially powerful, the nobility and gentry, those who shared and helped shape the church's distaste for revivalist excess. The united front of anti-evangelical clergy and the socially influential in some instances had the power to limit evangelical advance. When, for example, nonconformists began to intensify their home missionary efforts, high church clergy and the local gentry threatened to withhold poor relief from those who attended the ministry of itinerating evangelists or to expel them from church schools or tenancies. Just as significant as formal obstruction was the general climate of hostility created by men of "property and rank and influence" in a society marked by the downward percolation of ideas of correct behavior and by an educational system dominated by Anglican universities and church schools.

In contrast, America presented a much less deferential social order, while its educational institutions were commonly sustained by evangelical denominations for whom college revivals were a matter of custom and celebration. It is hardly surprising then that the expansion of revivalistic sects tended to occur where the parish system of the established church was failing to meet the needs of remote older settlements and untended new ones. Significantly, in Wales, where the parochial system was most inflexible, where there was a rooted tradition of expansive Calvinism and dissenting itinerancy, clusters of revivals on the American model became a feature of nineteenth-century popular religious life.

Historians of the American Awakening, aware that revivals have to be considered a part of a larger cultural process, have pursued a number of related themes. Did the revivals represent a challenge to the social order, or were they principally instruments of social control? Were they a force for cohesion in political culture, or for divisiveness and instability? Were they an irrational, emotional "enthusiasm" representing resistance to progress and a new capitalist order, or were they one of the means by which American modernity was achieved? It seems reasonable enough that those who have posed the questions should have looked within America itself for the answers. But given that Britain and America shared a common experience of awakening and even certain similarities in the roots of their revivals, we may possibly find in the British Awakening an additional perspective on these questions.

Mercifully, historians of the Second Great Awakening in America have on the whole moved away from the constricting approach that saw the movement essentially as a means by which a historic elite sought to maintain social and political control in a rapidly changing world. It might seem to Paul Johnson that the primary key to understanding the Rochester revival of 1830 was that its leaders were engaged in an effort to sustain their authority in a more market-oriented and democratic society. But it is not just the flowering of studies in black religion in the antebellum period that has encouraged us to view the Awakening as a movement of self-assertion by those men and women, black and white, who lacked social standing and political authority. Gordon Wood, in an interpretation that complements Donald Mathews's analysis of southern religion, approaches surging evangelicalism as an early nineteenth-century counterculture through which ordinary farmers, artisans, laborers, and their families expressed their independence of the world of the gentry and the well-to-do commercial and professional classes. We can recognize that social conservatives in church and state tried to turn revivals into instruments of control, but to see the Awakening as in some sense their creation misconceives both its mainspring and its function as a challenge to the status quo.

Interestingly, much the same interpretative thrust marks recent writing on the popular religious movement in Britain. Few would now choose to cast their lot with E. P. Thompson, at least to the extent of his conclusion that Methodist revivals acted as a means of dampening the aspirations of thwarted radicals, that revivalism was a diversion from the political struggle of class against class into a "chiliasm of despair." Thanks to the scholarship of W. R. Ward, we are in a much better position to recognize the significance of popular revivalism, and to see it as a dimension — not a suppression — of political radicalism. As in the United States, Methodism's democratic, egalitarian theology elicited a powerful response from socially marginal groups. From the 1790s to 1820s and beyond, the ecclesiastical and secular authorities, only too well aware of events in France, regarded revivalistic religion . . . certainly with suspicion, and often with terror. The established church, threatened through the phenomenal expansion of nonconformity with minority status and disestablishment, saw not just the excesses of religious enthusiasm but a dynamic challenge to its ecclesiastical control. This was certainly how Welsh revivalism should be interpreted, though in that case there was the added ingredient of fermenting nationalism. Thomas Laquer's study of the early Sunday school movement, closely related to popular revivalism, makes a similar thrust . . . in favor of the liberating motives and function underpinning popular evangelicalism. David Hempton's fine study of Methodism and politics serves to confirm the verdict. . . . Deborah Valenze's imaginative investigation of popular evangelicalism in pre-industrial England has skillfully recreated the world of cottage religion, in which autonomous men and women, including women preachers, resisted the controls of the new entrepreneurial order.

The challenge to the status quo on both sides of the Atlantic, however, remained within limits. In the first place, much of the revivalism of the early stages of the Awakening seems to have been unsympathetic to *direct* political action. The pietism of the revival preachers and those to whom they ministered . . . acted to insulate them against French revolutionary doctrine. Baptist and Methodist revivalists in particular, in Britain and America in the early decades of the century, commonly called on their hearers to

abjure the excitement of politics and concentrate on their own election, not that of political candidates. . . . Though it is clear that the respective political cultures of both
countries were powerfully shaped by the revivalist evangelicalism of the Awakening and
its legacies (contributing issue and style, and shaping constituencies), in neither case did
the surge of revivals take on a single political expression.

Second, whatever the challenge to the status quo, few historians of the British
Awakening have argued that revivals aggravated conflict between classes and sexes. The
explicit equality of individuals, the melting of differences of age, gender, social station,
or even race at the altar or anxious seat may have implicitly questioned social arrangements beyond the house, chapel, and campground; but in practice the revivalist's calling believers into a community of saints was more likely to soften social conflict. In his
study of South Lindsey, James Obelkevich concludes: "Farmers and laborers met on
equal terms in [Methodist] class meetings and farmers listened to sermons preached by
laborers and craftsmen; all of which implied a suspension of class divisions deepening
in the wider society." . . . David Hempton argues that revival-minded Methodists did
not throw up class-warriors as such; stressing that "Methodism both fostered radicalism
and opposed it," he finds the roots of the paradox "in the religious mind itself, with its
acceptance of authority on the one hand, and its desire to have justice and fair play on
the other."

Third, whatever the origins of the Awakenings may suggest about an implicit challenge to the new economic order, the fact is that over time evangelicals were able to
integrate themselves comfortably into the new entrepreneurial world, sharing in its philosophy and values. In the United States, by the later years of the Awakening the new
revivalism was no longer a movement of the fringes, and had itself become influential,
respectable, and middle-class. Nathan Hatch sees in revival theology and the practice of
ordinary Methodists and Baptists a religious counterpart to contemporary doctrines of
economic laissez-faire and individual self-help. In the blend of temperance and revivalism in antebellum America, Ian Tyrrell discerns both millennialist aspiration and, at a
more material level, an avenue for the upwardly mobile, independent-minded artisan.
A similar tale of "embourgeoisement" and enterprise marks early and mid-Victorian
nonconformity in Britain.

Certainly, revivalistic religion pulled in two directions. Some of the disruptive legacies of the early years of the Awakening remained: revivals could undermine orderly
working practices, through the exhaustion of mind and spirit that resulted from high
emotion, the multiplication of meetings, and long hours. In Scotland the Kilsyth revival
of 1839 seemed to lurch out of control as meetings were held at all hours in church,
churchyard, loom shops, factories, and market square. Over time, however, revival
meetings were held in the evening and over holidays to mitigate the worst effects of the
disruption. More fundamentally, Obelkevich sees Methodism promoting "modern attitudes to life and work" in its emphasis on sobriety, organization, and self-worth.
"Methodism acknowledged the infinite worth of the laborer's soul and his practical
worth as an active member of his society." He also argues that the voluntaryism of revivalist Methodists fostered "a new outlook, individual as well as collective, towards
money" and helped develop their business skills. Just as they did across the Atlantic,

revivals and temperance went increasingly hand in hand in Britain (despite the resistance of Wesleyan brewers and innkeepers), suggesting the grip of an ethic of self-help and economic self-improvement.

Revivalism in Britain, then, may have contributed to the emergence of a recognizably modern nineteenth-century economic order. To that extent it has much in common with the progressive, rational evangelicalism that Daniel Howe has persuaded us to contemplate in mid-nineteenth-century America. We may be encouraged to reject the idea of religious enthusiasm as primarily an irrational "movement of counter-enlightenment" and to see the "progressive" elements in revivalism's impact on culture outweighing the regressive. In both societies revivals were often the catalysts of progressive humanitarian and moral reform, drawing on and reinforcing established strains of millennial and perfectionist thought. Increasingly, . . . evangelicals came to look on the state as an agency by which socially and morally desirable ends might be accomplished. If there was an exception to this predicating of a "modernizing" and "progressive" transatlantic revivalist community, it was to be found within the antimission churches of the western and southern states; and in the defensive resistance of mainstream southern evangelicals to some (though by no means all) calls to use the state for reforming purposes. Certainly it was against the perceived archaism of southern culture, sustained by southern churches (and of course against the essentially "medieval" culture of Roman Catholic societies), that northern and British evangelicals . . . celebrated their own social advance.

These reflections prompt us to consider the role of revivals in creating and sustaining a sense of community, both locally and more widely. For although the conversions that were the primary end of revivals can be seen as the ultimate expression of Protestant individualism (indeed the transatlantic awakenings were but a part of a general burgeoning individualism in both cultures), the revivals themselves were only possible because geographically and psychologically displaced men and women corporately yearned for a shelter in which to "belong," or because, having created such a community, they sought to sustain, reinvigorate, and purify it. The revivals of the early phases of the awakenings in the 1790s and 1800s clearly fulfilled the former role; the camp meetings of the southwestern frontier and the protracted Methodist meetings in growing towns and cities created new social networks in a hostile world. Later on, at midcentury, the urban revivalism surrounding the Young Men's Christian Association may have worked in the same way for rural migrants to the cities. But by that date the adding of the "ism" to revival often meant less the overturning of an established hostile culture (though this was how the revivalists liked to perceive themselves) than the rededicating of essentially sympathetic communities that enjoyed an appetite for the nourishment of evangelical preaching and were attuned theologically to the importance of periodical "refreshing." This is what lay behind the convening of protracted meetings, the late-summer camp meeting in the South, or the "sasiwn," the annual outdoor association meeting in rural Wales, where thousands would turn out at the prospect of hearing one or more of the great folk heroes of Welsh society, the itinerant preachers. On these occasions, the community could share in pleasurable society, engage in social diversion and display, and celebrate and reassert its basic values and beliefs on an occasion whose centerpiece was the preaching of a gospel of repentance.

. . . [C]hurches that were born of revival and those that were reinvigorated by revival were pulled together into a larger community. Through the itinerating ministry, the synodical, associational, or conference structure of denominations, and the power of the religious press, the experiences of revival became events of regional and even national significance. British religious converts could regard themselves as part of a ramifying network of revival churches; by such means were localisms broken down and larger communities established. Obelkevich suggests that Methodism "tended to parochialize villagers. . . . [E]very Wesleyan was brought in contact with local preachers from other villages, and from the towns, and with the succession of itinerant ministers. The system promoted circuit mindedness, and beyond that, connection-mindedness." The effect was not limited to connectional churches but extended to those enjoying congregational autonomy and a stationed permanent pastorate; here too the experience of revival could and did act as a bonding agent. A corresponding thrust toward national integration is evident in the United States. The role of revivals and itinerancy in giving birth to a continental vision during the eighteenth-century colonial Awakening was as nothing compared to the capacity for national integration that Donald Mathews plausibly argues was a feature of the Second Great Awakening.

No discussion of the common elements of British and American experience should properly conclude, however, without pointing to legacies that were starkly conflicting. In Britain, the religious revivalism that reinforced the bonds of congregation and class meeting, and worked outward to cement larger communities, operated to mitigate intensities of social class, helping to neutralize one of the most potentially disruptive of social and political forces in an industrializing society, and contributed "cross-pressures" that helped sustain [a] "Peaceable Kingdom." Moreover, the converts of revivals, when they were able to vote, were drawn not only into the Whig/Liberal party that enjoyed a natural link with evangelical dissent, but also into "Protestant," anti-Catholic Toryism. Revival-sharpened anti-popery, particularly among Wesleyans, helped set up political cross-pressures that ensured that revival culture did not mesh straightforwardly with a single political party culture. Revivals came closest to acting as a centrifugal force where the cultural and political cohesiveness they helped create locally or regionally was not fully offset by balancing cross-pressures in the wider culture. Most obviously this was the situation in Wales, where revivals worked against a wider integration into British culture and helped cement the potent [Welsh] amalgam of dissent, economic disability, and incipient nationalism. . . .

One may then assert that, given Britain's social configurations, revivals there made for some degree of cultural integration, but it is less plausible to argue that they acted similarly to sustain national consensus in the United States. American revivals in the early decades of the century certainly confirmed a sense of national mission. Surely, it seemed, they represented divine approval of the Union and the country's republican arrangements. But after the major denominational schisms of the 1830s and 1840s (themselves both symptom and cause of mounting sectional polarization), revivals as affirmations of the community's basic values worked not toward national harmony but toward convincing each section that God was blessing its distinctive social arrangements. The experience of Methodist and Baptist revivals in the South in the later 1840s and 1850s suggested that the Almighty was smiling on the ecclesiastical and social arrangements of the slave states; a sense of a unique southern destiny paraded hand in hand with an emerging pro-slavery millennialism. And what northerner could doubt the significance of the unequal showering of grace on their churches in 1857 and 1858? The Republican party, as had its forerunner the Freesoilers, drank deeply at the well of evangelical revivalism; indeed, the triumph of the Republicans in 1860 has to be traced back, at one level, to the processes set in train by the Second Great Awakening.

The ensuing violent conflict, as we know only too well, was sustained on both sides by a moral intensity that owed much to a prior — and continuing — millennialist revivalism. British Victorian society did not lack moral crusades sustained by revivalistic fervor, whether against drink, slavery, corn laws, [or] Catholics. . . . But Britain's Peaceable Kingdom mercifully experienced nothing to match America's Holy War.

QUESTIONS TO CONSIDER

1. How, according to Carwardine, was the Second Great Awakening a response to changes in American society that took place between the Revolution and the Jacksonian era? What particular changes does he mention, and how did evangelical religion address them? What similar factors or pressures supported revivalism in Britain? In what ways were British churches and British society less receptive to religious revivals?

2. Historians have debated whether the rise of evangelical Protestantism posed a challenge to the existing social order in Britain and the United States, or whether its effects were conservative. What evidence and arguments does the author present on each side of this controversy? Did revivalism challenge established churches or become absorbed by them? Did it push believers toward political action or away from it? Did evangelical Protestantism foment class conflict or dampen it? How, according to Carwardine, was it linked to modern capitalist attitudes?

3. The author interprets religious revivals as both "the ultimate expression of Protestant individualism" and an important force for creating community. In what ways was the revivals' impact divisive? How did they unify believers or create a sense of community? How did revivals, according to Carwardine, promote the development of Britain as a "Peaceable Kingdom"? On the other hand, how did they heighten divisions in the United States that led to the Civil War?

4. Using Paul Johnson's account of "The Coming of the *Demos*" (Selection 13) as a reference point, compare the ways that Anglo-American politics and religion became democratized in the early nineteenth century. In what ways were the ideas and social forces that supported religious revivalism similar to those bringing political democracy? How were they different? How might religious revivals have paved the way for Jacksonian democracy in the United States or parliamentary reform in

Britain? Did social elites react in similar ways to political and religious upheavals? To what extent did democratic movements in politics and religion rely upon the personalities and actions of "great men"? What ideas about race, gender, or class limited these movements' inclusiveness?

5. Some historians see the Second Great Awakening as one phase of a continuing "populist impulse" that democratizes American Christianity in order to maintain its influence on the national culture. According to this view, nineteenth-century revivals set a pattern of religious innovation, theatrical preaching, and emotional faith that recurred in later "awakenings" and infused many ordinary Americans with a renewed religious spirit. What manifestations of "populist" Christianity do you see in today's United States? How are they similar to or different from nineteenth-century revivalism?

VIII

WESTWARD EXPANSION

Among the persistent myths that cloud American history is the notion that the pioneers moved westward into "virgin land." Like most frontiers, the American West was not a shifting boundary between settled and unsettled or "free" land, as the historian Frederick Jackson Turner famously defined it in 1893. Instead, it was a borderland between peoples. On one side, in the first half of the nineteenth century, were French traders, Spanish missionaries, Mexican settlers, and — far outnumbering the others — dozens of Native American tribes. Pushing relentlessly in their direction from the other side were the ranchers, farmers, and entrepreneurs of the young United States. Since many Americans believed that the westward expansion of their civilization was not just economic progress but the will of Providence, the outcome was often a collision, rather than the coexistence, of peoples.

The essays that follow use different comparative approaches to analyze two important conflicts that resulted from the Americans' continual move westward: Indian removal and the Mexican War. In the first selection, George M. Fredrickson juxtaposes the forced removal of American Indians to west of the Mississippi River in the 1830s with another episode of neo-European expansion proceeding simultaneously on another continent: the Great Trek of South Africa's white settlers to that colony's eastern frontier. Continuing the comparison between North America and South Africa begun in Selection 2, Fredrickson suggests why the new U.S. government strongly supported white encroachment on the lands of indigenous peoples, whereas in South Africa British colonial officials did not. In the second selection, a Mexican historian, Josefina Zoraida Vázquez, provides a fresh look at the war between Mexico and the United States in 1846–1848.

Vázquez embeds her comparative approach in analysis of a single event involving two countries. Her overview of the roots of the Mexican War in contrasting national cultures and her portrayal of its impact on both sides demonstrate the value of adopting a dual-perspective approach when studying international relations.

15

Expansionism on the American and South African Frontiers

George M. Fredrickson

Once we discard the myth of the open frontier, we can envision the West as an arena of cultural encounter and conflict, one whose context extends dramatically over time and space. The removal of eastern Indian tribes to lands west of the Mississippi in the 1830s becomes yet another unhappy chapter in the long European conquest of the New World (analyzed in Selections 1 and 2) that began with Columbus and Coronado and was continued for four centuries by Spanish, British, and French colonists and their descendants. More than this: the Americas take their place beside Australia, Asia, and Africa as continents with frontiers where European colonists expanded their empires of trade and settlement by dispossessing native peoples.

Selection 2 of this reader featured a comparison between the British North American colonies and the Dutch colony of South Africa taken from George M. Fredrickson's masterful study, White Supremacy. *This selection carries the story into the early nineteenth century, when the British controlled South Africa and the American colonies had become the United States. Recall that in the mid-1600s the Dutch settled the area around the Cape of Good Hope as a way station for their profitable Asian trade. Venturing out on their own as farmers and cattle growers, Dutch colonists induced the powerful Dutch East India Company, which controlled the colony, to help them enslave some of the native Khoikhoi (or Hottentots) and to put down rebellions as the remainder were forced into the arid interior. But settler expansionism continued to breed trouble. As they moved eastward, the white herdsmen, or trekboers, collided directly with another native African people, the Xhosas, and violence again erupted in a series of frontier wars. This was the situation the British inherited when they took over the Cape Colony during the Napoleonic Wars. (They acquired permanent sovereignty in 1814.) Angered by their British rulers, who abolished slavery and who refused to seize Xhosa lands, some twelve thousand Boers embarked upon a Great Trek (1835–1843) into the eastern interior. There they set up three Boer (or Afrikaner) republics, two of which (the Orange Free State and the Transvaal) held out against the British until the end of the century.*

The presence of two white groups with different nationalities and interests made the expansion process more complicated in South Africa than in the United States. So did the distance between the imperial center in London and its colony across the equator. But the most striking difference between the two frontiers was the British government's reluctance to take over native lands. In the United States, the full force of the state and federal governments bore down upon Native Americans. President Jackson, a veteran Indian hater who had waged war against the "Five Civilized Tribes" of the South, insisted that eastern Indians be moved beyond the Mississippi and threatened to use force if they did not consent. Under the Indian Removal Act of 1830, the Cherokee, Choctaw, Chickasaw, Creek, and Seminole tribes "voluntarily" exchanged their villages and farms for western lands. As many as one-third of them died as U.S. soldiers herded them along the "Trail of Tears" to Indian Territory.

Why did the United States officially support white expansionism while British officials in South Africa discouraged it, at least before the 1870s? Frederickson looks at geography, population ratios, and the relative strength of humanitarianism in the two lands as possible factors. At the essay's end, however, he telescopes outward to highlight the two frontiers' different stages of economic development and their contrasting international positions. The semi-subsistence life of South African herdsmen remained stagnant and relatively isolated from the world market, whereas American ranchers and farmers were connected almost immediately to the dynamic capitalist economy of the young United States and its thriving export business. If we imagine American frontiersmen raising cattle for easterners or selling cotton and wheat to the British, they begin to look like the advance guard of an expanding Euro-American civilization rather than inveterate loners escaping from it. In the terminology of political economist Immanuel Wallerstein, while South Africa remained on the "periphery" of the Europe-dominated world economy, the United States was rapidly integrating into its network as a "semiperipheral" trading partner. America's frontier ranchers and farmers provided essential commodities for the "core" European states and their emerging rival, the industrializing American Northeast. As capitalist entrepreneurs replace maverick adventurers like Daniel Boone and Davy Crockett in the revised western picture gallery, Fredrickson leaves us wondering whether yet another myth of the American frontier deserves to bite the dust.

GLOSSARY

AFRIKANERS   A more recent name for the Boers. Their language is Afrikaans, a derivative of Dutch. Today Afrikaners make up about 55 percent of South Africa's white population.

BOERS Descendants of the original Dutch colonists in South Africa.

CHEROKEES An Indian people of the American Southeast who spoke an Iroquoian language and lived in agricultural settlements. Half the tribe died in an eighteenth-century smallpox epidemic, but in 1827 they established themselves as the Cherokee Nation, with an elected, republican government. When gold was discovered on their lands, a fraudulent treaty obtained by whites forced them to move west to Oklahoma in 1838 along the Trail of Tears.

COLONIAL OFFICE The ministry responsible for governing Britain's colonies.

CREEKS A confederacy of fifty Indian tribes who lived a settled agricultural life, mainly in Georgia and Alabama. Aroused by white encroachment, they rebelled under the influence of Tecumseh in the Creek War of 1813–1814, but were defeated by Andrew Jackson and lost two-thirds of their territory. Eventually, they were moved to Indian Territory in Oklahoma.

DUTCH EAST INDIA COMPANY The company granted a monopoly on Dutch trade east of the Cape of Good Hope. Chartered by the Dutch government in 1602, the company had its own military and naval forces and was authorized to wage war or make peace within its domain. By compelling local Asian rulers to grant it trading privileges, the company routed its Portuguese rivals and dominated the spice trade for over a century.

FEE SIMPLE A privately owned estate of land that belongs to a person and his or her heirs until sold or willed away.

INDIAN REMOVAL ACT (1830) A federal law signed by President Jackson offering Indians in the Southeast land west of the Mississippi in exchange for their eastern holdings. Realizing that Jackson was prepared to send federal troops to remove them, the tribes negotiated nearly a hundred treaties, some of which were fraudulent, for such exchanges.

KHOIKHOI A native tribe of South Africa, called Hottentots by whites. They were a pastoral, transhumant society whose population was decimated as Dutch colonists took over their lands in the seventeenth century. Over time, many intermarried with whites and Asians to form a mixed-race group known as the Cape Coloreds. Others fled northward, where their descendants live in villages in present-day Namibia.

LOUISIANA PURCHASE Under President Thomas Jefferson, the acquisition by the United States of the Louisiana Territory from Napoleonic France for $15 million in 1803. Since this included not just New Orleans but also all the lands drained by tributaries of the Mississippi River westward to the Rocky Mountains and northward to British Territory, the Purchase doubled the area of the United States.

MANIFEST DESTINY The belief that God ordained the expansion of U.S. territory and influence throughout the North American continent.

METROPOLE The mother city of a colony: for the British North American colonies, London.

PONTIAC The chief of the Ottawa Indians who was responsible for an Indian uprising against British occupation of western lands at the end of the French and Indian War. During Pontiac's Rebellion (1763–1766), the Ottawa and allied tribes terrorized white settlers in western Pennsylvania, Maryland, and Virginia. Forced by his allies to seek peace, Pontiac signed a peace treaty with British authorities and was pardoned.

TIPPECANOE   The 1811 battle in which General William Henry Harrison, gover-
nor of the Indiana Territory, defeated an Indian confederacy led by the Shawnee chief
Tecumseh near Tippecanoe Creek, Indiana. Hailed as a great victory, the Battle of
Tippecanoe increased anti-British sentiment in the West (since the British supported
Tecumseh) and effectively broke Indian resistance to white settlement in the Ohio
Valley.

XHOSAS   A branch of the Nguni peoples of South Africa, formerly called Kafirs by
European colonialists. The Xhosas were farmers and cattle raisers who inhabited their
lands for centuries before European settlement. Traditionally they lived in patriarchal
clans governed by an elected chief and council. Today, over four million Xhosas live in
South Africa, most outside the "homelands" that the white government set aside for
them in the 1970s.

✮ ✮ ✮ ✮ ✮ ✮ ✮

At approximately the same time, shortly before or after 1770, the stream of
white settlers in both the American colonies and the Cape [Colony] began to
flow across or press upon certain geographical boundaries that the authorities
had hoped to maintain as at least semi-permanent dividing lines between European and
native society. The movement of American pioneers across the Appalachians and of
Boers into the vicinity of the Fish River in the eastern Cape inaugurated a new phase
of white-indigene confrontation that increased the prospect of endemic warfare between exposed settler communities and indigenous societies with a greater potential for
military resistance than those previously encountered.

In the 1760s, the land to the west of the Appalachian barrier that separated the
coastal plain from the interior of eastern North America, as well as areas on its northern and southern flanks, was still in the possession of independent Indian nations or
confederacies, ranging from the weakened but still intact League of the Iroquois in the
North to the powerful Creek Confederacy and the battered but unconquered Cherokee
nation in the South. In the Ohio Valley just west of the Alleghenies, a heterogeneous
group of tribes had gathered, some of whom had migrated from east of the mountains.
Despite their diversity of origin, these tribes possessed a capacity for collective resistance, as demonstrated by Pontiac's uprising against the British in 1763. It was the
movement of settlers to areas just south and north of the Ohio that set off the major
Indian wars of the revolutionary and post-revolutionary period. Not until the battle of
Tippecanoe in 1811 was the resistance of the Ohio Valley tribes broken for good.

In the eastern Cape, white settlers who crossed the Gamtoos River and pressed eastward toward the Fish in the 1770s collided directly with another expanding population,

the Xhosa branch of the Nguni-speaking peoples of southeast Africa. The Nguni had occupied the area now known as the Transkei as early as the sixteenth century, if not before, and had been slowly expanding westward since that time until some Xhosa offshoots arrived in the area just east of the Fish River at about the same time as the Boers. The Nguni peoples represented the southernmost vanguard of the great population movement of pre-colonial African history, the gradual drift of black communities speaking languages of the Bantu family into most of the continent south of the Equator. The Nguni had a much more highly developed economic, social, and political structure than the Khoikhoi; they combined cattle-herding with sedentary agriculture and were divided into chiefdoms that in the early nineteenth century ranged in size from 1,000 to 35,000. These political units were not larger because of a strong tendency for chiefdoms to divide as a result of disputes over succession. This practice weakened the capacity of the Xhosa to resist the European invaders, but that disadvantage was partly counteracted by their sheer weight of numbers, which was always greatly in excess of that of the white colonists. In any case, [Dutch East India] Company officials viewed with great alarm the beginnings of a conflict over land and cattle between the Boers and the numerically superior Xhosa on the eastern frontier.

In both the Cape and American colonies, the imperial or company authorities sought to avoid expensive new native wars by drawing lines on a map that would mark the limits of white settlements and protect the indigenous societies from disruptive white intrusion. When the British victory in the French and Indian War resulted in the removal of French forts in the Ohio region and raised the possibility that a flood of settlers from east of the mountains would now pour into Kentucky and the Middle West, the imperial government sought to avoid the wars that would inevitably result and preserve a regulated fur trade with the Indians by issuing the Proclamation of 1763. This edict prohibited settlement west of a line drawn roughly along the crest of the Appalachians, forbade Indians beyond the line to sell land without royal consent, and ordered colonial governors to punish white trespassers on tribal lands. Although the same desire for economy that was partly responsible for the policy in the first place prevented the imperial government from making the expenditures needed for effective implementation, even the relatively feeble enforcement efforts that were made irritated the colonists and became one of the grievances that led to the American Revolution.

Although the Cape came temporarily under British rule from 1795 to 1803 and then permanently after 1806, official frontier policy remained relatively constant. Whether British or Dutch authorities were making the effort, the aim was to draw a firm line of demarcation between the Boers and the Xhosa. But here the problem was even more intractable than in North America, not only because of the government's failure to commit resources necessary for enforcement but because there was no natural boundary at all. The rapidly migrating Dutch and the slowly drifting Xhosa arrived in the pasture lands west of the Fish River known as the Zuurveld at about the same time in the 1770s. Rivalry for pasturage and cattle theft by both sides resulted in the First Frontier War of 1779–81. Victories by white militia over some of the chiefs led to efforts by the government to induce the Xhosa to withdraw from the Zuurveld and recognize the Fish River as the boundary. But this policy failed and another war broke out in 1793.

Hopes for a negotiated settlement foundered because paramount chiefs east of the Fish, who were willing for reasons of their own to accept the boundary line, had no effective control over the sub-chiefs who had migrated across the river. Furthermore, the Fish was a meandering, shallow river that was easy to cross, and ejected groups could readily return. The British inherited this border problem and were forced to fight an unwelcome war in 1799, during which the hostile Xhosa were joined by rebellious Khoikhoi. It was not until 1812 that forces commanded by the British finally succeeded in driving the Xhosa out of the Zuurveld for good.

The goal of Dutch and British policy on the eastern frontier was similar to that of the British in North America just before the Revolution — the government hoped to limit white expansion and regulate contacts with the indigenous people in such a way as to maintain control over the frontiersmen and prevent inter-racial violence. Left to themselves, settlers were prone to engage in aggressive behavior that risked provoking native wars because they assumed that government forces would bail them out and that the resulting peace treaties would open up additional land for their own use. The attempts of the authorities to limit expansion and their failure to provide adequate protection from native attacks or raids on the frontier farms created intense dissatisfaction with the official native policy and weakened the allegiance of the Boers to the colonial government.

The attempt of the British to arrest the moving frontier in North America contributed to a similar spirit of dissension among the colonists. This policy is not usually regarded by contemporary historians as one of the most important causes of the American Revolution, but, if we recall that the stationing of a substantial British army in America and the taxation of the colonists for its support was necessitated in part by the need to police Indian-settler relations, then the policy of frontier containment takes on added importance as a precipitating factor. Furthermore, the Quebec Act of 1774, one of the "intolerable" acts that led to open hostilities, threatened to put a permanent limit on the expansion of the northern colonies by incorporating the region north of the Ohio into an enlarged Quebec colony that the Crown would rule directly and where the laws and Catholic religion of the French-speaking inhabitants would be respected. Support for an independence that would remove actual or potential restraints on American expansionism came not only from actual pioneers but, even more significantly, from men of influence and property on the seaboard who were involved in land speculation schemes west of the mountains. From a broader perspective, the effort to limit westward movement can be seen as one aspect of a comprehensive policy of imperial regulation that threatened to stifle the ambitions of an emerging capitalistic class in the colonies.

In South Africa, dissatisfaction with ineffectual or restrictive frontier policies was limited mainly to the border regions themselves, but it was sufficiently intense to provoke open rebellions that were a direct consequence of differing views on native policy. In 1795, complaints about the failure of the Company to drive the Xhosa out of the Zuurveld, provide security for frontier farms, and authorize punitive expeditions to recover stolen cattle inspired settler uprisings and abortive efforts to establish independent republics in the districts of Graaff-Reinet and Swellendam. The British, who were just taking over the colony at the time (as a war measure directed at the French and the new revolutionary republic in the Netherlands that was allied with them), quickly put down the insurrections by withholding supplies of ammunition; but a new uprising occurred in Graaff-Reinet in 1799. This one was also quickly suppressed, but not before it had unsettled conditions on the frontier to such an extent that a devastating war ensued with the Xhosa offshoots in the Zuurveld. The growth of a sectional settler consciousness thus antedated the British presence, but the imposition of foreign rule over the Dutch-speaking frontiersmen undoubtedly increased their sense of alienation from a government that seemed more interested in mediating and adjusting their conflicts with the Xhosa than in guaranteeing their safety and pushing their claims. If the American Revolution had some of the character of a white settlers' revolt against imperial native policy but involved a great deal more, the insurrections in the eastern Cape were — despite the relatively small numbers of whites involved — the first pure cases of settler rebellion against a metropole with different ideas about the treatment of indigenous peoples.

The fact that the American Revolution succeeded whereas the first attempts at settler independence in South Africa failed rather ignominiously made for different patterns of subsequent interaction between frontier whites and the central government. The newly established government of the United States proclaimed its jurisdiction over all Indians in its territory but wished to avoid the expense of military action against tribes that still had the capacity for sustained resistance. Furthermore, American statesmen were conscious of the fact that the new nation's self-justifying image as a virtuous republic would be tarnished in the eyes of a skeptical world if they permitted naked aggression against the Indians; consequently they characteristically professed the most benevolent intentions toward the red "children" of the "great white father" in Washington. Laws were passed in the first Congress governing intercourse between whites and Indians and establishing the principle that Indian land could be alienated only by the Indians' own consent and as a result of compensated transfers negotiated by the federal government and formalized by treaties. During the same period, Thomas Jefferson and others proclaimed a national commitment to the "civilization" of the Indian and his incorporation into American society with full citizenship rights. But the Jeffersonian ideal of Indian acculturation and assimilation was very conveniently tied to an expectation that Indians would lose most of their land. Only when they had been divested of their "surplus" hunting lands, Jefferson believed, would they be forced to become yeoman farmers and potential American citizens. It was also Jefferson who first conceived the idea of removing most eastern Indians to the trans-Mississippi West, a policy which became a theoretical possibility after the Louisiana Purchase of 1803.

The key to understanding American Indian policy between 1790 and 1830 is not the philanthropic and assimilationist rhetoric but the fact that the government was responsible to a white electorate convinced that the destiny of the nation and, in many cases, its own interests required the rapid extension of white settlement into areas still occupied by Indian nations. The extinction of Indian title and the removal of the Indians themselves were the generally accepted objectives; the only important differences of opinion were on the question of how rapidly and by what methods they should be carried out, and whether or not exceptions should be made for "civilized" Indians.

Widely distributed by the famous Currier and Ives firm, this popular lithograph, titled "Across the Continent," is a veritable allegory of Manifest Destiny. The railroad and telegraph lines penetrate the vast spaces of the West, bringing with them the beneficent forces of American civilization: farms, schools, and churches. The Indians, outnumbered and cast aside, can only watch in awed acquiescence. (Museum of the City of New York, The Harry T. Peters Collection.)

Between 1815 and 1824, a white supremacist policy of comprehensive Indian removal began to take shape. It did so in the context of growing disillusionment with Jeffersonian hopes that the Indians would voluntarily give up their "unnecessary" land and embrace white "civilization," and that white settlers would then accept them as members of their communities. These hopes were foundering as a result of the persistent and demoralizing pressure of white settlers on Indian lands, the reluctance of most Indians to abandon their traditional ways, and the refusal of state governments, particularly in the South, to give citizenship rights to "civilized" Indians who chose to accept the individual land allotments that were sometimes provided for in treaties. The state of Georgia was particularly adamant in its refusal to grant security of tenure to Indians holding land on a basis of individual ownership, despite the fact that relatively little acreage was involved. Georgia wanted nothing less than the extinguishment of all Indian land-holding within its borders in literal fulfillment of a pledge made by the federal government in 1802 that all tribal land within the state would become available for white occupancy as soon as the federal government could induce the Indians to relinquish title. Georgia's refusal signaled, according to the historian Reginald Horsman, the bankruptcy of the civilization and assimilation policy: "The logical conclusion of the civilization policy was land in fee simple and Indian citizenship, but the frontier states were unwilling to accept this." Faced with this reality, the Monroe administration proposed to

Congress a plan to remove virtually all eastern Indians "whether they liked it or not, whether they had become civilized or not," to designated areas west of Missouri and Arkansas.

Despite the establishment of this general policy, the pace of removal through negotiation during the 1820s remained too slow to satisfy the whites who coveted the Indian land. In 1828, Andrew Jackson, a veteran Indian fighter and long-time proponent of more coercive methods than the federal government had been willing to allow, was elected President with massive southern and western support. Between 1828 and 1831, the state of Georgia defied the clause of the Constitution giving the federal government exclusive responsibility for Indian affairs by unilaterally extending state law over the Cherokee nation within its borders and abolishing the tribal government. Jackson not only condoned this action but refused to enforce a Supreme Court decision disallowing it. Furthermore, he used his alleged inability to avert such state action as a way of bludgeoning other tribes to agree to removal treaties. The Indian Removal Act passed by Congress in 1830 gave him the funds and the authority to carry out the mass deportation of eastern Indians under federal direction, and during the next few years removal was carried out in ways that often caused great suffering to the migrating tribesmen. The refusal of the Cherokee leadership to agree to move voluntarily pricked the public conscience, particularly in the Northeast, because the Cherokees had gone further than any other Indian people in adopting the white man's way of life, even to the point of establishing a republican form of government and achieving literacy in their own language. But despite the fact that the traditional rationale for expropriating Indian land was inapplicable to the Cherokee because of the extent to which they had become agriculturalists on the white model, they were nonetheless rounded up by federal troops in 1838 and forcibly marched to Oklahoma. Because of their lack of preparation for the move and the brutal way it was carried out, an estimated 4,000 out of a total of 15,000 died on the way westward.

Events unfolded very differently on the eastern Cape frontier. Slowly driven back as the consequence of a series of border wars, the Xhosa were eventually forced to open up the portion of their territory between the Fish and Kei rivers to white settlement, and they saw the rest of it fall under British sovereignty in the late nineteenth century. But they were not displaced or removed to make way for an expansion of the kind of settler society that had developed in the western Cape. The main reason that they remained in *de facto* possession of most of their original territory and the predominant population group in the remainder was demographic. They always greatly outnumbered the white invaders and did not experience the disastrous loss of population as a result of white contact suffered by such other indigenous populations as the Khoikhoi and the American Indians. Their ability to maintain their numbers and the failure of the white population to grow rapidly as a result of the kind of massive immigration that occurred in the United States meant that they were never in danger of being overwhelmed by anything like the flood of settlers that populated much of the region between the Appalachians and the Rockies before the Civil War.

Despite their relative lack of numbers, South African frontiersmen shared some of the eagerness of their American counterparts to displace the indigenes in their immediate

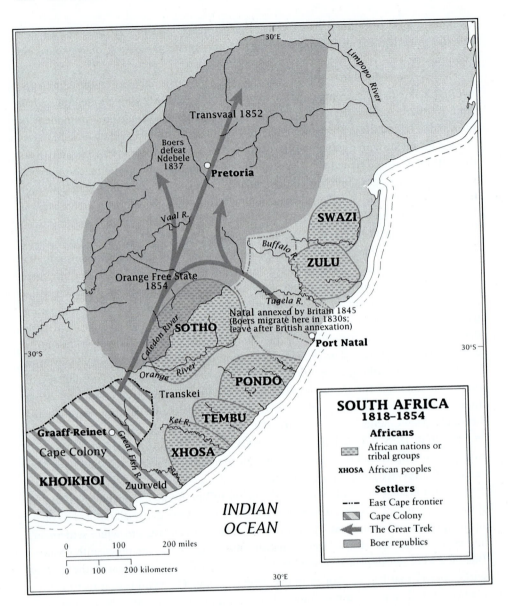

SOUTH AFRICA 1818–1854

Africans

African nations or tribal groups

XHOSA African peoples

Settlers

East Cape frontier
Cape Colony
The Great Trek
Boer republics

Transvaal 1852

Boers defeat Ndebele 1837

Pretoria

SWAZI

Vaal R.

Buffalo R.

ZULU

Orange Free State 1854

Tugela R.

Natal annexed by Britain 1845 (Boers migrate here in 1830s; leave after British annexation)

SOTHO

Caledon River

Port Natal

Orange River

PONDO

Transkei

Kei R.

TEMBU

Graaff-Reinet

XHOSA

Cape Colony

Great Fish R.

KHOIKHOI

Zuurveld

INDIAN OCEAN

0   100   200 miles

0   100   200 kilometers

Limpopo River

30°E

30°S

30°S

30°E

path, although their traditional reliance on native labor meant that they did not desire anything like the kind of wholesale removal that occurred in the United States. The fact that American expansionists had an adequate supply of black slaves to work the cotton plantations of the South, or enough family members and white hired hands to carry on the mixed farming that developed in the Middle West, meant that all Indians were dispensable. But in South Africa enough of the indigenous population had to remain in newly acquired white farming areas to provide the Boers with a labor force of a size they had come to regard as adequate. Nevertheless, South African frontiersmen were as interested as American settlers in gaining access to new lands and usually had hopes of expelling or encapsulating the "surplus" natives. The first step in what many must have hoped would be a continued eastward penetration was the establishment in 1819 of a "neutral zone" between the Fish and Keiskamma rivers, which was supposed to be vacant but in fact provided scope for white encroachment. This area quickly came to be known as the "ceded territory," and the government responded to the settlers' land hunger by granting them farms there.

By 1834, white farmers had occupied much of the "ceded territory" and some were intruding into areas explicitly reserved for the Xhosa. In that year the Xhosa launched a massive counterattack which involved devastating raids deep into the colony. But the British army crushed the invaders, and the settlers had good reason to anticipate a settlement that would give them access to much new territory. The British governor obliged by annexing the large area to the east of the "ceded territory" between the Keiskamma and the Kei, and he initially proposed that the hostile tribes be driven east of the Kei so that the whole region could be opened to white settlement. But the Colonial Office in London overruled the annexation itself and ordered that the entire area be retroceded to the Xhosa.

This determination to break an established pattern of dispossessing some of the Xhosa after defeating them in a "defensive" war resulted from a mixture of economic and philanthropic motives. From the point of view of the Colonial Office, territorial gains from one native war simply provoked another and were part of a never-ending sequence that placed an intolerable burden on the exchequer while bringing no tangible benefits to the British Empire. Furthermore, the humanitarian movement in England had begun to shift its interest from the emancipation of slaves to the protection of aborigines from brutal treatment by white settlers. Lord Glenelg, the Secretary of State for the Colonies, who made the decision to veto the new acquisition in South Africa, was close to the philanthropic lobby and quite prepared to believe the claim of some missionaries that the war had been an unjust one resulting primarily from illicit cattle raids and other provocative acts on the part of the Boers. But his action was probably conditioned more by fiscal considerations than by humanitarian idealism.

The Boer frontiersmen were bitterly disillusioned with British native policy. A number of grievances had been building up over the years concerning official interference with their own methods for controlling and disciplining the nonwhites who competed with them for land and cattle or worked as servants on their farms; the retrocession of the area that the governor had prematurely incorporated into the colony as "Queen Adelaide Province" was for some the last straw. The Great Trek — the mass migration of organized groups of Afrikaners in a northeasterly direction to regions beyond British control — had already begun, but it gained new recruits and a new sense of urgency after Glenelg's decision became known.

It is a curious and ironic coincidence that the Great Trek took place at almost precisely the same time as Indian removal in the United States. In one instance the indigenous population was forced to trek to make way for white farmers and planters, and in the other it was a substantial part of the settler population that did the trekking, partly at least because the government *refused* to provide access to the lands of natives in their immediate path. An explanation of the differing outcomes of what were in some ways similar situations may reveal much about the comparative dynamics of early-nineteenth-century white expansion in the two societies.

A large part of the explanation derives from the relative population density and demographic vitality of the Xhosa, making them of course a much more formidable obstacle to white expansion than the trans-Appalachian Indians. Also significant were the differing ways in which the settlers related to the frontier environment and envisioned its future economic development. Although there were some legendary American frontiersmen who moved on as soon as they could see the smoke from their neighbor's chimney, most migrated to the newly opened territories of the West with the desire to establish permanent homesteads, engage in sedentary agriculture, and "grow up with the country" as it became more populated, town-centered, and economically diversified. To typical settlers the frontier was a passing stage on the way to a recapitulation of the civilization they had left behind in the East. But for the Boer frontiersmen of the early nineteenth century a semi-subsistence pastoralism had become a permanent way of life. They neither desired nor anticipated the kind of economic "progress" that was eagerly awaited on the American frontier.

Since ecological conditions on much of the South African frontier were not only unsuitable for settled agriculture but did not even offer much promise for permanent occupation of the same pasture lands, survival often required a willingness to move on without leaving much behind except overgrazed wastelands. It was therefore quite natural for such a population of graziers to respond to any obstacle to their perpetual expansion — whether it was human or physical — by outflanking it and trekking off in a new direction. Their only ambition was to perpetuate their existing way of life wherever this could be done; for there was little sense on the South African frontier that white movement was part of a process of cultural and economic evolution that would culminate in the reproduction of a civilized society on the model of Europe or even of Cape Town. When conditions became difficult on the eastern frontier, they simply outflanked the Xhosa barrier by moving northeastward into regions where there seemed to be more open land and where they could continue their pastoral existence in a more secure environment. But that security turned out to be illusory; they soon came into conflict with other African peoples such as the Zulu, the Ndebele, and the Sotho, who were no more willing than the Xhosa to tolerate white encroachments. Consequently warfare with indigenous peoples continued to be a central element in the Boer experience.

Yet the Trek was more than a response to ecological and demographic circumstances. For those migrants joining the organized parties whose leaders proclaimed their desire to escape from British jurisdiction, it was also an act of political protest against the colonial government and its native policies. The . . . ideological conflict of Boer and Briton in the early-to-mid nineteenth century . . . [had many dimensions]; here it is enough to stress that the trekkers had a different relationship to constituted political authority than the frontier whites who coveted Indian land in the United States. The United States government was strongly susceptible to pressure from frontier expansionists, especially when Andrew Jackson, one of their most ardent spokesmen, occupied the White

House. Furthermore, the semi-autonomous state governments which impinged on the Indian frontier were totally dominated by the land-grabbing, Indian-removing mentality. But in the Cape effective political power was in the hands of British imperial authorities who were ethnically alien to the majority of the settlers and reluctant, in this period at least, to authorize the territorial expansion of the colony. Unlike the American frontiersmen who felt the power of a great nation behind them and considered themselves as archetypical exponents of American nationalism, the Boers were not only on their own but to some extent felt that they themselves were a persecuted ethnic group. Their constant complaint, almost inconceivable in the American situation, was that the government gave more consideration to native interests than to their own. This in fact was not strictly true, but the tendency of some British spokesmen, particularly missionaries, to blame the Boers whenever trouble broke out and to stigmatize their way of life as scarcely more civilized than that of their indigenous rivals cut deeply and made the Great Trek as much a reactive movement away from the British as a positive search for new opportunities. Comparing the kind of moving frontier associated with the Indian removal with that implied by the Great Trek is to juxtapose a situation where expansion of white settlement at the expense of indigenous peoples was seen as a legitimate fulfillment of a national destiny with one where it had more of the character of a divisive sectional or ethnic interest. This contrast should not be exaggerated, because Britain did in the end make a decisive contribution to the white colonization of South Africa; but in the era of the Great Trek, between the 1820s and the 1850s, such an intention was not at all clear.

These differences in the degree of commitment and legitimacy accorded to settler expansionism can be explained to some extent by noting the relative strength of missionary or humanitarian pressure groups. British policy-makers in the 1820s, 30s, and 40s paid respectful attention to a philanthropic lobby that stressed the mistreatment of the "aborigines" by the settlers and called for strong protective measures to keep native societies insulated from frontier whites so that missionaries could work for their conversion and civilization before they had been corrupted or degraded by the settlers. American missionaries working among the eastern Indians subscribed to much the same philosophy, but eventually most of them gave up hope of accomplishing the civilizing mission so long as a seemingly irresistible tide of white settlement encapsulated and then pressed inward on Indian territories east of the Mississippi. Ultimately, most of them acceded to the policy of Indian removal on the grounds that this would give them a second chance to nurture civilization and Christianization, in a more gradual and controlled fashion. This decision was based on a recognition that the government was unable or unwilling to take firm action to expel white intruders who plied Indians with alcohol and swindled them out of their lands and other resources.

A deeper explanation for the differing degrees of official or public support for settler expansionism in this era can be derived from the fact that South Africa and the United States were at radically different stages of economic development. The expropriation of Indian land in the Age of Jackson made a vital contribution to the growth of a dynamic capitalistic economy. Perhaps, as Michael Rogin would have it, Indian removal was an American form of what Marx called the stage of "primitive accumulation," a necessary prelude to free-market capitalism that involves the destruction by political or military means of precapitalist forms of holding land and using other natural resources so that these sources of wealth can be made available to emergent entrepreneurs. It is clear enough, as Ronald Satz has pointed out, that the "expectant capitalists" of the Jacksonian period put "unremitting pressure" on the government "to open new lands for sale and purchase." Hordes of land speculators, would-be timber and mining barons, and even slave-traders had vested interests in Indian removal that were perhaps even more influential than those of agrarian settlers. The strongest impulses of a market economy heading for industrial takeoff were thus enlisted behind Indian dispossession in the 1830s.

South Africa, on the other hand, was not experiencing rapid economic development or change at the time of the Great Trek. There was a market of sorts for agricultural commodities in Cape Town, but before the rise of wool as an export commodity between 1835 and 1845, it was still the sale of foodstuffs to passing ships that sustained most agricultural activity. The frontier pastoralists did send some of their cattle to market, along with such by-products as butter and tallow, but basically theirs was a semi-subsistence economy; such items as ammunition, coffee, sugar, and some clothing were all that they needed to purchase from the outside world. The expansion of the frontier opened no new sources of wealth for the enterprising; it simply extended and accentuated this pattern. Indeed, the farther the Boers wandered the less access they had to a market and the more self-sufficient they became. Nothing like the American pattern in which new lands were quickly exploited for commercial agriculture and tied in with expanding markets could develop in such a situation. Furthermore, before the beginnings of diamond-digging and gold-mining in the 1870s and 80s, South Africa had no known mineral resources to provide a foundation for industrialization.

From the vantage point of British imperialists of early to mid century, the Cape was an economically unsuccessful colony, and their only justification for being there at all was to control the sea lanes around the Cape of Good Hope to protect the passage to India. Consequently, there was no strong economic motive emanating from the metropole or even from commercial interests within the colony to expropriate native land or labor on a large scale in response to a grandiose vision of future economic development. The interest in further native dispossession or subjugation remained a local interest on the frontier, one which might involve the government in military actions but did not crucially concern the colony as a whole, to say nothing of the British Empire. No generally accepted ideology of "manifest destiny" — of the kind that sanctioned Indian removal and was central to American dreams of progress and prosperity — yet existed; but in the 1840s and 50s a special sense of mission began to emerge among the Afrikaner trekkers who were by then in the process of establishing their own republics. The idea that there was a divine plan to establish independent white Christian communities in what . . . [later became] Natal, the Orange Free State, and the Transvaal contained the seeds of an Afrikaner nationalism that would eventually lay claim to all of South Africa in the name of ethnic and racial supremacy.

QUESTIONS TO CONSIDER

1. What considerations shaped the policy of British imperial authorities toward indigenous peoples in their colonies? What forces restrained British expansion and dispossession of the natives? What happened when the British tried to draw a permanent line between white settlers and indigenous peoples in North America and South Africa? In what way were the American Revolution and the Boer insurrections of the 1790s similar? How does the author contrast the Great Trek with America's Indian removal?

2. What was the predominant idea behind early U.S. policy toward American Indians? Why does Fredrickson think that the policy of "civilizing" and assimilating Native Americans was doomed to fail? What role did Andrew Jackson play in removing Indian peoples to the West?

3. Why were the South African Xhosas able to withstand white expansionist pressures in the 1830s, whereas the American Cherokees were not?

4. How did nineteenth-century Americans identify westward expansion with progress? Did South Africans have an ideology of manifest destiny? Why or why not? How did the two countries' differing stages of economic development explain their policies toward settler expansionism?

5. In what ways, if any, has Fredrickson's comparative approach changed your image of the American frontier?

16

Mexicans and North Americans
on the War of 1847

JOSEFINA ZORAIDA VÁZQUEZ

By the 1830s, the westward movement of Americans pushed past the Louisiana Territory into Texas, which, along with the vast provinces of New Mexico and Upper California, the Republic of Mexico claimed as its Spanish inheritance. Thousands of Americans, mostly southerners, were permitted to enter Mexican lands but defied the law by retaining their slaves and refusing to become Catholics. In 1836, they rebelled against Mexican rule and, despite brutal reprisals by the Mexican general Santa Anna, won their independence. The issue of annexing Texas, complicated by war threats from Mexico and the slavery question, remained unresolved in American politics for the next eight years.

Democratic president James Polk, an ardent expansionist, saw the Texas question as a step toward fulfilling America's Manifest Destiny. Polk set his sights not only on Texas and Oregon (whose boundary with British Canada was under dispute) but also on California, which he regarded as too distant for Mexico to rule and hence ripe for takeover by England or France. Once Polk was elected in 1844, events moved swiftly. Early in 1845, Congress annexed Texas by joint resolution. Polk ordered American naval vessels to take up positions outside Mexican ports and sent U.S. forces under the command of Zachary Taylor to Corpus Christi. Meanwhile, he dispatched an emissary, John Slidell, to Mexico City with an offer to pay $5 million to settle the dispute over Texas, another $5 million for New Mexico, and up to $25 million for California.

Instability in the Mexican government worsened the already tense situation. The Mexican president, José Herrera, wanted peace but feared his people's wrath should he formally recognize Slidell. He equivocated by appearing willing to negotiate with the United States and at the same time ordering General Mariano Paredes y Arrillaga to subdue the Texans. Paredes promptly turned his army against Herrera, installed himself as president in January 1846, and rejected Polk's emissary. In response, Polk prepared a war message for Congress and issued an order sure to provoke the Mexicans. He ordered General Zachary Taylor's troops to cross the Nueces River (asserted by Mexico as the Texas boundary) and march 125 miles southward to the Rio Grande. A few weeks after Taylor's men entered the disputed territory, Mexican soldiers attacked them, and the United States declared war.

In a year and a half U.S. troops led by Generals Taylor and Winfield Scott overwhelmed the disorganized Mexican army. By the Treaty of Guadalupe Hildago (1848), Mexico recognized the Rio Grande as the boundary with Texas and ceded California and the New Mexico territory to the United States for $15 million and the assumption of $3.25 million in Mexican debts. The United States now controlled the Southwest, but the acquisition of new territory ignited a controversy over the extension of slavery that eventually led to the Civil War. As for Mexico, it suffered through more political and economic chaos, and had to endure episodes of foreign intervention (under the pretext of collecting debts) until 1867, when Benito Juárez finally freed the country from the French-imposed dictator, Maximilian.

The truism that every story has two sides is especially appropriate to foreign affairs. What historians in the United States call the Mexican War, Mexican writers call the "North American Invasion" or the "War of American Aggression." In this selection, Josefina Zoraida Vázquez, a distinguished Mexican historian, offers a glimpse of that other side. Vázquez makes it clear that she believes the United States provoked hostilities. But rather than condemn or defend either country, she tries to understand a war that both North Americans and Mexicans would like to forget, although for different reasons. Her explanation takes us back to the colonial period as she traces the roots of U.S. expansionism and the fragility of Mexican independence. In her most penetrating passages, she emphasizes the long-term causes of the war, its international context, and, finally, its psychological impact on the two nations. These are revealing themes not often found in U.S. history texts. Seeking to inform Mexican readers about the United States, Vázquez has at the same time given North American readers a new perspective on the histories of the two republics.

GLOSSARY

AUSTIN, STEPHEN F. (1793–1836)   An American colonizer who began planting settlements in Texas in 1822 and later worked for the Texas revolt against Mexico.

BUTLER, ANTHONY (1787–1849)   U.S. minister to Mexico appointed by President Jackson. A crude man and an indiscreet diplomat, Butler bungled the American attempt to purchase Texas from Mexico. Recalled in 1835, Butler remained in Mexico for another year, antagonizing Mexican authorities by challenging the secretary of war to a duel and encouraging the Texans to rebel.

COAHUILA   A state in northern Mexico just south of the Rio Grande. When Texas was Mexican territory, it was under Coahuila's jurisdiction.

FRENCH INTERVENTION IN MEXICO   In 1862, the arrival of French troops in Mexico, purportedly to collect debts, but in reality to establish an empire there. Napoleon III convinced the Austrian prince Maximilian to accept the crown as emperor of Mexico. Although supported by French troops and Mexican conservatives, Maximilian was unable to overcome the resistance of Mexican liberals led by Benito Juárez. The French withdrew in 1867, and Maximilian was executed.

GÓMEZ FARÍAS, VALENTÍN (1781–1858)   Vice president of the Mexican Republic. He pushed the Mexican congress to authorize in 1847 the seizure and sale of many Catholic Church properties in order to finance Santa Anna's armies. This led to a revolt by the Mexico City National Guard, which refused to march southward against the invading Americans.

HERRERA, JOSÉ JOAQUÍN (1792–1854)   Installed in 1844 as acting president of Mexico after Santa Anna was forced into exile. Herrera was prepared to accept Mexico's loss of Texas, but probably not to sell California and New Mexico to the United States. Under fire from Mexican nationalists, he refused to meet with President Polk's emissary, John Slidell. Shortly afterward, Herrera was deposed by a coup d'état led by General Paredes.

HISTORIOGRAPHY   All works by one country's historians, for example, Mexican historiography; alternatively, the accumulated historical writings on a particular subject, such as "the historiography of the Mexican War."

HOLY ALLIANCE   An agreement made in 1815 among the emperors of Russia and Austria and the king of Prussia to preserve European monarchies and the social status quo after the fall of Napoleon.

HUMBOLDT, ALEXANDER VON (1769–1859)   A German naturalist whose travels and experiments in Latin America from 1799 to 1804 laid the foundations for modern physical geography and meteorology.

JONES, THOMAS AP CATESBY (1790–1858)   A naval commodore who, mistakenly believing that the United States and Mexico were at war in 1842, landed a force that seized Monterey in California. His act was disavowed by President John Tyler, and apologies were made to the Mexican government.

LEWIS AND CLARK EXPEDITION (1803–1806)   An American expedition led by Meriwether Lewis and William Clark that explored the Louisiana Purchase and the land beyond to the Pacific Ocean. Its objectives were to find a land route to the Pacific, strengthen U.S. claims to the Oregon territory, and gather information on the Indians and the land.

MONROE DOCTRINE   The pronouncement by President James Monroe in 1823 that thereafter the Western Hemisphere was closed to further colonization or intervention by European powers.

MORMONS   Members of the Church of Jesus Christ of Latter-Day Saints, a religion founded in 1830 by Joseph Smith of New York. Smith claimed to have found and translated the Book of Mormon, an addendum to the Christian Bible, through angelic revelation. Hostility from neighbors forced the rapidly growing group successively westward. After Smith was murdered by a mob in Illinois, his successor, Brigham Young, led the Mormons in 1847 to Salt Lake City, Utah, which became a thriving Mormon settlement. Until 1890, the church sanctioned polygamy, or marriage of a man to more than one wife.

PAREDES Y ARILLAGA, MARIANO (1797–1849)   The leader of the Centralist faction in Mexico. He forcibly replaced José Herrera as president in January 1846 and took a strong anti-U.S. stance. Paredes ordered the attack on General Zachary Taylor's troops in disputed territory north of the Rio Grande. Defeats suffered by the Mexican army soon precipitated a rebellion by Federalist factions, and in July 1846 Paredes turned the government over to Vice President Gómez Farías.

PATAGONIA   The semiarid plateau that occupies the southern quarter of South America, mostly in Argentina, between the Andes Mountains and the Atlantic Ocean.

PHYSIOCRATIC THOUGHT   Theories of eighteenth-century French economists who argued that the source of all wealth was the land and its agricultural products.

SAN JACINTO   The decisive battle in the Texas revolution. In April 1836, the Texan army under General Sam Houston defeated one thousand two hundred Mexican soldiers and captured Santa Anna. Although Mexico refused to recognize the new republic of Texas, efforts to reconquer it were abandoned.

SANTA ANNA, ANTONIO LÓPEZ DE (1794–1876) The opportunistic general who ruled Mexico during most of the period from 1824 to 1855, shifting his allegiance from party to party. Defeated by the Texas rebels at San Jacinto in 1836, he returned to command the Mexican troops in the Mexican War.

THUCYDIDES (*circa* 460–400 B.C.) The Greek historian of Athens whose chronicle of the Peloponnesian War is a classic of analytical history.

WHIG PARTY One of the two main American parties between 1832 and 1854. It was the ideological successor to the Federalists and grew out of opposition to Andrew Jackson's Democratic Party. Daniel Webster and Henry Clay were its great leaders, but William Henry Harrison and Zachary Taylor its only elected presidents.

WILMOT PROVISO The amendment to an appropriations bill during the Mexican War that attempted to prohibit slavery in any territory the United States gained by the war. Introduced in 1846, the proviso never passed both houses of Congress, but it brought to a head the conflict between North and South over slavery.

✯ ✯ ✯ ✯ ✯ ✯ ✯

The war between Mexico and the United States is, without any doubt, a fundamental event in the history of the two countries. The conquered nation lost in that war a half of its territory, laying bare in the process the lack of national cohesion brought about by political pursuits that were at cross purposes and doomed to failure. The inability to meet the invasion with any degree of effectiveness conveyed a dramatic lesson which was to leave a profound mark upon the Mexican people, resulting in a more practical attitude, even in the lists of ideological warfare, which would continue for two more decades.

The United States emerged from the contest transformed into a continental nation. The great extensions of territory would permit an industrial and commercial expansion almost without parallel. But this same territory was to accelerate the regional conflict of which it was a harbinger. With the exception of Texas there was no slavery in the Mexican territories, and it was obvious that with the admitting of California as a free state in 1850 the crisis was inevitable. The drive across the continent and the discovery of gold in California postponed the conflict, but in doing so, only made it the more bloody.

The dimensions of the battles which followed the war of 47, in Mexico the Reform and the French Intervention, in the United States the Civil War, distracted attention, with the result that by comparison, despite its importance, the war of 47 was reduced to a minor status. This public downgrading does not serve as an adequate explanation for the limited attention which the event has received in the historiographies of the two nations. Doubtless, there exists the psychological element of failure among the Mexicans and of guilt among the North Americans. But the fact is evident: Mexican historiography is yet to produce the definitive "history" of the war, and North American historiography, which has so exhaustively studied the North American past, has, in great measure, put aside the "war with Mexico." . . .

. . . What is it that has made it so difficult to understand the history of this war? To the complexities which make it difficult to determine the real causes of any event are added in this case and on the North American side a puritan morality which has tended to avoid blame, or at least to throw it on special people or groups — the southern slave-holders, Polk, Mexico, the Democrat expansionists — all in an effort to avoid a sense of guilt. Secondly, there is the emergence of a phenomenon which is so difficult to classify, "Manifest Destiny." There is no doubt that this conception played a major role in overseeing the general plan by which, with a shove here and a shove there — by Polk, by the slaveholders, by the Texans, and by the Mexicans — a war was brought into being. In any event, the most difficult problem with this war, as with any war, is the problem of origins. Perhaps we need a Thucydides, who would probably take the question back to the basic nature of humanity, but we believe that the difficulty in gauging the war lies in the very clarity of its origins. Perhaps with this event, more than with others, one can observe that in the face of an obvious situation people seem bent on making it obscure. . . .

THE INEVITABLE WAR

The very conditions of colonization . . . were the elements that went into making the North American colony a new society, with all the dynamism that comes from throwing off the limitations imposed by a traditional order.

Those who colonized North America were obliged to emigrate because of religious persecution (particularly true of the leaders) or of the consequences of the economic transformation in England by which the rise of textile manufacturing led to a process through which farmers were displaced from their lands in order to make room for the raising of cattle. This whole mass of displaced people saw in the New World an alternative for survival, and they took the risk of selling themselves as indentured servants in order to pay their passage. The life which they had to confront was hard, both for masters and servants. It had to be built upon the same basic beginnings. The conscious intention of these men was to reproduce the society which they had left behind, but the American experience was leaving its mark on everything. The most extraordinary part of the venture was the availability of immense tracts of land, which in the eyes of those arriving Europeans became a veritable promise of a better life. Those same indentured servants, who in Europe would never have dreamed of being landowners, received, as payment for their term of servitude, a piece of land, and, since it was cheap, they could acquire more with a bit of work. Thus from the beginning there arose the lure of the lands farther off, toward the west, which always seemed richer than those they had already cultivated. Once they had struggled with the wilderness, it became easier to go off into the unknown, and since the immigrants kept coming, it was easy to sell off the land already possessed and to set off in search of yet better lands.

This scheme of things set the pattern for North American expansion, but independence and the industrial revolution brought new forces into play. The English textile industry with its demand for cotton stimulated the ambition to own "all the cotton lands of America of the North," which resulted in the colonization of Louisiana and Texas. The War of Independence and the discovery of the formula for "a perfect government" brought forth an apparition, a vision that would justify expansionism: "to extend the area of freedom," to extend its institutions to those unfortunate ones who have not known them and to those prisoners who remain in the clutches of tyrannical governments. Not everybody noticed the irony which was implied in much of this — such as in the case of Texas — whereby the area of freedom was extended by extending the area of slavery.

Physiocratic thought resulted in statesmen like Jefferson supporting the acquisition of new lands because they would assure the well-being of the nation, despite his fear that the growth of the country would put in jeopardy the liberty guaranteed by the Constitution. And if all this were not sufficient, the various forms of utopian or reformist thought, which proliferated during the first half of the nineteenth century, also served to stimulate the drive westward: to outdistance slavery, to set up more perfect societies, or even, as in the case of the Mormons, to preserve polygamy.

All of these elements combined to make of North America a dynamic society that nourished the ambition to dominate the lands to the west, to the north, to the south. The merchants, obsessive in their search for new markets, discovered first Santa Fe and later San Francisco, which was to provide a base for the opening up of the incredible Asiatic trade. In this same mode, statesmen like Jefferson, John Quincy Adams, and Jackson went on to lay the foundations for what was to become a spontaneous expansionism. Jefferson, for example, not only bought Louisiana but, after receiving Humboldt at the White House and obtaining from him a copy of the map of New Spain, sent forth the Lewis and Clark Expedition on its trek westward. This quest apparently reactivated the fears that the Spaniards had expressed ever since the founding of the new nation. During the presidency of Monroe, his Secretary of State, John Quincy Adams, a nationalist who wanted everything, south, north, west, managed to threaten the Floridas and Texas in such a way as to convince Spain to sign the Adams-Onís Treaty of 1819, by which the Floridas were obtained in exchange for the establishment of a boundary for Louisiana — which the North Americans had maintained included Texas — plus five million dollars. The North Americans also succeeded in getting the Spaniards to concede a northern limit of 42 degrees, which gave the North Americans a basis for claiming Oregon. Adams was convinced that all of North America was the "natural dominion" of the United States. All the Spanish possessions to the south and the British to the north would fall, little by little, under the control of the United States, and it is evident that this was the thinking behind the Monroe Doctrine of 1823.

The independence of the former Spanish colonies seemed to facilitate the task. Those who were discontented with the renunciation by the United States of Texas in the Adams-Onís Treaty saw those lands being opened up to colonization, and some people legally and others illegally began to enter upon those coveted lands. The North Americans kept up this continuous expansion, and the United States government followed their footsteps. Its first ministers in Mexico had instructions to buy Texas, a pursuit which greatly offended the Mexicans but which for the North Americans was a normal method of obtaining lands. (Hadn't they been doing this from the beginning? They had bought lands from the trading companies, from the Indians, from the French, and from the Spanish.)

Being unable to carry out Jackson's wishes in this matter of Texas, Anthony Butler then converted the individual claims of North American citizens, for damages suffered during the upheavals, into an instrument of diplomatic pressure against the Mexican government. So effective was this device that ultimately the claims were cited by Polk as being among the reasons for the declaration of war.

Meanwhile, in Texas the North American population had so surpassed the Mexican that everyone surmised what the immediate future would be. The dependency upon Coahuila, about which the Texans had complained so much, had in fact facilitated the colonization, because in Saltillo [capital of Coahuila] the concessions were easier to get since there did not exist there the consciousness of danger [of a pending Texas revolt] that existed in the capital of the republic.

Texas entered the decade of the 1830s with the certainty that independence was not far off. Stephen Austin made a final effort toward the establishment of Texas as a separate state, independent of Coahuila, but in reality he recognized the impossibility of accomplishing this. The atmosphere had turned antifederalist. An effort to straighten things out, which had not worked well in the republic, led the Mexicans toward a new formula of government, centralism. So now the Texans at least had the pretext they were looking for. The republic succeeded in vanquishing federalism in the state of Zacatecas, and it looked as though it would have the same success in Texas. On the second of March 1836, the Texan Declaration of Independence was signed and, with the fiasco at San Jacinto, it would swiftly acquire validity. Hundreds of North Americans crossed the Louisiana border to fight for the independence of Texas. The rebels received arms and support, but Jackson did not dare to go as far as extending official recognition.

The claims continued being used to pressure the neighboring republic, but in the face of the law, which Mexico, in its weakness, learned to wield as a defense, the United States had to accept arbitration. After long and vacillating deliberations, an agreement upon just claims was reached, and Mexico began to pay.

In the meantime, trade with Santa Fe had familiarized North Americans with regions west of Texas, and eyes began to be fixed upon California. Despite all the efforts of Mexico to prevent a repetition of the history of Texas, California was filling up with Americans. A North American squadron appeared along the coasts of the Pacific. The Mormons settled in Utah, and thousands of North Americans established themselves in Oregon. Expansionism was popular and spontaneous, but it cannot be denied that its impulses were coordinated, informally, from Washington. This can be demonstrated in the attitude of Commodore Jones, who in October 1842, believing that war had been declared, took the port of Monterey. Something such as this could only have happened as a result of secret instructions given in case hostilities were opened. Diplomatic apologies were given, and the matter ended there.

In the decade of the 1840s, expansionism became a veritable fever, which began to rationalize its urges. Some felt it was their obligation to extend democracy; others saw it as a fulfillment of the biblical mandate: "Increase and multiply and fill up the earth and subjugate it and be master over it." The militants clamored for Oregon (*Fifty-four forty or fight!* was their slogan) and Texas. Many thought about ways to acquire the Californias, too. The climate of this passion for lands was ready to become a genuine movement, which only needed a name. In 1845 John L. Sullivan coined the fortunate phrase: "Manifest Destiny," which expressed that vague conglomerate of ideas and sentiments that were used to justify North American ambitions and which he, himself, articulated into a veritable doctrine. Any neighboring people could establish self-government simply by contract, could solicit admission [to the Union], and if it were considered to be qualified, it would be admitted. Some people, such as the Mexicans, would, of course, have to be educated for some time to live in freedom, before being admitted. A decision so important could not be made hastily, and of course nobody should be forced to enter the system.

The popularity of the movement varied in the different regions of the country. The commercial East, interested in land speculation and in the establishments along the Pacific, and the frontiersmen were the most enthusiastic supporters of Manifest Destiny. In the North and in the East, where the abolitionists had entrenched themselves, there was considerable opposition to expansion because of the fear that it could serve to extend the "peculiar institution." The South never lacked enthusiastic expansionists, but since their leaders had become convinced that the new lands would favor the North and that, outside of Texas, they would not be slave territory, these leaders resisted the expansionist spirit. Despite the reservations which the South had toward this movement, one of the most popular interpretations of the war between Mexico and the United States accused the southern slaveholders of having provoked it in order to increase the number of slaveholding states. In much of northern and southern antiexpansionism there could be detected a strong tint of racism. There was fear that in having to absorb Mexicans, mongrel races, North American democracy would be brought to its ruin. "We cannot hope that a people who over many years have refused to obey their own laws will tranquilly submit to ours. If we take this semi-barbaric people under our jurisdiction, thousands of unlooked for evils will be the consequence." So said a member of the House of Representatives, while a senator affirmed that the Mexicans were "free men of a race superior to the Africans." But another stated: "We never dreamed of incorporating into our Union any but the Caucasian race — the free white race." But when the southerners were expansionists, their exalted form of expansionism made them into optimists and, although admitting a certain superiority for themselves, they expressed confidence in the long-term effects of education [upon the Mexicans] or that an avalanche of [European] immigration would assure the predominance of the Whites. The expansionists tried to keep the theme of slavery outside of the discussion, fearing

that it would throw a shadow upon the panorama. The antislavery forces, having become convinced during the war that the acquisition of new territories was inevitable,
proposed the Wilmot Proviso:

> Upon the condition that, and as the expressed and fundamental condition upon the acquisi-
> tion of any territory from the Republic of Mexico by the United States, by virtue of any
> treaty that might be negotiated . . . neither slavery nor involuntary servitude shall ever exist in
> that territory.

But those who have scruples are always the minority of the population. The popularity of the [expansionist] movement was such that the new type of politician who appeared in the decade of the 1830s and was symbolized by Jackson, responsive to popular
causes and attempting to interpret the popular will, found it very difficult to stay on the
sidelines of the movement and not try to capitalize on it. President Tyler, to increase his
popularity, openly supported the annexation of Texas, and during the election of 1844
the Democratic candidate, James K. Polk, based his campaign on the themes of Oregon
and Texas, which were the ones that excited the expansionists. At that time, the minimum that they were asking for was for the boundary to be set at Alaska and that all of
California be taken. There were even those who talked of going all the way down to
Patagonia. For such people, it was providential destiny that the institutions of North
America be extended throughout all the hemisphere.

In the first attempt, the annexation [of Texas] was rejected by the North American
Congress, and to avoid a second failure it was suggested that the measure be put before
a joint session of Congress where it could be passed by a simple majority. Said and done,
on March 1, 1845, the resolution was passed that provided for the addition (as it
was called thereafter) of the new state. On March 6, Juan Nepomuceno Almonte, the
Mexican minister in Washington, asked for his passport by way of protest. The British
diplomats, meanwhile, had convinced the administration of Herrera that there was no
other way to avoid total disaster than to recognize the independence of Texas on
the condition that it not join itself to any other country. On the fourth of June, the
president of Texas, Anson Jones, submitted to the Texas people the treaty proposed by
Mexico, but by now it was too late. The Texas unionist party succeeded on June 21st,
also by a joint resolution, in getting approval of annexation to the United States.

Polk was now the president, and with an expansionist in the White House, it was
easy to guess what was going to happen. A minimum of decorum prevented Polk from
attacking his neighbors straightaway. He tried to negotiate with Mexico over California
and with Great Britain over Oregon. An opportune moment and a compromise of 49°
instead of the hoped for 54°40′ solved the problem of Oregon without conflict, and the
treaty was signed in June 1846.

The negotiations with Mexico failed. The administration of General Herrera could
in no way receive Slidell, who was carrying a proposal for purchase. The seizure of
power by Paredes Arrillaga made a pacific arrangement all the more difficult. But behind it all lay the problem that there existed two different conceptions. The North
Americans considered that the Mexican properties were only nominal because the lands

were uninhabited. With the need that the Mexicans had for money, it seemed incomprehensible to the North Americans that they would not sell those empty lands, lands that they were bound to lose anyway. The governments of Herrera and Paredes understood perfectly well the impossibility of defending those areas, but they could not sell that which as Mexicans they considered to be the "national patrimony." In addition, the many insults and the offensive propositions which the North Americans had put forward had given popularity to the notion that it was now necessary to make answer to the North Americans with a show of arms.

Polk was ready for anything. The North American consul had precise instructions to repeat the pattern of the Texas episode, the method advocated by the defenders of Manifest Destiny. [Admiral] Stockton was in Texas trying to make the Texans provoke a war with Mexico so that the United States would find it necessary to intervene in order to protect its new state. President Jones botched the effort. This failure made Polk impatient, and he decided to order General [Zachary] Taylor, on January 13, 1846, to occupy the area between the Nueces and Rio Grande rivers, land which Texas claimed. As soon as news reached Washington that an incident had occurred on April 25th between troops of the two countries, Polk sent a message to Congress asking for a declaration of war (May 11, 1846). Polk claimed that Mexico had committed a series of offenses against and had caused injuries to North American citizens and their properties and that not content with this, Mexico "has finally invaded our territory and spilled the blood of our citizens on our own soil." Despite the opposition to some of the falsehoods contained in Polk's allegations — such as his claim as to where the boundary was — Congress voted a declaration of war by a vote of 40 to 2 in the Senate and 174 to 14 in the House. During the months which followed, the Whig party voiced its opposition to the war and its conviction that Polk was embarked upon a war of conquest. But even after the Whigs became, by the election of 1846, the majority party, they took no action to prove their opposition. When it came time to vote, they always approved more men and more money for the war. [Historian Frederick] Merk has clearly demonstrated the dilemma of the Whig party and the fear that they felt for the adjective "treasonous," which had buried the Federalists as a result of their opposition to the War of 1812 against the British.

Considerably after Matamoros was occupied by American troops (May 18, 1846) and Taylor had begun his penetration into the country, the Mexican government felt obligated to make a declaration of war, July 7, 1846. Article One of the congressional decree summarized Mexico's reasons: "The government, acting in defense of the nation, will repel the aggression which the United States of America has initiated and sustained against the Mexican Republic, having invaded it and committed hostile acts in various of the departments of its territory."

There was an element of the defensive in the tone of the declaration, which bespoke the fear that the several Mexican governments had felt toward a war about which they had done whatever possible to avoid. Nobody doubts that a great part of public opinion, at least that part which had an articulate voice, had been demanding war. But in spite of the popularity of the war, the country was unable to organize the defense, and the lack of war materials was such that it could not make real use of the dynamic leadership which Santa Anna undoubtedly had to offer, after his return from exile (September 14, 1846). The North Americans, who blockaded our coast, allowed free passage to the restless Santa Anna, sure that they would be able to buy his cooperation, a supposition in which they were apparently mistaken.

OBSTACLES TOWARD COMPREHENDING AN ENTIRE EPOCH

Something that all those who take it upon themselves to describe the Mexican insist upon is that for him there is a characteristic impediment toward regarding his past as really past. The [Mexican] historian himself cannot avoid this tendency and tries to change the past, falsifying what actually occurred. After four-and-a-half centuries, he does not accept the Conquest, and at the distance of a century-and-a-half he is incapable of coming to an agreement on the manner in which independence was arrived at. If this is the case with events in which the participants were "in house," it is comprehensible that we are incapable of assimilating the war of 47. The event was traumatic and still is, because we accept the loss of territory, the inevitability of the clash and its results, but we can only lament the ease with which the war was won and the total impotence in the face of the North American offensive. We do not understand all of this because we have not forced ourselves to come to an understanding. The historians have undertaken to set forth the various parties of the period and to accuse various of the sets of contenders of failure. Gómez Farías or Paredes Arrillaga, Santa Anna — the favorite villain — the army, or the church are the guilty ones. For ourselves, the case seems to be completely different, and in order to comprehend it we will make use of a comparison with the history of the United States. . . .

The United States began its revolution for independence by rising up against the British effort, as a result of the Seven Years War, to organize its empire recently acquired at the cost of France. The general methods used by the British, which were also applied to the three colonies [the north, middle, and southern groups of [colonies] in North America] which up until then had enjoyed autonomy, provoked a powerful reaction which led to independence (1776–1783). The colonies found themselves confronted with an England which, though victorious [in its European wars], was also bankrupt and in the middle of a struggle between political factions (1760–1770), which the colonies no doubt took full advantage of. England remained isolated. France was easy to conquer, being burdened by its alliance with Spain. The northern countries, seeing that the battle was being prolonged, formed the League of Armed Neutrality. Thus the international scene favored the North Americans. The simplistic manner in which we view the history of our neighboring country tells us that since the North Americans had experience in government, a group of exceptional citizens was able to find a magic formula, resulting from their own experience, which led them to a happy conclusion. There is an element of truth here, but in order to arrive at the Constitution of [1787] the North Americans had to undergo years of chaos and, when they finally achieved a political organization, thanks to the French Revolution and events which resulted from it, the United States was left alone until 1812, at which time, due to international affronts, it felt forced to declare war upon England. Notwithstanding the fact that it was distracted by its real enemy, Napoleon, England managed, with a small army, to launch a military drive against the United States which resulted in an occupation of the capital. But England was essentially concentrating upon its European interests and not upon the American territories. The politics of those years in the United States were also partisan and factional. The difference with our situation was that the country continued its way west and, open to steady immigration, it absorbed dynamic elements into its society.

Mexico came to its independence in 1821 after a long battle which had to a considerable extent weakened its socioeconomic structure. Furthermore, the economic debilitation had begun in 1804 when people of exceptional talents began, in an uninterrupted stream, to return to the [Iberian] Peninsula. The country, then, entered upon independence in a state of bankruptcy. It is . . . certain that there were . . . [some] people with political experience, because the first congresses were enriched by the experiences which the delegates had had at the Cortes [congress of Spain], many of them figures of importance in that institution, such as Ramos Arizpe. Nor can it be said that the choice of federalism was a mistake: . . . federalism, once rooted into our tradition, saved the integrity of the country, avoiding a repetition of the case of Central America. What turned out to be most surprising, in view of the experiences of our own times, was the extent to which federalism functioned effectively.

The difference with the United States was that Mexico faced a Spain sustained by the Holy Alliance, which neither England nor the Holy See [the pope] dared openly defy [by] recognizing its independence. Mexico was, until the following decade, bereft of protection and exposed in such a way that English, French, and North American ambitions warred on its territory ceaselessly. It was not left for a minute to put into practice the clear body of ideas developed by some of its men. Instead, shortly after its emancipation, Mexico had to face three international problems: the independence of Texas (international to the extent to which the United States was a participant, though not in an official capacity), the Pastry War [a short war with France], and the war with the United States. The lack of money and the low level of national sentiment, due to the briefness of its experience as a nation, completed the picture. The hoped for support from England never arrived. Its statesmen sought to prevent a war which the Mexicans . . . desired. But Paredes Arrillaga, who had seized power so that the Mexican government would present a firmer front to the United States, changed his opinion in taking over the responsibility for the situation.

QUESTIONS TO CONSIDER

1. The author says that North Americans have tried to avoid guilt for the Mexican War or have thrown the blame upon special groups, such as southern slaveholders. Why is this inadequate? Who or what does Vázquez think was responsible for the war? In what sense, according to Vázquez, was the Mexican War inevitable?

2. Describe how events of the preceding three decades led to the Mexican War. How was the Adams-Onís Treaty of 1819 related to the conflict? In what way did the

Texas independence movement lead to hostilities ten years later? How, according to Vázquez, did President Polk provoke the war?

3. The author attempts to view events from a dual U.S. and Mexican perspective. How did cultural differences between Mexicans and North Americans contribute to the coming of war? Why have both countries neglected thorough historical study of the war?

4. How did issues of slavery and race affect the controversy in the United States over acquiring Texas and Mexico? Why did the United States take over these lands in spite of North Americans' racially motivated fears?

5. Compare the political and economic situations of Mexico and the United States at independence. Would Vázquez agree with Anthony McFarlane (Selection 8) that North Americans were better prepared for independence? What weaknesses in Mexico's early history help to explain its quick defeat in the Mexican War? How did the international situation help the United States and hinder Mexico?

IX

FREE AND SLAVE SOCIETIES

A distinctive feature of America's westward expansion was its entanglement with a growing controversy over slavery. Competiton for western lands heated up a sectional rivalry between the North and South that had been simmering since independence. At its root was a conflict of economies and cultures. Although agriculture remained the foundation of the American economy in the first half of the nineteenth century, the nonslave states of the North increasingly invested their resources in industry, transportation, and finance, while southern states remained committed to slave plantations and subsistence farms. One historian has put it in a nutshell: the North expanded and developed, but the South merely expanded. While the North began an industrial revolution, southern growth was channeled into familiar economic patterns that eventually created the world's most extensive slave economy.

These contrasting sectional economies fed divergent lifestyles. Life in the North was urbanized, modern, impersonal, and egalitarian; life in the South was rural, traditional, personal, and hierarchical. The South's slave system became each section's defining point. Northerners criticized it as inefficient and un-Christian and championed their free-labor society as the modern, moral alternative. In response, southern whites dug in their heels, declaring that slavery was not just a "necessary evil" but a "positive good" in its maintenance of social stability and white supremacy. When such opposing visions of the good life and the American future collided in the western territories, the stage was set for civil war.

The essays in this chapter use comparative perspectives to examine key features that made northern and southern societies so different. In the first selection, three historians of technology, Grace R. Cooper, Rita J. Adrosko, and John H. White Jr., show how in the decades before the Civil War northerners "imported" an industrial revolution by adopting British technology, attracting European capital, and absorbing a cheap labor force in the form of millions of Irish and German immigrants. The South was linked to western Europe, but in a very different way: not as an imitator of industrialism but a supplier of crops, such as cotton, sugar, and tobacco, that kept Europe's factories humming and their workers awake. The South's role in the world economy and the slave society that supported it resembled Caribbean and South American plantation systems more than the North's free-labor capitalism.

In the second selection, Carl N. Degler compares slavery in the American South with its counterpart in the largest Latin American country, Brazil. Degler shows that, although everyday life was less harsh for slaves in the United States than for those in Brazil, by comparison with their Brazilian counterparts American blacks were trapped in the slave system. Stigmatized by their race and denied access to freedom, slaves in the South were harnessed indefinitely to a plantation order based upon white supremacy. Immigrants in the North were sometimes treated shabbily, as the first essay shows, but the North's free-labor society, in contrast to the society of the South, often made good on its promise of a better life ahead.

Importing a Revolution: Machines, Railroads, and Immigrants

GRACE R. COOPER, RITA J. ADROSKO, AND JOHN H. WHITE JR.

Two revolutions swept through the Western world in the nineteenth century, one political and the other industrial. The United States (along with France) pioneered the first, but it followed the commanding lead of England in the second. Thanks to English entrepreneurial know-how and capital, key inventions in the textile and iron industries, and a sprawling colonial market, Great Britain reached the industrial "takeoff" point by 1800 and became the world's chief producer of manufactured goods.

Yet in the remarkably short span of a generation, the United States began to catch up. Some of the basic ingredients were already here: abundant natural resources, an expanding domestic market, and a government that not only left capitalists alone but also promoted their enterprises through protective tariffs, land grants, and easy incorporation. But the young nation faced an acute shortage of capital, labor, and technology — crucial factors of production for an industrial economy. As a group of historians from the Smithsonian Institution shows in the following selection, all of these were imported from Europe.

England provided the technology. Its steam engines powered American riverboats and locomotives, and its textile machinery, duplicated by Samuel Slater, drove New England's mills. Engineers from Philadelphia and Baltimore, sent to inspect early British railways, returned to build facsimiles that chugged westward toward the lucrative Ohio Valley trade. But the Americans did not simply copy European machines; they transformed them into engines of democracy. Instead of expensive finished products, American factories put out cheap but useful goods that could be produced quickly and bought by the masses. Railroad builders cut corners and costs to build rapidly over the enormous American distances and to keep fares affordable. The sewing machine, ignored in Europe because of a surplus of cheap seamstresses, allowed American ready-made clothing to copy Parisian fashions for the urban middle class. This process of borrowing European technology and adapting it to mass markets and new commercial applications was repeated throughout the century. Outcompeting its teacher, the United States did to England in the 1800s what Japan was to do with American technology after World War II.

Capital for economic development, unavailable at home because agricultural expansion preempted it, also came from Europe. American railroads, for example, were financed largely by British, Dutch, and German investments in state securities or company stock. Thanks to a happy mixture of absentee capital and local control, the United States could boast as much railroad track by the 1850s as all of western Europe. By then, too, the great waves of German and Irish immigrants had ended the shortage of labor east of the Mississippi. Desperate Irish workers dug New York's Erie Canal, Germans were hired by the Illinois Central Railroad, Chinese laborers worked at the grueling Pacific end of the transcontinental line, and immigrant workers displaced native-born "mill girls" in the textile factories.

All these developments coalesced to create a booming demand for manufactured goods, efficient factories to produce them, and a far-reaching transportation network to distribute them. As the authors point out, the railroad, which became symbolic of the "go-ahead" spirit of the age, played multiple roles: it transported immigrants westward, offered them jobs, sold them land, sent their crops to market, and returned with their consumer purchases. The nation's economic growth coincided with spectacular individual success stories like those of Slater, the Cromptons, and Albert Fink, as well as millions of more modest climbs "from rags to respectability."

One momentous consequence, largely unforeseen, of this industrial takeoff was greater regional specialization. With poor soil and good waterpower, New England was the first to industrialize. By exporting manufacturing goods and technology, it played the role in America that England played in Europe. As the transportation network penetrated inland regions, western states increasingly sent their crops eastward over canals and railroads rather than down the Mississippi. Only the South maintained its preindustrial ways, concentrating on expanding its cotton production and slave system. Thus, as historian James McPherson has noted, "while the North and South as a whole were growing relatively farther apart, the eastern and western free states were drawing closer together." By heightening the differences between northern and southern societies and intensifying their rivalry for western lands, industrialism's uneven conquest of the country portended civil war.

There were other hidden costs to the nation's headlong rush to the industrial future. As the authors imply, Americans had to put up with an appalling rate of industrial and transportation accidents due to hasty or flimsy construction. Women and children were exploited in factories: when it opened in 1790, for example, Samuel Slater's mill had nine operatives, all children between the ages of seven and twelve. Wage cuts, increased hours, and poor working conditions led to the nation's first textile unions and strikes in the mills of Lowell, William Crompton's adopted city. Importing an industrial revolution in the early nineteenth century, Americans believed they could avoid Europe's working-class slums and its violent struggles between labor and capital. As the century wore on, they would learn otherwise.

GLOSSARY

ARKWRIGHT, RICHARD (1732–1792)   An English inventor best known for designing the spinning frame (1769), which helped to mechanize textile production and usher in the Industrial Revolution.

BALTIMORE AND OHIO (B&O)   The first railroad in the United States. The B&O Railroad was chartered in 1827 by Baltimore merchants eager to increase their share of the western trade. It opened in 1830 and crossed the Appalachian Mountains in the 1840s.

CARDING   Combing and paralleling fibers of cotton, flax, or wool. Carding, spinning, and weaving, the three basic operations of textile manufacture, were mechanized in the Industrial Revolution.

COLT PISTOL FACTORY   Pistol-producing factory in Hartford, Connecticut, established in 1836 by Samuel Colt, inventor of the revolver, or six-shooting pistol. Colt's company brought mass production by means of interchangeable parts to new heights.

ERIE CANAL   Human-built waterway, completed in 1825, that connected Buffalo on Lake Erie and Albany on the Hudson River, hence linking New York City to the West. Attempts by other states to duplicate the canal's success began a "canal boom" in the Jacksonian era.

INTERSTATE COMMERCE COMMISSION   A federal agency created in 1887 to regulate interstate railroad rates and investigate dishonest practices, such as "pools," or collusion, between competitors.

MASON-DIXON LINE   The boundary between Pennsylvania and Maryland, surveyed by Charles Mason and Jeremiah Dixon in the 1760s. Before the Civil War, it was the boundary between slave and free states; more loosely, it denoted the border between the North and the South.

SLATER, SAMUEL (1768–1835)   The British immigrant and entrepreneur who founded the cotton-textile industry in the United States.

YANKEES   In nineteenth-century America, a label for New Englanders or, more broadly, northerners; outside the country, a label for Americans generally.

* * * * * * *

In his propagandist essay *Common Sense,* Tom Paine argued for independence by noting that "Europe, and not England, is the parent country of America." Indeed, . . . peoples from many nations helped to build the thirteen colonies. This polyglot amalgamation continued to grow after the adoption of the federal Constitution. From 1790 to 1815, approximately 250,000 immigrants arrived. During the 1830s, 500,000 appeared, and by the 1850s the figure stood at more than 2.5 million. The *Democratic Review* (July 1852) described this as one of the wonders of modern times: "There has been nothing like it in appearance since the encampment of the Roman empire, or the tents of the Crusaders."

By 1860 there were almost 31,500,000 people living in the United States and of these 4,136,000 were foreign-born. Most had come from rural villages in Europe, and while a few left their homelands for religious or ideological reasons, the majority were prodded by the hope of improving their economic status. A Belgian observer wrote in 1846 that immigrants "did not leave their native villages to seek political rights in another hemisphere. The time of the Puritans and of William Penn is past. Theories of social reform have given way to a practical desire for immediate well-being."

The bulk of the foreign-born lived north of the Mason-Dixon line and east of the Mississippi in cities in New York State, which contained the greatest number, followed by Pennsylvania, Ohio, Illinois, Wisconsin, and Massachusetts. In New York City, Cincinnati, Chicago, Milwaukee, and Detroit, close to one-half the population came from Western Europe. The Irish were the most numerous: between 1830 and 1860 almost two million landed in eastern ports. Driven from their rural villages by the potato famines of the 1840s, they settled in city slums. More than one observer noted "this strange contradictory result, that a people who hungered and thirsted for land in Ireland should have been content when they reached the New World . . . to sink into the condition of a miserable town tenantry, to whose squalors even a European seaport could hardly present a parallel" (1855).

The Germans, 1,301,000 of them, spread across America from 1830 to 1860. Few found their way into New England, preferring instead to put their energy into Ohio, Illinois, Wisconsin, and Missouri, where they built farms and cities. The newcomers from England, Scotland, and Wales amounted to 587,775 in 1860. They moved about easily and quickly assimilated themselves into the social fabric. There were small groups of Norwegians and even a few Dutch.

Regardless of their nationality, most immigrants generally arrived penniless and ready to work, usually settling in areas where they could practice the skilled or semiskilled crafts they had learned in their homeland. Welsh miners made their way to the hard-coal fields of eastern Pennsylvania, while pottery makers of Staffordshire found

---

Reprinted from Peter C. Marzio, *A Nation of Nations: The People Who Came to America as Seen Through the Objects and Documents Exhibited at the Smithsonian Institution* (Washington, DC: Smithsonian Institution Press), by permission of the publisher. Copyright [1976] Smithsonian Institution.

employment in Trenton, New Jersey, or East Liverpool, Ohio. German craftsmen settled in numerous areas, including Cincinnati, where furniture was factory-made. British textile workers appeared in the mill towns where woolen or cotton goods were produced. It turned out that one of these English immigrants, Samuel Slater, was to have a share in starting the industrial revolution in America.

MACHINES

The industrial revolution had begun in England in the eighteenth century, and one of the earliest crafts to be affected was the spinning of cotton. Samuel Slater, who was eventually to be known as the father of cotton manufacturing in America, was born at Holly House, near Belper, England, in 1768. He was apprenticed to Jedediah Strutt after the death of his father in 1782, spending over six years learning how to operate the machines and oversee the mills at Milford, England. This was more than a routine apprenticeship, for Strutt was a family friend who treated Slater as a son.

Strutt was a partner of Richard Arkwright, who had given an early impetus to the industrial revolution by improving the machine spinning of cotton through an invention that used rollers traveling at increasing rates of speed to draw out the fibers. This dynamic period in England saw many mechanical inventions and improvements (and lawsuits over patent rights), and Slater was exposed to the best of the new high-speed, labor-saving machines. He served his apprenticeship faithfully, proving to be an excellent machinist as well as an efficient factory manager. Indeed, at this early period in the history of manufacturing, an industrialist had to be a man with a mechanic's sense of the practical and an entrepreneur's organizing prowess. Slater was learning both.

While Slater was serving his apprenticeship in England, several attempts were being made at Beverly, Massachusetts, and in other places throughout America to erect cotton carding and spinning mills. Time and again they failed. Americans, apparently, lacked the skills to start their own industrial revolution. More than one newspaper carried employment advertisements similar to this one appearing in the New York *Journal* of January 5, 1789:

> A person to act as manager and superintendent of the business of the society, whose office it shall be to devote his whole time and services to overseeing the different branches of the linen and cotton manufactures that may be established, take charge of the raw and manufactured articles, and fulfill the orders of the Director.

Almost every state sponsored societies for the encouragement of manufacturing and the useful arts, and many offered premiums for the introduction of efficient cotton machinery. As late as 1832, Calvin Collon's *Manual for Emigrants to America* was emphatic: "manufacturers *especially* will find employment."

This was surely the thrust of Alexander Hamilton's *Report on Manufactures,* which appeared in 1791. The foreign-born secretary of the treasury believed in the "promoting of emigration from foreign countries" because America needed the muscle power to build factories and the brain power to organize and automate the work. The introduction of "new inventions and discoveries . . . as may have been made in other countries, particularly those which relate to machinery" was thought by Hamilton and his advisers to be a basic need.

The difficulty of learning the art of cotton manufacturing was compounded by the laws of England, which forbade the export of models or plans of any machines. The laws, however, were circumvented when Samuel Slater departed for America in 1789, carrying neither models nor drawings, but with all the essential information in his brain.

Historians are at a loss to explain why this twenty-two-year-old Englishman, who had acquired some property and seemed to have a bright future in England, would leave. None of the explanations is sound. Just before his ship sailed, he posted a letter to his mother: he was beginning his New World adventure.

Slater arrived in New York in November 1789. He inspected the cotton products and mills of the area and quickly discovered what many already knew — the industrial revolution was still across the sea. Then he learned of Moses Brown and of the spinning mills he was attempting to build in Rhode Island. After a polite exchange of several letters, Slater found himself in Pawtucket.

The cotton business started by Moses Brown was operated by William Almy, his son-in-law, and Smith Brown, a kinsman. Impressed by Slater's obvious knowledge of the new cotton machines, Almy and Brown entered into a partnership with him, giving Slater half ownership and half the profits in exchange for erecting the Arkwright system in Pawtucket.

Slater not only built the machines from memory but made or supervised the making of the tools and parts as well. He also trained machinists according to English standards and instilled in these workmen a sense of professionalism and organizing skills. It was Slater's students who erected the first successful cotton mills in various parts of the country. George S. White wrote in 1836: "most of the establishments erected from 1790 to 1809, were built by men who had, either directly or indirectly, drawn their knowledge from Pawtucket, the cradle of the cotton business." . . .

[In the next generation, the Crompton family played a role similar to Slater's.] The Englishman William Crompton, born in Preston, Lancashire, left his family behind the first time he came to America at the age of thirty in 1836. He was already an accomplished weaver and mechanic with a thorough understanding of the pattern-weaving looms used in England's cotton manufacture. Crompton found a job with a Taunton, Massachusetts, textile mill. It is said he was asked to weave a certain type of patterned cloth, but, unable to do so with the looms available, he adapted one to produce the desired cloth. A patent was issued for his loom November 25, 1837. When the mill failed that same year, he returned to England, continued in cotton manufacture, and took out a British patent on his loom in the name of John Rostran, his English partner.

Perhaps American business opportunities seemed brighter to Crompton in 1839, for he once again moved to Taunton, this time emigrating with his family. To promote his looms, he launched a series of visits to New England cotton mills. This met with little success until Samuel Lawrence, who was in charge of the Middlesex Mills of Lowell, Massachusetts, asked Crompton to adapt his fancy cotton loom to weaving woolens.

A fashionable French patterned wool fabric called cassimere had attracted Lawrence and motivated his suggestion. Crompton completed his adaptation by 1840, and his subsequent success in developing and distributing the loom for weaving fancy woolens put America in a newly competitive position in this field.

Although patterned woolens had been power-woven before Crompton's time, the cams that controlled the looms limited the complexity of patterns; also, changing patterns was very complicated. Both these drawbacks were eliminated by Crompton's system, in which series of pegged bars, or lags, held together by links, controlled the weaving of patterns. These lags were capable of activating up to thirty loom harnesses and could easily be changed to accommodate new patterns.

William Crompton was naturalized an American citizen in the police court in Lowell, Massachusetts, on November 5, 1842, just three years after he had settled in this country. In 1849, an illness cut short his business career, which had been very active throughout the 1840s. Fortunately, his son George, though only twenty years old at the time, was willing and able to become involved in his father's business, which he subsequently took over completely.

George was ten years old when his father decided to move the family to America. William's business activities enabled him to provide his son with a good private education, which George supplemented with practical training in his father's mills and in the Colt pistol factory in Hartford. Once he took charge, George Crompton obtained more than thirty patents for improvements which increased the Crompton fancy loom's efficiency and speed. Over the years he also improved the quality of the loom's workmanship.

He began the manufacture of fancy looms in Worcester, Massachusetts, but in 1861, when the Civil War caused a reduction in the demand for looms, George turned to manufacturing gun-making machinery. In 1863–1864, when the need for soldiers' blankets and other textile supplies increased, he resumed the manufacture of plain and fancy looms for weaving woolens. He had to enlarge his works, and soon employed four hundred hands. Crompton looms won awards at both the Paris Exposition of 1867 and at the Centennial held in Philadelphia in 1876. Their use was widespread in Europe as well as in America.

Abetted by such technological advancements as Slater and the Cromptons provided, factories spread inexorably, for good and evil, throughout the nineteenth century. The many water sites in America provided abundant power, and the economics of the factory system lent itself to increasingly larger factories and machines requiring more and more semiskilled labor. The masses of immigrants filled this need. A government-sponsored report on the "condition of the Industrial Classes in the United States" observed in 1869:

> . . . foreign is every day replacing native skilled labour. . . . Indeed, the great number of foreign workmen employed in all the branches of American industries is very remarkable. . . . Nearly all the hands at present in American cotton, woolen, and worsted mills, and in the foundries and rolling-mills of the country, are of recent foreign extraction.

Factory life was better in America than in England, but it was far from ideal. In a letter written in 1837 from South Leicester, Massachusetts, to England, Jabez Hollingworth said:

> . . . this state is better calculated for manufacturing than farming. This causes it to be more like England, because where manufacturing flourishes Tyranny, Oppression, and Slavery will follow. . . . As to the manner of living there is not a King on earth that can live better. We have everything to eat that a reasonable man can wish for. We have beef or pork three times a day, potatoes, cheese, butter, tea and coffee and sometimes milk. . . .

But many immigrants, even before 1860, who worked in American factories and mill towns would not have compared their living standard to that of a king. The social statistics concerning crime, disease, and pauperism are far from precise for this period, but they frequently point to the immigrants' disadvantage. In Boston more than half the paupers between 1845 and 1860 were immigrants; at least 86 percent of the names on New York's relief rolls for 1860 appear to belong to immigrants.

The problems were most trying and most visible in the eastern cities. When the aristocratic New Yorker Phillip Hone wrote in his *Diary:* "All Europe is coming across the ocean; all that part at least who cannot make a living at home; and what shall we do with them? They increase our taxes, eat our bread and encumber our streets, and not one in twenty is competent to keep himself," he was expressing the thoughts of many who had found a comfortable spot in society.

RAILROADS

[Like factories] . . . the steam railroad came to North America from England. It was clearly an imported technology, but it became an American passion. By 1855 the northeastern United States was operating a dense network of lines. The South and Midwest were developing similar systems, and by 1869 steam cars reached the Pacific coast. . . .

Before we can understand why and in what form the railway came to America, something must be said of its origins. Its ancient beginnings were in the mines of Europe. It was many centuries before the railway's ability to move heavy loads with minimum power suggested the general carriage of goods and passengers. The public railway as we know it today was a late development, essentially a manifestation of the nineteenth century. We are indebted to the British for advancing the primitive industrial tramway into a sophisticated conveyance.

It is not surprising that the railway should emerge in Britain, which, by the mid-eighteenth century, was the dominant industrial power of the world. At this time the British were busy perfecting steam engines, textile machinery, iron bridges, and in general causing the mechanical arts to flourish as they did nowhere else. As the Italians are given to working stone, the English have always shown a facility for shaping iron; they have been described as a "ferruginous race."

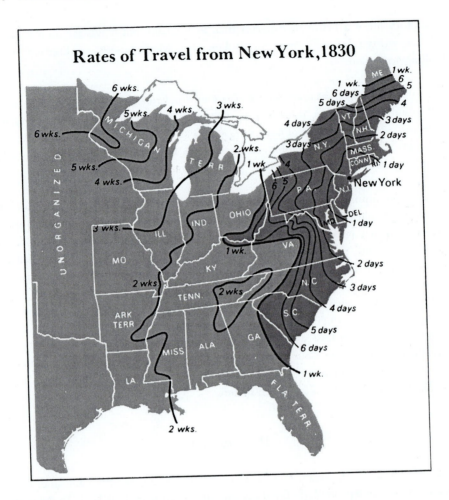

Rates of Travel from New York, 1830

To make the railway suitable for speedy long-distance travel, two basic reforms were necessary: a faultless track and mechanical power. Existing civil engineering techniques aided in the construction of level, straight lines. Iron rails, in use since the mid-1700s, offered a smooth, substantial path. And the steam engine, a reasonably compact, powerful machine, by 1800 was easily converted into a self-propelling vehicle. In 1825 these ingredients were brought together: mechanical land transport was at last realized on a commercial scale and easily outran its competition — the canal and the highway. England's railway revolution was under way.

Young America watched these developments with considerable interest. A vast, unsettled inland empire needed some form of communication, and to suit the temper of the energetic population, it had to be developed quickly. Arguments for a national system of highways, canals, and river improvements had been voiced since the beginning of the Republic, but little had been accomplished. Upstart advocates of the new British invention were received with considerable sympathy. They argued that canals were painfully slow and subject to spring floods and winter freezes, highways were equally

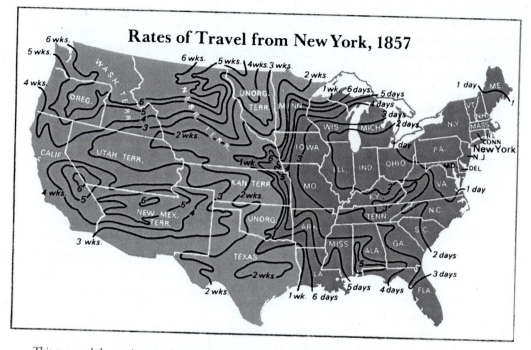

This map and the previous one (p. 278) show how the railroad dramatically decreased travel times in antebellum America. In 1830, a traveler from New York required nearly three weeks to reach the site of Chicago; by 1857 fewer than two days on the railroad were enough. Note that the east-west connection was far faster in the North than in the South, signifying the rapid development of the North and its growing ties to the West. Maps from David Herbert Donald, Liberty and Union *(Lexington, MA: D. C. Heath, 1978), pp. 4–5. Reprinted by permission of Houghton Mifflin Company.*

slow and were the most expensive form of freight haulage, but railroads were fast, cheap, and not subject to seasonal vicissitudes. The partisans mustered enough support so that some railway construction was under way by 1830. The first steam locomotive had been landed here a year before and others followed.

America was the first country outside Great Britain to give the steam railway a considered trial. Within two years we were not merely convinced, we were fanatical converts. We speak glibly today of America's love affair with the automobile, but we forget our earlier romance with the railroad. And it was no mere infatuation; it was a burning passion. We built railroads faster than anyone in the world. By 1850 we had outbuilt the British by 1,500 miles. The pace quickened to 2,000 to 10,000 miles a year thereafter. The system developed, as might be expected, from the settled east coast westward. The New England network was finished by 1850, and the Appalachian barrier was crossed a few years later. An east-west connection was made with the midwestern lines previously built. As the Civil War began, the northern states east of the Mississippi River were crisscrossed by rail lines and the South had a comprehensive system which lacked only a few important connections. . . .

The technology was borrowed directly and unashamedly from Britain. American engineers went overseas to copy what had been so painfully developed. William Strickland was sent over in 1825 by a group of Philadelphia worthies interested in bolstering their city's trade position against New York's recently opened Erie Canal. Horatio Allen went abroad three years later, and the Baltimore and Ohio sent their chief engineer and several assistants. The observations and reports of these men, together with several general texts on the subject, were all that was known of the railway in America. Moreover, the locomotives, rails, wheels, axles, and other necessary hardware were imported directly from Britain. That our pioneer lines were thus facsimiles of the British is not surprising. What is, is how fast the British plan was abandoned and a uniquely American style of construction and rolling stock came into being.

First to go was the method of roadway construction. The English conceived of a railway as a monumental civil engineering feat. Enormous cuts and fills, masonry viaducts, and lengthy tunnels produced level, direct roadbeds. Tracks were constructed with massive stone blocks as ties; iron chairs mounted on the blocks held wrought-iron rails. It was a railway intended to last for the ages, as indicated by the British term "Permanent Way." Such excellence, however, cost $179,000 a mile, a price Britain could afford but America could not.

America was looking for a provisional form of transit. We needed a cheap, easy-to-build railway. We had great distances to cover: centers of population were not only widely separated, but the land between was sparsely settled and traffic density was thus low. There was also a chronic shortage of both capital and labor.

The most obvious way to lower costs and hasten construction was to lower standards of construction. The elimination of extensive grading was the first economy: railroads would follow the natural rise and fall of the land. Tracks would go around hills rather than tunneling through. Wooden trestles took the place of masonry viaducts, and the track was fabricated from local timber, with only a thin iron strap for the running surface. The result was a decidedly inferior railroad. It was makeshift, dangerous, and expensive to operate and maintain. But it was wonderfully cheap to build; our costs were only one-sixth of the British plan.

Such economies were apparent to most American engineers after building only a few miles of track. Converts to the thrifty American plan were legion by the early 1830s. But a few stubbornly held to the old pattern, notably the Boston and Lowell Railroad. Financed by the Boston textile barons Nathan Appleton and Patrick Tracy Jackson, it could afford to build on the best plan. It was decided to copy exactly the finest railway in England, the Liverpool and Manchester. Grades were held to ten feet per mile; only broad curves were tolerated. The best wrought-iron edge rail was imported from England, and local quarries were pressed hard to produce some 82,000 stone-block ties. For all this, the project proved a failure. After the first hard frost the stone-block ties were heaved up, throwing the track out of alignment. Similar derangements were noted as far south as Delaware (the Newcastle and Frenchtown Railway). Stone-block ties were not suitable to the North American climate.

The American strap rail presented numerous problems too. It was admittedly an expedient: it was weak and could sustain slow speeds only; even conservative operating practice did not prevent its rapid deterioration. After only four years of service, the strap rails on the Philadelphia and Columbia Railroad were so dilapidated that they were reported "a fruitful source of injury to cars and engines." Passengers were wary of travel on strap-rail lines lest a "snake head" pierce the bottom of the car's floor. To reassure its passengers, one midwestern line advertised that the undersides of their cars were sheathed in iron to guard against loose bars. The defects of strap rail were recognized from the beginning, and most roads converted to some form of solid rolled rails as soon as they could afford to rebuild. This process was hastened in at least one instance by legislation when New York State passed a public law in 1847 requiring the elimination of strap rail. Most strap rail tracks were gone by the beginning of the Civil War.

From the 1830s, when steam railroads first became an important part of inland transport in America, provision was made to carry emigrating settlers westward. The service provided was economical but spartan, as might be expected. Some railroads used convertible boxcars outfitted with bench seats that could be removed for the eastward trip, when the cars carried merchandise. Such elementary comforts as lighting, heating, and toilet facilities were unknown in such boxcars. Even windows were considered a luxury.

As late as 1867 the Grand Trunk Railway of Canada was carrying immigrants in ordinary boxcars without seats. Some eight hundred to nine hundred German travelers were jammed at one time into a ten-car train, provoking a local newspaper reporter to state that he had never before witnessed such an inhumane or shameful scene. Within the folklore of railroading it is claimed that immigrant families would hire a freight car for the family members, their possessions, clothing, furniture, and, on occasion, livestock. Such caravans were called Zulu cars by contemptuous trainmen. . . .

Profit, not humanitarianism, was the guiding force of the transportation systems. Yet a few railroad managers felt immigrants deserved better conveyances, especially as the railroad network expanded westward in the 1850s and 1860s and journeys increased from jaunts of a few hours into three-thousand-mile treks that might occupy seven days. Even the hardiest Polish peasant looked longingly for a berth, a toilet, and a warm meal. For the aged, children and expectant mothers, a week-long cross-country rail trip under primitive conditions was nearly unendurable.

A modicum of comfort — even for the poor — did appear in the late 1870s when the Central Pacific Railroad introduced the immigrant sleeping car. While plain in finish, it provided the basic comforts necessary for overnight travel. Berths were offered, but the traveler was expected to furnish his own bedding. A common kitchen at one end of the car provided a place to prepare a warm meal, and provisions could be picked up along the line if the initial stock of food was insufficient. Station restaurants and dining cars, the latter common after 1885, were too expensive for immigrants. Even the ordinary coach traveler depended on a box lunch. . . .

The railroad's relationship to the immigrant extended beyond the one-way trip to the West. Like the European trading companies which, two hundred years before, had been granted vast tracts of real estate in the New World, the railroads were given millions of acres of western lands as an inducement to cross the continent with iron and steel. Railroads were thus also land companies, eager to sell a bit of the virgin territory to the hopeful newcomers. The St. Paul, Minneapolis, and Manitoba Railway nicknamed itself "The Nile of the American Continent"; not only could it transport you, as could the Egyptian Nile, but it terminated in a land rich as a delta — of "2,500,000 acres of the best wheat."

Western lands were nearly worthless when given to the railroad companies, but the opening of the railroads provided the catalyst of cheap transport that encouraged rapid settlement and a remarkable escalation in property values. Land began to sell rapidly. Six months after the Transcontinental Railroad opened, the Kansas Pacific R.R. alone sold nearly half a million acres. In 1870 the Burlington organized a land development office to sell 600,000 acres in Nebraska and Iowa. One hundred agents pushed for sales to American buyers, ten offices were opened in the British Isles, and literature was published and distributed in German, French, Bohemian, and Scandinavian. Prospective buyers, invited to inspect the land, were given a rebate on their tickets and provided with shelter in immigrant hotels specially built by the railroad. Credit was easy: ten years to pay at 6 percent interest and interest only payable during the first two years. Not many could resist such an attractive deal. In less than three years the Burlington sold half its land, some 300,000 acres, at a net profit of $7.50 per acre.

The railroad as a transporter and as a colonizer did not exhaust the relationship with the foreign-born. Access to market was essential for every immigrant farmer, and year after year, the railroads' ever-growing feeder lines penetrated the lives of the foreigners on the land.

The railroad was also a major employer in nineteenth-century America. The skilled and unskilled found work — managers, executives, and financiers, as well as track workers, firemen, and brakemen. It is common to think only of the lowest working ranks being filled by the immigrant, but some of the highest offices were held by foreign-born Americans, such as Albert Fink (1827–1897).

Fink began life with many advantages. He was distinguished in appearance, with a noble head and a tall, well-proportioned body. His manner was calm and thoughtful, he spoke clearly and to the point, and he was intelligent and carefully educated. He was not destined to be a failure.

He was born in Lauterbach, Germany, in 1827, and received a private school education. He studied architecture and engineering at Darmstadt Polytechnic School, graduating in 1848. The political revolution of that year, in which the democratic forces were defeated, prompted Fink's decision to emigrate to the United States, and in a typically methodical manner he began a rigorous study of the English language. In 1849 he found work with the Baltimore and Ohio Railroad's engineering department in Baltimore. The railroad was then pushing its main line over the Allegheny Mountains and required designs for countless new bridges and shop buildings. Fink showed great facility — particularly in preparing plans for iron bridges — and was soon advanced to a more responsible position.

In 1857 he left Baltimore to become an assistant engineer for the Louisville and Nashville R.R. Again Fink's skill and capacity earned him a promotion, and after two years he was made chief engineer. In 1865 he became general superintendent of the line and five years later was appointed vice-president. Fink's talents as an administrator equaled or exceeded his engineering abilities. His overview and understanding of railroad economics made him the logical choice to head the Southern Railway and Steamship Association, established in 1875 to coordinate rates and traffic between connecting and competing lines. The administration of such a complicated and potentially explosive arrangement called for tact, judgment, and a thorough knowledge of the transportation industry. Fink was so successful in dealing with the problems of the Southern Association that he was asked to supervise similar negotiations between the major northern trunk lines. He was a central figure in railroad traffic pooling operations until the Interstate Commerce Commission put an end to such arrangements. He retired from business in 1889 and spent his remaining years in the study of art, history, and philosophy, together with extensive travels abroad.

But Fink was the exception. The ordinary immigrant came with less education and fewer skills, prepared to handle a shovel but not a drafting pen. There was a middle echelon of locomotive engineers, machinists, and car painters who as skilled and semiskilled professionals earned good wages and sometimes rose to management positions. The greater number of railway workers, however, continued an unremitting grind of manual labor. The locomotive fireman not only stoked the firebox but worked long hours before and after the run, cleaning the engine. In the old South he was often a Negro, who had no hope, as was true elsewhere in America, of eventually taking the throttle as a locomotive engineer. The brakeman faced an even harder and certainly a more dangerous day than the fireman. He was expected to jump from car to car to wind up the hand wheels when the engineer whistled "Down brakes." A careless step and he was under the wheels. Between stops, he tended the heating stoves, refilled the lamps, and called the station names. Few men wanted this thankless job, and it was said that only the poor Irish could readily be signed on.

The trackworker did the heaviest, roughest work. From early in the morning to sunset he was lifting ties and rails, shoveling ballast, and rebuilding culverts and embankments. He would carry his weighty tools and supplies on a hand-pumped car, perhaps ten miles from his home station. It was an exhausting routine which continued winter and summer, fair weather and foul, and which only a strong, able-bodied man could endure. Many of the early lines were built and maintained by Irish day laborers.

In the Midwest in the 1850s, however, the Irish fell into disfavor. The Illinois Central Railroad, for example, found them too troublesome. Their excessive drinking and constant fistfights, which at times appeared to constitute minor riots, led the Illinois Central's labor agents to look for sober men with families who sought employment and hoped to buy a homestead — from the railroad, of course. The German immigrants filled the bill.

According to company records, the Germans were poor, less accustomed to the work, but more docile and reliable. The agents combed the eastern ports, promising high pay, cheap land, and good climate; they even arranged to transport German workers from New York City to Illinois for $4.75. One historian has estimated that between 1852 and 1856 the Illinois Central induced between five thousand and ten thousand immigrant workers to join the road gangs. Many of these did eventually settle on company lands, becoming successful farmers.

In the Far West the Central Pacific, desperate for construction crews, imported hands from China. Their efficient work is legendary. In the South before the Civil War,

Negroes worked as slaves on the lines in Dixie, and after the war they continued the same labor as free men.

Indeed, members of every immigrant group rode on trains, worked on track crews, purchased lands, and shipped goods with the railroads. For many newcomers, the railroad played a direct and continuing role in their American lives.

QUESTIONS TO CONSIDER

1. What technological advances did Samuel Slater and William Crompton introduce in America? How did these mechanics evade England's embargo on exporting machinery? Given the popularity of Thomas Jefferson's agrarian vision of America, how do you think nineteenth-century Americans felt about factories? How could industrialization be reconciled with traditional American ideals?

2. Compare railroads in nineteenth-century England and the United States. Why did railroads become "an American passion"? In what ways were America's railroads inferior to Britain's? How were they superior?

3. Railroads carried immigrants to the West, sold them land, and hired them as workers. Describe the spectrum of jobs available in nineteenth-century railroad work and the factors involved in getting them. How did employers' preference for Germans over Irish reflect ethnic stereotypes? How did American railroads become involved in real estate speculation? Did railroad companies exploit immigrants or assist in their adjustment to America?

4. Why did most immigrants avoid the American South? What evidence do the authors find of hostile attitudes toward immigrants among Americans?

5. What present-day analogies do you see to the nineteenth-century "transportation revolution"? Compare the impact of railroads before the Civil War with the effect of airplane travel after World War II or computers since the 1980s. Be sure to consider the impact of these new technologies upon industry and labor as well as their shrinkage of time and space. Explore the similarities and differences between the U.S. technological boom in the nineteenth century and the Japanese (or later, Korean and Chinese) in the twentieth century.

Slavery in Brazil
and the United States

CARL N. DEGLER

From the vantage point of the modernizing North, the South's "peculiar institution" seemed increasingly anachronistic. Yet slavery in the nineteenth-century American South was hardly unique. It shared essential similarities with plantation societies flourishing at the same time in the Caribbean and South America. All were brutal systems of human ownership and labor exploitation that passed down through generations. There were differences, too. The first historians who compared slavery in the United States with its counterpart in Latin America were so impressed by the long history of blacks' subordination in the American South and the extraordinary racial prejudice faced by African Americans that they pictured American slavery as uniquely severe, comparable perhaps only to a Nazi concentration camp in its violence and finality. By contrast, it was said, Spanish and Portuguese slavery was more liberal. Untainted by racial prejudice and free from the pressures of a booming capitalist economy, the burden of bondage in Latin America was further lightened by the protection that a paternalistic government and the Catholic Church extended to the slaves' humanity.

No doubt there is some truth in this contrast, but there is good reason to be skeptical. In the United States, an enduring plantation legend, peopled with the type of handsome masters, fluttering belles, and carefree slaves seen in the movie Gone With the Wind, *draped a deceptive romantic veil over the reality of southern slavery until modern historical studies lifted it. The contrast between evil North American and allegedly benevolent Latin American slavery suggests that historians rejected the Old South myth only to accept a similarly rosy picture of the "Big House" concocted by Latin American apologists for slavery. How useful is it, moreover, to argue over which nation's slavery was the worst? Weighing degrees of oppression is far less meaningful than finding similarities and differences in the kinds of oppression slaves faced, and assessing the consequences of these for each society.*

In this selection Carl Degler injects a healthy dose of clarity and common sense into the comparative study of slavery. Taking the United States and Brazil in the nineteenth century, he sorts the evidence into separate categories, analyzing information on legal codes, church activities, the physical treatment of slaves, slave revolts, and the incidence of manumission (the voluntary freeing of slaves). Overall, he finds that slavery in the United States was in fact less harsh than slavery in Brazil, but much harder for its victims to escape, especially by being granted their freedom. Due to the steady flow of slaves from Africa, Brazilian masters imported mainly young males and worked them until they dropped, inflicting types of punishment that were virtually unknown in North America. In the southern United States, the slave population continued to grow after the international trade officially ended in 1808 — a sign, Degler says, of the care planters took to maintain their "property." In North America, too, a balanced sex ratio allowed blacks to construct family networks that helped them to survive. The worst comparative feature of North American slavery was the southern states' virtual prohibition of freeing slaves. This was symptomatic, says Degler, of a society that indelibly labeled blacks inferior and, unlike Brazil, refused them a meaningful role in free society.

Degler's is certainly not the last word in this controversy. As you join the debate, you may want to think about divisions in slave environments that cut across national differences, such as those between urban and rural slavery, "boom" and "bust" economies, or large plantations and small farms. You might also consider whether Degler's emphasis upon black-white population ratios, like Winthrop Jordan's in Selection 6, begs the question of white prejudice, which remains a deeply rooted cultural habit. All the same, Degler's indictment of slavery in both the Americas rings truer than less balanced accounts. And his point that whites in the South were terrified by the thought of black freedom is a sobering reminder of the long road African Americans had to travel toward acceptance in a land they had helped build.

GLOSSARY

CHATTEL   A movable article of property.

INDENTURED SERVITUDE   Men or women bound to a master for a period of years, normally from three to seven. The master owned their labor and in return often paid for their passage to the colonies and provided food and shelter. Following their service, they were given money, tools and clothing, or land.

MANUMISSION   The legal process by which a master voluntarily freed his slaves.

MAROON   A runaway slave or descendant of runaway slaves. Also sometimes used to denote their hiding place.

PALMARES   A well-organized slave hideaway in northeastern Brazil that reached a population of twenty thousand before it was destroyed by Brazilian authorities in 1698.

PECULIUM   Property given by a master to a slave.

QUILOMBOS   The organized backcountry hideaways of runaway Brazilian slaves.

SECOND SEMINOLE WAR (1835–1842)   A war between U.S. troops sent by President Jackson and the Seminole Indians of Florida led by Osceola. The Seminoles resisted the government's attempt to move them west to Indian Territory. Osceola died in captivity in 1838, and after the Seminoles were defeated in 1842, most moved to Indian Territory.

STONO REBELLION   The first major slave revolt in North America. In 1739, seventy-five slaves gathered near the Stono River in South Carolina, killed some whites, and marched toward freedom in Spanish Florida. The colonial militia killed many of the Stono rebels and dispersed the rest before they reached Florida.

TURNER, NAT (1800–1831)   An African American slave who, believing himself divinely appointed, led a revolt in Virginia in 1831 that killed over fifty whites before he was captured and hanged. It was the most serious uprising in the history of slavery in the United States.

VESEY, DENMARK (1767–1822)   A freed slave in Charleston, South Carolina, who devised a conspiracy for a slave uprising in 1822. Informers divulged the plot, however, and thirty-five blacks, including Vesey, were captured and executed.

$$* \quad * \quad * \quad * \quad * \quad * \quad *$$

Until Frank Tannenbaum published his book *Slave and Citizen* [in 1947] it was generally thought that slavery, at least as legally defined, was much the same wherever it occurred, whether in ancient Rome and Greece, in medieval Europe, or in North and South America. And certainly in most times and places two common elements clearly differentiated slavery from other kinds of legally defined labor systems. The status of a slave lasted through his lifetime and was inheritable. In the seventeenth century, for example, indentured servitude was common, especially in the English colonies of North America, and though many elements of that status were similar to those of slavery, the term of service was limited, usually from four to seven years, and the status was not inheritable; a child born to a servant was free. One further element common to all systems of slavery, modern and ancient, was that the status was inherited from the mother. Thus the offspring of a slave woman and a free man was a slave whether in Brazil, the United States, or ancient Rome. Modern slavery, however, differed from the ancient form in one important way. It was imposed upon colored people only. In Brazil, as in the United States, white people were never slaves, though Indians were held as slaves in both places during the colonial period. To the implications of this fact we shall return later.

Frank Tannenbaum contended that despite these admitted similarities between the modern slave systems of North and South America, there were important differences between them. In Tannenbaum's view, the law of slavery in Latin America and the attitudes of the Roman Catholic Church toward the slave differed significantly from the laws and the religious practices in English North America. It was the differences in slavery, according to Tannenbaum, that explained the differences in the race relations of today. Because of the emphasis that Tannenbaum placed upon the role of the state and the church in differentiating the systems of slavery, the practices of slavery in the two places need to be examined in some detail. . . .

Neither Black nor White: Slavery and Race Relations in Brazil and the U.S. by Degler, Carl N., © 1971. Reprinted by permission of Prentice-Hall, Inc., Upper Saddle River, NJ.

WHO PROTECTS THE SLAVE'S HUMANITY?

In comparing slavery in Brazil and the United States, let us first look at the ways in which they were alike. (Although slavery has a long history in both Brazil and the United States, the basis of the comparison here will be slavery at its maturity in both places — that is, during the nineteenth century, if only because the evidence for making such comparisons is most abundant during that period.) . . . Tannenbaum . . . contrasts the legal definition of a slave as a chattel in the United States with the more ambiguous definition in Latin America. "In fact," Tannenbaum wrote, *"the element of human personality was not lost in the transition to slavery from Africa to the Spanish or Portuguese dominions.* He [the Negro] remained a person even while he was a slave. . . . He was never considered a mere chattel, never defined as unanimated property, and never under the law treated as such. His master never enjoyed the powers of life and death over his body, even though abuses existed and cruelties were performed."

Yet a comparison of Brazilian and United States law reveals striking similarities in the legal definition of a slave. Although by the nineteenth century the text of the law in the southern states of the United States defined a slave as chattel property, the judicial interpretations of that legal concept were not those that Tannenbaum assumed. The law always recognized that a slave was both a human being and a piece of property. The very fact, for instance, that slaves were legally responsible for any crime they committed immediately suggests that their status as chattel property was different from that of any other piece of property, even of an animate variety. The courts of the Southern states were quite explicit in their recognition of the humanity of the slave. "A slave is not in the condition of a horse or an ox," declared a Tennessee court in 1846. "His liberty is restrained, it is true, and his owner controls his actions and claims his services. But he is made after the image of the Creator. He has mental capacities, and an immortal principle in his nature that constitutes him equal to his owner but for the accidental position in which fortune has placed him. The owner has acquired conventional rights to him, but the laws under which he is held as a slave have not and cannot extinguish his high-born nature nor deprive him of many rights which are inherent in man." . . .

. . . [T]he position of the slave in a Brazilian court was not much different from that of the slave in the United States. No slave in Brazil could enter a complaint himself; it had to be done by his master or by the public authority. Nor could a slave make an accusation against his master. In fact, a slave could not give sworn testimony at all, only information. . . .

If the law in both Brazil and the United States defined the slave as at once a human being and a thing and limited his rights in court, there was also little difference in the way in which the law protected the slave's humanity. Tannenbaum, for example, has emphasized that in Latin America the law prohibited punishments and other kinds of treatment that would degrade or dehumanize the slave. Yet all the slave states of the United States in the nineteenth century enacted laws against the mistreatment or killing of slaves by masters. Kenneth Stampp, in his general study of southern slavery, . . . summarizes the legal situation as follows: "The law required that masters be humane to their slaves, furnish them adequate food and clothing, and provide care for them during sickness and old age. In short, the state endowed masters with obligations as well as rights and assumed some responsibility for the welfare of the bondsmen."

Because both societies had laws seeking to protect the humanity of the slave against his master's power to exploit, the important question is whether the state's law or the church's authority interceded between the master and the slave, in behalf of the latter. Generally historians of slavery in the United States have not put much weight upon the influence of the law, believing generally that the master on his isolated plantation was beyond the reach of the law. There are very few cases, for example, of cruel masters being summoned to court for violation of these laws. As . . . [a] Mississippi case of 1821 shows, occasionally masters were executed or otherwise punished for killing a slave and a cruel master did suffer the condemnation of his neighbors, if nothing else. All in all, however, the sanctions against mistreatment or even a high crime like murder of a slave were less rigorously applied than those against similar crimes against a white person in the United States. Informal controls over harsh or sadistic masters were probably more effective than modern commentators often recognize, but in the United States the law's protection of the slave's humanity is not impressive on the basis of the record.

A similar gap between law and practice seems to have prevailed in Brazil, too, where the power of the state or the church to affect the conditions of life of the slave was perhaps even more limited than in the more thickly settled and more highly organized United States. As Henry Koster, an English planter who lived for many years in Brazil, pointed out in the early nineteenth century, the Brazilian government was a weak reed on which to lean for anything, much less for control over the members of the slave-holding class. He tells, for example, of an instance in which one of his own slaves injured the slave of another man, but adds that nothing was done about the matter. The owner of the injured slave, Koster pointed out, might have pressed charges, if he was so minded, "but the law of itself seldom does anything. Even in the cases of murder the prosecutor . . . has it at his option to bring the trial forward or not; if he can be bribed or otherwise persuaded to give up the accusation, the matter drops to the ground." Occasionally, Koster writes, a cruel master was fined for maltreating his slaves, "but I have never heard of punishment having been carried farther than this trifling matter of correction." . . .

Sometimes it is said that an important distinction between the slave practices of Latin America and those of the United States is that in the former the Roman Catholic church protected the slave's humanity. . . . If Tannenbaum's assertion that the church in Latin America maintained a higher moral position for the slave than in the United States means that the Roman Catholic church intervened between master and slave in behalf of the latter, then it needs to be said that in Brazil, at least, the church's interest in and power to protect the slave's humanity was as limited as that of the state. For one thing, few plantations had priests on the premises; most of them saw a priest only once a year, when he came to legalize unions and to baptize. During the nineteenth century there simply were not sufficient priests in the country for them to be able to affect the daily life of the slave on the plantation, even if they had the interest to do so. And even where a priest was resident on a plantation, it seems doubtful that his will could withstand the master, on whom the priest depended so heavily. More important, there is abundant evidence that officially the church showed little interest in interfering with the institution of slavery, even in regard to matters that might seem to fall under the heading of moral behavior. Thus it was not until 1885 that the Archbishop of Bahia — the chief churchman in Brazil — ruled that no master could prevent a slave from marrying or sell him away from his spouse. Yet even at that late date — slavery was finally abolished in Brazil in 1888 — a slave could marry against his master's will only if the slave could demonstrate that he knew Christian doctrine — that is, the Lord's Prayer, the Ave Maria, the Creed, the Commandments, understood the obligations of holy matrimony, and was clear in his intention to remain married for life — a formidable set of requirements for an untutored slave! Furthermore, as in the United States, religion was used by the church in Brazil as a way to support slavery, not to weaken it. One priest told a group of planters, "Confession is the antidote to insurrection, because the confessor makes the slave see that his master is in the place of his father to whom he owes love, respect, and obedience." . . .

MANUMISSION: HOW EASY, HOW COMMON?

Perhaps the most frequently stressed difference between Latin American and United States slavery is the amount of manumission. Generally it is said that in Latin America manumission was both more common and easier than in the United States. . . .

On the Brazilian side of the comparison it needs to be said that prior to 1871, despite tradition and the assertions of some historians, there was no law requiring a master to permit a slave to buy his freedom, though many undoubtedly did. One American historian of Brazil made a search for such a law, but found none prior to 1871, when emancipationists insisted upon it, a fact that in itself suggests the practice of self-purchase was not as firmly protected as often is alleged. It is true, nevertheless, that Brazilian law contained none of the limitations on manumission that prevailed in the southern United States, especially after 1830. All of the southern states, for instance, threw obstacles in the path of the master who sought to free his slave, not the least of which was the requirement that all newly freed slaves must leave the state. Under Brazilian law, on the other hand, emancipation was legal in almost any form, whether by letter, by will, or by simple but explicit statement at baptism. . . .

Some commentators on slavery in the United States and Latin America assert that the slave's right to hold property in South America, as contrasted with the lack of such a right in the United States, made it easier for him to buy his freedom in Brazil than in the United States. Actually, the law in Brazil did not permit slaves to possess property — or a peculium — until near the end of the slave era. For as Perdigão Malheiro wrote in his treatise on slave law in 1866, "among us, no law guarantees to the slave his peculium." However, he goes on, most masters permitted slaves to keep whatever property they gathered, letting them use it as they saw fit. Generally, the same situation in law and in practice prevailed in the United States. Slaves' property was neither recognized nor protected by law in any of the southern states, but in practice most slave owners permitted their slaves to keep whatever property they earned from work on their own time. It was a cruel as well as a rare master in the United States, as in Brazil, who deliberately, if legally, confiscated earnings that his slave may have accumulated. . . .

Yet, . . . the balance must still come down on the side that sees [Brazil] as more liberal in this regard than the United States. In this aspect of slavery lies one of the principal differences between the two systems. The chief reason for drawing that conclusion is the considerably higher proportion of free Negroes in nineteenth century Brazil than in the United States. . . . According to the traditional estimates, in 1817–18 the number of slaves in Brazil was about three times that of free Negroes and mulattoes. This ratio may be compared with that in the United States in 1860, when the number of free Negroes reached its maximum under slavery. At that date there were eight times as many slaves as free Negroes in the whole of the United States and sixteen times as many slaves as free blacks if the comparison is made in the slave states alone. After abolition in the United States, the number of free Negroes in Brazil grew enormously. Thus in 1872 the number of free Negroes and colored was more than double the number of slaves! Here is certainly a striking difference between the two slave societies. How might one account for it?

Two explanations are worth looking at. One of these is that Brazilian masters freed the sick and the old, in order to relieve themselves of responsibility and financial loss. Frequent denunciations in newspapers and laws seeking to stop such practices leave no doubt that some masters were indeed freeing their infirm, aged, and incurably sick slaves. Yet it is difficult to believe that such practices, even as widespread and common as the sources lead us to believe them to be, could have been the principal source of the relatively large free colored population. Infirm, aged, or sick slaves simply would not have been numerous enough themselves or have been able to produce offspring in sufficient numbers to account for the great number of free Negroes and mulattoes in the society.

A more persuasive explanation is derived from the different processes of settlement and economic development in the two countries. . . . Negroes and mulattoes made up a majority of the population of Brazil prior to the last quarter of the nineteenth century. Whether as slaves or as free men, Negroes and mulattoes had a place in a society that was only sparsely populated and in a slave economy that concentrated upon staple production. The free blacks and mulattoes were needed to raise cattle, grow food, to serve as shopkeepers, craftsmen, peddlers, boatmen, and for a thousand other tasks. They filled the innumerable petty jobs, the interstitial work of the economy, that the constraints of slavery would not permit the slave to perform and that white men were insufficient or unwilling to man. . . .

In the United States the economic and demographic patterns worked in the opposite direction. . . . From the beginning of the settlement in the South, much less in the United States as a whole, there had always been more than enough white men to perform all the tasks of the society *except* that of plantation worker. . . . In the nineteenth century perhaps three-fourths of the cotton grown in the South came from plantations on which black slaves supplied the labor. Indeed, it seems clear now that without black slaves the great Cotton Kingdom of the South simply could not have developed as rapidly as it did. Off the plantations, however, unlike the situation in Brazil, white labor was more than ample for the needs and expansion of the economy. Indeed, throughout the antebellum years, as for years afterward, the South actually exported white people to the rest of the nation. . . .

REBELLIONS AND RUNAWAYS

Comparisons between Brazilian and United States slavery commonly emphasize the greater rebelliousness of slaves in Brazil. . . . [L]arge numbers of revolts by slaves were indeed not frequent in United States history. When one has counted the revolt at Stono, South Carolina, in 1739, that at New Orleans in 1811, and the Nat Turner upheaval at Southampton, Virginia, in 1831, the principal revolts have been listed. Others often cited, such as those led by Gabriel Prosser (1800) and Denmark Vesey (1822), never even came to a head; they remained conspiracies. Throughout the whole of the Civil War no major slave revolt took place, it is worth recalling, though controls at that time were, perforce, probably the weakest in the history of slavery.

Few and far between as the rebellions may have been in the United States, the contrast with Brazil is not as sharp as the usual comparisons often assert. The most often cited measure of the greater rebelliousness of Brazilian slaves, for example, is the great slave hideaway or *quilombo* of Palmares, situated deep in the backcountry of northeastern Brazil and counting 20,000 inhabitants at its height. For almost the whole length of the seventeenth century Palmares fought off the repeated assaults of governmental and other troops before it was destroyed in 1698. Many other *quilombos,* less spectacularly enduring or less well known than Palmares are equally well documented.

It is questionable, however, whether such collective runaways, no matter how long-lived or however large in scale, ought to be classed as slave rebellions. Generally, the *quilombo* neither attempted to overthrow the slave system nor made war on it. *Quilombolos* clashed with white society only when the whites sought to bring back the runaways or, as in the case of Palmares, acted to remove what the whites perceived as a threat to the unity of Brazilian society. The rulers of Palmares, on the other hand, would have been quite content to have remained aloof as an African state, separated by the forest from white society, if the government and whites in general had let them alone. . . .

In short, if the criterion is armed uprisings against slave holders, like that which took place under Nat Turner, then the total number of rebellions in Brazil is considerably smaller when the *quilombos* are not included. For as [Edison] Carneiro has pointed out, "The most used resource by black slaves in Brazil for purposes of escape . . . was without doubt that of fleeing to the forest, from which resulted the *quilombo.*" In Brazil, as in the United States, the commonest expression of slave unrest was the runaway, not the insurrectionist. . . .

. . . To admit that slave rebellions were few or even unimportant is not to indict Negroes for docility or racial suitability for slavery or any equally absurd charge to which rebelliousness is supposed to be the proper answer. Slave rebellions were extremely difficult as well as dangerous to plan and carry out at any time or place, regardless of the race of the slaves. Slave revolts were not common in antiquity, either. And when the slaves were readily identifiable as were Negroes, planning and organizing was even more difficult. Moreover, the difficulty stemmed not only from the fact that the preponderance of power was in the hands of the masters, but also from the psychological handicap that slavery imposed upon those raised under the system. Most slaves could not help but see slavery as a part of the natural order of the world. Once the difficulties, if not the dangers to the slaves, stemming from rebellion are appreciated, then there is no need to inflate relatively minor clashes between masters and slaves into rebellions, as is too often done, or to insist upon continuous violence when sporadic outbreaks were all that could be expected.

Yet even when these qualifications are taken into consideration, it is still accurate to see slave rebellions as more numerous in Brazil than in the United States. Among the good reasons for arriving at that conclusion are the series of bloody rebellions in and around the city of Bahia between 1807 and 1835, which have no analog in the history of United States slavery. . . .

The revolts in Brazil were not only somewhat more numerous, but were generally also larger in size. A mid-nineteenth century revolt in the province of Rio de Janeiro, for example, mobilized three hundred slaves and required federal troops to suppress it. In 1820 at least two revolts, involving several hundred slaves each, were reported in the province of Minas Gerais. On the other hand, of the three uprisings in the United States that have already been mentioned as the largest, only the one that occurred outside of New Orleans engaged more than a hundred slaves.

Similarly, *quilombos* or maroons in the United States were considerably fewer and smaller in size than those in Brazil. As far as the *quilombos* are concerned, probably the best explanation for the difference is simply the climate. Winter in most of the United States is much too harsh for a *quilombo* to survive for long; almost all of Brazil, on the other hand, lies in the tropics, which requires less substantial shelter and provides easier access to food for runaways than the changing seasons of the United States. Furthermore, even the frontier areas of the United States were too well settled and accordingly too well policed, especially after the seventeenth century, to provide safety for maroons for any length of time. The only example of a United States maroon's approaching the size and endurance of Palmares was the one that history calls the Second Seminole War. During that struggle in the 1830's runaway blacks and Indians held out against the United States Army for seven years. Significantly, the hideaway was located in the warmest part of the United States — Florida — and in an area then only thinly settled by whites.

THE INTERNATIONAL SLAVE TRADE AS CAUSE

The conclusion that on balance, revolts and *quilombos* were of greater frequency and size in Brazil than in the United States serves to introduce another difference between the two slave societies. That is the greater dependence of the Brazilians upon the African slave trade. There is good reason to believe, as we shall see, that the greater number of revolts and *quilombos* in Brazil is directly related to the continuation of the slave trade.

Although the slave trade from Africa to Brazil was supposedly ended in 1831 by treaty with Great Britain, the importation of slaves continued at high annual levels for at least another twenty years. Over 300,000 slaves, for example, entered Brazil from Africa between 1842 and 1851 alone. On the other hand, the importation of large numbers of slaves into the United States ceased in 1808, when the federal government prohibited the further importation of slaves. In fact, the importation of large numbers of slaves had slowed down considerably even before that date. Prior to 1800 each one of the slave states had itself prohibited importation at one time or another. Only in South Carolina was the slave trade open at the time it was closed for good by the federal government in 1808. It is therefore quite accurate to see the United States as ceasing to depend upon foreign importations even before the nineteenth century opened.

That Brazil kept open the slave trade while the United States closed it accounts for a number of differences in the nature of slavery in the two places. The larger size and number of *quilombos* in Brazil as compared with those in the United States was in part, at least, a consequence of the large number of African-born slaves in Brazil. As Raymond Kent has shown, the great *quilombo* of Palmares is most accurately seen as a reproduction of an African state, suggesting that it was African-born slaves who founded this greatest of Brazilian slave hideaways. . . .

Newly imported Africans also seem to have played a part in bringing about the greater number of rebellions in Brazil; some authorities have made the point quite categorically. Certainly it is plausible to see Africans as providing a basis for rebellions. Under any circumstances, as has been said, revolts were hard to organize and even more difficult to carry out, if only because success was so unlikely, that is, suicidal. But rebellions were especially difficult to organize under a system of slavery like that in the United States, where the slaves were principally native-born and thus almost entirely bereft of their African culture or identity. For some sense of slave unity, coupled with alienation from the master's society, would seem to be essential to the mounting of a revolt. But virtually all of the slaves in the United States were natives, raised from birth to be a part of the system. Native-born slaves were united by little more than their common degradation, while divided by their many personal connections with the whites among whom they lived. In Brazil, on the other hand, the presence of thousands of newly arrived Africans, who were resentfully hostile to their new masters and society while also united by their common African tribal culture, provided a basis for slave rebellions that was clearly lacking in the United States, especially after the Revolution. . . .

SLAVE REARING AS CONSEQUENCE

The endurance and even expansion of United States slavery, without any substantial additions from importations, is unique in the world history of slavery. Neither in antiquity nor in Latin America was a slave system sustained principally by reproduction of the slave population. The highest estimate reported for the smuggling of slaves into the United States after the official closing of the slave trade in 1808 was 270,000. For the fifty years prior to 1860 that works out roughly to 5,000 per year. Large as this figure is, it cannot account for the rather steady rate of growth in the slave population recorded in the census. For example . . . the average *annual* increase for the 1790's was 20,000 slaves, whereas that for the 1840's was 70,000. Both average figures far exceed even the highest estimate for annual importations from abroad. Thus these high annual increases can be accounted for only by recognizing that the principal source of the slave population in the United States during the nineteenth century was natural increase.

One consequence — as well as cause — of the dependence of United States slavery upon natural increase was that the ratio between the sexes was virtually equal — at least in the nineteenth century. The first census to differentiate slaves by sex was that of 1820. At that date the ratio of the sexes was 95 women to each 100 men, suggesting that a near balance between the sexes must have obtained even before the closing of the slave trade in 1808. By 1830 the ratio was 98 to 100 and by 1850 it was more than 99 to 100. All of these ratios, significantly enough, are close to those for the white population in 1800, which counted 95 women to 100 men. The ratio in 1850 was the same, though there had been some fluctuation in between. . . .

To speak of raising slaves in the United States South, however, ought not to be equated with arrangements on a stock farm, or at least not entirely so. It is true that examples have been found of plantations in which the women slaves far outnumbered the men, suggesting systematic breeding. And some planters have left personal records that clearly demonstrate that they bought females in order to translate the offspring into cash. . . . On the whole, however, examples of deliberate breeding are rare.

Much more commonplace was the recognition and expectation that the pairing off of the sexes would quite naturally result in offspring. . . .

By pairing off the sexes in . . . [common slave quarters] masters did more than disguise the fact that they were indeed breeding people. They also lessened discontent thereby and provided a check upon the slave's inclination to run away. A slave with offspring gave hostages to good behavior and docility.

If the kind of breeding that went on in the United States under slavery seems unexceptional and expected, the situation in Brazil reveals how unusual it really was. . . . [W]riters on slavery and commentators at the time make it clear that slave breeding on the scale achieved in the United States was not important to Brazilian slaveholders. . . . In fact, the very hours male and female slaves could be together . . . were deliberately limited. Some masters consciously restricted slave reproduction by locking up the sexes separately at night. . . . The reasoning of the slaveholders, as a contemporary reported it, was quite straightforward. "One buys a Negro for 300 milreis, who harvests in the course of the year 100 arrobas of coffee, which produces a net profit at least equal to the cost of the slave; thereafter everything is profit. It is not worth the trouble to raise children, who, only after sixteen years, will give equal service." . . .

Undoubtedly the steady stream of slaves from Africa accounts, at least in part, for the lack of interest in slave breeding in Brazil prior to 1851, when the trade ended. . . .

[There was also the fact that] infant mortality among slaves was . . . amazingly high. As one antislave-trade newspaper wrote in 1849, slaves "give us almost no children because the mortality among them is frightful in the first years, due to a thousand circumstances which are not strange to us." Even after the slave trade ended, the death rate of slave children was horrendous. One authority on the coffee country places it as high as 88 per cent. The census of 1870 revealed that in the city of Rio de Janeiro the mortality of slave children even exceeded births by 1.8 per cent and even that shocking figure must have been a minimum for the country as a whole because most slaves in Rio were domestics and presumably better cared for than agricultural slaves. . . .

One undoubted consequence of the continuance of the foreign slave trade was that Brazilian planters made no effort to balance the sexes among the slaves. Because male slaves were stronger and could serve in a greater variety of jobs than females, they constituted the overwhelming majority of the importations into Brazil. "What was wanted principally was labor," Perdigão Malheiro wrote in 1866, "not families." On some plantations there were no female slaves at all and on most, the males far outnumbered the females. One authority has estimated that for each Negro woman imported three or four males were brought in. . . .

The heavy imbalance between the sexes meant that once the slave trade was closed, Brazilian slavery began to decline, unlike the situation in the United States, where it flourished as never before *after* the closing of the foreign trade. The paucity of women, not to mention the Brazilian masters' lack of interest in breeding, insured that the reduction in the foreign supply of slaves would not be easily or quickly made up.

That same imbalance in Brazil may help also to explain the somewhat greater number of runaways in that country. In the United States, as has been suggested already, with slaves more or less divided into family units, for a male slave to run away meant serious personal loss, since he probably would have to leave woman and children behind. Such a consequence was much less likely in Brazil, where most slaves did not live in family units. . . .

A HARSHER SLAVERY

If the reader has gradually been concluding from the foregoing that the physical treatment of slaves in Brazil may well have been harsher than that in the United States, he is on the right track. . . .

There are several general reasons that suggest Brazilian slavery was physically harsher than North American. Perhaps the most persuasive is that slavery in the United States was able to endure and even expand on the basis of reproduction alone. At the very least, that fact offers testimony to a better standard of physical circumstances and care than a system of slavery that did not reproduce itself. It is true, to be sure, that the imbalance of the sexes in Brazil played a part in keeping down reproduction, but the recognized high mortality of slave children and the cost involved in caring for them probably account for the general reluctance to rear slaves in the first place. Masters had little incentive to breed slaves, which required that women be released from work to rear children, so long as the foreign slave trade promised to supply labor needs for the future. . . .

. . . Brazilians, in short, simply did not take care of their slaves well enough for them to reproduce, or at least for the children to survive, even when they had the incentive provided by the closing of the African trade.

A second general measure for comparing treatment of slaves in the United States and Brazil is that certain types of harsh treatment common in Brazil rarely occurred in the United States. A number of Brazilian sources, both during the colonial period and under the Empire in the nineteenth century, for instance, speak of the use of female slaves as prostitutes. In some cases their masters even lived off the earnings of such slaves. The practice, moreover, was sufficiently extensive for the Crown in the colonial period to legislate against the practice, though without success. This use of slave women as a source of income is virtually unknown in the history of slavery in the United States.

Another striking practice of Brazilian slavery that has little or no counterpart in the United States was the use of iron or tin masks on slaves, in order to prevent slaves from eating dirt or drinking liquor. The practice of using masks was sufficiently common in Brazil for pictures of slaves wearing them to appear in books of travel along with other references. Slaves in the United States also suffered from what we recognize today as dietary deficiencies that drove them to eat clay, and certainly many of them were addicted to liquor. Yet in the whole literature of United States slavery — and certainly northern abolitionists would have leaped upon such examples if they had been as common in the United States as they were in Brazil — I have yet to see a picture of a slave with a mask. Published references to the use of the mask for slaves in the United States are extremely rare, though they do occur.

Then there are two practices common among Brazilian slaves that have already been mentioned, but which are germane to a comparison with United States slavery. The first is the widespread practice among Brazilians, attested to by official and unofficial sources, of freeing ill, old, or crippled slaves in order to escape the obligations of caring for them. . . . In the literature of slavery in the United States, on the other hand, such charges were rarely heard from travelers, and historians have scarcely mentioned the issue and then only to discount it. "Only one instance has been noted of slaveholders shirking this responsibility [of caring for the old and incapacitated]," writes Charles Syndor in his thorough study of slavery in Mississippi. The instance was that of an idiot slave woman who was immediately taken in by a neighbor and eventually by the county.

The second practice of Brazilian slavery that has already been mentioned and which might be recalled here is that because of the heavy imbalance of the sexes most slaves in Brazil had neither sexual outlets nor the comforts of even a slave family relationship. To the extent that these deprivations constitute an element in the calculus of comparative treatment, the lot of the United States slave was easier than that of the Brazilian.

Finally, one other measure of comparative treatment might be mentioned, though it is not entirely clear how the facts ought to be interpreted. Suicides were apparently much more common among Brazilian than North American slaves. Nowhere in the secondary or primary literature on slavery in the United States, for instance, is much made of slave suicides, though, of course, they occurred. . . . On the other hand, suicides appear quite frequently in reports of travelers in Brazil. Visitors from the United States, significantly enough, were especially struck by the number of self-inflicted deaths by Brazilian slaves. "Suicides continually occur and owners wonder," wrote the American visitor Thomas Ewbank in the 1840's. Newspapers were constantly reporting such deaths, he goes on, citing from the newspaper three suicides by slaves in as many days. Another visitor from the United States a little later also commented on slave suicides, which, he observed, "are almost unknown in our southern states," but are "very frequent occurrences in the cities of Brazil."

As already pointed out, the meaning of the greater number of suicides is not entirely clear. Generally the travelers assumed it meant harsher treatment, a not unreasonable conclusion. Yet more frequent suicides could also have been the result of the larger number of Africans among the slaves. For as one of the North American visitors suggested, the African's "high spirit, refusing to bow to the white man," causes him to commit suicide. In any case, a higher incidence of suicide among slaves in Brazil does not suggest a milder form of slavery there than in the United States. . . .

. . . Simply on the basis of the comparison of physical treatment, it would appear that there is no reason to be confident that Brazilian slavery protected the humanity of the Negro who was a slave. On the contrary, insofar as physical treatment was concerned, it would seem that Brazilian slavery was less likely than United States slavery to give either the master or the slave an awareness of the Negro's humanity.

A second reason for making a comparison of physical treatment is to call attention to the importance of the slave trade in accounting for another of the differences between Brazilian and United States slavery. Brazilians simply did not have to treat their slaves with care or concern when new slaves were readily obtainable from outside the system. That the continuance of the slave trade had the effect of making the lot of the slave hard was clearly recognized in Brazil after the trade was stopped. Perdigão Malheiro in 1866, fifteen years after the closing of the trade, for example, asserted that the ending of the traffic had improved the treatment of slaves in Brazil. No longer, he wrote, do you "meet in the streets, as in other not remote times, slaves with their faces covered with a wire mask or a great weight on the foot." Slaves are now so well dressed and shod, he continued, "that no one would know who they are," by which he meant that they could not be distinguished from free blacks, because in the past slaves did not wear shoes. . . .

When the effects of the closing of the slave trade are thus explored it is readily evident that the question of harshness is more a function of the availability of slaves from abroad than a matter of different culture or social outlook. If on balance United States slavery was indeed milder, as the foregoing argues, then a large part of the explanation ought to be charged to the earlier closing of the slave trade. For once the trade was closed, slavery could survive as a going labor system only so long as it could replenish itself, and that required some attention to physical care of the slaves. . . .

WHO IDENTIFIES WITH NEGROES?

Further revealing of differences in attitudes toward Negroes and slaves in the United States and Brazil are the responses that the two societies made to the threat of slave insurrections. In both societies, it should be said, fear of slave revolts was widespread. One of the measures that whites in the southern United States took to forestall slave insurrections was to place restrictions upon free Negroes, who were widely believed to be fomenters of slave conspiracies and revolts. Thus the uncovering in 1822 of a plot among slaves, believed to be organized by the free Negro Denmark Vesey, caused South Carolina and other southern states to enact new and more stringent limitations on the free movement of Negroes. . . . Fear of the free Negro as a potential instigator of slave revolts was also a principal reason for the restrictions placed upon manumission in every one of the southern states during the nineteenth century. The most common limitation, significantly enough, was the requirement that all newly manumitted Negroes leave the state. Several of the southern states, at the very end of the antebellum era, so feared the influence of the free Negro that they enacted laws prohibiting manumission entirely; at least one state passed a law requiring the enslavement of all free Negroes found within the state after a certain date. White society in the southern United States saw a connection between the Negro slave and the free Negro; the important thing was, not that one was free and the other a slave, but that both belonged to the same race.

In a fundamental sense, Brazilian slavery was racially based, also. Only Negroes (and early in the colonial period, Indians) were slaves, though in Brazil, as in the United States, there was an occasional slave who was fairskinned and had blue eyes, so that he was a white in everything but status. In Brazil, however, the inferior status of slavery did not become as closely associated with race or skin color as it did in the United States. Although slaveholders in the United States viewed the free Negro as a potential threat to the slave system, their counterparts in Brazil envisioned the free Negro as a veritable prop to the system of slavery. Many, if not most of the *capitães de mato* — the bush captains or slave catchers — for example, were mulattoes or Negroes. "The men whose occupation it is to apprehend runaway negroes are," wrote Koster at the opening of the nineteenth century, "almost without exception, creole blacks." . . . And on the eve of abolition Anselmo Fonseca, the Bahian abolitionist, pointed out that the three props of slavery were the overseers, the *capitães de mato* and the public whippers of slaves. "Certainly two-thirds of the individuals who descend to such ignoble tasks," Fonseca complained, "are, in this province, and probably in the whole country, black men or of color." Moreover, many free blacks and mulattoes showed little, if any interest in abolition and some, according to the abolitionists, even actively opposed the end of slavery. In Brazil, in other words, more important than race in differentiating between men was legal status. The mere fact that a man was a Negro or a mulatto offered no presumption that he would identify with slaves.

The contrast is also evident in the ways in which slavery was defended in the two countries. At the height of the slave system in the United States, slavery was increasingly defended on racial grounds. From the outset, to be sure, the most common justification for slavery was the need for labor. But then during the 1830's as cotton became king, more and more southerners took up the argument that slavery was not only a necessary evil, as Thomas Jefferson had said, but a positive good. One of the reasons for accepting slavery as good was that Negroes were considered racially inferior to whites and therefore natural slaves. Sometimes the argument was couched in social terms, as in James Hammond's famous "mud-sill" speech in the Senate in 1858. "In all social systems there must be a class to do the menial duties," he argued, "to perform the drudgery of life. . . . Fortunately for the South, she found a race adapted to that purpose to her hand. A race inferior to her own, but eminently qualified in temper, in vigor, in docility, in capacity to stand the climate, to answer all her purposes. . . . We do not think that whites should be slaves either by law or necessity. Our slaves are black, of another inferior race. The *status* in which we have placed them is an elevation. They are elevated from the condition in which God first created them, by being made our slaves." At other times the racial defense of slavery was put in clear biological terms, with an assist from the Bible. "Aside and apart from Scripture authority," wrote Samuel Cartright in 1857, "natural history reveals most of the same facts, in regard to the negro that the Bible does. It proves the existence of at least three distinct species of the genus man, differing in their instincts, form, habits, and color. The white species having qualities denied to the black — one with a free and the other with a servile mind — one a thinking and reflective being, the other a creature of feeling and imitation, almost void of reflective faculties and consequently unable to provide for and take care of himself. The relation of master and slave would naturally spring up between two such different species of men, even if there was no Scripture authority to support it." . . . As these quotations attest, many hours of mental labor and many pages of print were consumed in developing and propagating a racial defense of slavery in the United States.

No such effort was made in Brazil. . . .

Brazilians . . . were not backward in defending slavery. But their most commonly voiced defenses were in behalf of the rights of property (slaves) and that the prosperity of the country depended upon slave labor. A number talked of slavery as a "necessary evil," as some North Americans had done in the early years of the Republic. Sometimes a slaveholder would admit publicly that he would be willing to see slavery abolished. . . .

THE HIDDEN DIFFERENCE

What may we conclude from this examination of slavery in Brazil and the United States? That there were in fact differences in the practices of slavery in the two countries there can be no doubt. That Brazil kept the foreign slave trade open longer than the United States was not only a difference, but a cause for several other differences, as we have seen. The two countries also differed markedly in their attitudes toward arming slaves and toward defending slavery on grounds of race. The explanations for these differences, however, are not to be found in differences in the laws of the two home governments nor in the attitudes and practices of the respective national religious persuasions. Neither the church nor the state in Brazil displayed any deep concern about the humanity of the slave and in any event, neither used its authority to affect significantly the life of the slave. . . . Much more persuasive as explanations for the differences are the demographic and economic developments and geographic circumstances in the two countries, that is, the differences in their respective historical experiences.

At the same time, there is yet something else that might be gained from this comparison. For there is a pattern behind some of the differences that becomes clear only as the individual differences are viewed together. Behind several of the divergencies in practice and ideology is the clear implication that in Brazil the slave may have been feared, but the black man was not, whereas in the United States both the slave and the black were feared. Thus the willingness of Brazilians to manumit slaves much more freely than North Americans is a result of their not fearing free blacks in great numbers, regardless of the fears they may have entertained about slave uprisings. Thus Brazilians did not feel it necessary to restrict manumission as North Americans did. In the United States, slavery was always a means of controlling dangerous blacks as well as a way of organizing labor. That is why most plans for emancipation, prior to the great abolitionist crusade, looked to expatriation to Africa or some other place once the Negroes were freed. Winthrop Jordan, in *White Over Black,* points out that the "earliest American suggestion of colonization included an observation that it was not safe to have Negroes free in America." The "warning" was published in 1715. As late as the Civil War, President Abraham Lincoln was still seriously considering the founding of a settlement in Central America for the blacks who would be freed by the war. Only the impracticality of resettling four million people caused him to give up the idea.

United States fear of Negroes is also highlighted in the contrast between the willingness of Brazilian slaveholders to use blacks as slave catchers and overseers, whereas in the United States, few white men, much less slaveholders, were prepared to put Negroes in such positions of authority. Nor is it accidental that a racial defense of slavery was developed in the United States and largely absent from Brazil. Such a defense followed almost logically from the fear of blacks and was quite consonant with the refusal to permit free blacks to be overseers and slave catchers. Although when one looks at the United States experience alone the development of a racial defense of slavery seems quite natural, the Brazilian experience compels us to realize that the development of such a defense was not a simple function of slavery, but the result of a special attitude on the part of whites toward blacks — an attitude derived from a particular history.

QUESTIONS TO CONSIDER

1. What evidence does Degler use to argue that in neither Brazil nor the United States did the church and government effectively protect slaves? Why is reliance solely upon legal statutes inadequate for the social historian?

2. Why were there many more free blacks in Brazil than in the United States? What conditions allowed freedmen to serve as shopkeepers and skilled laborers there but not in the southern United States? Why did laws in the American South restrict manumission? How did each society's propertied elite view free blacks?

3. On what basis does Degler conclude that slavery in Brazil was harsher than in the American South? How does he explain Brazilian slaves' lack of natural population increase? How was the situation of women, children, and families similar or different? Why were there more slave rebellions in Brazil than in the United States?

4. Would Degler agree or disagree with Winthrop Jordan's claim in Selection 6 that population ratios more than cultural factors affected each society's attitudes toward race? Where would Degler's essay fit in the controversy over whether slavery caused racial prejudice or prejudice caused slavery?

5. On the basis of Degler's evidence, why do you suppose that most southern leaders agreed to end the slave trade in 1808? Why might the abolition of slavery have occurred peacefully in Brazil, but required a civil war in the United States?

Transatlantic
Reform

Between 1830 and the Civil War, Americans' efforts to apply democratic ideals and religious values to their changing society produced an era of reform. Most American history texts portray the rise of antislavery, women's rights, and other reform movements as an entirely domestic affair. Yet the wave of reform that swept through the northern states was a transatlantic phenomenon, linked to counterparts in Britain and elsewhere in Europe. Arising from similar social conditions and often spread by political exiles or itinerant lecturers, these movements crossed national borders and intertwined as they grew. Abolitionist lecturers traded places in England and the United States to assist each other's causes. Women's rights conventions in America spawned imitators in Europe and drew lessons in turn from British feminists' campaign against restrictive marriage laws. British and French utopian socialists built communal experiments in the Mississippi Valley, while a Yankee scheme for the "League of Universal Brotherhood," an early version of the United Nations, attracted thousands of British and German supporters.

The transatlantic crusades for abolition, temperance, and peace culminated in huge international conventions held in New York, London, Paris, and Frankfurt in the 1840s and 1850s. Meanwhile, campaigns for women's rights gained momentum from the European revolutions of 1848 before collapsing in the 1850s when the achievements of those revolutions were reversed. Yet reform movements had lasting results as well, especially the agitation against slavery. British abolitionists successfully outlawed slavery in their nation's colonies in 1833, and French republicans followed suit in 1848. By forming new political coalitions, such as the Free Soil Party, that were committed to excluding slavery from the western territories, American abolitionists led the northern public toward a stance that spelled doom for the South's "peculiar institution."

The essays in this chapter take a distinctly transatlantic approach to two of the most important antebellum (pre–Civil War) reform movements: abolitionism and women's rights. The first selection, taken from Nathan I. Huggins's biography of Frederick Douglass, follows this courageous fugitive slave and eloquent abolitionist lecturer on a twenty-month speaking tour of the British Isles begun in 1845. In the second selection, Bonnie S. Anderson integrates the American women's rights crusade and its celebrated Seneca Falls Convention of 1848 into the larger story of the first international women's movement. The essays use different genres — an individual biography of Douglass versus a group portrait of the feminists — and they emphasize opposite vectors of influence — Europeans' impact on Douglass versus American feminists' impact abroad. But both accounts document transatlantic ties between nineteenth-century reformers and highlight decisive cross-cultural encounters that changed the course of history. Their broadly conceived narratives of abolitionism and women's rights demonstrate the value of situating the history of American social movements in a larger transnational context.

19

Apostle of Freedom

Nathan I. Huggins

Southern planters claimed that slaves were docile and content, but no American life provided more convincing and inspiring counterevidence than that of Frederick Douglass. Douglass was an escaped slave who moved audiences in the North with his testimony against the brutal institution, prodded President Lincoln to emancipate and arm the slaves, and after the Civil War became a distinguished spokesman for African American rights. Born into bondage in eastern Maryland in 1818, Douglass was treated better than many of his fellow slaves, in part because he may have been his owner's son. Still, as a young man he experienced enough of the horrors of slavery — including a year on the farm of a vicious slave-breaker named Covey — that he planned to escape. Through a kind mistress and some shrewd deception, Douglass learned to read. His confident bearing and his experience as a ship's caulker lent him a sufficiently independent air that when he boarded a northbound train in Baltimore armed with black seamen's papers, no one asked questions. Eventually Douglass's abolitionist contacts helped him to reach the port of New Bedford, Massachusetts.

Once in the North, Douglass discovered that "the promised land" was not completely free. He was placed in segregated pews at the local Methodist church and barred entry into the skilled shipyard trades — episodes he discreetly omitted from his first autobiography, The Narrative of the Life of Frederick Douglass, an American Slave *(1845), to avoid offending northern readers. Douglass began to attend antislavery meetings, and in 1841 he joined forces with William Lloyd Garrison, an outspoken and uncompromising white abolitionist editor whose paper,* The Liberator, *Douglass had read in Baltimore.*

Energized by moral zeal and religious convictions, American abolitionists were a contentious group whose movement was plagued by conflict and schisms. One key dividing line was drawn between those like Garrison who forswore political action in favor of moral pressure on slaveholders and northerners, and others who tried to infiltrate party politics. A parallel rift developed between radicals welcoming alliances with other reforms, such as women's rights and pacifism, and moderates fearful of diluting the cause or alienating mainstream audiences. In 1840 the Garrisonians and moderates split into competing antislavery societies whose backbiting hampered the movement's progress.

Douglass started out firmly in Garrison's camp, but as the following excerpt from Nathan I. Huggins's fine biography suggests, he began to change course during a revealing two-year sojourn in Great Britain in the mid-1840s. Traveling abroad gave the American a comparative and quite critical perspective on his own land. England's abolitionists were powerful enough to have convinced Parliament to emancipate slaves in the British colonies in 1833. As he met the movement's leaders and captivated British audiences, Douglass found himself for the first time treated as the equal of any white. He became acutely conscious of the extent of racism back home and lashed out at Americans both North and South for accommodating slavery. Even his relation to American abolitionists seemed tainted with racial prejudice. Tired of being supervised by Garrison and other white antislavery leaders, Douglass resolved to take an independent and distinctively African American stand against slavery and all forms of white supremacy.

Douglass's transatlantic journey proved to be a turning point both for him and the American antislavery movement. In 1847 he returned to the United States a free man in a double sense: having been purchased by British friends from his owners, he was physically free. But just as important, thanks to his awakening abroad, he was now determined to be "his own man" in the crusade against slavery and the long fight for black equality. In the late 1840s, Douglass began to explore political action as a means to eliminate slavery. Having decided that abolitionists should not repudiate the Constitution but use it, he helped to create the Free Soil Party, whose call to prohibit slavery in the territories eventually became a rallying cry for Abraham Lincoln and the Republican majority in the North.

GLOSSARY

AMERICAN ANTI-SLAVERY SOCIETY   Formed in 1833 by black and white delegates to an abolitionist convention in Philadelphia to convince the public that slavery was evil and to put pressure on Congress to take action against it. The society split in 1840 when anti-Garrisonians formed a rival group.

BURNT-OVER DISTRICT   An area in western New York that experienced rapid development in the 1820s and 1830s due to the Erie Canal. It was "burned over" by evangelical revivals and afterward spawned new religions, including Mormonism, and supported reform causes such as antislavery and utopian communities.

CHAPMAN, MARIA WESTON (1806–1885)   A Boston abolitionist who organized a female antislavery society in 1832, then became William Lloyd Garrison's ally and assistant.

CORN LAWS   Regulations dating from medieval times restricting imports of grain to England in order to maintain high prices. A popular campaign to repeal the restrictions of 1815 succeeded in 1846.

DU BOIS, W. E. B. (1868–1963)   An influential African American scholar and civil rights leader who was an early exponent of racial equality and a cofounder in 1910 of the National Association for the Advancement of Colored People (NAACP). In his later years, Du Bois promoted worldwide black liberation and African unity, eventually moving to Ghana.

FREE CHURCH OF SCOTLAND   A Presbyterian sect that broke off from the established Church of Scotland in 1843 protesting its lack of evangelical fervor and questioning the right of wealthy landowners to appoint church ministers. It did not rejoin until 1929.

GARRISONIANS   The American abolitionist faction that followed William Lloyd Garrison's doctrines. Garrisonians discouraged political organizing in favor of personal dissociation from the sin of slavery, and they linked abolitionism to kindred reforms such as pacifism and women's rights.

JIM CROW PRACTICES   Practices or policies of segregating or discriminating against blacks. In many northern states before the Civil War, free blacks were relegated to separate schools and railroad cars and prohibited from voting.

MANCHESTER SCHOOL   A group of nineteenth-century English economists, including John Bright and Richard Cobden, who advocated free trade and the laissez-faire doctrine of minimal government interference in economic matters.

MATHEW, FATHER THEOBALD (1790–1856)   An Irish priest who became an advocate of total abstinence from alcohol and lectured to enthusiastic audiences in England, Scotland, and the United States in the 1840s and 1850s.

O'CONNELL, DANIEL (1775–1847)   An Irish landowner and lawyer who led the fight in the 1820s to end British restrictions on Catholic officeholding. He was elected to Parliament in 1828, but only allowed to take his seat when the British government declared Catholic Emancipation in 1829. In Parliament, O'Connell worked to repeal the union of Great Britain and Ireland, to end official privileges for the Protestant Church of Ireland, and to gain greater access to landholding for the Irish.

PHILLIPS, WENDELL (1811–1884)   A prominent Garrisonian abolitionist and a noted orator who advocated immediate emancipation, full black civil rights, and the distribution of land to freed slaves. After the Civil War, Phillips agitated for temperance, woman suffrage, and labor rights.

TEMPERANCE REFORM   The Anglo-American movement of the nineteenth century to restrict the sale and consumption of alcohol. Initially relying upon voluntary pledges of abstinence, the movement increasingly tried to pass antiliquor legislation.

THIRTEENTH, FOURTEENTH, AND FIFTEENTH AMENDMENTS Reconstruction-era constitutional amendments that abolished slavery, gave African Americans citizenship and "equal protection of the laws," and outlawed denial of the vote on grounds of race.

THREE-FIFTHS CLAUSE The clause in the U.S. Constitution stipulating that a slave counted as three-fifths of a person for purposes of apportioning direct taxes and representatives in Congress.

✯ ✯ ✯ ✯ ✯ ✯ ✯

T he *Narrative of the Life of Frederick Douglass, an American Slave*, published in 1845, was the first of [Douglass's] three autobiographies. Revealing details of his life as a slave — the place of his enslavement, his original name, and the name of his master — took a special courage because it placed his freedom in immediate jeopardy. But [Douglass] refused to discuss his actual means of escape or name the friends who assisted him, for such information would add to the knowledge of slaveowners and their agents, making other escapes more hazardous.

More than an autobiography, the *Narrative*, like Douglass's oratory, was abolitionist polemic, contradicting the premises of the proslavery argument on every page. Slavery, rather than being a means of civilizing and Christianizing backward and pagan Africans, was shown to keep slaves unschooled and unlettered and ignorant of Christianity, except as it might serve the master and the institution. Slaveowners, rather than being gentle, Christian folk, were coarse men and women who dared not follow truly Christian teachings or their own humane and civilizing instincts.

Douglass hardly mentioned his grandmother or his half sisters and brother in this first autobiography. Ten years later, in *My Bondage and My Freedom*, he wrote about them at some length. But in the *Narrative*, he chose to emphasize how slavery undermined family feeling among slaves. It could not be otherwise when a system profited from the natural increase of its subjects, not their moral and circumspect behavior. Slavery also gave men absolute power over their female subjects; one could hardly miss the devastating implications for family life.

The point was clear. It was not a matter of good or bad men treating their subjects well or badly. It was not something one could reform simply with good will. The central evil was the ownership of human beings and the lack of freedom this imposed. That single enormity brought with it inevitable and ugly consequences. Good men and women were no better able to avoid doing evil as slaveowners than could their slave men and women become responsible, productive human beings while in chains. To be

Excerpt pp. 21–43 from *Slave and Citizen: The Life of Frederick Douglass*, by Nathan Irvin Huggins. Copyright © 1980 by Nathan Irvin Huggins. Reprinted by permission of Pearson Education, Inc.

an obedient slave meant to be something less than a man, and to be a good master meant to be a benevolent despot, but a tyrant nonetheless.

Real freedom — self-reliant, self-respecting, humanity dignifying freedom — was at bottom the issue, and there could be no substitute for it. Even the kindest, most gentlemanly masters denied this one essential. William Freeland was such a man, and Douglass praised him for being a Christian within the limits of the slave system. He was "the best master I ever had, *till I became my own master.*"

Freedom, too, was a matter of working for one's well-being and not having one's labor expropriated for the profit of others. Douglass became a more productive worker as he became more independent. . . . Freedom allowed him to be a self-reliant person, fully responsible for himself and his family. As for the slaveholders themselves, Douglass confirmed the suspicions of his Northern readers; slave labor spoiled the master class for efficient and productive labor in their own behalf. Slavery made work itself unrespectable.

There would be more than two dozen slave autobiographies published in the nineteenth century, but Douglass's *Narrative* would be the most widely read and the most influential. His celebrity as an abolitionist speaker helped, but it was also because the book was authentic and authoritative, and it was written in a style which managed to expose the ugliness and brutality of slavery without falling into bathos. While it showed how systematic oppression could diminish the quality of human life, it exemplified in the life of the narrator an irreducible human nature and an indomitable human spirit. The reader was not moved to pity for the slave but to anger at a system that oppressed him.

The slave narrative genre was much like the travel literature so popular with Americans at the time, introducing readers to an emotional and spiritual domain that was alien and unimaginable. It presented a world of experience foreign to the readers' clear sense of what was normal, moral, and civilized. There were no more telling arguments against slavery and for freedom than these personal expositions. In an age that celebrated the triumphant human spirit, autobiography was readily converted into effective political weaponry.

The very success of the *Narrative* placed Douglass's liberty in even greater jeopardy. His friends thought it wise for him to leave the country for a while and go to Great Britain. It was for his own safety, of course, but it was also thought that he could help mobilize British abolitionists to work in the American struggle. The British had abolished slavery in the West Indies in 1837. The men and women who had agitated long and hard for that result might help raise money and redirect their moral outrage at the United States.

The trip forced Douglass to leave [his wife] Anna and the children. The family had moved from New Bedford to Lynn, Massachusetts in 1842, shortly after the birth of their second son, Frederick Jr. Two years later, Charles was born. So Douglass, in going to England, left Anna with four children, one barely a year old. He expected the income from the American sales of the *Narrative* to take the place of what he would have earned from his lectures. To make ends meet, however, Anna went back to work; and the American Anti-Slavery Society helped out occasionally.

Frederick Douglass

This portrait of Frederick Douglass faced the title page of his second autobiography, My Bondage and
My Freedom, *published in 1855. The book was dedicated not to William Lloyd Garrison but to Gerrit
Smith, a political abolitionist and wealthy New York landowner who had given free blacks property from
his estate.*

On 16 August 1845 Frederick Douglass set sail for Liverpool aboard the Cunard
ship, *Cambria,* accompanied by five other abolitionists: the Hutchinson family (a singing
group) and James Buffum. Douglass was denied a first-class cabin and was forced to
travel steerage. He, nevertheless, made himself well-known to his fellow passengers, he
and his friends circulating his book on the promenade deck.

Several passengers asked the captain to arrange for Douglass to lecture. So on the last evening out, he gave a talk on the quarterdeck to a large audience. Two proslavery men heckled him and attempted to break up the meeting. They were restrained only after the captain knocked one down and threatened to put them both in irons. These incidents were the last reminders, for the twenty-month stay in Europe, of the passion and irrationality of American racism.

Douglass experienced in those months abroad what was common to Afro-Americans traveling outside the United States. For the first time in his life he felt himself accepted by the public as a man, nothing more or less. No longer did he have to wonder whether or not he would be served in restaurants and hotels or whether he would be given first-class seats on trains. He was warmly received not only on the lecture platform but in [t]he homes of many notables in Ireland, Scotland, and England. He could be seen in the company of women as well as men without evoking comment.

All of this was dramatically different from day-to-day life in the United States. For even in New England — thought the most liberal section of the country — he and all other black people were daily subjected to humiliating Jim Crow practices in schools, hotels, restaurants, and public transportation. Indeed, white abolitionists themselves were sometimes deeply ambivalent about race. Douglass might well have reflected that the British could better afford tolerance since blacks there were so few in number. But the contrast was too sharp for such speculation. There was quite a bit of irony in a nation's purporting to be the most enlightened and progressive in the world, yet being more despotic and tyrannical than all the monarchies.

Douglass arrived in Britain when the reform spirit there was at its height. While it had been ten years since the emancipation of slaves in the West Indies, abolitionists were still excited from their victory, and there were few who would now argue the proslavery side. If anything, the British were somewhat self-righteous in their attitude about slavery in the United States. They were also alive with demands for temperance and free trade legislation, resulting in the repeal of the Corn Laws in 1846. The debate over the issue of home rule for Ireland was at its most intense, and all of that British dominion was alive with agitation.

Douglass spent his first five weeks in Dublin promoting antislavery as well as lecturing on temperance and Irish home rule. He met the aging Daniel O'Connell, whose speech on Catholic emancipation had inspired him when he read it in *The Columbian Orator.* He also met the great Irish temperance reformer, Father Theobald Mathew, to whom he gave the temperance pledge. The meetings with O'Connell and other Irish reform leaders — all warm sympathizers with the cause of the American slave — would have great significance for Douglass in the years to come. Irish migration to the United States would reach its peak in the next decade, and it would be Irish immigrants who would be the greatest competitors with blacks for jobs. As they would press for their own rights, they would be some of the most vociferous opponents of political and economic rights for black Americans. Douglass would have cause to reflect on how quickly the oppressed could take on the role of oppressor.

Leaving Ireland, Douglass visited the industrial centers of England. In Birmingham and Manchester, he took active part in agitation to repeal the Corn Laws. Thrown into the excitement over free trade, Douglass learned much about the liberal economic theories of the Manchester school, which were to define his outlook on social and economic questions throughout his life.

Douglass was thrilled to find himself listened to and applauded for his reasoning and effectiveness as a speaker. True, he was notable because he was a black man who had lived as a slave in the United States; that gave him a special hearing. He was, however, more than a display for the antislavery cause. He was viewed as a shrewd interpreter of American society with trenchant opinions on all subjects of social reform.

There was something liberating for Douglass in taking up the fight for causes not his own. He wrote [William Lloyd] Garrison early in 1846, "I cannot allow myself to be insensible to the wrongs and sufferings of any part of the great family of man." It was not enough for one man to assert a common humanity with the rest of mankind, one had to act the part. "I am not only an American slave, but a man," he wrote, "and as such, am bound to use my powers for the welfare of the whole human brotherhood." A truly free man made everyone's cause of freedom his own.

At least some of Douglass's American abolitionist friends were uneasy about his growing independence while away from home. Some worried lest he fall under the sway of the London Anti-Slavery Committee, considered hostile to the Garrisonians. Wendell Phillips wrote Douglass alerting him to such dangers. Maria Weston Chapman was less direct. She wrote to Richard D. Webb, the publisher in Dublin who was to issue the British edition of Douglass's narrative. She warned Webb to keep an eye on Douglass since he was a man of small means and she worried that money would lure him away from his American friends. Webb apparently thought the best way to warn Douglass was to read him Mrs. Chapman's letter.

Douglass was offended that so little was thought of his integrity. His reply to Mrs. Chapman was sharp. He wrote that he was loyal to his Garrisonian friends, and had never given any of them reason to expect betrayal, especially not for personal gain. Shocked to learn that Mrs. Chapman thought he needed surveillance, he warned her, "If you wish to drive me from the Anti-Slavery Society, put me under overseership and the work is done." The image was calculated to shake an abolitionist's self-righteousness.

Whether or not Douglass would have a permanent overseer while abroad, his conduct was well observed and reported to members of the movement at home. He was not like other men; he had to be above reproach. Dr. J. B. Estlin, of Bristol, wrote Samuel May, Jr. of the many female admirers Douglass had in Britain. He was not sure exactly what it was in the man — his robust stature, his powerful voice, his serious mien, the hint of the exotic in him — but he was a sensation among English women. Some of them, Estlin feared, went beyond the bounds of "propriety, or delicacy as far as appearances are concerned." Estlin assured May that Douglass was, himself, always "guardedly correct, judicious and decorous," nevertheless he felt that this admiring attention from white women was cause for some concern. Estlin thought it might spoil him for his future role in the United States where the slightest association between a black man and white women was the subject of alarm and censure. Estlin also feared that after being in the company of "women of education," Douglass would "feel a void when he returns to his own family."

Such attention to his behavior must have been disturbingly suggestive of the oversight and unfreedom from which he had always been in flight. As he grew more confident, however, it became more clear to Douglass that he had to be his own man. Here was a source of friction that would ultimately cause a bitter rift with the Garrisonians. American abolitionism was rather strictly sectarian. There was little room especially among the Garrisonians for independence of thought and honest disagreement. For the time he was in Britain, however, there would only be hints of the problems yet to come.

In the summer of 1846 Garrison joined Douglass in England. Garrison hoped, with Douglass's help, to urge the establishment of an English antislavery society more friendly to him than he felt the British and Foreign Anti-Slavery Society to be. Both men seemed pleased to be reunited on the platform. They toured with great effectiveness and were gratified with the result.

The two men threw themselves into a raging controversy about the Free Church of Scotland which had broken with the Established Scottish Church in 1843. They raised money throughout Britain and America and received sizable funds from Southern Presbyterian churches. The Glasgow Emancipation Society challenged the propriety of accepting money from slaveholders and began a vigorous campaign to pressure the Free Church to Send Back the Money.

Officers of the Free Church argued that their deputies in America had merely avoided matters which were none of their concern. They had gone to gain support for the Free Church, not to pronounce upon domestic problems in America. While they recognized the system of slavery to be evil, they would distinguish between the character of the system and the "character of the persons whom circumstances have connected therewith." They saw no moral fault in accepting money from slaveholders, which, they felt, in no way suggested their support of the American domestic institution.

On 29 May 1846 Douglass spoke to an antislavery rally at Glasgow's city hall, denouncing the Free Church's behavior as mere opportunism. He was at the height of his rhetorical form. The American antislavery movement, he said, had worked hard — against a hostile and complacent public — to call slavery by its proper name, sin unmitigated. "Man stealing," woman beating, the expropriation of the labor of others, the denial of normal familial and religious development could hardly be called a nicer name. By accepting the money of slaveholders, the Free Church was conveniently ignoring the sinful source of the gift; they were not being neutral in a domestic issue but were working against the antislavery movement. By this implied fellowship with slaveholders the Free Church gave status and respectability to willful, self-serving sinners whose very lives and behavior represented the antithesis of Christianity. . . .

Adding to the agitation over the Free Church, Douglass and Garrison helped the critics of the church make Send Back the Money a slogan of sarcasm and contempt throughout Scotland and England. In the end, the Free Church kept the money but suffered considerable embarrassment in doing so. From the Americans' point of view, however, the issue brought fresh energy into the antislavery movement in Britain and made the necessary connection between the American institution and British behavior.

The hypocrisy of Christian churches over slavery had been a theme in Douglass's *Narrative*. While in Britain, his criticism grew more pronounced. Partly it was because he felt more free to speak, but mainly it was because he felt the strong urge to expose all American hypocrisy to the British.

This penchant embroiled him in a controversy with American clergymen who were in England to attend a world temperance convention in August 1846. While not delegates to the convention, both Douglass and Garrison were invited to attend. Douglass was asked to speak.

Being a temperance man, his sympathies were certainly with the delegates. He drew upon his experience as a slave and as an American to illustrate how alcohol destroyed the will and how slaveholders used whiskey to dull their slaves' sense of manhood and natural aspiration for liberty. Douglass went further, however. He criticized the American temperance movement for its remarkable failure to address the evils of drink in the slave system and for being inhospitable and even hostile to free Northern blacks in the temperance movement. He cited the experience of Philadelphia blacks who attempted to march in that city for the cause of temperance. They were set upon by an angry mob of whites who broke up their march. For all of their otherwise good intentions, Douglass charged, there were no American temperance crusaders who were willing to support such black men in their efforts at "self-improvement."

Douglass's remarks enraged the Americans there and caused Reverend Samuel Hanson Cox, of Brooklyn, to write an attack in the *New York Evangelist*. Douglass, Cox said, was an extremist, motivated politically and for money to shatter the harmony and single-mindedness of the temperance convention. "He lugged in antislavery or abolition . . ." To Cox it was a "perversion and an abuse" to call together thousands in order to be "conspicuous and devoted for one sole and grand object," but "with obliquity, open an avalanche on them for some imputed evil or monstrosity. . . . I say it is a trick of meanness!"

Cox was indignant that Douglass should hold America and Americans up for scorn before an international audience. White Americans were certainly not accustomed to being addressed by a black man who spoke "as if he had been our schoolmaster, and we his docile and devoted pupils." Douglass could hardly be his own man, Cox reasoned, when "the fact is, the man has been petted, and flattered, and used, and paid by certain abolitionists . . . till he forgets himself." Cox was certain that Douglass was doing his own cause more harm than good. Cox's own reactions might serve as a warning. "I came here his sympathizing friend — I am so no more, as I more know him."

Douglass was quick to respond, printing his letter to Cox and the speech in the *Liberator*. He suggested that the aggravating and intolerable insult to Cox was for "a Negro to stand upon a platform, on terms of perfect equality with a pure white American *gentleman!*" Were Cox a Christian, philanthropist, and abolitionist as he claimed himself to be, he would have been delighted to see a fugitive slave on the platform of a world temperance convention. He seemed rather to feel himself and his country "severely rebuked by my presence there." He could only suspect these to be Cox's feelings: "It may not be quite true. But if it be true, I sincerely pity the littleness of your soul."

Douglass insisted that his speech had been appropriate and invited his readers to judge for themselves. After all, he represented a people who were kept from moral and social betterment by the barriers of slavery and race prejudice. These evils would keep temperance or any other such reform from being effective among them. Certainly, he thought, a world temperance convention would want to know that.

. . . Cox's point had been condescending, perceiving Douglass as the pawn of others. "I acted on my own responsibility," Douglass wrote. "If blame . . . is to fall anywhere, it should fall on me." . . .

What troubled Douglass most were Cox's pretensions to being a Christian reformer with abolitionist sympathy. "Who ever heard of a true abolitionist speaking of slavery as an 'imputed evil,' or complain of being 'wounded and injured' by an allusion to it — and that, too, because the allusion was in opposition to the infernal system?" Cox's professions to the contrary, his letter made any claims as a reformer "brazen hypocrisy or self-deception."

The episode had been a welcome opportunity for Douglass to bring home the fact that the sin of slavery did not only rest on the heads of slaveholders in the South but also with liberal Northerners, like Cox, who were "artful dodgers" when it came to facing up to the realities of slavery. Douglass's attitude and tone while in Britain would echo the indignation of his letter to Cox. American society, its institutions, and its so-called reformers would be the subject of his withering criticism.

In the summer and fall of 1846 Douglass and Garrison toured Britain, sharing the platform. They worked very well together. On 17 August they spoke at the organizational meeting of the Anti-Slavery League for all England, launching an organization with which Garrison knew he could work.

His principal object accomplished, Garrison sailed for the United States in November. The departure of his friend saddened Douglass. He began to feel the length of time he had been away from his home and family. He had to give serious thought to going back.

English friends had offered to send for Anna and the children. They promised him that he would have a comfortable life if he chose to remain in England. He was a fugitive and had left his country partly out of fear of capture, but he had never intended to go into exile. The offer to help him resettle, while generous, did not appeal to him. In his farewell speech in London, 30 March 1847, he told an audience of over four hundred that he would return to the United States despite the hatred and insult that faced black men there at every turn. He saw his purpose and calling to share the plight of his fellow black Americans. He would "struggle in their ranks for that emancipation which shall yet be achieved by the power of truth and of principle"; that battle was in America, not in England. "I glory in the conflict," he exclaimed, "that I may hereafter exult in the victory. I know that victory is certain."

Still a fugitive, his return to America would be dangerous. [Although n]early two years had passed since the publication of the *Narrative,* it continued to command wide attention. Douglass's public role in Britain had drawn even more attention to himself. If his master had previously only wanted the return of his property, he would want now even more to have this celebrated fugitive under his control.

Several of Douglass's English friends chose to solve the problem by purchasing his freedom. Anna and Ellen Richardson raised a subscription and negotiated the sale. After Douglass's escape Thomas Auld had given ownership in him to Hugh Auld. It was arranged that £150 (approximately $700) be paid for his freedom. Thus Frederick Douglass, now approaching his thirtieth year, by the grace of Hugh Auld's signature, became a free man in the law of the United States.

The purchase of Douglass's freedom kicked up a small storm of controversy among some abolitionists who saw in the act an inconsistency with professed principles. Since abolitionists denied the right of one man to own property in another, there was nothing one could legitimately sell. In short, the purchase of Douglass implied the legitimacy of ownership in him and, therefore, was a proslavery act. The argument, itself, was not frivolous. Such were the grounds for denying the propriety of compensated emancipation. Was the good of freeing slaves fatally compromised by the expediency of compensating the masters for their loss? The British had compensated slaveholders in the West Indies, and some Northern states had paid slaveowners to free their slaves after the American Revolution. While it was a moot question, given the political atmosphere in the United States in the 1840s, still the principle could raise some heated debate.

Garrison defended the purchase as expedient, reasoning that it was wrong to consider the price paid as a *purchase*. Rather, it was a *ransom*. No one ever denied the right or propriety of paying thieves or kidnappers to gain a person's liberty. Why, he asked, should it be different in this case?

Whatever the principle, it did not trouble Douglass. In a letter to Henry C. Wright, published in the *Liberator* of 28 January 1847 Douglass defended the deal. He had not invited or encouraged the action of his friends, and he saw no reason why he should have discouraged them. There would have been a violation of principle, he wrote, if it had been done "*to make me a slave, instead of a freeman*" or "with a view to compensate the slaveholder for what he and they regarded as rightful property." Those who questioned the purchase were wrong in "confounding the crime of buying men *into slavery*, with the meritorious act of buying men out of slavery." The purchasers did not, as some of the critics claimed, presume to "establish my *natural right* to freedom"; he had that as a condition of his humanity. They merely, by the payment of money, removed social and legal obstacles to the exercise of those natural rights. It was an expediency, Douglass explained, nothing more. Had it been his money, he wrote, "I would have seen Hugh Auld *kicking*, before I would have given it to him." He would rather take his chances as a fugitive, paying money only as a last resort to avoid return to slavery. But he would not censure the judgment of his friends. . . .

On 4 April 1847 Douglass set sail from Liverpool to Boston aboard the Cunard steamer, *Cambria*. For the first time since landing in Britain, he was forced to confront Jim Crow practices. He was denied cabin accommodations because of his color, and he was obliged to take his meals alone and not mix with the other passengers in the salon. Douglass's friends complained to the company, and he wrote a letter to the London *Times*. He pointed out that during his entire sojourn in Britain he had enjoyed rights and privileges equal with other men until "I turned my face toward America." The Cunard line apologized in the press and vowed such a thing would never happen again.

Douglass thought this a victory despite the inconveniences to him. Like the Send Back the Money affair, the incident brought home to the British how they, too, were being corrupted by intercourse with a slave society.

Living abroad, Douglass was forced to confront the anomalous relationship Afro-Americans had to their native land. As slave or free, blacks could hardly be considered citizens of the United States. One could hardly be loyal to a nation that seemed to make one's people an exception to the rest of humanity; and loyalty to the United States meant that one honored slavery. Yet to forswear one's country would be to deny one's birthright. Douglass, like other Afro-Americans, struggled with this dilemma.

The Garrisonians had their own sense of loyalty. They honored the principles of the Declaration of Independence, but thought them fatally compromised in the Constitution. Those provisions that regarded a slave as three-fifths of a man, that obliged the national government to engage in the capture and return of escaped slaves, and that empowered the federal government to put down domestic insurrections made the entire nation complicitous in slavery. Thus, the union that was formed under the Constitution was corrupt and undeserving of allegiance.

Douglass shared these views and was unrestrained in his denunciation of the national union. In his farewell address in London, he emphasized that it was a mistake to think of the United States as divided between slave and free states, where the citizens of the latter were advocates of freedom and hostile to slavery. Northerners were the willing allies of slaveholders, and would "bring down . . . the whole civil, military, and naval power of the nation" to crush efforts of slaves to gain their freedom by force. The Northerner would nevertheless proclaim to the world, "let it be clearly understood that we hate slavery."

In returning to the United States Douglass planned "to unmask her pretensions to republicanism." He had no pride in the nation and did not think it deserving of praise: "No, she is unworthy of the name great or free." She stood upon the backs of three million people. Yet, the United States eagerly denounced European despotisms, calling Englishmen "a community of slaves, bowing before a haughty monarchy."

The people of the United States, he said, were "the boldest in their pretensions to freedom, and loudest in their professions of love of liberty," yet no nation exhibited a code of laws as "cruel, malicious, and infernal," as that of the Americans. "Every page," he proclaimed, "is red with the blood of the American slave."

Such strong language was not uncommon in an age of highly polemical oratory. The white Garrisonians were noted for their rhetorical vigor and audacity. But the matter of white men's citizenship was never in question. There was strong desire for black men to prove themselves "good Americans" rather than open themselves to the charge of disloyalty. It took special audacity, therefore, for Douglass to be forthright in denying loyalty to the United States.

He insisted that it was necessary to go outside the country to generate the kind of opinion that would destroy slavery. American slavery was so giant a crime, "so darkening to the soul, so blinding in its moral influence," so calculated to blast and corrupt normal human principles, "that the people among whom it exists have not the moral power to abolish it." No institution in America, neither the church nor the press, nor political parties could be counted on for reform. Since the United States lacked the conviction to overthrow slavery, he welcomed the aid of England.

Over fifty years later, W. E. B. DuBois was to sum up the Afro-American's dilemma as being a "twoness, — American, a Negro, two souls, two thoughts, two unreconciled strivings." Racism imposed on the Afro-American a duality that would continue to be impossible to reconcile. Racial oppression made one loyal first to one's race, but the dilemma evoked a persistent alienation.

Douglass would discover that the dilemma was much less troubling in the years before the Civil War. Before the war American government and institutions made themselves incompatible to Afro-American citizenship. That made it easier to be a critic and antagonist than it would be after the Thirteenth, Fourteenth, and Fifteenth Amendments had become part of the Constitution.

Whatever strain Douglass felt with the Garrisonians while he was abroad were minor. The question was natural, however, how well Douglass would fit back into the movement. He had already demonstrated a strong will and the desire to be his own man. He had become celebrated as a great speaker and reformer, not merely as an object on exhibition, but as a man whose brilliance and imagination could reshape issues. He had a gift for making white men and women sense a common humanity with him, and, through him, with the slave. Some of Douglass's American friends no doubt imagined that he would be content to pick up where he had left off: the same man only older, more experienced, and free. That was a vain hope.

Douglass had told his English friends that he would like to start a newspaper on his return to the United States. While he had some concern about his ability as a writer, he felt his strong talents were in publicity and that a successful paper, edited by a black man and former slave, would do more to counter prejudice and help the cause than anything else he might do. He was encouraged by English friends who promised to give more than two thousand dollars to the venture.

When he told his American friends about his plans, he got a chilling response. Both William Lloyd Garrison and Wendell Phillips advised against it, and in the strongest terms. Running a newspaper was very difficult for even the most experienced and well-financed editor. At best it was risky, almost destined to failure which could undo much that he had accomplished in building his reputation and poorly reflect on the whole race, giving support to those who insisted that blacks were incompetent. Finally, there were already enough abolitionist papers sharing a small readership. That fact alone could almost doom his paper from the start.

There was something to be said for the argument. There had been several efforts to establish a black newspaper, with no really lasting success. . . . Even the *Liberator,* after all, was never on secure financial footing. Garrison, his friends, and the American Anti-Slavery Society were often called upon to keep the paper afloat. At its height, it had a circulation of three thousand, of which two-thirds of its readers were black. Garrison and Phillips had reason on their side.

While their argument seemed solely in Douglass's interest, Garrison may also have wanted to avoid having another antislavery paper competing with the *Liberator.* Already there was the *Anti-Slavery Standard*. A paper by Douglass with his celebrity, however, might be more than the traffic would bear. Since the *Liberator's* readership was heavily black, it might well be undercut by a successful black paper appealing to a readership unable to support two papers.

On the other hand, Douglass had strong reason to assert himself as a black voice and as a black leader rather than as a principal spokesman for the Garrisonians. Blacks in the North had, in the 1840s, begun organizing and agitating for reform. Douglass himself had participated in one of the first national conventions of colored citizens, held in Buffalo in 1843. Issues pertaining to blacks were paramount. The civil rights of blacks in Northern states, for instance, the question of employment, education, and social improvement of the free black population were lively topics. Black men were raising questions about whether or not to foster black community action, at the risk of strengthening segregation, and whether or not it was in the interest of Afro-Americans to emigrate from the United States. While white reformers had opinions about these questions, it was black consensus that counted. A black man with pretensions of leadership would only weaken his position by being a mere spokesman for one of the several white abolitionist camps.

If Douglass wanted to be a leader among black people, the newspaper was a good idea. Not only could Douglass be his own man but, because of his influence with white abolitionists, he might be able to broaden their outlook to include questions of race relations in America beyond the single issue of slavery.

For the moment, however, Douglass was persuaded to abandon his plans. Aside from the strong opposition of Garrison and his desire not to alienate his friends, there was the fact that there were four black journals extant: the *Ram's Horn,* the *National Watchman,* the *People's Press,* and the *Mystery.* Since he and Garrison were to make a speaking tour of the West, Douglass had enough to occupy him for the moment.

The two men began what was to be a fateful tour in early August 1847. They encountered extremes of triumph and rude hostility. Douglass was lionized in a meeting organized by Philadelphia blacks. In Harrisburg, however, the audience was hostile and violent. As if Douglass needed a reminder that he was not in England, hardly a public place was willing to serve him, and since Garrison refused to eat where his companion could not, the two scarcely had a decent meal.

They were in considerable demand, and their speaking schedule reflected this. . . . The tour was exhausting. Most meetings were in the open air. Their voices and health suffered. Douglass was forced to cancel some appearances because of recurring inflammation of his tonsils.

In Cleveland, Garrison collapsed and was unable to continue. Douglass wanted to stay behind until they could continue together. Other engagements waited, however, and Garrison insisted that Douglass go on without him, promising to follow as soon as he was able.

Douglass went on to Buffalo. A week later, he learned that Garrison's condition was critical, and he began to reproach himself for having left his friend. He went on, nevertheless, attending meetings in Rochester and Syracuse. On 8 October Samuel J. May wrote Garrison that Douglass was deeply troubled on arriving at May's home and finding Garrison was not there: "His countenance fell, and his heart failed him."

Garrison was unimpressed by reports of Douglass's solicitude. His recent friend had "not written a single line to me, or to anyone else in this place, inquiring after my health." If that were not enough to cause him annoyance, Douglass resolved late in September that his original idea to start a newspaper was a good one. That decision had a chilling effect on their friendship.

In explaining his final resolve, Douglass wrote an English friend that it had been the western trip itself, his rude reintroduction to the bitterness and ugliness of racial prejudice that convinced him. More than ever, he felt that a journal, well managed and edited by a black man, would be the best weapon against slavery and racial prejudice. He had not brought the matter up to Garrison on the trip, and Garrison thought that inconsiderate and ungrateful. "Such conduct grieves me to my heart," Garrison wrote his wife. "His conduct about the paper has been impulsive, inconsiderate, and inconsistent with his decision in Boston."

Having decided to start his own newspaper, Douglass had to find a location. He thought it would be good to move away from the *Liberator* for reasons of circulation as well as for concerns about continued friction with Garrison. Douglass chose Rochester, New York. He had been led to believe he would be welcome there. The region — the "burnt-over district" of upstate New York extending through the Western Reserve — had been much affected by reform and revival movements. Also there was strong antislavery sentiment in the area. While the abolitionists of the region were more influenced by [moderates] Theodore Dwight Weld, Arthur and Lewis Tappan, and Gerrit Smith than by William Lloyd Garrison, they were also less doctrinaire and more likely to be tolerant of Douglass's views.

He had been promised help from his English friends, and $2,174 was made available to him. On 1 November 1847 Douglass moved his family to Rochester, and prepared for his new career. On the same date, the *Ram's Horn* announced the inception of a new publication, the *North Star,* to be published and edited by Frederick Douglass. "The object of *The North Star* will be to attack slavery in all its forms and aspects; advocate Universal Emancipation . . . promote the moral and intellectual improvement of the colored people; and to hasten the day of freedom to our three million enslaved fellow-countrymen."

Douglass declared a new independence. "I shall be under no party or society, but shall advocate the slave's cause in the way which in my judgment, will be best suited to the advancement of the cause."

This new declaration of independence, like his escape from slavery, was Douglass's claim to manhood and personal freedom. In this instance it was freedom from a role imposed and defined by those who called themselves his friends and yet considered his independence to be ingratitude. . . .

QUESTIONS TO CONSIDER

1. The author suggests that Frederick Douglass's slave narrative was much like the popular travel literature that introduced Americans to foreign lands. What similarities or differences do you see between slave autobiographies and accounts by travelers to

foreign countries? In what way was Douglass's own voyage abroad a transforming experience?

2. What issues did the "Send Back the Money" dispute over the Free Church of Scotland raise for British abolitionists? How were these issues similar to or different from those faced by American abolitionists? What were the arguments involved in the controversy over purchasing Douglass's freedom from his master? Did Douglass do the right thing by allowing his British friends to free him? Did his action contradict his stance in the Free Church dispute?

3. How did Douglass's trip to Great Britain force him to confront the dilemma of being black and American? How did it alter his view of the United States? How did other Americans react to his criticism of the United States, and why? Why did Douglass believe (at the time) that the Constitution was a proslavery document?

4. Why did Douglass decide to establish his own abolitionist newspaper? Why would an independent black press be useful or important in the North? Why did William Lloyd Garrison oppose Douglass's publishing plans? In what sense was Douglass's decision a "declaration of independence"?

5. Why do you think Douglass encountered less prejudice in Great Britain than in the United States? Why would Irish reformers such as Daniel O'Connell support Douglass's antislavery aims while most Irish immigrants in the United States opposed it? Does the story of Douglass's voyage suggest why British abolitionists were able to abolish colonial slavery peacefully, whereas in the United States opposition to slavery led to civil war?

The First International
Women's Movement

BONNIE S. ANDERSON

In America and western Europe during the early nineteenth century, fixed ideas about sexual difference prescribed the segregation of men's and women's roles. This ethic stemmed from the highly gendered work patterns that industrial work, commuting, and consumption had brought to middle-class lives. It replaced older, crude notions about women's inferiority with sentimental stereotypes that limited women's activities based upon the special "aptitudes" of their sex. The Victorian middle-class code assigned to men the public arenas of politics and the professions and gave women the more private tasks of childrearing, housekeeping, and churchgoing. This separation of roles, and the glorification of female domesticity that often accompanied it, reversed expectations for women's equality that had been built up by the American and French Revolutions. It spread through "respectable" society on both sides of the Atlantic, although foreign visitors such as Alexis de Tocqueville and Harriet Martineau noted that American women, even more than their counterparts in Europe, lived their lives separated from men, lost their rights upon marriage, and were placed on a pedestal in compensation.

Not all middle-class women in Europe and the United States accepted their prescribed role. Some found satisfaction and power in running the home, while others used the stereotype of female virtue to take on more public roles as charity workers, teachers, or temperance reformers. Beginning in the 1830s, however, a small but vocal minority of women shocked polite society by rebelling against the restrictive norms of the day, speaking out for equal rights, open access to politics and the professions, and (in some cases) a revolution in social arrangements favoring women's independence. Having served apprenticeships in antislavery, antichurch, or socialist movements, where they learned organizing skills but also experienced male domination firsthand, these women began building a movement of their own. Their efforts burst into bloom in the miraculous year of 1848 when the first woman's rights convention met in western New York, British and American activists set out to change the laws of marriage and divorce, and feminists in France and Germany demanded complete equality from new republican governments set up in the wake of popular revolutions that had toppled kings.

The dramatic rise of women's activism in the United States is usually portrayed as an isolated event, but Bonnie S. Anderson recasts it as part of a unified transatlantic story. Beginning with imprisoned French feminists who penned letters of solidarity to their American and British sisters, Anderson documents the close connections and striking parallels that made the feminist organizing of the 1840s and 1850s "the first international women's movement." Women activists in France, Britain, Germany, and the United States shared ideas and strategies, translated each others' manifestoes, and found inspiration in their courageous defeats and occasional victories. Using the new technology of railroads, steamships, telegraphs, and steam-powered printing presses, they disseminated feminist magazines and rushed to join each other's political struggles in times of crisis. Their influence coursed in both directions across the Atlantic: news of American women's rights conventions thrilled European feminists, while exiled German agitators such as Mathilde Anneke emigrated to the United States and found new audiences there. Exciting as it was, the feminists' heyday proved disappointingly brief. Riding the revolutionary wave of 1848, women's agitation peaked during the heady days when republican governments debated new constitutions, but it shared their fate when the resurgent forces of reaction restored authoritarian regimes in the 1850s. By 1860, says Anderson, the first international women's movement collapsed, although it would reappear toward the end of the nineteenth century as a more modest campaign centered on women's voting rights.

Anderson's book Joyous Greetings, *from which this essay is drawn, complements recent transnational studies of abolitionism, utopian socialism, and labor movements. Together with Frederick Douglass's story in Selection 19, these accounts show that the reform crusades of the antebellum years were not unique to America but instead were part of an interconnected transatlantic society. By implication, these essays question the traditional practice of stuffing historical events into national "containers" that prevent us from seeing their transnational connections and influences. As you read Anderson's essay, ask yourself what has been gained by placing the early women's rights movement in its larger international context. Her story also raises important and increasingly relevant questions about transnational identities: individuals' allegiances to communities beyond their own country. Under what historical conditions can bonds of gender, religion, class, or ethnicity overshadow allegiance to the nation? Is nationalism always a stronger force than such borderless solidarities? If connections forged by migration, social movements, or multinational corporations are leading Americans (and people of other nations) into international alliances or even toward "global citizenship," how will they reconcile their national and transnational commitments?*

GLOSSARY

BLACKWELL, ELIZABETH (1821–1910)   The first American woman to receive a medical degree, granted to her by Geneva College in 1849. Blackwell founded the New York Infirmary for Women in 1857 and expanded it into the first women's college for training doctors. After 1869 she taught and practiced in England, where she helped establish the London School of Medicine for Women in 1875.

CHARTISM   A worker's political reform movement prominent in Great Britain between 1843 and 1848. It aimed to enact a "people's charter" that called for a secret ballot, annual elections, and universal male suffrage.

DEROIN, JEANNE (1805–1894) A French feminist, socialist, and self-educated worker who linked women's emancipation to working-class struggles. Active in the Revolution of 1848, Deroin edited the monthly *L'Opinion des femmes* (Women's Opinion) and became the first woman to stand for election to the National Assembly. Deroin was imprisoned for six months in 1851 with Pauline Roland for promoting workers' organizations. Exiled the following year to London, she continued publishing her feminist writings in Britain.

DICKENS, CHARLES (1812–1870) Hugely popular British novelist whose works, such as *Oliver Twist* (1838) and *A Tale of Two Cities* (1859), were often printed in monthly installments before being published as books.

FOURIERIST MOVEMENT French and American movement based on the utopian socialist theories of Charles Fourier (1772–1837). Fourierists attempted to build model cooperative communities, called "phalanxes," to promote free expression, social justice, and women's equality. The Fourierist Victor Considerant first proposed woman suffrage in the French National Assembly in 1849, and Fourierist ideas about women's liberation from household drudgery influenced American feminists such as Elizabeth Cady Stanton.

FULLER, MARGARET (1810–1850) An American author and feminist whose *Woman in the Nineteenth Century* (1845) argued for the free development of women's abilities in accord with Transcendentalist ideals. Touring Europe in the late 1840s, Fuller joined the unsuccessful Roman republican revolt against the Papal States. She, her Italian husband, and their infant son were drowned in a shipwreck off New York's Long Island on her return to the United States in 1850.

GOLDMAN, EMMA (1869–1940) A Russian American anarchist and labor agitator who lectured widely in the United States and Europe. Jailed for two years for her outspoken opposition to American involvement in World War I, Goldman was deported to Russia during the Red Scare of 1919, but fled the Soviet Union in disillusionment in 1921.

HÉRICOURT, JENNY D' (1809–1875) A French feminist author who engaged in a widely publicized debate over women's role with anarchist P.-J. Proudhon and historian Jules Michelet in the 1850s. Héricourt lived in Chicago from 1862 to 1873 and wrote for American feminist periodicals.

KNIGHT, ANNE (1786–1862) An English Quaker abolitionist and feminist who advocated woman suffrage as early as 1847 and whose Sheffield Female Political Association was the first such group established in Britain. During the Revolution of 1848 in France, Knight moved to Paris to agitate for women's rights with French feminists.

LUDDITES Anti-industrial workers who rioted in England in the 1810s by destroying textile machinery, which they blamed for unemployment and low wages.

MARTINEAU, HARRIET (1802–1876) An English writer and reformer who visited the United States in 1834–1835. Her travel account *Society in America* (1837) was popular in England but controversial in the United States for its feminist and antislavery critique of American life.

MILL, HARRIET TAYLOR (1808–1858) The close associate and collaborator of John Stuart Mill, whom she married after her first husband died in 1849. An advocate of independence and equal opportunity for women, Mill wrote "The Enfranchisement of Women" (1851) and influenced many of her husband's works, including *The Subjection of Woman* (1869).

MILL, JOHN STUART (1806–1873)   A British philosopher and economist whose writings, including *On Liberty* (1859), tempered the self-interest of laissez-faire doctrines with humanitarian sentiments. Mill married Harriet Taylor in 1851, and largely due to her influence, he advocated women's emancipation in addition to parliamentary reforms and labor unions.

MOTT, LUCRETIA (1793–1880)   A Massachusetts teacher and a Quaker minister who made the transition to the lecture platform as a Garrisonian abolitionist and later as a women's rights advocate. Mott and Elizabeth Cady Stanton convened the Seneca Falls Convention on women's rights in 1848.

OTTO, LOUISE (1819–1895)   Orphaned at age sixteen and largely self-educated, a German feminist who joined the free-religion movement in the 1840s. She began publishing her weekly *Women's Newspaper* during the German Revolution of 1848–1849 and printed many news articles and manifestoes supporting women's equality. When the German state of Saxony banned female editors in 1850, Otto moved her newspaper to another state until ceasing publication in 1852. In later years she concentrated her publicity on women's education.

QUAKERS   The common name for the Society of Friends, a dissenting sect originating in seventeenth-century England. Quakers stood out for their beliefs in simplicity, equality, and pacifism, and they were often subject to persecution. The colony of Pennsylvania was established as a refuge for Quakers and a "holy experiment" in religious toleration.

ROLAND, PAULINE (1805–1852)   A French feminist, socialist, and sexual radical who turned to journalism and popular historical works to support herself and her children. Active in the campaign for workers' and women's rights during the Revolution of 1848, Roland was sentenced with Jeanne Deroin to six months in prison in 1851 for her political activities. When Roland resisted Napoleon III's takeover of the French republic in December 1851, she was arrested again and sent to a penal colony in Algeria. She died soon after her release the following year.

SAINT-SIMONIANS   The followers of French social philosopher Claude Henri de Saint-Simon (1760–1825). They organized a small but important movement in the 1820s and 1830s advocating the abolition of inheritance, public control of production, and women's emancipation. Saint-Simonianism developed into a bizarre cult in the 1830s, but its ideas influenced later socialists and feminists.

STANTON, ELIZABETH CADY (1815–1902)   American reformer who moved from abolitionism to feminism by organizing the first Women's Rights Convention at Seneca Falls, New York, in 1848. She promoted legal, educational, and economic equality for women, and joined these goals to the suffrage cause while president of the National Woman Suffrage Association from 1869 to 1890.

ULTRAMONTANIST   Supporting the power and authority of the pope in church and/or political matters.

WOLLSTONECRAFT, MARY (1759–1797)   An English radical whose unconventional private life and support for the French Revolution and women's rights brought her notoriety. She is most famous for *A Vindication of the Rights of Woman* (1792), which linked the natural rights theory underpinning the American and French Revolutions to feminism.

WRIGHT D'ARUSMONT, FRANCES ("Fanny") (1795–1852)   A Scottish American radical and feminist who was influenced by the ideas of the British utopian socialist Robert Owen. She founded Nashoba (1825), a short-lived colony for free blacks in Tennessee. After its failure, she was briefly married to William d'Arusmont, then wrote and lectured widely on women's rights, universal education, abolitionism, and birth control.

✷ ✷ ✷ ✷ ✷ ✷ ✷

In May 1851, two forty-five-year-old Frenchwomen, Jeanne Deroin and Pauline Roland, sat in a stone cell in Saint Lazare, the medieval prison for women in Paris. Wearing the convicted prisoner's uniform, a blue-checked neckerchief and a plain wool dress, they passed their time by writing. Leaders of the French women's movement, these close friends had already spent a year in jail for attending an unauthorized political meeting of the socialist Union of Workers' Associations, which they had organized.

As activists, journalists, and schoolteachers, Deroin and Roland had been pressing hard for women's complete political and social equality before they were arrested. In the revolutionary spring of 1848, Roland attempted to vote; Deroin wrote for and helped edit the *Voice of Women* (La Voix des femmes), a daily feminist newspaper whose offices became an organizing center. Believing in the power of group action, Deroin and Roland continually worked to bring women together: through newspapers and labor unions, in clubs and by petitions.

Almost from the beginning they had to fight their male associates for women's rights. Deroin wrote for a second newspaper in 1848, a monthly called *La Politique des femmes;* after a few issues appeared, the revolutionary government ruled that women could no longer participate in politics and the journal had to be renamed *L'Opinion des femmes.* Deroin then ran as a candidate for the legislative assembly in the spring of 1849. Criticized by French socialist P.-J. Proudhon on the grounds that just as men could not be wet nurses so women could not be legislators, Deroin retorted in print that "now we know what organ is needed to be a legislator." During their trial in November 1850, Deroin reported that her male socialist colleagues had "begged" her to hide her leadership role in the union. Although she could not deny being on the Central Committee, she played down her part for the sake of solidarity.

And now, in May 1851, Deroin and Roland composed a passionate letter, which they sent not to the "brothers" who have limited their achievements, but to their "sisters" abroad — two groups of women fighting for the same cause. A short draft of the letter goes to the Female Political Association in the industrial city of Sheffield, England; the other, a longer version, to "the Convention of the Women of America," which met in New England in October 1850. News of the English and American women's actions, declare Deroin and Roland, "has resounded even to our prison, and has filled our souls with inexpressible joy."

The Sheffield Female Political Association, the first in Great Britain, had been organized by Quaker feminist Anne Knight. A veteran English antislavery lecturer and organizer, Knight worked closely with Deroin in Paris during the 1848 revolution, publishing joint letters to prominent legislators asserting women's claims to equal rights. Knight supported Deroin's candidacy . . . ; when she returned to England early in 1851, she contacted the Sheffield women who had fought for the People's Charter, a six-point plan to make English politics more democratic. That February, Knight and the Sheffield women convinced the radical Earl of Carlisle to present a petition to the House of Lords for the vote by "adult Females." These actions created the solidarity Deroin and Roland felt for their "Sisters of Sheffield."

The bond with their "Sisters of America" came from the meeting of the first National Women's Rights Convention in the United States the year before. The American feminists at the convention represented nine states, but their view extended much further: "We are not contending here for the rights of the women of New England, or of old England, but of the world," declared Polish-born Ernestine Rose, who had lived in Berlin, Paris, and London before immigrating to New York. The convention endorsed "equality before the law without distinction of sex or color," and the opening address proclaimed that

> the reformation which we propose, in its utmost scope, is radical and universal. It is not the mere perfecting of a progress already in motion, a detail of some established plan, but it is an epochal movement — the emancipation of a class, the redemption of half the world, and a conforming re-organization of all social, political, and industrial interests and institutions.

In response, Deroin and Roland wrote that "your socialist sisters of France are united with you in the vindication of the right of Woman to civil and political equality." Explaining that they were convinced that these rights could be gained only "by the union of the working classes of both sexes to organize labor," the Frenchwomen entreated the Americans to carry on the struggle. "It is in this confidence that, from the depths of the jail which still imprisons our bodies without reaching our hearts, we cry to you — Faith, Love, Hope; and send to you our sisterly salutations," they concluded.

News of the women's rights convention was widely reported in the American press and its proceedings made their way to Europe in the few weeks it took a fast steamer to cross the Atlantic. Deroin and Roland were not the only Europeans to consider the news significant. The English philosopher and reformer John Stuart Mill wrote a long letter to his future wife, Harriet Taylor, describing the convention: "it is almost like ourselves speaking — outspoken like America, not frightened & servile like England — not the least iota of compromise — asserting the whole of the principle and claiming the whole of the consequences." Mill, a reader of Deroin's *Voix des femmes,* had been urging Taylor to finish a "pamphlet" she was composing on women's rights; the U.S. convention furnished its opening. In July 1851 the newly married Harriet Taylor Mill published her thirty-page essay, "Enfranchisement of Women," in the prestigious *Westminster*

Review. She began with an account of the Women's Rights Convention in Worcester [Massachusetts] and ended with the House of Lords petition. The bulk of the essay questioned "why each woman should be a mere appendage to a man" and concluded that "what is wanted for women is equal rights, equal admission to all social privileges; not a position apart, a sort of sentimental priesthood."

Harriet Taylor Mill's son, who was in America on a business trip, delivered copies of the essay to Lucretia Mott in Philadelphia in June 1851. Mott saw that the essay found wide distribution in the United States. A well-known Quaker minister and abolitionist, Mott had met a number of British feminists, among them Anne Knight, on an earlier trip to England. The second National Women's Rights Convention, which met in Worcester in October 1851, featured both this essay — which "vindicates every position which we assumed, and reaffirms and establishes the highest ground taken in principle and policy by our movement" as the opening address explained — and Deroin and Roland's letter, which was the centerpiece of the evening session of the first day. Three months after the convention, early in 1852, Deroin published an *Almanach des femmes* in Paris. The first article was a ten-page French précis [summary] of Harriet Taylor Mill's essay, entitled "Convention des Femmes en Amérique."

This web of feminist connections extended into Germany. From 1849 to 1852, German activist Louise Otto published a feminist weekly called the *Women's Newspaper* (Frauen-Zeitung). She covered some early American conventions, and in August and December 1851 printed two articles on "Johanna" Deroin. Otto praised Deroin for editing feminist journals, for insisting that male socialists renounce "all privileges of [their] *sex*," and for running as a candidate. Otto's countrywoman, Mathilde Franziska Anneke, who had gone into exile in the United States, reprinted Deroin and Roland's letter to the American women in the German-language feminist paper she published from New York in July 1852; October's issue featured an article on Ernestine Rose.

These women and their coworkers created the world's first international women's movement. They knew and learned from each other, they wrote and paid visits, they read the same books. They connected through conventions, periodicals, and correspondence. Reaching out to their counterparts in other nations, they sent "joyous greetings to the distant lands," as Emma Goldman wrote of Mary Wollstonecraft. In the middle of the nineteenth century, they demanded full equality in the economy, religion, and culture, as well as in law and government. In politics, they claimed not only the vote but the right to hold office, to govern, to serve on juries, to conduct the same public lives as men. They not only published but often did so in feminist journals they founded and edited, printed by women they recruited and trained. They fought in revolutions, voted illegally, and refused to pay taxes. They consistently spoke in public for "a cause which is still in its rotten-egg stage (I mean its advocates are apt to have rotten eggs and dirtier words thrown at them)," as English feminist Barbara Leigh Smith Bodichon wrote in her diary after visiting Lucretia Mott.

At the height of the Victorian era, these women dared to speak out in public about prostitution, forced marriage, the right to have sex or refuse it. They demanded that child custody be awarded to mothers instead of automatically going to fathers. They defined a new kind of marriage based on companionship and claimed the right to divorce if it failed. They saw prostitution not as a moral fault but as the direct result of an unjust economic system that forced women into only a handful of degraded and poorly paid jobs. They worried about all the victims produced by the undervaluing of women's labor: the housewives who toiled all day but did not "work," the women paid wages too low to live on, the prostitutes who worked the "fifth quarter of the day" to survive, the children who always suffered when their mothers were impoverished.

Holding prostitutes relatively blameless, they considered many "respectable" marriages to be legal prostitution, arrangements in which a woman with no other options sold herself to a single man. To remedy that situation, they worked to open new, better paid jobs for women, so that the average woman could secure the independence that feminists believed came only with the ability to support oneself. These early feminists insisted that women could do almost any job men did, and they founded the labor organizations and training centers, the colleges and medical schools necessary to realize their dreams. Inspired by the great scientific breakthroughs of their day — the telegraph, the railroad, industrial production — they believed they could create a peaceful, harmonious world without poverty for women and men of all races and classes.

Deroin and Roland sent out their letters in 1851, the heyday of this international women's movement. It had arisen two decades earlier, in the 1830s. During those years, key women in the United States, France, England, and, a few years later, in the German lands, developed a radical feminist outlook: they utterly rejected the traditional view that women's subordination was natural, God-given, and universal. They then insisted that women could and must redefine themselves, shaping new lives and claiming their own territory.

The demand for women's rights arose primarily from women who had been active in movements seeking to reform and improve society. Women who linked up with each other — on both national and international levels — often moved from supporting an initial radical cause, such as socialism, anti-slavery, or free religion into feminism because their ability to act was limited by men or other women in that cause. Like Deroin and Roland in French socialism, many women in radical movements became feminists both because those groups first allowed them room to grow and because the majority in these movements then sought to halt that growth. Women not previously active in such causes describe similar tensions, either within their own family or between a family that supported women's autonomy and a society that restricted it. Paradoxically, feminism required both nurture and opposition for its growth.

In France the cause that gave rise to feminism was socialism. The social problems created by the first phase of industrialization prompted many to question the equity of a system that rewarded factory owners with immense profits while pauperizing workers. On her fourth trip to England, in 1839, French socialist Flora Tristan criticized the "advances" of British industry:

Unless you have visited the manufacturing towns and seen the workers . . . you cannot appreciate the physical suffering and moral degradation of this class of the population. . . . they are all wizened, sickly and emaciated; their bodies are thin and frail, their limbs feeble, their complexions pale, their eyes dead.

Socialists differed from earlier protesters — the machine breakers known as Luddites — in that they believed industry could be made beneficial. "If at first I felt humiliated to see Man brought so low, his functions reduced to those of a machine," argued Tristan,

> I was quick to realize the immense advances which all these scientific discoveries would bring; brute force banished, less time expended on physical labor, more leisure for Man to cultivate his intelligence. But if these great benefits are to be realized, there must be a social revolution; and that revolution will come, for God has not revealed such admirable inventions to men only to have them remain the slaves of a handful of manufacturers and landed proprietors.

Tristan and other French feminists were inspired by the radical early socialism of the Saint-Simonian and Fourierist movements, which preached the equality of the sexes as essential to the creation of a peaceful future society in which workers would no longer be exploited. In 1831, male Saint-Simonians had called for "la femme libre," the "free woman" who would lead humankind to social and sexual liberation. Within a few months women in the movement formed their own group, published their own newspaper, and tried to redefine their own emancipation, since the movement's male leader excluded them from governing and emphasized the sexual side of liberation. "At bottom," one of them complained, "male Saint-Simonians are more male than they are Saint-Simonian." Most of the women who created a French feminist movement and linked up with international feminism — Jeanne Deroin, Pauline Roland, Suzanne Voilquin, Jenny d'Héricourt — had originally been followers of early male socialists.

The linkage of women's social emancipation with sexual license in the popular mind forced many socialist women, including Frenchwomen, to repudiate "the shameless picture of the 'femme libre' of the Saint-Simonians," as Louise Otto called it in 1843. Although Otto was known as "the red democrat," she, like many early feminists, found religion as important as socialism in leading her to feminism. Otto and many other women joined the radical new "free congregations" that arose in the German states during the 1840s. These congregations, which were free in that they belonged to no established church, either Protestant or Catholic, ranged from advocating a liberally defined Christianity to anticlerical secular humanism. "Our church is the world, our religion is reason, our Christianity is humanity, our creed is freedom, our worship, the truth," Louise Dittmar stated in 1845.

As feminists in other radical movements discovered, men in these free congregations both supported and limited women's rights. The creation of the first college "for the female sex" in Germany, for instance, can be traced in part to some women's outrage at being told in a public meeting of congregational delegates that females should not be allowed to teach in their kindergartens. A number of radical German feminists, like Dittmar, Louise Aston, and Mathilde Franziska Anneke, eventually rejected organized religion completely and questioned the double standard that judged women more harshly than men for rejecting religious faith. In 1847, Anneke wrote a long essay in support of Aston, exiled from Berlin the previous year, in part because she refused to say she believed in God. "Why do opinions which men have been able to hold for centuries seem so dangerous to the government when held *by women?*" asked Anneke, who titled her essay "Woman in Conflict with Social Conditions."

English feminist Elizabeth Pease questioned the same double standard in 1841: "It is thought most unaccountable for a *gentleman* to say he sees nothing wrong in [the democratic movement of] Chartism — but for a lady to do so is almost outrageous." The Chartist movement awoke women's hopes by demanding "universal suffrage" but frustrated them by being "too purblind or too poltron to proclaim that half the race are excluded," Harriet Taylor complained. Although Chartism provided some women with connections both in Britain and abroad . . . , it generally relegated women to a subordinate role.

So too did the antislavery movement. As with socialism and the free congregations, the contradictions faced by females in the antislavery movement led some English and American women to radical feminism. Abolitionism on both sides of the Atlantic enlisted women's help "in the labour of collecting and going from house to house for signatures to petitions" but excluded them from "the muster roll for the counsel-board," as Anne Knight complained. The turning point for many women came during the 1840 World Anti-Slavery Convention in London, when seven female American delegates, chief among them Lucretia Mott, were not allowed to take their seats. Elizabeth Cady Stanton, there on her honeymoon since her husband was a delegate, dated the beginning of the U.S. women's rights movement from this rebuff. The strong connections forged during that visit between American and British women developed into a vital link in the early international feminist movement.

The movements in which feminism began were themselves internationalist. Socialism, antislavery, and even the free congregation movement looked abroad for support in their struggles and for confirmation of their beliefs. "Our country is the world, our countrymen are all mankind," went the abolitionist motto and this expansive universalism carried over when women created their own movements.

Isolated in their own countries, feminists reached out to like-minded women in other lands. Lucretia Mott and Elizabeth Cady Stanton remained in correspondence for decades with the English radicals they met in 1840. When the American intellectual Margaret Fuller went to Europe in 1846, she naturally visited the English reformer Harriet Martineau and the French novelist George Sand. Feminists sent books as well as letters across the Atlantic. Mott mailed Sarah Grimké's *Letters on the Equality of the Sexes* to English friends; Margaret Fuller found Europeans familiar with her *Woman in the Nineteenth Century* when she traveled through Europe the year after it was published. "Pray let me have a few of your good books on this subject," wrote Anne Knight to the American abolitionists after recommending Scotswoman Marion Reid's 1843 *A Plea for Woman* to them. "These things ought to be sent darting off like lightning to all the world if possible."

Feminists constantly cited each other's achievements to prove their points. In the first article she signed with her own name, Louise Otto argued that women's participation in the state "was not just a right but a duty." She built her case by arguing that British and American women had used the laws and constitutions of their nations to participate more fully in political life than Germans. She also referred to the dictum first stated by the French socialist Charles Fourier: "From the position women occupy in a country you can see whether the air of the state is thick with dirty fog or clear and free: women serve as the barometers of states."

Early feminists drew on the same set of authorities, like Fourier or the eighteenth-century feminist Mary Wollstonecraft, to support their cause. French socialist Flora Tristan extolled Wollstonecraft's writings, and Mathilde Franziska Anneke translated parts of her *Vindication of the Rights of Woman* to make it accessible to German women. They drew examples of female achievement from the Bible, from history, from all eras and nations. Sarah Grimké praised French author and salonière Germaine de Staël in her letter on the "Intellect of Woman," as did Scotswoman Marion Reid in her *Plea for Woman.*

By 1847, hundreds of women in the United States, Great Britain, France, and the German states had become feminists: they believed that women were not innately inferior nor ideally subordinate to men, but oppressed by them. "I long for the time when my sisters will rise, and occupy the sphere to which they are called by their high nature and destiny," declared Lucretia Mott in a sermon the year after she returned from London. Throughout the 1840s Mott and others became convinced that they must work to change women's situation. "I came to the consciousness and to the knowledge that the position of women was absurd," recalled Anneke of this period. "So I soon began to do as much as I could, in words and print, for the . . . betterment of women."

The impending revolutions of the late 1840s strengthened feminists' ability to work for radical changes in women's situation. In German history, this period is called the Vormärz (before March), a time defined by the revolution of March 1848. People all over Europe expected a revolution. "While [the French king] Louis Philippe lives, the gases, compressed by his strong grasp, may not burst up to light," wrote Margaret Fuller in 1847, "but the need of some radical measures of reform is not less strongly felt in France than elsewhere, and the time will come before long when such will be imperatively demanded." In Germany especially, feminism added to the ferment of the period. "There is a vitality and a striving in our time which there has never been before," wrote Otto in 1847, "which women also are becoming aware of." In that year alone, four radical feminist texts appeared: Anneke's *Woman in Conflict with Social Conditions,* Dittmar's *Four Timely Questions,* Aston's novel, *From a Woman's Life,* and Otto's *Songs of a German Maiden.* . . .

Revolution was in the air, especially in the continental capitals — Paris, Berlin, Vienna, and Rome. Radical movements, for democracy, for socialism, for uniting Germany or Italy as nations, awaited the death of the French king as the signal to arise. As it happened, French democrats began the revolution on February 22. Within a few days, with hardly any bloodshed, the king had abdicated and the republic been proclaimed. The speed and ease of the overthrow seemed almost miraculous. "I heard the shout of the *people-king,* and the din of martial music and guns up the Champs Elysée from my window, and a man said, 'Louis-Philippe is no longer king,'" remembered Anne Knight. . . .

Revolutions quickly followed in the German and Italian states. "The electric current spread in all directions," remembered German feminist Malwida von Meysenbug, "Germany . . . now shuddered as from an underground fire. The news of [armed uprisings in] Vienna and Berlin followed swiftly. The prince of political darkness, Metternich, had fled!" The architect of international repression, Austrian foreign minister Prince Metternich, had masterminded the system of censorship, espionage, and armed intervention that supported the conservative monarchies of Europe between 1815 and 1848. "The news that a German Constituent Assembly would meet in Frankfurt filled me with nameless joy," continued Meysenbug. "The city was in boundless excitement. . . . Nature itself celebrated this festival of rebirth. Spring was unusually early and beautiful. . . . The railroads, the steamships incessantly brought crowds of joyful pilgrims, hastening to take part in the jubilee of freedom."

These revolutions released an explosion of feminist activism. In France and Germany, feminists seized the moment, using the new atmosphere of liberation to claim rights for themselves and their sisters. At the end of May 1848, Jeanne Deroin had helped to organize the Club for the Emancipation of Women, the Fraternal Association of Democrats of Both Sexes, and the Mutual Society for the Education of Women. She also wrote regularly for the *Voice of Women,* the feminist daily whose office became the center of another club for women. Louise Otto attended workers congresses and wrote numerous articles for the *Leipzig Workers Newspaper,* including a May address to the Saxon minister of the interior in which she insisted that women be included in any "reorganization of labor." One French group called themselves the Vésuviennes, the women of Vesuvius, after the only live volcano on the European mainland. Claiming the equal rights and duties of citizens, they explained that their name "marvelously portrays our position and more than any other expresses our thought." Images of lava, volcanoes, and underground fire appear in women's writings of this era, signifying the sense of pent-up energy released in an immense, satisfying explosion: "regenerative, not incendiary," the Vésuviennes promised. Nor was this explosive sense of liberation confined to places that actually experienced upheavals. Although economic prosperity and political reforms kept Great Britain safe from revolution, a number of English feminists applauded the uprisings across the Channel. "What wonderful times we live in," wrote Julia Smith, Barbara Leigh Smith Bodichon's aunt and Harriet Martineau's friend, to a correspondent in Germany that spring. "These last four weeks have had a century of history crowded into them. . . . The old routine is broken up & mankind *must* think & feel & search out new ways." . . .

1848 reverberated loudly in the United States, the first nation to recognize the new French Republic. Celebrations of reformers and immigrants erupted from New York to New Orleans. Abolitionists were especially buoyed by France's speedy decision to end slavery in all its colonies. Addressing the American Anti-Slavery Association in May, Mott argued that even though black bondage was still growing in America, "yet, when we look abroad and see what is now being done in other lands, when we see human freedom engaging the attention of the nations of the earth, we may take courage." Mott, like other radical feminists, believed freedom was universal: all must be free or none could be. We cannot separate our own freedom from that of the slave, continued

Mott. They are "inseparably connected . . . in France" and are "beginning to be so in other countries."

"Can man be free, if woman be a slave?" poet Percy Shelley had asked in 1818. Mott and other antislavery activists on both sides of the Atlantic had long connected abolitionism and feminism. Now, in the revolutionary summer of 1848, the "great events" in Europe seemed to "make possible the social reconstruction of reality, the reordering of things-as-they-are so they are no longer experienced as given, but rather as willed, in accordance with convictions about how things ought to be," as the historian Robert Darnton wrote about the first French Revolution.

In July 1848, Lucretia Mott traveled to upstate New York in part to investigate conditions among the Seneca Indians for her church; she later wrote that the Senecas were learning "from the political agitations abroad . . . imitating the movements of France and all Europe in seeking a larger liberty — more independence." This expansive climate and her visit sparked the first women's rights convention in the United States, when over three hundred people, two-thirds of them women, met at Seneca Falls, New York, on July 19 and 20. Mott, Elizabeth Cady Stanton, and three other female organizers appropriated the most revolutionary document in American history — the Declaration of Independence — as their text. Holding that "all men and women are created equal," they claimed a wide range of rights for women: better education, jobs, pay, and access to the professions (including religious leadership), moral authority, and self-determination, as well as complete political equality. By placing themselves in the position of the American colonists, feminists seized the revolutionary high ground. This forced men into the unenviable position of the tyrant King George III and the other tyrant kings so recently overthrown in Europe. Stanton made the connection explicit in her speech to the meeting. Men like to deny women "rights . . . the maintenance of which is even now rocking to their foundations the kingdoms of the Old World." Hostile newspapers, like the New York *Herald,* connected and condemned the actions of women in both societies:

> This is the age of revolutions. . . . [But] the work of revolution is no longer confined to the Old World, nor to the masculine gender. . . . Though we have the most perfect confidence in the courage and daring . . . of our lady acquaintances, we confess it would go to our hearts to see them putting on the panoply of war, and mixing in scenes like those at which, it is said, the fair sex in Paris lately took a prominent part.

Parisian women had played an active role in the so-called June Days, when the republican government closed the National Workshops established to solve unemployment, and then turned its weapons on the socialist working class when they protested. This violence signaled the end of the most radical phase of the revolution. Thereafter, conservative sentiments began to reassert themselves in France and elsewhere in Europe. In England and the United States, many sympathizers drew back once the revolution seemed to turn to violent class warfare.

Feminism, however, remained energized by the revolutionary spirit well into the 1850s. The years from 1848 to 1856 are the heyday of the international women's movement, as radical feminists, like Deroin and Roland from their prison cell, reached out to others like themselves. Just as national feminisms arose from the tensions between support and opposition, so international feminism came into full flower in a climate in which revolutionary ardor was being chilled, but not yet frozen, by conservative repression. Making the effort of their lives, feminists created an amazing array of radical institutions in these years.

In 1849, for instance, four feminist newspapers were founded: Louise Dittmar's *Social Reform* and Amelia Bloomer's the *Lily,* an American journal far more radical than its name, in addition to Jeanne Deroin's *Women's Opinion* and Louise Otto's *Women's Newspaper.* All emphasized solidarity with feminists in other nations, and in so doing often broadened their own claims for women. The *Lily,* begun as a temperance journal, evolved rapidly into a wide-ranging supporter of universal women's rights. It championed the reform of female clothing, frequently by citing instances of women wearing trousers in other societies. The *Lily's* cause gained wide publicity in Europe and became the subject of international feminist debate. Although she had doubts about dress reform herself, Louise Otto felt that international solidarity compelled her to join the discussion: *"New York — London — Paris —* the issue, which was only comical at the start, has now become serious and it is now time that we in Germany also have our say."

News of Elizabeth Blackwell's being awarded an M.D. degree from New York's Geneva Medical College in 1849 spread rapidly and emboldened feminists to extend their demands. In France, for instance, *Women's Opinion* argued that "the example of Miss Blackwell gives us the opportunity to return to the question of women doctors in France," which had arisen the previous year. Then Suzanne Voilquin had led the United Midwives to demand state funding, a radical action even in the revolutionary spring of 1848. A year later, Blackwell's achievement made Voilquin's seem tame — the French midwives demanded too little. They should have pushed for full medical training, argued Deroin's paper. "We salute in [Blackwell] the emancipator, who opens the breach through which others may follow . . . [in] this noble cause which is at the same time the cause of all women and of humanity." Bessie Rayner Parkes, then only twenty, met Blackwell in England that year and for the first time questioned "why should such a lucrative profession as medical attention of their own sex be denied women?" Parkes and her friend Barbara Leigh Smith (later Bodichon), founders of the English women's movement, became staunch supporters of Blackwell and raised money for her New York clinic from English feminists for years.

Excluded from most established institutions, feminists began to found the colleges and schools needed to actualize their dreams. "Thanks to the woman's movement some half-dozen medical colleges are now open to women and two schools of design are established," wrote Marianne Finch in her *Englishwoman's Experience in America* of 1853. English feminists created Bedford College for Women in 1849, the first English college to educate women to be more than governesses; Julia Smith and her niece Barbara Leigh Smith enrolled the first term. German feminists founded its equivalent in Hamburg in part to train women to teach in the radical kindergartens being established by the free congregations.

Feminists began to create larger groups and associations. A federation of German women, linking activists from the free congregations, was proposed in Otto's *Women's Newspaper.* In France, Deroin and Roland helped establish the Union of Workers Associations, an umbrella organization of 108 unions, a number of them all-female or combining both female and male workers. In the United States women's rights conventions, both local and national, began to meet on a regular basis, providing a nexus for the increasing numbers who attended, as well as the other American and European women who read about them and wrote letters of encouragement. Paulina Wright Davis, who had presided over the first two national conventions in Worcester in 1850 and 1851, proposed to the third national convention that "we should have a literature of our own, a printing press and publishing house, and tract writers, and tract distributors, as well as Lectures and Conventions. We must show the world that we are in earnest." The convention, now attended by 2,000 instead of the 263 who assembled the first year, did not fund a journal, but Davis was able to publish her internationally oriented *Una* from 1853 to 1855. "We shall not confine ourselves to any locality, set, sect, class, or caste," declared her opening editorial, "for we hold to the solidarity of the [human] race, and believe that if one member suffers, all suffer." The *Una* advertised Jeanne Deroin's *Women's Almanack,* published in both French and English in 1853, and a proposed English monthly, the *Woman's Advocate.* Articles about women in Europe appeared regularly, as did letters from England by both Marianne Finch and another woman who identified herself only as "a Friend of the Cause."

Finch had met and admired Paulina Wright Davis and other American feminists when she came to the United States in 1851. Travel often fostered a woman's feminism. Stepping out of her own society, being able to see it from a distance and to compare how women lived in other lands, enabled a woman to view the condition of women as mutable, not fixed and eternal. Harriet Martineau's chapter "The Political Non-Existence of Women" in her *Society in America* (1837), in which she used the Declaration of Independence and the U. S. Constitution to criticize the condition of women, was the most radically feminist of all her writings; Margaret Fuller's travel in Europe committed her more firmly to feminism and socialism.

Swedish novelist Fredrika Bremer's trip to the United States from 1848 to 1851 transformed her into an active international feminist. "Her religious and social views had, in America, been materially influenced," remembered Mary Howitt, Bremer's English translator and a friend of the Leigh Smiths. "An intense desire animated her to aid in the liberation of every oppressed soul; above all, to rescue her country-women from the dark and narrow sphere allotted them." Energized by her trip, Bremer rapidly published her two-volume *Homes of the New World,* in which she presented American feminists as the model for Europeans, particularly Swedes, to emulate:

> They resemble the most beloved women of our hemisphere; their grace of person is not less than their steadfastness in principle. But they have something more than the women of Europe. Their glance seems to me to embrace a larger world; their intelligence a larger activity; and their heart seems to me large enough to embrace and elevate the human community in all its spheres.

In 1854, Bremer published an international appeal in the London *Times* for women to form a peace alliance and began writing her explicitly feminist novel, *Hertha. Hertha* inspired legislation aiding women in Sweden and was widely admired in feminist circles abroad. . . . Travel facilitated feminism for Bremer, for the American and British women who met in London in 1840, for Barbara Leigh Smith and Bessie Rayner Parkes, allowed to journey unchaperoned through Europe in 1850, and for countless others.

Some women particularly embodied these international connections. Anne Knight in England and France, Lucretia Mott in Philadelphia, and Jenny d'Héricourt in Paris and then Chicago — all functioned as important nodes in the radical feminist network, traveling, corresponding, and seeking out like-minded visitors from other nations. . . .

Ernestine Rose personified, and saw herself as personifying, the international women's movement. Introduced at the Third National Woman's Rights Convention in Syracuse (1852) as "a Polish lady and educated in the Jewish faith," Rose, who had lived in Germany, France, and England before coming to the United States, repudiated those labels. "It is of very little importance in what geographical position a person is born," she began. "Yes, I am an example of the universality of our claims; for not American women only, but a daughter of poor, crushed Poland, and the down-trodden and persecuted people called the Jews, 'a child of Israel,' pleads for the rights of her sex." Rose, known as the "Queen of the Platform" for her skill in public speaking, lectured widely in the United States, not only at conventions but also on tours that ranged as far west as Michigan and southward to Virginia. She also served as the American movement's chief translator, able to communicate with Deroin and d'Héricourt in French and to render Anneke's German speech into English at the 1853 National Women's Rights Convention in New York.

Technological progress made all these connections increasingly easier, and the new inventions of the period facilitated the development of this international women's movement. When Harriet Martineau sailed to America in 1834, the shortest trip took a month; hers lasted forty-two days. Fifteen years later, Fredrika Bremer traveled from London to New York "on one of the great steaming Leviathans which cross the vast ocean in 12 or 14 days." "I hope to have it in my power to visit America next year," wrote a young German woman to the Worcester Convention in 1850. "Thanks to the invention of steam a voyage across the ocean is now a mere bagatelle!"

Steam also seemed to herald a new era on land: "To *be* free is nothing — to *become* free is heaven," wrote Louise Otto about the first German railroad, which opened near her town in 1839. "I consider myself to be Fortune's favorite because I experienced this at first hand. . . . The first locomotive was the path breaker of a new era for all." The railways emboldened Otto to journey alone throughout Germany at a time when few women traveled by themselves. Bremer declared that the railway police and "all the arrangements, at the stations, for the convenience of travelers" made England and the United States places where "a lady may travel alone in comfort." Increasing numbers of women began to journey and found they could do so in comfort without the previously requisite male escort to protect them. The United States set the tone here: Bremer and other female European travelers praised "that blending of brotherly cordiality and chivalric politeness," which made "the man of the New World . . . most agreeable" to encounter on a trip.

Ernestine Rose, photographed in New York City in 1858, personified the transatlantic character of the women's movement. Born in Poland, Rose lived in Germany, France, and England before coming to the United States in 1836. An outspoken opponent of slavery and organized religion as well as a lifelong feminist, Rose lectured widely in the United States and Europe. Her frequent travels and mastery of French and German made her an important contact between American and European feminists. (Library of Congress, #914080 LC-US262-52045.)

The new trains and steamships carried newspapers and novels, letters and periodicals as well as passengers. In 1848, the *New York Herald* sent *La Presse* in Paris a list of steamer departures so that news of the revolution could arrive as quickly as possible; people waited at the docks in New York City for the latest installment of Dickens's novels. By the 1840s the reading public mushroomed as increasing numbers of women and men gained in literacy, leisure, and income. Europe and the United States formed a single reading community that increasingly demanded new fare. With financial rewards to be reaped, the most sought-after books were rapidly translated and published abroad, often in pirated editions. Lengthy novels flourished, frequently printed in monthly install-ments. Monthly periodicals ran to about fifty pages of closely packed type a month. Shorter magazines and newspapers proliferated as nations lifted prohibitive stamp taxes and newspapers crammed long columns of tiny print into a four- or eight-page format. Even though few feminist journals existed before 1848, women managed to publish in left-wing periodicals and newspapers, although they usually did so anonymously or under male pseudonyms.

Most women's only writing beyond schoolwork was correspondence. Letters pro-vided one of the few ways in which a woman could learn to write as an adult, to pre-sent herself in prose as a full human being and so assume at least some of the authority of an "author." A number of feminists' first venture into print was either to publish let-ters originally written to friends or to write a letter intended for print to a newspaper or public figure. Anne Knight's lengthy dispatch of 1840 to the American abolitionist Maria Weston Chapman was reprinted on both sides of the Atlantic. Letters, both private and public, also sustained important connections among women in different nations; some correspondence networks among feminists lasted for forty years.

Before 1839, letters were expensive (the price rose with distance) and were usually paid for by the recipient. Harriet Martineau had to pay for the hate mail that followed her across the Atlantic after her American trip. But postal reform — the invention of a uniform, inexpensive stamp purchased by the mailer — made a tremendous difference. "Our greatest achievement, of late, has been the obtaining of the penny postage," wrote Martineau, "It will do more for the circulation of ideas, for the fostering of domestic affections, for the humanizing of the mass generally, than any other single measure our national wit can devise." The black one-penny stamp, with its profile of the young Queen Victoria, paid for a letter to cross the Atlantic. Senders could be more casual then. "I have no idea of thy husband's address — but, New York is, I suppose, suffi-cient," wrote one of Elizabeth Cady Stanton's English correspondents, and the letter arrived despite its lack of street or number.

By the mid-1840s, Knight had invented feminist labels printed in bright yellow, green, and pink, which she pasted to the envelopes of her domestic and overseas letters. These miniature broadsides crammed lines of tiny type into a two- by three-inch rectangle and ensured that a single missive could proselytize many. "Never will the nations of the earth be well governed," began one, "until both sexes . . . are fairly represented, and have an influence, a voice, and a hand in the enactment and adminis-tration of the laws."

Although feminists used the post to the fullest, it was the recent invention of the telegraph that excited their imaginations. The steam that powered trains, ships, and machinery could be seen and understood; electric telegraphy worked as if by magic. Invisible, almost instantaneous pulses connected humankind in a new network: if a cable could be run from Frankfurt to Berlin, from London to Glasgow, from New York to Philadelphia, then surely cables could connect the capitals to each other around the world. Developed in part to provide a signal fast enough to be useful in running the railroads, the electric telegraph spread in the 1840s at the speed of the lightning to which it was often compared. "In the electric Telegraph, we behold a system of nerves weaving itself over the surface of the earth," Fredrika Bremer wrote in 1851, the year after submarine telegraphic cable had linked England and France. "By these airy wires, nation is bound to nation."

. . . News traveled much more rapidly with the new technology. Until the telegraph it took days to send a message by stagecoach and packet from Paris to London, although in cases of extreme urgency a carrier pigeon could fly the distance in twenty-three hours if the weather was fair. Telegraphy shrank this to minutes. The Atlantic cable, briefly successful in 1858, seemed to complete the telegraph's "annihilation of space and time."

To many, these amazing technological triumphs signified a new moral era as well, a time in which people of good will could solve the world's age-old problems of injustice, poverty, and war. "The very first message transmitted to us across the Atlantic, by means of the mightiest instrument of man," declared Lucretia Mott in a sermon, "was a prophetic view of greater peace on earth" (Queen Victoria's greetings to President Buchanan). The blessings brought by the wonderful inventions, reinforced in many cases by the staunch confidence that God sanctioned innovation, heralded a new stage in human history — an era of progress. In "an age of changes like the present," Harriet Taylor Mill declared in her 1851 essay,

> it is the boast of modern Europeans, and of their American kindred, that they know and do many things which their forefathers neither knew nor did; and it is perhaps the most unquestionable point of superiority in the present above former ages, that habit is not now the tyrant it formerly was over opinions and modes of action, and that the worship of custom is a declining idolatry. . . .

But mid-nineteenth century visions of progress often excluded or ignored the female sex. "Our time is the time of progress," wrote Louise Otto in 1843, "as for the vaunted progress of women in the nineteenth century! Their situation has stayed almost completely the same." Arguing that women's position had stagnated or even deteriorated in recent times, feminists insisted that progress must include women. "So was it *once, now* it has become otherwise," wrote a German woman to an 1847 meeting of the radical free congregations in the small city of Nordhausen. "Even here the spirit of the age cannot remain still; it comes to slay ancient prejudice, and to elevate Woman to human dignity!"

In the United States, which increasingly prided itself on being the home of progress, feminists appropriated the concept for themselves. "A new era dawns upon us," concluded the final speaker at the Worcester woman's rights convention in 1851.

> Its approach is heralded by a thousand harbingers. The lightning coursing the telegraphic wires; the smoke-girt steeds rushing along our iron-rimmed ruts, are but embassies of a power

whose will will yet place freedom on something more than a theoretical basis, and give equality of privileges a being as well as a name.

To "great cheers" the speaker made the consequences clear: "We must agitate. Give woman knowledge — give mankind knowledge and their rights must follow. . . . The world is emerging into day. It is putting on shining robes of light!"

By the early 1850s, however, the repression that followed the European revolutions forced thousands of French and German radicals into exile. Anneke and her family came to the United States; Deroin and others moved to Britain. Just as the outbreak of revolution released an eruption of feminist activity, so reaction ended public feminism in France, Germany, and Austria. Laws were passed forbidding women (and children) from attending any political meetings; in 1851, the Prussian government outlawed kindergartens, which were seen as centers of radical indoctrination. Not only women's movements but also movements that had nourished feminism — socialism and the free congregations — went under. "Forbidding meetings of the 'Women's Circle for Needy Families' is no longer a novelty," went a Dresden woman's letter to Otto's *Women's Newspaper.* "But now they go so far as to keep individuals — not just groups — under surveillance and to hold them responsible for all they say and do which is not completely ultramontanist, reactionary, or 'gold-black.'" (The colors of the new German flag, minus the red.) By the end of that year, Otto had been forced to move her newspaper to a German state that had not passed the "Lex Otto" (a law forbidding women to edit newspapers, aimed specifically at her). The three other German feminist papers had already ceased publication.

Otto and other feminists managed to maintain their institutions — women's groups, journals, schools, and unions — longer than most other radicals within their beleaguered societies. But executions, arrests, harsh prison sentences, and censorship finally silenced the left. "The city is full of soldiers," reported Rose from Paris in 1856, "nor is this the worst; for at any rate you see them, you know who is near you. But there is a much more formidable army, an *espionage,* against which you cannot guard except by a dead silence on all subjects connected with political freedom."

The silence had been enforced by terror; from the summary execution of Robert Blum, the German hero of the revolution who had first published Louise Otto, to the sentencing of French socialists like Deroin and Roland to jail and transportation. Released from her first prison sentence at Saint Lazare in July 1851, Pauline Roland was rearrested six months later. Sentenced to prison in Algeria, she died from the harsh conditions in December 1852.

Those who were not silenced or dead, however, emigrated to freer societies, and some were able to contribute to women's movements in their new homes. . . .

. . . [W]hile feminism within the European continental nations ended abruptly, international feminism briefly benefited from the new connections and cross-fertilization forced by emigration. Exiles like Deroin carried on by insisting that the women's movement was international. "Since 1848," she wrote in 1853, "societies of

Women have been organized in France, in America, and in England — composed of females claiming their political rights. . . . We challenge all women to walk with us." In America, Mathilde Franziska Anneke demonstrated that feminists connected across national boundaries. Active in the German revolution, Anneke had published a radical, feminist newspaper and fought in the Baden uprising, before fleeing with her family to the United States. In April 1850, five months pregnant with her third child, she gave her first public lecture in Milwaukee. "The efforts of many American women became known to me," she remembered of that time, when she translated writings by Stanton and others into German, "I studied the worthy efforts of Fanny Wright d'Arusmont, Lucretia Mott, Ernestine L. Rose, Pauline Davis, and other highly esteemed women and strengthened myself thereby." In 1852, Anneke began to publish a *German Women's Newspaper* (in German, with some English translations) and embarked on an "agitation" tour for seven months, trying to recruit German immigrant women to feminism. The following year a group of American feminists invited her to be a delegate to the New York City Woman's Rights Convention in September 1853. Lucretia Mott introduced her at the meeting. With Rose translating her words into English, Anneke declared that she rejoiced when she learned that

> the women of America have met in convention, to claim their rights. I rejoiced when I saw that they recognized their equality; and I rejoiced when I saw that they have not forgotten their sisters in Germany. . . . The women of my country look to this [one] for encouragement and sympathy; and they, also, sympathize with this cause. We hope it will go on and prosper; and many hearts across the ocean in Germany are beating in unison with those here.

The severity of the European repression radicalized some American and English feminists. "I did not know before [her European trip with Bessie Parkes] how intense, how completely a part of my soul, were feelings about freedom and justice in politics and government," Barbara Leigh Smith wrote her Aunt Julia in 1850. "I did not think, when I was so glad to go to Austria, how the sight of people ruled by the sword in place of law would stir up my heart and make me feel as miserable as those who live under it." Leigh Smith and Parkes soon published their first and most radical feminist writings: *Remarks on the Education of Girls* and *A Brief Summary, in Plain Language, of the Most Important Laws Concerning Women*. Both stressed international examples of women's success and insisted that despite the temporary success of repression, "The genius of this age tears away one restriction after another which has hitherto crippled society. . . . It is for us to aid this work." American feminists especially continued to reach out to their embattled sisters in Europe. In 1853 and again in 1856, the Women's Rights Conventions established committees and passed resolutions of support for "the supporters of the cause of women . . . the worthy successors of Pauline Roland and Jeanne Deroin, who, in the face of imperial despotism, dare to tell the truth."

But what could they do? Brave words failed to prevent the triumph of "tyranny, by which every outcry of the human heart is stifled," as Anneke later declared. After 1856, radical feminism began to lose ground in the United States as well as Europe. Women's movements, as well as all left-wing activity, had been extinguished on the continent. "Whole nations are manacled and gagged; not allowed even to utter the cry of anguish," wrote an English socialist paper. "Behold . . . the fires of Liberty's altars quenched, the dial of Time reversed, the middle-age tyranny of priest and brigand reestablished." In the United States, the revolutionary momentum of the women's movement ebbed, overwhelmed by the crises impelling the nation to Civil War. When Barbara Leigh Smith Bodichon visited the United States on her honeymoon in 1858, she found that

> instead of any tendency to ameliorate the condition of the slave I see nothing but increasing barbarity in the laws and firmer barriers raised against the certain encroachment of the universal spirit of freedom. Here, as in Europe, laws to stifle this spirit increase in severity. Despotism seems dominant.

Bodichon and Parkes deliberately muted the radical feminism of their early years when they helped create the English women's movement in the late 1850s, reasoning that they could attract more supporters by not pressing for the vote or divorce. International connections weakened as radical feminists withdrew from public life or turned to other causes. While some Europeans, like Jenny d'Héricourt, continued to champion the U.S. women's movement as an example, the Americans transformed themselves into the "National Women's Loyal League" for the duration of the Civil War. Lack of support from abroad eroded radicalism at home. In both the United States and Europe the 1860s witnessed a return to purely national concerns and early international feminists felt the times to be against them. Three months before her death in 1862, the seventy-five-year-old Anne Knight had a friend transcribe an 1848 letter she had written with Jeanne Deroin into her diary. The letter demanded the emancipation of women for the good of humanity. Below it, Knight added her final entry: "It is 14 years ago & where are we now? Still heaving our agonized chests under the couchemar [nightmare] of a military despotism. . . . how long? Lord, how long?"

When national women's movements revived, as they did in the 1860s and 1870s, they were much less internationalist and far more conservative. International feminist organizations of the late nineteenth century focused more on suffrage, rather than the wide range of issues raised by the earlier movement. But the success of the first international women's movement should not be underestimated. It challenged the male dominance of Western culture and society in a way that would not be repeated until the late 1960s. It enabled some women to transcend national and class differences for feminist purposes in a period in which those differences intensified and increased. It created a coherent and convincing ideology that made wide-ranging claims for women's rights and equality, without surrendering a keen sense of women's difference from men. To advocate new roles for women required impressive courage and fortitude, "a heroism that the world has never yet recognized, that the battlefield cannot supply, but which woman possesses," as Ernestine Rose declared in 1856. The achievements of early feminists become all the more astonishing when we realize how unusual these women were in their own day.

QUESTIONS TO CONSIDER

1. How, according to the author, were the women's rights movements of Europe and the United States linked together between 1830 and 1860 into an international movement? How did the contemporary revolutions in printing, transportation, and communication support this linkage? What impact did transatlantic travel have upon women writers? Was this impact similar to or different from what happened to the abolitionist Frederick Douglass (Selection 19)? How did the American women's rights conventions influence European feminists? In what other ways did the women's movements of different nations influence one another?

2. Explain how mid-nineteenth-century feminism evolved out of women's previous ideas and experiences in reform and socialist movements. How did Saint-Simonian and Fourierist socialism inspire French feminists? How did campaigns for religious freedom or freedom *from* religion lead some European women toward feminism? In what ways did the antislavery movement in Britain and the United States become a bridge to women's rights agitation?

3. In what way did American feminists' "Declaration of Sentiments" at the Seneca Falls Convention in 1848 adopt the rhetoric and ideas of the American Revolution? How did the convention relate American women's stand to the revolutions that were shaking Europe that year? Was the feminists' linkage of their cause to democratic national revolutions appropriate? Was it a good strategy for their movement?

4. What forces and factors, according to the author, led to the decline of the transatlantic women's movement in the 1850s? Why did organized feminism last somewhat longer in the United States and Great Britain than on the European Continent? How, according to Anderson, were the post-1860s women's movements on both sides of the Atlantic more conservative than their predecessors? What events or factors hindered transnational feminist solidarity at the time? Why do you think feminism again became an international movement in the twentieth century?

5. How have our customs and laws changed since the 1850s in such areas as women's voting and officeholding, divorce and child custody, education, and the professions? To what extent are ideas about women's inferiority or fitness for domesticity still influential? In what ways did the focus on voting rights after 1860 change women's roles? Why has the achievement of suffrage fallen short of revolutionizing "woman's place" in Western society?

XI

THE CIVIL WAR

The Civil War was the most devastating event in American history. More than
six hundred thousand soldiers — nearly as many as all other American wars
combined — died in a four-year struggle between the North and South that
divided families and communities and threatened the nation's very existence.
No wonder then that so much effort has gone into analyzing every detail of the
political conflict that brought on the war and the battles that decided its outcome. With Civil War books appearing at the rate of one a day and films such
as *Glory, Cold Mountain,* and the PBS documentary *The Civil War* drawing huge
audiences, the story of the battle to save the Union and free the slaves retains a
unique hold on Americans' imaginations.

Yet while the Civil War may be unique in American history, how unique it
was in world history is still unclear. When historians stand back from the day-
to-day chronicling of the war, they ask larger interpretive questions. The responses to many of these can be enhanced by international comparisons. Was
the Civil War inevitable? One way to approach this question is to ask why it
took a civil war to abolish slavery in the United States, whereas most Latin
American countries ended slavery peacefully. Was the Civil War a "revolution,"
as Karl Marx suggested and historian Charles A. Beard claimed? Simply defining
what you mean by "revolution" entails comparing and generalizing from such
historical examples as the French and Russian Revolutions. How was the Union
able to defeat the secessionists? One response might be to compare the North's
resources, actions, and leaders not just to the South's but also to those of
nationalist governments elsewhere in the nineteenth century that put down
internal revolts or created a nation by force. Why did the Confederacy lose?
Ethnic nationalists in such places as Paraguay and South Africa in the nineteenth
century waged longer wars of resistance against powerful enemies, calling into
question the Confederates' vaunted will to fight. Was the Civil War a "total
war," as some military historians assert, or even "the first modern war"? To

situate the American conflict's tactics and weapons in the annals of warfare requires sweeping comparisons over time and place.

The essays in this chapter suggest two ways that international comparisons may help improve our understanding of the Civil War. In the first selection, Carl N. Degler interprets the American sectional conflict as a war to forge a nation out of a divided group of states. Thus, he finds striking similarities between the Civil War and wars of national unification that were raging in Germany, Italy, and Switzerland at virtually the same time. In the second essay, Brian Holden Reid and Bruce Collins conduct a lively debate over the South's conduct of the Civil War. Should the Confederates have resorted to guerrilla warfare, as the Boers of South Africa did at the century's end against the British? Why they did not, the authors say, may suggest an important distinction between the "War Between the States" and a war waged between profoundly different peoples.

Although the essays in this chapter focus on different topics, each makes claims about the strengths and weaknesses of southern nationalism that you should analyze and compare. In their recognition that the Civil War finally forged a nation out of separate states, these essays can also be tested against Peter J. Parish's analysis in Selection 12 of what made American nationalism different. Why, despite such promising ingredients and beginnings, did it take a horrific civil war finally to cement American nationhood? "Comparing the comparisons" may help you to construct a persuasive answer.

One Among Many: The United States and National Unification

CARL N. DEGLER

The Civil War transformed the national vocabulary in revealing ways. When the battles were finally over, Americans refashioned "the United States" from a plural to a singular noun: before 1861, they had said, "The United States are . . ."; afterward they said, "The United States is . . ." Torn by the social and economic divisions between North and South, the United States in 1861 was an "unfinished nation." It took the crisis of secession and the bloody war that suppressed it to create a unified nation out of the divided confederation the Founders had left behind.

In this selection, Carl Degler uses the concept of the Civil War as a nationalist struggle to ask fresh questions about this ever-fascinating subject. In his introductory section, Degler asks whether the southern states possessed the ingredients to become a nation in their own right. Of course, it is easy to say "no" in retrospect, for the South did not win its independence on the battlefield. But, says Degler, southerners saw themselves, and not northerners, as the legitimate heirs of the patriots of 1776. He points out that by the antebellum period the modernization of northern society had driven the sections apart and created a separate identity for stubborn traditionalists below the Mason-Dixon Line. And lest we doubt their sincerity, Degler reminds us that they fought long and heroically to defend their new nation in the "War for Southern Independence."

In the main section of his essay, Degler suggests provocative international comparisons between the Civil War and wars for national unification that were being fought in Italy, Germany, and Switzerland at nearly the same time. Italy's patchwork quilt of republics and dukedoms was sewn together too haphazardly and with too much foreign intervention to be comparable to the United States, Degler decides, although Lincoln did ask the Italian nationalist hero Garibaldi to lead one of the Union armies. Switzerland's civil war between Catholic and Protestant cantons in 1847 provides the closest parallel to the American conflict. But Degler's most striking comparison is his juxtaposition of Lincoln and Otto von Bismarck, the brilliant but ruthless Prussian prime minister who engineered the unification of Germany in the 1860s and 1870s by ignoring parliament and provoking a series of advantageous foreign wars. To Degler, Lincoln's determination to coerce the South back into the Union, his shrewd maneuvering at Fort Sumter, and his willingness to suspend northerners' civil liberties during wartime recall Bismarck's famous comment that great national questions are decided by "iron and blood."

As Degler concludes with a glance at Canada, whose federal constitution was adopted in the wake of America's Civil War, you may be left dizzied by the range of his references. But by then the questions he raised along the way should have opened new vistas and fired your imagination. In what sense was the United States an "unfinished nation" before the Civil War? Did the Confederacy possess the materials of a durable national identity? (Certainly you will want to assess Degler's answers to these questions against the theories of nationalism that Peter J. Parish presents in Selection 12.) Was the American hero Lincoln as ruthless a champion of nationalism as Bismarck? Does it necessarily take blood and iron to create a nation that will endure? Degler's stimulating questions and his graceful leaps over time and space illustrate comparative history at its provocative best.

GLOSSARY

BISMARCK, OTTO VON (1815–1898)   The Prussian prime minister and chancellor who masterminded the unification of Germany. He provoked war with Denmark in 1864 over the duchies of Schleswig and Holstein, then defeated Austria in 1866 and formed the North German Confederation, from which Austria was excluded. His ambitions collided with those of Napoleon III of France. Convinced that war was inevitable, Bismarck led France to declare it by editing a dispatch from the Prussian king so as to insult the French. The Franco-Prussian War ended in France's humiliating defeat in 1871, and Bismarck now brought the German states under the Prussian king, who became Emperor William I. As the German empire's first chancellor, Bismarck ruled until 1890 as virtual dictator.

CALHOUN, JOHN C. (1782–1850)   A South Carolina senator and vice president under John Quincy Adams and Andrew Jackson who was an ardent defender of southern agrarianism, slavery, and states' rights. He directed South Carolina's resistance to the Union in the Nullification Crisis of 1832–1833, promoted the extension of slavery into western territories, and defended the South's right to secede.

CAVOUR, CAMILLO (1810–1861)   A premier of Sardinia, a political moderate, and a shrewd realist who became the architect of Italian unification. Through complex maneuvers involving French intervention against Austria and the victories of Garibaldi's army in southern Italy, Cavour arranged for Sardinia's ruling house of Savoy to head the newly proclaimed Kingdom of Italy in 1861.

CRITTENDEN COMPROMISE (1860–1861)   A last-ditch effort to restore the Union after South Carolina's secession and to avert the Civil War. Senator John J. Crittenden of Kentucky proposed a constitutional amendment extending the Missouri Compromise line (36°30′) to California in order to divide free and slave states. Congress, dominated by Republicans after Lincoln's electoral victory, defeated it.

DAVIS, JEFFERSON (1808–1898)   The Democratic senator from Mississippi who, although initially cool to secession, was elected president of the Confederate States of America in 1861. Proud and determined, he was involved in many disputes with Confederate generals. His efforts to centralize authority met strong resistance from the Confederate Congress. Davis fled southward after Lee's surrender, hoping to rally southern civilians and soldiers, but he was captured by Union troops in Georgia in May 1865.

EMANCIPATION PROCLAMATION   The executive order issued by President Lincoln on January 1, 1863, that abolished slavery in remaining Confederate territory — but not in loyal slave states — as an "act of justice" and "a fit and necessary war measure" for suppressing the rebellion. The proclamation's immediate aims were to deplete southern manpower, enhance the Union cause abroad, and clear the way for recruiting black Union soldiers.

FIRE-EATER   A vehement spokesman for southern states' rights and a strong defender of slavery.

FORT SUMTER   The federal fort in the harbor of Charleston, South Carolina, where the Civil War began on April 12, 1861. Seeking to defend federal territory but not to start a war himself, President Lincoln informed Confederates that he would resupply the beleaguered Union garrison but unload no guns or ammunition. As the supply ships approached, Confederates opened fire and forced the Union commander to surrender.

FRANCO-PRUSSIAN WAR (1870–1871)   A war between France and Germany provoked by Bismarck as part of his plan to create a unified German empire. A string of German victories culminated in the Battle of Sedan, where the French emperor Napoleon III was captured. At the war's end, France was forced to pay a huge indemnity and to give up most of Alsace and Lorraine. The German empire was then proclaimed at Versailles.

FRENCH INTERVENTION IN MEXICO   In 1862, the arrival of French troops in Mexico, purportedly to collect debts, but in reality to establish an empire there. Napoleon III convinced the Austrian prince Maximilian to accept the crown as emperor of Mexico. Although supported by French troops and Mexican conservatives, Maximilian was unable to overcome the resistance of Mexican liberals led by Benito Juárez. The French withdrew in 1867, and Maximilian was executed.

FUGITIVE SLAVE LAW   A law, which was part of the Compromise of 1850 engineered in Congress by Henry Clay and Stephen Douglas, that included harsh measures meant to guarantee strict enforcement of the constitutional provision that runaway slaves be returned to their home state. Several northern states resisted the Fugitive Slave Law by passing "personal liberty laws" guaranteeing jury trials for alleged fugitive slaves, or otherwise complicating the law's enforcement.

GARIBALDI, GIUSEPPE (1807–1882)   A charismatic Italian patriot and soldier. Garibaldi took part in two failed republican uprisings in Italy, after which he fled to the Americas. Returning to Italy in 1851, he supported a united Italy under the Sardinian king, Victor Emmanuel. In a spectacular 1860 campaign, his army of one thousand volunteer "red shirts" conquered Sicily and Naples, then ceded them to the newly created Kingdom of Italy.

HABEAS CORPUS, WRIT OF   A court order demanding a court appearance to determine whether someone is being held in custody legally. This is a safeguard against illegal imprisonment guaranteed by the U.S. Constitution. Early in the Civil War, Lincoln suspended the writ of habeas corpus in Maryland and ignored a Supreme Court ruling declaring the act unconstitutional. During the war, Lincoln authorized the arrest of some fourteen thousand dissidents without any prospect for a trial.

JESUIT ORDER   An order of Roman Catholic priests founded in the 1530s by Saint Ignatius of Loyola and especially devoted to the pope. Fervent and highly disciplined, the Jesuits were a major force in the Counter Reformation, in European education, and in missionary work in Asia and the Americas.

JUNKERS   The landowning aristocracy of Prussia, whose traditional power Bismarck crushed and whose members he recruited into the army and government bureaucracy.

KOSSUTH, LOUIS (1802–1894)   A nationalist and a fiery orator who was a leader of the Hungarian Revolution of 1848 against the Austrian empire. He served as president of the new Hungarian republic in 1849, but was forced to resign after Russian troops intervened to help Austria. Thereafter, he went into exile, which included a much-publicized tour of the United States in 1851–1852.

MEIJI RESTORATION   In 1868, the surrendering of power to the young emperor Meiji (1852–1912) by the Japanese shogun (military dictator) after agitation by samurai warriors and nobles demanding a new government and stronger resistance to foreign economic powers. The restoration brought the downfall of feudalism, the establishment of a centralized administration, and the rise of westernizing leaders who made Japan a modern industrial state within a generation.

NULLIFICATION CRISIS   A constitutional crisis of 1832–1833 that began when South Carolina, led by John C. Calhoun, declared a federal tariff unconstitutional and thus null and void within its borders. President Jackson threatened force but later signed a compromise tariff bill passed by Congress, and South Carolina rescinded its nullification ordinance. Nullification was a forerunner of the doctrine of secession that brought the Civil War.

RHETT, ROBERT BARNWELL (1800–1876)   A U.S. representative and then senator from South Carolina. Rhett was a disciple of states' rights advocate John C. Calhoun. He became known as the "father of secession" for his early and uncompromising advocacy of an independent South.

RISORGIMENTO   The period of cultural nationalism and political activism in the nineteenth century that led to the unification of Italy.

SONDERBUND   The short-lived separatist confederacy of 1847 in Switzerland composed of three predominantly Catholic cantons.

TELL, WILLIAM   The legendary Swiss hero who allegedly led a Swiss revolt against the Austrians in 1308.

WATERLOO   The battle fought near Brussels, Belgium, in 1815 in which British and Prussian forces routed Napoleon's army, resulting in the French emperor's abdication and the end of the Napoleonic Wars.

YANCEY, WILLIAM L. (1814–1863)   A congressman from Alabama who was a leading proslavery "fire-eater" and an early advocate of secession. He later served in the Confederate Senate.

★ ★ ★ ★ ★ ★ ★

More than a century ago, between the years 1845 and 1870, the world witnessed a widespread efflorescence of nation-building, in the midst of which was the American Civil War. Some of those instances of people's seeking national identity and statehood remind us of the Confederacy inasmuch as they failed to achieve independence. The revolt of the Hungarians against their Austrian masters in 1848 under the leadership of Louis Kossuth was one such failure, though within two decades Hungarian nationalism achieved a kind of acknowledgment of national identity in the dual empire of Austria-Hungary. A more crushing failure was the experience of the Poles who rose in 1863 against their Russian rulers, at the very same time that the United States was struggling to suppress its own uprising in the South. Contrary to the Confederacy's fate, the Polish defeat would be reversed at the end of the First World War.

"One Among Many: The United States and National Unification," by Carl N. Degler, from *Lincoln the War President: The Gettysburg Lectures,* edited by Gabor S. Boritt, copyright © 1992, 1994 by Gabor S. Boritt. Used by permission of Oxford University Press.

Other instances of nation-building achieved their aims. In 1847 the Swiss cantons concluded their war for a Union under a new federal constitution and with a fresh and enduring sense of nationality. In 1860, Camillo Cavour of the kingdom of Sardinia with the assistance of France and the military help of Giuseppe Garibaldi brought into being the first united Italy since the days of ancient Rome. During that same decade of the 1860s a united Germany came into existence for the first time as well. Nor were the nationalist outbursts of that quarter-century confined to Europe. They also erupted in Asia, where a new Japan emerged in the course of the Meiji Restoration, in which feudal power was forever subordinated to a centralized state that deliberately modeled itself after the nation-states of Europe.

Looking at the American Civil War in the context of contemporary efforts to establish national identity has the advantage of moving us beyond the often complacent concern with ourselves that I sometimes fear is the bane of United States historians. The Civil War is undoubtedly a peculiarly American event, one central to our national experience. In its endurance, the magnitude of its killing, and the immense extent of its arena it easily dwarfs any other nationalist struggle of its century. Yet if we recognize its similarity to other examples of nation-building of that time we may obtain fresh insights into its character and its meaning, then and now.

First of all, let me clear the ground by narrowing our comparisons. Although the European and Asian instances of nation-building in the years between 1845 and 1870 are comparable to the American experience in that they all involve the creation or the attempt to create a national state, not all of them are comparable on more than that general level. The Meiji Restoration, for example, was certainly the beginning of the modern Japanese state but the analogy stops there since it did not involve a military struggle. The Polish and Hungarian national uprisings bear closer comparison to the Confederate strike for independence, but the differences in nationality between the oppressors and the oppressed (Austrians versus Hungarians; Russians against Poles) render dubious any further analogy to the Confederacy. After all, both the Hungarians and the Poles had been conquered by foreigners; each enjoyed a national history that stretched deep into the past, something totally missing from the South's urge to separate from the United States.

The Italian experience in nation-building comes closer to the North's effort to preserve the Union. A united Italy did emerge eventually from the wars of the Risorgimento and Garibaldi's conquests of Sicily and the Kingdom of Naples. Pertinent, too, is that Garibaldi, as an internationally recognized hero of Italian unification, was entreated by the Lincoln Administration to become a leading officer in the Union army. Yet, neither event offers much basis for comparison. The unification of all of Italy was, as English statesman William Gladstone remarked, "among the greatest marvels of our time," and simultaneously a kind of accident.

It was a marvel because Italy's diversity in economy, language, culture, and society between North and South and among the various states into which the peninsula had been divided for centuries made unification seem most unlikely. Cavour, who is generally considered the architect of Italian unification, came late to the idea of uniting even northern Italy much less the whole peninsula. That he always wrote in French because his Italian was so bad further illustrates the marvelous character of Italian unification. That the whole of the peninsula was united at all resulted principally from the accident of Giuseppe Garibaldi and his famous Thousand. Cavour had tried vigorously to prevent the irrepressible Genovese from invading Sicily only to have Garibaldi within a matter of months present Cavour's own King Victor Emmanuel of Sardinia with not only Sicily, but the Kingdom of Naples as well. Historian Denis Mack Smith has suggested that the limited energy expended in achieving the Kingdom of Italy is measured in the statistic that more people died in a single day of the Franco-Prussian War than died in all of the twenty-five years of military campaigns to unify Italy. In that story there is little to remind us of the crisis of the American Union.

Can a better analogy be drawn between our war for the Union and the story of German unification? When Otto von Bismarck in 1871 finally brought together into a single nation the heretofore independent states of Germany a new country was thereby brought into existence. The United States, on the other hand, had come into existence almost a century earlier. In 1861 it could hardly be counted as a fledgling state on a par with the newly created German Empire. To make that observation, however, is to read the present back into the past, that is, to assume that the Union of 1787 had created a nation. That, to be sure, . . . is the way in which many of us envision the Union, for which a war was necessary in order to excise the cancer of slavery threatening its survival. The unexpressed assumption here is that a *nation* had been endangered, that a sense of true nationhood already embraced the geographical area known as the United States. It was . . . the assumption from which Abraham Lincoln operated. That is why . . . Lincoln, unlike many other American political figures of his time, . . . never predicted a war over the Union. A nation does not go to war with itself.

Lincoln's view, however, was not that held by many people of the time, and especially not by Southerners. Suppose we look, then, at the era of the Civil War from the standpoint of the South, and not from the standpoint of him who conquered the region, and denied its essential difference from the rest of the United States. Southerners, it is true, unlike Poles or Hungarians, had originally agreed to join the Union; they were neither conquered nor coerced and they shared a common language, ethnicity, and history. Indeed, the South's sons were among those who drafted the Constitution of the Union, headed the resulting government, and even came to dominate it. Yet, as the early history of the country soon demonstrated, that Union was just a union of states, and not a nation in any organic sense. Paul Nagel in his study of the concept of Union points out that in the first twenty-five years of the country's existence the Union was generally seen as an experiment rather than as an enduring polity. It was, he observes, more a means to achieve nationhood than a nation itself.

Certainly the early history of the country reflects that conception of the Union. Within ten years of the founding of the new government one of the architects of the Revolution and an official of the administration, Thomas Jefferson, boldly asserted a state's right to nullify an oppressive act of Congress. Five years later those who objected to the acquisition of Louisiana talked openly of secession from the Union as a remedy for their discontent, and within another fifteen years even louder suggestions for getting out of the Union came in the course of the war against England. The most striking challenge to the permanence of the Union, of course, came not from New England, but from the South, from South Carolina in particular, during the nullification crisis of 1828–33. Just about that time, Alexis de Tocqueville recognized that if the Union was intended to "form one and the same people," few people accepted that view. "The whole structure of the government," he reported, "is artificial," rather than organic. It is true that in 1832 South Carolina stood alone, that not a single state of the South supported its defense of nullification, and some states, like Mississippi, actually branded nullification as naked revolution. But as Tocqueville had implied, that attitude began to change among Southerners as they recognized that their prosperity, racial security, and, in time, their very identity increasingly rested upon slavery. . . .

It is easy in retrospect to deny the existence of a true sense of national identity among Southerners before 1860, or by 1865. . . . For we know that once the war was over, that sense of difference among Southerners diminished precipitously — only a handful of Confederates found it necessary to leave the country after Appomattox. At one time historians described nationalism as an organic, almost naturally emerging feeling among a people. In time, it was contended, the feeling or sentiment reached sufficient strength to bring into existence a political framework that united power and feeling in a nation-state. Today, historians are more likely to see nationalism as a process, in the course of which flesh and blood leaders and followers creatively mold and integrate ideas, events, and power to bring a nation into being. That is what happened in the South during the years between nullification in 1832 and Sumter in 1861.

To bring nationalism into being, its proponents need materials to work with, events and personages around which to build and through which to sustain their incipient nationhood. For Southerners the underlying source of that nationalism, of course, was slavery, the wealth-producing capacity of which fixed the South as a region of agriculture and rurality at the very time that the North and West were increasingly diversifying their agriculture with trade, industry, and cities. Slavery, however, was more than a labor system; by the middle years of the nineteenth century, it had become a source of deep political and moral division in the country. . . .

Along with slavery as a source of Southern nationalism went social and economic differences, which, together with the election of an antislavery president, helped to convince many Southerners by 1860 that the Union they had joined in 1787 was not the Union in which they then found themselves. Not only had all the states at the time of the Revolution accepted slavery, but they had all been agricultural in economy, and rural in society as well as proud of their republican ideology that had been fashioned in the course of their joint revolt against Britain's central authority. It did not escape Southerners' attention that the American nationalism being fostered by the expanding urban and industrial economy of the North did not include them or their region. As a Texas politician told the correspondent of the London *Times* in early 1861, "We are an agricultural people. . . . We have no cities — we don't want them. . . . We want no manufactures; we desire no trading, no mechanical or manufacturing classes. . . . As long as we have our rice, our sugar, our tobacco, and our cotton, we can command wealth to purchase all we want." The South's prosperity, which slavery and the plantation had generated, only deepened the divisions between the regions and sharpened the recognition that Northerners were not like Southerners, that the South was a different place, that Southerners were strangers in the house of their fathers. As historian Allan Nevins later wrote, "South and North by 1857 were rapidly becoming separate peoples. With every passing year, the fundamental assumptions, tastes, and cultural aims of the sections became more divergent." . . .

This recognition of the Union's transformation since its founding is plainly reflected in Confederates' frequent insistence that their cause was but a rerun of the Revolution against England. It is surely no coincidence that February 22 and July 4 were official holidays of the Confederacy or that Jefferson Davis was inaugurated on Washington's birthday. In both 1776 and 1860, objections to political impositions by the dominant power were prominent, but an equally powerful source of the two revolutions was a sense of being alien, of being an outsider, a perception that independence would remove.

The existence of Southern nationalism, even the attenuated variety that I am asserting here, is admittedly not a settled issue among historians. Indeed, I suspect that most historians . . . think of its assertion in the late 1850s as a subterfuge, almost a trick played upon the mass of Southerners by a relatively few so-called Southern "fireaters" like [William] Yancey and [Robert Barnwell] Rhett. And certainly there were many men and women in the South in 1860 who spoke of themselves as Unionists. Lincoln, too, along with many other Republicans, thought Southern alienation from the North was but a ploy to gain concessions. Yet, despite such widely held doubts, in 1861 eleven Southern states withdrew from the Union and then proceeded to fight the bloodiest war of the nineteenth century to defend that decision. The proportion of Southerners who died in that struggle far exceeded that experienced by Americans in any other war and was exceeded during the Second World War only by the losses sustained by Germans and Russians. That straightforward quantitative fact, I think, provides the most compelling response to . . . doubts that Southerners were committed to winning.

We call the struggle the Civil War, some Southerners who accepted the Southern view of the Constitution, call it the War Between the States, and officially it is the War of the Rebellion. But it was, of course, really the War for Southern Independence, in much the same league, if for different historical reasons, as Poland's and Hungary's wars of national liberation around the same time. We know, too, that the South's determined struggle revealed how wrong Lincoln had been to believe in a broad and deep sense of Unionism among Southerners.

European observers of the time well recognized the incomplete nature of American nationalism, if Lincoln did not. William Gladstone, the English Chancellor of the Exchequer in 1862, could not conceal his conviction, as he phrased it, that "Jefferson Davis and other leaders of the South have made an army; they are making, it appears, a navy; and they have made what is more than either, they have made a nation." Soon after the war the great liberal historian Lord Acton, in a letter to Robert E. Lee, explained why he had welcomed the Confederacy. "I saw in State Rights," Acton wrote, "the only availing check upon the absolutism of the sovereign will, and secession filled me with hope, not as the destruction but as the redemption of Democracy. . . . I deemed that you were fighting the battles of our liberty, our progress, and our civilization; and I mourn the stake which was lost at Richmond more deeply than I rejoice over that which was saved at Waterloo."

In short, when the South seceded in 1860–61 that fact measured not only the failure of the Union, but, more important, the incomplete character of American nationalism. Or as historian Erich Angermann has reminded us, the United States in 1861, despite the Union of 1787, was still an "unfinished nation" in much the same way as were Italy and Germany.

True, a deep sense of nationhood existed among Americans, but it was confined largely to the North. Indeed, to acknowledge that nationalism is probably the soundest way to account for the remarkable explosion of popular support that greeted Lincoln's call for volunteers to enforce the laws in the South after the fall of Sumter. When we recognize that in 1860 only a truncated nationalism existed among Americans despite the eighty-year history of the Union, then the American Civil War suddenly fits well into a comparison with other nation-building efforts of those years. The Civil War, in short, was not a struggle to save a failed Union, but to create a nation that until then had not come into being. For, in Hegel's elegant phrase "the owl of Minerva flies at dusk," historical understanding is fullest at the moment of death. International comparison throws into relief the creative character of war in the making of nations, or, in the case of the Confederacy, in the aborting of nations.

For one thing, all of the struggles for national unification in Europe, as in the United States, required military power to bring the nation into existence and to arm it with state power. This was true not only of Italy and Germany, but of Switzerland as well, as I hope to show a little later. As Ernest Renan wrote in his 1882 essay "What Is a Nation?," "Unity is always realized by brute force. The union of North and South in France," he pointed out, "was the result of a reign of terror and extermination carried on for nearly a century" in the late Middle Ages. "Deeds of violence . . . have marked the origin of all political formations," he insisted, "even of those which have been followed by the most beneficial results."

The Italian wars of national unity may not present much of an analogy with the American war, but the course of German unification is revealing. Everyone is familiar with the role of the Franco-Prussian war in the achievement of the unification of Germany in 1871. Equally relevant for an appreciation of the American Civil War as struggle for nationhood was the Seven Weeks War between Austria and Prussia, which preceded the war with France and which culminated in Prussia's great military victory at Königgrätz or Sadowa in 1866. That war marked the culmination of Bismarck's determined efforts to exclude Austria from any united Germany in order that Prussia would be both the center and the head. By defeating Austria and creating the North German Confederation under the leadership of Prussia, Bismarck concluded what many observers at the time and historians since have referred to as a *Bruderkrieg,* a German civil war. For it was neither foreordained by history nor by the power relations among the states of central Europe that a *Kleindeutschland* or lesser Germany from which Austria was excluded would prevail over a *Grossdeutschland* or greater Germany in which Austria would be the equal or even the superior of Prussia.

At that stage in the evolution of German nationhood, the closest analogy to the American experience puts Prussia in the position of the Southern Confederacy, for it was in effect seeking to secede from the German Confederation, created at the time of the Congress of Vienna and headed by Austria. Just as Bismarck had provoked Austria into war to achieve his end, so Jefferson Davis and the South were prepared to wage war against their long-time rival for control of the North American Union.

Despite the tempting analogy, however, Jefferson Davis was no Bismarck. His excessive constitutional scruples during the short life of the Confederacy make that crystal clear. (If anything Bismarck was just the opposite: slippery in regard to any constitution with which he came into contact.) Davis's rival for domination of the North American continent — Abraham Lincoln — came considerably closer to Bismarck, including the Bismarck who by his innovative actions within the North German Confederation had laid the foundations of German industrialization.

Historians of the United States have not liked comparing Bismarck and Lincoln. As historian David Potter once wrote, "the Gettysburg Address would have been as foreign to Bismarck as a policy of 'blood and iron' would have been to Lincoln." It is certainly true that the Gettysburg Address could not have been a policy statement from Bismarck, though he boldly introduced universal manhood suffrage and the secret ballot in the new Germany, much to the horror of his conservative friends and to the consternation of his liberal opponents. And it is equally true that the Junker aristocratic heritage and outlook of the mature Bismarck stands in sharp contrast to the simple origins and democratic beliefs of Abraham Lincoln. But if we return to seeing the war and Lincoln's actions at the time from the standpoint of the South then the similarities become clearer. Once we recognize the South's disenchantment with the transformation in the Union of its fathers and its incipient nationalism, which slavery had sparked, we gain an appreciation of the incomplete nature of American nationalism. Lincoln then emerges as the true creator of American nationalism, rather than as the mere savior of the Union.

Given the immense carnage of the Civil War, not to mention the widespread use of iron in ordnance and railroads, that struggle in behalf of American nationality can hardly escape being described literally as the result of a policy of blood and iron. The phrase fits metaphorically almost as well. Reflect on Lincoln's willingness to risk war in 1861 rather than compromise over the issue of slavery in the territories. "The tug has to come, and better now, than anytime hereafter," he advised his fellow Republicans when the Crittenden compromise was before Congress. . . . Lincoln was determined to call what he considered the South's bluff, its frequent threat over the years to secede in order to extract one more concession to ensure the endurance of slavery. Convinced of the successful achievement of American nationhood, he counted on the mass of Southerners to rally around the national identity, only to find that it was largely absent in the region of his birth. Only military power kept even his native state within the confines of his nation. Bismarck had to employ no such massive power to bring the states of south Germany into his new Reich in 1870–71. Rather, their sense of a unified Germany bred over a quarter-century of common action brought Catholic Bavaria, Württemberg, and Baden immediately to Protestant Prussia's side when France declared war in 1870.

But then, unlike Bismarck, Lincoln was seeking to bring into being a nation that had lost whatever sense of cohesion its Union of 1787 may have nurtured. His task was more demanding and the means needed to achieve the goal were, for that reason, harsher, more deadly, and more persistently pressed than the creation of a new Germany demanded of Bismarck. Lincoln's commitment to nationhood rather than simply to the Union comes through quite clearly in an observation by James McPherson. In his First Inaugural, Lincoln used the word "Union" twenty times: "nation" appears not at all. (That description of the United States, of course, had long been anathema to the South.) Once the South had seceded, however, the dread word began to appear in his texts: three times in his first message to Congress. By the time of the Gettysburg Address, the term "Union" appeared not at all, while "nation" was mentioned five times. In his Second Inaugural, Lincoln used Union only to describe the South's actions in disrupting the Union in 1861; he described the war as having saved the "Nation," not simply the Union.

In deeds as well as in words, Lincoln came closer than Jefferson Davis to Bismarck. There is nothing in Lincoln's record that is comparable to Bismarck's famous "Ems dispatch" in which he deliberately edited a report on the Prussian king's reaction to a demand from the French government in such a way as to provoke the French declaration of war that Bismarck needed in order to bring the south German states into his unified Germany. Over the years, the dispute among United States historians whether Lincoln maneuvered the South into firing the first shot of the Civil War, has not reached the negative interpretation that clings to Bismarck's Ems dispatch. Yet Lincoln's delay in settling the issue of Sumter undoubtedly exerted great pressure upon the Confederates to fire first. To that extent his actions display some of the earmarks of Bismarck's maneuvering in 1870. For at the same time Lincoln was holding off from supplying Sumter he was firmly rejecting the advice of his chief military adviser, Winfield Scott, that surrendering the fort was better than provoking the Confederates into beginning a war. Lincoln's nationalism needed a war, but one that the other side would begin.

The way in which Lincoln fought the war also reminds us at times of Bismarck's willingness to use iron, as well as shed blood, in order to build a nation. Throughout the war Lincoln denied that secession was a legal remedy for the South, yet his own adherence to constitutional limits was hardly flawless. If Bismarck in 1862 in behalf of his king's prerogative interpreted parliamentary government out of existence in Prussia for four years, Lincoln's interpretation of the American Constitution followed a similar, if somewhat less drastic path. As Lincoln scholar James G. Randall remarked years ago, Lincoln employed "more arbitrary power than perhaps any other President. . . . Probably no President has carried the power of proclamation and executive order (independently of Congress) as far as did Lincoln." Randall then proceeded to list those uses of power: freeing slaves, accepting the dismemberment of Virginia by dubious constitutional means, providing for the reconstruction of states lately in rebellion, suspending the writ of habeas corpus, proclaiming martial law, and enlarging the army and the navy and spending public money without the necessary Congressional approval. "Some of his important measures," Randall points out, "were taken under the consciousness that they belonged within the domain of Congress. The national legislature was merely permitted," Randall continues, "to ratify his measures, or else to adopt the futile alternative of refusing consent to accomplished fact." Lincoln himself justified his Emancipation Proclamation on the quite questionable ground "that measures otherwise unconstitutional might become lawful by becoming indispensable to the preservation of the Constitution through the preservation of the nation."

That slavery was the spring and the river from which Southern nationalism flowed virtually dictated in Lincoln's mind that it must be extirpated for nationalist as well as humanitarian reasons. For many other Northern nationalists the fundamental role slavery had played in the creation of Southern nationalism must have been a prime reason for accepting its eradication. Few of them, after all, had been enemies of slavery in the South, much less friends of black people. Indeed, hostility to blacks on grounds of race in the 1860s was almost as prevalent in the North as in the South.

What the war represented, in the end, was the forceful incorporation of a recalcitrant South into a newly created nation. Indeed, that was exactly what abolitionist Wendell Phillips had feared at the outset. "A Union," he remarked in a public address in New York in 1860, "is made up of willing States. . . . A husband or wife who can only keep the other partner within the bond by locking the doors and standing armed before them, had better submit to peaceable separation." The United States, he continued, is not like other countries. "Homogeneous nations like France tend to centralization; confederations like ours tend inevitably to dismemberment."

A similar objection to union by force had been advanced by none other than that old nationalist John Quincy Adams. "If the day should ever come (may Heaven avert it)," he told an audience celebrating the jubilee of the Constitution in 1839, "when the affections of the people of these states shall be alienated from each other; when the fraternal spirit shall give away to cold indifference . . . far better will it be for the people of the disunited states, to part in friendship from each other, than to be held together by constraint." In Lincoln's mind, it was to be a stronger and more forceful nation, one which would mark a new era in the history of American nationality, just as Bismarck's proclamation of the new German Empire in the Hall of Mirrors at Versailles in January, 1871, constituted both the achievement of German unity and the opening of a new chapter in the history of German nationality.

The meaning of the new American nationhood as far as the South was concerned was its transformation, the rooting out of those elements that had set it apart from Northern nationalism. In the context of nation-building the era of Reconstruction can best be seen as the eradication of those aspects of the South that had lain at the root of the region's challenge to the creation of a nation. That meant ridding the South not only of slavery, but also of its undemocratic politics, its conservative social practices, its excessive dependence upon agriculture, and any other habits that might prevent the region from being as modern and progressive as the North.

Nowhere does this new nationalism appear in more strident form than in an essay by Senator Charles Sumner deceptively entitled "Are We a Nation?". The title was deceptive because there was no doubt in Sumner's mind that the United States was indeed a nation, and had always been. The essay was first given as a lecture in New York on the fourth anniversary of Lincoln's delivery of the address at Gettysburg. Sumner was pleased to recall Lincoln's reference to "a new nation" on that previous occasion, causing Sumner to remark that "if among us in the earlier day there was no occasion for the Nation, there is now. A Nation is born," he proudly proclaimed. That new nation, he contended, was one in behalf of human rights, by which he meant the rights of blacks, which the South must now accept and protect.

Interestingly enough, in the course of his discussion of nationhood, Sumner instanced Germany as a place where nationhood had not yet been achieved. "God grant that the day may soon dawn when all Germany shall be one," he exclaimed. In 1867 he could not know what we know today: that the defeat of Austria at Königgrätz the year before had already fashioned the character and future of German unity under Bismarck.

No single European effort at creating a new sense of nationhood comes as close to that of the United States as Switzerland's. Although the Swiss Confederation, which came into existence at the end of the Napoleonic era, lacked some of the nationalist elements of the American Constitution, it constituted, like the United States, a union of small states called cantons, which, again like the states of the American Union, had once been independent entities. And as was the case in the American Union, the cantons of the Swiss Confederation were separated by more than mountainous terrain. The role that slavery played in dividing the United States was filled among the Swiss by religion. The Catholic cantons of Uri, Schwyz, and Unterwalden had been the original founders of the confederation in the days of William Tell, while the Protestant cantons were not only the more recent, but more important, the cantons in which the liberal economic and social ideas and forces that were then reshaping European society had made the most headway.

Among the intellectual consequences of that modernity was a growing secularism, which expressed itself in 1841 in the suppression of all religious orders by the Protestant canton of Aargau. The action was a clear violation of the Federal Pact of 1815, but none of the Protestant cantons objected to it. The Catholic cantons, however, led by Lucerne, vehemently protested the overriding of their ancient rights. In this objection there is a striking parallel with the South's protest against the North's attacks on slavery and refusal to uphold the fugitive slave law; both slavery and a fugitive slave law, of course, were embedded in the original United States Constitution.

The Catholic cantons' response to the violation of the Confederation's constitution was that Lucerne then invited the Jesuit Order to run its schools, much to the distaste of the Protestants in Lucerne and the Protestant cantons in general. Some of the Lucerne liberals then set about to organize armed vigilantes or *Freischaren* to overthrow the governments in the Catholic cantons. The American analogy for these military actions that leaps to mind, of course, is "bloody Kansas" [where armed "free-stater" and proslavery groups fought over the expansion of slavery in 1856]. Nor was the guerrilla violence in Switzerland any less deadly than that in Kansas. When the canton government of Lucerne sentenced a captured *Freischar* to death, a group of his supporters invaded the canton and triumphantly carried him off to Protestant Zürich. More than one hundred died in the escapade.

Like "Bloody Kansas," the guerrilla phase of the Swiss conflict between old (Catholic) and new (Protestant) cantons deepened a sense of alienation between the two contending parties, which, in turn, led, almost naturally, to a move for separation from the Confederation. In December, 1845, seven Catholic cantons, including, interestingly enough, the three founding cantons of ancient Switzerland, formed what came to be called the *Sonderbund* or separatist confederation. Unlike the Southern states in 1860–61, the cantons of the *Sonderbund* did not proclaim secession, though they clearly saw themselves as resisting violations of traditional constitutional rights. Indeed, under the rules of the Swiss Confederation regional agreements among cantons were permissible, but the army the *Sonderbund* cantons brought into being, and the public stands they announced, strongly suggested to the rest of Switzerland that secession was indeed their intention. And so in July, 1847, the Diet [legislature] of the Confederation ordered the *Sonderbund* to dissolve, an act that precipitated the departure of the delegates of the *Sonderbund* cantons. Again, like the Confederacy, the *Sonderbund* sought foreign support (particularly from Catholic and conservative Austria), but it was no more successful in that respect than the Confederacy. In early November the Diet voted to use force against the *Sonderbund;* civil war was the result.

Although each side mustered 30,000 or more troops under its command, the war was brief and light in cost; it lasted no more than three weeks and fewer than 130 men lost their lives. The victory of the Confederation's forces resulted in the rewriting of the constitutional relations among the cantons. The new national government was to be a truly federal republic deliberately modeled after that set forth in the Constitution of the United States. The immediate postwar era in Switzerland exhibited little of the conflict that we associate with the Reconstruction era. But then, the Swiss civil war was short and if not sweet, at least not very bloody. Yet there, too, as in the United States, the winners deemed it essential to extirpate those institutions that had been at the root of the disruption of the Confederation. Before the cantons of the *Sonderbund* were accepted back into the Confederation they were compelled to accede to barring the Jesuit Order from all the cantons. The acceptance of the Order into Lucerne had been, after all, a major source of the cantonal conflicts that led to the civil war. A measure of the depth of the religious issue in the Swiss conflict is that almost a century and a half passed before the Jesuit Order was readmitted to Switzerland. And in that context it is perhaps worth remembering that a century passed before a president of the United States — Lyndon B. Johnson — could be elected from a state of the former Confederacy.

As happened with the Civil War in the United States, the *Sonderbundkrieg* — the war of the Separatist Confederation — marked the long-term achievement of nationhood. So settled now was the matter of Swiss national identity that when Europe erupted in 1848 in wars of national liberation and revolution, the new Swiss Federation, the embodiment of Swiss nationality, escaped entirely from the upheaval. No longer was there any question that Switzerland was a nation; just as after 1865 there could be no doubt that the United States was a nation. In both instances, war had settled the matter for good.

Finally, there remains yet one more comparison between America's achievement of nationhood through war and the unification of Germany. Contemporaries in 1871 and historians since often saw the creation of the *Kaiserreich* [the German Empire] something less than a comforting transformation of the European international scene. It is true that the new Empire did not include all European Germans within its confines. That is why Bismarck was seen as a *Kleindeutscher*. But never before had so many Germans been gathered within a single state and especially one with a highly trained and efficient army, as the quick defeat of Austria in 1866 and of France in 1870 forced everyone to recognize. The military presence of Prussia under Frederick the Great, once so formidable in central Europe, was easily surpassed by the new empire of his Hohenzollern descendants. It was an empire whose power would soon challenge its neighbors and the peace of Europe, despite Bismarck's original aim of hegemony without more war.

If nationhood through the agency of war meant a Germany of new power and potential danger to others, the achievement of nationhood by the United States during its civil war carried with it some strikingly similar aspects. Out of the war, the United States emerged, not only a nation, but also by far the strongest military force in the world of the time. But with the United States, as with the new German empire, military might was not the only source of a new tone in relations with other states. Nationhood brought a new self-confidence, even self-assertion, that ignited the apprehensions of neighbors. Even before its mighty victory over the South, the United States had been perceived in Europe as a rambunctious, even irresponsible Republic, challenging when not overtly rejecting the traditional ways of Europe and of international relations. As a European power, the new German empire aroused the fears of Europeans as the enhanced power of the United States, being separated from Europe by the Atlantic, never could. But those European powers which had interests in the New World soon found that the enlarged authority of the United States could well spell danger.

The first to sense it were the French, who had presumed to meddle in the internal affairs of Mexico while the United States had been preoccupied with suppressing the division within its own borders. The defeat of the Confederacy allowed the triumphant United States to turn upon the French for threatening American hegemony in the New World, a threat that never needed to be implemented since the Mexican forces themselves soon routed the meddling French. As far as the southern neighbor was concerned, the achievement of nationhood by the United States could be seen, temporarily, at least, as supportive rather than threatening.

For the neighbor to the north, the story was rather different. Ever since their founding revolution in 1776, Americans have thought that the most natural thing in the world would be for the English-speaking people to the north to join the United States. Though most Canadians, then as now, have rejected annexation, some Canadians have always thought it was natural and inevitable. The threat of annexation reached a new height during the Civil War, especially after some Confederate agents managed to mount a successful military raid from Canada against St. Albans, Vermont. The outrage expressed by the government in Washington, coupled with new talk of annexation aroused both Canadian nationalists and British statesmen to seek ways to counter Canada's vulnerability to the power of the newly emboldened American nation.

In the age of the American Civil War, the country known today as Canada, was a collection of diverse governmental and even private units, some of which were self-governing, but all of which were parts of the British Empire. The move to create a united Canada was spawned not only by a fear of annexation by the United States, but by an even more compelling insight from the American Civil War. It was the lesson that a vaguely defined federal system such as that of the United States could end up in civil war. The upshot was that the federal constitution drawn up in 1867 (technically known as the North America Act) to unite all of Canada under one government, placed all residual powers in the hands of the national government, a lesson derived from the perceived result in the United States of leaving to the states those powers not specifically granted to the federal government. As historian Robin Winks has remarked, "In effect the war had helped create not one but two nations."

But was the Canadian union established in 1867 a nation? Winks uses that term, but is it a nation in the organic sense that we have been talking about here? Listen to his own summary description of Canadian nationhood: "Born in fear, deadlock, and confusion, Canada grew into a nation that could not afford to exhibit the rampant nationalism usually associated with young countries, and even today [that is, in 1960], due to her mother, the nature of gestation, and the continuing pressures from her large, pragmatic and restless neighbor, Canada remains a nation in search of a national culture."

Canada, of course, was one of these countries that between 1845 and 1870 struggled to achieve a truly national identity. Does the Canadian example offer any further insight into the meaning of that era of nation-building in general or of Lincoln's nation-building in particular? The Canadian experience, I think, puts the cap on the argument I have been making throughout these remarks. . . .

. . . The Canadian union of 1867 is still jeopardized by ethnic and other differences, despite the efforts by some leading Quebeckers to smooth over the divergences between French-speaking and English-speaking Canadians. How then does the German or the Swiss, or the American road to nationhood differ from that of the Canadians? Obviously there are a number of cultural and historical differences, but one that grabs our attention in this comparison is that only Canada failed to experience a war of national unification. During the nullification crisis in 1832 John Quincy Adams remarked to Henry Clay that "It is the odious nature of the [Union] that it can be settled only at the cannon's mouth." But as Lincoln recognized and Ernest Renan reminded us, it was a nation, not merely a Union, that blood and iron brought into existence.

QUESTIONS TO CONSIDER

1. In what sense were southerners a "separate people" from other Americans? In what ways, according to Degler, were the North and South growing further apart? Does Degler think that the South possessed the materials of a viable nationalism? After reviewing the essay on American nationalism by Peter J. Parish (Selection 12), do you

think that Parish would agree that the United States was "an unfinished nation" before the Civil War? Do the theories of nationalism Parish presents support or refute the idea that the Confederacy was a good prospect for nationhood? Do you agree?

2. Compare Abraham Lincoln with Otto von Bismarck as national unifiers. How, according to Degler, did Lincoln pursue a policy of "blood and iron"? What differences do you see in their beliefs and actions? In what sense was Lincoln "the true creator of American nationalism, rather than the mere savior of the Union"?

3. What similarities does Degler see between the Swiss Confederation's war against the *Sonderbund* in 1847 and the American Civil War? How does the fact that the Swiss civil war was "short and . . . not very bloody" affect the analogy?

4. In what way was the nation of Canada a by-product of the American Civil War? How, according to Degler, is Canadian nationalism different from that of the United States?

5. Do American and world history support Degler's implied conclusion that the most binding kind of national unity is achieved by military force?

Why the Confederacy Lost

BRIAN HOLDEN REID AND BRUCE COLLINS

It is tempting to attribute the North's victory in the Civil War to its overwhelming superiority in manpower and resources. A lopsided numerical advantage in soldiers, railroads, ships, factories, guns, and money made the Union's triumph almost inevitable — at least according to Napoleon's aphorism that God is on the side of the heaviest battalions. But the Confederacy had advantages, too, less easily quantifiable but just as important: excellent generals and soldiers, high morale and clear war aims, the possibility of foreign intervention, and the need to fight only a defensive war rather than one of conquest and occupation. In fact, the Confederacy was in some ways in a better position to win independence than the frail and divided American colonies had been in 1776. Why, then, did it fail?

In this selection, historians Brian Holden Reid and Bruce Collins conduct a spirited debate on the causes of Confederate defeat in essays that originally appeared side by side in the popular magazine History Today. *Brian Holden Reid contends that southerners ultimately lacked the will to win the war. The Confederates, he claims, were revolutionaries who failed to take the drastic steps necessary to win their revolution, especially by resorting to guerrilla warfare to prolong the conflict and wear out the North. Pursuing an analogy to the South African Boer War of 1899–1902, in which a fighting force of some sixty thousand Afrikaners held a huge British imperial army at bay by using guerrilla tactics, Reid claims that southerners' reluctance to continue the fight in 1865 ultimately stemmed from their recognition that "Confederate nationalism was a fragile reed." Southerners were not nearly as different from other Americans as the Boers were from the British, and because they shared much with their Yankee brothers and sisters, they lacked the "rather-die-than-surrender" passion that wins revolutions.*

Bruce Collins, on the other hand, is impressed by how long and hard the Confederates resisted the superior Union forces that by 1864 were wreaking havoc on the South's land and economy. Like Reid, he finds analogies to the Boer War revealing, but Collins argues that southerners' traditional military training and their fear of anarchy on the plantations made guerrilla warfare unthinkable. Instead, Robert E. Lee's surrender at Appomattox Courthouse in April 1865 was a rational response to the increasingly devastating Union military victories. And like the Boers' laying down of arms, it also represented a shrewd gamble that the seceders' objectives might be achieved peacefully in the postwar political settlement.

Some background on the Boer War may help you assess the usefulness of each writer's comparative references. Recall from George M. Fredrickson's essay in Selection 15 that a segment of whites from the Dutch-speaking Cape Colony of South Africa gained freedom from British rule by trekking eastward to establish independent republics, the Orange Free State and the Transvaal, by the 1850s. These Boers (or Afrikaners) resisted British takeover attempts in the following decades. But Britain's desire to control the region's wealth — gold was discovered in the Transvaal in 1886 — and the Boers' refusal to enfranchise British immigrants working in the mines led to full-scale war in 1899. The fighting was fierce, and although it was billed as a "white man's war," both sides forcibly enlisted thousands of black soldiers. The Boers won early victories, but the tide turned in 1900 with the landing of heavy British reinforcements led by F. S. Roberts and Lord Kitchener. Outmanned but determined, the Boers resorted to guerrilla attacks. Kitchener responded by interning Afrikaners and blacks in "concentration camps," where more than thirty thousand died, and then combing the countryside for guerrilla outposts. When they finally agreed to surrender in 1902, the Boers accepted British sovereignty. Yet at the decade's end when the British created the Union of South Africa, they conceded the Boers self-government and racial supremacy in their provinces. Not unlike white southerners during Reconstruction, the Boers had lost the war but won the peace.

As you analyze Reid's essay and Collins's rejoinder, compare their assessments of southern society and the strength of southern nationalism with Carl Degler's in the preceding selection. From there, evaluate each writer's judgment of the Confederacy's wartime options, including the possibility of using the Boers' guerrilla tactics. When you also recall that the North had its share of military reverses and crises of will, yet still managed to win, you can glimpse how challenging the task of developing a convincing explanation of the Civil War's outcome — or any war's — can become.

GLOSSARY

ANTIETAM (SEPTEMBER 1862) A bloody Civil War battle in which Union troops under General George B. McClellan halted the northward advance of General Robert E. Lee's Confederate army in Maryland. This Union victory provided President Lincoln with the chance he was waiting for to announce his preliminary Emancipation Proclamation.

CAMPBELL-BANNERMAN, HENRY (1836–1908) A British Liberal Party statesman who, in opposition to Conservatives, advocated home rule for Ireland and leniency toward the Boers.

CHESNUT, MARY (1823–1886) The wife of South Carolina senator and planter James Chesnut. She kept a diary during the Civil War that suggests plantation mistresses' attitudes about slavery, race, men, and the Confederacy.

CORNWALLIS, LORD (CHARLES) (1735–1805) The English general who led British forces in the American Revolution and whose defeat at Yorktown ended the fighting.

FORREST, NATHAN BEDFORD (1827–1877) The Confederate cavalry commander infamous for his troops' massacre of black Union soldiers at Fort Pillow, Tennessee, in 1864. Forrest became the first grand wizard of the Ku Klux Klan in 1867.

HOBBES, THOMAS (1588–1679) An English philosopher, author of *Leviathan* (1651), who asserted that nation-states are created when people afraid of violence agree to surrender their natural rights and submit to the absolute authority of a ruler. States exist to maintain domestic order and repel external aggression.

KU KLUX KLAN The secret society, organized by ex-Confederates and led by Nathan B. Forrest, that terrorized southern blacks and their supporters during Reconstruction to maintain white supremacy and deny rights to the former slaves.

MORGAN, JOHN HUNT (1825–1864) A Confederate general famed for his daring cavalry raids behind Union lines.

SCOTT, SIR WALTER (1771–1832) A Scottish writer whose romantic novels of Scottish life and medieval European history were widely read in the nineteenth-century United States.

SHERMAN'S MARCH TO THE SEA The Union advance of sixty thousand soldiers, led by General William T. Sherman, from Atlanta to Savannah, Georgia, in November and December 1864. Sherman's devastation of the southern countryside ruined the region's economy and morale and earned him hatred in the South.

STUART, J. E. B. (1833–1864) The Confederate cavalry commander whose information on Union troop movements, gathered on bold raids such as the circling of General McClellan's army in June 1862, proved valuable to General Robert E. Lee. Stuart was killed during the Wilderness Campaign in Virginia in May 1864.

VELDT The grassy, undulating plateaus of southern Africa, suitable for growing potatoes and corn and for grazing cattle.

✯ ✯ ✯ ✯ ✯ ✯ ✯

BRIAN HOLDEN REID

A revolutionary war may be defined as the seizure of political power by armed force. The American Civil War was a good example of a revolutionary war — but one in which the side seeking to seize political power — the Southern Confederacy — failed to use revolutionary methods to its full advantage. What was the reason for this failure, and why did the Confederacy allow itself to be ground down in a war of attrition in a conflict in which the war aim on the Union side was nothing less than the unconditional surrender of the Confederate armies and the destruction of their warmaking potential? As nation states existed, according to Hobbes, either to maintain internal order or protect themselves from external aggression, this is the criterion by which to assess the strength of Southern society to resist invasion and the imposition on it of political measures, including ultimately the emancipation of slavery, which it had gone to war to resist. Indeed it could be suggested that by 1864–65 the

Brian Holden Reid and Bruce Collins, "Why the Confederacy Lost," from *History Today* 38, November 1988, pp. 32–41. Reprinted by permission of *History Today*.

Confederacy had no other justification for its existence other than to maintain armed forces in the field.

It was Napoleon, who was in a position to know, who said that in war moral factors are to the physical as three is to one. The study of social factors in the American Civil War presents a curious paradox. It is undoubtedly true that the Confederacy secured from its soldiers extraordinary courage, dedication and endurance, and the *élan* of Southern soldiers, their dash in the attack, the rebel "yell," were legendary. But there is another side to the coin: defeatism, desertion, war weariness, doubts about the validity of the Southern cause and guilt over slavery. These factors need to be taken into account and given their due weight beside the more glorious elements in histories of the Confederacy's gallant struggle against great odds. They certainly need to be related to a fundamental problem which emerges from a study of the South's participation in the Civil War. In the Confederate states the war opened decisively and abruptly in April and July 1861 with the bombardment of Fort Sumter and the victory at the First Battle of Bull Run. These events were celebrated with great popular enthusiasm. The war ended just as abruptly with the surrender of General Robert E. Lee at Appomattox in April 1865, but without a glimmer of enthusiasm — a gritty determination to fight on irrespective of the odds. Why was this? Why did the war not continue, perhaps in some irregular form? Popular support for opening a war is usually a gauge for some measure of support for continuing it after defeat appears inevitable. Why did the South fail to field guerrilla columns like the resolute Boer commandos of 1899–1902? It may be that Southern nationalism as a socially binding force in war was more apparent than it was real.

There are two ways in which one state can exert power over another using military force. They have been well codified by the German military writer, Hans Delbruck, and developed as a tool to analyze the American Civil War by Major General J. F. C. Fuller. The first is the strategy of annihilation. In accordance with the strategy, the enemy's armies are destroyed by rapid maneuver and battle. This strategic form con-forms to a more limited type of war and may be equated with the modern generic term, *blitzkrieg*. The second category is the strategy of exhaustion or attrition: belligerents attempt to wear one another down in a long drawn out struggle. It was in the South's interests, if its independence could not be secured quickly, to persuade the North that it could not win because of the unacceptable human and material cost. Or alternatively, the North could destroy the South because Confederate resources were insufficient to prevent Union armies occupying large areas of territory and their war-making potential; the South would also find it difficult to prevent the creeping disintegration of its armed forces through war weariness and despondency. The strategy of exhaustion adheres more to an unlimited kind of war — "total war." In both forms of strategy, geographical, economic and moral factors are crucially important. "Whereas in the first," commented General Fuller, "the aim is the decisive battle, in the second battle is but one of several means, such as maneuver, economic attack, political persua-sion and propaganda, whereby the political end is attained."

There is a long tradition in American writing which contends that the South had a distinct military tradition, that the South was a singularly militaristic region of the

United States. . . . [E]lements of a supposed Southern military tradition were shared by the North. Nonetheless, these martial attitudes are important because they assist in delineating the Southern reaction to strategic reverses irrespective of whether they were unique to this region or not. They can be distinguished with reference to three main themes.

Firstly, optimism mixed with fatal dread. As General J. E. B. Stuart told George C. Eggleston in 1861:

> I regard it as a foregone conclusion . . . that we shall ultimately whip the Yankees. We are bound to believe that anyhow; but the war is going to be a long and terrible one, first we've only just begun it, and very few of us will see the end.

There is a contradiction in Stuart's view: war consists in "whipping" the enemy. But this does not appear to be sufficient. Faith in an eventual Confederate victory rested on the moral strength of the Southern cause — not on the political and economic strength of the Confederacy. Yet the view propounded by Stuart did not take into account the effects on morale of a strategy of attrition. As he observed in 1864, "I would rather die than be whipped," a wish that was alas, fulfilled at the Battle of Yellow Tavern later that year.

Secondly, a romantic nineteenth-century heritage. This attitude dominated the Southern outlook and was personified by Stuart again, although many others saw themselves as dashing cavaliers — gentlemen at war. As gentlemen they were chivalrous, like knights of the Middle Ages, a spirit that was captured by groups such as the "Knights of the Golden Spurs." This romantic spirit fed on the novels of Sir Walter Scott, which were immensely popular in the South. It persuaded many that war could be viewed in a distinctly glamorous, even sentimental light, so that campaigns took on the character of a "quest," indeed a light-hearted "lark." Thus warfare came to be regarded as a game on an extended scale, such as Stuart's "Ride Around McClellan's Army," which captured the South's imagination in June 1862.

Thirdly, these attitudes engendered an enigmatic sense of triumph. The enemy would be "whipped" but his forces remained in the field despite the demonstrable superiority of Southern arms. The victories of Robert E. Lee reminded some Southern observers of the pyrrhic triumphs of Hannibal. Thus the final test would depend on the will of God.

These factors operated to sustain Southern morale while military operations appeared to favor the Confederacy. None of them, however, served to stiffen morale in a war of exhaustion. Despite their enigmatic asides to the contrary, most Southerners had expected a short war, or at least a longer war which conformed to the strategy of annihilation. This view contrasts clearly with the Boers of South Africa, for instance, who did not think in such European-orientated and romantic terms and were inured to the hardihood of the veldt.

Nevertheless a number of factors did operate in the South's favor. The Confederacy occupied a vast geographical area — certainly twice the size of South Africa which the British army had occupied with such difficulty in 1900–02. Clearly an army of occupation would have problems in holding down such an enormous area. Indeed it should be recalled that Sherman's "March to the Sea" did not constitute an occupation of territory, only a raid in which his forces traversed three Southern states, destroying warmaking potential *en route,* but making no effort to hold them down. Secondly, the Confederate armies, despite setbacks, were still in being in 1864–65. Their organization, equipment and performance in set-piece battles were a considerable advance over comparable efforts in the American Revolution. Here was a considerable source of experienced manpower if Confederate commanders had chosen to disperse their forces in guerrilla groups throughout the countryside and in the backcountry. Such a move would have been aided by the diffusion of the population over a great area and low wooded terrain, highly suitable for guerrilla warfare.

Finally, the importance of military time can hardly be underestimated in calculating the Confederacy's chances of survival. Time was on the side of the Confederacy, not in the sense that it required time to organize its resources (indeed time would dissipate these), but rather in that the South had to defer a military decision in the North's favor and assert its independence in the eyes of foreign powers. In other words, show to the world, and not least the federal government, that it could not be extinguished. Guerrilla action in the Carolinas against Lord Cornwallis in 1780–81 had achieved precisely this in the Revolution. But by 1865 a consensus had developed that the war should be ended. There had been a number of voices calling for the Confederacy to adopt a guerrilla strategy, the most famous being John Hunt Morgan, but these were a minority. How had this consensus taken such a firm hold? During the Boer War a mere 60,000 Boers had held at bay the might of the British Empire for two years, despite a much greater disparity of resources and the disadvantage of operating in a smaller theater of operations.

In considering why the South collapsed so decisively, it should be recalled that loyalty in wartime is usually shaped and inspired by a state's war aims. But it was not altogether clear *what* the South was fighting for. Was it defense of property rights as exemplified by the defense of slavery? Or was it the independence of the Southern states? In pursuit of independence and as a vital aid to the maintenance of its armed forces by saving manpower, the Davis Administration began to emancipate slaves in 1865 in return for their joining the Confederate army. Considering the gigantic gamble represented by secession and the impassioned rhetoric that had marked the Confederate states' ordinances of secession from the Union, and the fatal (and greatly exaggerated) threat that Southerners perceived faced the South's "peculiar institution" after the election of the Lincoln Administration in 1860, this desperate action five years later surely forms a *reductio ad absurdum* [reduction to absurdity] of the Confederate position and strengthened the voices of those who had claimed in 1861 that slavery was better protected *within* the Union than without.

In addition, there can be no doubt that Southern morale was volatile. It oscillated between extremes of depression and exultation. By 1864, after extensive territory — especially in the west — had been given up, a widespread feeling developed that so much had been sacrificed for nothing. As Mary Chesnut wrote in her diary:

> Think of all those young lives sacrificed! If three for one be killed, what comfort is that? What good will that do? ". . . The best and bravest of one generation swept away!" . . . literally in the tide of blood.

Many Southerners could not understand that the South could afford to trade space for time, so long as her armed forces retained their fighting power. Southern morale had not the sophistication or endurance to sustain the blows inflicted by a strategy of exhaustion. Every withdrawal, even if it made military sense, depressed and caused consternation. One newspaper editor commented:

> Courts of Heaven resound with one great prayer; the supplications of a sorrowing people for the return of *peace* . . . appalled at the dire calamities which war has inaugurated, the heart of a nation pants for relief.

Many Southerners were prone to think that withdrawals or defeats in battle were a heavenly sign of the Lord's displeasure with the sins of the South. This only served to weaken morale. Typical comments in the newspapers and the pulpits include, "Without special interposition we are a ruined people," and "God will avenge himself on this American people, if this unnatural fratricidal butchery continues much longer."

Confederate nationalism was a fragile reed. In a war against fellow Americans very few negative reference points existed for it to feed upon. Americans were not divided by any linguistic differences or fundamental cultural divergences of the type which so clearly differentiated the Boers from the British during the Boer War. The appeal of the Southern military tradition can be explained as an attempt to mark Southerners out as different from other Americans, inaccurately as it turns out. The only fundamental divergence that can be found concerns views about Negro slavery. But even here the Confederate Constitution imitated the Federal Constitution faithfully, save for additional clauses enshrining the protection of slavery. Yet by 1865, because of the pressure of Federal advances, the Confederate Government was beginning to emancipate slaves.

Finally, there was a widespread fear of what recourse to an uncontrolled revolutionary war would do to Southern society. This was especially strong among Confederate generals such as Robert E. Lee and Joseph E. Johnston, who were very keen to negotiate acceptable terms of surrender before guerrilla action developed on any sizeable scale. Irregular war might lead to the arming of blacks, and confirm the very worst Southern fears of race wars which had haunted whites before 1861. In the end, Southern leaders were not prepared to inflict guerrilla warfare on their people, who were in any case not prepared to carry its burdens.

In 1863 President Jefferson Davis claimed that Confederates:

> . . . Have added another to the lessons taught by history for the instruction of man; . . . they have afforded another example of the impossibility of subjugating a people determined to be free.

Actually, the opposite was the case: the Confederacy showed that whatever advantages had accrued to it, a rebellion may be crushed if the rebels show insufficient *will* to seek and secure their independence. Southerners simply lacked a sense of national identity during the war years. They staked a claim for independence which mortgaged too heavily their moral and psychological resources.

BRUCE COLLINS

Why the Southern Confederacy collapsed in April 1865 is naturally a question long debated by historians. Recent work on the subject has emphasized the lack of internal cohesion and sustained political will. It does not wholly concur in W. E. Gladstone's celebrated judgment of October 1862:

> Jefferson Davis and other leaders of the South have made an army; they are making, it appears, a navy; and they have made what is more than either, they have made a nation.

Instead, it sees feebleness of national spirit and fragmentation of political power as key contributors to Confederate defeat. In assessing this weakening of morale, Dr. Holden Reid has particularly focused on comparisons with the Boers' struggle against the British in 1899–1902 and on asking why the Confederates, unlike the Boers, failed to continue their fight for independence by guerrilla action once regular warfare had failed. The comparison of Confederates and Boers is most instructive, for the Boers resembled Southerners in conducting a farming people's war against fellow whites. The South African struggle may have been an imperial conflict but it was not a "colonial war" in the classic nineteenth-century sense, where British regulars and allied levies overwhelmed non-European forces, often defective in training and/or weaponry. Boers and Southerners saw themselves as gallant individualists trying to preserve a traditional agrarian order against spreading industrialism and "cosmopolitan" ideas. In many ways African subordination was less an issue for the Boers than slavery was for the Southerners, but Boers distrusted British policymakers' attitudes towards Africans. More generally, Boers and Confederates typically appear as opponents to national consolidation, advocates of localism, and upholders of increasingly anachronistic values. If one is thinking of nation-building and the role of war in it, and of morale, the comparison of Boers and Confederates is far from being strained.

Yet comparison in detail reveals important contrasts which in turn help explain Confederate collapse. The Boers undertook extensive, prolonged guerrilla campaigns against the British from late 1900 to May 1902 partly because that style of warfare matched their conceptions of armed struggle. The Boers had no experience of formal warfare worth the name; small-scale frontier policing operations were all they had engaged in. No West Point of the high veldt turned out regular officers. Although very well equipped in 1899–1900, they saw no virtue in giving battle in classic style. Their preferred dispositions against British regulars in the field took the form of large-scale ambushes, with the aim of doing damage from a distance rather than rushing enemy lines and seizing enemy positions. Even at the height of their success, their military organization creaked. At councils of war, at least in theory, corporals and cornets could outvote commandants. More important, the Boers lacked the manpower to sustain big battles once the British reinforced in strength. Their male population of arms-bearing age totaled only about 55,000. Their manpower losses in fighting *throughout* the war (about 7,000 killed) probably failed to match Confederate losses at Antietam. In terms of their training, past experience, and numbers, guerrilla warfare offered their *only* viable means of resistance once the British — to the surprise of some leading Boers — assembled an overwhelmingly superior army in South Africa during the winter of 1899–1900. From that point the Boers had little choice but to act, as was said at the time, as "the gadfly of regular armies." This was especially the case after no fewer than 13,900 men (of 35,000 initially raised) accepted Lord Roberts' terms for laying down their arms during March–July 1900. But when the Boers switched to guerrilla action they did so under existing leaders and with existing forces. The total number of *bittereinders* ["bitter-enders," or holdouts] who did not surrender until the war's end in 1902 (17,000) represented about half the strength of the initial Boer mobilization in 1899. They formed not so much a stubborn rump, as a principal campaign force.

The Confederates possessed a very different military background and very different military aspirations. Nothing in their past prepared them for Antietam, Gettysburg or the Virginia campaign from May 1864. Formal warfare American-style was, like General Zachary Taylor's nickname, rough and ready. The greatest battle fought on Southern soil before 1861 was New Orleans in 1815, a bizarre and triumphant affair of assorted American contingents against British regulars. Indian warfare required planning, manpower, and commitment to more than just brief forays, but, again, it scarcely imbued officers or men with European military codes of behavior. Yet Southerners entertained more formal ideas of warfare than the Boers. The crucial difference lay in the Mexican war of 1846–48 and in military education. The Southern states had provided a disproportionate contribution in manpower to the Mexican campaign, which required fairly elaborate planning and logistical organization. And Confederate generals were mostly West Point graduates. They believed in decisive battle. They boasted that Southerners enjoyed superior classic military skills to Northerners. Guerrilla warfare was neither desirable nor necessary; and it was scarcely honorable. To the Boers, it was formal warfare that seemed alien or aberrant.

Confederates' distrust of guerrilla warfare stemmed also from the nature of the war they waged. While secession was a revolutionary act, in overthrowing the constitutional Union established in 1787–89, politicians, not generals, created the Confederacy and they extended its area in the spring of 1861 because the North challenged its legitimacy, not because they conquered any territory. In that sense, the Civil War did not fit a major pattern of twentieth-century revolutionary wars in which armed struggle carries a political movement to power and then helps consolidate that movement's dominant position. The Confederates achieved their initial objectives by political means; they fought the war defensively to secure Northern recognition of their independence. This fact partly explains also why the Confederate government lacked sweeping domestic powers. Accustomed to controlling their individual states' affairs, presiding over properly administered state governments, and imbued with highly articulated ideas of state rights, Confederate leaders distrusted central authority. They also distrusted unstructured power. Ultimately they would rather work within a political structure dominated by their enemies than take their chance with informal government appended to and supported by guerrilla movements.

But did such reluctance to resort to informal means after 1865 suggest a lack of will? Like all armies, including the Northern, the Confederate forces suffered from periodic losses of confidence, desertions, and soldiers' resentment against their officers. These characteristics have to be seen against the nature of the war, one not lightly called the first modern war for its heavy casualties sustained in frontal infantry assaults upon well-secured positions strengthened by artillery, and for its mass mobilization of manpower. Desertions did not soar until autumn 1864, and did not reach epidemic proportions until early 1865, just before the surrender in April. The last returns of the Confederate armies gave 160,200 officers and men present, and no fewer than 198,500 absent from the flag. But by October 1864, the Confederate military cause was hopeless. The trans-Mississippi states of Arkansas, Louisiana and Texas had been virtually cut off from the rest of the Confederacy by the end of 1862. Those states in 1860 contained 1¾ million of the 9 million people of the Confederacy. Their isolation was no mean loss. The Confederacy was further fragmented when Sherman's army invaded Georgia and, on September 2nd, 1864, entered Atlanta. No Confederate army stood between Sherman and Lee's forces in Virginia. Sherman began marching northwards into South Carolina and subsequently into North Carolina in January 1865. The Confederate government controlled very little territory by then. No wonder men slipped away to rejoin and perhaps rescue their families and homesteads.

This final collapse must be seen against the preceding years of armed resistance. It was remarkable that the South fought for so long. By the end of 1862 the Confederate position was already grim. The border South had not seceded. Much of Tennessee had been lost. The Federals had captured the Confederacy's principal city and port, New Orleans. They also seized Norfolk, Virginia's main port, and blockaded the key remaining Confederate ports of Charleston, Mobile and Savannah. The international front offered no comfort, since no country recognized the Confederacy as a belligerent. One wonders if Northern refusal to recognize Confederate independence would have survived equivalent pressure: an effective Confederate blockade of the Atlantic seaboard ports, Confederate capture of New York City and Chicago, Confederate control of a belt of land cutting off everything west of Indiana from the rest of the North, and the establishment of pro-Confederate governments in southern Pennsylvania, southern Ohio, and southern Indiana. Given the panic and dismay Northerners evinced when faced with far more limited Confederate advances, it seems improbable.

The collapse of morale during the winter of 1864–65 must be seen against several facts. First, during the war about one in every three Confederate males of military age died in, or as a result of, war service. Many more received injury. That amounted to an unprecedented level of blood-letting in a major modern war. When one adds that by early 1865 very large tracts of the Confederacy had been invaded, it is little wonder that morale sank. Those still in arms had every reason to feel hopeless. For their part, the Boers did not sustain a level of casualties anywhere approaching that withstood by the Confederates. And their guerrilla campaign petered out when the British army devastated their farms and livestock and removed civilians into concentration camps. If, as in so many historical instances, we are to judge whether the jug was half full or half empty, it is surely right to conclude that, by any standard of comparison, the Confederate measure of resistance looks more full than empty. Bell Wiley, the pre-eminent historian of Johnny Reb, warts and all, concluded:

> Few if any soldiers have had more than he of *élan,* of determination, of perseverance, and of the sheer courage which it takes to stand in the face of withering fire.

This certainly was a view shared by the Confederates' opponents. Grant in his memoirs recorded:

> Up to the battle of Shiloh, I, as well as thousands of other citizens, believed that the rebellion against the government would collapse suddenly and soon, if a decisive victory could be gained over any of its armies.

Sherman justified the scorched earth campaigns of 1864–65 on the grounds that:

> We are not only fighting hostile armies, but a hostile people and must make old and young, rich and poor, feel the hard hand of war, as well as organized armies.

It was this combination of civilian depredations, loss of military manpower, and loss of territory that wrecked the Confederate, just as it wrecked the Boer, war effort.

But the loss of an attainable political objective was also vital. When the Boers' Assembly of the People debated submission to the British in May 1902, one of their generals, Jan Smuts, took as his theme the keynote of Lincoln's Second Inaugural: "to bind up the nation's wounds." From a military point of view, he told the Assembly, the contest could continue, for "We have still 18,000 men in the field, veterans, with whom you can do almost any work." But the Assembly had to consider not merely this army, but the Afrikaner people, those in concentration camps as well as the free, those who had already given their lives, and "those who will live after we are gone." Independence was an honorable objective; "But we may not sacrifice the Afrikaner people for that independence." The Boers' prolongation of the war after 1900 had been aimed at sapping British morale. Their dramatic raid into Cape Colony failed, however, to stir the "Dutch" population there to revolt. And, in Britain, although strong Liberal attacks on General Kitchener's concentration camps — "methods of barbarism" according to Campbell-Bannerman — surfaced in 1901, they failed to dent the Conservative Government's commitment to the war. By 1865, the Confederates faced a similar prospect of sacrificing the white South for an independence which could clearly not be attained. Invading the North had been tried and had failed to produce significant results. Confederate recourse to guerrilla fighting in 1865 would probably have stiffened Northern opinion even further politically against the Confederates and it is unlikely that the North would have refused the expenditure necessary to suppress guerrilla bands; the war, after all, had already cost enormous sums. Moreover, the last obvious chance for the Confederates to score a political settlement had already passed, just as the Boers' political strategy crumbled in 1902. For the Confederacy the last, best hope was the presidential election of 1864. If Lincoln had lost (and as late as August, before Atlanta fell on September 2nd, his prospects appeared by no means certain), some form of negotiated settlement might have been secured. Once Lincoln won re-election, then the Confederates had virtually no realistic political objective for which to fight. It was by no means illogical that Southern morale slumped after Atlanta's fall (the occasion of much public relief among Northerners) and after Lincoln's electoral victory in early November. Sherman set off from Atlanta on his march to the sea, and then inland, a few days after the Republicans' victory.

Behind these military and political events was a further cause of Confederate distress. However staunchly Confederate soldiers continued to fight the Yankees, their self-sacrifice could not stem the erosion of slavery at home. A recent study of wartime Georgia (by Clarence Mohr) shows how slavery became increasingly undermined, despite state politicians' efforts to maintain it in full force. Raids by the Federal navy drove coastal slave owners with their valuable chattels inland. Inflation drove up land prices and made it difficult for these migrants to purchase fresh lands. Inflation also cut back on paternalism as clothing and other items became "luxuries" for slave owners to bestow upon their work forces. The absence of white males on military service weakened racial control of the slaves. Rising demand for manufactured goods and urban services encouraged the hiring-out of slaves in towns, where, again, racial control became increasingly difficult. Slaves themselves exploited these openings to weaken the oppressive institution. Some ministers of religion began even to urge reform in the laws governing slavery. Finally, acute manpower shortages fostered proposals that slaves be armed and sent to war. As Howell Cobb, a former governor of Georgia and the United States Secretary of the Treasury, remarked in January 1865, "If slaves will make good soldiers, our whole theory of slavery is wrong." Georgia's experience was repeated throughout the South. If the very institution which Southerners left the Union to preserve against ultimate extinction was crumbling around them, it surely made more sense to uphold some vestige of white supremacy at home than to struggle for political objectives that, with Lincoln's re-election, were palpably unattainable. More generally, when the war ended, this collapse of traditional racial order was matched by the decline of settled relations between whites. Returning ex-soldiers indulged in a good deal of looting and lawlessness. Many Southerners saw any form of government as preferable to threatened anarchy.

Unfolding political circumstances also reduced possible pressures to continue resistance. Almost immediately after the Confederate surrender, Lincoln's assassination placed the vice-president, Andrew Johnson, in the White House. Johnson, a Tennessee Democrat before 1861, had been a wartime Unionist. While he often opposed the slave-holding planters as a social and political caste, his position towards the ex-Confederate leaders during 1865 shifted from hostility towards accommodation. So, too, Southern Unionists appointed to office within the shattered Confederacy lacked the numerical support and the ideological venom to press radical reform. Thus the political prospects in the former confederacy in the eight months following surrender resembled somewhat those obtaining in 1907–08 in South Africa. The ex-Confederates faced a leader who was no longer their wartime adversary, but a politician more amenable to their arguments. And many former secessionists accepted the need for cautious, conciliatory Southern leadership to restore the Southern economy and to safeguard social stability. Former Confederate leaders were soon winning elections to Congress. Interestingly enough, when Radical Republicans found this sort of reconstruction unacceptable and changed the very lenient rules of Andrew Johnson's political game, Southerners did indeed resort to armed resistance in 1868–71. But this took the form of widespread terrorism, directed by the Ku Klux Klan against black voting and office-holding.

Some efforts to continue the contest were made after Lee's surrender to Grant on April 9th. Jefferson Davis sought to fight on, possibly from across the Mississippi, but made it only to Georgia before being captured by Federal soldiers on May 10th. By then, it should have been clear that the Confederacy had fought itself to a standstill. Even the pugnacious Nathan Bedford Forrest refused to go on. "To make men fight under such circumstances," he said in early May from southwest Alabama, "would be nothing but murder." His force was massively outnumbered, even for informal conflict. "Any man who is in favor of a further prosecution of this war is a fit subject for a lunatic asylum." Given the whole range of social, political and military events in the previous six months, that was surely an apposite judgement.

QUESTIONS TO CONSIDER

1. In light of these essays and the previous selection by Carl Degler, evaluate Brian Holden Reid's contention that "Southerners simply lacked a sense of national identity during the war years."

2. Discuss the military, political, and social developments leading to the collapse of Confederates' morale in 1864–1865. What evidence do the authors use to determine the extent of southerners' commitment to the war? Did surrender in April 1865 demonstrate the Confederacy's lack of will?

3. Compare the situation of the Boers in 1899–1902 and that of the Confederates in 1861–1865. What were their war aims? How long had each people been independent? What distinctive military traditions did each have? Why did the Boers choose guerrilla warfare while the South rejected it? Why did each independence movement surrender? What, if anything, did the Boers and Confederates gain from the war?

4. What role did slavery play in the Confederacy's conduct of the war? Why did the Confederate government refuse to arm slaves until the very end of the war? In what sense was the Ku Klux Klan an ex-Confederate resort to guerrilla warfare?

5. Can you envision a scenario in which the Confederates would have won the Civil War? What conditions or events would have been necessary? What would have had to happen differently? Why did this scenario not take place?

EMANCIPATION AND
RECONSTRUCTION

As the Civil War ended, Americans were faced with the dual task of restoring the Union and securing the freedom of the former slaves. The first was a uniquely American problem, but the second was not. When the United States ratified the Thirteenth Amendment abolishing slavery in 1865, it followed an international trend that began with the Haitian Revolution in 1801, continued with British emancipation in the West Indies in 1833, and ended with Brazil finally freeing its slaves in 1888. Wherever emancipation happened, whether it was accomplished by black revolution, legislation, or civil war, it brought controversy over what economic and political role the freedmen would play in the new society. In the case of the United States, emancipation proceeded in the bitter aftermath of the Civil War and was complicated by the same sectional divisions that had caused that conflict. It was also compromised by impatience to restore the Union quickly and especially by the limits of white Americans' commitment to full equality for blacks. As Reconstruction developed, it became a struggle in which the nation briefly took two steps forward, then took one back. During the years of Radical Reconstruction (1867–1871), Republicans imposed sweeping egalitarian social and political changes on the defeated South, but failed to secure them against white southerners' return to power. As a result, although slavery was not reinstated, many of the gains freedmen made immediately after the war were reversed within a decade.

The selections in this chapter model two very different ways to weigh the successes and failures of American Reconstruction in comparative perspective. Eric Foner shows how emancipation in the United States, in a process very similar to that in the British West Indies, resulted in legal restrictions and economic dependency for the ex-slaves. But he also documents the Americans' unique attempt to grant freed slaves political rights. Although this "unfinished revolution" proved temporary, it did leave behind a legal framework that would lend critical support to future struggles for black equality. C. Vann Woodward is less optimistic. Denying that Reconstruction was at all revolutionary, Woodward undertakes a "counterfactual" comparison between what actually happened and what *might* have happened if northerners had been seriously committed to overthrowing the old southern order and achieving racial equality. The outcome of this imaginative experiment leaves Woodward doubtful that radical change was possible, given the pervasive nineteenth-century American commitment to white supremacy.

The issue of how "revolutionary" Reconstruction was should lead you to consider various kinds of revolutions that can provide models to measure Reconstruction against. The two essays in this chapter also give you an opportunity to assess the relative usefulness of "traditional" historical comparisons versus "counterfactual" analysis. What conclusions do Foner's comparisons between emancipation in the United States and in the West Indies support? Is Woodward's "what if" analysis equally reliable as history? Do his speculations about possible alternatives in the American past simply confirm Foner's conclusions, or do they add important new insights?

The Politics of Freedom

Eric Foner

No nineteenth-century change in the Western Hemisphere was as dramatic and far-reaching in its consequences as the abolition of slavery — or as controversial. What system of economic organization and what kind of social relations would replace slavery? Every plantation society undergoing emancipation witnessed bitter conflict over the role of the freedmen. Former slaves wanted control over their lives and ownership of land, while planters demanded a low-cost, disciplined labor force to continue tending and harvesting staple crops for export. In most cases the landed white elite retained the upper hand and used the law to coerce ex-slaves back to work. In Jamaica and Barbados, British colonial policy compensated owners and put the ex-slaves through a six-year system of "apprentice" farmwork. Planters in Trinidad and British Guiana turned instead to the importation of indentured laborers from India under five-to-ten-year contracts. Even Toussaint L'Ouverture, the black liberator of Haiti, conciliated the powerful planters by imposing a rigid system of forced labor upon the freedmen. Such policies did not always succeed. On larger Caribbean islands where land was available, for example, some former slaves managed to evade the system and become landowning peasants growing crops for local, rather than foreign, markets. But throughout the Caribbean the mass of ex-slaves were prevented from wielding political power either by outright exclusion or, in British dominions, by prohibitive property qualifications.

What about the United States? In the Reconstruction-era South, the same struggle took place between planters' prejudices and prerogatives on one side and the freedmen's aspirations on the other. But the United States was unique among postemancipation societies in granting freed slaves equal political rights — at least for a time. Here the struggle was complicated by divisions between slaveholders and non-slaveholders among southern whites and especially by the influence of northern Radical Republicans. Determined to make the South over in the North's free-labor image, these politicians joined with the emancipated slaves to create a unique, though short-lived, experiment in interracial democracy.

In this excerpt from his comparative study of emancipation, Nothing but Freedom, *Eric Foner surveys postwar conflicts in the South over labor laws, property rights, and taxes — all crucial to the future of blacks in the region. He traces the up-and-down fortunes of the freedmen during the three phases of Reconstruction. In 1865 and 1866, President Andrew Johnson pursued a lenient policy that restored ex-Confederates to economic and political power. One result of this "Presidential Reconstruction" was the infamous Black Codes, which reduced the freedmen to near-slave conditions. Outraged by Johnson's actions, Republican congressmen took control of the federal reins in 1867, forced southern states to accept black suffrage and civil rights in the Fourteenth and Fifteenth Amendments, and oversaw the election of biracial Republican regimes in the South. Gradually, however, conservative southern Democrats rallied under the banner of white supremacy and lower taxes and regained control of southern legislatures, ending Radical Reconstruction. These so-called Redemption governments put in place a new version of the South's "old regime" buttressed by repressive legislation that reversed important gains blacks had won. As Reconstruction wound down in the mid-1870s, the federal government, like British authorities in the West Indies, backed away from protecting the freedmen's civil rights and instead left intact a pattern of land distribution and black dependency essentially similar to the days of slavery.*

When the smoke of Reconstruction cleared, the outcome in the United States seemed depressingly similar to the Caribbean debacle. As in other postemancipation societies, slaves had won "nothing but freedom." Nevertheless, Foner points out, the unique U.S. experiment in Radical Reconstruction brought significant temporary advances in southern blacks' social and economic conditions. And — far more important — it put on the books federal laws and constitutional amendments that guaranteed freedom. Once enforced, these would support the struggle for racial equality during the "Second Reconstruction" a century later: the Civil Rights movement of the 1960s.

GLOSSARY

CONVICT LEASE SYSTEM   A legal provision by which the government hired out convicts to employers for low wages. In combination with vagrancy laws and excessive jailing of freedmen, this system was used to provide cheap black labor for planters and railroad companies.

COOLIE   Derived from Tamil and Urdu words for "hireling," a pejorative label for imported contract workers, especially from India or China.

ENCLOSURE   The process of enclosing, with fences, hedges, or other barriers, land formerly subject to common rights. The enclosure movement in eighteenth-century England was linked to the decline of the manorial system and the rise of commercial agriculture.

FOURTEENTH AMENDMENT   Formally adopted in 1868, the constitutional amendment that gave citizenship to all persons born or naturalized in the United States, including ex-slaves, and guaranteed them "the equal protection of the laws." As a key part of Radical Reconstruction, Congress required southern states to ratify this amendment in order to rejoin the Union. It took away congressional representatives from states that denied black males the vote.

FREEDMEN'S BUREAU   An agency of the army created by Congress in 1865 to oversee the condition of ex-slaves by providing food and clothing, establishing schools, and supervising labor contracts. Led by General O. O. Howard, the bureau had its role expanded by Congress in 1866 over President Johnson's veto.

MORANT BAY REBELLION   A freedmen's uprising in Jamaica in October 1865 in which angry blacks stormed a courthouse to protest the punishment of squatters, killing a magistrate and fifteen others. The colonial government retaliated by burning peasant villages, executing over four hundred blacks, and returning control of the colony to Britain.

PEONAGE   A system of involuntary servitude based on the indebtedness of the laborer (peon) to his or her creditor. It replaced slavery after emancipation in several Latin American countries and, for a time, in the United States.

POLL TAX   A uniform tax on adults that was levied in the South as a prerequisite for voting, thereby disfranchising many blacks and poor whites. The Twenty-fourth Amendment to the U.S. Constitution (1964) outlawed poll taxes in federal elections.

SHARECROPPING   A system of tenancy under which landowners gave blacks or poor whites a plot of land to work in return for payment of a share of the crops, usually from one-half to two-thirds, plus their debt to the landlord. In the long run, this system proved disastrous to sharecroppers because of falling cotton prices, high credit rates, and cheating by landowners and creditors.

TOUSSAINT L'OUVERTURE, FRANÇOIS DOMINIQUE (1743–1803)   Leader of the Haitian Revolution. A self-educated freed slave, he joined the rebellion of 1791 to liberate the slaves and played a key role in uniting the colony's blacks first against English and Spanish interference, then in an independence struggle against the French. He died in a French prison a year before the republic of Haiti became a reality.

WOOLSACK   A cloth-covered seat in the British House of Lords, reserved for the use of judges, especially the lord chancellor.

✯ ✯ ✯ ✯ ✯ ✯ ✯

At first glance, the scale, manner, and consequences of emancipation in the United States appear historically unique. The nearly four million slaves liberated in this country far outnumbered those in the Caribbean and Latin America. Although no abolition was entirely without violence, only in Haiti and the United States did the end of slavery result from terrible wars in which armed blacks played a crucial part. The economies of the Caribbean islands, tiny outposts of empire, had little in common with the nineteenth-century United States, where slavery existed within a rapidly expanding capitalist economic order.

Politically, the cast of characters in the United States was far more complex than in the West Indies. American blacks were outnumbered, even in the South, by whites, but this white population was divided against itself. There are few parallels in other postemancipation societies to the southern whites who cooperated politically with the freedmen, or the northerners, variously numbered at between twenty and fifty thousand, who moved into the South after the Civil War, carrying with them a triumphant free-labor ideology and, for a time, playing a pivotal role in political affairs. Nor were there counterparts to the Radical Republicans of the North, a group with real if ultimately limited political power, which sought to forge from emancipation a thoroughgoing political and social revolution, supplanting plantation society, as one put it, by "small farms, thrifty villages, free schools, . . . respect for honest labor, and equality of political rights."

Finally and most strikingly, the United States was the only society where the freed slaves, within a few years of emancipation, enjoyed full political rights and a real measure of political power. Limited as its accomplishments may appear in retrospect, Black Reconstruction was a stunning experiment in the nineteenth-century world, the only attempt by an outside power in league with the emancipated slaves to fashion an interracial democracy from the ashes of slavery.

Despite these and other exceptional features of their national experience, nineteenth-century Americans sensed that prior emancipations held lessons for the aftermath of slavery in this country. Their precise significance, however, was a matter of some dispute [for] . . . the experience of Caribbean emancipation was interpreted through the lens of rival American ideologies concerning race and slavery.

. . . To abolitionists, the West Indies revealed the dangers of leaving the fate of the emancipated blacks in the hands of their former owners. If British emancipation was open to criticism, it was for not going far enough. "England," the Boston cotton manufacturer and Republican reformer Edward Atkinson wrote, "after she had caused the negroes to cease to be chattels, stopped far short of making them men, leaving them subject to oppressive laws made entirely under the influence of their former owners."

Eric Foner, "The Politics of Freedom," in *Nothing but Freedom: Emancipation and Its Legacy* (Louisiana State University Press). Reprinted by permission of Louisiana State University Press.

The First Vote: *This lithograph appeared in* Harper's Weekly *in November 1867. It represents the uniquely American — but temporary — postemancipation policy of granting freed slaves equal political rights. Portrayed here are representative African American leaders in the South: an artisan, a member of the middle class, and a Union soldier.* (Harper's Weekly, *November 16, 1867.*)

His Boston colleague, railroad entrepreneur John Murray Forbes, likewise warned that Americans should take heed of "Jamaica's former experience in legislating the blacks back into slavery, by poor laws, vagrant laws, etc." Another abolitionist cited the Morant Bay "rebellion" of 1865 to demonstrate Britain's "grave mistakes" in attempting to create a halfway house between slavery and complete civil and political equality for blacks. Even Toussaint [L'Ouverture] now came in for censure, for what [abolitionist] Lydia Maria Child called "his favorite project of conciliating the old planters."

Toussaint's mistake, Child believed, lay in "a hurry to reconstruct, to restore outward prosperity," rather than attempting radically to transform his society on the basis of free labor principles. The implications of all these writings for American Reconstruction were self-evident.

Not surprisingly, white southerners drew rather different conclusions from the West Indian example. Opponents of Reconstruction seized upon Morant Bay and the demise of local self-government in the islands to illustrate the dangers of black suffrage and rule by "representatives of hordes of ignorant negroes." Democratic newspapers, north and south, were filled during the early days of Reconstruction with lurid reports of West Indian blacks sinking into a "savage state" when liberated from the controlling influence of whites. In Haiti, supposedly, they had reverted to barbarism, paganism, and even human sacrifice, and, said the New York *World,* "intimations of analogous phenomena have already reached us from the region of the lower Mississippi."

Most important, the West Indies demonstrated that plantations could not be maintained with free labor: "the experiments made in Haiti and Jamaica settled that question long ago." J. D. B. De Bow, the South's foremost economic writer, amassed statistics to demonstrate the collapse of the West Indian economies and the indolence of the blacks. Julius J. Fleming, the South Carolina journalist, noted, "It seems to be a conceded fact that in all countries where slavery has existed and been abolished the great difficulty in the way of improvement has been the very subject of labor." Certainly, the Caribbean example reinforced the conviction that American blacks must be prevented from obtaining access to land: otherwise, they would "add nothing to those products which the world especially needs." If the South were to escape the fate of Caribbean societies, it could only be through "some well regulated system of labor, . . . devised by the white man." The emancipated slave, the Louisville *Democrat* concluded after a survey of the West Indies, needed to be taught that "he is *free,* but free only to labor."

Whatever their ultimate conclusions, contemporaries were not wrong to draw parallels between American and Caribbean emancipations. For when viewed in terms of the response of blacks and whites to the end of slavery, the quest of the former slaves for autonomy and the desire of planters for a disciplined labor force, what is remarkable is the similarity between the American experience and that of other societies. As in the Caribbean and, indeed, everywhere else that plantation slavery was abolished, American emancipation raised the interrelated questions of labor control and access to economic resources. The plantation system never dominated the entire South as it did in the islands, yet both before and after emancipation, it helped define the quality of race relations and the nature of economic enterprise in the region as a whole. It was in the plantation black belt that the majority of the emancipated slaves lived, and it was the necessity, as perceived by whites, of maintaining the plantation system, that made labor such an obsession in the aftermath of emancipation. As Christopher G. Memminger, former Confederate secretary of the treasury, observed in 1865, politics, race relations, and the social consequences of abolition all turned "upon the decision which shall be made upon the mode of organizing the labor of the African race."

As in the Caribbean, American freedmen adopted an interpretation of the implications of emancipation rather different from that of their former masters. Sir Frederick Bruce, the British ambassador to the United States, discerned little difference between the behavior of American and West Indian freedmen: "The negro here seems like his brother in Jamaica, to object to labour for hire, and to desire to become proprietor of his patch of land." The desire for land, sometimes judged "irrational" when viewed simply as a matter of dollars and cents, reflected the recognition that, whatever its limitations, land ownership ensured the freedmen a degree of control over the time and labor of themselves and their families. Candid observers who complained blacks were lazy and shiftless had to admit that there was "one motive sufficiently powerful to break this spell, and that is the *desire to own land*. That will arouse all that is dormant in their natures." Equally a sign of the desire for autonomy was the widespread withdrawal of women from plantation field labor, a phenomenon to which contemporaries attributed a good part of the postwar labor shortage.

For the large majority of blacks who did not fulfill the dream of independence as owners or renters of land, the plantation remained an arena of ongoing conflict. In postemancipation east Africa, according to Frederick Cooper, "the smallest question — whether to plant a clove or cashew nut tree — became questions not just of marginal utility, but of class power." And so it was in the postemancipation South, where disputes over supervision by overseers, direction of the labor of black women and children, and work like repairing fences, ditches, and buildings not directly related to the crop at hand, followed the end of slavery. Emancipation ushered in a period of what that perceptive South Carolina planter William H. Trescot called "the perpetual trouble that belongs to a time of social change."

The eventual solution to the labor problem in the post–Civil War cotton South was the system of sharecropping, which evolved out of an economic struggle in which planters were able to prevent most blacks from gaining access to land, while the freedmen utilized the labor shortage (and in many cases, the assistance of the Freedmen's Bureau) to oppose efforts to put them back to work in conditions, especially gang labor, reminiscent of slavery. A way station between independent farming and wage labor, sharecropping would later become associated with a credit system that reduced many tenants to semipeonage. Yet this later development should not obscure the fact that, in a comparative perspective, sharecropping afforded agricultural laborers more control over their own time, labor, and family arrangements, and more hope of economic advancement, than many other modes of labor organization. Sharecroppers were not "coolie" laborers, not directly supervised wage workers. And whatever its inherent economic logic, large numbers of planters believed sharecropping did not ensure the requisite degree of control over the labor force. Sharecropping, complained one planter, "is wrong policy; it makes the laborer too independent; he becomes a partner, and has a right to be consulted." Such planters preferred a complete transition to capitalist agriculture, with a closely supervised labor force working for wages. A wage system did in fact emerge on Louisiana sugar plantations and many Upper South tobacco farms. But in general, sharecropping became the South's replacement system of labor after the end of slavery. "To no laboring class," said a southern senator, "has capital — land — ever made such concessions as have been made to the colored people at the South."

As in the Caribbean, the form of agrarian class relations that succeeded American slavery resulted from a struggle fought out on the plantations themselves. What made the American experience distinct was that the polity as well as the field became an arena of confrontation between former master and former slave. Here, emancipation occurred in a republic. In the British Empire, as one historian notes, "the question, 'does a black man equal a white man?' had little meaning in an age when few thought all white men deserved equality." In America, however, where equality before the law was the foundation of the political culture, emancipation led inexorably to demands for civil and political rights for the former slaves. In contrast to Caribbean peasants, moreover, whose major ambition seems to have been to be left alone, Afro-Americans demanded full participation in the political life of the nation. Nowhere else did blacks achieve a comparable degree of political influence after the end of slavery. "Their civil and political elevation," as a Tennessee congressman put it, "is unparalleled in the history of nations. . . . France and England emancipated their slaves, but the emancipated never dreamed that they should have letters of nobility, or should be elevated to the woolsack."

Black suffrage fundamentally altered the terms of the postemancipation conflict in the United States. Far more than in the Caribbean and Africa, where white planters, farmers, and mine owners monopolized local political power, state and local government in America became a battleground between contending social classes, including the black laborer. Southern planters, initially restored to local power during Presidential Reconstruction, sought to use the state to stabilize the plantation system and secure their control of the labor force. With the advent of Radical Reconstruction, the role of the state was transformed and the freedmen won, in the vote, a form of leverage their counterparts in other societies did not possess. Then, after Redemption, political and economic authority once again coincided in the South. If in the long run, planters, like their counterparts elsewhere, largely succeeded in shaping the political economy of emancipation in their own interests, by the same token Radical Reconstruction stands as a unique moment when local political authority actually sought to advance the interests of the black laborer. Many of the specific issues upon which postemancipation southern politics turned were the same as in the Caribbean and Africa: immigration, labor laws, the definition of property rights, taxation, and fiscal policy. The conflict over these questions, and its eventual outcome, reveal how much of postemancipation politics was defined by the "labor problem."

As in the Caribbean, some American planters advocated in the aftermath of emancipation that the government directly promote "the accumulation of population," to break the bargaining power of black labor. Immigration, said one observer, would solve two problems at once: "If you would control [the freedman's] political power, you must outvote him; and if you would control him as a laborer, you must fill the country with a more congenial and more reliable laborer."

Many southern states established agencies after the Civil War to encourage immigration from Europe, but the results were disappointing. Of the millions of immigrants landing in New York, Boston, and other northern cities, only a handful made their way south, a reflection, in part, of the ambivalent attitude white southerners communicated about their desire for immigration in the first place. Some reformers looked upon immigrants as prospective landholders; they urged planters to break up the large estates and make land available on easy terms to newcomers. Generally, however, immigration was intended not to undermine the plantation system, but to preserve it. A Republican newspaper was not incorrect when it concluded that the appeal for immigration, "when stripped of its verbosity, is about as follows: 'We have lands but can no longer control the niggers; . . . hence we want Northern laborers, Irish laborers, German laborers, to come down and take their places, to work our lands for ten dollars a month and rations of cornmeal and bacon.'"

"Immigration," a prominent North Carolina lawyer wrote in 1865, "would, doubtless, be a blessing to us, provided we could always control it, and make it entirely subservient to our wants." As in the Caribbean, many planters concluded that indentured laborers would admirably meet this need. West Indian experiments with "coolie" labor were widely publicized in the post–Civil War southern press, and Chinese contract laborers were known to be at work in mines, railroad construction, and large-scale agriculture in contemporary California. A commercial agency offered to deliver "coolies" under five-to-seven-year contracts to Mississippi planters in 1865, and two years later a few Chinese, dispatched from Cuba by southerners living there, arrived to labor in Louisiana sugar fields. Robert Somers, the traveling British correspondent, encountered a gang of some six hundred Chinese laborers, drawn from California, at work on the Alabama and Chattanooga Railroad in 1871; and a number of Chinese laborers were introduced into the Yazoo-Mississippi delta around the same time. But despite enthusiastic predictions of how the Chinese would transform the labor situation, . . . the total number of Chinese in the South never exceeded a handful. And many who were introduced proved less docile than anticipated, abandoning plantation labor to set up as small-scale merchants and truck farmers.

Compared with the situation in Trinidad and British Guiana, the need for imported laborers was less in the United States, and the obstacles to their introduction greater. Relatively few blacks had been able to abandon the plantations to take up independent farming. There was also the danger that meddling northerners would bestow the vote on the Chinese, further exacerbating political problems in the Reconstruction South. Blacks, moreover, exercising a measure of political power during Reconstruction, opposed the introduction of "coolies." And federal authorities warned that any effort to bring in laborers under long-term indentures would be deemed a violation of the 1862 statute outlawing the "Coolie Trade." During Reconstruction, Commissioner of Immigration A. N. Congar and Secretary of the Treasury George S. Boutwell promised that "all vigilance" would be exercised to suppress "this new modification of the slave trade."

As in the Caribbean, the effort to introduce Chinese labor in the postbellum South formed only one part of a broader effort to use the power of the state to shape the postemancipation economic order and create a dependent plantation labor force. "There must be stringent laws to control the negroes, and require them to fulfill their contracts of labor on the farms," wrote a South Carolina planter in 1865. "No one will venture to engage in agricultural occupations without some guarantee that his labor is to be controlled and continued under penalties and forfeitures." . . . [M]ost Southern whites accepted the fact that slavery was dead. But its dissolution, many believed, need not mean the demise of the plantation. "I am sure we will not be allowed even to contend for gradual emancipation," wrote Texas political leader and railroad promoter J. W. Throckmorton in August, 1865. "But I do believe we will be enabled to adopt a coercive system of labor."

The outcome of such pressures was the Black Codes of 1865 and 1866. Ostensibly, their purpose was to outline the legal rights to be enjoyed by the former slaves. Generally, blacks were accorded the right to acquire and own property, marry, make contracts, sue and be sued, and testify in court in cases involving persons of their own color. But the main focus of the laws was labor. As a New Orleans newspaper put it, with slavery dead, a new labor system must "be prescribed and enforced by the state."

First to rise to the challenge were the legislatures of Mississippi and South Carolina. The Mississippi Code required all blacks to possess, each January, written evidence of employment for the coming year. Laborers leaving their jobs before the contract expired would forfeit all wages up to that time, and the law empowered every white person to arrest any black who deserted the service of his employer. Any person offering work to a laborer already under contract was liable to a fine of five hundred dollars or a prison sentence. Finally, to ensure that no economic opportunities apart from plantation labor remained for the freedmen, they were forbidden to rent land in rural areas.

A vagrancy statute, enacted at the same time, imposed fines or involuntary labor on a bizarre catalog of antisocial types:

rogues and vagabonds, idle and dissipated persons, beggars, jugglers, or persons practicing unlawful games or plays, runaways, common drunkards, common night-walkers, lewd, wanton, or lascivious persons, . . . common railers and brawlers, persons who neglect their calling or employment, misspend what they earn, or do not provide for the support of themselves or their families, or dependents, and all other idle and disorderly persons, including all who neglect all lawful business, habitually misspend their time by frequenting houses of ill fame, gaming-houses, or tippling shops.

And an apprenticeship law permitted the binding out to white employers of black orphans and children whose parents were unable to support them, with "the former owner of said minors" enjoying "the preference." In case anything had been overlooked, all previous penal codes defining offenses of slaves were declared to remain in force, unless specifically altered by law.

South Carolina's Black Code was, in some respects, even more discriminatory. It did not prohibit blacks from renting land, but barred them from following any occupation other than farmer or servant except by paying an annual tax ranging from ten to one hundred dollars. Blacks were required to sign annual contracts, and there were elaborate provisions regulating such agreements, including labor from sunup to sundown, deductions from wages for time not worked, and a prohibition against leaving the plantation or entertaining guests upon it, without permission. . . .

The uproar created by this legislation led other southern states to modify the language and provisions, if not the underlying intention, of early legislation regarding freedmen. Virtually all the former Confederate states enacted sweeping vagrancy, apprenticeship, labor contract, and antienticement legislation. Florida's code, drawn up by a three-member commission whose report praised slavery as a "benign" institution whose only shortcoming was its inadequate regulation of black sexual behavior, made disobedience, impudence, or even "disrespect" to the employer a crime. Louisiana and Texas, seeking to counteract the withdrawal of black women from field labor, declared that labor contracts "shall embrace the labor of all the members of the family able to work." Apprenticeship laws continued to seize upon the consequences of slavery — the separation of families and the poverty of the freedmen — as the excuse for securing to planters the labor of black minors free of expense. Many localities supplemented these measures with vagrancy ordinances of their own.

The laws of the southern states concerning labor, *De Bow's Review* claimed in 1866, were as "liberal, generous, and altogether as humane and equitable as the legislation of any country in the world under similar circumstances." De Bow was not being entirely disingenuous, for despite their excesses, the Black Codes were not as severe as the *Code Rural* of Haiti or some of the statutes enacted in the British Caribbean after emancipation. Southerners, indeed, insisted that precedents existed even in free labor societies for strict legal regulation of the labor force. "We have been informed by a distinguished jurist, who is a member elect of the Virginia Legislature," reported a South Carolina newspaper, "that the 'labor laws' of England . . . contain just such provisions for the protection of the employer as are now needed . . . at the South." And, it is true, laws subjecting employees, but not employers, to criminal penalties for breach of contract remained on the British statute books until 1875, and were widely enforced. Draconian English vagrancy laws, however, had long since fallen into abeyance. . . .

The Black Codes are worth dwelling upon not because of any long-range practical effect — most provisions were quickly voided by the army or Freedmen's Bureau, or invalidated by the Civil Rights Act of 1866 — but because of their immediate political impact and what they reveal about the likely shape of southern economic relations if left to the undisputed control of the planters. As W. E. B. Du Bois observed, the Codes represented "what the South proposed to do to the emancipated Negro, unless restrained by the nation." The Codes persuaded many in the North that continuing federal intervention was essential if the fundamental rights of the freedmen were to be protected. They convinced southern blacks as well that their former owners could not be entrusted with political power. The "undisputed history" of Presidential Reconstruction, black Congressman Josiah Walls later recalled, explained why southern blacks refused to cast Democratic ballots, and stood as a warning "as to what they will do if they should again obtain control of this Government." But, as quickly as planters attempted to call forth the power of the state in their own interests, their political hegemony was swept away, and a new series of measures regarding labor was placed on the southern statute books.

Radical Reconstruction, in this respect, profoundly if temporarily affected the relationship of the state to the economic order. The remnants of the Black Codes were repealed and laws were passed seeking to protect blacks from arbitrary dismissal and to ensure payment for time worked. "There is a law now in this State," a black state senator from Florida told a congressional committee, "that allows a man to get what he works for." By the same token, planters' pleas for legislation "the more effectually to secure punctually the observance and performance of labor contracts" went unheeded. . . .

Equally important, the machinery of justice had, particularly in the black belt, been wrested from the planter class. As blacks and their white Republican allies took control of local courts, sheriff's offices, and justiceships of the peace, there were increasing complaints that vagrancy laws were unenforced, trespass was left unpunished, and efforts to discipline troublesome laborers enjoyed no support from the state. . . .

With Redemption, the state again stepped forward as an instrument of labor control. Georgia's Redeemer Governor James M. Smith was quite candid about the intention: "We may hold inviolate every law of the United States, and still so legislate upon our labor system as to retain our old plantation system." . . . Not all these measures, of course, were entirely effective. Black efforts to escape the clutches of tenancy and debt peonage persisted, and federal law placed limits on measures forthrightly designed to restrain the freedmen's mobility. The point is not that the law succeeded fully in its aims, but that the state's intervention altered the balance of economic power between black and white.

What one black political leader called "the class legislation of the Democrats against the race" embraced vagrancy laws, restrictions on labor agents, laws against "enticing" a worker to leave his employment, and criminal penalties for breach of contract. Apart from a few remaining enclaves of black political power, moreover, these laws were now administered by white sheriffs and judges who owed no political debt to the black community. Such legislation, as a Tennessee black convention noted in 1875, was calculated "to make personal liberty an utter impossibility and . . . place the race in a condition of servitude scarcely less degrading than that endured before the late civil war." As required by the Fourteenth Amendment, the statutes were, on the surface, color-blind — in this respect they differed from the Black Codes of Presidential Reconstruction. But as the Tennessee blacks commented, "a single instance of punishment of whites under these acts has never occurred, and is not expected." . . .

As far as most southern whites were concerned, the issue of property rights for the former slaves simply did not arise. As General Robert V. Richardson put it in 1865, "The emancipated slaves own nothing, because nothing but freedom has been given to them." Blacks, on the other hand, contended that freedom should carry with it a stake in the soil, a demand reminiscent of the aspirations of Caribbean freedmen, but legitimized in ways distinctively American.

Blacks in the Caribbean . . . had enjoyed under slavery the "right" to extensive provision grounds, the embryo of the postemancipation peasantry. Many American slaveholders also permitted blacks to keep chickens and sometimes hogs, to raise vegetables to supplement their diets, and to sell the products of their "kitchen gardens" to raise spending money. Slaves, Eugene D. Genovese contends, came to view these gardens as a right rather than a privilege, but they were far less extensive than their counterparts in the West Indies, and American slaves tended to market their corn, eggs, vegetables, and pork directly to the planter rather than at town markets as in Jamaica. Only in coastal Georgia and South Carolina, where the task system allowed slaves considerable time to cultivate their own crops and the planters were absent for much of the year, did an extensive system of marketing and property accumulation emerge under American slavery.

Blacks' claim to landed property in the aftermath of American emancipation, then, was not primarily legitimized as a "right" that had been recognized during bondage. Rather, it rested on a claim to compensation for their unrequited toil as slaves. . . .

. . . To blacks the justice of a claim to land based on unrequited labor seemed self-evident. It was not that blacks challenged the notion of private property per se; rather, they viewed the accumulated property of the planters as having been illegitimately acquired. . . .

In its most sophisticated form, this claim to land rested on an appreciation of the role blacks had historically played in the evolution of the American economy. This was the import of the remarkable speech delivered by freedman Bayley Wyat protesting the eviction of blacks from a contraband camp in Virginia in 1866:

> We has a right to the land where we are located. For why? I tell you. Our wives, our children, our husbands, has been sold over and over again to purchase the lands we now locates upon; for that reason we have a divine right to the land. . . . And den didn't we clear the land, and raise de crops ob corn, ob cotton, ob tobacco, ob rice, ob sugar, ob everything. And den didn't dem large cities in de North grow up on de cotton and de sugars and de rice dat we made? . . . I say dey has grown rich, and my people is poor.

Such an appeal, Georgia lawyer Elias Yulee responded, was "mere nonsense." As he informed Georgia blacks in 1868, "as well may the Irish laborer claim New York city, because by his labor all the stores and residences there were constructed. Or claim our railroads because they labored on them with their shovels and wheelbarrows."

Yulee's comment illuminates the paradoxical double quality of free labor. As Marx emphasized, free labor is not bound as serf or slave, but is also "free" in that it enjoys no claim to the means of production. As labor became free, E. P. Thompson has explained in a different context, so "labour's product came to be seen as something totally distinct, the property of landowner or employee." Emancipation thus demanded a sharper demarcation between property and labor than had existed under slavery (since the laborer himself was no longer property). And, while the distribution of land never did materialize, the conflict over the definition of property rights continued on many fronts in the postbellum South. . . .

Like their Caribbean counterparts, southern freedmen did not believe the end of slavery should mean a diminution of either the privileges or level of income they had enjoyed as slaves. The slave, after all, possessed one customary "right" no free laborer could claim — the right to subsistence. . . .

The "right" to subsistence, however, had no place in a free labor society. Indeed, the end of slavery required a complete overhaul of the law; in a wide variety of instances, what had once been "rights" were now redefined as crimes. Under slavery theft of food belonging to the owner had been all but universal. Virtually every planter complained of the killing of poultry and hogs, and the plundering of corn cribs, smoke houses, and kitchens by the slaves. Most planters seem to have taken a lenient attitude, particularly where the theft was for purposes of consumption (selling stolen food was another matter entirely). "I do not think a man ever prosecuted his own slave for a larceny," a South Carolina lawyer remarked after the Civil War. Most masters seem to have assumed that thievery was simply another of those inborn black traits that made slavery necessary in the first place. To slaves, on the other hand, as one freedman later recalled, theft simply followed the Biblical injunction: "Where ye labor there shall ye reap."

Under slavery the boundary between public and private authority had been indefinite; crimes like theft, looked upon as labor troubles, were generally settled by planters themselves. Abolition obviously required a restructuring and strengthening of the enforcement machinery. As George A. Trenholm, a prominent South Carolina merchant, explained soon after the end of the Civil War, " . . . Theft is no longer an offense against his master, but a crime against the State." Thus, in the transition from slavery to freedom, the criminal law emerged as a means of enforcing the property rights and demands for labor discipline of the landowner against the claims of the former slave.

Everywhere, the end of slavery witnessed a determined effort to put down larceny by the former slaves. In the United States as well, planters complained of the widespread depredations committed by the freedmen. No one was able to raise stock in South Carolina, according to one planter, because "the negroes have shot and stolen them all." In Louisiana the "thefts of animals by the 'colored gentlemen' who do not want to work," were described in 1868 as "appalling." . . .

[During the Redemption period], the southern criminal law was transformed to increase sharply the penalty for petty theft (and provide a source of involuntary labor for those leasing convicts from the state). There was precedent for such measures in the early Black Codes. South Carolina's criminal law as amended in 1865 had been, a southern writer noted, "emphatically a bloody code." It made every theft a felony punishable by death, the result of which, critics charged, was that convictions would be impossible to obtain. Severe criminal penalties for theft fell into abeyance during Reconstruction, but were revived by the Redeemers. South Carolina did not go to quite the extreme of 1865, but did increase the penalty for the theft of any livestock to a fine of up to one thousand dollars and a maximum of ten years in prison. In North Carolina and Virginia after Reconstruction, a black spokesman charged, "They send him to the penitentiary if he steals a chicken." Mississippi, in its famous "pig law," defined the theft of any cattle or swine as grand larceny, punishable by five years in prison. . . .

Such legislation made the convict lease system, which had originated on a small scale during Reconstruction, a lucrative business in the Redeemer South. Republicans were not far wrong when they charged of the system in Texas, "The courts of law are employed to re-enslave the colored race." . . .

A further example of the use of law to redefine class and property relations and enhance labor discipline is the evolution of legislation concerning liens and the control of standing crops. Crop liens as a form of agricultural credit had originated soon after the Civil War, but the early statutes made no distinction among suppliers — anyone who made advances could hold a lien on the crop. The Freedmen's Bureau and some military officials superimposed upon the credit system the requirement that laborers enjoy a lien superior to all others for their wages or share of the crop, and several states during Reconstruction enacted the laborer's lien into law. Some went further and prohibited the removal of crops from a plantation until the division and settlement took place before some disinterested party. As a result, control of the crop was somewhat indeterminate during Reconstruction.

As in so many other areas, what was an open question, an arena of conflict during Reconstruction, became a closed issue with Redemption. The right to property and terms of credit — the essence of economic power in the rural South — were redefined in the interest of the planter. Generally, landlords were awarded a lien superior to that of the laborer for wages or merchants for supplies. North Carolina placed the entire crop in the hands of the landlord until rent was fully paid, and allowed no challenge to his decision as to when the tenant's obligation had been fulfilled. In Texas the law prohibited the tenant from selling anything until the landlord received his rent. The law attempted to accomplish what planters by themselves had failed to achieve: the complete separation of the freedmen from the means of production, the creation of a true agricultural proletariat. Beginning with *Appling v. Odum* in Georgia in 1872, a series of court decisions defined the sharecropper simply as a wage worker, with no control of the land during the term of his lease, and no right to a portion of the crop until division. Croppers, said the court, enjoyed "no possession of the premises, . . . only a right to go on the land to plant, work, and gather the crop."

Conflicts over the legal definition of contract rights, liens and tenancy are familiar legacies of emancipation. Less well known, although equally important as an example of the reshaping of property relations, was the matter of fencing, an explosive political issue in parts of the postemancipation South because it directly involved the laborer's access to economic resources and alternative means of subsistence.

. . . The common law doctrine requiring that livestock be confined to the property of its owner, as in New England, did not apply in the slave states. Rather, the farmer, not the stockowner, was required to fence in his holdings. All unenclosed land, even if privately owned, in effect became public commons, on which anyone could graze his livestock. . . .

. . . Blacks, it appears, had a vested interest in existing southern fence laws, which allowed landless freedmen to own animals, grazing them on the property of others. . . .

. . . "All they need," said one writer, "is a little to plant, their diminutive gangs of stock can herd it about over the woods, and are no expense to them." Some freedmen, like the father of Nate Shaw, the protagonist of that classic of oral history, *All God's Dangers,* were able to subsist for a time entirely by hunting and the free ranging of their hogs, thereby avoiding wage labor altogether.

The first tentative steps to close the southern range had been taken during Presidential Reconstruction, directed at the black belt counties where most freedmen lived. Nothing more was done during Reconstruction, but with Redemption the legal offensive resumed. . . . Generally, the battle was fought out first in the black counties, although early efforts to enact local statutes were often defeated by the votes of black tenants and laborers. But fraud, state laws restricting the vote on fence issues to landowners, and statutes simply ending common rights in black counties without a popular vote, succeeded by the mid-eighties in enclosing most of the black belt, a severe blow to the ability of freedmen to earn a living independent of plantation labor. The conflict then shifted to the white upcountry, where bitter struggles were waged between agricultural reformers and poorer yeomen determined to preserve their customary rights. The closing of the open range was a long-drawn-out process; in some states it was not completed until well into the twentieth century. But, as with the analogous English enclosure movement of the eighteenth century, the result was a fundamental redefinition of property rights. Southern small farmers and tenants, black and white alike, might well echo the lament of the English rural laborer who had seen his access to the land legislated out of existence: "Parliament may be tender of property; all I know is I had a cow, and an Act of Parliament has taken it from me."

Much the same demise of customary rights allowing an alternative to plantation labor was reflected in another postwar development, the growth of laws to prohibit hunting and fishing on private property. Here, too, the pattern had been established in eighteenth-century England, where a series of game laws, including the infamous Black Act of 1723 making the hunting or stealing of deer and hares in royal forests capital crimes, redefined traditional practices as criminal offenses. Such laws were resented by those accustomed to hunt on privately owned land, and supported by large landowners who saw them as a means of counteracting the inclination to idleness among the poor, as well as preserving a much-esteemed sport.

In the pre–Civil War South, a sparsely settled region whose extensive woods harbored plentiful supplies of game, there were few restrictions on hunting and fishing by free men. Evidence suggests that a significant number of slaves also had experience hunting, trapping game, and fishing. . . .

Presidential Reconstruction witnessed legislative efforts to restrict blacks' rights to hunt and fish. The Black Codes of several states made it illegal to carry firearms on the premises of any plantation without the permission of the owner, defined hunting or fishing on private property as vagrancy, and imposed taxes on dogs and guns owned by blacks. Georgia in 1866 outlawed hunting on Sundays in counties with large black populations, and forbade the taking of timber, berries, fruit, or anything "of any value whatever" from private property, whether or not fenced. During Reconstruction these laws were repealed or went unenforced, while planter petitions for new trespass and game laws were ignored. . . . Nearly all black families, it seemed, owned shotguns which, as Cyrus Abram, an Alabama freedman, put it, were "a heap of service in shooting squirrels, birds, ducks, and turkeys, etc. That is the way we get a good portion of our meat." In the 1874 election campaign, however, armed whites confiscated the guns belonging to Abram and other freedmen. "My gun was a mighty loss to me," he told a congressional committee, "because it is so hard for a black man to get something to eat."

In the Redeemer period, scores of local ordinances and many state-wide measures were enacted, designed to secure white private property from trespass, thereby discouraging men like Abram from getting "something to eat" without plantation labor.

Georgia once again took the lead, restricting hunting and fishing in black belt counties, establishing hunting seasons for deer and fowl, and limiting the ownership of dogs. As in the case of fence laws, the redefinition of private property at the expense of customary rights provoked dissension, especially in white upcountry counties where the right to vote could not be as easily restricted or manipulated as in the black belt. . . . But those laws which applied in only the black counties faced weaker opposition, and represented a serious restriction on the opportunities for freedmen to earn an independent living.

In one final area, taxation, the relationship between the state and private property was also transformed after the Civil War. Before the war, landed property in the South had gone virtually untaxed, while levies on slaves, commercial activities, luxuries such as carriages, race horses, and gold watches, and licenses on professions provided the bulk of revenue. The result was that white yeomen paid few taxes — their tools, livestock, and personal property were generally exempted — while planters bore a larger burden, but hardly one commensurate with their wealth and income. The tax on slaves and luxury items drew money from the planter class, but the extremely low rate on real estate and the widespread practice of allowing the owner to determine the assessed value of his own land, meant planters could engross large holdings of unimproved land without incurring an added tax burden. . . .

With emancipation, the southern tax system became a battleground where the competing claims of planter and freedmen, as well as yeoman farmers and commercial interests, were fought out. In Presidential Reconstruction, planters, like their counterparts in other parts of the world, looked to taxation as one means of compelling blacks to offer their services in the labor market. Less well known than the Black Codes, the revenue laws of 1865 and 1866 formed part of the same overall attempt to create a dependent labor force. While taxes on landed property remained absurdly low (one-tenth of one percent in Mississippi, for example), heavy poll taxes were levied on freedmen, as well as imposts on the earnings of urban craftsmen. Because so much state revenue derived from taxes on individuals, an inequitable situation existed in which "the man with his two thousand acres paid less tax than any one of the scores of hands he may have had in his employ who owned not a dollar's worth of property." Not surprisingly, blacks resented a revenue system whose incidence was unfair, and from whose proceeds, as a North Carolina Freedmen's Bureau agent reported, "they state, and with truth, that they derive no benefit whatever."

Reconstruction witnessed a fundamental restructuring of the southern tax system. . . . The need to rebuild and expand the social and economic infrastructure of the South, coupled with the sudden growth of the citizenry resulting from emancipation, vastly increased the financial necessities of southern state governments. Moreover, with the fall of property values, tax rates had to rise, simply to produce revenue equivalent to that of the prewar years. But more significant than the overall rate of taxation was the change in its incidence. Every southern state adopted an ad valorem tax on landed and personal property, shifting the burden of taxation to property holders. The result was that planters and poorer white farmers, many for the first time, paid a significant portion of their income as taxes, while propertyless blacks escaped almost scot-free.

Democrats complained that apart from poll taxes, blacks contributed nothing to the support of the state, since generally a certain amount of personal property, tools, and livestock was exempted from the new levies. . . .

In some parts of the Reconstruction South, Republican lawmakers designed the tax laws to force land onto the market and stimulate the breakup of the plantation system. "The reformers complain of taxes being too high," said a South Carolina black leader. "I tell you they are not high enough. I want them taxed until they put these lands back where they belong, into the hands of those who worked for them." In this century a progressive land tax, often employed in the Third World, has proved an inefficient means of promoting a redistribution of landed property. The same seems to have been the case during Reconstruction, although the new tax system did seriously inconvenience those holding large tracts of land for purposes of speculation. One result of Reconstruction fiscal policy, it is true, was that vast acreages — one-fifth of the entire area of Mississippi, to cite one example — fell into the hands of the state for nonpayment of taxes. . . . State law often required that they be sold at auction in 40-acre plots, and there is some evidence of blacks acquiring land in this manner. The title to such holdings, however, was far from secure, since state laws generally allowed the former owner to redeem his property by paying the back taxes plus a penalty. . . . Where tax auctions did take place, the buyers tended to be neighboring white farmers, land speculators, or urban businessmen, who gathered up considerable expanses at a few cents per acre.

After Redemption, the southern tax system was transformed anew. First of all, the level of taxes was sharply reduced. The parsimony of the Redeemer regimes is notorious; in Louisiana, "they were so economical that public education and other state services to the people almost disappeared." But the reduction in taxes and expenditures did not affect all classes equally. Partly due to upcountry pressure, landed property enjoyed the sharpest decline in tax rates, while privilege and license taxes rose. The reduction in land taxes was not passed along to black tenants. As a black Louisiana politician complained, "The landowners get all the benefit and the laborers none from the reduction in taxes." Reconstruction laws exempting a certain value of property from taxation were replaced by exclusions only for specific items, such as machinery and implements utilized on a plantation. The result was that blacks now paid taxes on virtually every piece of property they owned — tools, mules, even furniture — while larger farmers had several thousand dollars exempted from levy. . . . Then, too, poll taxes — the most regressive form of revenue — remained in force. The result was that throughout the post-Reconstruction South, as in the postemancipation Caribbean, the poor bore the heaviest burden of taxation and received the fewest public services.

To reiterate the obvious, no one can claim that the complex structure of labor, property, and tax laws initiated immediately after the war, then dismantled during Reconstruction, and finally, with modifications, reinstated after Redemption, were completely successful in controlling the black laborer or shaping the southern economy. . . . Nor could any statute eliminate the colonial status of the South within the national economy, or counteract the slowdown in the rate of growth of world demand for cotton. But the post-Reconstruction legal system did have profound consequences for black and white alike, foreclosing economic possibilities for some, and opening opportunities for others. The issue, as Du Bois noted, was not so much whether the South could produce wealth with free labor — "It was the far more fundamental question of whom this wealth was to belong to and for whose interests laborers were to work."

In poverty, malnutrition, illiteracy, and a host of other burdens, the freedmen paid the highest price for the failure of Reconstruction and the economic stagnation of the plantation South. Even though these hardships were not confined to blacks, the freedmen were caught in a unique web of legal and extralegal coercions which distinguished their plight from that of the growing number of white sharecroppers. To the architects of the post-Reconstruction South, black poverty was a small price to pay for political peace and labor discipline. "I do not think that poverty disturbs their happiness at all," a Georgia editor told a congressional committee. Another Georgian took a slightly different route to the same conclusion: "The Nigger, when poverty stricken . . . will work well for you — but as soon as you get him up and he begins to be prosperous, he becomes impudent and unmanageable." For their part, blacks fully understood that their aspirations were incompatible with those of their former owners. "What motive has he to see you oppressed and down trodden?" a visiting congressman asked David Graham, an Edgefield County, South Carolina black leader in 1876. "In case I was rich, and all colored men was rich . . . ," Graham replied, "how would he get his labor? He couldn't get it as cheap as he gets it now. . . . His interest is in keeping me poor, so that I will have to hire to some one else."

Here, in the candid recognition of irreconcilable interests, lay a recipe for continuing conflict. And, indeed, it is the ongoing struggle over the definition of freedom and the control of labor that unites the experience of the American South with that of other postemancipation societies. Long after the end of slavery, the conflict would culminate in the enmeshing of blacks in a comprehensive system of segregation, disfranchisement, and, in many cases, virtual peonage, and the proletarianization of the agricultural labor force of the South. Here, as elsewhere, the adjustment to emancipation appears as a saga of persistence rather than change, stagnation rather than progress, the resiliency of an old ruling class rather than the triumph of a new order.

Yet if the ultimate outcome seems in retrospect depressingly similar to the Caribbean and South Africa experiences, by the same token it underscores the uniqueness of Reconstruction in the history of postemancipation societies, and the enduring changes American emancipation did accomplish. However brief its sway, Reconstruction allowed scope for a remarkable political and social mobilization of the black community, opening doors of opportunity that could never again be completely closed. If Reconstruction did not overturn the economic dominance of the planter class, it did prevent the immediate putting into place of a comprehensive legal and judicial system meant to define the political economy of emancipation solely in the planters' interests. Despite Redemption, the complete dispossession and immobilization of the labor force envisioned in 1865 and 1866 never was achieved, and blacks stubbornly clung to the measure of autonomy in day-to-day labor relations assured by sharecropping. Nor were plantation labor controls extended, as in twentieth-century South Africa, into industry, an outcome of great importance when employment opportunities opened for blacks in the North. And Reconstruction established a framework of legal rights enshrined in the Constitution that, while flagrantly violated in practice after Redemption, planted the seeds of future struggle and left intact a vehicle for future federal intervention in southern affairs.

Thus, a subtle dialectic of persistence and change, continuity and conflict, shaped America's adjustment to abolition. As in most other societies that experienced the end of slavery, black aspirations were, in large measure, thwarted and plantation agriculture, in modified form, survived. Yet for a moment, American freedmen had enjoyed an unparalleled opportunity to help shape their own destiny. The legacy of Reconstruction would endure as blacks continued to assert their claims, against unequal odds, to economic autonomy, political citizenship, and a voice in determining the consequences of emancipation.

QUESTIONS TO CONSIDER

1. What conclusions did Civil War–era Americans draw from the West Indian emancipation experience of the 1830s? How did their conclusions reflect each group's ideas about slavery and their expectations for the future?

2. How did the political context of emancipation differ in the United States from that in Caribbean societies? In what ways did the American ideal of equality, the granting of black suffrage, and the realities of national politics shape the nature of the conflict between white planters and ex-slaves?

3. Explain how the Black Codes showed what southern economic relations would look like if left completely under the planters' control. Why did the "solution" of importing immigrant plantation laborers not succeed in the South? Why was the former slaves' claim to land not recognized?

4. Planters and freedmen pursued their competing agendas in the southern political arena. Discuss how the two groups' ideas about property and subsistence rights differed. How did southern state laws reflect the victory of each group on these issues at different times? How did southern fence and game laws resemble the eighteenth-century English enclosure legislation? In what ways, according to Foner, did changing tax laws affect planters, independent farmers, and propertyless southerners?

5. In what sense was the system of sharecropping a compromise between the former slaves' desire for independence and the planters' demands for dependent wage laborers? How did landlords manage in the end to control sharecroppers?

Reconstruction:
A Counterfactual Playback

C. VANN WOODWARD

For a second opinion on Reconstruction, we turn from the hard evidence of Eric Foner's essay to the intriguing speculations of C. Vann Woodward, a distinguished historian looking back upon a half-century of Reconstruction scholarship, including his own. Like Foner, Woodward has compared Reconstruction to emancipations elsewhere and found a general pattern of limited gains for former slaves. But in this essay Woodward suggests a more imaginative and perhaps equally illuminating type of comparative history.

His starting point is the recognition that Reconstruction was a failure and that Americans always have a hard time coming to grips with failure. It will not do, Woodward says, to compensate by exaggerating Radical Reconstruction's partial and fleeting gains for blacks; nor, on the other hand, should Americans continue to berate our ancestors for falling short of the nation's lofty ideals. Instead, to arrive at a realistic assessment of Reconstruction, says Woodward, we need to seek comparative angles. First, understanding that emancipation in other nations did not lead to equality for their former slaves "removes the stigma of uniqueness" and should help Americans to live with their nation's failure. Second, we should dismiss the hyperbole that Reconstruction was a "revolution" and thus lower our expectations for it. Finally — and here Woodward hits his stride — we might ask whether Reconstruction would have succeeded if it had in fact been revolutionary.

What would have happened if the North had been seriously committed to revolutionizing the South and raising the ex-slaves to equality? Woodward is at his witty best when he compares what might have been with what actually happened — an exercise historians call "counterfactual" history. Moving historical figures around like chess pieces, Woodward has Ben Wade (a Radical Republican senator) replace an impeached President Johnson and sign into law a confiscation act that breaks up southern plantations and makes the land available to black homesteaders. As if this were not enough, Woodward next proposes to "liquidate white resistance" in the South down to "the last bed-sheeted Ku Kluxer." Finally, having killed off the planters and their allies, Woodward turns the South over to the Union army and northern reformers.

Would this revolution have succeeded? To address this question with evidence from the same period, Woodward recounts the depressing tale of how speculators undermined white homesteading in the West and how well-intentioned reformers were unable to prevent army violence and the triumph of white supremacy over the Native Americans. What actually happened in the West casts a long shadow over what might have happened in the South. At the essay's end, Woodward confesses himself "overcome with doubts" that even drastic revolutionary steps would have made Reconstruction successful. Reminding us that historians have to work with "human materials" and be true to the context of the past, Woodward seems to be saying — though he denies it — that Radical Reconstruction was doomed.

As you read Woodward's essay, ask yourself whether it demonstrates the usefulness of "counterfactual" analysis by highlighting aspects of the past not found in more conventional historical comparisons. You may find it ironic that Woodward the "armchair revolutionary" ends up more pessimistic than Foner the radical historian about the results of Reconstruction. Woodward, a master of irony, would be delighted. But the differing styles and conclusions of this chapter's two essays ought to challenge you to develop your own explanation of Reconstruction's successes and failures, and your own assessment of its implications for racial democracy today.

GLOSSARY

ARMSTRONG, SAMUEL (1839–1893)   A philanthropist and educator who worked for the Freedmen's Bureau after the Civil War. Armstrong helped establish the Hampton Institute in Virginia in 1868 to provide vocational training for former slaves and headed it until 1893.

CARPETBAGGERS   A derogatory term for northern whites who migrated to the South after the Civil War and became active Republicans. These included Union army veterans, businessmen, politicians, teachers, and missionaries.

COPPERHEADS   A derogatory term for northerners who actively sympathized with the Confederacy during the Civil War.

CROMWELL, OLIVER (1599–1658)   A forceful Puritan leader who emerged victorious in the English Civil War of the 1640s. One of the most controversial figures in English history, Cromwell defeated the Royalist forces of Charles I and Charles II and proclaimed England a republican commonwealth. He led an expedition into Ireland, where he began a policy of dispossessing the Irish. In 1653 he was named Lord Protector, or sole ruler, of England, Scotland, and Ireland, but the monarchy was restored shortly after his death.

DOUGLASS, FREDERICK (1817–1895)   An escaped slave who became an eloquent abolitionist and African American spokesman. In 1845 he published his first autobiography, and two years later he established a newspaper in Rochester, New York, which he edited for seventeen years, urging abolition through political activism. Committed to Radical Reconstruction, Douglass pushed for full black equality after the Civil War.

FREEDMEN'S BUREAU   An agency of the army created by Congress in 1865 to oversee the condition of ex-slaves by providing food and clothing, establishing schools, and supervising labor contracts. Led by General O. O. Howard, the bureau had its role expanded by Congress in 1866 over President Johnson's veto.

GRANT ADMINISTRATIONS (1869–1877) The two terms of President Ulysses S. Grant. They were characterized by corruption, special-interest legislation, and a gradual retreat from Radical Reconstruction.

HOMESTEAD ACT The 1862 law that opened millions of acres of western public land to settlers, who could receive ownership of 160 acres after five years of continuous residence or, alternatively, could buy the land after six months' residence at $1.25 an acre.

JACKSON, STONEWALL (THOMAS) (1824–1863) The Confederate general who became Robert E. Lee's ablest lieutenant. Jackson conducted brilliant campaigns in Virginia during the first half of the Civil War, but was mortally wounded by fire from his own troops at Chancellorsville.

KU KLUX KLAN The secret society, organized by ex-Confederates and led by Nathan B. Forrest, that terrorized southern blacks and their supporters during Reconstruction to maintain white supremacy and deny rights to the former slaves.

PRATT, RICHARD HENRY (1840–1924) A Civil War soldier transferred to the West during Reconstruction who became an influential Indian educator. He organized the Indian branch of the Hampton Institute in 1878 and the following year established the Carlisle Indian School, the first nonreservation federal school for Native Americans. Pratt was an advocate of assimilation who sought to root out tribalism and to end Native Americans' separate reservation status.

REDEEMERS Southern Democrats who rallied to regain control of their state governments and suppress Radical (or "Black") Reconstruction.

SCALAWAGS A derogatory term for white Southerners who supported the Republicans during Reconstruction. Never more than one-fifth of the South's white voters, they included backcountry farmers, financiers and businessmen, and a few philanthropic ex-planters.

STALIN, JOSEPH (1879–1953) The Russian communist who ruled the Soviet Union as virtual dictator from 1927 to his death. Stalin sent enormous numbers of citizens to their deaths during the forced collectivization of agriculture and in periodic mass purges of his critics and political foes.

STEVENS, THADDEUS (1792–1868) A powerful Radical Republican congressman from Pennsylvania. Stevens favored harsher Reconstruction terms than those of Presidents Lincoln and Johnson. He led the movement to impose military Reconstruction on the South in 1867 and was the most outspoken congressional advocate of confiscating Confederates' land.

STUART, J. E. B. (1833–1864) The Confederate cavalry commander whose information on Union troop movements, gathered on bold raids such as the circling of General McClellan's army in June 1862, proved valuable to General Robert E. Lee. Stuart was killed during the Wilderness Campaign in Virginia in May 1864.

SUMNER, CHARLES (1811–1874) An abolitionist senator from Massachusetts who was a leader of the Radical Republicans' Reconstruction program and active in the impeachment of President Johnson.

TORIES Also called Loyalists; American colonists who refused to renounce their allegiance to the British Crown after 1776. Many suffered physical abuse, disfranchisement, or confiscation of property, and about one hundred thousand were forced into exile in Canada, England, or the Caribbean.

WADE, BENJAMIN F. (1800–1878)   An Ohio senator and Radical Republican who led congressional oversight of the Civil War effort and opposed Lincoln's mild Reconstruction terms. As president pro tempore of the Senate, Wade would have succeeded as president had Andrew Johnson been convicted of impeachment charges in 1868.

WASHINGTON, BOOKER T. (1856–1915)   A young slave liberated by the Civil War who studied at Hampton Institute and became an instructor there in 1879. In 1881, he organized Tuskegee Institute in Alabama, which became a leading center for black industrial education. As a public spokesman for southern blacks, Washington advocated self-help and economic independence, but was criticized for accepting racial segregation and political disfranchisement.

✶ ✶ ✶ ✶ ✶ ✶ ✶

The ruins of two great failures dominate the landscape of American history. They stand close together in the middle distance, back to back, but separate and distinct. One is the ruins of the Confederacy, the South's failure to gain independence. The other is the ruins of Reconstruction, the North's failure to solve the problem of the black people's place in American life. The South's failure was the North's success and vice versa. Each can be and, of course, has been described by its opponents as simply the wreckage wrought in preventing acknowledged wrong. But from the standpoint of their supporters and champions there can be no doubt that each of these ruins represents a great American failure.

They stand out all the more conspicuously on the historical landscape because of their unique character. Failures and defeats on the grand scale are notoriously exceptional and uncharacteristic in the American experience. And so far, at least until very recent years, these two stand as the only instances of striking significance. They are surrounded by monuments of success, victory, and continuity, features far more familiar to the American eye. Some of these monuments — the Revolution, the Constitution, the two-party system, the parties themselves, the basic economic institutions, all still live and going concerns — are much older than the two historic ruins. This side of them in the foreground of American history stand more recent monuments in the traditional success style of the American Way, marred only somewhat by late twentieth-century exceptions. But the middle distance is still dominated by the two great historic failures.

The unavoidable responsibility of the historian is to explain these failures. But the strangeness and un-American character of failure seems to have inhibited or warped the fulfillment of the task. One evasive strategy of historians of the Confederacy has been first to acknowledge more or less candidly that the movement was misguided and perhaps destined to fail from the start and even to admit tacitly that it was best for all

concerned in the long run that it did fail. But then to dwell at length on the high moments, the ephemeral triumphs, the selfless devotion, the nobility of leadership, and the
hardships and suffering of the participants. Essentially romantic, the lost-cause approach
emphasized the glory and tragedy without too much attention to causes and consequences. Recent historians of the Confederacy have been addressing themselves more
and more to the causes of failure and less to the ephemeral triumphs. But for a long time
the South's refusal to face up to its own defeat contributed to the North's failure in accounting for the sequel to Appomattox.

Historians of Reconstruction have played variations on these Confederate themes
without exactly duplicating the order or the mood. For a long time they too started
with the assumption that the movement was misconceived and doomed to failure from
inception and that, all things considered, it was just as well that it did fail. Since failure
was regarded as both inevitable and fortunate, the problem of explaining it did not appear very challenging. With these more or less common assumptions, historians of the
old school divided mainly on how they distributed their sympathy and admiration
among the victims — the humble freedmen, the misguided idealists, the bumbling
Presidents, or the long-suffering Southern whites — and on their distribution of blame
among villains — Radical Republicans, Carpetbaggers, Scalawags, or black freedmen.
They were in substantial agreement, however, in their homage to the tragic muse.
Whether the spotlight was focused on the victims or the villains, the overriding preoc-
cupation was with tragedy. The best seller on the subject was entitled *The Tragic Era,* by
Claude Bowers. But whether as a cause for satisfaction or lament, there was little equiv-
ocation about the verdict of failure.

In the last few decades a shift has occurred in the common assumptions and preoc-
cupations about Reconstruction historians. Failure is no longer regarded as inevitable or
complete, the movement as misconceived, or the outcome as fortunate. On all these
matters there has occurred a reversal of attitude. The treatment is still fundamentally
tragic, but the reading of the tragedy has changed. The tragedy was not that a misguided
movement had caused so much unnecessary suffering, but that a noble experiment had
come so near fulfillment and failed. Furthermore, the impact of failure itself has been
blunted and the historical problem of explanation shelved by a new emphasis on the
positive accomplishments of Reconstruction.

Much of the attention of revisionists has been focused on correcting the excessively
negative picture painted by the old school and exposing the injustice and crudity of the
stereotypes. New studies have pictured the old abolitionists as persevering champions of
the freedmen. The collective portrait of the Radical Republican congressmen that
emerges from revisionist biographies and monographs is one of high-minded idealists
who rose above selfish political and economic interests. Studies of Northern teachers
and preachers who went to the South on missionary enterprises stress their seriousness
of purpose and the devotion and fearless dedication of their service. Carpetbaggers of
vision and courageous statesmanship have been sympathetically portrayed. Scalawags
of the new historiography appear to derive either from wealthy Southern aristocrats or
from sturdy Jacksonian yeomen, depending on one's school of revisionism or one's
technique of quantification. Among black leaders and statesmen revisionists have

discovered a gratifying amount of talent, ability, and vision. Swindlers, grafters, and corruption have been discounted by comparison with contemporaneous fraud and graft in Northern states. The result of all this has been a wholesale decimation of stock figures in the demonology of Reconstruction.

Praiseworthy achievements of Radical Reconstruction include not only the legislative and constitutional foundations for black citizenship, franchise, and civil rights, but the training and preparation of freedmen for political action. Radical state governments are also justly credited with framing laudable and often durable state constitutions and law codes, with providing relief and welfare for the distressed, with establishing public schools, and with inaugurating new public services. Scholars have pronounced the freedmen's economic progress during Reconstruction, given their low starting point, a tremendous success and enumerated with pride their gains in land and capital. Others have pointed out the general progress of the South in economic recuperation and growth. The emphasis here, as in so many other areas of revisionist history, is not on failures but on the successes of Reconstruction. . . .

The achievements of the revisionists are impressive. But as a contribution to explaining the failure of Reconstruction they tend rather to complicate than to solve the enigma. For if, as they have demonstrated, the statesmanship of the Radicals was all that inspired and their motivation all that pure, if the freedmen were so responsive and capably led, if government by the Scalawag-Carpetbagger-freedmen coalition was all that constructive, and if the opposition were indeed headed by a misfit in the White House who was out of touch with the electorate, then success would seem more indicated than failure. The paradox reminds me of the first historical problem I confronted as a boy. It went something like this: If Marse Robert [Robert E. Lee] was all that noble and intrepid, if Stonewall [Jackson] was all that indomitable and fast on his feet, if Jeb Stuart was all that gallant and dashing, and if God was on our side, then why the hell did we *lose* that war? . . .

. . . This brings me back to the old problem of failure. As I have remarked earlier, Americans have rather a thing about failure — about confronting it, confessing it, and accepting it, as well as about explaining it. It is noteworthy that the great bulk of work done by the revisionists has been on Andrew Johnson's administration, not on the two Grant administrations, that is, on the period where, paradoxically, the ephemeral successes and triumphs multiplied, not the period of twice that length when the failures piled up or became unavoidably conspicuous. This may be mere coincidence, but my guess is that it is more than that. Another tendency might be called the deferred success approach, the justification (or dismissal) of failure in the First Reconstruction on the ground that it prepared the way for success in the Second Reconstruction, or maybe a Third yet to come. Thus one historian writes that the failures of the First Reconstruction diminish to insignificance in comparison with successes of the Second in advancing equal civil and political rights for blacks and promise of further progress to come. This is a generational shift of the burden of responsibility. But it must be recognized as essentially another strategy of evasion.

One habit of mind that has complicated American ways of dealing with failure, apart from a relative unfamiliarity with the experience, has been the isolation of

American history from comparative reference. Comparisons have indeed been used with regard to Reconstruction, but they have been internalized. Lacking foreign comparisons, or indifferent to them, Americans have turned inward to compare professed ideals with actual practice. This has encouraged a strong moralistic tendency in our historical writing and controversy. Since the nation has advertised a commitment to some very lofty ideals and principles, the contrast between performance and principle has always been painful, and the application of absolute and abstract standards of judgment often sets up moral disturbance that clouds issues and distorts perspectives.

For more realistic perspective on the American experience of Reconstruction we need to turn to comparison with foreign experiences, including but not limited to those of the other twenty-odd slave societies in the New World that went through the post-emancipation ordeal. To avoid repetition [of an earlier essay] . . . I must be content with summarizing conclusions of the best informed authorities. The most important finding is that wherever slavery was widespread, emancipation was invariably followed by resort to drastic measures, including use of force, to put the freedmen back to work. The old masters of the American South were by no means alone in resorting to black codes and chain gangs. Old masters everywhere — West Indies, Latin America, Africa, Asia — took forceable steps to drive the freedmen back to work.

Furthermore, in those lands undergoing emancipation where the process of reconstruction was subject to outside control or supervision, whether from the crown, the mother country, an imperial or metropolitan administration, or as in the South the federal government under Northern control, such authorities proved quite ineffective in protecting the lives and rights of the emancipated. The universality of failure by authorities and oppression by old masters does not excuse or justify either the governments or the masters anywhere — especially not a government that had just fought a bloody civil war in the name of freedom. Reconstruction left a lasting blot on the American conscience and national history and continues to breed moral recrimination between regions and races. But at least the comparative context removes the stigma of uniqueness and places moral issues in a broader setting. That, I believe, is a legitimate use of history — not only to recover the past but to enable us to live with it.

Another type of comparison has often been used in interpreting Reconstruction, but not always with sufficient caution. To place a historical event in a category of events is to make a comparison. Thus, when Reconstruction is spoken of as a revolution, we are compelled to think of it in comparison with other revolutions. If we reserve the term "revolution" for the classic phenomena of England in the seventeenth century, America and France in the eighteenth century, and Russia and China in the twentieth century, then it is certainly misused when applied to the American Reconstruction of the nineteenth century. For in the last instance there were no mass executions, no class liquidations. No heads rolled. There were constitutional changes, to be sure, but they were insignificant compared with those in England, France, Russia, and China, and they were mainly effected through constitutional forms. The South's so-called Bourbons or Redeemers did not become proscribed and outlawed émigrés. They remained at home, retained their estates, took over from the ephemeral radical governments, and after their so-called counter-revolution they did not find it necessary to make very drastic changes in the system left them by the so-called revolution. All things considered, it would be better to abandon both the concept of revolution and that of counter-revolution in writing of Reconstruction as it *was*.

But in writing of what it *might* have been, what many hoped it would be, and of why Reconstruction failed, the concept of revolution seems indispensable. It should be fairly obvious that in order to succeed with the professed aims of full civil rights, equality, and justice for the freedmen, Reconstruction would have had to go much further in the way of revolutionary measures than it ever did. Even then it might have failed, for revolutions are not invariably successful nor are their innovations always lasting. It is not very helpful to prescribe revolution in the abstract without specifying the revolutionary program. Nor is it very realistic to imagine a revolutionary program without regard to the nature of the party and the people who would carry it out and the historical context in which they would have worked. Only by that means can we test the hypothesis that the failure of Reconstruction is to be explained by the lack of revolutionary measures.

One revolutionary measure, a favorite for the speculation over a century, is the confiscation of rebel estates and redistribution of them among the freedmen. This deserves serious consideration for a number of reasons. In the first place such a proposal was seriously made and had an able and powerful advocate in Thaddeus Stevens. The Stevens plan called for the confiscation of all rebel estates over $10,000 or over 200 acres. He estimated that this would result in the taking over of some 394 million out of 465 million acres in the rebel states. The redistribution would give 40 acres to each adult male freedman. This would take 40 million acres, and the remaining 354 million would be sold to the highest bidder and the proceeds allocated to pensions for Union veterans, damages and reparations, and enough left to retire three-quarters of the national debt. The plan was defeated, of course, but it has had later advocates such as W. E. B. Du Bois and various other Marxists.

Americans need no Marxist precedents, however, for there was ample precedent for the wholesale confiscation of the estates of disloyal elements of the population in the treatment of Tories during the American Revolution, and there was a spectacular contemporary example abroad in the distribution of some of the confiscated lands to emancipated serfs by the Czar of All the Russias in 1861. The American freedmen surely had as great a moral claim on the land on which they had toiled for 250 years. Furthermore if the federal government could overcome the legal and constitutional problems of confiscating the slave property of the planters, it surely could have justified confiscating their landed property as well. The planters would have objected strenuously, of course, but they would have been powerless to prevent the action had Congress been determined. Let us assume, then, that the Stevens Land Confiscation bill actually passed, that President Ben Wade signed it in the White House after President Johnson's removal by successful impeachment, and that the Fortieth Congress then brought to bear all its experience and wisdom in refining the legislation and President Wade marshaled the best talents for administering the land act. What would have been the consequences for the outcome of Reconstruction? Would this have converted a failure into a reasonable success?

No one can possibly say for sure, of course. What one *can* describe with some assurance, however, is the record of the same federal government, the same Congresses under the control of the same party in administering and distributing public lands elsewhere. Again we resort to the comparative approach, though this time the comparisons are drawn from domestic rather than foreign instances. The Reconstruction period coincided with the great era of public land distribution by the federal government according to the provisions of the Homestead Act of 1862 and other federal land laws placed on the books between 1862 and 1878. The public domain available for distribution under the Homestead and subsequent acts amounted to some 1,048,000,000 acres, more than half the total area of the nation and more than two and a half times the 394 million acres of confiscated rebel estates that would have been added to the public domain by the Stevens Act. This fabulous opportunity, without precedent in history, appeared to be the fruition of the American dream, the most cherished dream of reformers — free land for those who tilled the land.

What came of that dream in the administration of the Homestead Act is a matter of public record. We know that as things turned out the homesteaders got short shrift and proved to be the least favored of the various groups attracted to the western lands. The land-grant railroads alone got four times as much land as the homesteaders in the first four decades of the Homestead Act. In that period 84 percent of the new farms brought under cultivation were purchased or subdivided from larger holdings. Of the patents actually granted to homesteaders a great number were handed to pawns of speculators and monopolists, so that in all probability little more than one-tenth of the new farms were free in the homestead sense. Furthermore, the bona fide homesteader was typically shunted off into the poorest land and least desirable tracts, while the speculators pre-empted tracts closest to settlement and transportation and held them for resale at prices beyond the means of the class the Homestead Act was presumably designed to help. It is the opinion of Fred Shannon that, "In its operation the Homestead Act could hardly have defeated the hopes of the [land-reform] enthusiasts . . . more completely if the makers had drafted it with that purpose uppermost in mind."

While many of the same people who drafted and administered the Homestead Act for the West would in all probability have drafted and administered the Stevens Act for the South, it is only fair to remember that the Western land problem was complicated by variables absent from the Southern picture — granting that the latter had its own complications. But at least the South lay within the humid, forested longitudes, conditions that were far more familiar to Eastern lawmakers than . . . [the] Great Plains, and also the rebel estates provided a larger proportion of arable land, much more conveniently located in relation to the prospective homesteaders. Because of these advantages and the idealism said to have motivated Radicals in their dealings with freedmen (however inoperative it was in the same men's dealings with Western homesteaders) it is possible that the Stevens Act would have had a happier history than the Homestead Act and that the black freedmen would have actually entered into the promised land, peacefully and cheerfully, each one secure in the possession of his forty acres. And let us throw in an army mule apiece for good measure.

That outcome is conceivable and one would hope even probable. But in calculating the degree of probability one is forced to take into account certain other conditioning and relevant factors in addition to the western homestead experience. For one thing the Stevens Act as detailed by the Pennsylvania Radical set aside nine-tenths of the 394 million acres of confiscated rebel land for sale to the highest bidder — an open invitation to the speculator and monopolist. It is possible that these types might have behaved toward the black homesteaders of the South in much the same way they behaved toward the white homesteader in the West. If so the probability of success for the philanthropic part of the Stevens Act is appreciably diminished.

Prospects of success for the Stevens Act are also illuminated by the history of a Southern Homestead Act that actually *was* adopted by Congress. There were 47,700,000 acres of public land in five of the Confederate states in 1861, more than the amount of rebel estates set aside for freedmen by the hypothetical Stevens Act. In 1866 the Radicals pushed through a drastic bill applying exclusively to these lands, reserving them to homesteaders at 80 acres per holding, and favoring freedmen by excluding ex-Confederates from homesteading privileges. These lands were generally less accessible and less desirable than those of confiscated estates might have been, and as in the case of the Western act no provision was made for furnishing credit and transportation to homesteaders. These conditions probably explain why extremely few blacks seized upon this opportunity to double the elusive 40 acres. In that respect the act was a failure and, at any rate, Congress reversed the policy in 1876 and threw open this rich Southern empire to unrestricted speculation. There ensued a scramble of monopolists that matched any land rush of the Wild West, and the freedmen were thrust aside and forgotten. Admittedly this episode offers further discouragement for the chances of the revolutionary Stevens Act.

Determined revolutionists are not disheartened by reverses, however. They merely press forward with more heroic measures. Perhaps Thaddeus Stevens was not revolutionary enough. There is the problem of the rebel resistance to Radical Reconstruction and federal authority in the defeated states. My own researches have impressed me deeply with the seriousness of this resistance. It was often open, defiant, organized, and effective. White Southerners repeatedly insulted, persecuted, and sometimes murdered federal officials, army officers included. They scoffed at the law and ridiculed the courts. They did everything to black citizens the law forbade their doing and invented mistreatments that [the] law never thought of. How any self-respecting government put up with such defiance unless, indeed, it was at least subliminally sympathetic with the resistance, it is difficult to understand. With overwhelming power in its hands, even an ordinary respectable non-revolutionary government could have done better than this.

Let me remind you, however, that this is a revolutionary program that we are pursuing. Here Thad Stevens lets us down. He raises the question whether any Republican, Senator Charles Sumner included, really deserved the name "Radical." It is true that his rhetoric against the "proud, bloated, and defiant rebels" was violent enough, that he promised to "startle feeble minds and shake weak nerves," that he ridiculed "the prim conservatives, the snobs, and the male waiting maids in Congress," that he asked, "How can republican institutions, free schools, free churches . . . exist in a mingled community of nabobs and serfs," and that he thundered the promise to "drive her nobility into exile," or worse. But when it came right down to it he confessed that he "never desired bloody punishments to any extent." This admission of bourgeois softness proves that Stevens has exhausted his usefulness as a guide to revolutionary solutions.

It is becoming a bit tiresome (and it is entirely unnecessary) to be flanked on the left in speculative audacity. Armchair bloodbaths can be conducted with impunity by anyone, even a professor emeritus. Let us then pursue the logic of the revolutionary process on past Stevens and Sumner, past the Old Left and the New Left, and out to the wild blue — or rather infra-red — yonder. Let us embrace in our revolutionary program, along with the Stevens Act, an act for the liquidation of the enemy class. There is ample precedent for this in the history of revolutions. Even the American Revolution drove the Tories into exile. Mass deportation, considering the merchant marine's state of total disrepair in 1865, is unfortunately not a practicable option. That leaves available only the messier alternatives. It is true that the Alaska purchase from Russia made providentially available an American Siberia in 1867, but that would take care of relatively few, and again there is the tedious problem of transportation. The numbers are formidable, for the counter-revolutionary resistance extended beyond the planter class through a very large percentage of Southern whites. A few hundred thousand Northern Copperheads can be handled in concentration camps, but in Dixie harsher measures are indicated. Let no true revolutionary blanch at the implications. Remember that we must be cruel in order to be kind, that we are the social engineers of the future, that we are forestalling future bloodbaths, race riots, and relieving our Northern metropolitan friends of problems that trouble their thoughts and for a time threatened to destroy their cities. If our work is bloody our conscience is clear, and we do all that we do — compassionately.

Having liquidated the white resistance down to the last unregenerate lord of the lash and the last bed-sheeted Ku Kluxer, let us proceed unencumbered to build the true Radical Reconstruction. We will find it expedient to import managerial talent in large numbers to replace the liquidated white resistance, and place them in charge of agriculture, industry, railroads, and mines. They will doubtless come from the same states the carpetbaggers hailed from, but they must be carefully screened to eliminate the more objectionable types and certified as non-racists and non-Copperheads. We will also establish a permanent Freedmen's Bureau, perhaps modeled on the Indian Bureau, and place in command of it the very finest talent. If not General O. O. Howard, perhaps we can get the nomination of Frederick Douglass through a miraculously radicalized U.S. Senate, after a radicalized U. S. Grant had executed a Pride's Purge of half the members.

After these Draconian, Cromwellian, Stalinist measures had removed all resistance and interference from Southern and Northern racists and Kluxers and nightriders, silenced all Confederate orators, and shut down the last obstructionist press, the revolutionists should have had a perfectly free hand. What then would have been the consequences for fulfillment of Reconstruction purposes? Would these additional measures have converted failure into success? One would surely hope so after paying such a bloody price.

But again, no one can say for sure. And again we turn to the comparative method for possible illumination. I hope that I am sufficiently alert to the dangers of these comparisons. I realize that no analogy is complete, that no two historical events are identical, and that the risks of drawing conclusions by such reasoning are most formidable. I have tried to guard against such risks and to be very tentative about drawing conclusions, but I suspect I have already outraged respected historians by mentioning Grant in the same breath with Cromwell or Stalin. Nevertheless I shall take heart and venture one last excursion into the treacherous field of comparative or counterfactual history.

Once again the comparison is close to home and contemporaneous with the Reconstruction period. Moreover, the same electorates, the same congressmen, the identical presidents and judiciary, the same editorial chorus and clerical censors are involved in the one as in the other — one cast for two dramas. The second drama also has as its plot the story of reformers using the federal government to bring justice and rights and decent lives to men of color. This time the theater is in the West instead of the South and the colored minority is red instead of black. Since we have "controlled the variable" (as the quantifiers say) of Confederate slave owners' resistance in the South — with a regrettable amount of bloodshed to be sure — the two theaters are more readily comparable. For while the reformers in the West had their own problems, they were not encumbered by die-hard Confederate reactionaries, former owners and masters of the red people, and not dogged at every step by determined and desperate night-riders. In these respects they had a relatively free hand.

The personnel and policies of the white guardians of the blacks and the white guardians of the reds were often interchangeable. General W. T. Sherman moved from command of the Southern District to command of the Western District in 1867, from the final arbiter of the black freedman's destiny to final arbiter of the redskin's fate. Many other military officers including General O. O. Howard moved back and forth from South to West. While General Howard, who had been head of the Freedmen's Bureau, was serving as president of an all-black Howard University in 1872 he was dispatched by Grant to conclude a treaty with the Apaches; in 1874 he was placed in command of the Department of Columbia, and in 1877 he led a punitive expedition against the Nez Perce Indians. Black regiments served in West and South under the same white officers. In the educational field Samuel Armstrong of Hampton Institute, Booker Washington's mentor and model, took Richard Henry Pratt, the great Indian educator, as disciple and assistant, and the two of them integrated and taught black and red students at Hampton. Later Pratt took the Armstrong–Booker Washington gospel to Indian schools. The same missionaries, preachers, editors, and reformers often concerned themselves with the problems and destinies of both colored minorities.

What can be said, in view of the relatively free hand they had in the West, of the performance of the American reformers toward the Indian, as compared with their performance toward the Negro, when they did not have the free hand I have imagined for them? Was it any better? As a matter of fact the two problems were solved in much the same way. The red man like the black man was given to understand that the white man's will was supreme, that he had few rights the white man was bound to respect. He was promised land and the land was taken away. He was promised integration and then segregated, even more completely than the black man. He was degraded, exploited, humiliated, and because he offered more resistance he was cut down ruthlessly by military force or vigilante action. Idealists like Richard Henry Pratt who operated in both South and West were as frustrated in their efforts for the red man as they were with the black man. White supremacy forces were as triumphant over Eastern "Indian lovers" in Arizona and Colorado as they were over Northern "nigger lovers" in Mississippi and Alabama.

But this comparison is an outrage against established compartmentalizations of historical thought, a preposterous violation of respected conventions. Everyone knows what a "good Indian" was. And what but confusion of the undergraduate mind can possibly come from comparing Colorado and Alabama? I apologize for this travesty against sound canons of the profession. . . .

I owe further apologies. Having invited you to consider the causes of the failure of Reconstruction, I have produced nothing but negative results. While applauding the revisionists for their excellent work, I have questioned the emphasis on the idealism and sincerity of the Radicals and their ephemeral triumphs as an adequate indication of their ultimate failure. In the second place, I have raised doubts about moralistic and uniquely American explanations for post-emancipation failure in the protection of freedmen on the ground that much the same pattern of forced labor occurred everywhere in the world as a sequel to abolition. Thirdly, having embraced the Stevens policy of rebel land confiscation and redistribution, I am forced to admit that contemporaneous experience with federal administration of public lands discourages optimism about the freedman's chances. And finally, after eliminating Confederate resistance with bloody measures I am overcome with doubts, caused by belated reflections on the fate of the poor red man, that even these drastic steps would ensure success. With the candor I have urged upon other historians I am obliged to confess a failure of my own, the failure to find a satisfactory explanation for the failure of Reconstruction.

The problem remains unsolved. The assignment still goes begging. It deserves high priority among the unfinished tasks of American historiography. Those who next undertake the task will not, I hope, rely too uncritically on the received ideas, the shared moral convictions and political values of their own time to sanction their premises. They should give scrupulous attention to uniquely American conditions, but remember that the post-emancipation problem they attack was not unique to America. They may well profit from consideration of allegedly idyllic race relations on happy islands in the Caribbean sun, but remember that their home problem was environed by Protestant Anglo-American institutions of a temperate zone unblessed by Pope or tropical sun. They should give due weight to constitutional issues without fruitlessly pining for an English-type constitution to deal with states' rights, a Russian-type Czar to distribute land among the emancipated, or a Soviet-type commissar of security to liquidate mass resistance.

I hope those who accept this challenge will not take these reflections as the counsel of despair, or as intimation that Reconstruction was doomed to failure, or that our ancestors might not have done better by their experiment than they actually did. Nor should other historians be discouraged from revolutionary speculations by the inconclusive results of my own. Let them be as far-out left as is currently fashionable. But in the transports of revolutionary imaginings, arm-chair edicts, and dreams of glory, they would do well to keep in mind the human materials and the historic context of their problem. If they do this, they will face up to the fact that nineteenth-century Americans (and some in the twentieth century as well) were fatefully stuck with a perverse mystique of squatter sovereignty. The tenets of this perversion of the democratic dogma, this squatter sovereignty, were that whatever the law or the Constitution or the Supreme Court or world opinion or moral codes said to the contrary notwithstanding, the will of the dominant white majority would prevail. And where whites were not in the majority it would prevail anyway. How it was, and how early, we got stuck with a commitment to this caricature of democracy is a long story, a very long story, and the story did not begin in 1865, and the commitment was not confined to the South.

QUESTIONS TO CONSIDER

1. Why, according to Woodward, are interpretations of Reconstruction inadequate unless they see it as tragic? Why is it "a strategy of evasion" to say that the First Reconstruction prepared the way for the Second? What gains did the southern Reconstruction governments and the ex-slaves make, and why does Woodward discount them?

2. To what extent, if any, was Radical Reconstruction revolutionary in its goals or methods? What definition of "revolutionary" should be used in assessing it? How would Woodward and Eric Foner address these questions? How would you choose between their viewpoints?

3. Woodward makes a telling analogy between the treatment of ex-slaves in the South and Native Americans in the West. Why did the federal government (for a time) support black assimilation and enfranchisement, but simultaneously deny Indians citizenship and confine them to reservations? How, in the end, were these two "problems," according to Woodward, "solved in much the same way"?

4. What, at bottom, does Woodward blame for the failure of Reconstruction? human nature? capitalist greed? the sanctity of private property? the ineffectiveness of big government? white racism? Does Woodward's essay leave you with the impression that Reconstruction was doomed and that what happened was inevitable? Why or why not?

5. Has Woodward effectively demonstrated the usefulness of "counterfactual" analysis? Is this method "quackery," as one historian has charged, or are there benefits to speculating about options in the past? Are Woodward's analogies to the Homestead Act and Indian policy appropriate? Would anything have been different had Radical Reconstruction never occurred? What if the Confederacy had won the Civil War? What if Radical Reconstruction had *succeeded* and African Americans had had equal access to land, education, and the vote? How would subsequent American history have been changed?

CPSIA information can be obtained
at www.ICGtesting.com
Printed in the USA
FFOW03n2249130715
15141FF